AA

KEYGUIDE

AUSTRALIA

215

CONTENTS

259

145

79

288

CONTENTS | AUSTRALIA

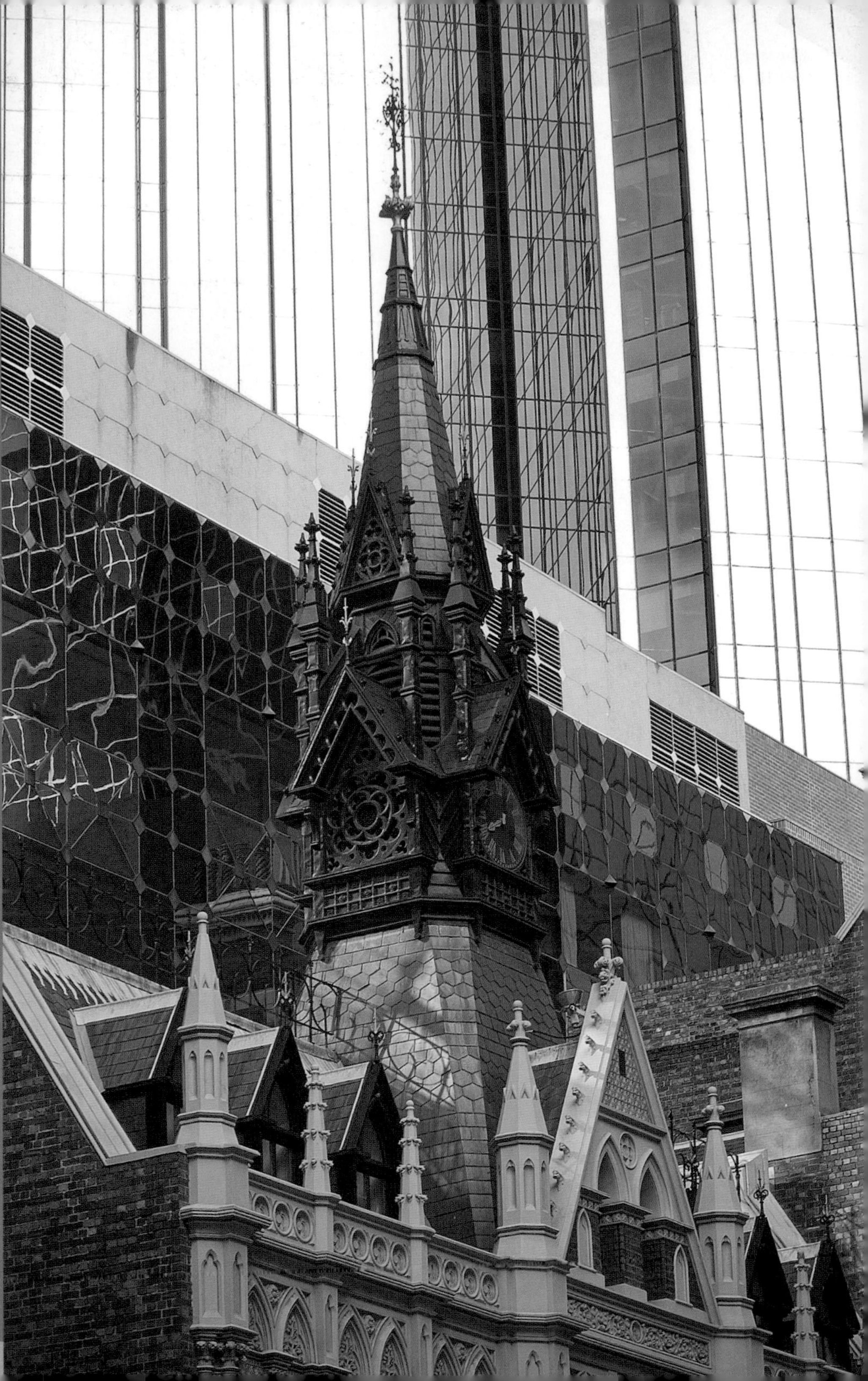

UNDERSTANDING AUSTRALIA

Understanding Australia is an introduction to the country, its geography, economy, history and its people. Living Australia gets under the skin of Australia today, while The Story of Australia takes you through the country's past.

UNDERSTANDING AUSTRALIA

It will take you more than a few days to grasp the depth and breadth of Australia; it can't be done just by spending a few days in Sydney or Melbourne. These are cosmopolitan cities where global culture has applied a universal veneer that takes some peeling back. The solid Victorian buildings and contrasting modern architecture remind you of many world cities, and the TV programmes are familiar to American and British audiences—with the best and worst on offer. Some city icons—the Sydney Opera House and Harbour Bridge, and the Melbourne Cricket Ground—distil something of the national character, but a real understanding of this country comes only through contact with the Australian people.

AUSTRALIANS

At the end of 2009 the Australian population was about 22 million, including Australians temporarily overseas. Population density is about 2.9 people per square kilometre (7.4 people per square mile); the United Kingdom has 100 times that level. Compared with other Western countries, though, Australia's population is increasing at quite a rate, mostly through immigration. Throughout the 20th century, waves of immigrants came from Europe, and more recently from Asia. Only 69 per cent of the population were born in Australia, and that includes Aboriginal Australians (3 per cent). Moreover, Australia's people are young compared to Europe: Around 36 per cent of the population are aged below 25 and only 13 per cent are over 65.

When it comes to religion, 75 per cent of the population profess Christianity, though the other major religions—Buddhism, Islam, Hinduism and Judaism—are represented in significant numbers.

A LUCKY COUNTRY?

Australians are not immune to the malaises of modern society: poverty, unequal distribution of wealth, and pressures on rural and city environments. But there is a peculiar optimism that pervades this multicultural society and a pride that many things have been done well. There is a feeling that things are generally OK. As far as visitors are concerned, friendly people can easily be found in the main cities, but it is the regional cities and towns and rural villages that seem to offer that quintessential Aussie experience—whether from a friendly nod or help with directions or by their relaxed air. It is not unknown for complete strangers to take you in their care and give you a tour of the local sights.

Above *Wildflowers in the Flinders Range in South Australia*
Opposite *Sydney ferries take part in the annual Australia Day Ferrython in January*

THE ECONOMY

Australia's Western-style capitalist economy is based on a wealth of natural resources and agricultural produce, service industries such as tourism, and a small manufacturing sector. The main exports are coal, gold, iron ore, alumina, petroleum products, meats, cereals, wool, wine and cotton. The agriculture and mining industries are competitive worldwide and manufacturing industries like car production have developed export markets. China is Australia's largest trading partner, followed by the EU, Japan and the USA.

Australia is the world's fourth-largest wine exporter, supplying about five per cent of the global market; the UK is their top market, taking 35 per cent of exports, while the US accounts for 31 per cent. Total wine exports by volume in 2004 were 750 million litres (198 million gallons).

POLITICS

The federal government is based on both the British and American democratic systems. A multiparty, elected parliament, led by the prime minister, is responsible for matters of national importance such as defence, foreign affairs, trade, treasury, social services and immigration. A governor-general, appointed by the British monarch on the advice of the prime minister, must give assent to all laws passed. Each of Australia's six states and two territories has its own elected representatives.

A CONTINENT

It's easy to underestimate the scale of Australia. The island continent has a land mass of 7.6 million sq km (3 million sq miles) and occupies five per cent of the earth's land area; it is the sixth-largest country in the world. If you travel between cities, particularly on the five-hour flight between Sydney and Perth, you start to appreciate the size. Beyond the mainland, Australia is surrounded by many thousands of small fringing islands and numerous larger ones, the largest being the southern island state of Tasmania.

Almost two-thirds of the continent belongs to the Western Plateau, covering the western and much of the central and northern regions of the country. Mostly flat and low, it is interrupted by spectacular individual features like Uluru (Ayers Rock), rocky strongholds like the Kimberley and Arnhem Land, and by rugged ridges like those of the MacDonnell and Flinders ranges.

The Great Dividing Range runs down the eastern coastline from Cape York in the far north to the hills of Victoria in the south; mountainous Tasmania is an extension of the range across Bass Strait. Although the mountains are not particularly high—Mount Kosciuszko in New South Wales is the highest at 2,230m (7,314ft)— they have a huge effect on climate, with the result that this area houses the bulk of the population.

Between the Western Plateau and the Great Dividing Range lies the Central Eastern Lowlands, running

north to south. River basins succeed one another, including the country's most extensive river system, the Murray-Darling-Murrumbidgee.

CLIMATE

In view of its size—Australia spans nearly 35 degrees of latitude—the earth's driest continent after Antarctica has a surprisingly small range of climates. The highest rainfall is in the tropical north, where temperatures stay high all year round, averaging 29°C (84°F) in summer and 24°C (75°F) in winter. The wettest recorded place is the summit of Mount Bellenden Ker in north Queensland, at a height of 1,555m (5,100ft). Average annual rainfall here is about 8,000mm (320in), but in 2000 an Australian record was set at 12,461mm (498in). Such rainfall occurs when warm, moist sea air rises over coastal ranges, cooling as it rises and then losing the moisture as rain.

Unlike the north, where the rain falls during the summer, temperate southern Australia experiences slightly higher rainfall in winter and spring, and there is more variation in average temperatures, between 24°C (75°F) in summer and 10°C (50°F) in winter, when snow falls on the highest peaks. Much of the interior is arid, with little rain, and the mostly dry Lake Eyre records an annual average of just 125mm (5in).

Inland temperatures soar to scorching heights—53°C (127.4°F) was recorded at Cloncurry in Queensland in 1889—although nights can be cold. The lowest recorded temperature, –23°C (–9.4°F), was in 1994 in the Australian Alps at Charlotte Pass, New South Wales.

MAKE THE MOST OF YOUR STAY

Most visitors opt for the flying triangle holiday—Sydney, Red Centre, Cairns—and miss the other bits. But many of the places off the beaten path are worth the extra effort or constitute a holiday in themselves—including World Heritage attractions such as Fraser Island, Shark Bay and the Tasmanian wilderness. Elsewhere, long coastlines, with uncrowded beaches and mountain ranges, interspersed with towns and cities, provide scenery, outdoor dining and cultural options away from the noise of well-known cities. Or retreat to the hinterland communities among the hills of the Great Dividing Range, and the small outback towns beyond the mountains.

A QUICK TOUR

Australia is divided into six states and two territories. New South Wales's tourist regions famously include Sydney and surrounds, where urban icons such as the Opera House and the Harbour Bridge are within striking distance of the Blue Mountains and the Hunter Valley vineyards. Farther north, Queensland has Cairns, the

focus of activity for Great Barrier Reef tours, tropical rainforests and outback adventures, but also the Gold and Sunshine coasts, with world-class beaches. Island-hopping and yacht cruising are a good way to see the Whitsundays.

Remote Darwin and tropical Top End have major attractions. Kakadu National Park is a World Heritage Site, while Uluru-Kata Tjuta National Park (Ayers Rock and the Olgas) and the MacDonnell Ranges epitomize the arid Red Centre. Just as remote are Broome and the Kimberley in the north of Western Australia: Discover the romance of pearling days and rugged mountain scenery. Busy Perth is the commercial heart of the southeast of Western Australia.

Adelaide and the Barossa Valley vineyards have a European charm, though South Australia's wines are distinctly Australian. Melbourne is cosmopolitan and the rest of Victoria has mountains, desert and a fertile coastline. Few international visitors see Tasmania, but its scenery is on a grand scale.

Below *Sydney Opera House and Harbour Bridge at dusk*

WESTERN AUSTRALIA

NORTHERN TERRITORY

QUEENSLAND

SOUTH AUSTRALIA

NEW SOUTH WALES

*ACT

VICTORIA

* Australian Capital Territory

TASMANIA

AUSTRALIAN CITIES AT A GLANCE

SYDNEY

Take a cruise on the glorious harbour, check the scene at Bondi Beach, sample some of Sydney's Asian cuisines and revel in the wild glories of the Blue Mountains.

CANBERRA

View some of Australia's most treasured icons in the National Museum of Australia, see the extraordinary flora in the National Botanic Gardens and have a look at parliamentary democracy Australian style from the Visitor's Gallery in the national parliament.

MELBOURNE

Hop aboard the St. Kilda tram and have an ice cream on the pier, explore the city's markets and the lovely gardens around the city centre, walk the Golden Mile Heritage Trail and roar with the crowd at an AFL game.

BRISBANE

Take a stroll through the city's historic heart, catch the ferry out to Stradbroke Island for a swim, cuddle a koala in the Lone Pine Koala Sanctuary and explore the lovely South Bank Parklands.

DARWIN

Wander through the botanic gardens, check out some of the city's Aboriginal art galleries and take an evening stroll around the marina at Cullen Bay and then stay for a leisurely dinner.

ADELAIDE

Admire the historic buildings along North Terrace, wander the aromatic aisles of Central Markets, finger the greenery in the botanic gardens and shop for fiery opals in the city's gemstone galleries.

PERTH

Sign up for a Swan River cruise, walk through King's Park, spend some time on the city's gorgeous beaches, take a trip to Rottnest Island to admire the quokkas and explore historic Fremantle.

HOBART

Stroll through history in the streets of Battery Point, take in the bustling waterfront around Constitution Dock, browse the stalls at the Salamanca Place Market and make a meal of the island's wonderful seafood and cool-climate wines.

THE BEST OF AUSTRALIA

BEST OF NEW SOUTH WALES

Blue Mountains (▷ 105–108) Great landscapes, activities and fresh air are just a couple of hours away from Sydney

Sydney Harbour (▷ 78–79) Get the sea-level view on a ferry ride from Circular Quay.

Sydney Opera House (▷ 82–83) Book as early as you can for performances.

BEST OF AUSTRALIAN CAPITAL TERRITORY

Parliament House (▷ 111–112) Canberra's billion-dollar government home is not just a fine modern building, it is also a showcase for Australian art.

BEST OF VICTORIA

Ballarat (▷ 133) The creek running through the reconstructed Sovereign Hill gold-mining town is seeded with gold—try your hand at gold panning.

Federation Square (▷ 142) Melbourne's vibrant cultural hub is a focus for many events.

Great Ocean Road (▷ 136–139) This classic route weaves around breathtaking cliffs, quiet bays and wild surf beaches.

BEST OF QUEENSLAND

Cairns and the Tropical North (▷ 177–178) Queensland's northern capital, tropical rainforest and a fabulous scenic drive to Cape Tribulation.

Great Barrier Reef (▷ 182–184) Over 1,200km (744 miles) long, this is the world's largest coral reef system.

Whitsunday Islands (▷ 191) Keen sailors can navigate

an archipelago of 74 forested islands with sandy beaches for world-class food and luxury relaxation.

BEST OF NORTHERN TERRITORY

Alice Springs (▷ 210) A good base for driving through Watarrka National Park and the MacDonnell Ranges, taking in spectacular gorge scenery.

Kakadu National Park (▷ 212–213) Ubirr and Nourlangie Rock are among the best accessible Aboriginal rock art sites in the Top End.

Uluru (Ayers Rock) (▷ 215–218) Vast and dramatic, this is justifiably one of Australia's greatest and most mysterious attractions.

BEST OF SOUTH AUSTRALIA

Adelaide Hills (▷ 238) Beautiful scenery, natural bushland and pretty gardens surrounding Adelaide.

Barossa Valley (▷ 239) The home of many of Australia's best-known and award-winning wines.

BEST OF WESTERN AUSTRALIA

Margaret River (▷ 264–265) You may be interested in award-winning wines or excellent surfing, but also consider visiting the caves, the forests and the beaches.

Rottnest Island (▷ 268) On a cool day, explore the Indian Ocean coastline on a bicycle.

BEST OF TASMANIA

Cradle Mountain–Lake St. Clair National Park (▷ 288) Keep an eye open for wallabies, wombats, possums—or possibly an elusive platypus.

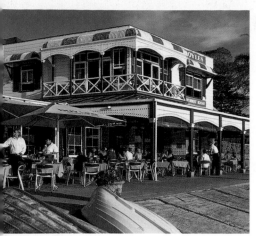

Port Arthur (▷ 292) For a taste of convict life.
Strahan and west coast (▷ 293) Strahan's waterfront sports complement one of the world's last great wilderness areas.

BEST EATING

Cafe Zuppa (▷ 124) This Katoomba café in the Blue Mountains is a great, inexpensive place to be refreshed and to relax.
Ottoman Cuisine (▷ 125) For the best Turkish dishes, come to Canberra.
Doyle's On The Beach (▷ 95) Relish the superb view from Watsons Bay across Port Jackson to Sydney Harbour with fine seafood and great wines.
Rockpool (▷ 96) Not just Sydney's but one of Australia's best restaurants—but go with a friend who's paying.
The Stokehouse (▷ 164) Dine on superb seafood in a Melbourne suburb with the backdrop of Port Phillip.
Thy Thy 1 (▷ 164) Dine on a budget at this popular Melbourne Vietnamese restaurant.
e'cco Bistro (▷ 202) Simple, stylish food in a glamorous Brisbane setting.
Mermaids Café and Bar (▷ 203) Good, informal meals beside a Gold Coast surfing beach in Burleigh Heads.
Ochre Restaurant (▷ 203) Bush tucker at its best in the centre of Cairns.
Sounds of Silence (▷ 226) Top-notch outback barbecues in view of Uluru (Ayers Rock)—at a price.
Citrus (▷ 252) Innovative Modern Australian restaurant in Adelaide—famous for its breakfasts.
Black Rock Café (▷ 280) After visiting Kalbarri National Park, take a rest and look out over the Indian Ocean.
Sail and Anchor (▷ 280) An Aussie pub that brews its own beer and commands fine views over Fremantle.
Stillwater at Ritchie's Mill (▷ 303) Fine dining with local produce to the fore in a historic riverside millhouse in Hobart.
Windsor (▷ 167) Afternoon tea at Melbourne's grand 19th-century hotel is a genteel occasion.

BEST SHOPPING

David Jones (▷ 157) The department store branch on Bourke Street, Melbourne, has most major Australian brands and an excellent food hall.
Eumundi Markets (▷ 186) This huge Saturday morning Queensland arts and crafts market gets crowded, so arrive early.
The Rocks (▷ 76) *The* place in Sydney for quality Australiana—Akubra hats, Driza-Bone coats and opals—and a lively weekend market.
Salamanca Market (▷ 299) For Tasmanian gifts and bargains, head for Hobart's harbour on a Saturday.

BEST STAYING

The Crown and Anchor Inn (▷ 129) A tranquil 19th-century inn gazing across the South Pacific Ocean.
Hyatt Hotel (▷ 129) Art deco luxury in the midst of Canberra parkland.
Peppers Guest House (▷ 129) The luxury and the Hunter Valley scenery in New South Wales are hard to beat.
The Russell (▷ 100) Victorian-style accommodation in The Rocks, Sydney.
The Queenscliff Hotel (▷ 167) Victorian-era hotel, set in parkland, facing Port Phillip.
Robinsons in the City (▷ 167) Melbourne's only central guest house provides a friendly alternative to the large hotels.
Cape Trib Beach House (▷ 205) Basic accommodation where the tropical rainforest creeps down to the beach.
Gagudju Crocodile Inn (▷ 229) A refreshing rest stop for tourers in the immense Kakadu National Park, Northern Territory.
Cradle Mountain Lodge (▷ 304) This luxurious retreat looks out across Tasmania's famed World Heritage wilderness area.

Opposite *Walkers at Dove Lake near Cradle Mountain in Tasmania*
Above *Doyles On The Beach at Watson's Bay, Sydney*
Below *A brightly coloured aquatic resident of the Great Barrier Reef*

BEST EXPERIENCES

At night the stars in the outback are so big and bright it's almost as if you could touch them.

Book a guided tour to explore tropical rain forest if you want to see crocodiles, fruit bats, pythons, birdwing butterflies and cassowaries.

Climb to the top of Kings Canyon in Watarrka National Park for a spectacular view of the desert.

Enjoy a glass of Australian wine while looking across the vineyard, or take a winery tour to understand the production process.

For those who don't want to get their feet wet there are a number of dry options to see the Great Barrier Reef, from semi-submersibles and glass-bottomed boats to scenic flights in a helicopter.

Hot-air balloons offer a unique view of the Australian landscape, and each state has a variety of options.

If you cannot stomach witchetty grubs, then try the nuts and fruits on an Aboriginal-led forage for bush tucker in the outback.

If you don't have the opportunity—or the courage—to meet Australia's wildlife in its natural setting, a visit to an Australian wildlife sanctuary or zoo is the next best thing.

If you've never been surfing, then take a lesson at on the beach; there are opportunities in most states

It is surprisingly easy to see kangaroos in rural areas if you're around at dawn or dusk—ask a local for the best places.

Savour the fusion of European and Asian cooking styles in any of the state capitals.

Several historic prisons are now tourist attractions—a visit gives a good idea of the harsh reality of the lives of the first European settlers.

Tackle the spectacular mountains and forests of the Tasmanian wilderness via a range of trails, from the five-day Overland Track to one-hour strolls on paths suitable for wheelchairs and buggies (strollers).

View the deep canyons, valleys and sheer cliffs, and take in the aroma of eucalypts from a lookout in the Blue Mountains.

Walk the 9.4km (6-mile) circuit around the base of Uluru (Ayers Rock) to appreciate its overwhelming size and magnificence.

You may not think of Australia as a major cheese-making nation, but boutique cheese manufacturers produce several world-class varieties.

Below *Bushwalking near The Three Sisters rock formation in the Blue Mountains*
Opposite *Historic beach houses at Brighton, near Melbourne*

LIVING AUSTRALIA

URBAN AND RURAL AUSTRALIA

Although one of the world's most urbanized nations, Australia still gets plenty of mileage out of trading on the proud heritage of its rural past. However, the nation has changed from the days when it supposedly 'rode on the sheep's back'. Over three-quarters of Australia's population is concentrated on the coastal strip from north Queensland to Adelaide, and 85 per cent of the population live in state or territory capitals or in cities of more than 100,000 people. Continued migration has only intensified this trend, as almost all new arrivals settle in the cities. Rural Australia is alive and kicking, though, despite poor commodity prices, successive droughts, the trials of access to education and the general tyranny of distance. No doubt country people have generations of tenacity built into them. And they are the most friendly folk you're likely to encounter—perhaps it is because they are isolated, but more likely it's because as members of smaller communities, they have had to work together to get by. Everyone pitches in when there's a bushfire, and if your tractor breaks down, a neighbour is likely to help out. So don't be afraid to get to know the people in the country—you never know when you'll need some help!

LIVING SUSTAINABLY

Each Australian creates more than 1.4 tonnes of litter a year. Up until the 1950s relatively little waste was produced. There wasn't much packaging, most containers were reused or refilled, and food scraps were used as garden compost.

Nowadays, consumer products come in more and more packaging and disposable containers are the norm. Plus it's nearly always cheaper to buy a new product than fix a broken one.

Local councils are encouraging residents to separate their waste so that it can be disposed of in a sustainable manner or recycled in a number of different ways. The next goal is to reduce consumption generally, but ultimately, sustainablility means a return to the ways of the past.

Clockwise from above *Cattle mustering taking place on an Outback station; The Macquarie Apartments in central Sydney; Sydney is a modern urban landscape*

LANDCARE

During the past two decades a green revolution has swept rural Australia. Communities have banded together to form Landcare groups and taken on the task of repairing an environment that has suffered degradation through over-clearing, bad farming practices, the damming of rivers and excessive irrigation. The loss of topsoil to wind and water erosion, and increased salinity caused by rising water tables, have the potential to devastate huge areas; about 70–80 per cent of irrigated land in New South Wales is affected by salinity problems. Salinity is also a threat to the health and productivity of many river catchments, and can be economically ruinous to the rural and urban communities that live in them. Now government agencies are funding Landcare and the future looks brighter.

URBAN RENEWAL

For the past 50 or so years, most Australian city dwellers have been realizing their dream to own a plot of land. A brick-veneer home with a big backyard for gardening and recreation completes the picture. So suburb after suburb of 1,000sq m (10,760sq ft) house blocks have been created and they stretch out to the mountainous limits of cities like Sydney and Melbourne. Today, with rising prices, shortages of available land, lower birth rates and the move towards single-person households, the trend is to build medium- and high-density housing in areas well served by public transport. New housing in the city centre and suburbs is now predominantly multi-level apartments. As suburbs of old terrace (row) houses become gentrified in central Sydney and Melbourne, life returns to the city centre.

CAR MANIA

Since the end of World War II, increased affluence has led to the rise and rise of the motor vehicle. Today, Australia has the second-highest level of car ownership in the world—one car for every 2.2 people. Cars are destroying the ambience of major cities, especially Brisbane and Sydney, where geography works against efficient transport routes. Despite talking public transportation, governments are building super roads to handle the traffic. As fast as these roads are built, they become congested —car culture shapes the cities and the nation. Australia has the third-highest rate of fuel consumption per capita in the world. So until the Aussie's love affair with the car subsides, a brown pall of pollution will often hang over major cities.

THE OUTBACK

'Where is the outback?' This is the first question many visitors to Australia ask. Unfortunately, there's no one particular place to point to and, apart from Victoria and Tasmania, each state has its outback regions.

Of course, the Red Centre is in the outback, but how far inland from Australia's huge coastline does the outback begin? Some people define this somewhat mythical place as where you get a wave from a driver coming in the opposite direction, while others simply say it's 'back of beyond'. Others assume they have arrived when they see lots of 'Eat Beef, You Bastards!' stickers on the back of dusty vehicles! However, since the concept of the outback implies remoteness and a sparse population, you'll certainly know when you've arrived!

ABORIGINAL AUSTRALIA

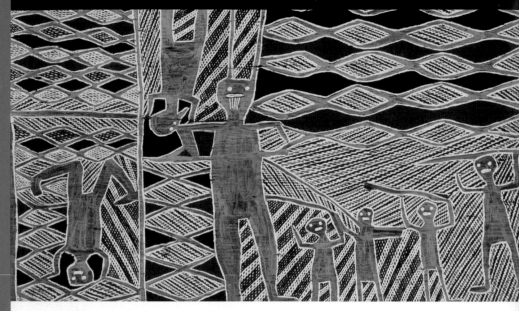

Aboriginal Australia has a complexity that defies stereotypes. Its people are living in the 21st century with traditions that go back more than 40,000 years and they are coping more or less well depending on how they have adapted to the changes. The major push from traditional Aboriginal people has been to return to their homelands—the places from which they either voluntarily left or were forcibly removed. For urban Aboriginal people of mixed descent, the continual re-appraisal of their heritage has meant coming to terms with fragments of their past while keeping a foot in the realities of present-day Australia. Aboriginal people have had to make compromises in order to face the reality of modern times. Many of them maintain cultural practices such as dance or art by forging new ways that synthesize the past with the present. The energy of this raw artistic renaissance is a cultural phenomenon which has both enlivened Australian culture and given back pride to a people who for too long have suffered the patronage of a white society determined to forget the injustices of the past.

ABORIGINAL LANGUAGES

Languages are inextricably linked to cultural and spiritual identity and are connected to creation stories, cultural laws and traditional practices. Prior to colonization, there may have been as many as 250 Aboriginal languages and about 700 dialects. Fewer than half remain today; many are known to a handful of the elderly, and only about 30 are spoken regularly. While their communities are reviving some languages, many are threatened. In remote areas, relative isolation from Western influences has resulted in the continued use of local dialects, while indigenous languages are taught to many school children. With Aboriginal bands like Yothu Yindi performing many songs in their own languages, the future for some surviving languages looks brighter.

Clockwise from above *An Aboriginal bark painting depicting ritual dance, from Yirrkala in Arnhem Land; Cathy Freeman is an Australian national hero; Bush tucker: bush raisins*

ABORIGINAL BUSH TUCKER

While the use of bush ingredients is fashionable in a range of city restaurants all around the country, to Aboriginal people they were sustenance and survival.

From the rainforests of north Queensland, with its myriad fruiting plants, to the dry deserts of the Red Centre where plants are scarce, local people have a vast store of knowledge of what to collect or hunt and where to find it.

It is common for children to accompany their older family members to gain an intimate knowledge of the land, the seasons, plants and animals, and the collection skills necessary to exist in often harsh terrain.

While some foods can be eaten straight from the plant, many poisonous fruits require leaching for days in streams before preparation can begin.

Guided tours allowing you to find and taste a variety of bush tucker are available in many centres.

STOLEN GENERATION

From the late 19th century to the 1960s, Australian governments had a policy of removing part-Aboriginal children from their homes in order that they could be raised as part of white society. Exact numbers were uncertain, but tens of thousands of babies and children were removed, often by force. As these young people grew up, their sense of grief was a personal burden, and political pressure forced a federal inquiry in 1995. The report, *Bringing Them Home*, published two years later, branded the policies as genocide and called for an official apology, compensation for those affected, and the establishment of a national Sorry Day. In 2008, shortly after the Australian Labor Party won a federal election, the then Prime Minister Kevin Rudd made a formal apology to Australia's indigenous people that spoke of removing a 'stain from the soul of Australia'.

ABORIGINAL MUSIC

Yothu Yindi put the reconciliation of Aboriginal people in the limelight with their 1991 hit song 'Treaty'. Combining sounds of Western rock with songs and performances that go back in time, the band has adapted the ancient song cycles of Arnhem Land, mixing instruments such as didgeridoos and clapsticks with electric guitars. Its shows feature adaptations of traditional mythology, but songs that include Dreamtime or sacred content are first approved by clan leaders. Yothu Yindi has been described as 'the most beautiful blend of indigenous and modern music to emerge from the world's music scene'. As band leader, the charismatic Mandawuy Yunupingu, 1992 Australian of the Year, and a school principal, says: 'It is not colour of skin that defines our identity but the culture into which we were born.'

CATHY FREEMAN

Born in Mackay, north Queensland, in 1973, Cathy Freeman became the first Aboriginal track and field athlete to represent Australia. She was named Young Australian of the Year in 1991, and she has created new Australian and Commonwealth records in the 400m and 200m sprints. She won gold medals in the 1990 and 1994 Commonwealth Games in Canada, and silver in the 1996 Atlanta Olympic Games.

At the 2000 Sydney Olympic Games, Cathy lit the Olympic flame and her running career came to a splendid peak when she took the gold medal in the 400m event.

In July 2003 Freeman announced her retirement from competition. Today she backs the Catherine Freeman Foundation, which brings opportunity and hope to indigenous people around Australia.

SPORTING AUSTRALIA

Without a doubt, most Aussies are obsessed with sport. The Sydney 2000 Olympics, in which Australia excelled, presented a sports-loving people to the world. The entire nation comes to a standstill for the annual Melbourne Cup: Elaborate lunches, complete with champagne and fancy hats, are all the rage, and everyone has a bet on the horses, hoping to back the winner. Melbourne and Adelaide even proclaim a public holiday for the event. The prestigious race, run over 3.2km (2 miles), is held on the first Tuesday in November. But Australians participate in sports as well as watch them, and on any weekend in the appropriate season you'll find plenty of junior and amateur cricket, soccer, basketball, netball, hockey, tennis and golf competitions going on. Suburban bowls grounds attract any number of retired older folk, while the bays and harbours are packed with sailing crafts of all kinds competing in club events. And Aussies on holiday are always likely to start up a friendly family game of cricket or touch soccer on the beach. Generally, all comers are welcome, so feel free to join in!

AUSSIE RULES

The home-grown football game is Australian (Aussie) Rules. The game originated in Victoria in the 1850s and has been described as a cross between rugby, soccer and Gaelic football. Melbourne is the home of Aussie Rules, although Hobart, Perth and Adelaide are also strongholds. Teams from Brisbane, Sydney, Adelaide and Western Australia compete with Victorian teams in a national competition. The top eight compete to play in the grand final at the end of the season in September, when Melbourne is infected with an extra dose of sporting fever. More than 80,000 spectators pack the Melbourne Cricket Ground, and it's a special experience to watch this tactical and athletic sport, while sitting among cheering fans.

Clockwise from above *The Alice Springs Camel Cup; Collingwood play Carlton in an Aussie Rules match; Ricky Ponting at the Sydney Cricket Ground*

AUSTRALIAN INSTITUTE OF SPORT

When Australia fared poorly at the Montreal Olympics in 1976, the federal government decided to set up a sports institute. Based in Canberra and opened in 1981, the AIS provides athletes with world-class training facilities, specialist coaching, state-of-the-art training equipment, and access to sports medicine and sport science. It conducts 35 programmes in 26 sports around Australia. With accommodation for 350 residents on site, the Canberra facility supports archery, artistic gymnastics, basketball (men and women), boxing, netball, rowing, soccer (men), swimming, athletics (including athletes with disabilities), volleyball (men and women) and water polo (men). Of the record 58 medals that were won at the Sydney Olympics, 32 came from current or former institute athletes.

TENNIS

Melbourne plays host to a grand slam event, the Australian Open, for two weeks in January and February each year, and tennis has long been a favourite Aussie sport, for players and spectators alike. Although recent greats have included Pat Cash and Pat Rafter, there was a feeling that the sport was in decline after the 1950s and 1960s when the likes of Rod Laver, Ken Rosewall and John Newcombe dominated world men's tennis, and the 1960s and 1970s when Margaret Court and Evonne Goolagong Cawley dominated the women's game. Now Lleyton Hewitt, recognized by his trademark back-to-front hat and regular fist pumps, is one of the top players. Highly ranked female players include Samantha Stosur, who reached the final of the 2010 French Open, and Jelena Dokic. Keep an eye out for emerging talent, including Benjamin Mitchell and Sean Berman.

CRICKET

No cricket contest is as keenly followed as an Ashes series between Australia and England. The prized 'Ashes' refer to a tiny urn believed to contain the charred remnants of a stump bail. This harks back to 1882, when Australia beat England for the first time on their home soil, and a sports newspaper ran a mock obituary for English cricket which had 'died' and stated that: 'The body will be cremated and the ashes taken to Australia'.

After England won in Australia the following year, the mythical Ashes became reality when the urn was presented to the victorious captain. England currently holds the Ashes after beating Australian 2–1 in the 2009 competition. The revered Ashes are kept at cricket's spiritual home, the Marylebone Cricket Club (MCC) at Lord's in London.

CASEY STONER

Australia has produced some huge talents in motorcycle racing, and Casey Stoner is one of the best. At 14, after a promising career in junior races, Casey relocated to Europe, which offered far better prospects to develop his racing skills. Following a string of successes in the 125 and 250cc classes, Stoner entered MotoGP in 2006, the most prestigious motorcycling events. In the 2007 season, Stoner had his first MotoGP win. That same year he secured Ducati's first MotoGP World Championship. The 2009 season was a disaster for Stoner, who fell prey to a mystery illness. His return to form came too late in the season to make an impression on the points leaders and he finished fourth overall, with every promise of a spectacular return to MotoGP racing in 2010.

CULTURAL AUSTRALIA

Australia's cultural achievements are often overshadowed by its success in the sporting arena. Until recent years, Australian writers, musicians, actors, artists and dancers who aspired to international recognition were forced to travel overseas—especially during the 1960s and 1970s. Today, world-class actors such as Russell Crowe are able to work in the US or Europe and still make Australia their home. And the 'cultural cringe', which once caused Australians to defer to artistic and intellectual achievements in Europe and the US, has mostly disappeared. Australia has made a solid contribution to the world popular music scene with bands such as Australian Crawl, INXS, AC/DC and Midnight Oil, and there are enduring solo performers, such as Kylie Minogue and Nick Cave, who have a solid international reputation. Modern Aboriginal art has become very popular, and the influential Papunya Tula artists, who took body decoration and sand paintings based on Dreamtime stories and applied them in a series of dots and lines on canvas, are responsible for starting one of the 20th century's great art movements. Author Peter Carey, whose acclaimed novel *True History of the Kelly Gang* (2000) won the 2001 Booker Prize, is today the exception rather than the rule, in that he makes New York his home.

Clockwise from above *Sydney Dance Company in Rafaela Bonachela's 2009 work 'we unfold'; actress Cate Blanchett with her husband Andrew Upton; Kylie Minogue started her career in Melbourne*

PAUL JENNINGS

Children's writer Paul Jennings has managed to work his way into the hearts of millions of children worldwide. Born in England in 1943, and arriving with his family in Australia as a boy of six, Jennings trained as a teacher before studying speech pathology and lecturing in special education. His first book, *Unreal*, published in 1985, was an instant success. Since then he has written 20 collections of quirky and humorous short stories, including *Unseen* and *Unbelievable*, and has co-authored *Wicked*.

Jennings' empathy with children—a frequently asked question is 'How do you know what it's like to be me?'—arises out of his varied teaching experiences, plus the fact that he is the father of six children.

KYLIE MINOGUE

Pop diva Kylie Minogue has come a long way since her days as Charlene in early episodes of the Melbourne-based TV soap *Neighbours*. Her two 1987 pop hits, 'Locomotion' and 'I Should Be So Lucky', followed in the next year by 'Got To Be Certain', set her on the path to success.

In the 1990s, Kylie moved from pop to club music and reinvented herself. With punk legend Nick Cave, she performed the beautiful ballad 'Where the Wild Roses Grow', which went to number two in Australia. In 2000 she wowed audiences worldwide at the closing ceremony of the Sydney Olympic Games.

Since 2005, Minogue has overcame breast cancer and she now lives in London. Her album X, recorded in 2007, was nominated for a Grammy.

CATE BLANCHETT

The most applauded and admired of Australia's current actors is Cate Blanchett. Born in Melbourne in 1969, Blanchett's first major role was in the 1993 production of David Mamet's *Oleanna*, for which she won the Sydney Theatre Critics' Best Newcomer Award. Four years later, she made her international film debut in the role of an Australian nurse captured by the Japanese Army during WWII in *Paradise Road*. Since then she has played Queen Elizabeth I in *Elizabeth*, Galadriel in *Lord of the Rings* and played the part of Bob Dylan in *I'm Not There*, winning numerous awards along the way. In 2008 Cate Blanchett and Andrew Upton, her playwright husband, become joint Artistic Directors of the Sydney Theatre Company.

ABORIGINAL ART

As custodians of Dreamtime stories, Michael Nelson Jagamara and Billy Stockman Tjapaltjarri keep their culture alive by passing the stories on through their art. Jagamara, born at Pikilyi in Central Australia in about 1947, is Australia's most prominent Aboriginal artist. He created a mosaic for the forecourt at Parliament House in Canberra, and his 8m (26ft) painting adorns the foyer of the Sydney Opera House. Before becoming a painter, he was a buffalo shooter, truck driver and drover. Japaltjarri, born in about 1925, was one of the founders of the Papunya Tula art movement, the spark that led to the renaissance of Aboriginal Art in the 1970s. Jagamara and Tjapaltjarri visited the US in 1988 and have had many international exhibitions. Their art has engendered a sense of pride and renewed cultural identity among Aboriginal people.

DANCE

For almost 40 years, Graeme Murphy has been a seminal figure as a choreographer and director in the world of Australian dance. Murphy became Artistic Director of the Dance Company (NSW) in 1976, which later became the Sydney Dance Company. Over the next 30 years, he consolidated its reputation as Australia's premier contemporary dance company. During this period he directed for Opera Australia and created choreography for The Metropolitan Opera in New York. In 2007, Murphy left the Sydney Dance Company to work on other projects, including several ballets for The Australian Ballet, Baryshnikov's White Oak Project, the Canadian Opera Company and the Bavarian State Ballet. The new Artistic Director of the Sydney Dance Company is 2004 winner of the Place Prize for Choreography, Raphaela Bonachela.

NATURAL AUSTRALIA

From the coral formations of the Great Barrier Reef to the gorges, rocky outcrops, and sandy plains of the dry outback, Australia has a wealth of natural wonders. Unique plants and animals have evolved on this ancient continent and its surrounding islands since they were isolated by sea from the mega-continent of Gondwana more than 50 million years ago. Today's distinctive flora and fauna, including the eucalypts, have developed over the millennia on a continent once completely covered in rainforest. Fortunately for the traveller, many of Australia's best parks and reserves are easily accessible. Within the boundaries of major towns and cities are many parks, gardens and bushland reserves that give the short-term visitor a good overall picture of Australia's plants and animals. Less than an hour's drive from state capitals are superb scenery and diverse ecosystems ranging from coastal heathlands and riverine estuaries to mountain forests. Even many World Heritage-listed places, such as Fraser Island, are not far off the beaten path. A variety of animals can be seen in the wild and there are any number of quality wildlife parks and zoos with koalas, kangaroos, dingoes, wombats, emus, crocodiles (and more) on view.

EUCALYPTS AND FIRE

Eucalypts, known as gum trees, are the most common trees in Australia. Consisting of more than 500 species, they once thrived in rainforests and developed a resistance to fire through aeons of natural and man-made conflagrations. When managed fires lit by the Aboriginals ceased, the land was cleared and settled and the remaining forests were protected as timber reserves and national parks. Fire was generally excluded and fuel levels often built to intolerable levels. While regular controlled burning has reduced the risk, each year there are hundreds of major bushfire outbreaks caused by lightning strikes or careless humans. Even cities may be ringed by fires, and water-bombing aircraft are used to save life and property.

Clockwise from above *Anglesea Golf Club, Victoria, is famous for its large population of kangaroos; A termite mound on the plains of Old Mornington, in the Kimberley; Cane toads are an introduced pest*

CROCODILE ATTACKS

Crocodiles have been a protected species in Australia since 1971, and, as a result, numbers have increased dramatically in parts of northern Australia in recent years. So who would ignore prominent signs warning against swimming in crocodile-infested waters? And who would swim at night? Kakadu National Park tour leaders, apparently.

When a 24-year-old German tourist, swimming in a waterhole with her tour group, was killed by a crocodile in 2002, she was a victim of complacency. Witnesses heard her scream and she vanished beneath the water. Next day, rangers found the offending 4m (13ft) croc about 2km (1 mile) up river and harpooned it. Since 2000, ten people have been killed by crocodiles.

TASMANIAN TIGERS

Naturalists have concluded that when the last known thylacine, or Tasmanian tiger, died in a Hobart zoo in 1936, it was the end of the line for a unique family of carnivorous marsupials that had lived in Australia for millions of years. The 1.5m (5ft) thylacine was native to Tasmania, but existed on the mainland before becoming extinct there thousands of years ago. Common even around the beginning of the 20th century, thylacines were hunted to extinction in Tasmania because they were a threat to sheep. Or are they extinct? The most recent possible sighting was in 1995, when a Parks and Wildlife Service officer thought he saw one in the east of the state, but there are about a dozen unconfirmed sightings each year. So watch this space.

FRASER ISLAND

Mass tourism is not without its problems. When Fraser Island, the world's largest sand island, was added to the World Heritage register in 1992, unique rainforests and half the world's perched freshwater lakes received permanent protection.

Also preserved were cliffs of coloured sands, mangroves and coastal heathlands, as well as eastern Australia's purest population of dingoes. For the dingoes, increased visitor numbers meant more food to scavenge, and the visitors were only too keen to feed 'tame' dingoes. All this came to a head when a nine-year-old boy was killed by dingoes in 2001; since then, dozens of dingoes have been shot by rangers.

The goal now is to find some compromise between the rights of the people who visit Fraser Island and the rights of these protected animals.

CANE TOADS

These amphibians, with a dry warty skin and poison glands, were introduced from Hawaii to Australia in 1935 to control scarab beetles that were infesting sugar cane fields. Cane toads have now spread from far northern New South Wales, across coastal and savanna Queensland, to Western Australia. Although they have poisoned many native animals that have tried to eat them, there is evidence that animals are adapting to their presence, and their menace status is somewhat over-rated. The toads average 10–15cm (4–6in) in length, with one female measuring a record 24cm (9.5in), and their habitats range from sand dunes and coastal heath to rainforest and mangrove margins. However, they are most abundant in open clearings in urban areas where artificial lighting attracts plenty of insects.

MONKEY MIA

Shark Bay, 850km (530 miles) north of Perth, is one of only a handful of regions in the world to meet all four criteria for World Heritage listing. In the shallow waters of the Shark Bay Marine Park, with its abundant marine life and vast seagrass meadows, where dugong graze and manta rays, turtles and whales come in to feed, are the dolphins of Monkey Mia, which visit the beach each morning to interact with visitors. They are fed freshly caught local fish under the strict supervision of national park rangers. Since these are wild animals that must support themselves, no more than one-third of each dolphin's daily food requirement is provided, but visitors are surprised when they sometimes get offered fish that the dolphins themselves have caught!

THE ENDANGERED CASSOWARY

Perhaps fewer than 1,000 of the southern cassowary remain in the wild. An adult bird can be up to 1.5m (5ft) tall and has a coarse, black plumage that contrasts with the distinctive red and blue neck.

Cassowaries range from Paluma, north of Townsville, to north of Cairns. The heavier, taller female bird is the dominant sex, and the male incubates the eggs and rears the chicks for between 9 to 12 months.

While cassowaries have a measure of protection under World Heritage listing, attacks by domestic dogs, hits by speeding motor vehicles and the clearing of adjacent habitats are pushing this flightless bird towards extinction. As the gene pool shrinks, so does their chance of survival in the wild.

BIRDING IN THE CITY

There are many large parks in urban Australia where you can watch birds. Birds congregate in logical places, so look for them around water areas on a hot day, flowering trees and shrubs, and even places where humans are likely to feed them, such as at the seaside.

Willie wagtails are very common, and can be seen chasing other birds away from their nests. Flowering eucalypts soon attract screeching rainbow lorikeets, and the shrill cry of the sulphur-crested cockatoo is commonly heard in urban areas. Perhaps the most common sound in the early morning, the loud laughing call of the kookaburra, signals the start of the day for these scavenging birds. Watch out, though—they're liable to steal food from your picnic!

WORLD HERITAGE AUSTRALIA

Australia's natural heritage is recognized by 17 UNESCO World Heritage listings. Queensland's Great Barrier Reef, Wet Tropics rainforests, Riversleigh fossil fields and Fraser Island are all listed. The subtropical rainforests of the Lamington Plateau, in southern Queensland, are part of the Central Eastern Rainforest Reserves that extend into New South Wales. West of Sydney is the Greater Blue Mountains Area, and in southwest New South Wales is the Willandra Lakes Region Aboriginal cultural site. The Tasmanian Wilderness has rugged mountain scenery. Seagrass meadows mark Shark Bay in Western Australia, and Purnululu National Park in the same state contains the Bungle Bungle Range. Kakadu National Park and Uluru (Ayers Rock) are in the Northern Territory. The iconic Sydney Opera House joined the list in 2007.

Above *Hardy Reef is part of the Great Barrier Reef*
Opposite *Aboriginal rock painting at Nourlangie Rock in Kakadu National Park*

THE STORY OF AUSTRALIA

At the time of white settlement, the Aborigines of Australia did not form a unified cultural entity, as has been reported for nearly two centuries. Rather, they lived across a series of distinct, complex societies, which incorporated at least 600 language groups and employed a variety of technologies and cultural practices. The first Australians crossed over to the northern part of the continent from Indonesia around 70,000 years ago, an estimation confirmed by the 60,000-year-old remains found at the World Heritage-listed Mungo site in outback New South Wales. As the population increased, small family groups began to scatter in search of new hunting grounds, settling most of the continent within 2,000 or 3,000 years, but leaving the harsh desert lands of the interior until last. Most groups lived a semi-nomadic, hunter-gatherer lifestyle, but each employed distinct survival techniques in response to the environmental conditions of the area they occupied. Spiritual belief and tribal law were also directly influenced by the specifics of the landscape, which led to great cultural diversity. Trade, inter-marriage and a complex web of family relationships maintained contact between different groups. Around 5,000 years ago, some groups began refining their food-gathering techniques to include the building of fish traps, the use of harvesting techniques and the processing of some foods to remove toxins.

DREAMTIME
The Dreamtime refers to the creation period of Aboriginal spiritual belief. Stories of the Dreamtime vary greatly, but the notion of an Ancestral Spirit is a common thread. For the tribes of the southeast corner of the continent, this figure was known as Bunjil—also Baiami, Nurelli and Nurrundere depending on the region. During the Dreamtime, Bunjil, with the aid of other spirits, created the landscape, its vegetation and animals, as well as the people, their laws and religion. He then ascended to the heavens, where he lives as a star. In a rock shelter in the Grampians in central Victoria, there is a painted image of Bunjil: It shows a human-like figure with two dingoes and is said to be an impression left by the spirit when he squatted down to rest.

Clockwise from above *Traditional subsistence—kangaroo hunting; grass trees in central Australia; the face of one of the last-surviving Aboriginal Tasmanians*

LIFESTYLES IN VICTORIA

The Gunditjmara people of Lake Condah, Victoria, enjoyed a fairly stable existence. They had a plentiful supply of fresh fish, which they caught by building traps and engineering canals. Because they did not have to move often to find food, they built stone houses and lived in permanent settlements. By contrast, the Jaitmathang, who lived in the Victorian Alps, moved in accordance with the seasonal availability of food resources. They built small huts made of stringybark that could be erected quickly to provide some protection from the cold. Bogong moths—large, fleshy creatures—were an important food source and bogong-feasting ceremonies, which involved hundreds of people from a number of clans, were held regularly.

RELATIONSHIP WITH THE LAND

Aboriginal people were —and still are—linked to their land by powerful stories. These serve to mark out territory, advise on the availability of resources, chart routes through deserts, and preach caution and conservation. From the Adnyamathanha people of the Flinders Ranges in South Australia comes a tale about the creation of the region's spiky grass trees around the chasms of Weetooltla Creek. A greedy woman was climbing high on the rocks looking for arta, the edible substance at the core of the plant. She fell and was dashed to pieces on the rocks. These pieces became the spiky flares of these distinctive grass trees—and a permanent reminder of the need to take care while negotiating a dangerous landscape.

ROCK ART

At the Ubirr Art Site in Kakadu National Park, one of the largest repositories of rock art in Australia—if not the world—is a representation of the wily Namarrgarn Sisters. They are depicted pulling apart taut pieces of string, which, according to the Gundjeihmi people of the region, they used as a means of sending down sickness into people's bodies. There is a tale told about them that is used to warn children against the dangers of crocodiles. One sister turned herself into a crocodile as a joke. The other tried it as well, and soon they both decided to become crocodiles permanently so that they could eat anyone at any time. The palms that are found around the springs in the area grew from the teeth the 'crocodile' sisters pulled from their mouths.

THE PALAWA

Tasmania's Aboriginal people, descendants of mainland Aborigines, are known as Palawa. They migrated to the island some 35,000 years ago. At the time of European settlement it had a population of more than 4,000.

In the early 1830s, George Augustus Robinson sent the last 130 tribal Aborigines to the bleak shores of Flinders Island, in the Bass Strait, for their own 'protection'. In 1847 the 47 survivors were relocated to Oyster Cove, near Hobart. The last full-blood Aborigine, Truganini, died in 1876, but many mixed-race descendants of Aborigines and white seal hunters from the Bass Strait islands lived on. In recent years, they have asserted their heritage and, controversially, the right to make claims on land in Tasmania.

Australia existed as a place in the imagination for many centuries before it was discovered. The ancient Greeks referred to an unknown continent called Utopia of the South, and Chinese classics described a mythical southern land with black pygmies. Before the earth was known to be round, cartographers based their knowledge about the existence of a great southern mass on the fact that the disk-like earth would surely tip over if there were not something there to balance the great bulky continents of the north. Dutch colonization of the East Indies opened the way to discovery by accident more than design: Ships blown off course on the voyage to Java sighted land, and some were wrecked on the coast of Nova Holland. Between 1642 and 1644 Dutchman Abel Tasman charted large parts of what had become known as New Holland. In the late 17th century, the Englishman William Dampier explored and partially mapped the northwest coast of the continent. In the late 18th century British strategists made the discovery of the southern land a priority, convinced as they were that they would find a continent larger than Asia supporting a population of 50 million, and that subsequent colonization of such a place would give them trade advantages over other European nations.

Clockwise from above *The replica of* The Bounty *in Campbell's Cove, Sydney; statue of Captain Cook in Sydney; early map of Botany Bay*

THE COMING OF COOK

In 1768, the British government gave Lieutenant James Cook (1728–79) command of the *Endeavour*. His goals were to chart the transit of Venus and establish the eastern extent of the great southern land, which was still very much the subject of speculation in the scientific community.

Despite the scientific nature of the mission, political and strategic interests were at work. Cook, on finding the coast, made contact with the Aboriginal inhabitants, described plants and animals, named prominent features and laid down charts. Then, at a flag-raising ceremony at Botany Bay in April 1770, he claimed the entire east coast on behalf of King George III and the British Empire.

TRANSPORTATION TO A PENAL COLONY

In the 18th century, poverty, harsh laws and the imposition of long prison sentences created a chronic shortage of space in the prisons of Britain. In May 1787, under the command of Admiral Arthur Phillip, the First Fleet, comprising 11 ships carrying 1,487 people—759 of them convicts—set sail. They set up camp on the shores of what would come to be known as Sydney Harbour which, according to Phillip, was 'one of the finest harbours in the world'. Despite Phillip's upbeat assessment, the landscape was thought universally appalling by all who landed there, with one officer moved to comment: 'In the whole world there is not a worse country than what we have seen of this.' The alien nature of the landscape was to prove a deterrent to escape, and no jails were built for many years.

CLAIMING THE CONTINENT

Fear that the French and Dutch would come and claim a piece of the vast Antipodean continent forced the British into some pre-emptive colonial action, which included the establishment of a penal settlement in Van Diemen's Land, later Tasmania, in 1803.

Over the next 50 years, approximately 60,000 convicts—more than a third of Australia's convicts—were sent to this remote, chilly place, which soon gained a reputation for violence and lawlessness.

Many prisoners worked on buildings and infrastructure, examples of which survive. From 1830, re-offending prisoners from other prison colonies were housed in the dreaded confines at Port Arthur, the sandstone ruins of which stand today in eerie splendour overlooking the Tasman Sea.

CIVILIZING THE COLONY

Governor Lachlan Macquarie ruled the colony from 1808 to 1821. Along with his wife Elizabeth, he made an unprecedented attempt to transform a rough and ready prison colony into an ordered, elegant and benevolent society. He opened up new lands, established villages, set aside land for parks and commissioned fine public buildings in the belief that quality architecture would raise the moral tone of the community.

In his belief that men were basically good, he treated the convicts with fairness and compassion. But this attitude annoyed the wealthy settlers whose prosperity depended upon a compliant convict workforce. They lobbied England and Macquarie was eventually recalled after an unfavourable inquiry into his administration.

EXPLORING THE INTERIOR

The colonists, driven by curiosity and a greed for grazing land, set out to explore and claim the vast interior. Despite successes, the explorers who failed have had the strongest hold on the popular imagination, and none more so than Burke and Wills. These two, along with a large party and too much equipment of the wrong kind, set out in 1860 to cross the continent from south to north. They came within several kilometres of the north coast, but turned back thinking that it was much farther away than it was. They made the 1,600km (992-mile) journey back to base camp only to find that the party, after many patient months, had packed up and departed that morning. They eventually perished, but not before rejecting offers of help from Aborigines.

WHITE SETTLEMENT 1825–1900

When Captain Cook's botanist, Sir Joseph Banks, proposed the east coast of Australia as an ideal place for a penal colony, he felt confident enough about his recommendation to say 'if the people formed among themselves a Civil Government, they would necessarily increase'. Banks's hope that something good could emerge from what must have been one of the most unpromising beginnings of any nation, bore fruit. The British government played its part, not just by sending more prisoners and some fairly eccentric characters to govern them, but with its programme of assisted immigration. From 1832 money raised from the sale of colonial land paid the passages of emigrants from the British Isles. Preference was given to skilled workers, farm workers and single women. The colonies obtained much-needed labour and the mother country was relieved of some 'surplus' population. The other factors at work were a mix of design and good luck. The success of various agricultural pursuits, particularly sheep farming, the phenomenon of the gold rush, and the development of an identifiable national character—pioneering, hardy and humorous—all helped to ensure that, by the 1860s, Australia—then consisting of six colonies—was not only functioning economically, but flourishing socially and politically as well.

Clockwise from above *Rippon Lea Estate in Elsternwick, Victoria; bushranger Ned Kelly fights the law, 1878; panning for gold at Sovereign Hill, Ballarat.*

CONVICT LEGACY

The 160,000 or so convicts transported to Australia formed a mixed bag. Some were career criminals of the lower orders; some considered themselves political prisoners; and others were skilled professionals. In the last category was Francis Greenway, an architect whose legacy is the Georgian colonial buildings that survive in and around Sydney. He was convicted of forgery in 1814 and transported to Australia for a 14-year term. He designed some 40 buildings, including St. James Church and the Hyde Park Barracks in central Sydney. Governor Macquarie pardoned him in 1819. His image has appeared on one of the notes of the national currency, which may make him the only convicted forger in history to have enjoyed such an honour.

THE FATE OF THE ABORIGINES

The losers in the Australian story of this period were the Aboriginal peoples of the continent. Many died as a result of exposure to disease and alcohol. And some were killed by whites in a series of massacres.

The most infamous massacre took place in June 1838 at Myall Creek in western New South Wales, when 12 men killed 28 Aborigines. Unusually, the perpetrators were rounded up and charged.

The trial generated great public interest and opinion was sharply divided. Many agreed with the official line of the defence—that the killing of Aborigines did not constitute a crime. Others were outraged at the barbarity of the massacre— the victims included women and very young children. Seven of the men were convicted and hanged.

A CITIZEN OF THE COLONY

William Charles Wentworth personified the ideals of early Australian society. Born in 1790, two years after the first settlement, he was the son of a convict mother and surgeon father. In 1813, he was one of a team of three to cross the Blue Mountains, opening up valuable grazing land beyond. He married Sarah Cox, also of convict stock, with whom he already had a number of children. He became wealthy and set his large family up on an estate at Vaucluse (now open to the public). Despite his assets, Wentworth and his wife had a tenuous relation with Sydney society, which tended to cling to propriety and the prejudices of class. He was a passionate advocate of the independence of the colonies, long before it was a fashionable cause.

GOLDEN AGE

The discovery of gold in 1851 transformed the colonies. Thousands came from all around the world, and the population of the region exploded. In Melbourne and central Victoria, the first area where gold prospectors congregated, ornate public buildings and lush parklands began to grace previously functional streetscapes.

An armed insurrection occurred on the goldfields when, in 1854, miners led by Peter Lalor rose up against the inequities of laws governing mining fees—34 miners and 6 soldiers were killed in what is now known as the Eureka Uprising. The ringleaders were brought to trial for high treason, but public opinion and the press were on their side and they were acquitted.

Shortly after the uprising, the licensing system was reformed. The events of the time marked the beginning of the end of colonial rule and the birth of the myth of the Australian sense of 'a fair go'.

BUSHRANGERS

Bushrangers were both feared and admired in the 19th century. Some, like Mad Dan Morgan, were vicious criminals; others, like Ned Kelly, were maverick youths with social ideals. Of the more benign variety was Martin Cash. Known as the 'Gentleman Bushranger', he came from Ireland as a convict in 1827. Sentenced for property crimes in Australia, he was sent to the supposedly escape-proof Port Arthur, from which he escaped with two colleagues. Charged with murdering a policeman, he was sentenced to hang. Escape this time came in the form of a reprieve, just an hour before his date with death; rumour had it that the good matrons of the colony lobbied hard on behalf of this notorious ladies' man. Sentenced to the grim penal colony of Norfolk Island, he became a reformed character and, on his release, wrote a bestseller dealing with his adventures on the wrong side of the law.

THE COMING NATION 1901–1945

Australia's transition from penal colony, to a free, democratic society has been relatively untroubled. In 1856 all the Australian colonies—except Western Australia, which waited until 1893—received bicameral legislatures. Legislative Assemblies (the lower houses) were elected. Legislative Councils (upper houses), seen as a bulwark against democratic excesses, were elected on a high property franchise in Tasmania, South Australia and Victoria; in New South Wales and later Queensland the governor appointed members for life. The British government retained the right to veto legislation. The need for uniform immigration and tariff legislation, concerns about threats from Germany and Japan to the north, and a desire on the part of many to be free from the British and self-determining as a nation, were the driving forces behind the federation movement. The foundation of the Australian Labor Party in 1891, and the rise of the coalition parties of the right to defend the propertied classes against threats of socialism, established the present two-party system. Newly federated in 1901, Australia had the capacity and fortitude to take on the challenges of the first half of the 20th century: the Great Depression, two world wars, enormous social change and the continuing challenge of nation building.

Clockwise from above *Colonies to country—politicians gather in 1890 for Melbourne's Australasian Federation Conference; women begin to stand out in Victorian society; Australia's war dead are honoured at the Cenotaph in Martin Place, Sydney*

FEDERATION

Visionaries began advocating a union of the Australian colonies in the 1840s. In 1889 the New South Wales premier, Henry Parkes, made a strong case for federation, saying that 'what the Americans had done by war, the Australians could bring about in peace without breaking the ties that held them to the mother country'. Voters from the six separate self-governing colonies of New South Wales, Queensland, Victoria, Tasmania, South Australia and Western Australia accepted federation through a referendum held in 1899. In January 1901 the governor general proclaimed the Commonwealth of Australia in Centennial Park in Sydney. As fireworks exploded, crowds gathered to celebrate the newest nation on earth.

THE OTHER HALF

The much-vaunted egalitarianism of the Australian bush and the gold fields did not apply to women. Admiration for women was conditional on their remaining uncomplaining as they bore large numbers of children in extraordinarily isolated circumstances. But when a feminist voice emerged, it was loud and effective. South Australia gave women the vote in 1894—only the second province in the world to do so. Prominent feminists emerged into the public sphere, including the indomitable Vida Goldstein, who rose to national prominence as a campaigner for women's rights and better working conditions (in 1894, New South Wales's 90,000 female breadwinners earned half what their male counterparts did). Women voted for the first time federally in 1903, but it was not until 1921 that the first woman, Edith Cowan, was elected to an Australian parliament.

THE ANZAC TRADITION

The Allied landings at Gallipoli on 25 April 1915 have come to be regarded as the symbolic beginning of Australian nationhood. Stories about the Australian and New Zealand Army Corp (Anzac) have a greater hold on the collective imagination than do the events of settlement or federation.

Under what is now seen as flawed British command, 2,000 of the 16,000 men who landed on that first day were killed—a devastating number given the countries' small populations.

Among the heroes of the campaign was stretcher bearer John Simpson Kirkpatrick, a former cane cutter and miner. Using a donkey, he rescued hundreds of injured soldiers at the frontline and delivered them back to the beach for evacuation. Over a period of three-and-a-half weeks he continued his life-saving efforts until he too was shot and killed. In total, 60,000 Australian men and women died in World War I.

DEPRESSION RELIEF

The construction of the Sydney Harbour Bridge, one of the symbols of modern Australia, provided some relief from the economic depression of the early 1930s. It was designed by John Bradfield and employed 1,400 workers. Its massive 503m (1,650ft) steel arch earned it the nickname 'coathanger'. The project, although popular, was also controversial: In the working-class Rocks district 800 homes were destroyed to make way for the structure; 16 workers died in accidents; and country people complained that the bridge was a symbol of the 'vampire city…sucking the life-blood out of the country'. The 1932 opening ceremony was disrupted when a disgruntled right-wing royalist rode in on horseback and cut the ribbon ahead of the left-wing premier Jack Lang.

INVASION

Australia joined the European war in 1939, but resources were soon redeployed closer to home in response to Japanese aggression. In 1942, Australia came close to being invaded. The country's most remote and northerly city, Darwin, had become a strategic naval, air and supply base.

On 19 February 1942, 200 Japanese planes flew towards the city. A priest on Bathurst Island saw the planes overhead and made frantic radio calls to the air force, but these were ignored. In that first attack, 240 people were killed, ships were sunk and almost every Allied plane was destroyed.

During 1942 and 1943 some 60 more raids took place, by which time much of the civilian population had decamped to the bush or southern cities.

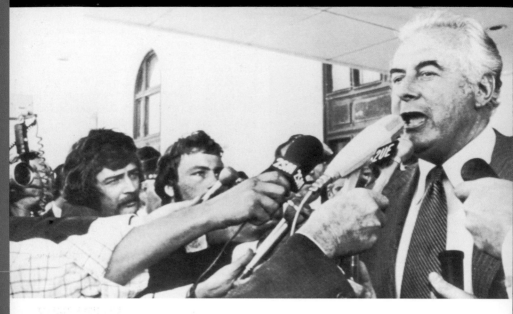

During the 1930s, immigration had virtually ceased and the birth rate had fallen to the lowest level in Australia's history. But war in the Pacific brought home the threat of invasion, and by the war's end, everyone from Halls Creek to Hobart knew that Australia, with its population of 7.5 million, had no hope of defending an area the size of Europe and bordered by a coastline of nearly 60,000km (37,200 miles). Under the guidance of former engine driver Joseph Chifley, prime minister from 1945 to 1949, the catchcry was 'populate or perish' and a massive immigration programme was put in place. The economy expanded as governments initiated large national projects to keep pace with the growing population. Of these, none was bigger than the Snowy Mountains Hydro-Electric Scheme, which diverted water inland to power generating stations and employed large numbers of newly arrived migrants. Despite the almost visionary economic and political developments that were taking place, mainstream society for the first 30 years after the war was deeply conservative: Governments banned unsuitable books, the Communist Party was very nearly voted out of existence, women left their jobs when they married, black people were barred from rural swimming pools. When change came, which it did in 1972 with the election of Gough Whitlam, it was radical and wide-ranging.

WHITE AUSTRALIA

An official 'White Australia Policy' was introduced in 1901. The government could exclude non-white or undesirable immigrants by using a dictation test in an unfamiliar European language. In 1934, a left-wing Czech writer took the government to the High Court when he was set a test in Scottish Gaelic. After World War II Australia had no choice but to relax its 'standards'. In 1947 it signed an agreement to take displaced persons from European camps, and by 1968 more than 800,000 non-English-speaking Europeans were living a version of the Australian dream. At first non-whites were not among them but the notion of 'White Australia' was gradually abandoned, and by the early 1970s the country was ready to receive refugees from war-torn southeast Asia.

Clockwise from above *Prime Minister Gough Whitlam addresses reporters after his dismissal by the Governor-General in 1975; new power—the Murray 1 hydroelectric power station in the Snowy Mountains; Italian migrants arrive in Sydney in 1956*

COMMUNISM AT HOME AND ABROAD

Australia was gripped by anti-communist fever in the 1950s and 1960s, but not always to a point that defied reason. In 1951, the conservative Prime Minister, Robert Menzies, attempted to ban the Communist Party. A referendum was held and the 'no' vote won by a narrow 53 per cent. A disgruntled Menzies claimed the people had been 'misled by a wicked and unscrupulous "No" campaign'.

Anti-communism helped convince Australians to join America's war in Vietnam, but US power to motivate public opinion wore thin. The realities of conscription—64,000 young men were conscripted and 15,000 were actually deployed—the seeming futility, if not abject failure, of the Vietnam campaign, and the growing divisions on the domestic front, convinced Australians that communist aggressors in foreign places were a low priority.

'IT'S TIME'

In 1972 Australia voted in Gough Whitlam and his Labor government, thereby ending 23 years of conservative rule. Whitlam's tenure was brief but spectacular. He granted recognition to China, abolished conscription, ended Australia's involvement in Vietnam, ran inquiries into Aboriginal land rights, legislated for equal pay for both sexes and pensions for single mothers, created a universal health-care system and introduced free tertiary education. His radical programme was thwarted by a hostile Senate and undermined by incompetence in his government. When the Senate blocked essential legislation in 1975, the Governor-General, John Kerr, sacked Whitlam and appointed the opposition leader to head an interim government. Despite the unpopularity of the move, and the subsequent demonizing of Kerr, Whitlam was defeated at the polls one month later.

INDIGENOUS AFFAIRS

In a referendum in 1967, 90 per cent of white Australia voted to count Aboriginal people—Australia's first inhabitants—as Australian citizens, a right that had previously been denied them. Despite the benevolence of the result, the fact that such a referendum was necessary speaks of the sorry history of white–black relations. Since the 1970s, land rights for Aboriginal people has been seen as a positive way forward, and court decisions of the 1990s opened the way for vast tracts of Crown land to be transferred to traditional owners. But it remains to be seen whether native title will enable remote Aboriginal communities to find salvation in closer economic and spiritual ties with traditional lands, and thus overcome two centuries of discrimination and dispossession.

ENVIRONMENTALISM

Since 1788, a common attitude towards the environment has been 'if it moves, shoot it, if it doesn't, cut it down'—a not untypical pioneer sentiment.

The battle for the Franklin River marked a shift in the nation's green consciousness. In the late 1970s the Tasmanian government decided to dam the mighty Franklin to generate electricity. Conservationists swung into action: They targeted government seats, ran a non-violent blockade, and argued that there was no economic need for the massive project.

Hearing the publicity, Australians who had rarely taken a walk in the bush now began discussing the ecological value of old-growth forests. The issue was resolved in the High Court and the area is now protected as a World Heritage Site.

INTO THE 21ST CENTURY

Australia's population grew from 7.6 million in 1947 to 22 million in 2009, mainly through immigration. Those born overseas account for more than a quarter of the population and are drawn from over 100 different countries; they have contributed greatly to the cultural diversity of the nation. With the exception of Canberra, all major Australian cities are located on the coast; Australians holiday on the coast, retire there and engage in fantasies about dropping out of mainstream society and leading a simple life in Byron, Broulee or Barwon Heads. At the beginning of the 21st century, Australians are starting to look beyond life in the suburbs to the long-neglected inner city. A great trading nation, Australia had a painful period of adjustment to economic rationalism and deregulation during the early 1990s. More recently, Australia's vast mineral and agricultural resources have underwritten its prosperity.

Above *Café culture in Sydney Harbour*

CULTURED EXPORT

One of Australia's best-known characters is Barry Humphries. An actor and comedian of exceptional talent, he has long conquered British audiences and, more recently, persuaded a hitherto mystified American public to love his alter-ego character, suburban Melbourne housewife and mega-star Dame Edna Everage.

Dame Edna made her stage debut in a rural Australian town in 1955, and now, more than 50 years later, she is dazzling audiences, physically and metaphorically, all round the world.

Dame Edna's official website claims her to be 'probably the most popular and gifted woman in the world today: housewife, investigative journalist, social anthropologist, talk show host, swami, children's book illustrator, spin doctor, Megastar, and Icon'.

THINKING GLOBALLY, ACTING LOCALLY

Australians like to think of themselves as environmentally aware, and are concerned that their huge southern continent doesn't suffer further species extinction. When national icons such as rainforests, coastlands, and wilderness areas come under pressure from developers, or when nuclear power is proposed, thousands take to the streets in protest. While a conservative government failed to ratify the Kyoto Protocol in 1997, when the Labor Party came to power in 2007, the new leader, Kevin Rudd, signed the document. In June 2010 Rudd stepped aside and was succeeded by Julia Gillard, the first woman to lead Australia. Gillard continued to ensure that environmental issues were high up on the agenda when she formed a coalition government after an election in August 2010.

ON THE MOVE

On the Move gives you detailed advice and information about the various options for travelling to Australia before explaining the best ways to get around the country once you are there. Handy tips help you with everything from buying tickets to renting a car.

ARRIVING

FLYING TO AUSTRALIA

Australia's national carrier is Qantas. Many other international airlines fly to the state capitals, including British Airways (which shares schedules with Qantas), Singapore Airlines, Malaysia Airlines and Cathay Pacific. Qantas, Jetstar, Tiger Airways and Virgin Blue provide domestic flights.

STOPOVERS

You can plan your trip independently with the help of travel guides, brochures and the internet, or online travel specialists such as Travelbag in the UK (www.travelbag.co.uk) can provide a tailored itinerary and arrange stopovers.

A stopover on a long-haul flight can be a good idea: The additional cost is usually not great, and the break helps you to get used to the new time zone. Popular choices for travellers to Australia are Bangkok, Singapore and Hong Kong.

If you know of a hotel you want to stay at, you can arrange your stopover direct by phone or

ARRIVAL AIRPORTS

AIRPORT	LOCATION	TRAIN	BUS/COACH
Sydney	9km (5.5 miles) S of city centre	Airport to Central Station (15 min); every 15 min Mon–Thu 5am–12am, Fri–Sun 5am–1am adult one-way A$15.20	Airporter (tel 02 9666 9988) to hotels in Darling Harbour, Kings Cross, city centre (A$12.60)
Melbourne	25km (15.5 miles) NW of city centre	None	Skybus (tel 03 9670 7992) to Spencer Street Station; every 30 min 6am–12am, hourly 12am–6am. Adult one-way A$16
Brisbane	13km (8 miles) NE of city centre	Airport to Brisbane City Station (Airtrain; 22 min); adult one-way A$14.50. AirtrainConnect to the Gold Coast; every 30 min (72-min journey) A$26.60	Airport to city centre (tel 07 3358 9700); every 15 min 5am–7.30pm, every 30 min 7.30pm–10.45pm. Adult one-way A$14. Airport to the Gold Coast; daily every hour A$40. Airport to the Sunshine Coast; daily every 2 hours 6.10am–6.35pm A$48
Cairns	8km (5 miles) N of city centre	None	Australia Coach to city centre and hotels. Adult one-way A$10. Coral Coaches to Port Douglas. Adult one-way A$32
Perth	12km (7.5 miles) NE of city centre	None	Airport City Shuttle to city centre. Adult one-way A$20. Fremantle Airport Shuttle to hotels (tel 08 9335 1614). Adult one-way A$35

via the web, or you can ask your travel supplier to arrange it (you are not restricted to the hotels in a company's brochure).

Remember to check passport, visa and health requirements in the stopover country.

AIRPORT FACILITIES

All Australian airports offer the same general facilities to arrivals, though larger airports may provide a wider range. Expect the following services in the arrivals area:

» Accommodation information desk
» Automatic teller machines (ATMs)
» Currency exchange
» Duty-free and tax-free shopping
» Lost and found desk
» Luggage trolleys (usually free but sometimes a small charge of around A$3—coins needed)
» Pharmacy
» Porterage services
» Post office or mailbox
» Rental car agencies
» Shopping and refreshment facilities
» Taxi ranks
» Telephones
» Toilets and showers
» Tourist information
» Wheelchairs and assistance for disabled travellers—call the airport administration offices or your airline staff before travelling if you have special requirements.

AIRPORTS

Sydney

Terminal and transportation information is online at www.sydneyairport.com.au.

Transfers

» The international and domestic terminals are 1.6km (1 mile) apart—a shuttle bus operates between them.
» A train station at the airport provides a fast, easy way of getting to the city, although the suburban trains used for this service are far from luggage-friendly.
» A single-journey ticket takes you to Central Station (15 minutes), where you can change trains if you are staying in the suburbs. Tickets for multiple journeys are also available. Tickets can be used on other forms of transport, including the Manly ferry (▷ 56).
» Leaving the airport by car is simple; it is a straight run into the city and the entire route is clearly marked.

Melbourne

The airport's efficient website (www.melair.com.au) has an interactive map of the airport.

Transfers

» Airport shuttle buses: For information or to arrange a hotel pick-up, tel 03 9670 7992.
» Taxis are metered and, while negotiation is uncommon, drivers may be happy to agree a fare in advance. Fares to the city are publicized as being A$50, but this can rise to A$65 with GST and a surcharge for paying by credit card. Automatic tolls are in operation along the City Link and these are reflected in the taxi fare. Pre-booking a taxi incurs a A$3.00 booking fee, and departing passengers must pay a A$2 taxi parking fee.
» Maps are available at the airport to help drivers going into Melbourne. The best route from the airport to the city is the City Link freeway. Follow signs from the airport to City Link, then after the Bolte Bridge take the left-hand lane and then one of the exits to the city (e.g. City Road exit). After leaving City Link follow the signs to the city centre.

City Link is a toll road and a City Link pass must be purchased before or after travelling. A City Link pass can be purchased before or up to midnight three days after travel; tel 13 26 29 for credit card purchases (A$12.40 for one day of unlimited travel). City Link passes can also be purchased from a post office. Failure to obtain a pass will incur a fine.

Brisbane

Brisbane has fast links to the Sunshine Coast in the north and the Gold Coast and northern NSW to the south, via the Gateway Arterial Highway. The website www.brisbaneairport.com.au is useful for checking arrivals and departures and internal flight planning.

Transfers

» The shuttle connecting the domestic and international terminals runs about every 15 minutes. It's free for airline ticket holders in transit, A$3.00 for non-travellers.
» For more general information on coach services call Coachtrans: tel 07 3258 9700.

USEFUL WEBSITES	
Qantas	www.qantas.com
British Airways	www.britishairways.com
Singapore Airlines	www.singaporeair.com
Malaysia Airlines	www.malaysiaairlines.com
Cathay Pacific	www.cathaypacific.com

TAXI	CAR
About A$40 to city centre; passengers pay road toll charges	South Dowling Street from airport to city centre
About A$55 to city centre; 30 min	Tullamarine Freeway from airport to city centre
About A$35 to city centre. About A$200 to Gold Coast. About A$325 to Noosa	Kingsford Smith Street from airport to city centre
About A$40 to city centre; 15 min. About 1 hour to Port Douglas: A$150	Sheridan Street from airport to city centre
About A$35 to the city centre; 30 min. About A$60 to Fremantle	Great Eastern Highway/Tonkin Highway from airport to city centre

» AirtrainConnect is a door-to-door rail service to accommodation on the Gold Coast. About every half-hour: adult A$26.60, child A$4.90.

» Passengers departing by taxi must pay an additional A$1 on top of the charge.

Cairns

All flights and terminal information can be found at www.cairnsport. com.au.

Transfers

» A five-minute walk along a covered walkway takes you from the international to the domestic terminal. Alternatively, a shuttle bus (Australia Coach) connects the two: cost A$2.

» Shuttles leave for Cairns from immediately in front of the arrivals area at both terminals.

» Most major hotels in Cairns provide a courtesy coach service to and from the airport—check with your hotel in advance.

Perth

The official website contains all the airport information: www.perthairport.com.au

Transfers

» In addition to the airport shuttle buses, Transperth routes 37 and 39 operate between the domestic terminal and Perth city centre: every half-hour during the day, hourly after 6pm and all day Sunday. Journey time about 35 minutes.

» If you drive into the city, all routes are well signed from the airport and traffic generally is light.

GOODS AND SERVICES TAX (GST)

Visitors to Australia can claim back Goods and Services Tax (GST) paid on items above A$300. A purchase must be made within 30 days of the date you are due to leave Australia.

» At Sydney Airport you can claim back GST on the spot in a designated refund booth (you will be given cash or a cheque which you can convert at one of the currency exchange facilities, or you can request a credit payment). The items in question must be available for inspection, so keep them in your hand luggage.

» For passengers departing Australia on international flights, all Australian airports offer GST-free (duty-free) shopping. The GST-free prices are at point of purchase—no paperwork, no minimum spend requirement.

» There are more than 2,000 shops in Australia that allow passengers departing on international flights to buy GST-free goods. More than 60 shops in The Rocks area in Sydney operate this system.

TAXI RANKS AND CAR RENTALS

	TAXI RANK	AVIS	CAR RENTAL BUDGET	HERTZ
Sydney	South end of International Terminal	13 63 33	1300 362 848	13 30 39
Melbourne (Tullamarine)	Arrivals ground floor level	13 63 33	1300 362 848	13 30 39
Brisbane	Domestic Terminal and Arrival Level 2 International Terminal	13 63 33	13 362 848	13 30 39
Cairns	Arrivals hall; free taxi phones in Arrivals hall	13 63 33	13 362 848	13 30 39
Perth	Outside Arrivals hall	13 63 33	13 362 848	13 30 39
		www.avis.com	www.budget.com	www.hertz.com

CRUISES

If you dislike flying, or simply wish to avoid jet lag, you may want to consider visiting Australia as part of a world cruise. Visitors arriving in Australia by air can still take advantage of the many cruises that call at the major cities, all of which are located on the coast. Trips range from the height of luxury on one of the largest liners, to a 'small ship' cruise. The choice is greatest around the Queensland coast and the Great Barrier Reef.

Cruises to Australia depart from many ports around the world, including Southampton, New York and Los Angeles; ports of call in Australia are frequently combined with Asian destinations. Cruise ships also ply the Tasman Sea between Australia and New Zealand. The website at www.cruisecritic.com provides useful background about many of the cruise lines, their ships and tips on life at sea.

P&O
Tel UK 0845 678 0014
USA +1 877-828-4728
For up-to-date information on P&O's Australian cruises, go to www.pocruises.com.au.
Example cruises:
Sydney–Auckland via Melbourne, Hobart, Milford Sound, Dunedin, Christchurch and Wellington (7 nights)
Sydney–Bangkok via Cairns, Darwin, Indonesia, Malaysia, Singapore and Vietnam (18 nights)

Cruise options and the following information are on the P&O websites (see above):
Accommodation; activities; booking; dining; dress code; embarkation; entertainment; facilities for children; health and fitness; luggage; money matters; prices; tours and hotels for shore visits; travel documents.

CUNARD
Tel Australia 02 13 24 41
UK 0845 071 0013
Germany +00 800 180 84 180
USA and Canada +1 800 728 6273
www.cunard.com
The following give an idea of some of the cruises available and the destinations that these luxury ships visit around the world.

World Cruise
Southampton–Southampton
Sea cruising and ports of call around Australia:
Tasman Sea; Auckland; Bay of Islands; Melbourne; Sydney; Brisbane; Cairns and Great Barrier Reef; Torres Strait; Arafura Sea; Darwin; Timor Sea.
Includes an overland excursion to Uluru (Ayers Rock)
Polynesian Cruise
Los Angeles–Sydney
Honolulu, Hawaii; Pacific Ocean; Papeete, Tahiti; Moorea, French Polynesia; Auckland; Bay of Islands; Melbourne; Tasman Sea; Sydney
Australian/Asian Cruise
Sydney–Hong Kong
Sydney; Brisbane; Great Barrier Reef; Cairns; Torres Strait; Arafura Sea; Darwin; Timor Sea; Flores Sea; Makassar Strait; Kota Kinabalu, Malaysia; South China Sea; Manila, Philippines; East China Sea; Nagasaki, Japan; Kobe, Japan; Taipei, Taiwan; Formosa Strait; Hong Kong

SMALL SHIP CRUISES
Captain Cook Cruises
Tel Australia 02 9206 1100
www.captaincook.com.au

This family-owned company runs a number of different cruises around Australia and the Fiji Islands, including:
Great Barrier Reef
Three, four or seven nights
Sydney Harbour
Daily, and two-night Weekend Explore cruise
Murray River
Three, four or seven nights, or weekend cruise (on 120-passenger paddlewheeler)
Fiji Islands
Three, four or seven nights
Fiji Sailing Safari
Three or four days, on a tall ship

Sunlover Cruises
Tel Australia 07 4050 1333, 1800 810 512
www.sunlover.com.au
Sunlover's reef cruises are centred around Cairns:
One-day Reef cruises
Two-day Reef and Rainforest cruise
Two-day Reef and Daintree Tour
Sunlover Cruises has links to Sunlover Helicopters, who offer one-day Fly and Cruise tours
Tel 07 4035 9669
www.sunloverheli.com.au

GETTING AROUND

INTERSTATE AIR TRAVEL

Most of Australia's tourist destinations are located in or near the coastal regions, among the large states, or are a great distance inland. Air travel between states or inland is often the best form of transport to make the best use of your available time.

Qantas, Jetstar, Tiger Airways and Virgin Blue operate a range of domestic flights to popular but remote destinations such as Alice Springs, Uluru, the far north and the Kimberley. There is also a wide choice of flights available up and down the length of the east coast, connecting the popular tourist attractions of Sydney, the Gold Coast and the Great Barrier Reef.

QANTAS/JETSTAR
Head Office and
Customer Relations:
Qantas Centre203 Coward Street
Mascot, NSW 2020
Tel 02 9691 3636
Information and reservations
within Australia: tel 13 13 13
Holiday packages: tel 13 14 15
www.qantas.com
www.jetstar.com.au

Qantas operates domestic flights within Australia—some under the Qantas banner, others under the company's no-frills brand, Jetstar. Holders of a Qantas international flight ticket can book the discounted Boomerang Pass for internal flights within Australia and New Zealand.

(The pass is also available when travelling with other airlines—check with your travel agent when booking.)
» Must be purchased before you depart.
» You must book a minimum of two or a maximum of 10 flights.
» Reductions apply for children.
» The Australian continent is divided into four zones for booking—a single fare entitles you to travel within one zone only; a multi-zone fare allows travel in further zones.
» Airpasses may save money off full fares, but cheaper, discounted local fares are often available.

Sample fares
When booked in the UK:

Single fare zone £110 per flight
Multi-fare zone £140 per flight

VIRGIN BLUE
Head Office (administration only):
PO Box 1034
Spring Hill
Brisbane, QLD 4000
www.virginblue.com.au
Information and reservations: tel
13 67 89
email: reservations@virginblue.
com.au
Group bookings (10 or more): tel
13 67 00

Virgin Blue operates no-frills flights throughout Australia. The emphasis is on booking by phone or online. The interactive map on the company's

website enables you to click on a destination and receive advice on how to get there.
» To find which of the airlines fly to your chosen destination, check the table below.

TIGER AIRWAYS
Head Office
Terminal 4, Tullamarine Airport, VIC 3045

Information and reservations: tel 03 9335 3033
www.tigerairways.com/au

» Tiger Airways is a Melbourne-based, low-cost airline operating flights to all Australian capitals, except Darwin, and a number of popular holiday spots.

Distance / flight chart:

From \ To	1	2	3	4	5	6	7	8	9	10
Adelaide (ADL)	305	215	505	135	330	500	110	315	150	550
Alice Springs (ASP)	455	230	245	155	500	235	330	255	055	
Brisbane (BNE)	215	155	410	425	220	525	130	500		
Cairns (CNS)	340	230	500	320	745	250	315			
Canberra (CBR)	545	245	100	535	045	500				
Darwin (DRW)	705	405	350	420	545					
Hobart (HBA)	110	550	150	705						
Melbourne (MEL)	400	120	500							
Perth (PER)	400	245								
Sydney (SYD)	325									
Uluru (AYQ)										

Distances (km):
1315
1619 1963
2130 1453 1390
969 1948 954 2074
2619 1305 2848 1673 3139
1170 2455 1789 2888 848 3739
640 1858 1379 2311 468 3130 616
2112 1976 3604 3429 3081 2650 3014 2698
1163 2018 751 1971 235 3152 1038 705 3279
1303 333 2216 1786 2072 1419 2473 1907 1643 2175

REGIONAL FLIGHTS

STATE	LOCATION	SYDNEY	MELBOURNE	BRISBANE	CAIRNS	PERTH	ADELAIDE
NSW	Albury	QS					
	Armidale	QS		QS	QS		
	Canberra ACT	QS, VB	QS, VB	QS, VB	VB	VB	QS, VB
	Coffs Harbour	QS, VB	VB	QS, VB			VB
	Sydney		QS, VB, JS, TA	QS	QS, VB, JS	QS, JS	
	Tamworth	QS					
VIC	Melbourne	QS, VB, JS, TA		QS, VB, JS, TA	QS, VB, JS	QS, JS, TA	QS, JS, TA
	Mildura		QS				
QLD	Brisbane	QS, VB, JS, TA	QS, VB, JS, TA		QS, VB, JS	QS, VB, TA	QS, VB, TA
	Cairns	QS, VB, JS	QS, VB, JS	QS, VB		VB	VB, JS
	Gold Coast	QS, VB, JS, TA	QS, VB, JS, TA	VB, JS, TA	QS, VB, JS	QS, VB, JS, TA	VB, JS, TA
	Longreach			QS			
	Mackay	VB, JS	QS, VB	VB, JS	QS	QS, VB	VB
	Mount Isa			QS			
	Rockhampton	VB, JS	VB	VB, JS			VB
	Roma			QS			
	Townsville	QS, VB, JS	VB, JS	QS, VB, JS		VB	VB
WA	Broome	QS, VB	QS, VB	QS, VB	QS, VB	QS, VB	QS, VB
	Kalgoorlie	QS	QS	QS	QS	QS	QS
	Perth	QS, VB	QS, VB	QS, VB	QS, VB		QS, VB
	Port Hedland	QS	QS	QS	QS	QS	QS
NT	Alice Springs	QS, VB, TA	QS, VB, TA	VB, TA	QS	QS, TA	QS, VB, TA
	Uluru (Ayers Rock)	QS	QS	QS	QS	QS	QS
	Darwin	QS, VB, JS	QS, VB, JS	QS, VB, JS	QS, VB, JS	QS, VB, JS	QS, VB
SA	Adelaide	QS, VB, JS, TA	QS, VB, JS, TA	QS, VB, JS, TA	QSVB, JS	QS, VB, JS	
TAS	Hobart	QS, VB	QS, VB, TA	QS, VB, TA		QS, VB, TA	QS, VB, TA
	Launceston	QS, VB, TA	QS, VB, TA			QS, VB, TA	QS, VB, TA

For a more leisurely and comfortable alternative to flying between the states, Australia's long-distance trains offer first- and economy-class compartments, sleeping berths and reclining seats.

Reservations are advisable: Bookings can be made up to nine months in advance, or when you arrive in Australia. The rail map at www.railaustralia.com.au highlights the route and extent of the main lines. (Note: There are no passenger trains in Tasmania.)

RAIL AUSTRALIA

PO Box 445
Marleston Business Centre
Marleston, SA 5033
Tel 08 8213 4592
email: reservations@railaustralia.
com.au, www.railaustralia.com.au

RAIL PASSES

An **Austrail** pass (best purchased outside Australia before you travel as it will be considerably cheaper— contact your travel agent) gives unlimited economy-class travel on rail networks and some coaches. The price is A$801 for six months unlimited travel on Traveltrain, Countrylink and Great Southern Rail Services.
www.traveltrain.com.au

A **Great Southern Railway Pass** allows six months of unlimited travel on the Indian Pacific, the Ghan and the Overland. Prices start from A$690, with reductions for students and backpackers.
Great Southern Railway Tel 13 21 47; www.gsr.com.au.

The **East Coast Discovery Pass** from CountryLink provides economy travel between Melbourne and Cairns. Significant reductions are available on many routes when you book at least 15 days in advance.
CountryLink Reservations
PO Box K349
Haymarket, NSW 1238
Tel 13 22 32
Germany +31 35 69 55 155
UK 08701 210 606
USA +1 310 643 0044 ext. 420;
www.countrylink.info

NEW SOUTH WALES

CountryLink (see above) is the long-distance passenger rail and coach operator for regional NSW, serving Canberra, Melbourne and Brisbane. Trains run from Sydney to Melbourne and Brisbane.

For information on routes, timetables and fares call at the CountryLink Travel Centre in the town where you are staying. Many are dedicated CountryLink offices; others are agencies within travel agents' offices.

VICTORIA

The Ghan covers 2,979km (1,847 miles) from Adelaide to Darwin.

This 53-hour trip is one of the great train journeys of the world. You can stop off at Alice Springs, which is 18 hours from Adelaide.
Tel 13 21 47; www.gsr.com.au

SOUTH AUSTRALIA

The **Overland** runs four times each week from Melbourne to Adelaide (10 hours), including a daytime service from Adelaide to Melbourne. Regional and interstate connections depart from Adelaide's Keswick terminal. Tel 13 21 47
www.trainways.com.au

WESTERN AUSTRALIA

The ocean-to-ocean 4,352km (2,698-mile) **Indian Pacific** route runs between Sydney and Perth via Adelaide, twice each week in each direction.

At 70 hours, this is one of the world's longest train journeys—a holiday in itself.
Tel 08 8213 4592, 13 21 47;
www.gsr.com.au

QUEENSLAND

The **Queenslander** follows a tropical, coastal route between Brisbane and Cairns (32 hours). Unlike any other journey in Australia, this is the one to choose if you want a mix of rainforests, coastal ranges and Pacific reef scenery.

Complete your journey to the north of Queensland with a trip on Queensland Rail's **Kuranda Scenic Railway** (▷ 177), with its station adorned with tropical plants.
www.railaustralia.com.au

The **Spirit of the Outback** combines part of the lush Queenslander coast route from Brisbane to Rockhampton with a journey through the harsh outback to Longreach—the best of both worlds (24 hours).

Queensland Rail
Tel 07 3235 1133, 1300 131 722;
www.traveltrain.qr.com.au

The modern *Tilt Train* runs not far from Queensland's coast between Brisbane and Cairns. The journey takes 25 hours and there are three trains each week, through the beautiful tropical scenery of north Queensland.

The 1,681km (1,042-mile) route has stops at all the major coastal cities, including Gympie, Maryborough, Bundaberg, Gladstone, Rockhampton, Mackay and Townsville.
Bookings: tel 1300 131 722;
www.traveltrain.qr.com.au

AUSTRALIAN CAPITAL TERRITORY

Canberra's train station (for interstate services only) is located to the south of the Parliament area, in Kingston. There are direct trains to Sydney, however, for trains to Melbourne you must first drive the 60km (37 miles) to the nearby town of Yass and take a train from there.

RENTING A VEHICLE

Australia has an enormous number of car rental firms offering new or used models. Daily rates are not high but many agreements are restricted to driving within a limited area; you may not be allowed to take the vehicle on unsealed (unmetalled) roads or beyond a particular town.

Rates may increase at peak holiday periods and you must expect to pay more for unlimited mileage. Also you may have an unpleasant surprise when you collect a 4WD vehicle or camper van—there will probably be a 'bond' to pay of several hundred dollars, which may not have been explained at the outset, plus 'government duty'.

RENTING
To rent a vehicle you must hold a current driving licence and, preferably, an International Driving Permit. These must be carried with you when you drive.

If you are a young or inexperienced driver, check the minimum requirements for age and driving experience before you travel; generally drivers must be 21 or over and must have held a licence for at least three years.

If you have any problems with a rental vehicle you must contact the rental company to arrange any breakdown assistance (▷ 46).

It is possible to collect a rental vehicle in one state and return it in another. This can be expensive, however, because the vehicle has to

be driven back to its state of origin (clearly known by the distinctive state number plates).
Sample rates for rentals
Small car: A$50–A$70 per day
Large car: A$70–A$90 per day
4WD: A$100–A$125 per day

Most car rental companies have deals with various associations whereby discounted rates are available for their affiliates. Travellers should investigate possible links to such associations.

RENTING A CAMPER VAN OR MOTORHOME (RV)
If you decide to 'go bush' during your holiday, a camper van or 4WD may be more appropriate to cope with country roads and the immense distances in greater comfort.

Camper vans and motorhomes are available for rent in all the states. All are equipped with cutlery and crockery, a range of cooking utensils, sleeping bags, pillows and towels, plus optional awnings. Some de luxe vehicles have showers and toilets.

Minimum rental period is usually seven days; savings are offered on rentals of three weeks or longer. There are restrictions concerning travel on unsealed roads and the contract may not cover unlimited mileage—important if you plan to cover a large distance.
Sample mid-season rates
Camper van 2/3 berth:
A$820–A$1,190 per week
Motorhome 4 berth:
A$1,180–A$1,500 per week
Motorhome 6 berth:
A$1,450–A$1,950 per week

Britz Australia specializes in tourist rental—their white, orange-banded vehicles often stand out in remote areas. Britz has depots in Sydney (NSW), Melbourne (VIC), Brisbane, Cairns (QLD), Alice Springs, Darwin (NT), Adelaide (SA), Broome, Perth (WA) and Hobart Airport (TAS).
Tel 1800 331 454, 03 8379 8890;
www.britz.com.au

Maui operates throughout Australia. Tel 1300 363 800;
www.maui-rentals.com

RENTING A MOTORCYCLE
Rental rates for motorcycles are between A$150–A$300 per day or A$600–A$1,600 per week, depending on engine size. A refundable credit card deposit of about A$2,500 is required.

You must have an International Motorcycle Licence. A helmet is compulsory; you can rent a helmet, gloves and wet/cold-weather gear.

GREY NOMADS
If you are touring in the north of Australia in 'winter', you may encounter 'grey nomads' or 'geriatric gypsies'—retired people from the cooler states who follow the sun throughout the year, gravitating north in winter. Campsite society is generally very congenial.

ROAD ROUTINE

People routinely drive great distances in Australia: It's not unusual to drive for an hour and a half just for a lunch engagement.

Most visitors adjust to the scale of the country and make the epic journeys part of their holiday.

Vehicles, private or rental, are geared to the road conditions. The majority are automatic and have air conditioning, which makes driving much more comfortable and allows you to keep windows closed when driving through dusty areas.

The main highways are straight sealed (metalled) roads and you can cover long distances reasonably quickly. Coastal and mountain roads can be winding. Roadhouses provide welcome comfort stops, and are usually sited about every 100km (62 miles). They supply most necessities, as well as fuel.

BREAKDOWN ASSISTANCE

The Australian Automobile Association (AAA) represents the seven state motoring organizations that provide roadside assistance. AAA is also a member of the Alliance Internationale de Tourisme (AIT), through which national motoring organizations assist each other's members. Check with your organization before travelling that they are a member of AIT. Whichever Australian state you are travelling in, call 13 11 11 for assistance. Remember to carry your organization's membership or road service card.

AAA

Tel 02 6247 7311;
www.aaa.asn.au

DRIVING ON UNSEALED ROADS

Travelling in remote parts of Australia often means driving on unsealed roads for long distances, and these involve special hazards. The main danger is that tyres have far less traction than on sealed roads. Wheels are more likely to lock up under brakes, which makes braking and cornering especially dangerous. Travel at a slower speed than you would on a sealed road, and avoid braking in corners. Another hazard is stones thrown up by the wheels of passing vehicles, which can shatter your windshield. Keep well clear of the rear of other vehicles travelling in the same direction. When another vehicle approaches from the opposite direction, pull to the left side of the road as far as practicable, and slow down.

DRIVING IN TASMANIA

Fuel is more expensive in Tasmania than in cities on the Australian mainland (typically 10–20c per litre more). In places like Strahan it can be 10c per litre more expensive again.
NB See table opposite to work out the distance in km (green) and estimated duration in hours and minutes (blue) of a car journey.

TIPS

» Before setting out on a long journey, ensure your vehicle is in top condition.
» Make sure you have a good, up-to-date map—a scale of at least 1:200,000 in built-up areas, and at least 1:1,000,000 for country driving.
» Plan your journey in advance, building in stops to counteract the effects of tiredness, boredom and loss of concentration.
» Freeways in Australia may have exits to the right as well as the left.
» Take great care when overtaking road trains—make sure you can see for at least 1km (0.6 mile) ahead of the road train before pulling out, and

ROAD SIGNS

Take care at country rail crossings that lack gates

Emergency phones are found beside highways

Cyclists sometimes share paths with pedestrians

Yellow signs warn of potential danger

On toll roads, signs give drivers advance notice of charges

Work out the freeway exit you need well in advance

All speed limits are given in kilometres per hour

signal your manoeuvre in good time. When you are overtaken by a road train, your vehicle may be buffeted by the slipstream as it passes; if it is safe, pull over to the left of the highway and let it pass.

» Avoid driving at night in the outback. Look out for kangaroos, especially at dawn and dusk. Other animals that can cause damage to your vehicle include wombats, camels, emus and buffalo

» Do not be tempted to drive off-road unless you have an appropriate vehicle, expertise and access to local knowledge.

» Roads in the outback may be closed at certain times of year; for example, in the Northern Territory during the Wet, from November to April, or in New South Wales and Victoria, from May to the end of August, when roads in the high country may be snowbound. Check with the local tourist office or parks office before starting your journey; important traffic information is usually found on prominent display boards. Flash floods are another hazard; avoid camping in or too close to riverbeds.

» Always carry plenty of water in case of breakdown in remote areas. Hardware stores and supermarkets stock insulated water carriers of all sizes. If you are going to camp in an area with no facilities, you will need a large water container, available from camping shops.

» If touring in the outback for a few days, stock up at the supermarket before you leave town. Roadhouses and hotels may provide meals but they probably won't have a shop selling provisions.

» Carry ample fuel (gas) when driving in the outback, as fuel stations are few. Ensure your tank is full before setting out. Many 4WD vehicles have a supplementary fuel tank—fill this too.

» Heavily laden vehicles are at risk of 'bogging' in soft ground—take care where you stop or park.

» If your car breaks down in the outback, build a shelter that provides some shade, stay with your vehicle and summon assistance. Never leave the vehicle to attempt to walk out of the bush.

Distance chart (km):

	Adelaide	Alice Springs	Brisbane	Broken Hill	Broome	Cairns	Canberra	Coober Pedy	Darwin	Esperance	Exmouth	Kalgoorlie-Boulder	Mackay	Melbourne	Mount Gambier	Mount Isa	Perth	Port Augusta	Port Macquarie	Rockhampton	Sydney	Townsville
Alice Springs	1535																					
Brisbane	2105	3004																				
Broken Hill	511	1644	1543																			
Broome	3239	1704	4979	3348																		
Cairns	2964	2421	1709	2460	4100																	
Canberra	1192	2669	1249	1092	4373	2971																
Coober Pedy	848	691	2902	956	2395	3127	1988															
Darwin	3018	1492	3422	3130	1861	2857	4162	2178														
Esperance	2182	3102	4236	2291	2936	5537	3322	2413	4587													
Exmouth	3919	3018	5973	4027	1384	5428	5059	4150	3178	2148												
Kalgoorlie-Boulder	2176	3096	4230	2285	2185	5531	3317	2407	3978	408	1812											
Mackay	2765	2405	972	2203	4084	753	2225	3096	2826	4895	5397	4890										
Melbourne	723	2265	1673	839	3965	3080	660	1576	3741	2911	4648	2905	2334									
Mount Gambier	435	1961	2094	947	3674	3500	1073	1282	3453	2617	4354	2617	2754	438								
Mount Isa	2657	1122	1911	2318	2801	1346	2960	1813	1544	4223	4115	4217	1315	3387	3092							
Perth	2689	3618	4752	2806	2225	5248	3631	2929	4017	926	1259	594	5410	3427	3134	4739						
Port Augusta	305	1229	2361	415	2933	3665	1447	541	2715	1876	3613	1870	3020	1035	742	2351	2390					
Port Macquarie	1770	3246	581	1304	5190	2308	648	2558	3933	3892	5629	3887	1562	1231	1651	2421	4407	2017				
Rockhampton	2428	2737	639	1865	4416	1085	1887	3428	3159	4551	5730	4546	338	1995	2344	1648	5065	2676	1224			
Sydney	1408	2885	987	1308	4589	2709	284	2206	4209	3531	5268	3526	1962	869	1289	2697	4046	1656	387	1627		
Townsville	3150	2067	1360	2113	3754	373	2608	2766	2479	5177	5068	5171	390	2716	3143	986	5693	3304	1946	724	2347	
Wyndham	3386	1851	3788	3494	1112	3223	4369	2542	972	3977	2425	3228	3192	4115	3821	1909	3266	3080	4297	3523	4736	2862

DRIVING REGULATIONS

STARTING OFF

In Australia you drive on the left. In order to drive you must hold a current licence and, preferably, an International Driving Permit. You may drive in Australia for a limited period (such as a holiday) on your own licence.

UK drivers who don't have the new photocard licence should consider obtaining one, as photo-licences are the norm in Australia. For this reason an International Driving Permit (IDP), although not required by law, is recommended. You must carry your national licence, with the IDP if taken, when driving.

Front and back seat belts must be worn and small children must be seated in an approved child seat or restraint appropriate to their size and height. These can be hired from car rental companies, as they must meet the strict Australian standards.

The use of hand-held mobile (cell) phones is forbidden, whether you are on the move or stationary in traffic.

Many drivers in Australia habitually 'undertake' (overtake on the left on a freeway); there has been a campaign to persuade drivers to overtake only on the right.

You must come to a complete stop at a STOP sign.

SPEED LIMITS

Rules of the Road and speed limits vary from state to state. Make sure you know those that apply to the state you are in, as traffic police are exceedingly zealous and will pursue and prosecute offenders.

Speed limits are generally signed alongside roads, including freeways. Speed and red-light cameras are used throughout Australia and fines are high.

SPEED LIMITS

ROAD	LIMIT
Cities and suburbs unless otherwise signed	50kph (31mph); 60kph (37mph) on major arterial roads
Near schools	40kph (23mph)
Suburban roads	up to 80kph (49mph)
Freeways	100kph (62mph) or 110kph (68mph); 80kph (49mph) on busier sections and near signals
Highways within built-up areas	up to 100kph (62mph)
Country roads	100kph (62mph)

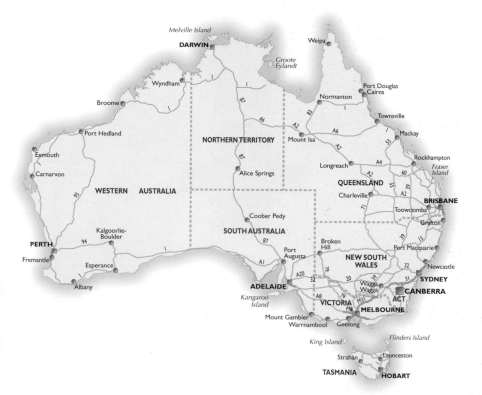

ALCOHOL LIMIT

The maximum legal blood-alcohol level is 0.05, or 50 milligrams per litre. The limit is enforced with random breath tests on any road at any time—even freeways. On-the-spot fines are issued, payable within 28 days, or you may be required to make a court appearance.

For learners, provisional licence holders—P plates are compulsory for newly qualified drivers—and drivers under 25 who have held a licence for less than three years, the limit is zero: No alcohol at all may be consumed before driving.

ROAD ACCIDENTS

All road accidents involving injury or vehicle towing must be reported to the police at once, or within 24 hours. Your rental contract provides the procedures to follow after an accident. In Western Australia all accidents must be reported if damage exceeds A$1,000, if drugs or alcohol are involved, or if there is any dispute.

DRIVING INTERSTATE

Regulations may change when you cross state boundaries. While road signs indicate an 'honour system', do not be surprised to find your vehicle being checked thoroughly for any fruit or vegetables, flowers and seeds, as these are not allowed to be taken from one state to another. Information on how road rules differ from state to state is available from the National Transport Commission, www.ntc.gov.au.

DRIVING WITH TRAMS

Special regulations apply in central Melbourne when driving in streets

where trams operate.

» No vehicle may overtake a stationary tram at a recognized tram stop, unless there are barriers between the tram and the road. You must stop level with the rear of the tram and wait for people to get on and off.

» Give way to trams moving into or across a roundabout.

» Do not pass on the right of a tram (unless tram tracks are at or near the far left side of the road).

» Buses travelling along the tram tracks must be treated as trams.

» Continuous yellow lines on the road give priority to trams at all times. You may cross a broken yellow line and drive on the tram tracks, but you must not pull out in front of or delay a tram.

PARKING

Signs indicate when and where parking is permitted. You must park pointing in the same direction as the flow of traffic to allow your rear reflecters to be seen. 'No Standing' means 'No Waiting'.

TIPS

» UK visitors can obtain an International Driving Permit (IDP) by calling the AA on 0870 600 0371 or at www.theAA.com. Click on 'Advice and Information' and then 'International Driving Permit', located under 'Travelling Abroad.'

» The speed limit for open roads is 110kph (68mph) in Northern Territory.

» New South Wales has different speed limits for Learner, Provisional and Unrestricted licence holders; in the Australian Capital Territory the speed limit is the same for all.

» Speed limits are lower for cars towing trailers and some other vehicles. Check with the motoring organization in the state(s) you intend to visit.

» Roadside cameras are in use, and police frequently set up roadside 'speed traps'.

» Many urban areas have speed restrictions lower than 60kph (37mph).

MAKING IT EASY—THE HOOK TURN

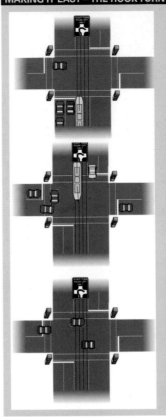

In Melbourne and Canberra, regulations stipulate when to make a hook turn at an intersection (usually to avoid right-turning traffic blocking tram lines). In Melbourne, hook turn signs are found at some intersections in the central business district. The signs may be at the side of the road or hung from wires. A driver turning right at an intersection with traffic lights and a hook turn sign must do as shown here:

1 Approach the intersection in the left lane
2 With a green light, move straight ahead to the far left corner of the intersection box and wait until traffic clears, and traffic lights change to green on the road you are entering
3 Complete the right turn and continue straight ahead.

In Melbourne a cyclist can make a hook turn at any intersection—not just at signed hook turn intersections. When turning right at an intersection in Canberra, cyclists have the option of making a hook turn, rather than a normal right turn. This may be safer on roads where there is heavy traffic.

www.path.unimelb.edu.au/~bernardk/victoria/melb/hook_turn.html

ABORIGINAL LAND

Apart from public roads, you need to obtain a transit permit to travel on other roads through Aboriginal land. You must not use tracks off the road for sightseeing. Aboriginal land, which is privately owned, is marked on road atlases. Further conditions about access are explained on application or are noted on the Land Council websites. A permit is also required to visit an Aborigine community.

Central Region (area south of Tennant Creek)	Northern NT Region	
Permits Officer	Permits Officer	197 St. Georges Terrace
Central Land Council	Northern Land Council	PO Box 7770
31–33 Stuart Highway	45 Mitchell Street	Perth, WA 6850
PO Box 3321	Darwin, NT 0810	☎ 08 9235 8000
Alice Springs, NT 0871	☎ 08 8920 5178	www.dia.wa.gov.au
☎ 08 8951 6211	www.nlc.org.au	
www.clc.org.au		**South Australia**
⊙ Mon–Fri 8–12, 2–4; closed public holidays	**Western Australia**	Anangu Pitjantjatjaraku
	Department of Indigenous Affairs	Yankunytjatjara Land Council
	1st Floor Capita Centre	PMB 227 Umuwa
		via Alice Springs, NT 0872
		☎ 08 8950 8110

LOCAL/URBAN TRAVEL

BUSES

NEW SOUTH WALES
Sydney
Sydney Buses are run by State Transit, which also runs CityRail and Sydney Ferries (▷ 55, 56). Tickets are available from ticket agents and from the Sydney Buses Ticket and Information Offices at Circular Quay and Wynyard. Pick up a bus information leaflet to check which 'sections' (zones) you need to travel, or see the zone maps displayed in bus and train stations.
Tel 13 15 00; www.131500.com.au

» You validate the magnetic stripe ticket when you board the bus, by dipping it in the green machine on board.
» When travelling with a companion, you can 'dip' your ticket the correct number of times to pay for that person.
» If you travel only occasionally on Sydney Buses, purchase a single fare from the driver.

Multiple Journeys
For multiple trips, there is a range of discount ticket options. Prices depend on sections travelled—each section is based on a nominal length of 1.6km (1 mile).

TravelPasses
TravelPasses are colour-coded according to price, with red covering the central section, and pink and purple the outer zones:

TravelPass	Weekly	Quarterly
Red	A$38	A$418
Pink	A$53	A$583
Purple	A$60	A$660

TravelPasses can be used on buses and trains too.

Sydney DayTripper
The DayTripper allows all-day travel on 'Blue and White' Sydney Buses, CityRail trains within the suburban area, and Sydney Ferries. You can buy tickets on the buses or at CityRail ticket offices or Sydney Ferries ticket outlets.
Tel 13 15 00
Fare: Adult A$17, child A$8.60

TravelTen
Available only from agents (usually newsagents/newsstands) displaying the Sydney Buses Ticket Kiosk flag: tickets cover 10 journeys.

TIP
» In Sydney, the best-value ticket is the Day Tripper (A$17), which allows unlimited travel on government-operated buses and ferries and CityRail trains in the city and suburban area (within certain limits).

VICTORIA
The Metlink website provides maps and the latest information about Victoria's buses, trains and trams: www.metlinkmelbourne.com.au
Purchase a MetCard in advance, you will not only save time queuing to buy public transportation tickets, but you will also money, depending on the number of zones to be travelled (1–3) and period of use (hourly to monthly); tel 13 16 38 (metropolitan and regional).

Melbourne
Melbourne's integrated transportation system allows you to use tickets interchangeably on trains, trams or buses. Tickets are available at the outlets mentioned

below. The exception is single fares or 'short journeys'.

Single Fares

A 'short trip' consists of up to two sections (several stops) on trams and buses within Zone 1. You purchase tickets from the driver (A$3.70).

Multiple Journeys

The wide choice of Metcard ticket options must be pre-purchased from various outlets, including newsagents, chemists and coffee bars—look for the blue Metcard Sales flag. Tickets can also be purchased at train stations, including Spencer Street and Flinders Street. The vending machines at stations take notes, coins and debit cards. In addition, you can buy tickets at the Met Shop at Melbourne Town Hall, on the corner of Little Collins and Swanston streets.

You can also buy a Metcard over the phone by credit card.
Tel 1800 652 313
⊕ Mon–Thu 8.30–6, Fri 8.30–9, Sat 9–1.

Metcard unlimited travel within Zone 1

Daily Metcard   A$6.80
Weekly Metcard   A$29.40
Monthly Metcard   A$109.60

Melbourne Trams

The famous Melbourne trams are a symbol of the city, but it can be daunting to board one immediately upon arrival without knowing how the system works. Don't bother watching the locals as most of them have Metcard tickets (see above) and may not be familiar with the on-board ticket machines.

TIPS

» Trams warn of their approach by ringing a bell. They run down the middle of the road and you have to walk out to board them at the signed tram stops.
» They operate Mon–Sat 5am–12am, Sun 8am–11pm, about every 12–15 minutes; more frequently on busy routes, less on quieter routes.

» It is important to know which tram route you need to take, and where you want to get off. Tram guides are displayed on the tram stops, or a map of the popular routes is available from the Met Shop at Melbourne Town Hall. If in doubt, ask the driver to let you know when you reach your destination.
» For short journeys, buy a ticket on board: Get on and then move to the centre of the tram and select the 'Short Trip' buttons on the machine (don't try to select the Zone as well). Cost for a short journey is about A$3.70. These tickets are automatically validated for that trip—other tickets, which can be purchased in advance, must be validated on board. The machines take coins only.
» If you are going to use the trams frequently, it is more economical to buy a daily or weekly Metcard. For information on Metcards, see 'Buses,' ▷ 52. Tickets can be ordered by phone on 1800 652 313, as for buses.

City Circle Trams

Several old maroon-and-cream trams have been renovated to provide the free—yes, there is no charge—City Circle tram service that tours the perimeter of the city-centre grid. An excellent way to see the city on a rainy or an uncomfortably hot day.

Park and Ride

Park at either Telstra Dome or Melbourne Museum and purchase tickets from the parking attendants for tram travel to the city. From Melbourne Museum, trams 86 and 96 run from the corner of Nicholson and Gertrude streets to Bourke Street. From the La Trobe Street entrance of Telstra Dome, tram 86 goes to Bourke Street and tram 48 travels to the city via Flinders Street.
Tel 13 16 38;
www.yarratrams.com.au
⊕ Parking Mon–Fri 7–7

TIPS

» Melbourne's NightRider buses are intended to enable people to get

home safely late at night. A free taxi booking service is available on the buses, and you can use the on-board mobile phones to arrange for someone to meet you off the bus.
» There are several ways to save money with a Metcard: a 10 x 2-hour Metcard gives ten trips for less than the price of nine.
» If you have mobility difficulties, remember that there is a tall step up to board the old City Circle trams. The newer types on the other routes are more easily accessible.
» A 'shopper's off-peak daily' ticket represents good value at A$4.10. Use them Mon–Fri 9–4.30 and after 6, Sat–Sun and public holidays all day. For senior citizens the price falls to only A$1.40.
» In Melbourne, a Daily Metcard for an adult costs A$6.80 and allows unlimited train, tram and bus travel for one day within the city area.

AUSTRALIAN CAPITAL TERRITORY

The Action Bus is the key to travelling around Canberra. Routes range around the four bus interchanges: City, Woden, Tuggeranong and Belconnen. Catch a bus from any other stop by signalling the driver.

Timetables are available from the bus interchanges, newsstands, 'Canberra Connect' Shopfronts, the Canberra Visitor Centre or the website. Tickets can be purchased from the driver or from the above locations.
Tel 13 17 10;
www.action.act.gov.au
Single journey (purchase tickets from driver)   A$3.80
Multiple journeys (pre-purchased tickets)
Daily   A$7.40
Faresaver 10   A$24.50
Weekly   A$27.00
Monthly   A$89.00

WESTERN AUSTRALIA
Perth

Perth's buses are operated by Transperth. The city's integrated transportation system means that tickets can be used on trains, buses and ferries. Two types of ticket are available: cash tickets and Multiriders. Buses run Mon–Fri 6am–11.30pm; reduced services Sat–Sun and public holidays. Tel 13 62 13; www.transperth.wa.gov.au

Cash Tickets

Buy a cash ticket from the bus driver when you start your journey.

Multirider Tickets

These must be bought in advance, from newsagents or from the Transperth InfoCentres at: Perth City Busport, Mounts Bay Road; Plaza Arcade, between Murray and Hay streets; Wellington Street Bus Station; Perth Railway Station, 376 Wellington Street.

For sample fares, see 'Urban Trains', ▷ 55.

CAT

Transperth's Central Area Transit (CAT) system operates frequent free buses around central and suburban Perth and Fremantle.
» Look out for the Black Cat logo.
» There are Blue, Red and Yellow CAT routes for Perth, and Orange for Fremantle.
» Colour-coded bus stops tell you which CAT to board, and lighted displays tell you when the next bus is due.
» The CAT system is accessible for wheelchair users.

TIPS

» If you are sightseeing only in Perth city centre, travel on any Transperth service is free at all times within the Free Transit Zone in the Perth Central Business District (CBD).
» Perth's DayRider ticket gives unlimited all-day travel on all Transperth services Monday to

Friday after 9am, Saturday, Sunday and public holidays all day.

SOUTH AUSTRALIA
Adelaide

Adelaide's bus and tram services are provided by TransAdelaide, which also run the trains (▷ 55). TransAdelaide tickets are of three types: Singletrip, Multitrip and Daytrip.
Tel 08 8210 1000
www.transadelaide.com.au

Singletrip

A Singletrip ticket pays for one journey. A Zone Singletrip ticket allows you to travel anywhere on the transport system within a two-hour period. Buy these on board the tram.

Multitrip

A Multitrip ticket must be bought in advance; the ticket gives you ten trips for about the price of seven. Tickets can be bought at a range of outlets including newsagents and convenience stores displaying the Metroticket sign; selected post offices and post office agencies; Adelaide Railway Station; the Passenger Transport Information centre, at the corner of King William and Corrie streets.

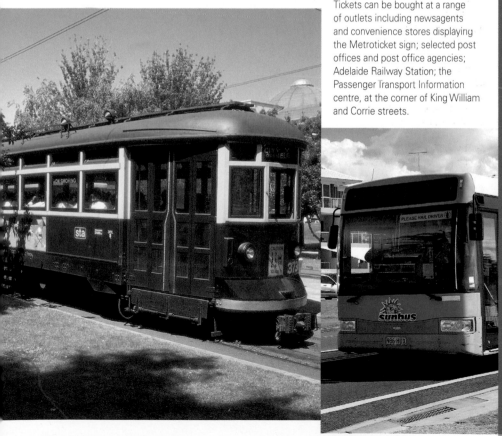

Daytrip

Daytrip tickets can be bought either in advance or on board the trams. As the name suggests, the ticket allows you to travel throughout the city for a whole day. At weekends and public holidays you can take two children under 15 free on your adult ticket.

Sample fares

Single trip (short journey)	A$2.60
Multitrip (short journey)	A$15.90
Daytrip	A$8.30

Free Bus Service

The free Bee Line bus service (No. 99B) runs in a loop from Victoria Square via King William Street and North Terrace.
» Frequent service from 8.27am (starts 10.00am Sat–Sun)
» Board at any stop on the route— look for the bee symbol.

QUEENSLAND
Brisbane

Brisbane's integrated transportation system of buses, trains and ferries incorporates the services of some private transportation operators who match their fares to those of Brisbane Transport.
Tel 13 12 30;
www.transinfo.qld.gov.au

» Tickets are obtainable from bus and ferry drivers and from agents ('ticket resellers')—the majority of agents are provided by newsagents.
» The TransInfo website Journey Planner works out routes, fares and timetables. Transport route maps are also available on the website, including one showing Brisbane's five fare zones.

Sample fares

Single (1 zone)	A$2.40
Daily (2 zone)	A$5.80
Weekly (2 zone)	A$23.20

Brisbane Loop

This two-way circular downtown route stops either way beside the Brisbane River at Wharf Street, Riverside, Eagle Street Pier and Stamford Plaza.

The clockwise service then goes from Stamford Plaza via Alice Street (Botanic Gardens), George Street (Government Precinct, Queen Street Mall) and Adelaide Street (City Hall, Central Station).

The counter-clockwise goes from Wharf Street via Ann Street (Central Station, City Hall), William Street (Queen Street Mall, Government Precinct) and Margaret Street (Botanic Gardens).

» You can download an excellent transportation map with timetables from www.translink.com.au.

TASMANIA

Bus services In Burnie, Hobart and Launceston are run by Metro.

The main bus station for Hobart is in Franklin Square, right by the main post office. Buses run every 15–30 minutes on major routes, and maps and timetables are on the website.
Tel 13 22 01;
www.metrotas.com.au
» Buy single trip and daily off-peak tickets from the bus driver.
» Discounted Ten Trip or Ten Day tickets can be bought from most newsagents, some convenience stores, and the post office at Macquarie Street, Hobart. Passengers must validate their ticket each time they board the bus at the validating machine next to the driver; the machine will return your ticket with the travel details and a display shows how many trips or days are left on the ticket. The driver can help if you have any ticket difficulties.
» Wheelchair-accessible buses operate on some routes; visit www.metrotas.com.au for details.

URBAN TRAINS
Sydney
Metropolitan trains are operated by CityRail, which also runs day trips to tourist destinations such as the Blue Mountains and Newcastle. Trains from the airport arrive at Central Station.
Tel 13 15 00;
www.cityrail.info

» There are eight stations in the city centre: Central, Town Hall, Wynyard, Circular Quay, St. James, Museum, Martin Place and Kings Cross. If you ask for a ticket to the city, your ticket allows you to get off at any one of them. You can also return from any station in the city with a return ticket.
» Trains run every 2–3 minutes in both directions on the City Circle line to Central, Town Hall, Wynyard, Circular Quay and Museum stations. Trains to the suburbs and the airport station run every 10 minutes at peak times and every 15 at other times. Single, return and off-peak return tickets are available.
» The www.cityrail.info website includes all timetables, a full list of facilities at each station, and a fare calculator showing all fares and concessions for all destinations on the network.

Sample fares for short journey
Single
Adult A$3.20   Child A$1.60
Round-trip
Adult A$6.40   Child A$3.40
Off-peak round-trip
Adult A$4.40   Child A$2.80

Sydney Monorail
The monorail follows a loop route through the city to Darling Harbour, Powerhouse Museum, and back.
Tel 02 8584 5288;
www.metromonorail.com.au

» Runs every few minutes Mon–Thu 7am–10pm, Fri–Sat 7am–12am, Sun 8am–10pm.
» One fare for all journeys–A$4.80.
» City stop on the corner of Pitt and Market streets.

» The widely available free Visitor Guide includes a route map.

Light Rail
A tram runs from Central Station to Darling Harbour, calling at several stops including the Casino, the Convention Centre and the Fish Market.
Tel 02 8584 5288

» The circuit takes approximately 15 minutes.
» Prices vary according to zones: a full fare round trip is A$6.40.

Melbourne
The main stations in Melbourne are Flinders Street, serving local metropolitan lines, and Spencer Street, for country and interstate travel.
The metropolitan lines are operated by M-Train and Connex.
VicTrip timetable info:
tel 13 16 38 (daily 6am–10pm)

M-Train:
www.movingmelbourne.com
Connex:
www.connexmelbourne.com.au

» Fares are divided into zones, as for trams (n50), and tickets may be bought at the same outlets.
» Route maps are included in the widely available free Visitors' Guide.

Sample Metcard fares
2-hour Zone 1
Adult A$3.70
2-hour Zone 2
Adult A$2.80
2-hour all zones
Adult A$5.80
See also Tips, ▷ 52.

V/Line
V/Line trains go from Melbourne to Geelong, Ballarat, Bendigo, Echuca, Seymour, Wodonga, Traralgon and Sale. In the metro area V/Line trains connect with some of the outer stations of Zone 2. A train network map is on the V/Line website.
Tel 13 61 96;
www.vlinepassenger.com.au

Perth
Transperth trains run from the main station on Wellington Street to Fremantle—a 30-minute journey including stops. Other lines run north to Joondalup, east to Guildford and Midland, and south to Armadale.
Tel 13 62 13
www.transperth.wa.gov.au

» Buy tickets on the platform from machines (coins—change given). The cost depends on the zones travelled. Tickets are valid for 2 hours (3 hours from zones 5–8) and can also be used on Transperth buses and ferries. Route maps are in the widely available free Visitors' Guide.
» You can also buy a Smartrider card, a cash-free method of payment, that can be used on buses, trains and ferries. Value is stored on the card and is deducted as you travel, giving you a discount of up to 25 per cent.
» Smartrider cards are available from Transperth Infocentres at the main bus and train stations in Wellington Street and at Plaza Arcade, and most newsagents.

Sample adult fares
	1 zone	2 zones
Cash	A$2.40	A$3.60
Familyrider	A$8.80	N/A
DayRider	A$8.80	N/A

Adelaide
Trains and trams in the metro area are operated by TransAdelaide (▷ 53).
Tel 08 8210 1000;
www.transadelaide.com.au

Brisbane
Train services in the city centre and suburbs are operated by Queensland Rail Citytrain.
Tel 13 16 17;
www.qr.com.au

Canberra
There are no local train services available in Canberra; visitors use the buses (▷ 52) or rent a vehicle.

FERRIES

Sydney

Ferries depart from the wharves at Circular Quay, where signs and notice boards indicate services to Manly Beach, Darling Harbour, Watsons Bay, Rose Bay, Double Bay, the North Shore and Balmain.

Tickets are obtained from the Sydney Ferries booking offices on wharves 2, 3, 4 and 5, from information offices, and from local newsagents. Tickets can also be used on buses and trains.

Sydney Ferries

Tel 13 15 00;
www.sydneyferries.nsw.gov.au

Matilda Cruises
Rocket Harbour Express

Aquarium Wharf, Pier 26
Wheat Road, Darling Harbour
Tel 02 9264 7377
www.matilda.com.au

» Darling Harbour (Aquarium)–
Circular Quay–Opera House–
Watsons Bay–Taronga Zoo–Darling
Harbour (Harbourside)
» Mon–Sun 9.30am–4.15pm
» Buy tickets on board or book online

Melbourne

Ferries run half-hourly from
St. Kilda to Williamstown, and from
Southgate to Williamstown featuring
a cruise along the Yarra. Buy tickets
on board.
Tel 03 9506 4144

Ferries run on the hour between
Queenscliff Harbour and Sorrento
Pier, daily 7–6.
Tel 03 5258 3244;
www.searoad.com.au

Adelaide

Ferries to Kangaroo Island are run by
Kangaroo Island SeaLink. The ferry
departs from Cape Jervis daily at
9am and 6pm; also at 12pm, 3pm
and 9pm when there is sufficient
demand.

SeaLink office

440 King William Street,
Adelaide
Tel 08 8202 8688, 13 13 01;
www.sealink.com.au

Sample fares

Adult one way   A$41
Adult return   A$82
Passenger vehicle return   A$160
Journey time 45 minutes.

Brisbane

Brisbane Transport operates the
ferries that ply across and along the
Brisbane River. The Inner City Ferry
Service and the Cross River Ferry
Service cross the central section of
the river between North Quay and
Mowbray Park.

CityCats link the University of
Queensland (St. Lucia) and Bretts
Wharf (Hamilton).

For timetables, routes and fares:
tel 13 12 30, 07 3215 5000;
www.transinfo.qld.gov.au

Perth

Transperth ferries operate between
Barrack Street jetty (near Swan River
Bell Tower) and Mends Street jetty
in South Perth (near Perth Zoo);
daily 6.50am–7.24pm (also Fri–Sat
6.50–9.15pm in summer)
Tel 13 62 13;
www.transperth.wa.gov.au

Rottnest Ferry

Ferries operate to Rottnest Island
from Perth (Barrack Street jetty),
Hillarys Boat Harbour north of the
city, or Fremantle.

Ferries from Hillarys daily 8.00,
10.30 and 3 (also Friday 6pm).
Hillarys Fast Ferries
Tel 08 9246 1039;www.
hillarysfastferries.com.au

Sample return fares

From Perth, Adult   A$77
From Fremantle, Adult   A$38

Tasmania

Apart from air travel, the major link
to Tasmania is the Bass Strait Ferry
Service. Two large roll-on-roll-off
vehicle ships operate between
Melbourne and the East Devonport.

Accommodation options range
from family cabins to a lounge seat.
Fares are from A$110–A$194 (one
way, seat, no cabin) depending on
the season. Crossings are every
night at 9pm, except for Sundays
during winter (journey time 9 to
11 hours), and daily (at 9am) from
21 Dec to 15 Jan and at weekends
until mid-Feb. The standard car fare
is A$79 (one way).
Reservations: tel 1800 634 906;
www.spiritoftasmania.com.au

TIP

» The SydneyPass 3-, 5- and 7-day
inclusive sightseeing tickets allow
unlimited travel on:
    All regular bus, ferry and train
    services
    Harboursights cruises
    Sydney and Bondi Explorer buses
They are available from ferry ticket
offices, and visitor information
centres.
www.sydneypass.info

BICYCLING IN AUSTRALIA

Road traffic is generally light in many parts of Australia, which makes bicycling an ideal way to go sightseeing. Some cities have dedicated cycleways, and there are routes in the surrounding countryside and the national parks—families are frequently seen out bicycling together. However, there are always risks from other traffic and you must observe all safety regulations that apply to the state you are visiting.

Beyond the cities there is much fine touring country, but only the very experienced should venture into the dry centre by bicycle, and all safety and survival precautions must be taken, together with extensive forward planning.

BICYCLE HELMETS

Bicycle helmets are compulsory for both children and adults; they must conform to approved designs and fit correctly. Local bicycle dealers can be found in the Yellow Pages: www.yellowpages.com.au.

NEW SOUTH WALES
Sydney

There are bicycling maps at www.rta.nsw.gov.au. The ongoing Bikeplan 2010 project is creating a series of bicycle routes across the state.

AUSTRALIAN CAPITAL TERRITORY
Canberra

Except in the rush hour, Canberra's roads are not too busy and bicycling is a good way to to cover the distance between the city and the attractions around Lake Burley Griffin.

» Bicyclists are permitted to ride two abreast.

» When turning right at an intersection a hook turn (▷ 50) may be safer on roads where there is heavy traffic.

» Brochures about cycling in the ACT are available from the Government Shop Front and other outlets: tel 13 22 81; www.canberraconnect.act.gov.au.

VICTORIA
Melbourne

Bicycle maps and information on where to ride are available at www.vicroads.vic.gov.au. Nearly 300km (186 miles) of disused rail lines across Victoria have been turned into recreational routes.

QUEENSLAND
Brisbane

Brisbane City Council promotes bicycling: there are 500km (310 miles) of city 'bikeways', with 1,200km (744 miles) more in development. You can download maps of the bikeway network from www.ourbrisbane.com, under the website's Transport tab.

NORTHERN TERRITORY
Alice Springs

Alice Springs has some 25km (15.5 miles) of paved bicycle track. A map of the bicycle network is available from the Town Council offices or www.alicesprings.nt.gov.au/community/sport_rec.asp.

SOUTH AUSTRALIA
Adelaide

The city's wide roads and flat terrain make it ideal for bicycling. There are also the popular parklands encircling the city. Torrens Linear Park has bicycle trails linking the city to the sea and the Adelaide Hills; Linear Park Bike Hire, Elder Park (adjacent to Torrens Lake).

A set of eight Bikedirect maps covers the Adelaide area from Gawlor in the north to Willunga in the south, showing bicycle routes and lanes. These are available free from good bicycle shops, or download from www.transport.sa.gov.au.

WESTERN AUSTRALIA
Perth

Bicycle tracks run alongside most city and suburban roads, and also throughout Kings Park (▷ 267) and all along the Swan River frontage. Bicycles can be hired at points along the river, in Kings Park, and most importantly on Rottnest (▷ 268), where vehicles are banned. Maps of Perth's bicycle network are available from the Bicycle Transportation Alliance: tel 08 9420 7210; www.multiline.com.au/~bta.

» The 42km (26-mile) cycleway that runs along both sides of the river from Perth to Fremantle is the longest in Australia.

TASMANIA
Hobart

Tasmania is a rewarding place to bicycle although most towns are quite hilly. Traffic is light and bicyclists are permitted to ride two abreast on roads. Bicycle rental is hard to find outside of organized tours; enquire at bicycle shops.

Hobart has a bicycle track from the Cenotaph by the Domain to Glenorchy (city to northern suburbs). In Devonport a track goes along the Mersey River, past the Bluff to the Don River.

BICYCLE WEBSITES

www.bicycles.net.au
Lists of all bicycle shops, clubs and organizations, plus a calendar of events. There are links to tour operators in Australia who cater for bicyclists.

www.bikesa.asn.au
Good list of South Australian and national links.

www.pedalpower.org.au
Represents Pedal Power ACT Inc, an Australian Capital Territory bicycling organization, but there are links to tours throughout all the states.

VISITORS WITH A DISABILITY

Access for people with disabilities in Australia has improved significantly and remains a priority. Hotels, airlines, tourist attractions and transportation carriers usually provide access facilities. However, it is always best to check in advance whether your particular need can be met at the site you plan to visit.

NDS
The head office of the National Disability Services (NDS) is in Canberra, but each state and territory has an office. All are listed on www.nds.org.au.

DRIVING
Car Rental
There are few suitable vehicles available for rent for people with disabilities, so drivers should bring their own hand-held controls and have them adjusted for a standard vehicle on arrival. State paraplegic and quadriplegic groups can assist with the fitting of controls. It is best to contact vehicle rental firms in advance.
» Disability Hire Vehicles specializes in vehicle rental for the independent disabled traveller:
49 Hession Road, Oakville, Sydney, NSW 2765
Tel 02 4573 6788;
www.disabilityhire.com.au

PARKING
Reciprocal disabled parking rights exist for overseas visitors for up to three months. For information, contact NDS (above).

SYDNEY
» www.cityofsydney.nsw.gov.au includes an access guide to public toilets, ATMs, buses, train stations, taxi ranks and parking.
» All taxi firms have vehicles that can accommodate wheelchairs.
Tel 02 8332 0200
» Ferries, trains and some buses have lifts and ramps. Tel 13 15 00
» The City of Sydney website has maps and information specifically for people with disabilities.
www.cityofsydney.nsw.giv.au/AboutSydney/

MELBOURNE
» TADAS provides equipment and facilities, and computers for visitors to access information:
Travellers Aid Disability Access Service, Level 2, 169 Swanston Street, Melbourne, VIC 3000 (lifts via alcove two shops south of Bourke Street Mall).
Tel 03 7690 9654, 03 9654 5412 (telephone typewriter),
www.vicnet.net.au/~tadas/home
» The Victorian government is working to make all trains, trams and buses fully accessible for all users. A first step is the Tram 109 project, creating 'Superstops' with raised platforms to fill the gap between the door and platform.

CANBERRA
» Information for visitors with mobility, visual and hearing impairments is available from:
Canberra Visitor Centre,
330 Northbourne Avenue,
Dickson, ACT 2602
Tel 1300 554 114;
www.visitcanberra.com.au

PERTH
» All buses on CAT routes and Circle routes in the city are accessible, as are buses displaying a blue wheelchair symbol. A special taxi service for wheelchair users is available daily 24 hours. Book 24 hours in advance: tel 13 62 94.
» To rent a wheelchair, or an electric scooter, contact the Independent Living Centre. Tel 08 9381 0600
www.ilc.com.au

BRISBANE
» The Access Brisbane website has a searchable database of accessible facilities in the city: www.brisbane-stories.webcentral.com.au/access

» www.e-bility.com gives an overview of accessibility in Queensland.

ADELAIDE
» Adelaide claims its has the nation's highest percentage of accessible buses and taxis within each fleet. The yellow free buses, the Bee Line (▷ 54), have special ramps and low floors. Bus and taxi details are described at www.service.sa.gov.au, under Services.
» Access Cabs
Tel 1300 551 156
» Units at bus interchanges, stations and major stops provide timetable and route information featuring Braille, engraved signs and push-button recorded details.

TASMANIA
» Information is available from:
Department of Health and Human Services, GPO Box 125B, Hobart, TAS 7001
Tel 13 799 530;
www.dhhs.tas.gov.au/disability/services/index.html
» Taxi companies in each city have disabled access vehicles:
Hobart and Southern Maxi Taxis
Tel 03 6227 9577
Taxi Combined (Devonport)
Tel 03 6424 1431
Maxi Taxi (Launceston)
Tel 13 22 27

HELPFUL WEBSITES
www.youreable.com
The Travel tab has good checklists for travellers.

www.accessibletravel.co.uk
This UK travel agency specializes in accessible holidays.

www.translink.com.au
This website has a wealth of information for travellers with disabilities in Australia.

REGIONS

This chapter is divided into eight regions of Australia (▷ 59–304). Places of interest are listed alphabetically in each region.

Australia's regions

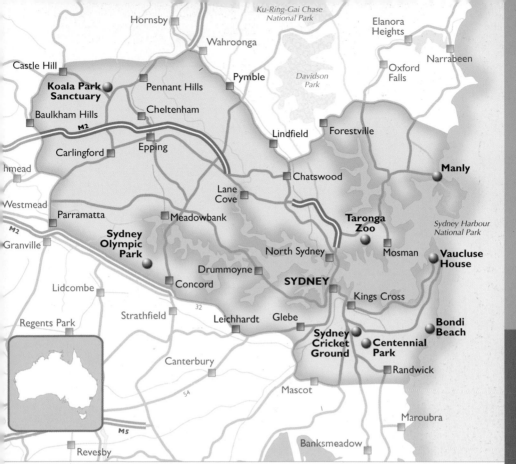

SYDNEY

Sydney is the biggest, oldest and most cosmopolitan city in Australia, and one of the most vibrant and exciting cities on the planet. Endowed with a sparkling harbour, dazzling beaches and a sunny, Mediterranean climate, its setting alone has guaranteed Sydney a place among the world's glamour cities. Grafted onto those natural splendours is an impressive array of worldly treasures, including splendid museums and galleries, a spirited nightlife, sophisticated shopping, a relaxed lifestyle and an architectural heritage that ranges from the sandstone cottages of the convict days to the glistening white sails of the Sydney Opera House. Sydney is also one of the most racially diverse cities on earth.

Over the past few decades the city's original Anglo-Irish population has been diluted and enriched by successive waves of immigrants, initially from southern Europe and later from all parts of Asia, from North and South America and the South Pacific. Sydney people come from everywhere, and this alphabet soup of nationalities can be seen in what Sydney eats and an exotic festival calendar. For the traveller looking for glamour, good looks, location, lifestyle, scenery and sunshine, no other Australian city comes close.

Despite its obvious charms, Sydney also has quite a few secrets—hidden beaches, quiet places to watch the sunset, waterfront restaurants that the locals would prefer you didn't know about and golf courses with the 'Made in Heaven' brand name. Sydney is also Australia's business capital and a financial landmark in the Asia-Pacific. One of the world's leading service economies, Sydney is prominent in the finance and business service industries and information and communications technology.

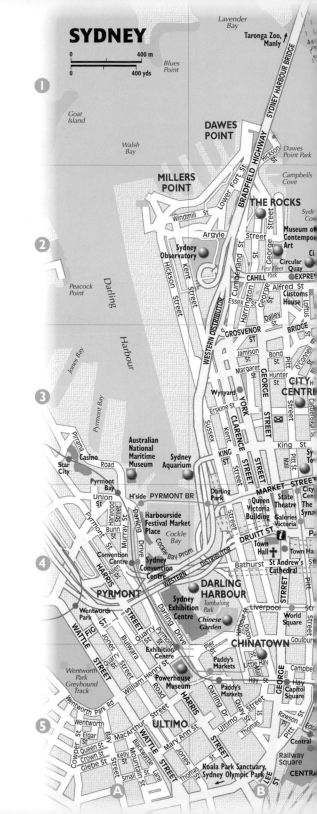

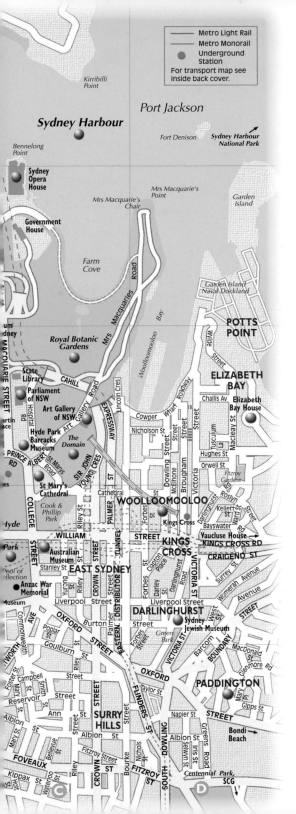

Metro Light Rail
Metro Monorail
● **Underground Station**
For transport map see inside back cover.

Kirribilli Point

Port Jackson

Sydney Harbour

Fort Denison ↗ *Sydney Harbour National Park*

Bennelong Point

Sydney Opera House

Mrs Macquarie's Point

Mrs Macquarie's Chair

Garden Island

Government House

Farm Cove

Woolloomooloo Bay

Garden Island Naval Dockland

POTTS POINT

um dney

Royal Botanic Gardens

State Library

Parliament of NSW

CAHILL

Lincoln Cres

ELIZABETH BAY

Challis Av **Elizabeth Bay House**

Art Gallery of NSW

Cowper

Wharf Roadway

Nicholson St

Hyde Park Barracks Museum

The Domain

Dowling Street

McElhone Street

Brougham Street

Victoria Street

Tusculum La

Macleay Street

Hughes St

Orwell St

Fitzroy Gardens

St Mary's Cathedral

Cathedral

WOOLLOOMOOLOO

Palmer

Forbes St

Roslyn

Kellett St

Cook & Phillip Park

Riley St

Kings Cross

Darlinghurst

Bayswater Rd

Vaucluse House →

WILLIAM STREET

KINGS CROSS

KINGS CROSS RD

Australian Museum

Stanley St

EAST SYDNEY

Crown Street

Clapton Place

CRAIGEND ST

VICTORIA ST

Surrey St

Surrey St

Womerah Avenue

Pool of Reflection

Anzac War Memorial

Yurong St

Liverpool Street

Forbes St

Darley St

Darlinghurst Road

Liverpool Street

Avenue

Museum

OXFORD STREET

Poplar St

Burton Street

DARLINGHURST

Street

Green Park

Sydney Jewish Museum

West Street

Goulburn

Barcom

MacDonald St

Glenmore Rd

BOUNDARY

Commonwealth Ave

Riley St

OXFORD

FLINDERS ST

Taylor St

PADDINGTON

Mary Pl

Gipps St

Foster St

Campbell Street

Reservoir St

Smith St

Mary St

Ann St

Napier St

STREET

Greens Road

Bondi Beach →

Albion St

Bellevue St

SURRY HILLS

Albion St

Albion St

Iris St

Sewin St

FOVEAUX

Kippax St

Holt St

Riley St

CROWN ST

Bourke Street

Nichols St

FITZROY

SOUTH DOWLING

Centennial Park,

SCG

Ⓒ   Ⓓ

REGIONS SYDNEY • CITY MAPS

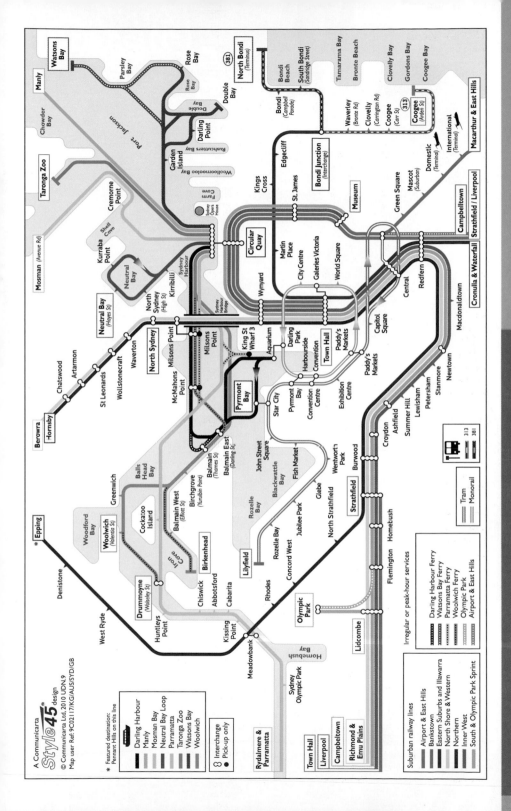

ART GALLERY OF NEW SOUTH WALES

www.artgallery.nsw.gov.au

The state's premier art gallery is one of Australia's very best. There is an excellent collection of Australian, Aboriginal, Asian, American and European paintings, sculptures, photographs, prints, drawings and other works of art. If you're short of time, join the free guided tour to avoid missing the highlights, which include the Yiribana Gallery with its noted collection of Aboriginal and Torres Strait Islander art.

🖸 63 C3 ✉ Art Gallery Road, The Domain, Sydney, NSW 2000 ☎ 02 9225 1744 (enquiries); 02 9225 1790 (What's-on Line) 🕐 Daily 10–5 (also Wed 5–9pm) 🖐 Free; charge for exhibitions 🚌 441 from Queen Victoria Building; Sydney Explorer bus (stop 6) 🍴 🖵 🏛

AUSTRALIAN MUSEUM

www.australianmuseum.net.au

Don't be put off by the Victorian classical facade and the old-fashioned glass-case displays in some of the galleries: This is an excellent museum of humankind and natural history. It's a particularly good place to discover Aboriginal culture, as well as Australia's ecology, and unique plant and animal life. Hands-on displays and insect costumes for dressing up are among the attractions for children. A self-guided one-hour tour points out the best features.

🖸 63 C4 ✉ 6 College Street, Sydney, NSW 2000 ☎ 02 9320 6000 🕐 Daily 9.30–5 🖐 Adult A$12, child (5–15) A$6, under 5 free 🚇 Museum (City Circle Line) 🚌 Sydney Explorer bus (stop 7) 🍴 🖵 🏛

AUSTRALIAN NATIONAL MARITIME MUSEUM

▷ 68.

BONDI BEACH

▷ 69.

CENTENNIAL PARK

www.centennialparklands.com.au

This 220ha (540-acre) parkland is Sydney's green lung, a favourite spot for picnics, kicking a football and walking the dog. The names dates from 1888, the centenary of Sydney's foundation, when this was proclaimed a public space for the enjoyment of the people, and its groves of mature fig trees, avenues of palms and formal gardens bear witness to the foresight of its architects. The lower end of the park was originally a wetland of creeks, swamps, springs, sand dunes and ponds fed by groundwater, and from 1837 to 1859 this supplied Sydney with most of its water, via an underground pipe along Oxford Street. Today this is a lush area of palm-fringed lakes and water-loving paperbark groves.

The park has a rich birdlife, most notably a large population of ibis, which are prone to stealing picnics. This is also Sydney's all-purpose social velodrome, a great place to ride a bike, rollerblade, jog or just walk through lovely parkland. On summer nights, Centennial Park becomes the venue for the Moonlight Cinema (www.moonlight.com.au), one of Sydney's two outdoor film theatres. On Grand Drive close to Oxford Street, Centennial Park Dining is a chic café/restaurant.

🖸 Off map 63 D5 ✉ Oxford Street and Lang Road, Paddington NSW 2021 ℹ Centennial Parklands Dining, Grand Drive ☎ 02 9339 6699 🕐 Main gates open Apr and Sep–Oct daily 6–6; May–Aug 6.30–5.30; Oct–Mar 6am–8pm 🚌 Frequent bus services run along Oxford Street between the city and Bondi Junction

CHINESE GARDEN AND CHINATOWN

▷ 70.

CITY CENTRE

This is the main shopping precinct and home to some of Sydney's Victorian architectural treasures. This is also the site of the gleaming, glassy towers of the city's central business district, often abbreviated in Sydney-speak to CBD. In this compact area you'll find the Sydney Tower, the city's tallest building, Aurora Place, designed by the noted architect Renzo Piano, and the grandiose, sandstone-fronted banks and the former General Post Office that scowl down on Martin Place.

Shopping in the area has recently been reinvigorated with the reopening of the Centrepoint complex, while traditionalists might prefer the elegant, cloistered confines of the Strand Arcade.

Sydney's Victorian architecture reaches its zenith along George Street, between Market and Druitt streets where the sprawling Queen Victoria Building takes up an entire city block. Originally the city's produce market, this is now a major shopping plaza. Across Druitt Street, Sydney Town Hall was built between 1873 and 1888, and the grandiose, wedding-cake facade reflects a diversity of classical styles.

🖸 63 B3 ✉ Bounded by George, Bridge, Macquarie and Park streets 🚇 Town Hall, Wynyard and St. James stations lie adjacent to this district 🚌 Many bus routes pass along George and Macquarie streets

Opposite *The Australian Museum is a fun day out*
Above *The Classical facade of the Art Gallery of New South Wales*

INFORMATION

www.anmm.gov.au

✚ 62 A3 ✉ 2 Murray Street, Darling Harbour ☎ 02 9298 3777 ☀ Daily 9.30–5 (also 5–6pm in Jan) ✋ Free for galleries; adult A$10–A$32, child A$10–A$17 for admission to ships including the *Endeavour*, *James Craig* and *Onslow*. 🚌 443 from the city 🚇 Metro Monorail to Harbourside 🚢 From Circular Quay to Pyrmont Bay 🚻 🎫

Above *HMAS* Vampire *houses a permanent museum at the Australian National Maritime Museum*

AUSTRALIAN NATIONAL MARITIME MUSEUM

Australia's long and intimate association with the sea is chronicled in this riveting display of artefacts, paintings and boats of all descriptions, from dugout canoes to a jet-powered hydrofoil and a historic collection of naval vessels.

Galleries inside the waterside museum explore the seafaring history of the Eora, the original inhabitants of the region around Sydney Harbour, the coming of the first European explorers, the convict and immigrant eras of the 19th century, Australia's naval history and the sea as a playground for sport-loving Australians. Among the highlights in the Navigators gallery are various pieces of navigation apparatus from the era of maritime exploration, artefacts recovered from early shipwrecks and a ceiling of twinkling stars and a recreation of the night sky that was one of the few navigation aids for early seafarers on long journeys across the Pacific.

THE SHIPS

Among the floating exhibits moored at the front of the museum in Darling Harbour is the destroyer HMAS *Vampire*, Australia's largest museum vessel and the last of the country's big gun ships, and the *Tu Do*, a fishing boat that arrived in Darwin with 31 refugees fleeing Vietnam in the aftermath of that country's civil war.

The floating collection also includes HMAS *Onslow*, an Oberon class submarine. Launched in 1968, the submarine offers a fascinating, behind-the-scenes look into the cramped and hot world of the submariner. Also on display is an Australian-built replica of HMB *Endeavour*, the vessel sailed by James Cook on his first voyage to Australia and a magnificent evocation of life aboard an 18th-century sailing ship.

BONDI BEACH

Big, bold and beautiful, this is where Sydney sheds its clothes and most of its inhibitions. A 1km (0.6-mile) curved strip of golden sand between two rocky headlands, Bondi is the most celebrated beach in the country and also the closest ocean beach to the city centre, a stretch of golden grains where Sydney comes to bare it all. The sands become very crowded during the summer months, particularly over the Christmas/January break. A great time to visit is during winter when cliffside walks are a pleasure.

BONDI STYLE

As well as the essential ingredients—booming surf, seagulls riding the breeze, the smell of sun-block—Bondi has a style all its own. This is see-and-be-seen territory, and nobody is ever too tanned, too thin or too muscled. Bondi also has a vibrant café and restaurant culture.

Campbell Parade, which runs along the back of the beach, is a near-continuous strip of outdoor cafés and gelato bars. The streets behind Campbell Parade are home to beachwear and fashion boutiques for acquiring the instant dressed-down look that Bondi requires.

SCENIC WALKWAY

Winding south from the beach across a succession of sea-sculpted sandstone headlands, the Scenic Walkway takes you on a roller-coaster ride past the swimmers in the Bondi Icebergs pool to Tamarama Beach—'Glamarama' to the locals—Bronte Beach and eventually all the way to Coogee Beach, with refreshment stops and sparkling views all the way. The real estate along the walkway is some of Sydney's glossiest.

INFORMATION

www.waverley.nsw.gov.au

✚ Off map 63 D5 ℹ Leaflets available at the Bondi Pavilion, beachfront; Sydney Visitor Centre, 106 George Street, The Rocks ☎ 02 9240 8788 🚉 Bondi Junction 2km (1.2 miles); frequent bus services to the beach and Bondi Explorer bus

Below *Enjoying the weekend sun at Bondi Beach*

INFORMATION

www.chinesegarden.com.au

✚ 63 B4/B5 ✉ Corner Pier Street and Harbour Street ☎ 02 9240 8888 ◷ Apr–Sep daily 9.30–5, Oct–Mar 9.30–5.30 💵 Adult A$6, child (4–14) A$3 🚃 Chinatown stop, buses along George Street

CHINESE GARDEN AND CHINATOWN

As soon as you enter the Dixon Street pedestrian plaza through the traditional red lion gates, the shops, flashing neon calligraphy, vitality and scent of Asian cooking transport body and soul to the Orient. Chinese have been prominent in the Sydney community ever since the first wave of migrants arrived from China during the gold rush days of the mid-19th century.

THE PLACE TO EAT

This compact section of the city was once home to the Chinese traders and fruit and vegetable sellers who worked at the adjacent Central Markets, now more commonly known as Paddy's Market. Today, the main activity of the area is dining. From Peking duck to Mongolian lamb, Japanese *teppanyaki* to spicy Malay soups and Indonesian stir fries, this is where Sydney comes to eat Asian. Thai cuisine is one of Sydney's favourite Asian foods, and for lovers of the fiery, piquant dishes of the Thai kitchen, the standard can be high. Thai restaurants have nibbled their way into the fringes of Chinatown, so much so that a section of Campbell Street between George and Wentworth has been nicknamed Thai town.

THE PLACE TO SIT

On the southern edge of the Darling Harbour precinct, bordering Chinatown, the Chinese Garden is a cool, green sanctuary. Created by Chinese landscape architects and gardeners, the garden relies on classical concepts using the four key elements of water, plants, stone and architecture, creating a harmonious balance that is the essence of every Chinese garden. Willows stroke the water, while paddling ducks fracture the reflections of the tiled pagoda roofs. A 45-minute audio tour, available at a cost of $4, provides detailed information about the design philosophy and history of the garden. The garden also incorporates a tea pavilion.

Below *The Chinese Garden of Friendship has a dramatic cityscape backdrop*

DARLING HARBOUR

Opened in 1988, this former port and industrial area is Sydney's premier specially built entertainment district,. Lawns, gardens, palm tree groves, fountains, waterways and marinas soften the bold architectural outline. The area is a magnet for visitors and locals alike. New Year's Eve celebrations and many of the Sydney Festival events are held here.

THE HARBOUR

Harbourside is the main shopping and dining complex. One of the best shops is the Gavala Aboriginal Art Centre. The Outback Centre on Darling Walk specializes in Aboriginal arts and crafts, with Aboriginal musical and dance shows several times daily.

Cruises operate from the Aquarium Wharf and nearby King Street Wharf, and fast jet boat rides and water taxis depart from in front of Harbourside. Heritage sights include Pyrmont Bridge, a 1902 steel and timber structure, the world's oldest surviving electrically operated span bridge; and the *South Steyne*, a 1938 steam ferry that now houses a floating restaurant.

THE ATTRACTIONS

Major attractions include the Australian National Maritime Museum (▷ 68), Sydney Aquarium, IMAX Theatre, Sydney Wildlife World and Chinese Garden (▷ 70). The Metro Monorail runs from the city to Darling Harbour, Chinatown and back, while the Metro Light Rail operates from Central Station to Darling Harbour, the Sydney Fish Market, Glebe and other inner west suburbs.

Sydney Aquarium (daily 9am–10pm, admission charge) on Aquarium Pier is Australia's largest. This dazzling facility displays the creatures that live in Australia's rivers and oceans in their various habitats, including saltwater crocodiles from Australia's tropical rivers and the multicoloured marine life from the Great Barrier Reef. One highlight is the see-through tunnels that take visitors for a fish-eye view of sharks and stingrays. There are over 650 species in displays, others include turtles, eels, seals, fairy penguins and platypus.

Sydney Wildlife World (daily 9am–10pm) is right next to the Aquarium. Opened in 2006, there are exhibits on nine different habitats from all over the continent of Australia. Visitors can get nose-to-nose with some of Australia's animal icons, including koalas, wallabies, snakes and birds, and there's a huge butterfly habitat with thousands of delicate winged beauties.

INFORMATION

www.darlingharbour.com
www.sydneyvisitorcentre.com
✚ 62 B4 🛈 Sydney Visitor Centre, Darling Harbour ☎ 02 9240 8788, 1800 067 676 ⏰ Daily 9.30–5.30 🚉 Town Hall (City Circle line)

Above *Sydney's Monorail runs through Darling Harbour*

DARLING HARBOUR
▷ 71.

ELIZABETH BAY HOUSE
www.hht.nsw.gov.au

In its heyday this sandstone villa, built in Greek revival style, was known as the finest house in the colony, and it remains one of Sydney's best examples of colonial architecture. There are also excellent views of the harbour from McElhone Park in front of the house, a vestige of the former grounds. It was built in 1835–39 for Alexander Macleay, the Colonial Secretary of New South Wales, and his family, after their arrival from England in 1826.

A video in the cellar explains the history of the building and the occupants. Six rooms are open on the ground floor and an upper level includes bedrooms and a morning room, all furnished in period style. The staircase is a particular feature.
✚ 63 D3 ✉ 7 Onslow Avenue, Elizabeth Bay, NSW 2011 ☎ 02 9356 3022
🕐 Fri–Sun 9.30–4 ✋ Adult A$8, child A$4, under 5 free 🚇 Kings Cross (Eastern Suburbs line) 🚌 311 from Circular Quay, the city or Kings Cross ❓ Historic Houses Trust Ticket Through Time gives admission to the Trust's 11 museums/historic houses; adult A$30, child A$15

HYDE PARK BARRACKS MUSEUM AND HYDE PARK
www.hht.nsw.gov.au

The attractive three-storey Barracks is one of Sydney's oldest buildings, built by convicts in 1817–19. It was designed by the ex-convict Francis Greenway, the architect of many of Sydney's most attractive Georgian buildings. The former prison now contains a museum of convict and early settler history. Galleries feature archaeological objects found on the site and stories of the former inhabitants. The Greenway Gallery hosts changing exhibitions on Australia's convict and penal colony history (▷ 29). Just south of the museum, Hyde Park is the city centre's largest green area, with its formal gardens, tree-shaded seating, fountains and statues. The area was declared public land as early as 1792 and it has been an official park since 1810. Take a walk to the moving art deco Anzac War Memorial at the southern end of the park.
✚ 63 C3/C4 ✉ Hyde Park Barracks Museum, Queens Square, Macquarie Street, Sydney, NSW 2000 ☎ 02 8239 2311
🕐 Museum: daily 9.30–5; park: daily 24 hours ✋ Museum: adult A$10, child A$5, under 5 free; park: free 🚇 St. James (City Circle line) 🚌 Sydney Explorer bus (stop 4) 💻 Museum and park 🏛

KOALA PARK SANCTUARY
www.koalapark.com

The sanctuary, 4.1ha (10 acres) of rainforest, eucalypt forest and gardens, is not just for koala fans. Other native animals include kangaroos, wallabies, wombats, dingoes, emus, echidnas, possums, cockatoos and kookaburras. You can feed kangaroos, pat dingoes and cuddle koalas. There are also shows involving koalas (daily 10.20, 11.45, 2), wombats (daily 2) and sheep shearing (daily 10.30, 2.30).
✚ 355 W13 ✉ 84 Castle Hill Road, West Pennant Hills, NSW 2125 ☎ 02 9484 3141 🕐 Daily 9–5 ✋ Adult A$19, child (4–14) A$9, under 4 free 🚇 Pennant Hills, then private bus service (Glenorie Buses) to the park 💻 🏛 🚌 25km (15.5 miles) northeast of the city via the Hills Motorway (Metroad 2)

Above left *The splendid staircase at Elizabeth Bay House*
Above right *Hyde Park Barracks*

MANLY AND THE NORTHERN BEACH SUBURBS

www.manlytourism.com

Manly has been a popular seaside resort since the late 1840s, when the first paddle-steamer ferry service to the city began. The present scenic ferry ride across Sydney Harbour is a major attraction in itself. Stretching from Manly to Palm Beach are 21 golden sandy surf beaches, headlands, lagoons and lakes, and beachside suburbs.

Manly has surfing, North Fort and the Royal Australian Artillery Museum (Wed and Sat, Sun 11–4), the Oceanworld aquarium (daily 10–5.30), Manly Art Gallery and Museum (Tue–Sun 10–5), Manly Waterworks fun pool and waterslide complex (Sat, Sun 10–5), plus walks and great harbour views from North Head, part of Sydney Harbour National Park (▷ 79).

Nearby is Palm Beach, known for its long surf beach, boating and ferry rides, cafés, restaurants and smart shops, and a walk to the lighthouse in Ku-ring-gai Chase National Park.

➕ 355 W13 ℹ Manly Visitor Centre, Manly Wharf, Manly, NSW 2095 ☎ 02 9976 1430 🚢 Ferry or fast JetCat from Circular Quay to Manly. There are then bus services to the other beachside suburbs

MUSEUM OF CONTEMPORARY ART

▷ 74.

MUSEUM OF SYDNEY

www.hht.nsw.gov.au

The MOS explores the stories of Sydney and its people—from early Aboriginal times to the present day. The stone and glass structure stands on the site of Sydney's first Government House, the foundations of which can be seen through a glass panel in the floor. Three levels of themed galleries focus on Sydney's indigenous and other people, history and environment. The displays are more imaginative than those of more traditional museums; some, perhaps, are rather avant garde and unsatisfying.

➕ 62 B3 ✉ Bridge Street, Sydney, NSW 2000 ☎ 02 9251 5988 🕐 Daily 9.30–5 💷 Adult A$10, child (under 5s free) A$5 🚇 Circular Quay (City Circle line) 🚌 Any Circular Quay bound bus 🚇 🏛

PADDINGTON

This is Sydney's prettiest suburb, a hillside village of Victorian two-floor terrace houses, with a taste for galleries, gourmet delicatessens, smart patisseries and fashion boutiques. Originally a working-class suburb, Paddington has been progressively gentrified since the 1970s, and today it has become a favourite haunt for lawyers, media high-flyers and anyone else who can afford the high price of local real estate.

Spilling down from the spine of Oxford are long rows of Victorian terrace houses with their distinctive wrought-iron balconies. Oxford Street, the suburb's main thoroughfare, is Sydney's fashion catwalk and there are plenty of sidewalk cafés to provide a vantage point. The street is at its liveliest on Saturdays, with Paddington Village Bazaar, a leafy churchyard selling fashions, food, jewellery and accessories.

➕ 63 D5 ✉ Oxford Street 🚌 Along Oxford Street from the city

PARLIAMENT OF NEW SOUTH WALES

www.parliament.nsw.gov.au

This has been the home of the New South Wales State Parliament—the Legislative Assembly (Lower House) and Legislative Council (Upper House)—since 1829 (▷ 32). The original building was the northern wing of the Rum Hospital, built by convict labour between 1812 and 1816 on the profits of the lucrative rum importation trade. You enter through the simple but very attractive verandah of this original building. The present parliamentary chambers date from the mid-19th century. You can watch the proceedings from the public galleries on sitting days.

➕ 63 C3 ✉ Macquarie Street, Sydney, NSW 2000 ☎ 02 9230 2111 (general enquiries); 02 9230 3444 (tour information and reservations) 🕐 Mon–Fri 9.30–4; closed public holidays 💷 Free. Tours (on non-sitting days only—call in advance) 9.30, 11, 12.30, 2, 3, 4 🚇 Martin Place (Eastern Suburbs line) or St. James (City Circle line) 🚌 Sydney Explorer bus (stop 4)

Left *The exterior of the Museum of Sydney*

INFORMATION

www.mca.com.au

🕂 62 B2 ✉ 140 George Street, The
Rocks, NSW 2000 (main entrance on
Circular Quay West) ☎ 02 9245 2400
(general enquiries) 🕓 Daily 10–5
✋ Free; charge for special exhibitions
Ⓢ Circular Quay (City Circle line)
🚌 Any Circular Quay bound bus 🖥 🏛

MUSEUM OF CONTEMPORARY ART

Australia's bespoke venue for modern art, the MCA is the only public museum
in the country dedicated to exhibiting, interpreting and collecting contemporary
art from across Australia and around the world.

PRIME POSITION

Set in a peerless position on the brink of Circular Quay, the museum opened in
1991 as a result of a bequest made to Sydney University for the purchase and
exhibition of contemporary art. Housed in the former home of the Maritime
Services Board, the portly, bunkerlike brown facade gives no hint of the
revolutionary ferment that goes on within. This is contemporary art in all its
diversity—performance, sculpture, photography and video as well as painting.
Its specialities are confrontation, and provocation. Visitors will often find
themselves baffled, amused and quite possibly irritated by the artworks they
see displayed—although seldom unmoved.

EXHIBITS

Although it has a permanent collection of around 4,500 works of art, little of
this is on display, as the museum concentrates on changing exhibitions. Recent
exhibitions have included a moving kaleidoscope of coloured lights 'painted'
onto a white wall, a model of the Sydney Harbour Bridge constructed from
glitter, cardboard, glue and shells, banners with slogans, flags made from
seersucker fabric and a porcelain bust painted in the style of a Chinese willow-
pattern plate.

Under the direction of Scottish-born Elizabeth Ann Macgregor since 1999,
the MCA has made enormous strides in making contemporary art more
accessible to the people of Sydney, implementing a free admissions policy
that has resulted in massive growth in visitor numbers. In 2007, the MCA was
named Sydney's favourite museum, beating more established institutions.

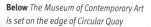

Below *The Museum of Contemporary Art
is set on the edge of Circular Quay*

POWERHOUSE MUSEUM

www.powerhousemuseum.com

This is one of Australia's most popular museums, housing thousands of items from the vast Museum of Applied Arts and Sciences collection. The museum, to the south of Darling Harbour, is in a former power station. The exhibits and galleries are on four levels; imaginative displays cover social history, decorative arts, music, technology, design, industry, transportation and space exploration. There are more than 200 fun interactive exhibits. Exhibitions are a regular feature and free 45-minute guided highlight tours are usually available (11.30, 1.30).

🕂 62 A5 ✉ 500 Harris Street, Ultimo, NSW 1238 ☎ 02 9217 0111 (enquiries) 🕐 Daily 10–5 ✋ Adult A$10, child (5–15) A$5; free after 4; additional charge for exhibitions 🚊 Metro Light Rail to Haymarket (from Central Station) or Metro Monorail to Powerhouse Museum 🖥 🚇

THE ROCKS AND CIRCULAR QUAY
▷ 76.

ROYAL BOTANIC GARDENS
▷ 77.

ST. MARY'S CATHEDRAL

www.stmaryscathedral.org.au

This is the city's largest church, the seat of the Archbishop of Sydney and the spiritual centre for the city's Catholic community. Since its foundation in 1788, Sydney has always had a significant Catholic population due to the large number of Irish among the convict population. Built in sandstone from quarries in nearby Pyrmont, the Gothic Revival church is reminiscent of the great medieval cathedrals of Europe. Completed in 1928, the church measures 106m (348 feet) in length, and the central tower rises to 46m (151 feet). The spires, which were only added in 2000, rise to 75m (246 feet). Inside, the cathedral has three levels of arched openings along its length, a typical feature of a Gothic cathedral. Notable features

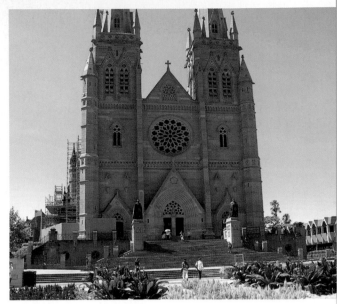

Above *St. Mary's Cathedral is the seat of the Archbishop of Sydney*

include the High Altar and screen, the terrazzo mosaic floor and the stained-glass windows.

🕂 63 C3 ✉ College Street and St. Mary's Road, Sydney, NSW 2000 ☎ 02 9220 0400 🕐 Daily 8–7 🚊 Museum (City Circle line) 🚌 Sydney Explorer bus (stop 7)

SYDNEY CRICKET GROUND

www.sydneycricketground.com.au

Known to locals as the 'SCG', the Sydney Cricket Ground is one of Australia's most famous sporting venues. In summer this 44,000-seater stadium is a venue for state and Test cricket; at other times the SCG is used primarily for exciting Aussie Rules Football games (▷ 18)—it is the home ground of the Sydney Swans team. On weekdays a twice-daily Sportspace Tour goes behind the scenes to visit dressing rooms, the players' tunnel, the SCG Members' Pavilion, the Walk of Honour area and SCG Museum.

🕂 Off map 63 D5 ✉ Driver Avenue, Moore Park, NSW 2021, 3.5km (2 miles) southeast of the city ☎ Ticketek (tickets to sporting events) 13 28 49; Sportspace Tours 02 9360 6601 🕐 Mon–Fri tours 10 and 1 (excluding public holidays and event days); Sat generally for sporting events ✋ Admission to events varies. Sportspace

Tours: adult A$29.00, child A$19.00 🚌 372–377, 390 or 391 from Circular Quay 🚶 20-minute walk or buses 372, 393 or 395 from Central Station 🖥 🚇

SYDNEY HARBOUR
▷ 78–79.

SYDNEY JEWISH MUSEUM

www.sydneyjewishmuseum.com.au

This small museum tells the moving story of Jewish people in Australia from the first days of European settlement—there were 16 Jews on the First Fleet in 1788. In a wider context it explains Jewish culture and traditions, documents the Holocaust and its aftermath, and serves as a memorial to the Jews who perished in World War II. A particular highlight of the museum is the Children's Memorial and 'Reflection and Remembrance', telling the stories of Australian Holocaust survivors.

🕂 63 D4 ✉ 148 Darlinghurst Road, Darlinghurst, NSW 2010 ☎ 02 9360 7999 🕐 Mon–Thu, Sun 10–4, Fri 10–2; closed Sat and Jewish holidays ✋ Adult A$10, child (4–16) A$6 🚊 Kings Cross (Eastern Suburbs line) 🚌 324 or 325 from Circular Quay to Kings Cross 🖥 🚇

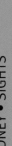
INFORMATION

www.sydneyvisitorcentre.com
www.therocks.com

✚ 62 B2 ℹ Sydney Visitor Centre
✉ Level 1, The Argyle Centre, The
Rocks, Sydney, NSW 2000, ☎ 02 9240
8788 or 1800 067 676; 1902 222 222 (The
Rocks Infoline) 🕔 Daily 9.30–5.30

TIP

» Walking is the best way to explore the
area—a A$1 map/guide is available from
the Sydney Visitor Centre.

HIGHLIGHTS

» Museum of Contemporary Art (▷ 74)
» Sydney Observatory (daily 10–5)
» Susannah Place Museum (Sat, Sun
10–5), 19th-century houses; The Rocks
Pub Tour (Mon, Wed, Fri, Sat 5pm), a
walking tour of historic hotels

THE ROCKS AND CIRCULAR QUAY

The Rocks is Australia's oldest 'village', where the convicts of the First Fleet
set up their tents in January 1788.

Both The Rocks and the Circular Quay area are set around Sydney Cove,
about 1km (0.6 mile) north of the central area. It's very easy to walk round,
and there are plenty of colonial buildings, narrow streets, cobbled lanes such
as Nurses Walk and Suez Canal, museums and galleries, shops, cafés and
restaurants, and great views of the harbour, Sydney Harbour Bridge and the
Opera House.

THE ROCKS

The Rocks, at various times, has been the domain of convicts and soldiers,
lawless sealers and whalers, brothels, rough inns and gangs of thugs, and the
gentry. The area was also the site of Australia's first fort, hospital, windmill and
wharves. Despite much demolition in 1900 and again in the 1960s, the area still
has historic streets and lanes, and many buildings dating from the 1820s
to the 1840s.

The built heritage includes Cadmans Cottage (1816) which is now an
information point for Sydney Harbour National Park, Campbells Storehouses
(1839–90), the Argyle Stores (1828), Sydney Observatory (1858) and the
Garrison Church (from 1840) at Argyle Place. Among the atmospheric pubs are
the Lord Nelson Hotel (1834) and the Hero of Waterloo (1844) at Millers Point,
and The Fortune of War (1922), Orient Hotel (1844) and Mercantile Hotel (1915)
along George Street.

The area is packed with arcades, galleries and souvenir and gift shops. The
Rocks Market takes over the upper end of George Street on weekends, and
there are free musical performances, street theatre and live bands in the pubs.
The Sydney Visitor Centre has a free History of The Rocks display and The
Rocks Discovery Museum in Kendall Lane (daily 10–5) presents an interactive
collection of archaeological artefacts and images that tell the area's story.

CIRCULAR QUAY

Fronting Sydney Cove, this was the area in which the British flag was first
raised by Governor Phillip in 1788 (▷ 29). It has since become the city's ferry
and cruise boat hub, much frequented by visitors. The Overseas Passenger
Terminal at Circular Quay West has fashionable restaurants and bars, while
East Circular Quay has waterfront shops, restaurants, bars, cafés, a hotel and
a cinema. The Sydney Opera House (▷ 82), Museum of Contemporary Art
(▷ 74) and the Justice and Police Museum are in this area.

Above The First Impressions *sculpture by*
Bud Dumas in The Rocks area of Sydney

ROYAL BOTANIC GARDENS

This is a tranquil place to walk and relax within the heart of the city. Founded by Governor Lachlan Macquarie in 1816, the gardens incorporate the land used for Australia's first farm, established by members of the First Fleet in 1788. When the first convict-settlers, troops and administrators reached Sydney, it was essential to establish gardens and the damp, sandy spot on the edge of the cove was the chosen spot. The first attempt was a miserable failure, and for a couple of years the colony hovered on the brink of starvation.

Now covering 30ha (74 acres) on the shores of Sydney Harbour, the Royal Botanic Gardens contain one of Australia's best collections of native and introduced plants. Among the themed areas are the Rose, Herb, Oriental and Succulent gardens, and also the Sydney Fernery and the Palm Grove. A free guided tour (Mar–end Nov daily 10.30) picks out the highlights and explains more about the area's history.

ROUND AND ABOUT

To the north, the gardens wrap themselves around the horseshoe curve of Farm Cove. The lovely palm grove at the centre of the gardens is infested with grey-headed flying foxes, which hang upside-down from the branches in squabbling menageries. Although they destroy the trees, they are an endangered species and attempts to relocate them have failed. Nearby is Cadi Jam Ora, a garden with some of the plants once used by local Aboriginal people. The waterside path leads to Mrs Macquarie's Point, which has a sublime view of the Opera House and Sydney Harbour Bridge.

To the south of the botanic garden, The Domain is a broad area of lawns used extensively by city office workers for lunchtime sporting competitions. Beyond the eastern and southern boundaries are The Domain parklands.

The Sydney Tropical Centre is another feature not to miss: There are two large modern glasshouses that contain palms, orchids and a large range of other tropical plants.

INFORMATION

www.rbgsyd.nsw.gov.au
✚ 63 C3 ✉ Mrs Macquaries Road, The Domain, Sydney, NSW 2000 ☎ 02 9231 8111/8125 ⊕ Gardens: daily 7–dusk; Sydney Tropical Centre: daily 10–4 ♿ Free. Sydney Tropical Centre: adults A$2.20, child A$1.10 ⊕ Circular Quay (City Circle line) 🚌 441 from the Queen Victoria Building (York Street bus interchange) to the Art Gallery of NSW
🍴 ♿ 🚻 ♿

Below *The Pyramid Building of the Sydney Tropical Centre in the Royal Botanic Gardens*

INFORMATION

www.sydneyvisitorcentre.com
www.nationalparks.nsw.gov.au
Sydney Visitor Centre
🕂 63 C1 ✉ 1 The Argyle Centre, The
Rocks, Sydney, NSW 2000 ☎ 02 9240
8788 🕔 Daily 9.30–5.30 ❓ Sydney
Ferries: 13 15 00. Sydney Harbour
National Park: 02 9247 5033 🚉 Circular
Quay (City Circle line). From here ferries
depart for destinations all around the
harbour and along the Parramatta River.
For the Harbour Bridge walkway, Circular
Quay or Milsons Point (station on the
northern side)

INTRODUCTION

Sydney's harbour, bridge and opera house are known the world over. The
Sydney Opera House is not only Sydney's most distinctive landmark, it is the
city's—and perhaps Australia's—most important venue for the performing arts.
A walk beside the shoreline is a must for visitors to the city.

From the South Pacific Ocean, a 317km (230-mile) shoreline extends
inland around the harbour, beneath Sydney Harbour Bridge and west along
the Parramatta River. The harbour is surrounded by tall office buildings, port
facilities, cruise ship terminals, beaches, bays, headlands and, of course, the
suburbs of Sydney residents. Yet most unusual for a major city is the survival
of extensive areas of bushland, which are preserved in the Sydney Harbour
National Park. The best place to start exploring the harbour is the water
itself—take one of the ferries from Circular Quay to view the many coves and
beaches and get close to the spectacular waterfront houses and seemingly
remote bushland. After viewing the Bridge and visiting the Opera House don't
miss out on exploring the Royal Botanic Gardens (▷ 77) and parts of the
Sydney Harbour National Park.

Sydney Harbour (the official name is Port Jackson) was bypassed by Captain
Cook on his 1770 exploration of Australia's east coast, but in 1788 the ships,
crew and convicts of the First Fleet, disappointed by the barren surrounds
farther south at Botany Bay, entered the waterway and set up their tents in
the area now known as The Rocks. Since those times, the harbour has been
vital for communication and transportation and it is now also a great attraction.
Bennelong Point is named after an Aboriginal man who lived there in the late
18th century. In 1955 this site, then a tram depot, was chosen as the setting
for the Opera House.

WHAT TO SEE

SYDNEY HARBOUR BRIDGE

www.pylonlookout.com.au
This distinctive steel arched structure, with its pairs of stone pylons at
each end, is a Sydney icon. The rounded shape has led to its nickname of
the 'Coathanger'. Construction began in 1923 and it was opened in March
1932. It is still the bridge with the longest span in relation to its width. The

Above A view of the harbour from
Lavender Bay in North Sydney

main span is 502.9m (1,650ft) long and 48.8m (160ft) wide and carries two rail tracks, a walkway, a cycleway and eight road lanes. The top of the arch is 134m (440ft) above sea level. The bridge is still a vital link between the north and south sides of the harbour, but due to increasing traffic it has been supplemented by the Sydney Harbour Tunnel, constructed in the early 1990s.

There are several ways to experience the bridge. To view it from below, walk from Campbells Cove in The Rocks to Dawes Point, or take a ferry across the harbour to Milsons Point. The bridge walkway from The Rocks to the Pylon Lookout allows you to see the structure close up, and gives good city and harbour views. The exhibition in the Pylon Lookout describes the history and construction of the bridge, and there is a great view from the top (200 steps).

Thousands of Sydneysiders cross the bridge daily on foot, and this is a fine walk on a sunny day. There are footpaths on both the eastern and western side of the bridge. The eastern side has the views, while cyclists whiz across the western side. To access the stairways to the bridge, begin at Argyle Street in The Rocks and climb the Argyle Stairs, which are just a short walk above the intersection with Harrington Street. The walk across the bridge takes about 20 minutes. At the end, walk down the stairs to Milsons Point and cross back under the bridge. Stop off at the café in the shadow of the bridge and return to the city by ferry, with an upward glance to admire the underbelly of the bridge as you go. This is not her Hollywood side, but all that steel, hefted into the heavens, is a sight to inspire.

The most exciting way to see the bridge is on a day or night BridgeClimb tour (3.5 hours; tours every 10 minutes from early morning to evening; night climbs by demand), which takes you along catwalks and ladders to the very top of the structure. The climb might be expensive, but it is well worth the price—book in advance.

🔲 62 C1 ✉ Pylon Lookout, via Cumberland Street, The Rocks, Sydney, NSW 2000 ☎ 02 9240 1100 🕐 Daily 10–5 💷 Adult A$9.50, child (8–12) A$4 ❓ BridgeClimb booking: 02 8274 7777; www.bridgeclimb.com 💷 Adult A$198/295, child (12–16 accompanied by adult) A$128/195

SYDNEY HARBOUR NATIONAL PARK

www.npws.nsw.gov.au

Scattered around Sydney Harbour to the east of the bridge, the national park takes in islands, headlands, beaches, bushland, bays and historic Aboriginal and colonial sites. These relatively unspoiled areas are a remarkable feature for any metropolis, but their close proximity to the city makes them particularly unusual.

Try to sample at least one area of the national park. The easiest access is by taking a ferry from The Rocks to either Manly (▷ 73) or Watsons Bay, both of which are on peninsulas between ocean and harbour. The Manly Scenic Walkway is a spectacular 10km (6-mile) coastal walk from Manly to the Spit Bridge at Middle Harbour (it takes 3–4 hours to do the entire route, but the walk can be shortened). South Head, with great views of the harbour, ocean and North Head, is a 1.5km (1-mile) walk from Watsons Bay, and it can be combined with a visit to the beach at Camp Cove. Closer to the city, the north side Chowder Head/Bradleys Head section is south of Mosman near Taronga Zoo (▷ 80). Perhaps the best way to enjoy the park is to take a short walk, laze on a beach or picnic area, and enjoy the views.

Fort Denison, an island north of The Domain and Royal Botanic Gardens, was formerly a place of convict punishment and then a military fort in the 19th century. Access to Fort Denison is via the National Parks and Wildlife Service tours only.

🔲 Off map 63 D1 ✉ Sydney Harbour National Park Information Centre, Cadmans Cottage, 110 George Street, The Rocks, NSW 2000 ☎ 02 9247 5033 🕐 Cadmans Cottage Mon–Fri 9.30–4.30, Sat–Sun 10–4.30; most of the national park is open daily 24 hours 💷 Most sections free; fees vary for tours to Goat Island, Fort Denison and the Quarantine Station at North Head; landing fees for Shark Island, Clark Island and Rodd Island: A$5 per person (under 5s free)

Below *Visitors climbing the bridge will be rewarded with a stunning view of the harbour*

SYDNEY OBSERVATORY

Perched on the summit of Observatory Hill, this handsome sandstone building was originally a signal station, built in 1848. Every day at exactly 1pm, a ball would drop from the mast of the square tower so that ships' masters in the harbour could set their chronometers, which were crucial for calculating longitude on long Antipodean voyages. Later in the century this became a full astronomical observatory, but as Sydney grew the city's brightening night lights made astronomy more and more difficult.

Since 1982, Sydney Observatory has been a museum of astronomy, with an imaginative 3-D Space Theatre that takes visitors on a conducted tour of the universe. At night, the Observatory's enthusiastic astronomers take visitors on a viewing tour of stars, galaxies and planets through a sophisticated, computer-controlled 40cm (16-inch) reflecting (mirror) telescope. Times for the tour vary depending on sunset times throughout the year.

✚ 62 B2 ✉ Observatory Hill, The Rocks, NSW 2000 ☎ 02 9921 3485 🕐 Daily 10–5, and every night at varying times, bookings required for night sessions 🖐 Adult A$7, child (4–15) A$5 🚌 Millers Point, The Rocks Train: Circular Quay

SYDNEY OLYMPIC PARK

▷ 81.

SYDNEY OPERA HOUSE

▷ 82–83.

SYDNEY TOWER

www.sydneytower.myfun.com.au
The views from the Observation Deck of Sydney's tallest building, 250m (820ft) above street level, are fantastic—on clear days you can see as far away as the Blue Mountains, about 90km (56 miles) away. It's also a good way to orientate yourself to the city. OzTrek, a virtual tour complete with headphones and a commentary in English and several Asian languages, provides an introduction to Australia's culture, history and geography, but it's only a sideshow to the main experience.

A major attraction is the Skywalk—a guided walk around an outdoor viewing platform, 268m (292 yards) above the city. It is also a great place to visit at sunset as the views are outstanding.

✚ 62 B3 ✉ Podium Level, 100 Market Street, Sydney, NSW 2000 ☎ 02 8251 7800 🕐 Daily 9am–10.30pm (also Sat 10.30–11.30) 🖐 Adult A$25, child (5–16) A$15, under 5 free (admission to both OzTrek and the Observation Deck) 🚇 St. James or Town Hall (City Circle line) 🚌 Sydney Explorer bus (stop 14) 🍴 🛒 🏛

TARONGA ZOO

www.taronga.org.au
Taronga is Australia's premier zoo, set in 28ha (69 acres) of beautiful landscaped gardens, native bushland and foreshore on the northern side of Sydney Harbour. There are buses from the city to Taronga Zoo, but the best way to arrive is by ferry from Circular Quay; if you take this option, then purchase an economical ZooPass, which includes the return ferry fare, entrance to the zoo, the bus trip to or from the main entrance, and a ride on the Sky Safari cable car.

The zoo is home to around 340 species of marsupial, mammal, bird, fish and reptile, totalling more than 2,600 individual animals. From Australia there are koalas, dingoes, kangaroos, wallabies, echidnas, platypuses, wombats, Tasmanian devils, crocodiles and snakes, and bird species such as pelicans, emus, fairy penguins, kookaburras, lyrebirds and a variety of different parrots. Exotic animals include giraffes, snakes, reptiles, elephants, snow leopards, orang utans, lions, tigers, red pandas, Kodiak bears and sun bears.

✚ Off map 62 B1 ✉ Bradleys Head Road, Mosman, NSW 2088 ☎ 02 9969 2777 (general enquiries) 🕐 Daily 9–5 🖐 Adult A$41, child (4–15) A$20, under 4 free. ZooPass: adult A$48, child A$23.50 🚌 247 from the city centre, Wynyard Station 🛳 Ferry from Circular Quay 🛒 🏛

VAUCLUSE HOUSE

www.hht.net.au
Dating from 1827, this Gothic Revival mansion was originally the home of William Charles Wentworth. It is one of only a few large historic houses in and around Sydney. Wentworth was a famous Australian explorer and barrister, the founder of the University of Sydney, and the 'Father of the Australian Constitution'. The three-floor house is furnished in mid-19th-century style. It is surrounded by 11ha (27 acres) of grounds and gardens, only a fraction of the estate's original 200ha (494 acres).

✚ Off map 63 D4 ✉ Wentworth Road, Vaucluse, NSW 2030 ☎ 02 9388 7922 🕐 Fri–Sun 9.30–4 🖐 Adult A$8, child A$4, under 5s free 🚌 325 from Circular Quay, central Sydney and Kings Cross; Bondi Explorer bus (stop 9) 🛒 🏛

WOOLLOOMOOLOO

The name is derived from a local Aboriginal word, probably meaning either a young black kangaroo or a place of plenty, but either way it's a tongue-twister. Woolloomooloo has seen huge changes since the time when it was a bustling and colourful shipping yard. The world's longest timber-piled building, the Finger Wharf is a relic from Sydney's early commercial shipping industry. In 2000, it was transformed into a marina lined with waterfront cafés, swanky restaurants and a stylish hotel. Nearby, Harry's Café de Wheels is a Sydney legend, a roadside food stall that sells meat pies to shift workers, taxi drivers, actors and visiting rock stars. Opened in 1938 to serve sailors and workers at the Woolloomooloo dockyards, the name, 'Café de Wheels' came from a city ordinance that required mobile food caravans to move a minimum of 12 inches per day. Woolloomooloo's wharves are used by ships of the Australian navy, which has its base at Garden Island, at the end of Cowper Wharf Road, and by vessels of allied navies.

✚ 63 D4 ✉ Cowper Wharf Road, Woolloomooloo, NSW 2011

SYDNEY OLYMPIC PARK

Olympic Park was the focus of Sydney's highly successful Olympic and Paralympic Games in 2000 and is now a world-class sporting and leisure venue. The site takes in seven parks and 15 sporting and other venues, and many festivals and special events are held here. Bicentennial Park and The Parklands adjoin the site—a large area of grass, trees and open space. Bicentennial Park consists of 100ha (247 acres)—these include wetlands, mangroves, parkland, fountains, playgrounds, bicycle paths and walkways.

Although Sydney Olympic Park can be reached by train, the best way to arrive is by RiverCat ferry along the Parramatta River from Circular Quay. Once at the site, various tours are available, including a 60-minute guided coach tour, and behind-the-scenes visits to the Aquatic Centre and Telstra Stadium. Look out for the SOP Sports Centre, home of the New South Wales Hall of Champions, a museum dedicated to the state's champion athletes; Sydney Showground, used primarily for the Royal Easter Show, a mainly agricultural festival; the Sydney SuperDome, a major musical, concert and sports venue; and the Sydney International Tennis Centre, which is open to anyone keen for a game.

If you feel like cooling off, jump in at the SOP Aquatic Centre. In addition to two Olympic-size pools, there is a waterslide and other fun aquatic areas, a gym and a café.

INFORMATION

www.sydneyolympicpark.com.au
⊕ Off map 62 A4 🚹 Sydney Olympic Park Visitor Gateway, 1 Showground Road, Sydney Olympic Park, NSW 2127 ☎ 02 9714 7888 🕐 Daily 9–5, Park: daily 24 hours; venues vary 🚊 Olympic Park

Above *The stadium at Olympic Park still attracts the crowds*

SYDNEY OPERA HOUSE

Dazzling, dramatic, bold and beautiful, Sydney Opera House is one of the great buildings of the 20th century, a focal point for the city that surrounds it and a potent icon for modern Australian culture.

EXTRAORDINARY DESIGN

The NSW government launched an international competition for an opera house in 1955 to be built on the site of former tram depot on Bennelong Point. The competition was won by Danish architect Joern Utzon, whose extraordinary design was brilliant but problematic. Nothing like it had ever been attempted before. The technology to cast the soaring sails and to join enormous sheets of glass into vast, seamless walls did not exist at the time. Nevertheless, Utzon's concept caught the judges' imagination, and construction of the giant podium began in 1958, and the Opera House was completed 14 years later in 1973.

From the start, the contractors faced a cost blowout, a problem that was to plague the Opera House throughout its construction. Projected to cost A$7 million and take four years to erect, the building would eventually require A$102 million and 15 years. Utzon resigned in 1966, long before the building was completed and a team of Australian architects then took over. Utzon has never returned to see his masterpiece, but he was a consultant for its refurbishment during the early 2000s.

PERFORMANCE

Officially opened by Queen Elizabeth II in 1973, this soaring architectural marvel is now Sydney's premier venue for all the performing arts, home to the Australian Ballet, the Sydney Dance Company and the Australian Opera Company. The Opera House contains five performance spaces, and the outside forecourt is also used for entertainment. Its arching 'shell' or 'sail' roofs, covered with more than a million Swedish-made ceramic tiles, and dramatic stepped terraces are recognized the world over.

The Opera House is now an essential stop on a visit to Sydney. You can join a tour of the interior, attend a performance or just admire the architecture. There are also shops and four restaurants and cafés. The location, too, is spectacular: Bennelong Point juts out into Sydney Harbour with views across Sydney Cove to the Harbour Bridge. The most popular tour, the Front of House, takes you into the various theatres and theatre foyers. These are the Concert Hall (seating 2,679 people) and Opera Theatre (seating 1,547), both under the main roof, and three smaller spaces (The Studio, Playhouse and Drama Theatre) on the lower level. The less frequent Backstage tour takes visitors into technical areas, rehearsal rooms and other behind-the-scenes spaces normally reserved for performers and crew, including the dressing rooms used by the stars.

The Opera House does not have its own resident company, but is used by various companies that perform opera, ballet, classical music, theatre, modern dance and other art forms. These companies include some of Australia's best, such as Opera Australia, the Australian Ballet, Sydney Symphony Orchestra, Bell Shakespeare Company, Sydney Dance Company and Sydney Theatre Company. Jazz and contemporary music concerts are also held in the building. On site is the celebrated Guillaume at Bennnelong, one of Sydney's finest restaurants (▷ 95).

Since its opened, the Sydney Opera House has become one of the world's busiest performing arts centres. More than 45 million people have enjoyed over 100,000 performances, and an evening at the Opera House is a highlight of any visitor's experience of Sydney.

INFORMATION

www.sydneyoperahouse.com
✚ 63 C2 ✉ Bennelong Point, NSW 2000 ☎ 02 9250 7777 (general enquiries and box office: Mon–Sat 9–8.30); 02 9250 7250 (tours) ◉ Performances mostly evenings; tours daily 9–5 ✋ Front of House tour daily 9–5, departures generally every 30 minutes (no pre-booking), one hour duration. Adult A$35, child A$24.50. Backstage tour, most days at 7am (bookings essential), two hours' duration. $150 including breakfast (Note: no child price—children under 12 are not permitted)

REGIONS   SYDNEY • SIGHTS

Opposite *A view of the Bridge from between the sails of the Opera House*
Below *An interior view of one of the larger performance spaces*

WALK

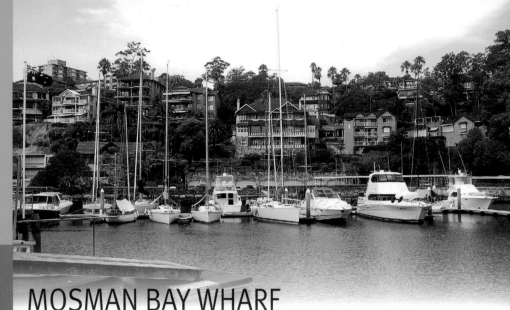

MOSMAN BAY WHARF
TO CREMORNE WHARF

This easy walk along the shoreline of Mosman Bay takes in magnificent views of Sydney and its harbour (▷ 66–83). Suburban houses blend with bushland and yacht anchorages, and signs along the route explain the history of the Aboriginal inhabitants.

THE WALK

Distance: 2.25km (1.5 miles)
Allow: 35–45 minutes
Start at: Mosman Bay Wharf
End at: Cremorne Wharf
How to get there: Ferries from Circular Quay (see map ▷ 62, B2) to Mosman Bay, Mon–Sat every 30 mins, Sun hourly

★ On the crossing to Mosman Bay you pass by Fort Denison, built in the 1840s to protect Sydney from naval attack. From the Mosman wharf, head past the café and turn left to walk along the foreshore of the bottom end of Mosman Bay. Across the water is a marina and Mosman Rowing Club.

❶ About 100m (110 yards) from the wharf, on the land side, is a sculpture of HMS *Sirius*, the principal naval escort ship of the First Fleet, which arrived in Port Jackson (Sydney Harbour) on 26 January 1788. Across the road is Mosman's oldest building, The Barn, built as a whaling store-house in 1831.

Walk towards the tall palms of Reid Park and follow the foreshore path as it curves around the head of the bay. Walk through the parking area of Mosman Rowing Club.

❷ Smartly dressed visitors can sign in at the Mosman Rowing Club for a drink and have lunch or dinner in the restaurant, or enjoy bistro-style snacks or barbecue meals on the verandah overlooking the yachts in the marina.

Climb the steps just past the rowing club entrance. Walk along the path, with harbour views to your left, and over a timber bridge. You enter a dense grove of trees where the path splits: Take the left-hand path up a short flight of steps and past some houses.

❸ You are now on the eastern side of Cremorne Point. Some of the larger houses on the Point are examples of the local arts and crafts style (known as Federation), dating from the early 20th century. These and other traditional buildings have made the Point a Heritage Conservation Area.

A path leads down to the Sydney Amateur Sailing clubhouse; another

turn-off leads to Old Cremorne Wharf. The path soon passes the Lex and Ruby Graham Gardens.

Opposite Moored boats at Mosman Bay
Above left Deep-fried calimari is on the menu at Mosman Rowing Club
Above right Across the harbour from Mosman Bay

❹ The tropical foliage of Lex and Ruby Graham Gardens, a community garden established in 1957 by the Grahams, a local couple, was developed over nearly 30 years. Palms and tree ferns mix with exotic and native shrubs. Tracks through the gardens lead down to the water.

On from the gardens, a row of impressive old apartments is on your right. The main harbour comes into view ahead. Take the path to the left into a small park, pass the playground and continue through bushland, from where there are great views of the city. Continue 200m (220 yards) along the path to the southerly Robertsons Point.

❺ At Robertsons Point, the view of Sydney Harbour opens up before you. If you wish, scramble down to a small white lighthouse on the shoreline. The peninsula was once occupied by the Cammeraygal people. Colonial settlement came only slowly after 1830.

Walk back to the playground. A path to your left leads to steps that go steeply down to the road below. Directly ahead is Cremorne Wharf where you can wait for the next city-bound ferry.

Uphill from the wharf there is an excellent picnic area that has a public swimming pool on the harbour's edge. Both the picnic ground and the pool have magnificent views over Shell Cove to the city.

WHEN TO GO
All year round.

WHERE TO EAT
MOSMAN ROWING CLUB RESTAURANT
🕒 Tue–Sun 12–3, Wed–Sun 6–9; breakfast Sun 8.30–10.30. Also bistro and barbecue meals daily 12–3.30, 6–9).

PUBLIC TOILETS
Park above Cremorne Point Wharf and at Mosman Wharf.

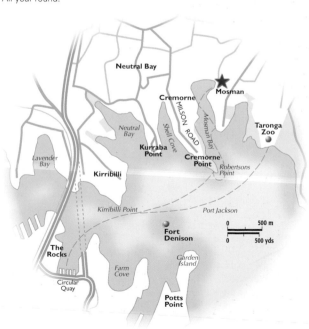

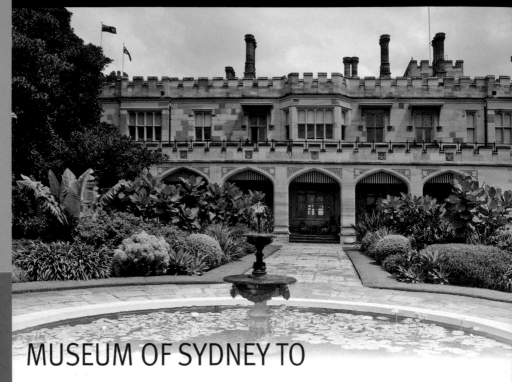

MUSEUM OF SYDNEY TO
MRS MACQUARIE'S CHAIR

This first part of this walk explores Australia's history with a stroll along Macquarie Street, named after a far-sighted early governor, then wanders through the green glories of the Royal Botanic Gardens.

THE WALK
Distance:
Allow: 4 hours
Start at: Museum of Sydney
End at: Mrs Macquarie's Chair
How to get there: Bus, ferry or train to Circular Quay and walk to the Museum

The Museum of Sydney (▷ 73) charts the city's history, from the era of the Eora Aboriginal people to the present. Artefacts, pictures, audio and digital technologies tell the story of Sydney's gradual evolution, from a wilderness populated by hunter-gatherers to penal settlement to cosmopolitan metropolis. The museum is built on the site of the original Government House, which was unearthed by accident in 1983.

★ From the museum, walk up Bridge Street to Macquarie Street and turn right. The castellated building behind the equestrian statue of King Edward VII is the Sydney Conservatorium. It was designed as the stables for Government House, which lies behind it. When it was built in 1819, the cost caused an outrage among Governor Macquarie's superiors in London, and eventually helped bring about his downfall.

Walk uphill along Macquarie Street.

❶ The classical sandstone building on the opposite corner of the Bent Street intersection is the State Library of NSW. The library houses some of the most important archives of Australiana. Inlaid in the marble floor of the foyer is a reproduction of Abel Tasman's 17th-century map of Australia.

Continue along Macquarie Street.

❷ Behind the iron railings on the left, the Parliament of New South Wales (▷ 73) is the seat of the NSW State Government, originally the north wing of the General Hospital and Dispensary. The British Government had refused to fund a hospital so Governor Macquarie granted the builders the right to import 60,000 gallons of rum. Since rum was a precious commodity in thirsty Sydney, the city got a free hospital, known as 'The Rum Hospital', which subsequently became the State Parliament.

Continue along Macquarie Street.

❸ Hyde Park Barracks (▷ 72) was Sydney's original lock-up. Before it was completed in 1819, most convicts were left free to wander the streets, and Sydney was a dangerous place after dark. The Barracks is now a museum.

Turn left to follow the curve of College Street, and left again at the back of St Mary's Cathedral into Prince Albert Road, which becomes Art Gallery Road.

❹ The Art Gallery of New South Wales (▷ 67) has a collection of works by all major Australian artists. The gallery also has a well-respected Asian Collection, which includes many fine works from Japan, China and South-East Asia.

Walk past the gallery across the bridge that spans the Eastern Distributor and take the steps leading down into the Royal Botanic Gardens. Take the first path right and left at the bust of a woman.

❺ The Royal Botanic Gardens (▷ 77) are a serene wonderland, a treasury of tropical and temperate flora, lawns, ponds, shady trees and some of Sydney's finest views.

From the palm grove, walk past the ponds toward the water and follow the curving path alongside Farm Cove to Mrs Macquarie's Point for a classic Sydney view.

Around the point is Garden Island naval base and chiselled into the rock is Mrs Macquarie's Chair, named after the wife of Governor Macquarie, who would drive here in her carriage to admire the scenery.

From here you can either catch a Sydney Explorer Bus or walk back to the city via the Opera House.

Opposite *Government House is situated within the Royal Botanic Gardens*
Above *Mrs Macquarie's Chair has a splendid view of the harbour*

WHEN TO GO
All year round.

WHERE TO EAT
THE HYDE PARK BARRACKS CAFÉ
The Botanic Gardens Café (near the Visitor Centre Daily 8.30–4.30).

✉ Queen Square ☎ 02 9222 1815
🕐 Mon–Fri 8–3, Sat–Sun 10–3).

PUBLIC TOILETS
In the NSW State Library, the Art Gallery, and near the visitor centre in the Royal Botanic Gardens.

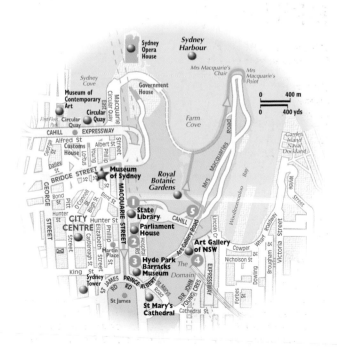

WHAT TO DO

SHOPPING

AUSTRALIAN ABORIGINAL ART GALLERY

www.jintaart.com.au

This gallery sells works by many leading Aboriginal artists from the Central Desert region. There is also a large range of artefacts and objects that make great gifts.

✉ 283 George Street, NSW 2000 ☎ 02 9299 4953 ⏰ Mon–Sat 9.30–6.30, Sun 11–6

AUSTRALIAN GEOGRAPHIC

www.australiangeographic.com.au

An offshoot of *Australian Geographic Magazine,* this store celebrates the natural world with books, posters, scientific instruments, games and cuddly soft toys.

✉ Shop 34, Queen Victoria Building, 455 George Street, Sydney, NSW 2000 ☎ 02 9257 0086 ⏰ Mon–Fri 9–6, Sat, Sun 10–5 🚊 Town Hall, Galeries Victoria (Monorail)

DAVID JONES

www.davidjones.com.au

A Sydney institution, the David Jones department store has been

trading since 1838. Selling Australian and international goods of all kinds, the two DJ buildings are beautifully decorated and offer courteous, almost old-fashioned, service that is rare in the 21st century.

✉ Elizabeth and Market streets, and Castlereagh and Market streets, Sydney, NSW 2000 ☎ 02 9266 5544 ⏰ Mon–Fri 9.30–6 (also Thu 6–9pm), Sat 9–6, Sun 10–6 🚊 St. James 🚊 City Centre (Monorail)

DFS GALLERIA

www.dfsgalleria.com

DFS Galleria is one of the largest department stores in Australia selling duty- and GST-free goods. It has four floors of Australian and international goods, including wines, opals, clothing, jewellery, perfumes, cosmetics and electronic equipment. Brands include Tiffany and Co. and Burberry of London.

✉ 155 George Street, The Rocks, NSW 2000 ☎ 02 8243 8666 ⏰ Mon–Fri 11–9, Sat, Sun 10–9 🚊 Circular Quay (CityRail)

DONE ART AND DESIGN

www.done.com.au

One of the most popular tourist

shops in The Rocks, Done Art and Design sells clothes, swimwear, homewares and souvenirs—all with designer and artist Ken Done's trademark vibrant designs.

✉ 123 George Street, The Rocks, NSW 2000 ☎ 02 9251 6099 ⏰ Daily 10–6 🚊 Circular Quay (CityRail)

EQ MARKETS

www.eqmoorepark.com.au

The market has stalls selling movie memorabilia, collectables, clothing, gifts, houseware, toys, art and crafts. There is also an interesting Farmers' Market here Saturday and Wednesday. There are many dining options, a playground and a cinema complex.

✉ Lang Road, Moore Park, NSW 1363 ☎ 02 9383 4333 ⏰ Wed, Sat, Sun 10–3.30 🍴 🚌 372–377 from Circular Quay 🚕

FLAME OPALS

www.flameopals.com.au

By buying their opals direct from the miners and manufacturing their own jewellery, Flame Opals offer competitive prices and a wide selection of stones. Buy them unset or as jewellery.

✉ 119 George Street, The Rocks, NSW 2000 ☎ 02 9247 3446 ◷ Mon–Fri 9–6, Sat 10–5, Sun 11.30–5 ⊡ Circular Quay (CityRail)

GOODWOOD SADDLERY
www.goodwoods.com.au
Australian bushmen's gear such as Akubra hats, Drizabone coats and R. M. Williams boots can be found at this saddlery southwest of the city centre.

✉ Unit 19/1 Hordern Place, Camperdown, NSW 2050 ☎ 02 9519 8844 ◷ Mon–Fri 9–5, Sat 9–4 ⊡ Central Station then 1461 bus

HARBOURSIDE SHOPPING CENTRE
www.harbourside.com.au
An extensive fashion and gift shopping complex, with an accent on Australian-made clothing and souvenirs. Check out Australian Craft Galleries for fine, handcrafted glassware.

✉ Darling Harbour, Sydney, NSW 2000 ☎ 02 9281 3999 ◷ Daily 10–9 ⊡ Harbourside (Monorail)

NATIONAL MARITIME MUSEUM
www.anmm.gov.au/store.htm
The museum shop has maritime books, gifts and souvenirs. You can buy some unusual gifts including compass cufflinks, lighthouse-shaped egg cups, and clocks in the form of submarines.

✉ 2 Murray Street, Darling Harbour, NSW 2000 ☎ 02 9298 3777 ◷ Daily 9.30–5 ⊡ Harbourside (Monorail) ⊡

PADDINGTON MARKETS
www.paddingtonmarkets.com.au
Head to Sydney's best market, in fashionable Paddington and with more than 250 stalls, for jewellery, crafts, fashions, accessories and unusual gifts. The markets are a great place to people-watch and meet the locals, and there is also live entertainment and good food.

✉ 395 Oxford Street, Paddington, Sydney,

NSW 2021 ☎ 02 9331 2923 ◷ Sat 10–4 (until 5 in summer) ⊡ 380 from Circular Quay and City Centre

QUEEN VICTORIA BUILDING
www.qvb.com.au
Sydney's most opulent shopping mall, housed in a magnificent 1898 building that takes up an entire city block, offers five levels of clothing, accessories, jewellery, antiques, gift and souvenir shops. There are also many cafés and restaurants, beautiful stained-glass windows and historic exhibits. Come here to shop 'til you drop or just to admire the Victorian architecture.

✉ 455 George Street, Sydney, NSW 2000 ☎ 02 9264 9209 ◷ Mon–Sat 9–6 (also Thu 6–9pm), Sun 11–5 ⊡ Town Hall ⊡ Galeries Victoria (Monorail)

R. M. WILLIAMS
www.rmwilliams.com.au
This famous bushman outfitter sells shirts, hats, moleskins, drills, jeans, oilskins and boots. There's another branch at 389 George Street.

✉ 71 George Street, The Rocks, NSW 2000 ☎ 02 9247 0204 ◷ Mon–Sat 10–6, Sun 10–5 ⊡ Circular Quay (CityRail)

SOH STORE
www.sydneyoperahouse.com
Located underneath the Opera House, this shop offers an unusual range of gifts—official SOH merchandise, including books, CDs, videos, clothing and more.

✉ Lower Concourse, Sydney Opera House, Bennelong Point, Sydney, NSW 2000 ☎ 02 9250 7543 ◷ Mon–Fri 9–5.30, Sat, Sun 10–4 ⊡ Any Circular Quay bound bus ⊡ Circular Quay

STRAND HATTERS
www.strandhatters.com.au
This hat shop specializes in Australia's Akubra hats; more than 60 styles are available. Other brands include Barmah, and Montecristi panamas. The staff will help fit, shape and steam your hat.

✉ Strand Arcade, 412 George Street, NSW 2000 ☎ 02 9231 6884 ◷ Mon–Fri 8.30–6 (also Thu 6–8pm), Sat 9.30–4.30, Sun 11–4 ⊡ Town Hall (CityRail)

SURF, DIVE AND SKI
www.sds.com.au
This long-established outlet sells everything representative of surf culture, including boards, fins, wetsuits, waterproof watches, casual wear and sunglasses. You'll find all the brands here including Quiksilver, Rip Curl and Aquabella.

✉ 462 George Street, NSW 2000 ☎ 02 9267 3408 ◷ Mon–Fri 9–6, Sat 9–6, Sun 10–6

SYDNEY AIRPORT
www.sydneyairport.com
There are now more than 150 stores at Sydney Airport's international terminal, including such famous names as Gianni Versace, Oroton, Angus & Coote, Virgin Music, and Done Art and Design. All goods are available duty- and GST-free.

✉ International Terminal, Sydney Airport, Mascot, NSW 2020 ☎ 02 9667 9111 ◷ Daily 6am–10pm ⊡ ⊡

SYDNEY'S PADDY'S MARKETS
www.paddysmarkets.com.au
Tourists and locals rub shoulders at the largest and most traditional market in Sydney, within walking distance of Darling Harbour. More than 800 stalls sell everything from souvenirs to sheepskins, clothes to cosmetics and sporting goods to CDs. There's also a Paddy's Market at Flemington in western Sydney.

✉ Corner Thomas and Hay streets, Haymarket, NSW 2000 ☎ 1300 361 589 ◷ Thu–Sun 9–5 ⊡ Powerhouse Museum (Monorail) ⊡

ULLADULLA ABORIGINAL ART GALLERY
www.ulladullaaboriginalart.com.au
One of Australia's best Aboriginal galleries, with a good selection of paintings, ceramics, statues and gifts, such as didgeridoos and carvings. Both traditional and contemporary art are represented, and the works come from various parts of Australia.

✉ Shop 13, Opera Quays, 2 East Circular Quay, Sydney, NSW 2000 ☎ 02 9251 0511 ◷ Daily 10–7 ⊡ Any Circular Quay bound bus ⊡ Circular Quay

ENTERTAINMENT AND NIGHTLIFE

CAPITOL THEATRE
www.capitoltheatre.com.au
This lavish theatre was originally a market building. In 1927 the interior was remodelled to create the present theatre, which now stages large-scale musicals and some classical music concerts.
✉ 13 Campbell Street, Haymarket, NSW 2000 ☎ 13 61 66 🚊 Haymarket (Light Rail) ⬛

CITY RECITAL HALL
www.cityrecitalhall.com
Just off Martin Place, this is a 1,200-seat venue for chamber orchestras and soloists.
✉ Angel Place, NSW 2000 ☎ 02 8256 2222 🚊 Martin Place Wynyard (CityRail) ⬛

DENDY OPERA QUAYS
www.dendy.com.au
Art-house films in comfortable surroundings.
✉ 2 East Circular Quay, NSW 2000 ☎ 02 9247 3800 🕐 Daily, phone for session times 🖐 Adult A$15, child A$10 🚊 Circular Quay (CityRail) ⬛ Fully licensed

ENMORE THEATRE
www.enmoretheatre.com.au
The 1,600-seat Enmore, a few kilometres from central Sydney, hosts rock acts.
✉ 130 Enmore Road, Newtown, NSW 2042 ☎ 02 9550 3666 🚊 Newtown ⬛ ⬛

ENSEMBLE THEATRE
www.ensemble.com.au
The Ensemble is a small theatre just over the Harbour Bridge. Mainstream productions by well-known playwrights.
✉ 78 McDougall Street, Kirribilli, NSW 2061 ☎ 02 9929 0644 🚊 North Shore 🚊 Milsons Point 🚢 Kirribilli Wharf from Circular Quay 🖐 A$25–A$75 🍴

LA PREMIERE AT HOYTS AT THE EQ
www.hoyts.com.au
Five of the cinemas here have La Premiere areas, with private two-seat sofas, where you can have a glass or two of wine while watching a movie.
✉ Bent Street, Moore Park, NSW 1363 ☎ 02 9332 1300 🚊 Moore Park, from Central Station 🕐 Daily from 12pm ⬛

LG IMAX THEATRE
www.imax.com.au
The IMAX cinema presents eye-popping movies (some in 3-D) on an eight-floor screen.
✉ 31 Wheat Road, off Southern Promenade, Darling Harbour, NSW 2000 ☎ 02 9281 3300 🕐 Daily 10–10 🖐 From A$19.50 adult, A$14.50 child 🚊 Darling Park (Monorail), Convention (Light Rail), Town Hall (CityRail) ⬛

LYRIC THEATRE
www.starcity.com.au
Part of Star City Casino, the Lyric stages international musical productions.
✉ 80 Pyrmont Street, Pyrmont, NSW 2009 ☎ 13 28 49 (Ticketek, for bookings) 🚌 Explorer bus (stop 19) 🚊 Star City (Light Rail) ⬛ ⬛

MOONLIGHT CINEMA
www.moonlight.com.au
Outdoor movies in the park on summer evenings.
✉ Centennial Park (Woollahra gate), Oxford Street, NSW 2000 🕐 Dec–end Feb, 8.30; tickets at gate from 7pm 🚌 3.5km (2 miles) southeast of Sydney

THE SHOWROOM
www.starcity.com.au
Part of Star City Casino, this 1,000-seat theatre hosts mostly musical performances. International stars Michael Crawford, kd lang and Tony Bennett have played here.
✉ 80 Pyrmont Street, Pyrmont, NSW 2009 ☎ 13 28 49 (Ticketek, for bookings) 🚌 Explorer bus (stop 19) 🚊 Star City (Light Rail) 🍴 ⬛ Snackbar ⬛

SYDNEY ENTERTAINMENT CENTRE
www.sydentcent.com.au
Sydney's largest indoor venue is the place to see the big-name rock acts and large-scale productions. Its central location at Darling Harbour means that it is easy to get there.
✉ 35 Harbour Street, Darling Harbour, NSW 2000 ☎ 02 9320 4200 🚌 Explorer bus (stop 16) 🚊 Haymarket (Light Rail), Powerhouse Museum (Monorail) 🍴 ⬛

SYDNEY OPERA HOUSE
See page 82.

WHARF THEATRE
www.sydneytheatre.com.au
This converted cargo-ship wharf houses two theatres where productions by the Sydney Theatre Company are staged.
✉ Pier 4, 5 Hickson Road, Walsh Bay, NSW 2000 ☎ 02 9250 1777 🚌 430 from city centre 🚊 Circular Quay (CityRail) 🍴 ⬛

TWILIGHT AT TARONGA
www.zoo.nsw.gov.au
Family-orientated concerts are held outdoors at Taronga Zoo in late summer months.
✉ Taronga Zoo, Bradleys Head Road, Mosman, NSW 2088 ☎ 13 28 49 (Ticketek, for bookings) 🕐 Performances Feb–end Mar Fri–Sun most evenings 🚢 Taronga Wharf ⬛

ARQ
www.arqsydney.com.au
Sydney's finest DJs, drag performers, and entertainers.
✉ 16 Flinders Street, Darlinghurst, NSW 2010 ☎ 02 9380 8700 🕐 Thu–Sun 10pm–late; closed Mon–Wed 🚌 380, 394, 🖐 Cover charge at weekend

THE BAR AT SIR STAMFORD
A nightspot with lavish decor on an Edwardian theme.
✉ Sir Stamford Hotel, 93 Macquarie Street, Circular Quay, NSW 2000 ☎ 02 9252 4600 🕐 Mon–Fri 3–12am, Sat 12–12, Sun 12pm–10 🚊 Circular Quay (CityRail)

THE BASEMENT
www.thebasement.com.au
Operating since the early 1960s, this is Sydney's best live jazz, blues and funk venue, featuring local artists and international acts from all over the world. The Basement is also a restaurant, serving lunches

during the week and pre-show dinners nightly.

✉ 29 Reiby Place, Circular Quay, Sydney, NSW 2000 ☎ 02 9251 2797 🕐 Mon–Fri 10–5.30 and 7.30pm–late, Sat, Sun 7pm–late; performances from 9.30pm ✋ From $20 🚌 Any Circular Quay bound bus 🚊 Circular Quay

CARGO BAR AND LOUNGE
www.cargobar.com.au
A lively place for a drink or dance; the upstairs lounge here has a more relaxed atmosphere. Great views over Darling Harbour.

✉ 52–60 The Promenade, King Street Wharf, NSW 2000 ☎ 02 9262 1777 🕐 Sun–Wed 11.30am–12am, Thu–Sat 11.30am–4am 🚌 Bus, train or ferry to King Street Wharf

COHIBAR
www.cohibar.com.au
On two levels, CohiBar serves up great harbour views, cocktails and, on weekends, urban funk and harmonic jazz.

✉ Shop 359, Harbourside, Darling Harbour, NSW 2000 ☎ 02 9281 4440 🕐 Daily 10am–late 🚊 Harbourside (Monorail)

CUSTOMS HOUSE BAR
Lively bar in the historic Customs House opposite the ferry wharves at Circular Quay.

✉ Customs House, corner Loftus and Bridge streets, Circular Quay, NSW 2000 ☎ 02 9259 7317 🕐 Daily 11am–late 🚊 Circular Quay (CityRail)

ESTABLISHMENT
www.merivale.com
Establishment, the bar in a boutique hotel near Circular Quay, attracts a sophisticated crowd who love the restored 19th-century interior.

✉ 252 George Street, NSW 2000 ☎ 02 9240 3000 🕐 Mon–Fri 11am–late, Sat 6pm–late 🚊 Circular Quay (CityRail)

HARBOUR VIEW HOTEL
www.harbourview.com.au
One of Sydney's favourite heritage pubs; true to its name, it has great harbour views.

✉ 18 Lower Fort Street, The Rocks, NSW 2000 ☎ 02 9252 4111 🕐 Daily 11–11

HEARTBEATS CRUISING NIGHTCLUB
A nightclub harbour cruise with DJs playing a mix of music.

✉ Harbourside Jetty, Darling Harbour, NSW 2000 ☎ 02 9602 0321 🕐 Departs Sat 10.30, returns 1am 🚊 Darling Park (Monorail)

HEMMESPHERE
www.merivale.com
Large leather club chairs define this stylish cocktail bar.

✉ Level 4, 252 George Street, NSW 2000 ☎ 02 9240 3040 🕐 Tue–Sat 6–late (also Tue–Fri from 12pm)

HUGO'S LOUNGE
www.hugos.com.au
The long, sleek, black bar is the feature of Hugo's Lounge.

✉ 33 Bayswater Road, Kings Cross, NSW 2011 ☎ 02 9357 4411 🕐 Thu–Sun 8pm–3am 🚌 325, 327 🚊 Kings Cross

LONGRAIN
www.longrain.com
Inner-city Surry Hills is home to two stylish bar/restaurants. This is one of the best, located in an old warehouse. Live music from Tuesday to Saturday.

✉ 85 Commonwealth Street, Surry Hills, NSW 2010 ☎ 02 9280 2888 🕐 Lunch: Mon–Fri 12–2.30; dinner: Mon–Sat 6–late, Sun 5.30–10 🚊 Central Station

LORD NELSON BREWERY HOTEL
www.lordnelsonbrewery.com
Built in 1841, the Lord Nelson is the oldest pub in Sydney. Sample the pub's own beers, produced in its micro-brewery.

✉ Corner Kent and Argyle streets, The Rocks, NSW 2000 ☎ 02 9251 4044 🕐 Daily 11–11 🚊 Wynyard or Circular Quay (CityRail)

THE NEWPORT ARMS HOTEL
www.newportarms.com.au
This family-orientated pub in a Northern Beaches suburb stages live music and an outdoor screen showing sport. There are also views over Pittwater.

✉ 2 Kalinya Street, Newport, NSW 2105 ☎ 02 9997 4900 🕐 Mon–Sat

10am–12am, Sun 10–11 🚌 From Wynard Station (CityRail): L87, L88, L89 or L90

ORBIT LOUNGE BAR
www.summitrestaurant.com.au
This chic bar, 47 floors up in the Australia Square building, has sensational panoramic views over Sydney.

✉ Australia Square, 264 George Street, NSW 2000 ☎ 02 9247 9777 🕐 Mon–Fri 10am–late, Sat, Sun 5–late

Q BAR/THE EXCHANGE HOTEL
This is one of the most popular gay venues in Sydney, with some of the best DJs in town.

✉ 34–44 Oxford Street, Darlinghurst, NSW 2010 ☎ 02 9331 2956 🕐 Wed–Sat 9pm–late 🚊 Museum

SOHO BAR AND LOUNGE
www.sohobar.com.au
Located in an art deco hotel, this bar features Yu nightclub, where you can party all night.

✉ 171 Victoria Street, Potts Point, NSW 2011 ☎ 02 9358 6511 🕐 Mon–Thu 10am–3am, Fri–Sun 10am–6am

Below Hoyts Cinema Complex

STAR CITY

www.starcity.com.au

Sydney's casino has six bars, seven restaurants, two theatres, 1,500 poker machines and more than 200 gaming tables.

✉ 80 Pyrmont Street, Pyrmont, NSW 2009 ☎ 02 9777 9000 🕐 Open daily 24 hours 🚌 Explorer bus (stop 19) 🚉 Star City (Light Rail)

THE WORLD BAR

www.theworldbar.com

Housed in a converted terrace in Sydney's favourite nightlife zone, this busy, buzzy bar/nightclub is a class act with multi-level rooms that offer different moods and music that swings from hip hop to deep house to tech.

✉ 24 Bayswater Road, Kings Cross, NSW 2011 ☎ 02 9357 7700 🕐 Daily from 9 From A$12 🚌 325, 327 🚉 Kings Cross

SPORTS AND ACTIVITIES

BRIDGECLIMB

www.bridgeclimb.com

A guide leads a small group on an exhilarating and informative climb to the top of the Sydney Harbour Bridge. Climbers must be over 12 and physically fit.

✉ 5 Cumberland Street, The Rocks, NSW 2000 ☎ 02 8274 7777 🕐 Daily. Closed Dec 30–31 ✋ From A$188 (adult) 🚉 Circular Quay (CityRail)

HARBOUR JET

www.harbourjet.com

Zoom around spectacular Sydney Harbour on a jet-boat. You'll see the sights and experience head-spinning manoeuvres.

✉ Shop 191 Harbourside, Darling Harbour, NSW 2000 ☎ 1300 887 373 🕐 Tours depart at various times ✋ Adult from A$65, child from A$45 for 35-minute Jet Blast tour 🚌 443 from Circular Quay 🚢 Ferry from Circular Quay

MANLY SURF SCHOOL

www.manlysurfschool.com

Learn to surf with a qualified instructor at Manly Beach. All the necessary equipment is provided.

✉ North Steyne Surf Club, North Steyne, Manly, NSW 2095 ☎ 02 9977 6977

🕐 Daily 9–3 ✋ A$60 (two hours), private lessons A$90 (per hour) 🚢 Manly Wharf (regular ferries from Circular Quay)

THE ROCKS GHOST TOUR

www.ghosttours.com.au

Take a lantern-led stroll through dark and narrow passageways to haunted houses where creaking floorboards and squeaky doors betray an eerie presence. Tours are led by Rocks locals, some of whom have a family history that dates back to the earliest days of European settlement in the area.

✉ Cadman's Cottage, 110 George Street, The Rocks, NSW 2000 ☎ 1300 731 971 🕐 Apr–Sep daily at 6.45pm; Oct–Mar 7.45pm ✋ Adult A$38, child A$29 🚌 Circular Quay 🚉 Circular Quay 🚢 Circular Quay

SHARK DIVE XTREME

The opportunity of a lifetime—the chance to dive with sharks in Oceanworld, Manly's famous northside harbourfront aquarium. After a comprehensive briefing, divers are kitted out in wetsuits and scuba gear and plunge into a huge tank with huge grey nurse sharks, giant stingrays, sea turtles, wobbegong sharks and moray eels. Divers are accompanied by a dive master throughout, and this experience is safe even for first-time divers.

✉ West Esplanade, Manly NSW 2095 ☎ 02 8251 7877 🕐 Daily 10–5.30 ✋ A$185–A$250 🚢 Manly

SKYWALK

www.skywalk.com.au

Thrillseekers can take a guided walk around Sydney Tower's outdoor viewing platform, 268m (880ft) above the city. The views are simply sensational.

✉ Sydney Tower, Podium Level, 100 Market Street, Sydney, NSW 2000 ☎ 02 9333 9222 🕐 Regular departures daily 11–10pm ✋ From A$65 adult, A$45 child (10–16 years only) 🚉 St. James

SYDNEY BY SAIL

www.sydneybysail.com

Get afloat on Sydney Harbour with

learn-to-sail courses, charters and overnight trips.

✉ National Maritime Museum, 2 Murray Street, Darling Harbour, NSW 2000 ☎ 02 9280 1110 🕐 Office, daily 9–5 ✋ Three-hour harbour cruises from A$150, learn-to-sail courses from A$495, social racing from A$75 🚌 Explorer bus (stop 20) 🚉 Harbourside (Monorail) 🚢 Pyrmont Wharf

SYDNEY CRICKET GROUND (SCG)

www.sydneycricketground.com.au

One-day international and Test cricket matches are held here (▷ 75); Australian Rules football takes over in winter.

🚌 Moore Park ✋ Cricket: adult from ✉ Driver Avenue, Moore Park, NSW 2021 ☎ 02 9360 6601; Ticketek 02 9266 4800 for event details and tickets A$46, child from A$21. Australian Rules: adult from A$35, child from A$22 🚌 🚉

SYDNEY EXPLORER

www.131500.com.au

The Sydney Explorer bus follows a circular route, allowing you to hop on and off at stops along the way. Covering 27 central attractions and with an on-board commentary, buses depart every 20 minutes.

☎ 13 15 00 🕐 First bus departs Circular Quay at 8.40am, last bus at 5.22pm ✋ Adult A$39, child A$19, family A$97

SYDNEY OLYMPIC PARK AQUATIC CENTRE

www.aquaticcentre.com.au

Two 50m swimming pools, water slides, spray jets and other fun water activities.

✉ Olympic Boulevard, Sydney Olympic Park, NSW 2127 ☎ 02 9752 3666 🕐 Mon–Fri 5am–8.45pm, Sat, Sun 6am–7.45pm (6.45pm in winter) ✋ Adult A$6.80, child A$5.50, family A$20 🚌 From Lidcombe and Strathfield 🚉 Olympic Park 🚢 Homebush Bay (by Rivercat) 🚌

SYDNEY OLYMPIC PARK TENNIS CENTRE

www.sydneyolympicpark.com.au

You can play on one of 16 courts at this world-class tennis venue, or watch state, national and international tournaments.

Rod Laver Drive, Sydney Olympic Park, NSW 2127 ☎ 02 8746 0888 ⊕ Courts: Mon–Fri 7am–9pm, Sat, Sun 8–5 ✋ A$22 an hour 8–5, A$26 an hour 5–9pm 🚌 From Lidcombe and Strathfield 🚉 Olympic Park and Rivercat 🚢

FOR CHILDREN
LOLLIPOPS PLAYLAND
www.lollipopsplayland.com.au
A multifloor funhouse with giant mazes, tunnels, cargo nets, ball pits and more.
✉ The Entertainment Quarter, Driver Avenue, Moore Park, NSW 1363 ☎ 02 9331 0811 ⊕ Daily 9.30–6 ✋ Adult A$5, child (1–2) A$10, (2–9) A$14 🚌 Moore Park 🚢

SYDNEY AQUARIUM
See page 71.

COCKATOO ISLAND
www.cockatooisland.gov.au
Largest of all the harbour islands, Cockatoo Island is a former prison island that adds flesh and bones to Sydney's fascinating history. Retrace the city's convict heritage, its social history and shipbuilding industry on a guided or self-guided tour of the island's convict prison and guardhouse, the underground grain silos, the two dry docks and the immense industrial workshops and their cranes, jetties and slipways. A ferry service operates daily between Circular Quay and Cockatoo Island.
✉ Sydney Harbour Daily, but check ferry timetable ☎ 02 8969 2100 ✋ Ferry: Adult A$5.20, child A$2.60

MANLY SEA KAYAKS
The cockpit of a sea kayak is an ideal way to explore Sydney Harbour. It's travel in the slow lane, hugging the shore—and it's amazing what secrets the shoreline holds. Hire a kayak from Manly Kayaks and you can paddle around the headlands and visit some of the beaches that few people will ever get to, or join a group tour.
✉ East Esplanade, Manly, NSW 2095 ☎ 1300 529257 ⊕ Daily 9–1 hour before sunset ✋ Single kayak $30 for 2 hours, double $60 for 2 hours 🚢 Manly

FESTIVALS AND EVENTS

JANUARY
SYDNEY FESTIVAL
www.sydneyfestival.com.au
Sydney Festival is the main performing arts festival, strong on outdoor events such as Symphony in the Park.

MARCH
MARDI GRAS PARADE
www.mardigras.org.au
Sydney's Mardi Gras celebrates all things gay and lesbian with parades of outrageous floats.

APRIL
ROYAL EASTER SHOW
www.eastershow.com.au
Agriculture is the theme at the Royal Easter Show at Sydney's Homebush Showground.

MAY
SYDNEY WRITERS' FESTIVAL
www.swf.org.au
Local and international authors take part in the Sydney Writers' Festival.

ROSEMOUNT AUSTRALIAN FASHION WEEK
www.afw.com.au
Rosemount Australian Fashion Week, in Sydney, shows off the spring/summer collections of Australia's leading designers.

JUNE
SYDNEY FILM FESTIVAL
www.sydneyfilmfestival.org
The Sydney Film Festival shows all kinds of films from Australia and overseas.

AUGUST
SUN-HERALD CITY TO SURF
www.sunherald.com.au/city2surf
Thousands take part in the Sun-Herald City to Surf, a 14km (9-mile) fun run that starts in the city and finishes at Bondi.

Right *On stage at Sydney Festival*

SEPTEMBER
SPRING RACING CARNIVAL
www.ajc.org.au
The Australian Jockey Club stages its Spring Racing Carnival at the Royal Randwick Racecourse.

NOVEMBER
SCULPTURE BY THE SEA
www.sculpturebythesea.com
Art meets a delectable slice of nature when the sea-sculpted sandstone headlands between Bondi Beach and Tamarama become the backdrop for this annual sculpture exhibition. Australia's largest annual outdoor free sculpture show, the dramatic setting encourages artists to unleash their imaginations and construct works from the realms of fantasy.

DECEMBER
SYDNEY TO HOBART YACHT RACE
www.cyca.com.au
On Boxing Day, thousands line Sydney Harbour for the start of the world-famous but gruelling Sydney to Hobart Yacht Race.

NEW YEAR'S EVE
Spectacular fireworks against a harbour backdrop set Sydney's New Year's Eve festivities apart. Crowds gather in central Sydney and other places around the harbour with views.

EATING

PRICES AND SYMBOLS

The restaurants are listed alphabetically (excluding Le, La and Les). The prices given are the average for a two-course lunch (L) and a three-course dinner (D) for one person, without drinks. The wine price is for the least expensive bottle.

For a key to the symbols, ▷ 2.

AQUA DINING

www.aquadining.com.au
The Modern Australian cuisine features dishes such as Pacific oysters with a verjuice dressing, and grilled wild barramundi fillet with green vegetables. The wine list is extensive. Reservations advised.
✉ North Sydney Olympic Pool, cnr Paul and Northcliff streets, Milsons Point, Sydney, NSW 2061 ☎ 02 9964 9998 ⊕ Mon–Fri 12–2.30, Mon–Sat 6.30–10pm ✋ L A$80, D A$95, Wine A$48 🚉 Milsons Point ⛴ Circular Quay to Milsons Point

BILLS

www.bills.com.au
Bill Grainger created a whole new trend in Sydney eating when he opened his namesake Darlinghurst café with the Texas-size table in the middle.

Mostly white and well polished, bills continues to dazzle with silky service and presentation straight from a glossy food magazine. The scrambled eggs are a local legend, but the honey ricotta pancakes with honeycomb butter and maple syrup are simply scrumptious.
✉ 433 Liverpool Street, Darlinghurst, NSW 2010 ☎ 02 9360 9631 ⊕ Mon–Sat 7.30am–3pm, Sun 8.30–3 ✋ B A$20, L A$35, Wine A$36 🚌 Victoria Street, Darlinghurst

BILLY KWONG

www.kyliekwong.org
Diners sit on stools, and can't book, but still the crowds pile in for celebrity chef Kylie Kwong's organic, biodynamic take on Chinese cuisine, such as caramelized pork belly and crispy skin free-range chicken.
✉ Shop 3, 355 Crown Street, Surry Hills, NSW 2010 ☎ 02 9332 3300 ⊕ Daily 6–11 ✋ D A$45, Wine A$38 🚌 Crown Street

BLACKBIRD CAFÉ

www.blackbirdcafé.com.au
This is a large, buzzing, all-day diner-style café. The eclectic fare includes breakfasts, pastas, pizzas, salads and some Asian options.
✉ Balcony Level, Cockle Bay Wharf, Darling Park, Sydney, NSW 2000 ☎ 02 9283 7385 ⊕ Daily 9am–late ✋ Dishes A$20–A$25, Wine A$25 🚉 Town Hall 🚝 Monorail to Darling Park

BONDI TRATTORIA

www.bonditrattoria.com.au
Lively café above Bondi Beach. Breakfasts are popular, with bacon and eggs, but also poached fruits, pancakes and muesli creations; plus a good range of pizzas, pastas, daily fish specials and kangaroo dishes. The wine list is reasonable.
✉ 34 Campbell Parade, Bondi Beach, Sydney, NSW 2026 ☎ 02 9365 4303 ⊕ Mon–Fri 7am–late, Sat, Sun 8am–late ✋ B A$12, L A$30, D A$35, Wine A$40 🚌 378 from Central Station, 380, 382 and L82 from Circular Quay and city 🚉 Bondi Junction then buses 380, 382 or L82 🚗 8km (5 miles) east from the city

CAPTAIN COOK CRUISES

www.captaincook.com.au

On a cruise around Sydney Harbour, with entertainment in the evenings, the food is Modern Australian: examples are smoked salmon with a herb salad, and skinned ocean trout fillet with minted cucumbers, salsa, light mayonnaise, crushed potatoes and wilted Chinese greens. Vegetarian options and children's portions are available, as are reduced-fat and low-salt dishes. The range of Australian wines is extensive. Reservations essential.

✉ Depart Jetty 6, Circular Quay, Sydney, NSW 2000 ☎ 02 9206 1122 🕐 12.30 departure for lunch cruise, 5 for sunset dinner, 7 for starlight dinner 🍴 L from A$69, D from A$82, Wine A$24 🚃 Circular Quay 🚌 Any bus to Circular Quay

CASA ASTURIANA

www.casaasturiana.com.au

Authentic Spanish meals are served in this informal 'Spanish Quarter' establishment. Expect good tapas, seafood paella, and a choice of Spanish wines.

✉ 77 Liverpool Street, Sydney, NSW 2000 ☎ 02 9264 1010 🕐 Daily 12–3, 5–11 🍴 L, D A$45, Wine A$24 🚃 Town Hall 🚌 Monorail World Square

CHAT THAI

www.chatthai.com.au

This is heaven incarnate for lovers of authentic Thai food in all its sweet, sour and spicy glory—however it's not for those new to Thai food. There's a no-booking policy, and the never-ending crowd testifies to its success. Sign your name at the door and go for a stroll around Chinatown. Service is brisk but friendly.

✉ 20 Campbell Street, Haymarket, NSW 2000 ☎ 02 9211 1808 🕐 Daily 8am–1am 🍴 L A$25, D A$30, Wine BYO 🚌 Monorail Capital Squarer

CHINTA RIA — TEMPLE OF LOVE

www.chintaria.com

Vibrant Asian restaurant enlivened by blues, jazz and soul music. The cuisine is Malaysian with Chinese and Indian influences and features laksas, satays, noodle dishes, curries and tofu dishes. The wine list is fairly limited; BYO corkage A$6 per bottle. Reservations advised.

✉ The Roof Terrace, Cockle Bay Wharf, Darling Park, Sydney, NSW 2000 ☎ 02 9264 3211 🕐 Daily 12–2.30, 6–11, Sun 6–10 🍴 Entrées A$7–A$9.50, large dishes A$17–A$29, desserts A$6.50, Wine A$25 🚃 Town Hall 🚌 Metro Monorail from City Centre to Darling Park

DIN TAI FUNG

This is heaven on earth for dumpling lovers. The World Square restaurant is part of a Taipei-based global chain, and the crowds at the front door tell the story. Silky, gossamer-thin and beautiful to behold, the dumplings are moistened with an infusion of pork stock and they come in tantalizing combinations. The beef soup and fried rice are every bit as sensational. There's entertainment while you wait, by way of an assembly line of white-clad dumpling makers working in a cloud of steam.

✉ Shop 11, Level 1 World Square Shopping Centre, 644 George Street, Haymarket, NSW 2000 ☎ 02 9264 6010 🕐 Daily 11am–10.30pm L A$25, D A$30, Wine BYO 🚌 Haymarket 🚃 Town Hall

DOYLE'S ON THE BEACH

www.doyles.com.au

The seafood menu is usually served with fries, rice or mash; salads or roast vegetables are available for an additional cost. Try the Tasmanian ocean trout or the yellowfin tuna. The extensive wine list includes wines by the glass. Reservations are advisable.

✉ 11 Marine Parade, Watsons Bay, Sydney, NSW 2030 ☎ 02 9337 2007 🕐 Daily 12–3, 6–9.30 🍴 L from A$60, D from A$80, Wine A$32 🚌 324, 325 from city 🚢 Circular Quay to Watsons Bay lunchtimes; water taxis evenings 🚌 10km (6 miles) from the city

FLYING FISH

www.flyingfish.com.au

The double-decker restaurant does nothing to hide its blue-collar origins. It's all there in its muscular glory—the skeletal framework of huge beams and bare timber walls that chart its evolution from former cargo wharf.

Chef Peter Kuruvita is a fish man, and his Sri Lankan heritage shows although it's a restrained presence, adding delicacy and grace to the subtle seafood dishes. A sunset cocktail outside on the comfy couches is highly recommended.

✉ Jones Bay Wharf, 19–21 Pirrama Road, Pyrmont, NSW 2007 ☎ 02 9518 6677 🕐 Tue–Fri 12pm–10pm, Sat–Sun 6.30pm–10.30pm L A$55, D A$70, Wine A$45 🚃 Light Rail, Sydney Casino

GOLDEN CENTURY

www.goldencentury.com.au

A large, bustling and very popular Cantonese seafood restaurant. Crabs and lobsters are offered fresh from the tank and steamed fish is among the house specials.

✉ 393 Sussex Street, Sydney, NSW 2000 ☎ 02 9212 3901 🕐 Daily 12pm–4am 🍴 L from A$20, D from A$30 🚃 Town Hall 🚌 Metro Monorail to World Square

GUILLAUME AT BENNELONG

www.guillaumeatbennelong.com.au

One of Sydney's finest dining venues. Guillaume Brahimi is one of Australia's most respected chefs and he serves Modern Australian cuisine with French influences. His signature dish is an entrée of basil-infused tuna. Other tempting items are confit of Atlantic salmon on braised endive with red wine sauce, and chocolate soufflé with almond milk ice cream. Reservations are essential.

✉ Sydney Opera House, Bennelong Point, Sydney, NSW 2000 ☎ 02 9241 1999 🕐 Thu, Fri 12–3, Mon–Sat 5.30–late 🍴 L A$70, D A$90, Wine A$45. Tasting menu A$180. Pre-theatre menu 5.30–7: A$63 for two courses, A$75 for three courses 🚃 Circular Quay 🚌 Any bus to Circular Quay

HARBOURKITCHEN & BAR

www.harbourkitchen.com.au

The restaurant's menu features

seasonal Modern Australian cuisine and an extensive cellar of Australian and imported wines. The view of Sydney Harbour is spectacular.

 7 Hickson Road, The Rocks, Sydney, NSW 2000 ☎ 02 9256 1660 ⏰ Daily 6.30am–11pm 🖐 B A$40, L A$65, D A$85, Wine A$32 🚇 Circular Quay 🚌 Any bus to Circular Quay

HYDE PARK BARRACKS CAFÉ

www.hydeparkbarrackscafé.com.au
A great place to stop for lunch across the road from Hyde Park. Choose from pastas, salads, fillet of beef and various seafoods.

✉ Queens Square, Macquarie Street, Sydney, NSW 2000 ☎ 02 9222 1815 ⏰ Mon–Fri 8–3, Sat, Sun 10–3 🖐 B A$12, L A$48.

THE MALAYA

www.themalaya.com.au
A Sydney institution, The Malaya is on the first floor of the King Street Wharf complex, with an open kitchen. The food is mostly Malaysian, but with Chinese, Indonesian and other Asian influences. Particularly famous for its laksas, other signature dishes include beef rendang and satays. The wine list is fairly limited. Reservations recommended.

✉ 39 Lime Street, King Street Wharf, Sydney, NSW 2000 ☎ 02 9279 1170 ⏰ Mon–Sat 12–3, daily 6–9 🖐 L, D A$40, Wine A$30 🚇 Wynyard Station 🚊 Metro Monorail Darling Park

MAMAK

www.mamak.com.au
Be prepared to join the queue (line) that spills out onto Goulburn Street because Mamak is one of the hottest acts in town. In fact this no-frills restaurant has reminded diners just how satisfying the authentic, street-hawker version of Malay cooking can be, with an accomplished *nasi lemak* and several different versions of roti, a specialty of the house.

✉ 15 Goulburn Street, Haymarket, NSW 2000 ☎ 02 9211 1668 ⏰ Tue–Sun 12pm–3pm, 6pm–10.30pm 🖐 L A$20, D A$30, Wine BYO

MARIGOLD CITYMARK

www.marigold.com.au
A large restaurant on two levels. Classic Chinese fare, the specialty *yum cha* lunches, has more than 100 varieties of dim sum. The à la carte menu includes mud crab in chilli sauce, deep-fried spicy salt and pepper prawns, steamed scallops in their shell with black bean sauce.

✉ Levels 4 & 5, 683 George Street, Haymarket, Sydney, NSW 2000 ☎ 02 9281 3388 ⏰ Daily 10–3, 5.30–12 🖐 Entrées A$8–A$15, mains A$18–A$45, *yum cha* lunch A$15–A$25 per person, Wine A$32 🚇 Central Station or Town Hall 🚊 Metro Monorail to Powerhouse Museum

OPERA BAR

www.operabar.com.au
A long bar-café in a spectacular location at the foot of the Sydney Opera House, with live entertainment nightly and on weekend afternoons. While specials change, examples of the Modern Australian bistro menu are duck and mushroom risotto with peas and chives, poached chicken salad with coriander (cilantro), mint and lime, or roast capsicum and tomato soup with parmesan toast.

✉ Lower Concourse, Sydney Opera House, Bennelong Point, Sydney, NSW 2000 ☎ 02 9247 1666 ⏰ Daily 11.30am–1am 🖐 Dishes A$17–A$29, desserts A$12, Wine A$32 🚇 Circular Quay 🚌 Any bus to Circular Quay

PIZZA E BIRRA

The pizzas might have come straight from Naples and the menu is a list of classics from the Italian kitchen, but don't expect a quiet meal at this buzzy, glass-walled bistro. The 'birra' comes from the restaurant's own Hopping Mad Brewery.

✉ 500 Crown Street, Surry Hills, 2010 NSW ☎ 02 9332 2510 ⏰ Mon–Wed 5.30–11, Thu-Sat 1–12, Sun 12–11 🖐 L A$40, D A$55, Wine A$24 🚇 Crown Street

ROCKPOOL

www.rockpool.com
Owned by Neil Perry, a celebrity chef, Rockpool is one of the

Below *Marron salad with truffle at Tetsuya's, Kent Street, Sydney*

country's best-loved restaurants. Innovative Modern Australian cuisine features gourmet produce such as Tasmanian lobster and Redgate Farm partridge and a large range of seafood such as snapper, red emperor and seared tuna studded with anchovy and roast garlic with bone marrow and red wine sauce. There is an extensive wine list including local and imported vintages. Reservations are advised during the week and essential at weekends).

✉ 107 George Street, The Rocks, Sydney, NSW 2000 ☎ 02 9252 1888 ⏰ Tue–Sat 6–11 🍴 D A$130, tasting menu A$195, Wine A$45 🚇 Circular Quay 🚌 Any bus to Circular Quay

SAILORS THAI CANTEEN
www.sailorsthai.com.au
A lively, canteen-style café featuring an enormous stainless steel communal table. The innovative Thai food includes stir-fried marinated beef with ginger, black fungus and Asian celery, rice noodles with pork and Asian broccoli, curry of grilled fish, Pad Thai noodles, and desserts such as pomegranate and smoked coconut sorbets. There is a small wine list.

✉ 106 George Street, The Rocks, Sydney, NSW 2000 ☎ 02 9251 2466 ⏰ Mon–Sat 12–10 🍴 Dishes A$17–A$29, Wine A$30 🚇 Circular Quay 🚌 Any bus to Circular Quay

SAILORS THAI POTTS POINT
www.sailorsthai.com.au
It's Thai food with a difference, but still rendered with an eye to authenticity. There's power as well as delicacy in the interplay of flavours in the spiced rice balls with minced chicken, peanuts and ginger, mint and coriander, spicy seduction for the tongue in the dish of green papaya salad with peanuts, dried prawns, spicy and sour dressing, coconut rice and sweet pork.

✉ 71A Macleay Street, Potts Point, NSW 2011 ☎ 02 9361 4498 ⏰ Daily 6pm–10pm, Friday 12–3pm 🍴 L A$35, D A$55, Wine A$39 🚇 Potts Point 🚉 Kings Cross

SEAN'S PANAROMA
www.seanspanaroma.com.au
The ocean view across Bondi Beach accompanies a changing Modern Australian menu. This charming, small restaurant has a limited wine list or BYO (corkage A$8).

✉ 270 Campbell Parade, Bondi Beach, Sydney, NSW 2026 ☎ 02 9365 4924 ⏰ Sat, Sun from noon, Wed–Sat from 6pm 🍴 L A$40, D A$65 🚇 Bondi Junction 🚌 7km (4.5 miles) southeast from the city

SPICE TEMPLE
www.spicetemple.com.au.
The latest offering from Sydney uber-chef Neil Perry of Rockpool fame, who indulges his long-standing passion for Chinese food with subtle and silky flavour combinations sourced from the Chinese regional cuisines of Yunnan, Jiangxi, Guangxi, Xinjiang, Sichuan and Hunan. Complexity and well-rounded richness are key on a menu saturated with tantalizing choices.

✉ 10 Bligh Street, Sydney, NSW 2000 ☎ 02 8078 1888 ⏰ Mon–Fri 12–11, Sat, Sat 6–11 🍴 L A$55, D A$65, Wine A$44 🚇 Wynyard 🚉 Wynyard

SUMMIT RESTAURANT
www.summitrestaurant.com.au
On the 47th floor of the Australia Square building, the innovative Modern Australian cuisine at this revolving restaurant features local seafood, lamb, chicken and vegetarian dishes. There is an extensive wine list. Reservations are advised.

✉ Level 47, Australia Square, 264 George Street, Sydney, NSW 2000 ☎ 02 9247 9777 ⏰ Mon–Fri 12–3, Mon–Sun 6–9.30. Orbit Bar daily 5–late 🍴 Set-price menus L A$65, D A$99; bar snacks A$8–A$19 🚇 Wynyard Station 🚌 Any bus to Circular Quay (alight at Wynyard Station)

SYDNEY FISH MARKET
www.sydneyfishmarket.com.au
The many places to eat within the complex include Christie's Seafoods, Claudio's Quality Seafoods, Fish Market Sushi Bar, Doyles and the Fish Market Café.

Seafood of all types include fish and chips, sushi and sashimi, freshly shucked oysters, chilli mud crab, and grilled or fried fish. Pizzas, breakfasts and coffee are also available at a couple of the cafés. All accept BYO.

✉ Bank Street, Pyrmont, Sydney, NSW 2009 ☎ 02 9004 1100 ⏰ Daily 7–4 🍴 From A$6 for single sushi to A$45 seafood platter 🚉 Fish Market

TETSUYA'S
www.tetsuyas.com
The fusion of Japanese, French and Modern Australian cuisines comes at a price, but then this is innovative cooking. Enjoy the finest veal, salmon and Tasmanian ocean trout. Reservations essential.

✉ 529 Kent Street, Sydney, NSW 2000 ☎ 02 9267 2900 ⏰ Sat 12–2.30, Tue–Sat from 6pm 🍴 Tasting menu $195 per person 🚇 Town Hall

WHARF RESTAURANT
www.thewharfrestaurant.com.au
This waterfront restaurant, part of the Sydney Theatre Company complex, is known for its Modern Australian cuisine, including offerings such as ricotta and zucchini (courgette) dumplings, salt-and-pepper squid, and imaginative duck, seafood and meat dishes. Reservations recommended, especially for dinner.

✉ Pier 4, Hickson Road, Walsh Bay, Sydney, NSW 2000 ☎ 02 9250 1761 ⏰ Mon–Sat 12–3, 6–late 🍴 L A$50, D A$65, Wine A$27 🚇 Circular Quay 🚉 Circular Quay

UNIVERSAL
www.universalrestaurant.com
Celebrity chef Christine Manfield elevates small-plate dining to an elegant art form, drawing rave reviews for the firecracker flavours she dishes up at her inside/outside restaurant in Darlinghurst's Republic apartment building.

✉ 2 Courtyard Palmer Street (between Burton and Liverpool streets), Darlinghurst, NSW 2010 ☎ 02 9331 0709 ⏰ Mon–Sat 6pm–11pm, Fri 12pm–4pm 🍴 L A$50, D A$70, Wine A$49 🚇 Taylor Square

STAYING

PRICES AND SYMBOLS

Prices are for a double room for one night including breakfast, unless otherwise stated. All the hotels listed accept credit cards, unless otherwise stated. Note that rates can vary widely throughout the year.

For a key to the symbols, ▷ 2.

AARONS HOTEL

www.aaronshotel.com.au

A clean hotel representing good value by Chinatown. The bedrooms are a good size; family rooms accommodate up to six; the more expensive Executive Rooms have their own small private courtyard. The restaurant, Café Nine, serves food from 6.30am–late.

✉ 37 Ultimo Road, Haymarket, Sydney, NSW 2000 ☎ 02 9281 5555 ③ All year 🛏 A$119–A$230; breakfast not included ① 94 ⑤ 🚌 At the southern end of the city next to Chinatown and near Central Station, just south from Darling Harbour

BLUE SYDNEY

www.tajhotels.com/sydney

Set on the historic Finger Wharf at Woolloomooloo, this converted warehouse has been transformed into a slick, sleek and suitably dark designer hotel, although the soaring dimensions and exposed beams and joists recall its blue-collar origins. Guest rooms are arranged atrium-style around the hotel's central well.

✉ Cowper Wharf Road, Woolloomooloo, NSW 2011 ☎ 02 9331 9000 ③ All year 🛏 A$265–A2,690 ① 10 ⑤ 🚿 Indoor 🍴 🚌 Woolloomooloo

CAMBRIDGE SYDNEY HOTEL

www.cambridgehotel.com.au

This top-value accommodation is just a few minutes' walk from Oxford Street. Check the 'Red Hot Web Rates'.

✉ 212 Riley Street, Sydney, NSW 2000 ☎ 02 9212 1111 ③ All year 🛏 A$110–A$285 ① 170 🚿 Indoor 🍴

ESTABLISHMENT HOTEL

www.merivale.com

Luxurious and intimate, this boutique hotel is part of the empire of Sydney nightclub supremo, Justin Hemmes.

Guest rooms are moody and elegant with sculptural lighting and configurations that make a refreshing change from the standard hotel room layout.

✉ 5 Bridge Street, Sydney, NSW 2000 ☎ 02 9240 3100 ③ All year 🛏 A$280–A$1,050 ① 31 ⑤ 🍴 🚈 Circular Quay

FOUR POINTS BY SHERATON

www.fourpoints.com/sydney

Most of the 630 rooms including 45 suites have balconies; some rooms have been specially designed for visitors with mobility problems. Decorated in stylish modern tones, facilities include a choice of dining rooms, plus a historic pub dating from the 1850s.

✉ 161 Sussex Street, Darling Harbour, Sydney, NSW 2000 ☎ 02 9290 4000 ③ All year 🛏 From A$245 (city views)–A$363 (harbour views) ① 630 ⑤ 🚌 On the west side of the city, beside the aquarium

FOUR SEASONS HOTEL SYDNEY

www.fourseasons.com/sydney

At the base of The Rocks, The Four Seasons is almost invariably rated the city's finest in international business traveller surveys.

Rooms are large and luxurious and bathrooms are decorated in an opulent but restrained style. Request a room with a view of the harbour on one of the upper floors for a memorable stay.

✉ 99 George Street, Sydney, NSW 2000 ☎ 02 9250 3100 ③ All year 🛏 A$375–A$5,650 ① 531 ⑤ 🚿 Indoor 🍴 🚈 Circular Quay 🚌 Circular Quay 🚈 Circular Quay

Opposite *The exterior of the Hilton Sydney*

THE GRACE SYDNEY

www.gracehotel.com.au

At the heart of the city's shopping and business district, this restored hotel retains traces of its art deco origins. Room furnishings are warm-toned and the hotel is especially popular with package groups. Despite the busy location, rooms are quiet, especially those overlooking the central well of the building.
✉ 77 York Street, Sydney, NSW 2000 ☎ 02 9272 6888 🖐 A$170–A$495 🕐 All year 🕐 382 🈯 🈺 George and King streets 🈁 Wynyard

HILTON SYDNEY

www.hiltonsydney.com.au

A landmark hotel at the heart of Sydney's central shopping district, the hotel now has almost 600 rooms and suites, a health club and spa, swimming pool and business centre. Dining options are the Glass Brasserie and a café, and there are three bars, including the famous Marble Bar.
✉ 488 George Street, Sydney, NSW 2000 ☎ 02 9265 6045 🕐 All year 🖐 A$315–A$419 (standard or deluxe room), excluding breakfast 🕐 577 🈯 🏊 Indoor heated 🈁 🈺 Town Hall

THE HUGHENDEN HOTEL

www.thehughenden.com.au

On the leafy main street of one of Sydney's prestige eastern suburbs, this hotel is ideal for visitors looking for accommodation with character at a reasonable price. Refined and gracious, the historic property has a wide choice of rooms, all with en suite bathrooms. This is also a hub for musical and literary events.
✉ 14 Queen Street, Woollahra, NSW 2025 ☎ 02 9363 4863 🕐 All year 🖐 A$168–A$350 🕐 36 🈯 🈺 Oxford Street Woollahra

HOTEL IBIS DARLING HARBOUR

www.accorhotels.com.au

This large, modern hotel is a good-value option. All rooms have TV and videos, tea/coffee-making facilities, fridge, radio, hairdryer, iron and STD/ISD phone. The hotel restaurant serves breakfast and dinner.
✉ 70 Murray Street, Pyrmont, NSW 2000 ☎ 02 9563 0888 🕐 All year 🖐 A$184–A$244; breakfast A$17.50 extra or ask for 'dollar breakfast' special 🕐 256 🈯 🈺 Metro Monorail to Harbourside or Convention stops at Darling Harbour 🈁 1km (0.6 mile) from city centre on the west side of Darling Harbour

INTERCONTINENTAL SYDNEY

www.sydney.intercontinental.com

This sleek, sophisticated, multilevel hotel rises from the honey-coloured sandstone facade of the historic Treasury Building. It's also near the harbour and within easy walking distance of Circular Quay, the Opera House, and the central business district. The best views are from the rooms facing north, which overlook the Harbour Bridge, or from the rooms on the eastern side of the hotel.
✉ 17 Macquarie Street, Sydney, NSW 2000 ☎ 02 9253 9000 🕐 All year 🖐 A$243–A$4,784 🕐 509 🈯 🏊 Indoor heated 🈺 🈁 Circular Quay 🈁 Circular Quay

KIRKETON BOUTIQUE HOTEL SYDNEY

www.kirketon.com.au

The strong sense of design is obvious from the moment you step through the big glass doors and into a minimalist foyer. Rooms are a study in simplicity, decorated in creamy tones, and although dimensions are tight, those who don't mind suffering in the name of fashion will find plenty to please.
✉ 229 Darlingshurst Road, Darlinghurst, NSW 2010 ☎ 02 9332 2011 🕐 All year 🖐 A$135–$239 🕐 40 🈯 🈺 Kings Cross 🈁 Kings Cross

MEDINA GRAND HARBOURSIDE

www.medina.com.au

Despite its water views and central location, tariffs at this apartment-style hotel are good value. Accommodation consists of studios and one-bedroom apartments at King Street Wharf, with the attractions and restaurants of Darling Harbour on the doorstep. Rooms are large and bright, and each has a kitchenette, although decor and furnishings are purely functional.
✉ 55 Shelley Street, King Street Wharf, Sydney, NSW 2000 ☎ 02 9249 7000 🕐 All year 🖐 A$180–A$535 🕐 114 🈯 🏊 Indoor 🈺 🈁 Town Hall

MEDUSA

www.medusa.com.au

A small and finely tuned temple to style, this modernist hotel sits close to Sydney's naughty nightlife district of Kings Cross, and closer still to the cafés and restaurants of bohemian Darlinghurst. Colours are splashy and super-saturated, and the furnishings might have come direct from Milan. Each room has a kitchenette.
✉ 267 Darlinghurst Road, Darlinghurst NSW 2010 ☎ 02 9331 1000 🕐 All year 🖐 $270–A$420 🕐 17 🈯 🈺 Kings Cross 🈁 Kings Cross

METRO APARTMENTS ON SUSSEX

www.metrohotels.com

Enjoy the excellent views of Darling Harbour from these apartments, which are in two adjacent buildings on the west side of the city. They include fully serviced one-bedroom suites and apartments. King Street has 10 apartments, rooftop pool and barbecue facilities; Sussex Street has 30 apartments. All sleep up to four people and have a balcony, fully equipped kitchen, living and dining area, shower and bath.
✉ 132–136 Sussex Street, Sydney, NSW 2000 and 27–29 King Street, Sydney, NSW 2000 ☎ 02 9290 9200 🕐 All year 🖐 A$150–A$330 excluding breakfast 🕐 40 🏊 King Street only 🈯 🈁 Wynyard, Darling Park Metro Monorail 🈁 On west side of the city, one block from Darling Harbour and King Street Wharf

OBSERVATORY HOTEL

www.observatoryhotel.com.au

The backstage location in a quiet street in The Rocks disguises Sydney's most patrician hotel, from the same stable as the Hotel

Cipriani and the Venice Simplon Orient-Express..

Regency-style furnishings with accents of Venice and the Orient emphasize the hushed, privileged atmosphere and determinedly personal service. The day spa is one of Sydney's finest.

✉ 89–113 Kent Street, Sydney, NSW 2000 ☎ 02 9256 2222 ⏰ All year ✋ A\$430–A\$3,790 ⓘ 100 🈳 🏊 Indoor 🗦 🚌 Circular Quay 🚇 Circular Quay 🚢 Circular Quay

PARK HYATT

www.sydney.park.hyatt.com

Glossy, glamorous and the only Sydney hotel with absolute harbour frontage, this is a favourite with visiting mega-stars. The luxury hotel wraps itself around the waterfront in a prime location opposite the Opera House.

The hotel is high on personal attention—including a butler service and check-in on every floor. Inside, the restrained decor blends classical works with contemporary Australian artworks.

✉ 7 Hickson Road, The Rocks, Sydney, NSW 2000 ☎ 02 9241 1234 ⏰ All year ✋ A\$650–A\$4,500 ⓘ 163 🈳 🏊 Indoor 🗦 🚌 Millers Point 🚇 Circular Quay 🚢 Circular Quay

QUAY GRAND SUITES

www.mirvachotels.com

The one- and two-bedroom suites at this all-suite hotel are spacious, elegant and designed to take advantage of the exceptional views across Circular Quay on one side, and the Royal Botanic Gardens on the other. All suites have balconies and a lounge and dining area separate from the bedroom.

✉ 61 Macquarie Street, Sydney, NSW 2000 ☎ 02 9256 4000 ⏰ All year ✋ A\$359–A\$579 ⓘ 70 rooms 🈳 🏊 Indoor 🗦 🚌 Circular Quay 🚇 Circular Quay 🚢 Circular Quay

RADISSON PLAZA HOTEL

www.radisson.com

The heritage-listed sandstone facade gives no clue of the stylish, contemporary hotel that lies within.

At the centre of the business district and a five-minute stroll from Circular Quay, this crisp property offers a choice of atrium rooms or more expensive deluxe rooms on upper levels with balconies.

✉ 27 O'Connell Street, Sydney, NSW 2000 ☎ 02 8214 0000 ⏰ All year ✋ A\$270–A\$4380 ⓘ 362 🈳 🏊 Indoor 🗦

RAVESI'S

This small boutique hotel offers sculptural, uncluttered rooms overlooking Australia's most famous beach. Rooms are airy and spacious, and decorated in coffee and cream colours. There is a range of room options, including larger split-level suites. The café/bar downstairs is a popular style scene so light sleepers might want to look elsewhere.

✉ Campbell Parade and Hall Street, Bondi Beach, NSW 2026 ☎ 02 9365 4422 ⏰ All year ✋ A\$249–A\$350 ⓘ 12 🈳 🚌 Bondi Beach

RENDEZVOUS STAFFORD HOTEL SYDNEY

In a quiet but central location in Sydney's historic precinct, these studios, apartments and terrace houses offer particularly good value for anyone looking for self-catering accommodation. Rooms are simple but pleasant. Try to get a room on the fourth floor or higher as they have excellent views across Circular Quay.

✉ 75 Harrington Street, The Rocks, Sydney NSW 2000 ☎ 02 9251 6711 ⏰ All year ✋ A\$230–A\$379 ⓘ 61 🈳 🚌 Circular Quay 🚇 Circular Quay 🚢 Circular Quay

THE RUSSELL

www.therussell.com.au

This delightful Victorian building has been renovated to provide boutique-style accommodation. The sitting room and its bar, furnished in period style, opens on to a balcony over George Street. There is also a rooftop garden.

The bedrooms are all furnished in Victorian style. Acacia Restaurant serves breakfast, lunch (Mon–Fri) and dinner.

✉ 143A George Street, The Rocks, Sydney, NSW 2000 ☎ 02 9241 3543 ⏰ All year ✋ A\$155–A\$315 ⓘ 29

SHANGRI-LA HOTEL SYDNEY

This is Sydney's tallest hotel, and harbour-view rooms offer outstanding panoramas. The Shangri-La is a leading Asian hotel chain and rooms are decorated with a soothing, subdued Oriental theme. On the 36th floor, the glass wall of the Blu Bar on 36 offers an exceptional view in the evening.

✉ 176 Cumberland Street, The Rocks, Sydney, NSW, 2000 ☎ 02 9250 6000 ⏰ All year ✋ A\$450–A\$ ⓘ 563 🈳 🏊 Indoor 🗦 🚌 Millers Point 🚇 Circular Quay 🚢 Circular Quay

SHERATON ON THE PARK

www.starwoodhotels.com

Directly opposite Hyde Park, the Sheraton has all the features and amenities of an international five-star hotel. Rooms are decorated in a classic palette of creams and earthy tones, and the plush Sheraton SweetSleeper beds bring comfort to the most jet-lagged traveller.

✉ 161 Elizabeth Street, Sydney, NSW 2000 ☎ 02 9286 6000 ⏰ All year ✋ A\$280–A\$4,360 ⓘ 557 rooms 🈳 🏊 Indoor 🗦

SIMPSONS OF POTTS POINT

On a quiet street just a few minutes' stroll from Kings Cross, this hotel retains many decorative features from its Victorian origins, including stained-glass windows and a grand cedar staircase. Rooms are comfortable and decorated in modestly opulent period style.

✉ 8 Challis Avenue, Potts Point, NSW 2011 ☎ 02 9356 2199 ⏰ All year ✋ A\$235–A\$425, breakfast included ⓘ 14 🈳 🚌 Potts Point 🚇 Kings Cross

SIR STAMFORD AT CIRCULAR QUAY

www.stamford.com.au

In an elegant building on Sydney's finest colonial-era street opposite

Opposite *The Tower Room of The Westin Sydney*

the Royal Botanic Gardens, this hotel offers a patrician sense of style with its chandeliers, old-fashioned oil paintings, reproduction antiques, marble floors and personal service. Suites here are excellent value.

✉ 93 Macquarie Street, Sydney, NSW 2000 ☎ 02 9252 4600 🕒 All year ✋ A$197–A$3,080 ⓘ 105 ♿ ⛱ Heated outdoor ⛲

SYDNEY HARBOUR MARRIOTT AT CIRCULAR QUAY
www.marriott.com.au

Bright, eye-catching rooms with a splashy colour scheme sets this apart from the norm at the city's elite hotels. The hotel is well equipped for the business as well as the leisure traveller and its performance is ballasted by the tried-and-tested Marriott formula.

✉ 30 Pitt Street, Sydney, NSW 2000 ☎ 02 9259 7000 🕒 All year ✋ A$269–A$3,000 ⓘ 550 ♿ ⛱ Indoor ⛲

TRICKETTS BED & BREAKFAST
www.tricketts.com.au

A quiet location in a historic suburb, easy access to the city and great value make this one of the picks of Sydney's bed-and-breakfast

accommodation. The Victorian character of this converted mansion is evident throughout, and the house is decorated in an opulent style. Guest rooms are vast and each has a bathroom.

✉ 270 Glebe Point Road, Glebe, NSW 2037 ☎ 02 9552 1141 🕒 All year ✋ A$185–A$245 ⓘ 2 🚌 Glebe Point Road

VICTORIA COURT HOTEL
Set on a leafy street in Potts Point, this small, smart hotel is appealing for more than just its reasonable rates. Created from the amalgamation of two terrace houses, the Victoria Court recalls its Victorian ancestry, yet all rooms have en-suite bathrooms.

The glass-roofed conservatory, where a complimentary buffet breakfast is served, is a particularly attractive room.

✉ 122 Victoria Street, Potts Point, NSW 2011 ☎ 02 9357 3200 🕒 All year ✋ A$135–A$275 ⓘ 22

THE WESTIN SYDNEY
www.westin.com/sydney

This deluxe hotel occupies two buildings—a modern 31-floor tower,

and the beautifully restored Sydney GPO building, dating from 1887.

Facilities include a 24-hour business centre, health club, hair salon, boutiques, the Lobby Bar and Lobby Lounge, the Mosaic Restaurant and a basement-level food court.

✉ 1 Martin Place, Sydney, NSW 2000 ☎ 02 8223 1111 🕒 All year ✋ A$330–A$1200+ (suite). 'Best available' rates start from A$305, excluding breakfast ⓘ 416 ♿ ⛱ Indoor heated

THE YORK APARTMENT HOTEL
www.theyorkapartments.com.au

This hotel offers a choice of studio apartments and one- and two-bedroom apartments in a prime position, at a considerable discount over the price of hotel accommodation of similar standard in the area. Although the rooms are slightly bland, they are comfortable, spacious and well equipped, with kitchens, balconies and laundry facilities.

✉ 5 York Street, Sydney, NSW 2000 ☎ 02 9210 5000 🕒 All year ✋ A$190–A$360 ⓘ 123 rooms ♿ ⛱ Heated outdoor ⛲ 🚌 Circular Quay 🚆 Circular Quay 🚢 Circular Quay

NEW SOUTH WALES AND ACT

New South Wales is the fifth largest of Australia's states, yet with a landmass of 801,428 square km (309,433 square miles), it's more than three times the size of the United Kingdom, or bigger than Texas. It's also the most populous state in Australia, yet with just 8.5 per square kilometre (22 per square mile), its population is a shadow of the 670 people who live in every square mile of the UK. In the US, that would be equal to the desert state of Nevada, which ranks 42nd in the list of US states' population density.

Most of that population lives along the eastern seaboard. To the west are the hills of the Great Dividing Range, which vary in height from a few hundred metres to more than a thousand. Further west the great plains begin, becoming progressively drier as they advance into the outback. The state encompasses a diversity of landscapes, from subtropical rainforests to the glacier-carved valleys that surround Australia's highest mountain peaks, from ancient volcanoes to parched red sands.

New South Wales has a little of many of the diverse experiences that Australia has to offer. Just to the west of Sydney are the Blue Mountains, part of a World Heritage region and the ideal place to experience Australia's flora, fauna and its scenic majesty. To the north is the Hunter Valley, one of the country's premier winegrowing regions. Farther west is the outback, rich with Aboriginal heritage and the soul-stealing magic of the desert, while the coast is a treasure from end to end, the perfect backdrop for any beach lover.

In the state's south is the Australian Capital Territory, site of Canberra, the national capital. Canberra is Australia's largest inland city, created by an act of parliament as a model city, carved from the blank slate of what was once sheep pastures. As well as a political capital, it is also a showcase of national aspirations, home to many of Australia's premier cultural, artistic and sporting institutions.

BLUE MOUNTAINS

INTRODUCTION

The Blue Mountains is a superb World Heritage wilderness area with truly magnificent scenery and within easy reach of Sydney.

The region begins around 75km (46 miles) west of Sydney and extends west to Mount Victoria, 140km (87 miles) from the city. These are not really mountains, rather a high plateau that has been weathered over many millions of years. The area is visited primarily for its superb sandstone cliff, canyon and valley scenery, much of it encompassed by the Blue Mountains National Park. This wilderness can be enjoyed from many spectacular lookouts, or more actively by bushwalking or adventure sports such as abseiling (rappelling), canyoning, horseback riding, rock climbing and 4WD tours. There are several day trips available from Sydney (your hotel or tourist office can supply details), but most visitors rent a car and explore at will.

Although Aboriginal people lived in the area for tens of thousands of years, the Blue Mountains proved impenetrable to the earliest Europeans. Explorers found a route through the mountains only in 1813. After the arrival of the railway from Sydney in the 1860s the region became a retreat for Sydneysiders, particularly during the summer. The Blue Mountains National Park was established in 1959 and is significant for its outstanding biodiversity of plant and animal communities—there are some 90 species of eucalypts. The Wollemi pine, one of the world's rarest plants, was discovered north of the Blue Mountains in 1994.

The entire region—the Greater Blue Mountains Area—was designated a World Heritage Area by UNESCO in November 2000. This wilderness is conserved in seven national parks (Blue Mountains, Kanangra-Boyd, Wollemi, Gardens of Stone, Nattai, Yengo and Thirlmere Lakes) and the Jenolan Caves Karst Conservation Reserve.

WHAT TO SEE

LOWER BLUE MOUNTAINS

Glenbrook marks the eastern approach to the national park, with a visitor centre, short bushwalks, and Aboriginal rock art in Red Hands Cave about 5km (3 miles) to the southwest. The Norman Lindsay Gallery and Museum, former home of artist and author Norman Lindsay (1879–1969), is at Faulconbridge,

INFORMATION

www.visitbluemountains.com.au
www.nationalparks.nsw.gov.au
✚ 354 V13 ℹ Blue Mountains
Visitor Information Centres, Great
Western Highway, Glenbrook, NSW
2773; Echo Point, Katoomba, NSW 2780
☎ freecall 1300 653 408 ⊘ Daily 9–5
🚉 Glenbrook, Springwood, Wentworth
Falls, Leura, Katoomba, Blackheath,
Mount Victoria, Lithgow

Opposite *The picturesque Dangar Falls are a few kilometres from Dorrigo, NSW*
Above *The Three Sisters rock formation is near Katoomba*

TIPS

» Visit during the week as at weekends the park becomes crowded (mostly with Sydneysiders looking for an escape), and accommodation is more expensive.

» For a serious bushwalk, ensure you have maps, water, food and suitable clothing. Contact the National Parks and Wildlife Service at Blackheath for advice: 02 4787 8877.

16km (10 miles) farther west along the Great Western Highway (daily 10–4). Continuing along the highway, Wentworth Falls has a golf course and Wentworth Falls Lake just north of the town, some short bushwalks and of course the falls themselves to the south.

✉ Great Western Highway, 68km (42 miles) west of Sydney

UPPER BLUE MOUNTAINS
LEURA

Leura is perhaps the most picturesque Blue Mountains village. The delightfully old-fashioned main street is lined with cafés, arts and crafts shops, boutiques, delicatessens and bakeries. In addition to a golf course and some fairly easy bushwalks, the main attractions are large gardens and superb views of the Blue Mountains National Park.

The Everglades Gardens (spring and summer 10–5, autumn and winter 10–4) were designed by the Danish-born master gardener Paul Sorensen in the 1930s. The Leuralla NSW Toy and Railway Museum and Gardens (daily 10–5) are based around an Edwardian mansion, the former home of Dr. H. V. Evatt, an Australian politician who became president of the United Nations in 1948. As the name suggests, there are attractive gardens, and a large collection of toys, dolls, trains and NSW Railways memorabilia. South of Leura, Sublime Point lookout has wonderful views of the Jamison Valley and surrounds—arguably better than those at the more famous Echo Point at Katoomba.

✉ Great Western Highway, 108km (67 miles) west of Sydney, 3km (2 miles) east of Katoomba

KATOOMBA

Katoomba is the region's largest town, a good base for bushwalking, rock climbing and abseiling (rappelling) in the Blue Mountains National Park. Bushwalks range from an hour or so along the clifftop to the long (three-day) and arduous Six Foot Track walk to Jenolan Caves. For gentle browsers there are galleries, craft shops, cafés and restaurants, including the Paragon, an ornate café established in 1916 but renovated in 1925 in art deco style. The

Below A view over the rooftops of Katoomba
Right Learning to abseil in the Blue Mountains

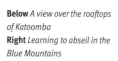

Edge cinema (▷ 123) has a six-floor-high screen that shows a spectacular film on the Blue Mountains and its scenery. Katoomba Street, the long, steep main road, leads south 1km (0.6 mile) to Echo Point, the region's most famous lookout, with celebrated views of the deep forested Jamison Valley, cliffs, ridges and the Three Sisters rock formation. Nearby Scenic World (daily 9–5) incorporates the Skyway cable car (equally great views) and Scenic Railway (which descends to the valley floor). The forest boardwalk at the base of the Scenic Railway is ideal for those who wish to see the lush valley, but who lack the equipment for a serious bushwalk.

The Hydro Majestic Hotel at Medlow Bath, 7km (4 miles) northwest, is not just a hotel but a tourist attraction in itself. Built in 1904, it stands on an escarpment overlooking the Megalong Valley.

✉ Great Western Highway, 111km (69 miles) west of Sydney

BLACKHEATH

The small town of Blackheath is not particularly attractive in itself but it is the main access point for the spectacular Grose Valley and the northern section of the Blue Mountains National Park. The town has a golf course, a good selection of cafés, craft and antiques shops, and a famous sourdough bakery.

The Blue Mountains Heritage Centre is a couple of kilometres away from the main street on Govetts Leap Road, just within the national park boundary (daily 9–4.30). It's a good start for tourist information and walking tracks, and there is a shop and displays on the national park. Nearby Govetts Leap Lookout has awe-inspiring views of Bridal Veil Falls and the deep forested Grose Valley with its dramatic sandstone cliffs. There are equally good views from Evans Lookout, about 3km (2 miles) southeast of the heritage centre; the landscape is quite different from that of the Katoomba–Leura region.

To the south of Blackheath, the agricultural Megalong Valley has a number of horseback-riding establishments. Reached along Megalong Road after 10km (6 miles), the Megalong Australian Heritage Centre (daily 9–5) presents horseback riding, sheep shearing and Clydesdale horse demonstrations. Retracing your steps to Blackheath and going about 1km (0.6 mile) north brings

Below *Hanging Rock overlooks the Jamison Valley*

you to Bacchante Gardens (daily 9–4), a woodland garden that's particularly good in autumn. Mount Victoria, along the Great Western Highway, is a small village with a few antiques shops and spectacular views from the lookouts at nearby Mount York and Mount Piddington.

✉ Great Western Highway, 12km (7.5 miles) northwest of Katoomba

JENOLAN CAVES

www.jenolancaves.org.au

First discovered by Europeans in the 1830s, Jenolan Caves is a subterranean world of limestone caverns and underground rivers, and stalagmites and stalactites. Even today the location is remote, some 60km (37 miles) south of Lithgow, and there is no public transportation to the area: You have to drive or join a coach tour. The guided tours explore up to nine spectacular caves, lasting from one to two hours.

Lucas Cave is the most popular, with the widest and highest chambers. The Orient Cave is richly decorated with delicate crystalline formations. In all, the Jenolan karst cave system has as many as 300 caverns. Four are used for adventure caving. Experienced tour guides for adventure caving can be booked in advance.

Above ground, the scenery is equally impressive, a mixture of bushland, rock formations, eucalypt forests, pools, rivers and waterfalls. Rugged attractions include adventure caving and abseiling (rappelling). Otherwise the Jenolan Karst Conservation Reserve has walking tracks and scenic lookouts. To experience this isolated area properly it is best to overnight at Jenolan Caves House (a restored 1920s hotel) or one of the less expensive accommodation options.

✉ Jenolan Caves, NSW 2790 ☎ 02 6359 3911 🕐 Tours depart regularly at set times daily 9.30–5.30 (phone to check; bookings advisable). There are evening tours on Saturdays at 7.30 or 8pm and in school holidays when the caves may open later—call to check 🖐 Prices vary according to the number of caves visited: adult A$27–A$40, child A$18.50–A$25; two-hour night tours A$40 per person

MOUNT TOMAH BOTANIC GARDEN

www.mounttomahbotanicgarden.com.au

Lithgow is an unattractive coal-mining town at the western foot of the Blue Mountains. From here the Bells Line of Road meanders east through the northern section of the national park via Mount Tomah, and makes an alternative scenic route to and from Sydney. The only way to reach Mount Tomah is by driving or joining a coach tour.

About 10km (6 miles) east from Lithgow at Clarence is the Zig Zag Railway (daily train rides at 11, 1 and 3; tel 02 6355 2955). You can ride a steam or vintage rail motor along the steep zigzagging 1860s rail line, a masterpiece of engineering in its day.

Occupying a 1,000m (3,280ft) ridge that overlooks the northern Blue Mountains region, 38km (23.5 miles) east from Lithgow, Mount Tomah is the cool climate garden of Sydney's Royal Botanic Gardens (▷ 77). It is one of the Blue Mountains' highlights. The 28ha (69-acre) gardens include lawns, woods, a formal garden, a rock garden and a pond. Of particular interest are the native and exotic plant collections. The shady Gondwana Forest Walk passes some of Australia's unique plants and trees.

The on-site Mount Tomah Restaurant serves modern Australian cuisine and is an attraction in its own right. (Many people come here primarily for lunch rather than to visit the gardens.) If you have time, follow a sealed road west of Mount Tomah. It branches north to the small village of Mount Wilson and the Cathedral of Ferns, where there is a short walk through shady woodland.

✉ Bells Line of Road, Mount Tomah, NSW 2758 ☎ 02 4567 2154 🕐 Apr–end Sep daily 10–4; Oct–end Mar 10–5 🖐 Adult A$5.50, child (4–16) A$3.30

Above *Wentworth Falls are south of the town named after them*

CANBERRA

INTRODUCTION

Australia's meticulously planned capital city is unlike any other in the country, and is the home of many national galleries, museums and other institutions.

After the federation of the Australian colonies in 1901 there was fierce rivalry between Sydney and Melbourne for the status of capital city. As a compromise, Canberra was chosen in 1908 as the site for the capital, in a 'neutral' farming region some 300km (186 miles) from Sydney and 600km (372 miles) from Melbourne. In 1911 an international design competition for the cityscape was won by American architect Walter Burley Griffin. Construction began in 1913 and the Parliament moved to Canberra in 1927. Over the last 90 years, Canberra's straight avenues and circular streets have been planted with more than 10 million trees and shrubs to produce an attractive and elegant city. The main sights are clustered near Parliament House, to the south of Lake Burley Griffin, while the commercial area is to the north.

INFORMATION

www.visitcanberra.com.au

🚹 357 U14 🚹 Canberra Visitor Centre, 330 Northbourne Avenue, Dickson, ACT 2602 ☎ 1300 554 114 (calls from all parts of Australia) 🕐 Mon–Fri 9–5, Sat, Sun 9–4 🚉 Canberra, 4.5km (3 miles) southeast of the city. The journey from Sydney takes 3 hours 15 minutes; from Melbourne (no direct rail link) about 8 hours

WHAT TO SEE

AUSTRALIAN INSTITUTE OF SPORT

www.ausport.gov.au/ais/

This sprawling complex on the north-west edge of the city is the engine room of Australia's sporting success. It's a place of sweat, toil and dreams, where visitors on one of the AIS's guided tours might bump into some of the stars of the swimming pool or a famous cyclist in training. The facility's 90-minute tours are guided by athletes who are in training at the institute, and who can give you the inside story on just what it means to perform at this level. See how you measure up against Australia's finest with Sportex, an interactive facility that assesses your performance as a golfer, rower, wheelchair basketball player or skier.

✉ Leverrier Crescent, Bruce, ACT 2617 ☎ 02 6214 1010 🕐 Daily 9–5 ✋ Tours: Adult A$16, child A$9

Above *New Parliament House is set into Capital Hill*

TIP
» Canberra's ACTION bus network makes it easy to get around and the Daily (A$7.40) and Off-Peak Daily (A$4.50) tickets are good value. Tel 13 17 10 for details.

THE AUSTRALIAN NATIONAL BOTANIC GARDENS

This 90ha (222-acre) garden at the foot of Black Mountain is the most complete garden of Australian native flora, with about 99,000 plants representing more than 6,800 species from Australia's rainforests, deserts, alpine meadows and scrublands. The Main Path is an easy stroll of 1.5km (1 mile) that takes around an hour. You can also walk to the summit of Black Mountain from here, a 90-minute round trip. During January and February each year the gardens host a Summer Concert Series on weekends starting at 6pm.

✉ Clunies Ross Street, Acton, ACT 2601 ☎ 02 6250 9450 🕐 Daily 8.30–5

AUSTRALIAN WAR MEMORIAL

www.awm.gov.au

The domed building at the end of Anzac Parade is one of the world's best war museums and makes a very rewarding experience. The site includes The Hall of Memory, Tomb of the Unknown Australian Soldier, the Roll of Honour (naming more than 100,000 service men and women who have died during war) and a courtyard with the Eternal Flame and Pool of Reflection. There is a Discovery Room for children with hands-on exhibits, and sound-and-light shows in the Object Theatre in Anzac Hall.

✉ Treloar Crescent, Campbell, ACT 2612 ☎ 02 6243 4211 (enquiries) 🕐 Daily 10–5

BLUNDELL'S COTTAGE

This is one of 27 cottages built on the 1,600ha (3,952-acre) Duntroon sheep station, the original landholding on which Canberra now stands. Made from fieldstone in 1858, the cottage originally consisted of four rooms and was set above the flood level of the Molonglo, the river that was dammed in 1963 to create Lake Burley Griffin. George Blundell was a bullock driver who worked for the Campbells, the family that occupied Duntroon, moving wool and supplies between Duntroon and Sydney. Blundell lived in the house from 1874 with his wife, Flora, yet it wasn't until their eighth child was born that they added the two rooms at the back of the house. The cottage was used as a dwelling until 1958.

✉ Wendouree Drive, Russell, ATC 2600 ☎ 02 6272 2900 🕐 Daily 10–3 ✋ Adult A$7, child A$5

Below The National Carillon on Lake Burley Griffin
Right The National Museum of Australia stands beside Lake Burley Griffin

NATIONAL GALLERY OF AUSTRALIA

www.nga.gov.au

This is Australia's premier art gallery, with a permanent collection of more than 100,000 Australian, Aboriginal, European, American, Asian and other works. Of particular note is the Aboriginal and Torres Strait Islander collection, and the Asian art collection.

✉ Parkes Place, Parkes, ACT 2600 ☎ 02 6240 6502 (enquiries) 🕐 Daily 10–5,

NATIONAL LIBRARY OF AUSTRALIA

www.nla.gov.au

Australia's largest collection of library material, the archive includes books, maps, journals, letters, sheet music, magazines, newspapers, ephemera, films, videos, oral history media, more than 500,000 photographs and around 40,000 works of art.

✉ Parkes Place, Parkes, ACT 2600 ☎ 02 6262 1111 (enquiries) 🕐 Exhibition Gallery: daily 9–5; Main Reading Room: Mon–Thu 9–9, Fri, Sat 9–5, Sun 1.30–5

NATIONAL MUSEUM OF AUSTRALIA

www.nma.gov.au

The nation's social history museum has galleries relating to the land, the nation and the people. Exhibits range from Aboriginal bark paintings to a convict's jacket.

✉ Lawson Crescent, Acton Peninsula, ACT 2600 ☎ 02 6208 5000 🕐 Daily 9–5

OLD PARLIAMENT HOUSE

www.moadoph.gov.au

Completed in 1927, Old Parliament House was the home of Australia's Federal Parliament until 1988. The building now contains the Museum of Australian Democracy, dedicated to the history of democracy in Australia.

✉ King George Terrace, Parkes, ACT 2600 ☎ 02 6270 8222 🕐 Daily 9–5

PARLIAMENT HOUSE

www.aph.gov.au

Parliament House is one of Canberra's most popular attractions. The Australian Federal Parliament moved to this modern building from the nearby Old Parliament House in 1988. Free tickets for the public galleries are available

Below *The Australian National Botanic Gardens are in Acton, Canberra*

for Question Time when Parliament is in session. The building also contains paintings, sculptures and other artworks.

✉ Capital Hill, ACT 2600 ☎ 02 6277 5399 (enquiries) ⏱ Daily 9–5

QUESTACON—THE NATIONAL SCIENCE AND TECHNOLOGY CENTRE

www.questacon.edu.au

Australia's leading interactive science and technology centre turns education into great fun for all ages. Most of the exhibits are hands-on and irresistible for both adults and children.

✉ King Edward Terrace, Parkes, ACT 2600 ☎ 02 6270 2800 ⏱ Daily 9–5

NATIONAL FILM AND SOUND ARCHIVE

www.nfsa.afc.gov.au

Subtitled The National Screen and Sound Archive, the museum concentrates on Australia's moving image (television and film) and recorded sound (radio and music) heritage. A film theatre presents screenings.

✉ McCoy Circuit, Acton, ACT 2601 ☎ 02 6248 2000 ⏱ Mon–Fri 9–5, Sat, Sun 10–5

MORE TO SEE

AUSTRALIAN INSTITUTE OF SPORT

The national training centre offers guided tours and an interactive sports exhibit gallery.

✉ Sports Visitors Centre, Leverrier Crescent, Bruce, ACT 2617 ☎ Tours: 02 6214 1444 ⏱ Mon–Fri 8.30–5, Sat, Sun and public holidays 10–4

BLACK MOUNTAIN TOWER

View ACT from this communications tower on Black Mountain.

✉ Black Mountain Drive, Acton, ACT 2601 ☎ 02 6219 6111, 1800 806 718 ⏱ Daily 9–10

CANBERRA SPACE DOME

The night sky is recreated in a domed theatre.

✉ Hawdon Place, Dickson, ACT 2602 ☎ 02 6248 5333 ⏱ Planetarium sessions Tue–Sat 7–8.30pm

Above left *The Captain Cook memorial jet on Lake Burley Griffin*
Above right *Hot-air ballooning over the Old Parliament House*

NATIONAL ZOO & AQUARIUM

Australia's second-largest private zoo is good for big cats.

✉ Scrivener Dam, Yarralumla, ACT 2611 ☎ 02 6287 8400 ⏱ Daily 10–5

BLUE MOUNTAINS
▷ 104–108.

CANBERRA
▷ 109–112.

CENTRAL COAST
www.visitcentralcoast.com.au
The Central Coast has been an escape for Sydneysiders since the railway arrived in the late 1880s. There are just peaceful towns and villages, with beautiful coastal and bushland scenery. Attractive seafront towns include Ettalong, Terrigal and The Entrance, and there are sandy beaches and surf at Umina, Avoca, MacMasters and Toowoon Bay. Of the seven national parks in the area, Brisbane Water, Bouddi and Wyrrabalong have coastal walkways and wildlife. Inland there are lakes and waterways at Brisbane Water, Tuggerah Lake, Budgewoi Lake and Lake Munmorah. Among the wildlife sanctuaries, the Australian Reptile Park (daily 9–5) has native and imported animals.
✚ 355 W13 ℹ️ Central Coast Visitor Centre, 52 The Avenue, Mt Penang Parklands, Kariong, NSW 2250 ☎ 1300 130 708 🕙 Daily 9–5 🚉 Gosford; Woy Woy (southern region); Tuggerah and Wyong (northern region and the lakes)

COFFS HARBOUR AND DORRIGO NATIONAL PARK
www.coffscoast.com.au
A major beach resort and popular holiday area, and crowded during the summer holidays, Coffs Harbour is graced by golden sandy beaches. Attractions include watersports, cruises, a marine park, oceanarium, zoo, botanic garden, art gallery and white-water rafting on the nearby Nymboida River. Inland, near the picturesque town of Dorrigo, is the 11,902ha (29,398-acre) Dorrigo National Park within the Central Eastern Rainforest Reserves World Heritage Area. There are trails, picnic areas, waterfalls and the Dorrigo Rainforest Centre; explore the rainforest's paths, or take it all in from the Skywalk boardwalk above the canopy.

✚ 353 W11/X11 ℹ️ Coffs Coast Visitor Information Centre, cnr Pacific Highway and Maclean streets, Coffs Harbour, NSW 2450 ☎ 02 6648 4990; (local call rate) 1300 369 070 🕙 Daily 9–5 🚉 Coffs Harbour

EDEN AND THE FAR SOUTH COAST
www.sapphirecoast.com.au
This beautiful, unspoiled region is 465km (288 miles) from Sydney, , but a visit could be combined with a tour to Melbourne (▷ 140–149) or the Snowy Mountains. The 'Sapphire Coast' has some of the state's most attractive beaches, where watersports, fishing, whale-watching cruises, river cruises and coastal walks are popular. Eden, the southernmost town of New South Wales, has had a long whaling history. To the north and south of the town, Ben Boyd National Park is a beautiful environment of beaches, visible geology and historic buildings. Farther north Bermagui, Tathra and Merimbula, and Pambula Beach, all have secluded beaches.
✚ 357 V14 ℹ️ Eden Gateway Centre, Princes Highway, Eden, NSW 2551 ☎ 02 6496 1953 🕙 Daily 9–5

HAWKESBURY REGION
www.hawkesburytourism.com.au
This low-lying region northwest of Sydney was settled in the early 1790s. The area's most important feature is the Upper Hawkesbury River, which winds from the Great Dividing Range to the ocean north of Palm Beach. Other than Richmond, the area's main commercial town, most of the historic towns and villages are picturesque. Windsor

was laid out in 1810; its old buildings include the Macquarie Arms hotel, St. Matthew's Church, Courthouse and the Observatory. Pitt Town, Wilberforce and Castlereagh are small farming towns, also founded in 1810.
✚ 354 V13 ℹ️ Hawkesbury Visitor Information Centre, Ham Common, Hawkesbury Valley Way, Clarendon, NSW 2756 ☎ 02 4578 0233 🕙 Daily 9–5 🚉 Windsor, Clarendon or Richmond

HUNTER VALLEY
▷ 114.

JERVIS BAY AND THE SHOALHAVEN REGION
www.jervisbaytourism.com.au
www.shoalhavenholidays.com.au
Shoalhaven is an unspoiled South Coast beach-resort region. It includes the town of Nowra, Jervis Bay and the coastline south to Ulladulla. The best area is Jervis Bay, a large inlet famous for its dazzling white sand, blue waters and wildlife such as migrating whales and resident dolphins. Other attractions include national parks, bushwalking, Aboriginal culture at Wreck Bay, and more than 90km (56 miles) of surf. Nowra dates from the 1850s and is the region's largest town. Stop for Australia's Museum of Flight (daily 10–4), cruises on the Shoalhaven River, wineries and historic houses. North of Nowra, the village of Berry is renowned for its art and craft shops, antiques outlets and cafés.
✚ 357 V13 ℹ️ Shoalhaven Visitor Information Centre, Princes Highway, Nowra, NSW 2541 ☎ 02 4421 0778, 1300 662 808 🕙 Daily 9–5 🚉 Bomaderry

Below *Whale watching near Merimbula on the Far South Coast*

INFORMATION

www.winecountry.com.au

355 W12 Hunter Valley Wine Country Visitor Information Centre, 455 Wine Country Drive, Pokolbin, NSW 2325 02 4990 0900 Mon–Sat 9–5, Sun and public hols 9–4 (later in summer) Maitland, 27km (17 miles) from Cessnock

TIP

» The valley is extremely popular at weekends. Visit during the week when the area is quieter and accommodation is generally less expensive.

HUNTER VALLEY

Take the opportunity to sample some fine wines in one of Australia's premier wine-growing regions.

The Hunter Valley is Australia's oldest winegrowing region. Vines were first planted here in the 1820s and the broad valley is now one of the nation's best-known wine areas. There are more than 120 wineries and cellar doors, most located around the hamlets of Pokolbin, Lovedale, Broke and Rothbury, with some closer to Cessnock and the village of Wollombi in the south. Cessnock is the region's largest town, founded on coal mining. Maitland, Morpeth and Wollombi are notable among the early colonial settlements, the historic village of Wollombi having changed little since the 19th century.

WEEKEND ESCAPE

The valley is a popular weekend escape for Sydneysiders and people from the Central Coast and the Newcastle regions. Numerous restaurants offer fine modern Australian cuisine, while a variety of musical events (jazz, blues and opera, for example) are held at wineries throughout the year. Art, craft and antiques shops are found all around the valley. Among the activities are golf, tennis, hot-air ballooning, tandem skydiving, horseback riding, carriage rides around the wineries, bicycling and 4WD vehicle tours.

WINERIES

There are too many to mention in detail, but suggestions are:
Brokenwood Wines—excellent shiraz.
Ivanhoe Wines—a small boutique winery.
Lakes Folly Vineyard—some of the area's best reds.
Lindemans—reliable for all wine varieties.
Tulloch Wines—particularly good for sparkling wines.
Tyrrell's Vineyards—a long-established family-owned winery.
Wyndham Estate—established in 1828, producing quality wines.

Northwest of the main Hunter Valley region, around the village of Denman, the Upper Hunter Valley is another winery area; best wineries here are Arrowfield Wines and Rosemount Estate.

Below *The green rolling hills near Pokolbin are typical of the Hunter Valley in Spring*

KIAMA AND THE JAMBEROO VALLEY

www.kiama.com.au

Within easy reach of Sydney, the small town of Kiama has excellent sandy surf and swimming beaches, and many historic buildings. Its most famous attractions are the 1887 Kiama Lighthouse and the Blowhole, through which the sea spurts when the conditions are right.

To the south, Gerringong and Gerroa have further beautiful beaches, including the Seven Mile Beach, ideal for surfing.

🚹 354 V13 🚶 Kiama Visitor Information Centre, Blowhole Point, Kiama, NSW 2533 ☎ 02 4232 3322, (local call rate) 1300 654 762 🕙 Daily 9–5 🚉 Kiama

KOSCIUSZKO NATIONAL PARK

www.nationalparks.nsw.gov.au

At almost 675,000ha (1.66 million acres), Kosciuszko is the largest national park in New South Wales. It also contains Australia's highest mountain, Mount Kosciuszko at 2,228m (7,308ft). This highland wilderness, part of the Great Dividing Range and within the Snowy Mountains, is known for its winter skiing and summer bushwalking. The largest ski resorts

in the region are Perisher Blue and Thredbo, with smaller facilities at Charlotte Pass, and Mount Selwyn. Check weather warnings before bushwalking or cross-country skiing.

🚹 357 U14 🚶 Snowy Region Visitor Centre, Kosciuszko Road, Jindabyne, NSW 2627 ☎ 1800 004 439 🕙 Daily 8.30–5 🖐 Park A$27 per vehicle per day (A$16 per vehicle in summer) 🚌 Coaches from Sydney and Canberra call at Cooma, Jindabyne and Thredbo (and Skitube railway in winter); bus from Cooma airport 🚉 🚃

MURRAY RIVER

www.echucamoama.com

The Murray River flows for 2,700km (1,678 miles) from the Great Dividing Range of New South Wales to the ocean in South Australia—it is Australia's longest and most important waterway. The forest and wetlands of Barmah State Forest and Barmah State Park, north and east of Echuca-Moama are highlights, as is the slow stretch along the Victoria border from the old river ports of Echuca-Moama and Barham to Swan Hill. Here the route takes in forests, lakes and farming scenery, Aboriginal and European history, paddle-steamer cruises, houseboat holidays and fine local

foods, including cheeses and yabbies (freshwater crayfish).

🚹 356 S14 🚶 Echuca-Moama Visitor Information Centre, 2 Heygarth Street, Echuca, VIC 3564 ☎ 03 5480 7555, Freecall 1800 804 446 🕙 Daily 9–5

MYALL LAKES NATIONAL PARK

www.nationalparks.nsw.gov.au

This popular national park consists of tranquil lakes, forests and 40km (25 miles) of sandy surf beaches. The lakes cover 10,000ha (24,700 acres) and form the largest natural fresh or brackish water system on the state coast. The landscape includes rainforest, paperbark swamps, heath and dry eucalypt forests—home to goannas, possums, kangaroos, swamp wallabies and many birds. It's an ideal place for canoeing, boating, most watersports, walking—or relaxing.

🚹 355 W12 ✉ NSW National Parks and Wildlife Service, The Lakes Way, Pacific Palms, NSW 2428 ☎ 02 6591 0300 🕙 Park: daily 24 hours. Office: Mon–Fri 8.30–4.30 🖐 A$7 per vehicle per day

Above left *A restored paddle-steamer on the Murray River*
Above right *The Blowhole and lighthouse at Kiama*

INFORMATION

www.armidaletourism.com.au
www.tamworth.nsw.gov.au
✚ 353 W11 ℹ️ Armidale Visitor
Information Centre, 82 Marsh Street,
Armidale, NSW 2350 ☎ 02 6772 4655
🕐 Daily 9–5 🚉 Armidale, Tamworth
and Glen Innes

TIP

» Be prepared for chilly nights in
winter—though log fires and a
welcoming atmosphere make up for
any discomfort.

NEW ENGLAND

New England is a superb upland rural and wilderness area with several national parks, spectacular scenic drives and historic towns and cities.

The region is in northern New South Wales and is primarily a farming area high on the Great Dividing Range. It is known for its cool climate and distinct seasons. The region was first settled by farmers in the early 1830s, and the main towns are Armidale, Glen Innes, Inverell and Tamworth. Apart from farming, New England's prosperity is based on minerals and tourism.

TOWNS

Armidale is home to the University of New England and is renowned for its gardens, historic buildings (including two cathedrals) and genteel atmosphere. Among the museums and galleries, the New England Regional Art Museum (Tue–Sun 10.30–5) has an excellent collection of Australian art. The Saumarez Homestead is a magnificent 1860s National Trust property (Sep to mid-Jun daily 10–4; guided tours at 10.30 and 2).

Inverell is a small town long associated with farming and mining—the area still produces most of the world's blue sapphires. Attractions include Copeton Waters State Park (a large lake and its surroundings) and a fossicking reserve, where visitors can search for gemstones.

The main claim to fame of the large agricultural town of Tamworth is its annual Country Music Festival, which draws thousands of people each January. The Australian Country Music Foundation Museum (Mon–Sat 10–2) may explain why.

NATIONAL PARKS

Oxley Wild Rivers NP and New England NP are part of the large Central Eastern Rainforest Reserves of Australia World Heritage Area. Oxley Wild Rivers has rivers, waterfalls, gorges and Australia's largest area of dry rainforest, and New England is renowned for its wet and dry rainforest, caves and cliffs.

Guy Fawkes River NP is northeast of Armidale, a rugged and remote wilderness, with rivers and some challenging walks.

Cathedral Rock NP lies east of Armidale. It is known for its sub-alpine heath, huge granite boulders and eucalypt forests.

Above *Wheat harvesting at Baan Baa,*
near Narrabri in New England

OUTBACK NEW SOUTH WALES—BROKEN HILL

www.visitbrokenhill.com.au
Broken Hill is about 1,160km (719 miles) northwest of Sydney. It's a three-day drive from the state capital along Route 32—but a visit to any of the state's outback towns is recommended for a different perspective on Australian life. A train or plane to Broken Hill is quicker.

This rugged country—mostly dry and very hot in summer, exceptionally flat with long straight roads and scattered settlements. The only contrast in scenery is provided by low hills, and rivers such as the Darling and Lachlan.

Broken Hill (population 25,000) developed after the discovery of silver in 1883. Mining is still the major industry and there are above-ground and underground mine tours. The town also has museums, galleries, an Afghan mosque (1891), Aboriginal art and craft outlets, and the Living Desert Reserve, with trails, lookouts and sculptures. Broken Hill is on Central Standard Time, 30 minutes behind the rest of NSW.

Menindee is a small town, 110km (68 miles) southeast of Broken Hill, beside the Darling River and the Menindee Lakes system, with fishing and boating. Nearby Kinchega National Park is a 44,000ha (108,680-acre) reserve with lakes, Aboriginal sites, the historic Kinchega woolshed and waterbirds. The remote, World Heritage-listed Mungo National Park, about 350km (217 miles) southeast of Broken Hill, has evidence of at least 40,000 years of Aboriginal occupation. Its famous feature is the Walls of China, a long crescent dune that has been eroded over thousands of years.

⊞ 347 R12 🚹 Broken Hill Visitor Information Centre, cnr Blende and Bromide streets, Broken Hill, NSW 2880 ☎ 08 8080 3560 🕔 Daily 8.30–5 🚉 Menindee or Broken Hill

PORT MACQUARIE

www.portmacquarieinfo.com.au
Port Macquarie is one of the best North Coast holiday towns. The small city traces its origins to a penal settlement founded here in 1821. St. Thomas's Church is one of Australia's oldest churches. Other attractions include surfing, fishing, cruises on the Hastings River (dolphin-spotting trips), beach camel rides, skydiving, parasailing and wineries.

⊞ 355 W12 🚹 Port Macquarie Visitor Information Centre, cnr Clarence and Hay streets, Port Macquarie, NSW 2444 ☎ 02 6581 8000, (local call rate) 1300 303 155 🕔 Mon–Fri 9–5.30, Sat, Sun 9–4 🚉 Wauchope

PORT STEPHENS AND NELSON BAY

www.portstephens.org.au
With more than 20 sandy beaches and the vast Port Stephens bay, this area likes to describe itself as a 'Blue Water Paradise'. The sheltered bay is flanked by several small settlements, including the main town of Nelson Bay. The appeal of the area is that of an old-fashioned holiday resort. The surrounds consist of heath, forest and rocky headlands, in particular don't miss the walk to the headland of Tomaree National Park for great views of the coast.

Port Stephens has a large resident population of bottlenose dolphins, and the area is on the seasonal (May–end July) whale migration route—cruises to see these creatures are very popular. The 30km (18.5-mile) Stockton Beach is remarkable for its massive sand dunes.

⊞ 355 W12 🚹 Port Stephens Visitor Information Centre, Victoria Parade, Nelson Bay, NSW 2315 ☎ 02 4980 6900, Freecall 1800 808 900 🕔 Daily 9–5

SOUTHERN HIGHLANDS

www.southern-highlands.com.au
The Southern Highlands is an attractive upland farming region to the southwest of Sydney. There are old towns and villages, large country houses, antiques shops, art galleries, craft shops, gardens, golf courses, historic pubs, good-quality restaurants, and cafés and tea rooms. Unlike Sydney, the Highlands experience four distinct seasons, and winter snow is not unknown. In the late 19th century, wealthy Sydneysiders built rambling country houses here to escape the hot, humid summers.

Berrima is one of Australia's best-preserved Georgian villages, founded in 1829 and retaining many historic buildings. Apart from its parks and gardens, and antiques and craft shops, the commercial town of Bowral is known for the Bradman Museum (daily 10–5), in honour of the cricketer Sir Donald Bradman, who spent his boyhood here and played for the local club.

Morton National Park is ideal for bushwalkers; particularly good is the view of the waterfall and valley from Fitzroy Falls. Speleologists will be interested to note that several of the Wombeyan Caves are open to the public and self-guiding tours are available (daily 8.30–5).

⊞ 354 V13 🚹 Tourism Southern Highlands, 62–70 Main Street, Mittagong, NSW 2575 ☎ 02 4871 2888, (local call rate) 1300 657 559 🕔 Mon–Fri 9–5, Sat, Sun 9–4 🚉 Mittagong, Bowral, Moss Vale, Exeter and Bundanoon

Above *Swimming in the surf at Flynns Beach, Port Macquarie on the North Coast*

DRIVE

BLUE MOUNTAINS ROUND TRIP

This circular drive explores the two sides of the Blue Mountains (▷ 104–108): the wild world of canyons, cliffs and forests, which can be sampled from lookouts and bush tracks; and the civilized world of welcoming towns, villages and gardens.

THE DRIVE

Distance: Approximately 310km (192 miles)
Allow: 1 day or stay overnight
Start at: Central Sydney
End at: Central Sydney

★ Follow the Metroad 4 and 5 signs from the heart of the city to reach Parramatta Road (Metroad 4), which connects with the Western Motorway (M4) near Strathfield. After about 35km (22 miles) the M4 ends, becoming the Great Western Highway (National Route 32), which begins a gradual climb into the mountains. Beyond Springwood, turn right to visit the Norman Lindsay Gallery and Museum.

❶ The artist and writer Norman Lindsay (1879–1969) was infamous in the 1920s and 1930s for his bohemian lifestyle and paintings of voluptuous nudes. His rambling home is now a gallery and museum of his works and life (daily 10–4).

Return to the highway, turn right and head to the town of Wentworth Falls. Past the traffic lights, turn left on to Falls Road and follow signs to the Wentworth Falls picnic area.

❷ Lookouts near the picnic area give magnificent vistas of the forested Jamison Valley and Wentworth Falls. Tracks from the lookouts include some strenuous descents into the valley, as well as moderately demanding walks and easy strolls along the cliff top.

Rejoin the highway and drive west for 6km (3.5 miles) before turning off to the left to reach Leura (▷ 106).

❸ Leura is a small town with a picturesque main commercial street,

The Mall. You can explore The Mall's cafés, tea rooms, restaurants, galleries and gift shops, as well as the nearby residential streets with their attractive old weatherboard houses and well-tended gardens.

From the main street, turn on to Cliff Drive, which soon leads to Echo Point. This is the most popular, and sometimes crowded, viewpoint in the mountains, a cliff-top perch overlooking the expanse of Jamison Valley. From the viewing platform not far from the Visitor Centre there is a vista of cliffs, eucalypt forest and the Three Sisters, a dramatic rock formation.

From Echo Point you can detour to the busy main street of Katoomba, where there is a plentiful supply of art, craft and antiques shops, as well as a good range of cafés and

Opposite Mount Tomah Botanic Garden near the town of Mount Wilson

restaurants. Otherwise continue on Cliff Drive for a short distance to Scenic World. This is the home of the Scenic Skyway and Scenic Railway, which take you either high above or deep into the valley (▷ 107). There is also a walk from here (▷ 120).

From Scenic World, continue along Cliff Drive and then follow Narrow Neck Road, which brings you to the highway west of Katoomba.

❹ The grand Hydro Majestic Hotel dominates the village of Medlow Bath. Originally constructed in 1904 as a spa for well-off Sydneysiders, it was rebuilt as a tourist hotel in the 1920s. Now restored, it is a good spot for refreshments, or an overnight stay.

Continue along the highway for about 7km (4 miles) to the town of Blackheath (▷ 107). Turn right on to the main street and follow signs to Govetts Leap Lookout.

❺ From Govetts Leap Lookout there are superb views of the deep, forested Grose Valley and its sandstone cliffs. Local legend has it that a bushranger named Govett galloped over the cliff to escape pursuing mounted police, so giving his name to this place.

From Blackheath, continue west on the highway for 5km (3 miles) to Mount Victoria, which consists of not much more than an old pub, tea rooms and a few antiques shops.

Turn off the highway and follow signs to the hamlet of Bell, 10km (6 miles) along the Darling Causeway. Once you reach Bells Line of Road (State Route 40), turn right to Bilpin and Kurrajong. This route back to Sydney has far less traffic than the Great Western Highway. About 8km (5 miles) east of Bell, turn left to the village of Mount Wilson.

❻ Sydney's well-to-do founded Mount Wilson in the late 19th century as a cool retreat from the city's hot and humid summers. They built grand homes with large gardens planted with English trees and shrubs. Many of these gardens are open to the public. One area with many large tree ferns is known as the Cathedral of Ferns.

Back on Bells Line of Road, about 15km (9 miles) from the Mount Wilson turnoff, the next stop is Mount Tomah Botanic Garden.

❼ Mount Tomah Botanic Garden is the cool-climate branch of the Royal Botanic Gardens, Sydney (▷ 77). Paths wind through impressive plantings of native and exotic species. The Australian plants include the rare Wollemi pine, which was discovered only in 1994.

Drive east on the Bells Line of Road through the small rural settlements of Bilpin and Kurrajong Heights— with their orchards and roadside fruit stalls—and on to North Richmond, Richmond and Windsor.

From here, the fastest route back to Sydney is Metroad 2 (Windsor Road and Old Windsor Road), which becomes the M2 Motorway closer to the city. This route and its continuation (Metroad 1) take you over the Sydney Harbour Bridge and back to the city itself.

WHEN TO GO
All year round. Traffic is heaviest at weekends, when Sydneysiders go on day trips to the mountain towns.

WHERE TO EAT
There are plenty of cafés and restaurants throughout the Blue Mountains, particularly in Leura, Katoomba and Blackheath.

Passing through Katoomba, the Paragon Restaurant (daily, generally 9.30–5.30) and Café Zuppa (7am–10pm), both on Katoomba Street, provide breakfasts and a good choice of snacks and meals in a casual setting.

Other suggestions are the spectacular Hydro Majestic Hotel at Medlow Bath and the Mount Tomah Botanic Garden.

PRINCE HENRY CLIFF WALK
AND THE THREE SISTERS

This scenic Katoomba walk follows a cliffside path along the northern edge of the Jamison Valley, within the Blue Mountains National Park (▷ 104–108). Lookouts give superb views of the valley's dense forest and sandstone outcrops.

THE WALK

Note: Although not long or difficult, the route is classified as moderate because it includes several sets of steps, some of which are fairly uneven and steep.

Distance: Approximately 3km (2 miles)
Allow: 1.5 hours
Start at: Scenic World, Katoomba; see map ▷ 119
End at: Echo Point, Katoomba

★ Take a train from Sydney Central to Katoomba; bus or taxi from station to Scenic World

At Scenic World, face the Three Sisters fountain, walk diagonally across the yard to your left and

down a path until you come to the Prince Henry Cliff Walk sign. Follow this path to an intersection, turn left and walk through bushland before crossing a bridge. Walk up the steps to enter a park, part of Katoomba Falls Reserve. Follow the sign for Echo Point and descend more steps. The main track leads to the left, but climb the steps to the lookout.

❶ This lookout has a commanding view of the Jamison Valley, 300m (984ft) below. Orphan Rock, an outlier of the sandstone escarpment, is straight ahead and Katoomba Falls is to your left.

Go back to the main track, which heads away from the Jamison

Valley. You soon reach a pool and Katoomba Cascades.

❷ This area of parkland surrounds the fast-flowing Katoomba Falls Creek, which downstream from here tumbles down the cliff to become Katoomba Falls. The cool, shady gully, surrounded by ferns and rocks, is a good spot for a break.

Cross the creek using the stepping stones, walk up some fairly steep steps, and turn right to reach the grassy Katoomba Falls Park. Follow the signpost to Echo Point, walking through forest and heathland and under the Scenic Skyway cable car wires. You soon reach Cliff View Lookout with more views of the

Jamison Valley. Turn left and continue on the gravel track, fringed by heath on the right and weathered sandstone rocks on the left. The path then heads downhill to Wollumai Lookout.

❸ Wollumai Lookout is where you get your first view of the Three Sisters, three sandstone pillars that are all that remain of an eroded cliffline. An Aboriginal legend claims that the rocks are the daughters of a man who turned them to stone to protect them from the attentions of a bunyip (monster), but was unable to change them back again.

Follow the track down to Allambie Lookout, then into a eucalypt forest and past a rock overhang before heading up steps and a steep metal staircase to the Lady Darley Lookout for another good view. Keep following the sign to Echo Point, through more forest and heath before emerging near the top of a cliff. Continue on the track, which brings you to the Echo Point parking area and on to the fenced lookout at Echo Point itself.

❹ The view from Echo Point is one of the highlights of the Blue Mountains. It takes in a huge sweep of the Jamison Valley. The natural monoliths, Mount Solitary and the Ruined Castle, rise like islands in a sea of trees. The Three Sisters are nearby.

Turn left at the lookout and follow the track under a stone arch. You can turn right for a short detour (which later rejoins the main track) to see more valley views from Spooners Lookout, or keep going along a forested hillside. The main track then leads down some steps and through another archway to a lookout directly behind the Three Sisters.

❺ From here there are excellent views to the left, along the escarpment edge. You should be able to make out Sublime Point, just south of Leura.

Return to Echo Point by the same track. Here you will find a Blue Mountains Visitor Information Centre (daily 9–5), public toilets and the Three Sisters World Heritage Plaza, containing shops, eating places and the Blue Mountains World Heritage Exhibition. A number of other walking tracks start from Echo Point; most include very steep sections.

You can return to Scenic World by taxi, on foot along Cliff Drive (20–30 minutes), or by the Trolley Tours tourist bus service, which stops at Echo Point (daily 10–5; all-day pass A$20). To return to Katoomba, take a taxi or shuttle bus, or walk through town (about 30 minutes).

WHEN TO GO
All year round. The path is very popular at weekends, so try to go on a weekday.

PLACES TO VISIT
Scenic World, ▷ 107, 118.
Blue Mountains, ▷ 104–108.

WHERE TO EAT
Early in the walk, Katoomba Falls Café serves snacks and drinks, and there are food outlets in the Three Sisters World Heritage Plaza at Echo Point. Public toilets are available at Scenic World and Echo Point.

Opposite *Orphan Rock near Kataoomba*
Below *Part of the famous Three Sisters rock formation*

WHAT TO DO

ADAMINABY

REYNELLA KOSCIUSZKO RIDES

www.reynellarides.com.au

Experienced guides lead you and your mount through the mountains of Kosciuszko National Park. Farmstay accommodation is available.

✉ Reynella, Adaminaby, NSW 2630
☎ 02 6454 2386, 1800 029 909
⊙ Alpine Horseback Safaris operate Oct–end Apr 🖐 From A$1100 for three-day/four-night ride and from A$1760 for five-day/six-night ride

BROKEN HILL

RED SANDS GALLERY

The gallery, in an old homestead, features the works of local artists who are inspired by the landscape. Also furniture, ceramics and gifts.

✉ 355 Wolfram Street, Broken Hill, NSW 2880 ☎ 08 8088 7734 ⊙ Tue–Sat 10–4

CANBERRA

NATIONAL GALLERY OF AUSTRALIA SHOP

www.nga.gov.au

The gallery shop sells good-quality prints, books and postcards.

✉ Parkes Place, Parkes, ACT 2600 ☎ 02 6240 6420 ⊙ Daily 10–5 🔲

QUESTACON SHOP

www.questacon.edu.au

The gift shop at Questacon, the science and technology museum, sells educational and fun toys for children of all ages; there are also books and CD-ROMs.

✉ King Edward Terrace, Parkes, ACT 2600
☎ 02 6270 2800 ⊙ Daily 9–5 🚌 34 🔲

CANBERRA THEATRE CENTRE

www.canberratheatre.org.au

The Centre presents performing arts groups and entertainers from Australia and abroad.

✉ London Circuit, Canberra, ACT 2601
☎ 02 6275 2700 🔳

THE STREET THEATRE

www.thestreet.org.au

This is Canberra's prime location to see local artists performing in experimental theatre, music and dance.

✉ Cnr Childers Street and University Avenue, Canberra, ACT 2601 ☎ 02 6247 1223 🔲 🔳

ALL BAR NUN

www.allbarnun.com.au

Popular with everyone from students

to executives, All Bar Nun has one of the biggest ranges of international and domestic beers in Canberra.

✉ 1 Macpherson Street, O'Connor, ACT 2602 ☎ 02 6257 9191 ⊙ Mon–Thu noon–late, Fri–Sun 8am–late

CASINO CANBERRA

www.casinocanberra.com.au

This is a European-influenced 'boutique' casino that also features entertainment areas.

✉ 21 Binara Street, Canberra, ACT 2601
☎ 02 6257 7074 ⊙ Daily noon–6am

WIG & PEN

www.wigandpen.com.au

This atmospheric, British-style pub at the heart of the city is also a microbrewery that produces ten different beers.

✉ Canberra House Arcade, Alinga Street, Canberra, ACT 2600 ☎ 02 6248 0171 ⊙ Mon–Wed 12–10, Thu 12–11, Fri 12–12, Sat 2–12, Sun 2–8

CENTRAL COAST

ETTALONG BEACH WAR MEMORIAL CLUB

www.ettalongbeachclub.com.au

This club has bars, restaurants and

live entertainment most nights of
the week.

✉ 51–52 The Esplanade, Ettalong,
NSW 2257 ☎ 02 4343 0111 🕐 Sun–Thu
7am–3am, Fri, Sat 7am–4am

COFFS HARBOUR
COLORADO
www.coloradogroup.com.au

This branch of the Colorado chain,
in the Park Beach Plaza, sells tough
and functional leisure and outdoor
clothing, boots and accessories.
It's a good place to buy gear for
exploring the rainforest national
parks in the area.

✉ Shop 38, Park Beach Plaza, 253 Pacific
Highway, Coffs Harbour, NSW 2450
☎ 02 6650 9631 🕐 Mon–Fri 9–5.30,
Sat 9–4, Sun 10–2

LIQUID ASSETS ADVENTURE TOURS
www.surfrafting.com

Rafting on the Nymboida River, one
of the country's best white-water
rivers. Sea-kayaking, surf rafting and
surfing trips are also available.

✉ 38 Marina Drive, Coffs Harbour, NSW
2450 ☎ 02 6658 0850 🕐 Call for details
of departures 🤚 $160 for a one-day
rafting trip

THE BIG BANANA
www.bigbanana.com

A massive concrete banana is the
symbol of this theme park. There's
a banana plantation, ice rink and
toboggan rides.

✉ Pacific Highway, Coffs Harbour, NSW
2450 ☎ 02 6652 4355 🕐 Daily 9.30–4.30
🤚 Free; fee for activities 🖥

HUNTER VALLEY
CAPERCAILLIE WINE COMPANY AND GALLERY
www.capercailliewine.com.au

The Capercaillie Wine Company
is one of the newest and smallest
wineries in the Hunter Valley. Buy
wines and browse the gallery, which
has fine glass, ceramics, silks,
timbers and original paintings.

✉ 4 Londons Road, Lovedale, NSW 2325

FESTIVALS AND EVENTS

MARCH
CANBERRA BALLOON FIESTA
www.canberraballoonfiesta.com.au

Canberra Balloon Fiesta is the
southern hemisphere's biggest
gathering of hot-air balloons.

SEPTEMBER
THE MUDGEE WINE CELEBRATION
www.mudgeewine.com.au

The Mudgee Wine Celebration
at Mudgee in the Central Ranges
includes public tastings, arts
and markets.

FLORIADE
www.floriadeaustralia.com

Floriade is a colourful Canberra
flower festival.

☎ 02 4990 2904 🕐 Mon–Sat 9–5,
Sun 10–5

JAMBEROO
JAMBEROO ACTION PARK
www.jamberoo.net

Enjoy waterslides, bobsleds, racing
cars, speed boats, a chairlift, train
ride and mini-golf.

✉ Jamberoo Road, Jamberoo, NSW
2533 ☎ 02 4236 0114 🕐 Sep–end Apr
Sat, Sun, school and public holidays 10–5
🤚 Adult A$37, child (4–12 years) A$29
(under 4 free) 🍴 🖥

KATOOMBA
THE EDGE
www.edgecinema.com.au

The Edge is a 40-minute
documentary about the rugged
attractions of the Blue Mountains,
shown to dramatic effect on a six-
floor screen.

✉ 225 Great Western Highway,
Katoomba, NSW 2780 ☎ 02 4782 8900
🕐 10.20–5.30 🚆 Katoomba 🤚 Adult
A$14.50, child A$10 🍷 🏛

BLUE MOUNTAINS ADVENTURE COMPANY
www.bmac.com.au

OCTOBER
JAZZ IN THE VINES
www.jazzinthevines.com.au

Jazz in the Vines is a jazz festival in
late October at Tyrrells Wines in the
Hunter Valley

OPERA IN THE VINEYARDS
www.operainthevineyards.com.au

Opera in the Vineyards is the
Hunter Valley's annual feast of
wine, food, music and song at the
Wyndham Estate winery, a two-hour
drive north of Sydney. Held in late
October every year, Australia's
premier opera singers lead the
festivities.

Climbing, mountain-biking,
canyoning, abseiling and
bushwalking for all skills.

✉ 84A Bathurst Road, Katoomba, NSW
2780 ☎ 02 4782 1271 🚆 Katoomba
🤚 Abseiling (rappelling) A$105–A$310;
rock-climbing A$175 (one day); canyoning
A$165–A$235; mountain-biking A$125 (half-
day), A$190 (one day)

WOLLONGONG
BEACH BAR
www.novotelnorthbeach.com.au

The Beach Bar of the hotel has
views over the Pacific and live music
most nights.

✉ Novotel North Beach Hotel, 2–14
Cliff Road, North Wollongong, NSW 2500
☎ 02 4226 3555 🕐 Wed–Sun 3pm–late
🚆 North Wollongong (City Rail)

CASTRO'S NIGHTCLUB
www.castros.com.au

Sleek and sophisticated, this
lesbian, gay and transgender-friendly
nightspot draws in the crowds
for cocktails, drag shows and a
throbbing disco.

✉ 5 Victoria Street, Wollongong, NSW
2500 ☎ 02 4227 2058 🕐 Wed–Sat 9–late
From $12

PRICES AND SYMBOLS

The restaurants are listed alphabetically (excluding Le, La and Les). The prices given are the average for a two-course lunch (L) and a three-course dinner (D) for one person, without drinks. The wine price is for the least expensive bottle.

For a key to the symbols, ▷ 2.

BELLINGEN

THE OLD BUTTER FACTORY CAFÉ

www.belligen.com/butterfactory/cafe
This relaxed café is part of a complex that includes an alternative-therapy centre, and serves breakfasts, light lunches and afternoon teas.
✉ 1 Doepel Lane, Bellingen, NSW 2454 ☎ 02 6655 2150 ✪ Daily 9–5.30 ✋ Meals from A$8.50 🚌 On State Route 78 from the Pacific Highway to Dorrigo

BLUE MOUNTAINS

CAFÉ ZUPPA

✉ 36 Katoomba Street, Katoomba, NSW 2780 ☎ 02 4782 9247
This trendy café has free papers and a piano. Generous breakfasts and main meals are available daily. Choose from pancakes, maple syrup and strawberries; muesli, yogurt and fruit; a full fry-up before 11.30am or an all-day breakfast; and grilled

barramundi fillet or cannelloni crêpes with ricotta and spinach for lunch or an evening meal.
✪ Daily 7.30am–11pm ✋ Breakfast A$5–A$10, main meals A$20

DARLEY'S

www.lilianfels.com.au
This renowned restaurant is in Lilianfels Resort (▷ 128), a country hotel dating from the 1880s. The Australian country cuisine has French influences and relies on quality regional produce. The wine list is devoted to native vintages.
✉ Lilianfels Avenue, Echo Point, Katoomba, NSW 2780 ☎ 02 4780 1200 ✪ Tue–Sat from 6.30pm, Sun 10–1.30pm ✋ Breakfast A$65, L A$78, D A$95, Wine $35

ESCA BIMBADGEN

www.bimbadgen.com.au
This smart restaurant attached to the Bimbadgen Estate winery serves generous portions of Modern Australian fare. Entrées might include grilled quail or Gruyère soufflé and mains of pan-roasted spatchcock, chargrilled ocean trout or loin of lamb. There is a great selection of local wines. Reservations are essential.
✉ Bimbadgen Estate, 790 McDonalds Road, Pokolbin, NSW 2320 ☎ 02 4998

4666 ✪ Daily 12–3 ✋ L A$60, Wine A$25 🚌 7km (4.5 miles) west from Cessnock

LOCHIEL HOUSE

www.lochielhouse.com.au
In the foothills of the Blue Mountains, this rustic cottage specializes in beautiful, exquisite food with tantalizing flavours derived largely from locally grown herbs and vegetables, nuts, cheeses and fruits.
✉ 1259 Bells Line of Road, Kurrajong Heights, NSW 2758 ☎ 02 4567 7754 ✪ Thu–Sat 12–3, 6–9, Sun 12–3 ✋ L A$55, D A$75, Wine A$39

MOUNT TOMAH BOTANIC GARDEN RESTAURANT

The Mediterranean-style menu includes soups, salads, sandwiches and grilled and roasted meat, poultry and seafood dishes. Good vegetarian options and children's menu. Good wheelchair access. BYO wine.
✉ Bells Line of Road via Bilpin, Mount Tomah, NSW 2758 ☎ 02 4567 2060 ✪ Nov–end Mar daily 10–4; Apr–end Oct 10–3 ✋ L A$25

ROBERTS RESTAURANT

www.robertsrestaurant.com
The menu at this heritage building includes handmade pastas, crisp

fried brains, oysters, and mains such as venison steaks, rack of lamb, milk-fed veal and exotic fungi. Vegetarians are not particularly well catered for. The wine list emphasizes local wines. You will need to reserve ahead.

✉ Halls Road, Pokolbin, NSW 2320 ☎ 02 4998 7330 ⏰ Daily 12–2.30, 7–9.30 ✋ L A$60, D A$75, Wine A$35

SOLITARY

Overlooking the Kings Tableland and Mount Solitary, this sophisticated restaurant is in a heritage-listed weatherboard Blue Mountains cottage. The menu includes quail, lamb, swimmer crab and barramundi.

✉ 90 Cliff Drive, Leura Falls, NSW 2780 ☎ 02 4782 1164 ⏰ Daily 12–4.30, Fri, Sat from 6pm ✋ L, D A$55 🚌 Five minutes' drive from Katoomba

THE SWISS COTTAGE

www.swisscottage.com.au
The restaurant is famous for its fondues and rösti, but the menu might also include stuffed mushrooms and octopus salad to start, King Island Scotch fillet and *saucisson vaudois* to follow, with desserts such as death by chocolate or fresh strawberries and kirsch ice cream. Extensive selection of Australian wines or BYO. Reserve ahead for a table.

✉ 132 Lurline Street, Katoomba, NSW 2780 ☎ 02 4782 2281 ⏰ Wed–Sun lunch from 11, dinner from 6 ✋ L A$32, D A$50, Wine A$21 🚉 Station at far end of Katoomba High Street, a good walk away

VICTORY CAFÉ

This consistently good Blue Mountains café offers everything from enormous breakfasts (served all day) and great coffee and cakes to excellent burgers, curries, laksas, steaks and other main meals. BYO.

✉ 17 Govetts Leap Road, Blackheath, NSW 2785 ☎ 02 4787 6777 ⏰ Daily 8.30–5 ✋ L A$20

VULCAN'S

Just off the Great Western Highway close to the Blue Mountains National Park, Vulcan's offers slow-cooked country flavours in simple, rustic surroundings. BYO, A$2.50 corkage per person. Reserve ahead.

✉ 33 Govetts Leap Road, Blackheath, NSW 2785 ☎ 02 4787 6899 ⏰ Fri–Sun 9am–11.30pm ✋ L A$45, D A$55

CANBERRA

ARTESPRESSO

Running well ahead of the pack of Canberra restaurants, this modern Australian bistro serves consistently fine food with Mediterranean flavours to the fore. However the acoustics of the brittle interior can turn a conversation into a shouting match on busy nights.

✉ 31 Giles Street, Kingston, ACT 2603 ☎ 02 6295 8055 ⏰ Mon–Fri 12–3, 6–9, Sat 6–9 ✋ L A$50, D A$65, Wine A$31

BOATHOUSE BY THE LAKE

www.boathousebythelake.com.au
A Modern Australian menu and local Riesling complement the stunning view over Lake Burley Griffin to Capital Hill. It's a detour from the city but the outside dining area is perfect for a relaxing lunch.

✉ Grevillea Park, Menindee Drive, Barton, ACT 2600 ☎ 02 6273 5500 ⏰ Mon–Fri 12–2, Mon–Sat 6–10 ✋ L, D A$65, Wine A$25 🚌 3km (2 miles) southeast of the city

THE CHAIRMAN AND YIP

www.thechairmanandyip.com
The cuisine is essentially Cantonese but Thai, Japanese and other influences make up the fusion menu. Try stir-fried tiger prawns, duck, or salmon with wasabi and spinach sauce. There is a good Australian wine list or BYO (corkage A$6.50).

✉ 108 Bunda Street, Canberra, ACT 2601 ☎ 02 6248 7109 ⏰ Mon–Sat 12–3, 5.30–11 ✋ L, D A$50, Wine A$28 🚌 Any bus to city centre

FIRST FLOOR

www.firstfloor.net.au
A large, popular, buzzing (noisy) restaurant, serving Modern

Australian cuisine with international influences. Typical dishes may include South Coast oysters, Thai red curry of shredded beef fillet, pumpkin, Chinese broccoli and Hokkien noodles or fresh prawn and scallop risotto. There is always a selection of vegetarian options; the wine list is extensive. Reserve ahead to ensure a table.

✉ Green Square, Jardine Street, Kingston, ACT 2604 ☎ 02 6260 6311 ⏰ Thu–Fri 12–2, Tue–Sat 6–10.30 ✋ L A$40, D A$50, Wine A$25 🚌 38, 39, 80 🚗 4.5km (3 miles) southeast from the city

GUS' CAFÉ

www.guscafe.com.au
Breakfasts include a huge plate of bacon, eggs, sausages, tomato, onion and mushrooms on focaccia bread, while main meals include pasta, nachos, salads, sirloin steaks, stroganoff and fish dishes. There are good vegetarian options. Moderate wine list; BYO corkage A$3 per bottle.

✉ Shop 8, Garema Arcade, Bunda Street, Canberra, ACT 2601 ☎ 02 6248 8118 ⏰ Daily 8am–11pm ✋ B A$7–A$14, L A$20, D A$40, Wine A$20 🚌 Any bus to city centre

OTTOMAN CUISINE

www.ottomancuisine.com.au
At this Turkish restaurant, chef/owner Serif Kaya prepares innovative food, such as *Narli karides* (king prawns pan-sautéed with a savoury pomegranate sauce), *Dana kulbasti* (tender slices of veal with mild spices, served on eggplant (aubergine) and baby spinach with tangy lemon sauce) and baklava pastries. The wine list is extensive; BYO corkage A$8. Reservations are essential.

✉ Cnr Broughton and Blackall streets, Barton, ACT 2600 ☎ 02 6273 6111 ⏰ Tue–Fri 12–3, Tue–Sat 6–10 ✋ L A$40, D A$60, Wine A$30 🚌 34, 35, 36 🚗 4km (2.5 miles) southeast from the city, near Capital Hill

SAMMY'S KITCHEN

A noisy and crowded restaurant that serves good-value food in a no-frills environment: the cuisine is Chinese and Malaysian. Entrées and soups include garlic king prawns, satay sticks, spring rolls and hot and sour soup; plus a range of laksas, rice dishes and noodle dishes, as well as curries, stir-fries and hotpots. The wine list is limited; BYO corkage A$3 per bottle. Reserve for dinner.

✉ Garema Centre, Bunda Street, Canberra, ACT 2601 ☎ 02 6247 1464 ◷ Daily 11.30–2.30, 5–10.30 ◷ L A$25, D A$35, Wine by theglass or BYO 🚌 Any bus to city centre

SILO BAKERY
www.silobakery.com.au
Silo is a small bakery/café. Popular are breakfasts, snacks such as soup, sandwiches, cakes and coffee, as well as lunches. Silo is also a cheese shop, selling wonderful pastries, coffee, sourdough bread and a good range of cheeses. A wide range of wines is available. Lunch reservations are essential.

✉ 36 Giles Street, Kingston, ACT 2604 ☎ 02 6260 6060 ◷ Tue–Sat 7–4 🖐 B A$13, L A$22, Wine A$33 🚌 38, 39, 80 🚌 4.5km (3 miles) southeast from the city, near Parliamentary Triangle

CENTRAL COAST
THE COWRIE
www.thecowrie.com.au
Set high on a hill overlooking Terrigal, this award-winning restaurant specializes in fine seafood. Dishes such as a sashimi tasting plate, wild barramundi fillet and fresh oysters and lobster. Meat, chicken and vegetarian options are also available.

✉ 109 Scenic Drive, Terrigal, NSW 2260 ☎ 02 4384 3016 ◷ Daily 12–2.30 and 6pm–late 🖐 L A$37 for two-course set menu, including a glass of wine; D A$75, Wine A$30

ELIZAN'S
www.ulladullaguesthouse.com.au
Part of the Ulladulla Guesthouse Elizan's provides fine French dining with a Modern Australian style. Try the tender Milton beef or peppered kangaroo steaks. The wine list includes local wines. Reservations are advised.

✉ 39 Burrill Street, Ulladulla, NSW 2539 ☎ 02 4455 1796, 1800 700 905 ◷ Daily breakfast 8.30–10, Thu–Tue dinner from 6.30 🖐 D A$50, Wine A$30

COFFS HARBOUR
MANGROVE JACK'S CAFÉ
www.mangrovejackscafe.com.au
A fashionable café serving breakfasts, lunches and evening meals. Seating is mostly outdoors. Breakfast may include pancakes, omelettes, fruit salads and sausages; lunch may be pumpkin risotto, BBQ eye-fillet steak or burgers; evening meals (reservation advised) have a Modern Australian bent, and include oysters and catch of the day.

✉ Coffs Promenade, 321 Harbour Drive, Coffs Harbour, NSW 2450 ☎ 02 6652 5517 ◷ Sun, Mon 7.30am–3pm, Tue–Sat 7.30am–9pm 🖐 L A$25, D A$45, Wine A$30

TIDE & PILOT BRASSERIE
Right on the marina, with two separate eating areas. The lower deck is informal for breakfast and lunches, with the most popular fare being fresh fish and chips. Upstairs (reservations advised) has a relaxed, intimate atmosphere, with options such as seafood risotto and a wide selection, including lobster, at the seafood bar. Steaks, lamb and similar dishes are also available. Australian wines include several 'champagnes'.

✉ 1 Marina Drive, Coffs Harbour, NSW 2450 ☎ 02 6651 6046 ◷ 7am–9pm; closed some Sun evenings: call to check 🖐 L A$25, D A$50, Wine A$25

HUNTER VALLEY
CHEZ POK
www.peppers.com.au
The menu, with French, Asian and Italian influences, might include calf's liver or vegetarian wontons followed by chargrilled beef medallions or pan-fried reef fish. For dinner, home-baked bread accompanies roasted and pan-fried meat, seafood and game dishes. A good but pricey selection of local wines. Reserve ahead.

✉ Peppers Guest House, Ekerts Road, Pokolbin, NSW 2320 ☎ 02 4993 8999 ◷ Daily 7–9 🖐 L A$50, D A$70, Wine A$40

MOLINES BISTRO
www.bistromolines.com.au
Now transplanted to a new location, Robert Molines continues to dazzle as he continues to pay homage to the full-flavoured provincial cooking of Italy and France.

✉ 749 Mount View Road, Mount View, NSW 2325 ☎ 02 4990 9553 ◷ Thu–Mon 12–3, Fri–Sat 6.30–10 🖐 L A$65, D A$80, Wine A$43

NEWCASTLE
CUSTOMS HOUSE HOTEL
www.customshouse.net.au
A stylish pub-restaurant where meals range from snacks such as burgers and Caesar salad to pastas and hearty steak, fish and duck dishes. Prices are very reasonable, and the hotel offers set-price two- or three-course menus.

✉ 1 Bond Street, Newcastle, NSW 2300 ☎ 02 4925 2585 ◷ Mon–Sat 12–3, 6–9, Sun 12–3 🖐 Snacks A$15, L A$42, D A$48, Wine A$18

NEW ENGLAND
INLAND CAFÉ
At this modern, chic café, the menu includes a wide choice of cakes, coffees and pastries, plus good lunchtime meals that change seasonally, such as Thai-style chicken and Hokkien noodles or light beer battered barramundi fish fillets, as well as soups and sandwiches. Limited vegetarian options.

✉ 407 Peel Street, Tamworth, NSW 2340 ☎ 02 6761 2882 ◷ Mon–Fri 7–5.30, Sat 7.30–5, Sun 8–4 🖐 L A$25

JEAN PIERRE'S
The Modern Australian menu, with strong French and Mediterranean influences, includes venison, rabbit and duck as well as good local beef. The tender twice-roasted duck is delicious!

✉ 110 Marsh Street, Armidale, NSW 2350

☎ 02 6772 2201 ⏰ Tue–Sat 6.30–late
✋ D A$55 🚗 Right on the main street

PEPPERMINTS COFFEE LOUNGE
On the block south from Main Street, just behind Bi-Lo. Specializes in all Australian-grown coffees, tasty home-made scones and cheesecakes, plus sandwiches, burgers, doughnuts and snacks.
✉ 215 Grey Street, Glen Innes, NSW 2370
☎ 02 6732 5914 ⏰ Mon–Fri 8.30–5
✋ B A$10, L A$15

PORT MACQUARIE
SIGNATURES BAR
On the menu at this brasserie are local oysters, the catch of the day, and regulars such as barramundi fillet and local T-bone steaks; plus several imaginative vegetarian dishes. There is a good selection of Australian Hunter Valley wines.
✉ 2/72 Clarence Street, Port Macquarie, NSW 2444 ☎ 02 6584 6144 ⏰ Daily 12–2.30, 6–9 ✋ L A$25, D A$45, Wine A$17

SOUTHERN HIGHLANDS
CENTENNIAL VINEYARDS RESTAURANT
www.centennial.net.au
This is country dining at its finest. The french doors spring open to a big veranda with vineyard views, there's a huge fireplace for winter warmth and a bistro-style menu that sings on the palate.
✉ 250 Centennial Road, Bowral, NSW 2576 ☎ 02 4861 8722 ⏰ Wed–Mon 10–5
✋ L A$55

ESCHALOT
www.eschalot.com.au
In a patrician dining room in a historic sandstone house, the menu revels in complex, multi-layered flavours. Much of the produce is sourced from the restaurant's own gardens.
✉ 24 Old Hume Highway, Berrima, NSW 2577 ☎ 02 4877 1977 ⏰ Wed–Sat 6–10, Fri–Sun 12–3 ✋ L A$50, D A$65

HORDERN'S
www.milton-park.com.au
About a 90-minute drive southwest from Sydney. Hordern's hotel restaurant uses the best local ingredients in a Modern Australian menu touched by French provincial finesse. Main courses include salmon, venison and duck, and the wine list is mostly Australian with a selection of fine reds.
✉ Horderns Road, Bowral, NSW 2576 ☎ 02 4861 1522 ⏰ Daily 12–2.30, 7–9
✋ L A$62, D A$75, Wine A$30

KATERS RESTAURANT
www.peppers.com.au
Modern Australian cuisine highlighting fresh produce from the district. Magnificent garden and bushland views and excellent friendly service. A 90-minute drive south of Sydney
✉ Pepper's Manor House, Kater Road, Sutton Forest, Southern Highlands, NSW 2577 ☎ 02 4860 3102 ⏰ Daily 7am–10am, 12–2.30, 6.30pm–9pm
✋ B A$30, L A$55, D A$65, Wine A$25

WOLLONGONG
CAVEAU
www.caveau.com.au
Chef Peter Sheppard has carved out an enviable reputation for his French-accented, modern Australian menu, while the degustation menu draws rave reviews for his elegant Wollongong restaurant. Look out for the mouth-watering cheese board.
✉ 122–124 Keira Street Wollongong, NSW 2500 ☎ 02 4226 4855 ⏰ Tue–Sat 6–10 ✋ D A$75, Degustation A$95

LAGOON SEAFOOOD RESTAURANT
www.lagoonrestaurant.com.au
In a secluded waterfront location, this is a brisk and breezy showcase for the culinary talents of Jonni and Andrew Harrison, who use bush herbs and fresh produce to bring out the natural flavours of their seafood menu.
✉ Stuart Park, North Wollongong, NSW 2500 ☎ 02 4226 1677 ⏰ Daily 12–9
✋ L A$45, D A$60, Wine A$30

LORENZO'S DINER
www.lorenzosdiner.com.au
Modern Italian cuisine is the forte at this stylish, modern dining room, with an ever-changing menu that makes good use of the local farms, fields and seas.
✉ 119 Keira Street, Wollongong, NSW 2500 ☎ 02 4229 5633 ⏰ Wed–Fri 12–3, Tue–Sat 6–10.30 ✋ L A$55, D A$70

Below *Try peppered kangaroo steaks at Elizans in Ulladulla*

STAYING

HYATT HOTEL CANBERRA

PRICES AND SYMBOLS

Prices are for a double room for one night including breakfast, unless otherwise stated. All the hotels listed accept credit cards, unless otherwise stated. Note that rates can vary widely throughout the year.

For a key to the symbols, ▷ 2.

BERRY

BROUGHTON MILL FARM

www.broughtonmillfarm.com.au
This guesthouse comes with luxury trimmings and wonderful food, set in rich, rolling meadows against the forested backdrop of the coastal escarpment. Each of the guest suites opens directly to the gardens, and each has a private sitting room and full bathroom. The guesthouse has a tennis court, solar heated pool, water gardens, more than a hectare (2.5 acres) of grounds, a games lawn and a private picnic area.
✉ 78 Woodhill Mountain Road, Berry, NSW 2535 ☎ 02 4464 2446 🖐 A$220–A$280 🛈 5

BLUE MOUNTAINS

BLUE MOUNTAINS YHA

www.yha.com.au
This pleasant hostel has retained many original art deco features. There is a lounge area and games

room, plus a spacious eating and cooking area. The largest dorm rooms sleep eight people, and there are double and twin rooms, many with private bathrooms.
✉ 207 Katoomba Street, Katoomba, NSW 2780 ☎ 02 4782 1416 🖐 A$27.50–A$98/116 (double/family room with private bathroom) 🛈 25

THE CARRINGTON HOTEL

www.thecarrington.com.au
Several generations of British royalty have favoured this grand hotel, built in the 1880s and National Trust-listed, which offers all mod cons and spa.
✉ Katoomba Street, Katoomba, NSW 2780 ☎ 02 4782 1111 🖐 A$129 (traditional room)–A$450 (Carrington Suite) 🛈 64

ECHOES BOUTIQUE HOTEL AND RESTAURANT

www.echoeshotel.com.au
Perched on the very brink of the Jamison Valley at the cliff end of Katoomba, this small hotel brings sophistication, luxury and fine dining to the traditional charms of the Blue Mountains guesthouse. Set in cool-climate gardens, there's a spa, sauna and underfloor heating, within an airy, two-storey building with acres of glass.

✉ 3 Lilianfels Avenue, Katoomba NSW 2780 ☎ 02 4782 1966 🖐 A$350–A$695 🛈 14

LILIANFELS RESORT & SPA

www.lilianfels.com.au
This luxurious hotel has a gym and a swimming pool. The rooms have been individually decorated, with marble bathrooms. The hotel's restaurant, Darley's (▷ 124), is renowned for French cuisine.
✉ Lilianfels Avenue, Echo Point, Katoomba, NSW 2780 ☎ 02 4780 1200 🖐 A$310–A$670 💲 ⬛ Indoor heated 🛈 85 🚗 90-minute drive from Sydney, just next to The Three Sisters rock formation

BYRON BAY

BYRON AT BYRON

www.thebyronatbyron.com.au
Created in a former paperbark wetland just south of Byron Bay, this handsome resort wraps itself around a sweeping poolside complex that houses the reception area, the gym, the spa, tennis courts and restaurant. Guest rooms are large and each has a screened veranda as well as kitchen facilities. Opaque sliding glass screens separate the lounge from the bathroom and bedroom.

✉ 77–97 Broken Head Road, Byron Bay, NSW 2481 ☎ 1300 554 362 🖐 A$385–A$425 ⓘ 92 🚗 2.5km (1.5 miles) south of Byron Bay ≋ Outdoor ⊠

CANBERRA

THE BRASSEY OF CANBERRA
www.brassey.net.au
At this colonial brick building, some rooms have period furnishings; the standard rooms are more contemporary. All have minibars, tea/coffee-making facilities, irons, hairdryers and internet connections. The Belmore Restaurant provides a hot buffet breakfast, lunch (Friday only) and dinner; also a Garden Bar.
✉ Belmore Gardens and Macquarie Street, Barton, ACT 2600 ☎ 02 6273 3766 ⓒ All year 🖐 A$151–A$178 ⓘ 78 ⓢ 🚗 6km (4 miles) southwest of city, 1km (0.6 miles) from Parliamentary Triangle

CROWNE PLAZA
www.ichotelsgroup.com
Reliable, modern, city centre hotel with an atrium lounge and bar. The restaurant, Redsalt, serves Modern Australian lunches and dinners daily, and Binara One serves tea, coffee, drinks and cocktails. All the bedrooms have internet access, colour TV, and minibars. Suites, interconnecting rooms and non-smoking rooms are available.
✉ 1 Binara Street, Canberra, ACT 2601 ☎ 1800 899 960 ⓒ All year 🖐 A$215–A$475 excluding breakfast ⓘ 295 ⓢ ≋ Outdoor heated ⊠

FORREST HOTEL AND APARTMENTS
www.forrestinn.com.au
A good range of moderately priced accommodation, with modern furnishings. The apartments (one- and two-bedroom, sleeping up to five people) include a full kitchen, dining area and lounge.
✉ 30 National Circuit, Forrest, ACT 2603 ☎ 02 6295 3433 ⓒ All year 🖐 A$135–A$160 (motel room), A$180–A$220 (two-bedroom apartment) excluding breakfast ⓘ 76 motel units, 28 apartments ⓢ 🚗 35, 36, 39 🚗 4km (2.5 miles) south of city, immediately south of Capital Hill

HYATT HOTEL
www.canberra.park.hyatt.com
The originl building dates from the 1920s and has been restored to its opulent art deco style. The luxurious bedrooms have marble bathrooms, full business facilities, minibar, hairdryer, iron and ironing board. There are also a number of suites. The Promenade Café serves breakfast, lunch and dinner; the Tea Lounge serves traditional afternoon tea.
✉ Commonwealth Avenue, Yarralumla, ACT 2600 ☎ 02 6270 1234 ⓒ All year 🖐 A$235–A$585 excluding breakfast ⓘ 249 ⓢ ≋ Indoor ⊠ 🚗 31, 32 🚗 3km (2 miles) south of city, near Parliamentary Triangle

COFFS HARBOUR

BREAKFREE AANUKA BEACH RESORT
www.aanuka.com.au
With its own beach, this hotel is very good value. Rooms include studios and two- or three-bedroom villas, some with spa baths. There are bars and restaurants, as well as several swimming pools, tennis courts, a gymnasium and a 'massage and rejuvenation retreat'.
✉ Firman Drive, Diggers Beach, Coffs Harbour, NSW 2450 ☎ 02 6652 7555 ⓒ All year 🖐 A$185–A$348 excluding breakfast ⓘ 135 ⓢ (all rooms) ≋ Three outdoor, one indoor ⊠ 🚗 2km (1.2 miles) north of Coffs Harbour

EDEN

THE CROWN AND ANCHOR INN
www.crownandanchoreden.com.au
At this bed-and-breakfast all bedrooms have private bathrooms and there is a guest lounge.
✉ 239 Imlay Street, Eden, NSW 2551 ☎ 02 6496 1017 ⓒ All year 🖐 A$165–A$200 ⓘ 5

HUNTER VALLEY

PEPPERS CONVENT
www.peppers.com.au
This statuesque former convent was transplanted to one of the loveliest parts of the Hunter Valley and elevated to five-star status, and in the process, set a new benchmark

for boutique accommodation in the area. Throughout, the hotel is furnished and decorated in an opulent country style. Guest rooms hark back to another era with queen- or king-size beds enveloped in gauzy mosquito nets, a classical, country-style decor and palatial dimensions.
✉ Halls Road, Pokolbin, NSW 2320 ☎ 02 4998 7764 ⓒ All year 🖐 A$399–A$585 ⓘ 17 ⓢ ≋ Outdoor heated

PEPPERS GUEST HOUSE
www.peppers.com.au
Luxury accommodation and fine dining at Chez Pok (▷ 126). The rooms in this traditional building have modern amenities, as do the four rooms in the separate, self-contained homestead. There is a spa and sauna, and massages are available.
✉ Ekerts Road, Pokolbin, Hunter Valley, NSW 2320 ☎ 02 4993 8999 ⓒ All year 🖐 A$324–A$436; Homestead A$985. Meals extra ⓘ 48 ⓢ ≋ Heated 🚗 At Cessnock, turn left at first T-junction, then first right; after 6km (4 miles), turn left on to Broke Road. Ekerts Road is 5km (3 miles) along Broke Road on the left

TOWER LODGE
www.towerlodge.com.au
Setting a new benchmark for luxury in the Hunter Valley wine-growing district, each of the suites has its own distinct personality, enhanced by a fine collection of antiques, treasures and collectables set against rich fabrics and recycled timbers. There's also a heated pool, and an Italian-inspired piazza at the centre surrounded by a loggia.
✉ Halls Road Pokolbin, NSW 2320 ☎ 02 4998 7022 ⓒ All year 🖐 A$550–A$700 ⓘ 12

JERVIS BAY

JERVIS BAY GUESTHOUSE
www.jervisbayguesthouse.com.au
With just four rooms, one with its own spa and each with a private veranda, this is a quiet spot for a relaxing break.
✉ 1 Beach Street, Huskisson, NSW 2540 ☎ 02 4441 7658 ⓒ All year 🖐 A$195–A$255 ⓘ 4 ⓢ

VICTORIA

Victoria is the smallest of Australia's mainland states, slightly smaller than the United Kingdom, or about the same size as the US state of Minnesota.

It was in Victoria that most of Australia's rich gold discoveries of the mid-19th century took place. This coincided with the taste for architectural ornament typical of the Victorian era, and the state has a rich legacy of fine public buildings and stately homes built from the fortunes won on the goldfields. It was these fortunes that also attracted the attention of some of Australia's most notorious bushrangers, and larceny looms large in the state's history.

This wealth also made Melbourne the largest and most opulent city in Australia. By the 1880s, Melbourne was the second largest city in the British Empire after London, and the logical choice for the nation's capital between the time of federation in 1901 and 1927, when the political capital shifted to Canberra. Melbourne prides itself on its lifestyle, and Melbourne is often awarded the title of the most liveable of Australia's capitals, especially by those who live there.

The surroundings of Melbourne offer a diversity of experiences that might come as a surprise to many visitors, such as the lushly forested Dandenong Ranges, the beaches and golf courses of the Mornington Peninsula, Melbourne's seaside playground, and the vineyards of the Yarra Valley, source of some of Australia's finest cool-climate wines. Slightly farther afield, the Great Ocean Road is the most spectacular coastal drive in the country.

One of the lesser-known glories of the state is its forests. The high rainfall along the coast provides ideal conditions for temperate rainforests that are richly furnished with forests of soaring mountain ash, one of the world's tallest trees.

BEECHWORTH

www.beechworth.com

The small town of Beechworth nestles in the foothills of the Victorian Alps in the northeast of the state. Beechworth is one of Victoria's best-preserved gold-rush towns, close to the Rutherglen, Milawa and Beechworth wine regions. Gold was discovered in the area in 1852. Many early buildings are preserved, while the nearby hamlets of Yackandandah and Chiltern are little changed since the 19th century.

The impressive Beechworth Court in the Beechworth Historic and Cultural Precinct (daily 9–5) is complete with its original furniture and fittings; Ned Kelly, Australia's most notorious bushranger was committed to stand trial here, accused of murder.

✚ 356 T14 🛈 Beechworth Visitor Information Centre, Ford Street, Beechworth, VIC 3747 ☎ 1300 366 321, 03 5728 8065

BALLARAT

www.ballarat.com.au

Gold is still extracted from the site of the world's biggest gold rush, which began in 1851.

On 21 August 1851 gold was discovered near Sovereign Hill. Fortune-hunters flocked to Ballarat from across the world, carving out a rough and ready and defiantly independent community. The wealth from Ballarat resulted in the rapid growth and prosperity of Melbourne and the colony of Victoria, and also a miners' revolt against British rule, the Eureka Stockade Rebellion.

The goldfields are realistically recreated at Sovereign Hill, 2km (1.2 miles) south of the town (Oct–end Mar daily 10–5.30; Apr–end Sep 10–5). The 25ha (62-acre) outdoor museum has more than 60 working period buildings, including banks, saloons, steam-driven battery houses and even an undertaker. Costumed actors and local volunteers provide a living reflection of the times, with street theatre staged all day. Modern fortune-seekers can pan for gold in creeks and there is a tour of underground mines. After sunset a sound-and-light show, Blood on the Southern Cross, re-enacts the Eureka Stockade Rebellion. Entrance to Sovereign Hill includes the Gold Museum, next door.

In East Ballarat, about 1km (0.6 mile) from Sovereign Hill, is the Eureka Centre (daily 9–4.30), on the site of the 1854 rebellion: Ballarat's miners took up arms against the unjust goldfields administration by the British colonial government. The overnight battle, when miners built their own stockade and many died during the fight, is regarded as a struggle against injustice and oppression. Nearer the middle of town is the grand 1884 Ballarat Fine Art Gallery (daily 9–5). The gallery has superb Australian prints and drawings, and its collection of colonial and Heidelberg School paintings is also particularly good.

✚ 356 S15 🛈 Ballarat Visitor Information Centre, The Eureka Centre, cnr Rodier and Eureka streets, Ballarat, VIC 3350 ☎ 03 5320 5741 🕔 Daily 9–5 🚉 Ballarat

❓ The Ballarat Eureka Pass gives entry to Sovereign Hill, the Gold Museum, the Ballarat Fine Art Gallery and the Eureka Centre; adult A$42, child A$19

BENDIGO

www.bendigotourism.com

Gold was found in Bendigo in 1851, and from 1870 to 1880 the area was thought the richest goldfield in the world. The 19th-century boom-town architecture includes the former post office, now the visitor centre. The Chinese prospectors who flocked to the Bendigo goldfield are celebrated in the Golden Dragon Museum and Classical Chinese Gardens (daily 9.30–5). Mining heritage continues at the Central Deborah Gold Mine on Violet Street, with tours below the city. Many of Bendigo's attractions are linked by vintage trams, which give a recorded commentary. Stop off at View Street for the Bendigo Art Gallery (daily 10–5).

✚ 356 S14 🛈 Bendigo Visitor Information Centre, 51–67 Pall Mall, Bendigo, VIC 3550 ☎ 03 5434 6060, 1800 813 153 🕔 Daily 9–5 🚉 Bendigo

BRIGHT AND MOUNT BUFFALO NATIONAL PARK

www.brightescapes.com.au

Bright is a peaceful town in the Ovens Valley below Mount Buffalo and the Victorian Alps. The resort attracts trout fishermen, bicyclists and walkers in spring and summer, skiers in winter, and anybody for its autumn foliage. The many deciduous trees in the town are a legacy of the pioneers who planted avenues of elms, chestnuts, poplars and scarlet oaks.

West of Bright, the 31,000ha (76,570-acre) Mount Buffalo National Park has cliffs, steep granite tors, waterfalls and ski fields. Visitors walk and rock climb in summer, and ski from late June to September. The terrain is also well suited to caving and hang-gliding.

✚ 357 T14 🛈 Bright Visitor Centre, 76a Gavan Street, Bright, VIC 3741 ☎ 1300 551 117

Opposite *Evidence of gold mining is apparent in Bendigo*
Below *Sovereign Hill in Ballarat is a recreated gold town*

INFORMATION

www.visitvictoria.com
www.dandenongrangestourism.com.au
⊞ 356 T15 ⓘ Dandenong Ranges
Visitor Information Centre, 1211 Burwood
Highway, Upper Ferntree Gully, VIC 3156
☎ 03 9758 7522, 1800 645 50 ⊕ Daily
9–5 🚋 Ferntree Gully, Belgrave

TIPS

» Take advantage of the picnic, barbecue
and swimming facilities at Emerald
Lake Park on the Puffing Billy scenic
railway line.

THE DANDENONGS

The Dandenongs have been a cool summer retreat for Melburnians for more
than 150 years.

The bush-covered Dandenong Ranges stretch north for 30km (19 miles)
from Ferntree Gully in Melbourne's east, through the hill village of Olinda in the
heart of the Ranges to Lilydale and the start of the Yarra Valley wine-growing
plains. Tall mountain ash forests blend with some of Australia's most beautiful
gardens, where exotic flowers and trees meld with native species. Visit in late
winter and early spring when the hills are full of daffodils, camellias,
rhododendrons and azaleas.

HIGHLIGHTS

At the southern end of the Dandenongs near Belgrave is Puffing Billy,
Australia's oldest preserved steam railway and one of Melbourne's best-
loved icons (departures daily 10.30, 12; additional trains in summer and on
weekends). The 25km (15-mile) journey goes east through thick forests and
fern-filled gullies to Emerald Lake Park and Gembrook. Break the journey at the
Steam Museum at Menzies Creek station.

The region, however, is best explored by car and on foot. The Mount
Dandenong Tourist Road zigzags north from Ferntree Gully to Montrose;
the landscape is heavily forested, with few village communities. Much of
the region is protected within the 3,200ha (7,904-acre) Dandenong Ranges
National Park, which has picnic grounds and walking tracks, and plays an
important role in protecting its population of lyrebirds, notable for their
distinctive long tail feathers. The 30-minute walk to Sherbrooke Falls, near
Olinda, is popular. For a longer walk of some seven hours, the 17km (11-
mile) Dandenong Ranges Tourist Track runs southeast from the hill village
of Sassafras along the cool Sassafras and Menzies creeks, across mountain
ridges to Clematis. Maps are available from the Parks Victoria website
(www.parkweb.vic.gov.au) and from the Dandenongs Ranges Visitor
Information Centre.

In contrast to the wild landscape of the Dandenongs are its gardens.
The 40ha (99-acre) National Rhododendron Gardens cascade down a hillside
near Olinda (daily 10–5). An astounding display of 250,000 daffodils, 3,000
camellias, 12,000 azaleas and 15,000 rhododendrons bloom from June
through to December.

Below *Puffing Billy winds through the
thick forests of the Dandenongs*

Above *The Boroka Lookout over the Grampians National Park*

DAYLESFORD AND HEPBURN SPRINGS

www.visitdaylesford.com

These two towns arose during the 1850s gold rush, and became spa resorts in the late 19th century, drawing visitors to the area's mineral springs. Water from each of the 70 springs has its own distinctive taste—no visit is complete without trying some. Bathing in the springs is popular, and the various spa resorts provide a range of treatments. Day visits should also include the Sunday markets, antiques shops, galleries, cafés and lakeside restaurants.

✚ 356 S15 🛈 Daylesford Visitor Information Centre, 98 Vincent Street, Daylesford, VIC 3460 ☎ 03 5321 6123 🕓 Daily 9–5 🚌 Ballarat then regular bus services to Daylesford

GEELONG

www.greatoceanrd.org.au
www.geelongaustralia.com.au

Victoria's second-largest city was built on wool: Within four years of the first sheep being grazed on Victorian pastures in 1836, wool was being exported from Geelong to British mills. See and hear the story (great 'yarns') at the National

Wool Museum, housed in an 1872 stone wool store near the seafront on Moorabool Street (daily 9.30–5). The waterfront of Corio Bay is ideal for strolling. At Steampacket Quay is an 1892 steam carousel, with 36 carved wooden horses and two chariots. If it's hot, try the art deco sea baths at Eastern Beach. On the headland above, Eastern Park contains the Botanic Gardens. West of the beaches and the city's central area, wide tree-lined Pakington Street is Geelong's answer to Melbourne's café society and love of ethnic food.

✚ 356 S15 🛈 Geelong Visitor Information Centre, 26 Moorabel Street, Geelong, VIC 3220 ☎ 1800 620 888 🚋 Geelong

THE GRAMPIANS

www.thegrampians.com.au

The Grampians are the western foothills—still over 1,000m (3,280ft) high—of the Great Dividing Range, which stretches down the east coast of Australia. Halls Gap is the main tourist focus of the region, at the base of the spectacular Pinnacle Lookout. Ararat, on the east side of the region, is the only town in Australia founded by

Chinese immigrants, following their discovery of the Gum San (Hill of Gold) goldfield in 1857. The Gum San Chinese Heritage Centre highlights the contribution of Chinese culture to the development of Australia (daily 10–4.30).

Bunjil's Shelter east of Pomonal is the most important of the area's many Aboriginal rock art sites, stunningly depicting Bunjil, the traditional creator of Gariwerd (the Grampians). Brambuk—the National Park and Cultural Centre, 2km (1.2 miles) south of Halls Gap—traces the history of the local Aboriginal people from ancient times to the present day. The same building also hosts the Grampians National Park Visitor Centre, perhaps the best introduction for newcomers to the park. Both are open daily 9–5.

✚ 356 R15 🛈 Halls Gap Visitor Information Centre, Centenary Hall, Grampians Road, Halls Gap, VIC 3381 ☎ 03 5356 4616, 1800 065 599

GREAT OCEAN ROAD

▷ 136–139.

HEALESVILLE SANCTUARY

www.zoo.org.au

Go to Healesville Sanctuary for native animals and authentic bush sights and smells. Expect close encounters with dingoes, kangaroos, wombats and duck-billed platypus, as well as brightly feathered native birds, all in a natural bush setting within the Yarra Valley (▷ 151). There are 200 species of bird, mammal and reptile, some of which—kangaroos, emus and wallabies—roam freely. You can also see echidnas and wombats at play— or asleep—and glimpse possums, flying foxes and tiny sugar gliders. There is a beautiful koala area, and a reptile house for viewing Australian snakes and lizards. Don't miss the Birds of Prey Presentation—a wedgetail eagle soars low over the crowd.

✚ 356 T15 ✉ Badger Creek Road, Healesville, VIC 3777 ☎ 03 5957 2800 🕓 Daily 9–5 💰 Adult A$24, child A$12.10, under 4 free 🚌 Coach tours from Melbourne daily 🖥 🏛

GREAT OCEAN ROAD

INTRODUCTION

Winding round hair-raising bends, passing through clifftop tunnels and climbing steep forest-clad hills, Victoria's famous tourist drive snakes and weaves around 250km (155 miles) of spectacular cliffs, scenic lookouts, beaches and rainforests. The Great Ocean Road follows a sprawling stretch of coastline in Victoria's southwest, with spectacular lookouts and vistas. It runs between Torquay on the Surf Coast and the town of Warrnambool on the west coast, taking in the highlights of Lorne, Apollo Bay, the Loch Ard Gorge, the Twelve Apostles and Port Campbell, a distance of more than 250km (155 miles). Torquay is 100km (62 miles) southwest of Melbourne via Geelong. Apart from striking views across the Bass Strait and the Southern Ocean, the Great Ocean Road region has laid-back coastal towns and maritime villages, and there are plenty of opportunities for bushwalking, swimming, surfing, fishing and whale-watching. One of the most visited stretches is the Port Campbell National Park, home to the stunning Twelve Apostles rock stacks, chilling Loch Ard Gorge and the windswept Bay of Islands near Warrnambool.

The Great Ocean Road is an epic in both scope and history. The main eastern section linking Anglesea and Apollo Bay was built from 1918 to 1932. Key mover was Geelong businessman and mayor Howard Hitchcock, who saw it as a way of employing soldiers returning from World War I; the road would create a lasting monument to those who died and also provide a tourist route. The high cliffs, bad weather and rocky terrain made it back-breaking toil, using picks and shovels—and the occasional explosive—and horses and drays. On 26 November 1932 the route was officially opened by a cavalcade of official vehicles, with bands and waving schoolchildren lining parts of the route. People using the road initially paid a hefty toll between Aireys Inlet and Lorne, but the levy was abolished in 1936.

WHAT TO SEE

SURF COAST

www.visitsurfcoast.com

The first 12km (7-mile) stretch of the Great Ocean Road between Torquay and Anglesea is Victoria's famous Surf Coast. The beach town of Torquay is widely regarded as Australia's surfing capital. The fun Surfworld Museum (daily 9–5) on Beach Road focuses on surfing history and culture, while alongside are two temples of surfing wear, the Rip Curl and Quiksilver factories. Nearby Bells Beach is one of the world's greatest surf beaches, hosting the Rip Curl Pro and Sunsmart Classic, which attracts many of the world's best boardriders each Easter. Sit on your board—they can be rented in town—out on the break and watch surfgear millionaires mix with drop-out surfies. Nearby Jan Juc is another world-famous surf beach.

Beyond the Surf Coast proper, Anglesea, Aireys Inlet and Fairhaven are popular holiday towns, all with their own surf beaches and lifesaving teams. Lorne is a thriving area of cafés, restaurants, boutiques and stylish accommodation, ringed by the cool gullies, rainforest and waterfalls of surrounding Angahook-Lorne State Park. A walk in the state park inland from Lorne takes you to the lovely cascading Erskine Falls. From Lorne, the Great Ocean Road twists and turns, marked by stunning lookouts, constant sea views and descents into the little beach holiday hamlets of Wye River, Kennett River and Skenes Creek, before the relaxing and picturesque haven of Apollo Bay is reached.

🔁 329 T17 ℹ️ Torquay Visitor Information Centre, Surf City Plaza, Beach Road, Torquay, VIC 3228 ☎ 03 5261 4219 🕓 Daily 9–5

INFORMATION

www.greatoceanroad.org

🔁 356 S15 ℹ️ Great Ocean Road Visitor Information Centre (Geelong), Stead Park, Princes Highway, Corio, VIC 3214 ☎ 1800 620 888 or 03 5275 5797 🕓 Daily 9–5 🚌 Geelong, then regular bus services down the Great Ocean Road to Warrnambool

Opposite *The Twelve Apostles have been formed over the last 20 million years*

» It might appear that the Great Ocean Road, starting 100km (62 miles) from Melbourne and stretching for more than 250km (155 miles), can be easily driven in a day. Be warned: The route is slow and winding, and there are many distracting views and things to see.

» Day bus tours from Melbourne are often the only way many visitors get to see the beauty of the Great Ocean Road. Do it if you must, but seriously consider renting a car to explore and enjoy this magnificent route at your own pace and time, preferably over at least two days.

Below *Triplet Falls is one of many cascades in Otway State Forest near Warrnambool*

APOLLO BAY

Spread around a sweeping beach, bay and harbour, with the lush Otway Ranges rising behind, Apollo Bay is a popular and peaceful overnight or weekend stop along the Great Ocean Road. Its popularity revolves around its main beach, right in front of the town, its Saturday morning art and local produce market, its local fishing fleet, which keeps the town well supplied with lobsters and fish, and its cultural bent—there are resident artists, sculptors and the Apollo Bay music festival in March.

Part of the pleasure of Apollo Bay is to eat crays and fish straight from the boats on the jetty and the fishermen's co-op. From Apollo Bay, the Great Ocean Road turns into a magnificent inland drive through the thick, cool rainforest and mountain ash bush of the Otway National Park. Close to the settlement of Beech Forest, the Otway Fly is an elevated metal walkway that rises to a height of 25m (82ft) to convey a bird's-eye view over the canopy of myrtle beech, blackwood and mountain ash trees as it follows the silvery trail of Youngs Creek.

⊞ 356 S15 ℹ Great Ocean Road Visitor Information Centre, 100 Great Ocean Road, Apollo Bay, VIC 3233 ☎ 03 5237 6529 🕐 Daily 9–5

CAPE OTWAY

www.lightstation.com
About 20km (12 miles) west of Apollo Bay is the turnoff to one of Australia's most rugged points, Cape Otway. Not surprisingly, this is the location of Australia's oldest surviving lighthouse, built in 1848. After climbing the heights of Lavers Hill, in the heart of the Otways, the Great Ocean Road descends back through farmland to beaches and clifftops on the entirely different southwest coastline. After the hamlet of Princetown the green volcanic plains collide with tall limestone cliffs and the wild Southern Ocean.

Rising from the coast into the steep ranges east of Cape Otway, Great Otway National Park is a temperate rainforest where soaring messmate, manna gums and mountain ash climb from an understorey of ferns. The Otway Ranges also has an exceptional hiking/cycle trail in the Old Beechy Rail Trail, which follows the line of a narrow-gauge railway built more than a century ago. Although the rails and sleepers have been removed, the narrow cuttings, track formation and features such as the water reservoir still conjure up the ghosts of the original railway.

⊞ 356 S15 ✉ Cape Otway Lightstation, Cape Otway Lighthouse Road, Cape Otway, VIC 3233 ☎ 03 5237 9240 🕐 Daily 9–5 ✋ Adult A$15.50, child A$7.50

THE TWELVE APOSTLES

www.visit12apostles.com.au
Port Campbell National Park protects much of the southwest coastline alongside the road, which over 20 million years has been battered to form a series of striking natural features. The main stop is the unforgettable Twelve Apostles, the isolated rock stacks marooned off the coast, sculpted by surging seas and the wild storms that howl in from the frigid waters north of Antarctica. There are not actually 12 stacks; the formations are in a continual state of erosion as the ocean wears away the soft limestone. But no matter what their number, the Apostles are among the true natural icons of Australia and remain captivating however often you see them. At dawn, the stacks glow golden against a blue-grey sky; in the late afternoon the sunlight filters through the sea haze, dramatically silhouetting the Apostles against the fading light.

The Twelve Apostles Interpretative Centre was designed to blend into the environment. It contains information about the area's history and Port Campbell National Park, and explains how nature has shaped the coastline. There are boardwalks and lookouts on the clifftop overlooking the Apostles, with display boards describing features of the unique coastal landscape and its flora.

Other eroded limestone arches, caves and island stacks worth looking at here include Pudding Basin Rock, Island Arch, the Razorback, Muttonbird Island, Thunder Cave, the Blowhole, Bakers Oven, the collapsed London Bridge and the Grotto.

✚ 356 R15 ℹ 12 Apostles Interpretative Centre, near Port Campbell, VIC 3233 ☎ 13 19 63 or 03 5598 6089 ⏰ Daily 9–5 ✋ Free

LOCH ARD GORGE

About 5km (3 miles) on from the Twelve Apostles are the plunging, eerie depths of the Loch Ard Gorge. This is the haunting, tragic scene of the *Loch Ard* shipwreck. The vessel foundered on Mutton Bird Island reefs in 1878, and only two people survived: Tom Pearce, a cabin boy, and Eva Carmichael, aged 18, who was sailing to Australia from Ireland with her well-to-do family. At Loch Ard Gorge you can see where the disaster unfolded, walk the beach where Tom and Eva struggled ashore, and see the monument to the Carmichael family in the clifftop cemetery where the few bodies recovered from the shipwreck are buried. Nearby Glenample Homestead (Thu–Mon 11–5.30), where Tom and Eva recuperated from their shipwreck trauma, has displays telling the story of the *Loch Ard* tragedy and its survivors.

✚ 356 R15 ✉ Loch Ard Gorge, near Port Campbell, VIC 3233 ✋ Free

SHIPWRECK COAST

www.visit12apostles.com.au

More than 700 ships are thought to have sunk along Victoria's Shipwreck Coast—the coastline between Princetown in the east and Port Fairy in the west—mainly in the late 19th century, victims of wild weather, human error and the rocky coast. Hundreds of people lost their lives. While much wreck evidence is at the bottom of the sea, some relics are displayed at museums and on the foreshore at many towns along the Great Ocean Road, including Port Campbell, which also has a lovely surf beach. A Discovery Walk heads west from the town.

ℹ 12 Apostles Visitor Information Centre, 26 Morris Street, Port Campbell, VIC 3269 ☎ 03 5598 6089 ⏰ Daily 9–5

WARRNAMBOOL

www.warrnamboolinfo.com.au

The spectacular part of the Great Ocean Road, and the Port Campbell National Park, ends at Peterborough. Just west of the town is the Bay of Islands Coastal Park, a 32km (20-mile) coastal strip that stretches almost to Warrnambool. Its spectacular ocean views and offshore stacks are equal in beauty and majesty to their more famous cousins, the Twelve Apostles, up the coast, and the park is much quieter and more deserted, too. The Great Ocean Road arrives at the major city of Warrnambool through farmland. Overlooking Lady Bay, Warrnambool was a busy port in the 19th century, its history recalled at the lively Flagstaff Hill Museum with its re-created maritime village (daily 9–5).

Warrnambool's other draws are the giant southern right whales that calve every year off Logans Beach from late May to the end of September, and the majestic Tower Hill Game Reserve (daily dawn–dusk), 15km (9 miles) west of Warrnambool, where the bowl of an extinct volcano is a beautiful haven for kangaroos, koalas, emus, waterbirds and bushwalkers. Port Fairy, 28km (17 miles) west of Warrnambool, is a fishing village, with beautifully preserved colonial buildings and whalers' cottages. Although Port Fairy is not exactly undiscovered, many overseas visitors don't call in at the village after their tour of the Great Ocean Road. Consider making it an overnight stay, as it is a real gem, nestled beside the Moyne River.

✚ 356 R15 ℹ Shipwreck Coast/Warrnambool Information Office, Flagstaff Hill, 23 Merri Street, Warrnambool, Victoria 3280 ☎ 03 5564 7837, 1800 637 725 ⏰ Daily 9–5

GREAT OCEAN ROAD BY BUS

Return bus services operate along the Great Ocean Road between Geelong and Apollo Bay. V/Line and McHarry's Buslines provides regular services between Geelong, Lorne, Apollo Bay, Port Campbell and Warrnambool. However, these bus services are not daily, so check with V/Line to plan schedules. There is a public bus from Geelong Station down the Great Ocean Road every Friday; departing the station about 9.55am, it arrives in Lorne at 11.20am, Apollo Bay at 12.30pm, the Twelve Apostles at 3.05pm and Warrnambool at 5pm.

Below *Loch Ard Gorge in Port Campbell National Park was the scene of the* Loch Ard *shipwreck*

MELBOURNE

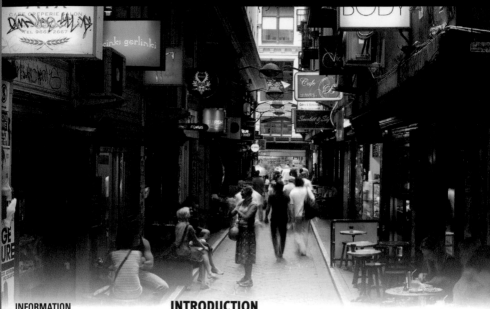

INFORMATION

www.visitvictoria.com

www.thatsmelbourne.com.au

🔣 Melbourne Visitor Centre, cnr Flinders and Swanston streets, Melbourne, VIC 3000 ☎ 03 9658 9658 ⊕ Daily 9–6

INTRODUCTION

Australia's second-largest city is very different from Sydney, with which it has always had a friendly rivalry. Melbourne is far more 'European', with grand Victorian buildings, atmospheric lanes full of shops and cafés, and many parks and gardens. The dynamic city centre, with its bustling Chinatown, includes several functioning Victorian-era theatres. Melbourne was founded in 1835. The discovery of gold in Victoria came soon after, and by the 1880s the city was booming. Melbourne today is a lively city with more than 4,000 restaurants and a sophisticated cultural and nightlife scene.

WHAT TO SEE

THE ARTS CENTRE

www.theartscentre.com.au

Unlike its Sydney counterpart, the Opera House, Victoria's Arts Centre has most of its performance spaces and art treasures concealed underground. The landmark 162m (531ft) tubular white spire is lit at night by blue neon tubing and laser lights. The Centre's theatres and halls host the Melbourne Theatre Company, Opera Australia, the Australian Ballet and the Melbourne Symphony Orchestra. It is also a popular venue for choirs, small chamber orchestras and international performing artists. The plush, four-tiered State Theatre, effectively Melbourne's Opera House, has the world's second-largest stage. The Centre also exhibits Australian art, including massive Aboriginal works. The Performing Arts Museum (Mon–Sat 9–11, Sun 10–5) celebrates the magic of the stage. Half-price tickets for some shows only are available on the performance day from the HalfTix box at the Town Hall (corner of Swanston and Collins streets). Don't miss the Sunday market (10–5), with 150 art and craft stalls, in the undercroft of the Melbourne Concert Hall.

✚ 149 B3 ✉ 100 St. Kilda Road, Melbourne, VIC 3004 ☎ 03 9281 8000 ⊕ Concert Hall building closed until performance times. Theatre complex Mon–Fri 8am–12am, Sat 9am–12am, Sun 9–5 💲 Public spaces free. Front of House tours (one hour, A$15): Mon–Sat 11, Backstage tour (90 min, A$20): Sunday 12.15; not appropriate for children under 12 🚊 Any tram along Swanston Street 🚉 Flinders Street 🍴 🛍 🏛

Above *Centre Place is one of Melbourne's favourite shopping precincts*

AUSTRALIAN CENTRE FOR THE MOVING IMAGE
www.acmi.net.au

On the north, city-side of Federation Square, the Australian Centre for the Moving Image projects visions from early cinema to the latest digital media. Containing displays relating to the Australian screen industry, including interactive hands-on features, the ACMI also has two multi-format cinemas screening unusual and historic films and documentaries.

149 B2 ☒ Federation Square, cnr Flinders and Swanston streets ☎ 03 8663 2200 ◷ Daily 10–6; cinema screenings throughout the day and until 11pm ✋ Free. Cinemas: adult A$11–A$12, prices vary according to screenings

BIRRARUNG MARR

Birrarung Marr is the first new park to be added to Melbourne's inner city for more than a century. It stretches from the river's edge of Federation Square down between Batman Avenue and the Yarra River to reach the Melbourne Park complex. Birrarung is the name the local Wurundjeri people gave to the river, meaning 'river of mist', while Marr means 'side of the river'. The 8ha (20-acre) park is designed more for strolling and quiet sitting than for its floral displays. Federation Bells in the park consist of 39 bells ranging in size from a handbell to one weighing a tonne. The bells are computer controlled and ring several times daily. From Federation Square, you can follow the Yarra River beside Birrarung Marr to Melbourne Park and the MCG (▷ 143). Find out when the free lunchtime concerts are on and join the locals for an entertaining lunch.

149 C2 ☒ Batman Avenue ☎ Federation Bells ringing, information hotline 03 9658 9658, Mon–Fri 6.30am–7pm ◷ Daily 24 hours ✋ Free

THE BLOCK ARCADE

Forming a short, narrow, covered laneway between Collins Street and Little Collins Street, the Block Arcade is the very picture of Victorian elegance. Among its decorative features are a domed roof of etched glass roof with wrought-iron and timber supports, and a mosaic floor. Today, the arcade is home to some of the city's most exclusive retailers. The Hopetoun Tea Rooms in particular are a Melbourne institution, evoking the genteel manners and style of a bygone era.

149 B2 ☒ 282 Collins Street, between Swanston and Elizabeth streets ☎ 03 9654 5244 ◷ Mon–Wed 10–6, Thu–Fri 10–9, Sat–Sun 10–5 🚋 Trams 11, 42, 48

CHINATOWN, CHINESE MUSEUM
www.chinesemuseum.com.au

During the 1850s more than 40,000 Chinese left Guandong province to the north of Hong Kong for Victoria and the lure of the goldfields. Melbourne's Chinatown dates from the early 1850s and is the longest continuous Chinese settlement in the Western world. It's a bustling precinct near the eastern end of Little Bourke Street, an area dominated by restaurants, cafés and Asian grocery stores.

The Chinese Museum has items and photographs from the gold-rush days. The precinct explodes with fireworks and dancing dragons during the Chinese New Year Festival (January or February) and the Autumn Moon Lantern Festival (September).

149 B2 ☒ Chinese Museum, 22 Cohen Place, Chinatown, Melbourne, VIC 3000; information desk for Chinatown inside the Chinese Museum ☎ 03 9662 2888 ◷ Daily 10–5 ✋ Adult A$7.50, child A$5.50 🚋 Tram 86 or 96 to Exhibition Street 🚉 Parliament Station

COMO HISTORIC HOUSE AND GARDEN
www.comohouse.com.au

Como was built on Toorak Hill in 1847, 4km (2.5 miles) from the young city. It was Melbourne's first colonial mansion, an unusual mix of Regency and

TIPS
» Travelling by tram is one of Melbourne's delights. Make use of the free City Circle tram, and buy Daily Metcard tickets for regular services.
» To gain an insight into the sporting culture, attend an Australian Rules Football game (Apr–end Sep) or cricket match at the MCG.
» Explore Melbourne's lanes and arcades, the location of some of the best shops and cafés (▷ 156–160, 162–165).

REGIONS VICTORIA • SIGHTS

Below *A dragon procession at the annual Chinese New Year Parade*

Italianate styles surrounded by gracious gardens running down to the river. From 1865 to 1959 it was lived in by the Armytage family, who owned a string of grazing properties in western Victoria and Queensland. Como gives an insight into the lifestyle of the wealthy during the mid- to late 1800s, when the city's population ballooned from 77,000 to more than 600,000.

✚ Off map 149 C3 ✉ Cnr Williams Road and Lechlade Avenue, South Yarra, VIC 3141 ☎ 03 9827 2500 ⊙ Daily 10–4 ✋ Adult A$12, child A$6.50, family A$30 🚋 Tram 8 (stop 34) 🚆 South Yarra then tram 8 east 🔲 🏛

FEDERATION SQUARE

www.fedsquare.com; www.visitmelbourne.com; www.melbourne.vic.gov.au

The size of a city block, Melbourne's vibrant hub is both the city's piazza and cultural focus. It's also the place to start your visit to Melbourne with information, sights and plenty of wonderful places to sit and watch the world go by. Federation Square is such a popular and essential addition to Melbourne, both for visitors and locals, that it is hard to imagine how the city lived before it. It's a great place to begin any trip to the state capital. The Square is built atop the commuter railyards, between the slow-flowing Yarra River and the main retail and business parts of the central business district(CBD). Opened in November 2002, the Square commemorates the centenary of the founding of the Commonwealth of Australia.

At the core is the open space of the Square itself, paved in pink and ochre sandstone cobbles from the remote Kimberley region of Western Australia (▷ 261). Sections of the paving form a giant artwork, with stories and events that have taken place on or near this site through the centuries, chiselled into the stone. From here there are views over the Yarra River to Southgate and The Arts Centre (▷ 140). Capable of hosting 20,000 people, the Square is the focus for much of Melbourne's busy calendar of festivals, events and promotions, while its tiered steps have become the new meeting place for Melburnians, as well as a great space to watch sports matches on the giant digital screen; key tennis matches are relayed direct from the Australian Open in January (▷ 161). Restaurants, cafés and bars embellish the atmosphere.

✚ 149 B2 ✉ Federation Square, Melbourne, VIC 3000 ☎ 03 9658 9658 ⊙ Daily 9–6 🚋 City Circle tram; Flinders Street Station stop 🚆 Flinders Street ⛴ Williamstown ferry stops at Southgate, just across Princes Bridge from Federation Square. Melbourne River Cruises boats or river water taxis ply upstream or downstream on the Yarra and moor alongside Federation Square at Princes Wharf ❓ Multilingual facilities, interpretative multimedia, internet access, accommodation and tour booking service

GOLD TREASURY MUSEUM

www.citymuseummelbourne.org

The Old Treasury Building was built as gold wealth turned Melbourne into a rich and substantial city. Located as close as possible to Parliament House (1855–56), the Treasury was built to house the offices of the colony's leaders, and to store the bullion pouring in from the colony's goldfields. Exhibitions recall the city's history, gold-rush days, architecture and 19th-century life.

✚ 149 C2 ✉ Old Treasury Building, Spring Street, Melbourne, VIC 3000 ☎ 03 9651 2233 ⊙ Mon–Fri 9–5, Sat, Sun 10–4 ✋ Adult A$8.50, child A$5 🚋 Trams 12, 31, 42, 109, 112, City Circle 🚆 Parliament 🏛

HEIDE MUSEUM OF MODERN ART

www.heide.com.au

Australian art underwent a revolution during the 1930s, 1940s and 1950s when controversial works emerged from a small artistic community on the banks of the Yarra River. Heide, the Bulleen home of wealthy art benefactors John and Sunday Reed, is now a public art museum, featuring the work of Sidney Nolan, John Perceval, Arthur Boyd, Joy Hester and Albert Tucker,

Above *Como House is one of Victoria's favourite historic houses*
Below *Federation Square has given the city a new focus*

among others. Visitors can explore the original Victorian farmhouse (Heide I) and 1960s modernist house (Heide II), along with extensive new spaces, all showcasing an outstanding collection of contemporary and modern art. This is a cultural destination of national significance.

✚ Off map 149 C1 ✉ 7 Templestowe Road, Bulleen, VIC 3105 (10km/7 miles northeast of Melbourne) ☎ 03 9850 1500 🕐 Tue–Sun 10–5 💵 Adult A$12, under 12s free. Gardens and Sculpture Park: free 🚆 Heidelberg (Hurstbridge line) then 🚌 291 ▣ ⌘

IMMIGRATION MUSEUM
www.museumvictoria.com

Over the past 200 years people have journeyed to Australia from all over the world, seeking a better life, a new start or to escape conflict in their homeland. The Immigration Museum, housed in the 1876 Customs House on the northern bank of the Yarra River, relives their stories through images, interactive screens, voices, memories and belongings.

Visitors can use the museum's resources to research their family's origins in Australia, to look up the passenger shipping lists, or even discover whether their relatives were convicts, unwillingly shipped out to Australia from Britain in the First Fleet (▷ 29).

✚ 149 B2 ✉ Old Customs House, 400 Flinders Street, Melbourne, VIC 3000 ☎ 03 9927 2700 🕐 Daily 10–5 💵 Free to ground floor (Immigration Discovery Centre). Exhibitions: adult A$6, under 17s free 🚋 Tram 48, 55, 70, 75, City Circle tram, any tram along Flinders Street 🚆 Flinders Street ▣ ⌘

Above *The Journeys Gallery houses a 17m (56-foot) replica of an immigrant ship at the Immigration Museum*
Below *The neo-Grecian Shrine of Remembrance is a Melbourne landmark*

KINGS DOMAIN AND THE SHRINE OF REMEMBRANCE
www.shrine.org.au

The parklands of the Kings Domain have been beloved of Melburnians for more than 130 years: gravel paths meander across lawns, down tree-lined avenues and through well-tended gardens. Adjoining the Domain are the Royal Botanic Gardens (▷ 146). The Shrine of Remembrance stands on a slight rise, about 1.5km (1 mile) south of the city. Completed in 1934, it commemorates the 114,000 Victorians who volunteered, and the 19,000 who died, in World War I. Other memorials have been added for World War II and the campaigns in Korea, Vietnam and the Persian Gulf. The Visitor Centre hosts exhibitions.

✚ 149 C3 ✉ St. Kilda Road, Melbourne, VIC 3000 ☎ City of Melbourne Council 03 9658 9658; Shrine of Remembrance 03 9654 8415; Sidney Myer Music Bowl 03 9658 9960 🕐 Daily 24 hours; Shrine of Remembrance: daily 10–5 💵 Free 🚋 Any tram from Flinders Street Station down St. Kilda Road 🚆 Flinders Street ▣ ⌘

MELBOURNE AQUARIUM
www.melbourneaquarium.com.au

Melbourne Aquarium overhangs the Yarra River beside Kings Bridge. Within are thousands of creatures from the cold and wild Great Southern Ocean, where 85 per cent of marine species are found nowhere else in the world. This is the place to see sea dragons, cuttlefish, moray eels, giant crabs and sharks, as well as reef and school fish. There are also Australian species from many other freshwater and marine habitats.

✚ 149 A3 ✉ Cnr Flinders and King streets, Melbourne, VIC 3000 ☎ 03 9923 5999 🕐 Daily 9.30–6 💵 Adult A$32.50, child A$18.50 🚋 City Circle tram; trams 109, 112 from Spencer Street; any tram from Flinders Street 🚆 Spencer Street, Flinders Street 🍴 ▣ ⌘

MELBOURNE CRICKET GROUND (MCG)
www.mcg.org.au

Established as a cricket oval in 1853, the MCG is one of the world's great sports stadiums, seating more than 90,000 people. The 'People's Ground' is famous as the birthplace of Australian Rules Football in 1858, the main venue of the 1956 Melbourne Olympic Games, and the scene of international Test cricket

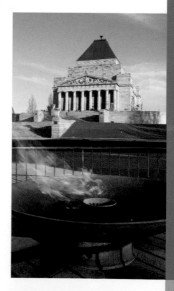

Above *View the fish of the Melbourne Aquarium from below*
Below *You can see cricket in the summer months and Aussie Rules in the winter at the MCG*

matches. Watching a game of Aussie Rules Football on a Friday night, Saturday afternoon or Sunday afternoon (Apr–end Sep) will give a glimpse into the role sport plays in the Australian psyche. In the early 2000s the MCG underwent a major redevelopment, in time for the 2006 Commonwealth Games. In addition to the creation of a new stand, the stadium's many collections and exhibitions have been expanded to form the National Sports Museum.

✚ Off map 149 C2 ✉ Gate 1, Jolimont Terrace, Jolimont, VIC 3002 ☎ 03 9657 8867 🕐 Daily tours (on non-event days) every half-hour 10–3 ✋ Matches at MCG: adult from A$20, child from A$5.20. Tours at MCG: adult A$15, child A$11 🚋 Trams 48, 75 🚆 Jolimont ▣ 🏛

MELBOURNE MUSEUM
www.museumvictoria.com.au

Melbourne Museum, in Carlton Gardens, uses the latest technology to give visitors an insight into Australia's flora, fauna, culture and way of life. Touch a fossil in the Evolution Gallery (DNA, dinosaurs and Darwin); sense the look, sounds and smells of a mountain ash forest in the Forest Gallery; or take a look at the new imaging technology in the Virtual Room. The Children's Museum thrives in the bright Big Box Gallery, and Australia's only interactive cinema game, ICE (Immersion Cinema Experience), is a hit with teenagers.

✚ 149 C3 ✉ 11 Nicholson Street, Carlton, Victoria, VIC 3053 ☎ 13 11 02, 03 8341 7777 🕐 Daily 10–5 ✋ Adult A$8, child free to 16 years 🚋 Trams 86, 96; City Circle 🚆 Parliament 🍴 ▣ 🏛

MELBOURNE ZOO
www.zoo.org.au

The 22ha (54-acre) zoo in Royal Park, Parkville, is known for its authentic recreations of animal habitats. More than 350 rare species are on display, many of them endangered. The large animal enclosures represent different climatic habitats (rainforest, bush and savannah), including the Big Cat Complex, the Arboreal Primate Enclosure, the Great Flight Aviary and the beautiful Butterfly House, and the popular Trail of the Elephants. To see Australian animals at their best you should go to Healesville Sanctuary in the Yarra Valley (▷ 151).

✚ Off map 149 A1 ✉ Elliott Avenue, Parkville, Victoria, VIC 3052 ☎ 03 9285 9300 🕐 Daily 9–5 ✋ Adult A$24.40, child A$12.10, under 4 free 🚋 Trams 55, 68 🚆 Royal Park from Flinders Street 🍴 ▣ 🏛

NATIONAL GALLERY OF VICTORIA AUSTRALIA
www.ngv.vic.gov.au

Housed within the Federation Square's main building, the Ian Potter Centre, the gallery presents the most extensive collection of Australian art in the nation: traditional and contemporary indigenous art, and art from the colonial period through to the present. International art is held at the National Gallery of Victoria International on St. Kilda Road, a 10-minute walk away (▷ 145). The idea of an Australian-only art gallery has proved an enormous hit, and should not be missed, while its architecture is a triumph of daring. The 20 sub-galleries flow chronologically: Australian indigenous art, traditional and contemporary, is on the ground level. Famous works include paintings by Wurundjeri elder William Barak, painted around 1890–1900; the early works by contemporary Limmen River artist, the late Ginger Riley Munduwalawala; and the much-loved *Big Yam Dreaming* by Emily Kame Kngwarraye of the Central Desert.

On the second level are paintings from Australia's late 19th-century Impressionist movement (Tom Roberts, Fred McCubbin, E. Phillips Fox and Arthur Streeton) and art from the mid- to late 20th century (Fred Williams, Russell Drysdale, Sidney Nolan and John Brack). The 1964 work by Sidney Nolan, *Landscape (Salt Lake)*, is exhibited here. The third level is used for temporary Australian exhibitions.

The glass-shell Atrium acts both as a forecourt to the National Gallery of Victoria Australia and a public festival and event space. It leads down to the riverside BMW Edge, an indoor amphitheatre designed for small music, cabaret and corporate events, which has stunning views across the Yarra River through its glass walls.

🚩 149 B2 ✉ Federation Square, Melbourne, VIC 3000 ☎ 03 8620 2222 🕐 Tue–Sun 10–5. Free guided tours daily 11, 3 ✋ Free. Charge for exhibitions

NATIONAL GALLERY OF VICTORIA INTERNATIONAL

www.ngv.vic.gov.au

The revamped 1968 gallery houses the state's international collection of European paintings, Asian art, decorative arts, textiles, photographs and sculptures. Australian art is now on show at the Federation Square gallery (▷ above), a 10-minute walk away. Inside the St. Kilda Road gallery you first meet a water wall, where water cascades down glass sheets. Works include Egyptian, Pre-Columbian, Greek and Roman antiquities. There are Asian art galleries, and European paintings and sculpture from the 14th to the 17th centuries. Late 20th-century art is also featured.

🚩 149 B3 ✉ 180 St. Kilda Road, Melbourne, VIC 3004 ☎ 03 8662 2222 🕐 Mon, Wed–Sun 10–5 ✋ Free. Charge for exhibitions 🚌 Trams 3, 5, 6, 8, 16, 25, 64, 67, 72 🚉 Flinders Street 🍴🛍️🏛️

OLD MELBOURNE GAOL

www.nattrust.com.au

Built in 1841, Victoria's oldest surviving prison housed hardened murderers and criminals. Its most infamous resident was bushranger Ned Kelly, who was imprisoned here and hanged on 11 November 1880. This dehumanizing place, where the prisoners were kept in solitary confinement, was the scene of 136 hangings until the prison closed in 1929. The prisoners' grim stories are retold using contemporary newspapers, photographs, letters, audio recordings and death masks—including Kelly's. The Old Melbourne Gaol runs a candle-lit night tour that is not for the faint-hearted. Tests for paranormal activity in mid 2003 supposedly detected the faint sounds of a woman's voice.

🚩 149 B1 ✉ Russell Street, Melbourne, VIC 3000 ☎ 03 9663 7228 🕐 Daily 9.30–5. Night tours Mon, Wed, Fri, Sat from 8.30 (7.30 in winter); bookings: Ticketek 13 28 49 ✋ Adult A$20, child A$11, family A$49. UK National Trust members free. Night tours: adult A$25, child A$16.50 🚌 Trams 23, 24, 30, 34; City Circle 🚉 Melbourne Central

POLLY WOODSIDE MELBOURNE MARITIME MUSEUM

www.pollywoodside.com.au

From 1835 until about 1970 almost all Melbourne's immigrants arrived by sea. The city remains the biggest port in Australia, and many of the city's inhabitants live around Port Phillip. This maritime heritage is preserved in one of the warehouse sheds that once lined the Yarra River, where old clipper boats and steamships tied up after perilous voyages from Europe. Historic photographs, models and film capture the early sailing days. The key exhibit is the newly restored three-masted iron barque, the *Polly Woodside*. Built in 1885, the vessel made 16 voyages around Cape Horn before sailing for 20 years around the Pacific.

🚩 149 A3 ✉ Lorimer Street East, Southbank, VIC 3006 ☎ 03 9656 9800 🕐 Daily 10–4 ✋ Adult A$12, child A$6.50. UK National Trust members free 🚌 Trams 96, 109; City Circle 🚉 Spencer Street 🛍️🏛️

RAAF MUSEUM

www.raaf.gov.au

In 1913 the Australian Flying Corps (later the Royal Australian Air Force) was formed at Point Cook. The first Australian pilots trained three years later in a

Above *Melbourne Zoo is well known for its gorilla enclosure*
Below *The three-masted* Polly Woodside *now sits in dry dock*

Maurice Farman bi-plane and this same plane is in the museum, along with more than 20 other aircraft from little Tiger Moths to Phantom fighter jets. There is also an excellent collection of RAAF memorabilia, film footage and photographs from the two world wars, Korea and Vietnam.

➕ Off map 149 A3 ✉ RAAF Williams Base, Point Cook Road, Point Cook, VIC 3027, 20km (12 miles) southwest of Melbourne ☎ 03 9256 1300 🕐 Tue–Fri 10–3, Sat, Sun 10–5 🖐 Free 🚌 Werribee Park Shuttle from The Arts Centre, St. Kilda Road 🏛

RIPPON LEA ESTATE
www.ripponleaestate.com.au
Rippon Lea is one of Australia's great 19th-century estates that has survived largely intact, and is the largest mansion of its period open to the public. It was built and enlarged between 1868 and 1903 by one of Melbourne's leading businessmen and politicians, Frederick Thomas Sargood. Along with the garden, the atmosphere conjures up Victorian England rather than the young colony, and the house is remarkable for its polychrome brickwork, oak and mahogany parquetry floors, stained-glass windows, rich European wallpapers and gilt decorations. This was the backdrop for family gatherings and huge society parties. In 1938 the then owner, Louisa Jones, modernized the house, and much of the furniture of this glamorous period is retained in the mansion today. During summer, plays are often performed outdoors in the garden and grounds.

➕ Off map 149 B3 ✉ 192 Hotham Street, Elsternwick, VIC 3185 ☎ 03 9523 6095 🕐 Daily 10–5 🖐 House and garden: adult A$12, child A$9. Garden: adult A$7, child A$3. UK National Trust members free 🚋 Tram 67; buses 216, 219 🚉 Ripponlea 🅿 🏛

ROYAL BOTANIC GARDENS
www.rbg.vic.gov.au
Established in 1846, the Royal Botanic Gardens are the pride of Melburnians and renowned as one of the finest examples of 19th-century garden landscaping in the world. The rolling 36ha (89 acres) are both a botanic garden and a public park, with broad sweeps of grass, lakes, tall riverside eucalypts, acacias and native hoop pines, rainforest, palms, cacti and woodland. There are more than 12,000 species of native and exotic plants. The gardens also hold the national camellia collection, planted in a mass bed near the equally stunning rhododendron and magnolia gardens.

The Children's Garden (near the Observatory Gate) has touching and feeling plants, as well as a beautifully carved storytelling tree.

➕ Off map 149 C3 ✉ Birdwood Avenue, South Yarra, VIC 3141 ☎ 03 9252 2300 🕐 Mon–Fri 9–5, Sat–Sun 9.30–5 🖐 Free 🚋 Trams 3, 5, 8, 16, 64, 67 to interchange of St. Kilda and Domain roads 🅿 🏛

ROYAL EXHIBITION BUILDING AND CARLTON GARDENS
www.museumvictoria.com.au/reb
The Royal Exhibition Building is one of Australia's most important 19th-century buildings. It was completed in 1880 as the central attraction of the Melbourne International Exhibition, which ran for eight months and attracted 1.3 million visitors. Apart from the Eiffel Tower in Paris, it is the only structure to remain from the series of grand international exhibitions held around the world from 1850 to 1890. The Classical basilica was designed by the Melbourne architect Joseph Reed, and the dome's shape reflects that of Florence Cathedral (Duomo); within the dome allegorical figures depict Peace, War, Federation, Government and the four seasons.

The first Commonwealth Parliament of Australia was opened here on 9 May 1901. Since then it has been a hospital during the Spanish influenza outbreak of 1919, a concert hall, and a venue for the 1956 Melbourne Olympic Games—it has now returned to its role as an exhibition space. The surrounding Carlton

Above *A statue of Queen Victoria surveys the Royal Botanic Gardens*
Below *The Royal Exhibition Building dates from 1880*

Gardens contain a grand Victorian marble fountain, an ornamental lake and formal avenues of shady elms. In 2004 the building and Carlton Gardens were inscribed as a World Heritage Site.

➕ 149 C1 ✉ Nicholson Street, Carlton, VIC 3053 ☎ 13 1102 or 03 8341 7777 ⏱ REB by tour only (1 hour): daily 2pm from Melbourne Museum foyer. Carlton Gardens: daily 24 hours 🎫 Tour: adult A$5, child A$3.50. Gardens: free 🚋 Trams 86, 96, City Circle tram

ST. KILDA AND LUNA PARK
www.portphillip.vic.gov.au

The bayside suburb of St. Kilda pulsates with activity 24 hours a day. St. Kilda is so full of tourist attractions that it is sometimes easy to forget how beautiful and special it is. The elegant pier, the Moorish palace-style baths and the fine restaurants balance the old-fashioned rides at Luna Park, live music at the famous Esperance (Espy) Hotel and the ubiquitous backpacker joints. On weekends, Melburnians walk, cycle and skate along the palm-lined foreshore or sit in an outdoor café, enjoying the panorama of Port Phillip. Many of the suburb's 19th-century mansions have been converted into smart apartments.

A walk along the 1857 pier is a must, with its views of the bay and the city skyline, and the historic café/kiosk perched at the end. Next to the pier is the St. Kilda Sea Baths, opened in 1850 and still Melbourne's only indoor heated seawater pool (Mon–Fri 6am–10pm, Sat, Sun 7am–9pm). Farther along the beach, the much-loved Luna Park is an institution. First opened in 1912 and upgraded in 2001, it was modelled on New York's Coney Island; the smiling face entrance and the timber and iron Scenic Railway are both classified historic monuments. Away from the foreshore, much of the activity is concentrated on the two main action strips of Fitzroy and Acland streets. Fitzroy Street is renowned for its cafés, pubs, restaurants and bars, and is one of the city's most interesting eating and drinking streets. Acland Street is more eclectic, with a mix of restaurants, Continental cake shops, book and record shops, and retro clothing boutiques. The oldest and the best café is Monarch (No. 103); enjoy one of the many treats from a window seat. On Sundays there is a popular open-air arts and crafts market along the Upper Esplanade. Note that this is probably one area of Melbourne where walking alone after dark, away from Fitzroy and Acland streets, is not advisable.

➕ Off map 149 B3 ☎ Port Phillip Council 03 9209 6777 🚋 Trams 16, 96

ST. PAUL'S CATHEDRAL
www.stpaulscathedral.org.au

The Anglican cathedral is one of Melbourne's most visited landmarks. St. Paul's stands on the site where the first public Christian services in Melbourne were led by Dr. Alexander Thomson in 1836. St. Paul's Parish Church was built here in 1848–52 and demolished in 1885 to make way for the present cathedral. The neo-Gothic cathedral was designed by the British architect William Butterfield, who steadfastly refused to visit Melbourne. He resigned from the project in 1884 and the building was completed by Joseph Reed, who also designed many of Melbourne's other public buildings.

The cathedral was consecrated on 22 January 1891, but the spires were not begun until 1926, and then to the design of John Barr of Sydney rather than Butterfield's plan. The building's interior is remarkable for its polychrome stonework, marbles, rich mosaics and stained glass. However, it is the church's musical contribution to Melbourne that is unsurpassed: The choir, organ and bells repay any visit. The peal of 13 bells can be enjoyed from a café on Federation Square or Southgate, on Wednesdays between 6.30pm and 9pm.

➕ 149 B2 ✉ Cnr Flinders and Swanston streets, Melbourne, VIC 3000 ☎ 03 9653 4333 ⏱ Sun–Fri 8 until after Evensong (about 6), Sat 8–5 (6 in summer) 🎫 Free 🚋 City Circle tram; any tram along Swanston or Flinders streets, or St. Kilda Road 🚉 Flinders Street 🏛

Above *Luna Park, in St. Kilda, is the oldest theme park in Australia*
Below *St. Paul's Cathedral was built in Gothic-transitional style*

SCIENCEWORKS MUSEUM

www.museumvictoria.com.au/scienceworks

A ferry ride away from central Melbourne, the award-winning Scienceworks Museum is based around the 1880s Spotswood Pumping Station, which has enormous working steam pumps that once rid Melbourne of its sewage. But don't be misled, Scienceworks Museum is one of the most compelling you'll come across.

The main aim of this fascinating museum is to answer the question: What is science? In the Sports Works section, there are fun activities that test your fitness and athletic skills: race against the Olympic 400m sprint champion, Cathy Freeman (▷ 17); see how well your heart and lungs are working; or throw balls, ride bicycles and pump iron. In the House Secrets section you can explore the science behind food, everyday objects and the animals in our homes. These and similar hands-on displays engage children of all ages in the fascination of science, while educating adults into the bargain. Melbourne Planetarium recreates the night sky on a domed ceiling, and takes you on a simulated three-dimensional journey through space to the moon, stars, galaxies and beyond.

✚ Off map 149 A3 ✉ 2 Booker Street, Spotswood, VIC 3015 ☎ 03 9392 4800, 13 11 02 🕒 Daily 10–4.30 💵 Scienceworks and the Planetarium: adult A\$13, child A\$4. Scienceworks only: adult A\$8, child free 🚢 Ferries from Southbank to Williamstown stop at Scienceworks (40-min trip), tel 03 9682 9555 💻 🏛

SOUTHBANK

www.southgate-melbourne.com.au www.crowncasino.com.au

The 15-minute walk along the south promenade of the Yarra River from Princes Bridge to Spencer Street Bridge takes in the two arts and leisure precincts of Southbank. Unless you are interested in gambling, the main reason to visit either Southgate or the Crown Complex is for a meal or coffee, and the lovely views across the Yarra River to central Melbourne. The Southgate complex, just 100m (328ft) from Princes Bridge and Federation Square (▷ 142), has shops, wine bars, art galleries and gourmet food and wine shops; opened in 1992, it was quickly embraced by Melburnians as the city's hottest restaurant location. At weekends there is live music in the forecourt. Ferries and cruises depart up- or downstream. There is also an enjoyable bicycle route along the Yarra River that takes you right out of the city. The main route is 33km (20 miles) and links with other routes going farther out. All sections of the path can also be walked. You can rent bicycles and helmets at Federation Square.

The nearby Crown Complex is not only a casino, but also contains restaurants, cafés, cinemas, late-night dance and club venues, and exclusive brand stores such as Burberry, Prada, Louis Vuitton, Versace and La Perla. Brash and flash, it's more a night destination, especially for keen gamblers, though some of Melbourne's best Asian restaurants are here. The Crown's 14 cinemas include the world's first four Gold Class cinemas, complete with reclining chairs and table service.

✚ 149 B3 ✉ Crown Entertainment Complex, Whiteman Street, Southbank, VIC 3006 ☎ Southgate customer information: 03 9699 4311. Crown: 03 9292 8888 🚊 Trams 96, 109, 112, City Circle 🚉 Spencer Street and Flinders Street

WILLIAMSTOWN

www.visithobsonsbay.com.au

The pretty seaport lies on a peninsula between the mouth of the Yarra River and the beaches of Port Philllip. Port Gellibrand or Williamstown began life in 1835 as a suitable place to unload cargo from Tasmania for the fledgling Melbourne settlement. Within five years the sheltered harbour had 100 buildings and was Melbourne's main port. Seafaring traditions continue in the yacht clubs, shipyards, port, naval dockyards and sea and river cruises. The suburb is now a heritage area, preserving its beautiful churches, pubs and timber cottages. Modern life fills the cafés, bars and seafood restaurants clustered around the maritime precinct of Nelson Place.

Every third Sunday of the month a craft market is held in Commonwealth Reserve on Nelson Place; the Message Tree here was used to pin messages for those disembarking from sailing ships. The 1876 Customs House is currently closed, but ferries still dock at Gem Pier, built by convicts in 1839. The relaxing river ferry to Williamstown stops at the Scienceworks Museum.

The World War II minesweeper, HMAS *Castlemaine*, moored at Gem Pier, has a maritime museum on board (Sat, Sun 12–5).

🛈 Hobsons Bay Visitor Information Centre, cnr Nelson Place and Syme Street, Williamstown, VIC 3016 (9km/6 miles southeast of city) ☎ 03 9399 8641 🕐 Daily 9–5 🚆 Williamstown; from Flinders Street change at Footscray 🚢 Ferries leave Melbourne Southgate quay every half-hour to Williamstown (50-minute river trip); also from St. Kilda at weekends

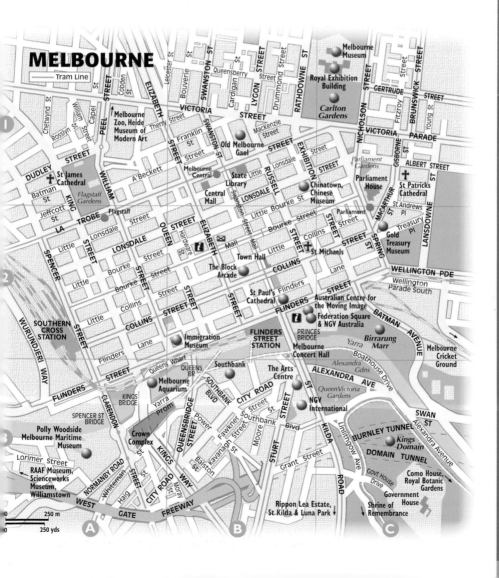

Above *Every night Little Penguins waddle onto Summerland Beach on Phillip Island*

MORNINGTON PENINSULA

www.visitmorningtonpeninsula.org
Melburnians come to Mornington Peninsula to laze on the beach, fish in Port Phillip, walk along the ocean cliffs and relax. The southern 'back' beaches facing Bass Strait are prone to dangerous tides and rough seas, though there is good rock fishing, diving in calm weather and surfing. The 'front' beaches facing the bay are calm, gently sloping and sandy are ideal for swimming, sailing and windsurfing.

Mornington Peninsula National Park runs along the ocean coast from the 1859 Cape Schanck Light Station (open for tours, tel 03 5988 6184 for details) to Point Nepean, where Fort Nepean was a vital part of Victoria's defences from the 1880s. Sorrento is the heart of the peninsula, a village with elegant eateries, boutiques, galleries and shops. The ferry leaves here for Queenscliff across The Rip seaway (daily 7–6). Near Dromana on the front shore, the 314m (1,030ft) mound known as Arthurs Seat looks over the bay and peninsula. The gardens at Ashcombe Maze near Shoreham (daily 10–5) are popular with children.

➕ 356 S15 ℹ️ Mornington Peninsula Visitor Information Centre, 359B Point Nepean Road, Dromana, VIC 3936 ☎ 03 5987 3078 🚉 Frankston then twice-daily bus connection to Portsea

MOUNT MACEDON

www.visitmacedonranges.com
Many of Melbourne's wealthy families built summer retreats in the Mount Macedon range in the late 1800s, creating magnificent gardens within the bush. Some of these English-style woodland gardens are open all year. Mount Macedon itself rises to more than 1,000m (3,280ft)—drive up to the summit for spectacular views and walks.

To the north across the volcanic plains is Hanging Rock (daily 8–6), a small steep volcanic plug rising 105m (344ft) from the surrounding bush. The rock was made famous as the setting for Joan Lindsay's novel, *Picnic at Hanging Rock*, and a subsequent film, about the strange disappearance of three schoolgirls in 1900.

➕ 356 S15 ℹ️ Woodend Visitor Information Centre, High Street, Woodend, VIC 3442 ☎ 03 5427 2033 🚉 Woodend then bus or taxi to Mount Macedon and Hanging Rock

PHILLIP ISLAND

www.visitvictoria.com
www.phillipisland.net.au
Reached by a bridge, low-lying Phillip Island is just 26km (16 miles) long and 9km (5.5 miles) wide. The island faces Western Port bay to the north and the Bass Strait to the south. Cowes, on the bay side, is the largest town. From here,

weather permitting, boat trips go to Seal Rocks, where Australia's largest colony of fur seals lives. A clifftop walk also gives views of the seals, and a path leads down to the spectacular Blowhole. The three main tourist attractions—Penguin Parade, Churchill Island and the Koala Conservation Centre—are managed by the Phillip Island Nature Park (tel 03 5951 2830), and a combined entry ticket is available. Each night at dusk (around 8 in summer, 5–6 at other times of year) dozens of groups of Little Penguins return to Summerland Beach to rest and to feed their young—the breeding season is from August to late March—after fishing in the waters off Phillip Island. Pre-book and remember to bring warm clothing. At the Koala Conservation Centre (daily 10–5.30), a thick section of bush is home to 900 koalas; raised boardwalks provide a treetop aspect of them. For walkers, the route to Cape Woolamai is the best of 15 tracks around the island.

➕ 356 S15 ℹ️ Phillip Island Visitor Centre, Phillip Island Tourist Road, Newhaven, VIC 3925 ☎ 03 5956 7447

RUTHERGLEN

www.visitwangaratta.com.au
www.rutherglenvic.com.au
Wine-makers have taken advantage of the fertile land and mild climate around Glenrowan, Rutherglen and Wahgunyah since the early 19th century. There are numerous wineries in the area and they offer cellar-door tastings. Rutherglen's main street is lined with historic buildings, antiques shops and restaurants. South of Rutherglen, the main town of Wangaratta is famous for its annual jazz festival (November).

Little Glenrowan is the site of the siege where the bushranger Ned Kelly and his gang made their last stand on 28 June 1880, dressed in their distinctive hand-forged armour. Kellyland is a cinematic and theatrical portrayal of the siege (daily 9.30–4.30).

➕ 356 T14 ℹ️ Rutherglen Visitor Information Centre, 57 Main Street,

Rutherglen, VIC 3685 ☎ 02 6033 6300 🚆 Wangaratta; connecting bus service to Rutherglen

WERRIBEE PARK

www.visitvictoria.com/mansion
www.zoo.org.au

The mansion and magnificent formal garden at Werribee Park testify to the success of the early Australian pastoralists. The Victorian Italianate house was built by brothers Thomas and Andrew Chirnside between 1874 and 1877, based on the plan of an English country estate. The main bedrooms, billiard room, reception rooms and servants' quarters are open. The adjacent State Rose Garden has 4,500 rose varieties, which are at their best from November to March. In the north of the park, the 200ha (494-acre) Open Range Zoo is formed around the picturesque Werribee River. An hour-long bus safari tours the fields where grassland animals from Africa, Asia, North America and Australia roam free. Endangered species include the Mongolian wild horse and the white rhinoceros. Try to visit in the morning, when the animals are more active.

🔼 356 S15 ✉ K Road, Werribee, VIC 3030 ☎ Mansion: 13 19 63. Zoo: 03 9731 9600 🕐 Mansion: Nov–end Mar Mon–Sun 10–5; Apr–end Oct Mon–Fri 10–4, Sat, Sun 10–5. Zoo: daily 9–5 💷 Mansion: adult A$14, child A$8. Zoo: adult A$24.40, child A$12.10. Combined Heritage and Wildlife Pass: adult A$34.60, child A$18.10, family A$79.70 🚌 Shuttle from Flinders Street station daily 9.30 🚆 Werribee then bus 439 💻 🏧

WILSONS PROMONTORY NATIONAL PARK

The 'Prom', as the southernmost point of the Australian mainland is called, is the most loved national park in Victoria. It has great spiritual significance to local Aboriginal people, who know the area as Yiruk or Wamoom. The granite promontory, with a 130km (81-mile) coastline, is the vestige of a land bridge that linked Australia to Tasmania up to 15,000 years ago, when the sea level rose. In 1859 a

lighthouse was built on South East Point to mark the Prom's position in the turbulent waters of Bass Strait.

The small settlement of Tidal River, 30km (19 miles) inside the park boundary, is the focus for tourism and recreation. The camping ground here fronts Norman Bay, a popular swimming spot, while the white 'squeaky' sands of Squeaky Beach are only a half-hour walk away. The Lilly Pilly Gully nature trail circuit is an easy walk (two to three hours) through banksias, casuarinas and gum trees, down into a cool rainforest gully and back to Tidal River. The views from Mount Oberon, south of Tidal River, are spectacular. Birding is magnificent, with more than half of all Victorian bird species found in the park; tame crimson rosellas flock around Tidal River. Wombats, echidnas and koalas are all commonly seen too.

🔼 356 T15 ✉ Wilsons Prom National Park Office, Tidal River, VIC 3960 ☎ 13 19 63 🕐 Park: daily 24 hours. Office: daily 8.30–5 💷 A$10.50 per car, per day, plus charges for camping and overnight hikes (reserve well in advance) 💻 🏧

YARRA VALLEY

www.visityarravalley.com.au
www.wineyarravalley.com

The Yarra Valley, within the area of Dixons Creek, Yarra Glen, Coldstream and Healesville, is the home of the Victorian wine industry. The state's first vineyard was planted here in 1837, at what is now Yering Station. There are more than 50 wineries in the valley, growing a range of grape varieties, though it is the Chardonnay and Pinot Noir grapes that receive the highest accolades. Almost all the major wineries are open daily (usually 10–4), when guests can sample varieties from the current vintage and tour the wineries. Harvest in the Yarra Valley is from March to the end of May. Wineries offering both tastings and restaurant meals include De Bortoli's at Dixons Creek (daily 10–5) and De Bortoli's restaurant (daily 12–5, and Sat for dinner), Yering Station, south

of Yarra Glen (Mon–Fri 10–5, Sat, Sun 10–6), and Domaine Chandon on the Maroondah Highway (daily 10.30–4.30).

The broad farming valley is now as famous for its food as for its wine, and you can find good local produce at the farmers' market at Yering Station winery (third Sunday of every month) or at the Yarra Valley Pasta shop in Healesville. This former forest town is better known for the nearby Healesville Sanctuary, the best place in Australia to view native animals in the bush (▷ 135). Just 2km (1.2 miles) east of the sanctuary is Badger Weir picnic area, within the Yarra Ranges National Park. Short walks loop amid tree ferns and mountain ash forests, or alongside babbling creeks.

Worth a detour is Mont de Lancey (Wed–Sun 10–4.30), a late 19th-century homestead in the south of the Yarra Valley at Wandin North (Wellington Road).

🔼 356 T15 ℹ Yarra Valley Visitor Information Centre, Harker Street, Healesville, VIC 3777 ☎ 03 5962 2600 🕐 Daily 9–5 🚆 Lilydale then bus to Healesville

Below *The view towards the Great Dividing Range from the tasting room at Domain Chandon winery in the Yarra Valley*

DRIVE

ALONG THE GREAT OCEAN ROAD

Hugging the rugged coastline of southwest Victoria for most of its 250km (155-mile) route, the Great Ocean Road (▷ 136–139) is one of the world's most spectacular coastal roads; it was completed in 1932. The route takes in wild surf and beautiful beaches, massive cliffs and impressive rock formations, spectacular rainforests and abundant wildlife, and busy resort towns and sleepy holiday hamlets.

THE DRIVE

Distance: 300km (186 miles) from Torquay to Warrnambool, plus drive to and from Melbourne
Allow: 2 days
Start at: Melbourne
End at: Melbourne

★ Drive from Melbourne to Geelong, 75km (46.5 miles) down the Princes Freeway (M1), crossing the Westgate Bridge and heading around the edge of Port Phillip Bay. In Geelong (▷ 135), follow the Great Ocean Road signs through the town, and then go 21km (13 miles) on the Surf Coast Highway to Torquay. The Great Ocean Road—route B100—begins in this resort town.

❶ Anglesea is a small holiday town at the mouth of the Anglesea River. Just west of town, the local golf course supports hundreds of kangaroos and wallabies. You can see them from Golf Links Road.

The Great Ocean Road sweeps west for 9km (6 miles) to Airey's Inlet,

where the Split Point Lighthouse has wonderful views of the Bass Strait and the Otway Ranges. Drive 5km (3 miles) west through Fairhaven to Eastern View, a stretch of road marked by long sandy beaches and holiday homes. About 2km (1 mile) past Eastern View there is a signed turnoff to Cinema Point, one of the road's highest vantage points. The road then winds its way back to sea level to enter Lorne.

❷ The flourishing holiday town of Lorne, between Loutit Bay and the cool Otway forests, has mild weather, lovely beaches and a touch of café culture. There are beautiful waterfalls and cool fern gullies to explore in nearby Angahook-Lorne State Park.

From Lorne, the road twists along a cliff edge. Continue to Kennett River.

❸ At the holiday hamlet of Kennett River, walk or drive to the Grey River picnic ground to try to spot koalas in the trees. If none can be found,

take a short detour by turning right up the hill on Grey River Road, and drive for about 4km (2.5 miles) until surrounded by bushland.

Return to the Great Ocean Road and head west to Apollo Bay.

4 Apollo Bay nestles in the foothills of the Otway Ranges, which descend to a sweeping arc of golden beaches. There is plenty to do here (▷ 138), and the town is a good place to stay overnight. For coastal panoramas, try Marriners Lookout (on Marriners Lookout Road).

After Apollo Bay, the road climbs into the cool-climate rainforest of Otway National Park, whose attractions can be sampled at Maits Rest, and the Otway Fly. About 20km (12 miles) from Apollo Bay, turn left on to a road that leads to Cape Otway.

5 Cape Otway, reaching into the wild Southern Ocean, is marked by Australia's oldest lighthouse, which can be visited (▷ 138). The ocean views are sensational, especially from the cliff walk.

Back on the Great Ocean Road, it is 33km (20 miles) to the town of Lavers Hill, the highest point on the road, and another 7km (4 miles) to Melba Gully State Park.

6 Melba Gully State Park protects a very beautiful area of cool-climate rainforest. The short Madsen Track wanders past tree ferns, waterfalls,

mosses and fungi above a canopy of tall myrtle beech, messmate and blackwood trees.

The road enters the heathlands of Port Campbell National Park, fringed by cliffs that rise up to 70m (230ft) high. Soon the weathered stacks of the Twelve Apostles come into view; pull in to the parking area.

7 The rock pillars of the Twelve Apostles—the wave-eroded remains of the old cliffline—stand like sculpted chess pieces in the sea (▷ 138). They are among a range of stunning natural features along this part of the coast.

One such feature is Loch Ard Gorge, a short distance to the west. In 1878, the sailing ship *Loch Ard* was wrecked here. The Twelve Apostles Interpretative Centre puts the nature and history of the coast into perspective.

Head west for about 11km (7 miles) to Port Campbell.

8 Port Campbell is a pretty village located beside a sheltered beach. The short Port Campbell Discovery Walk leads west from the town, giving excellent views of the cliffs to the east.

About 25km (15.5 miles) west of Port Campbell, the main road dog-legs to the right. Go straight ahead on to a side road that leads to the Bay of Islands Coastal Park.

9 Along the coast here are dozens of little islands and rock stacks that seemingly float offshore from the cliffs. Besides stunning vistas, there are some easily accessible and safe swimming beaches.

Rejoin the Great Ocean Road, and head west to Warrnambool, the official end of the road. The return to Melbourne inland by the Princes Highway (National Route A1; about 3–4 hours) passes the volcanic Lake Corangamite, the largest saltwater lake in Victoria.

WHEN TO GO
All year round. November to the end of March is the best time of year for swimming.

WHERE TO EAT
Apollo Bay: Bay Leaf Café, 161 Great Ocean Road.
Lorne: Qdos Gallery and Café, 35 Allenvale Road; Kosta's Taverna, 48 Mountjoy Parade.
Port Campbell: Waves Café Bar Restaurant, 29 Lord Street.

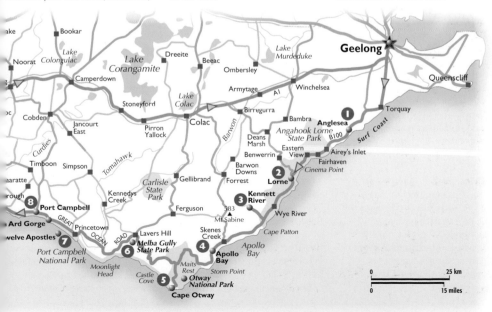

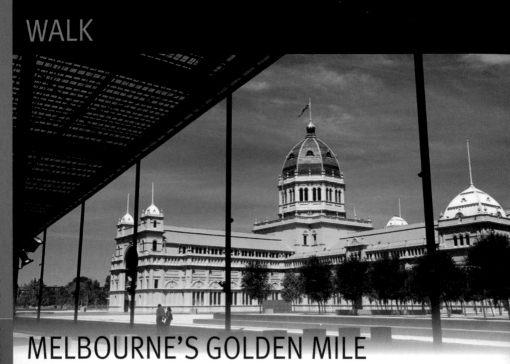

MELBOURNE'S GOLDEN MILE

The gently undulating Golden Mile Heritage Trail, marked by 2,700 circular brass discs, follows part of the street grid pegged out by the official town surveyor, Robert Hoddle, soon after Melbourne (▷ 140–149) was founded in 1835.

THE WALK

Distance: 4km (2.5 miles)
Allow: 2–3 hours
Start at: Immigration Museum, cnr William and Flinders streets; see map ▷ 149, B2
End at: Royal Exhibition Building/ Melbourne Museum, Victoria Street, Carlton

★ Take the City Circle tram to the start point near the Yarra River on the steps of the Immigration Museum on Flinders Street. You will see the trail's brass markers embedded in the footpath about every 1.2m (4ft).

❶ The imposing Customs House (now the Immigration Museum, ▷ 143) was built on bustling Queen's Wharf by gold rush immigrant J. J. Clark in 1873–76. Hundreds of thousands of hopeful gold diggers disembarked here from England, Ireland, China and California.

From the museum, turn right up William Street and left at Flinders Lane. John Batman, Melbourne's founder, supposedly came ashore here in 1835 from Tasmania and declared it was 'the place for a village'. The sturdy bluestone buildings along Flinders Lane were formerly dockside warehouses. Turn right into King Street up the hill, then right into the grand boulevard of Collins Street.

❷ Just next to the Rialto Towers, with its sky-high restaurant, is the magnificent former Rialto Hotel (now InterContinental Melbourne The Rialto) and the nearby Olderfleet offices, two of Melbourne's best examples of 19th-century neo-Gothic architecture.

Detour left up William Street, past the grey stucco façade of the grand Australian Club, and right into Little Collins Street, the heart of the legal

profession (often referred to as 'Chancery Lane' after the equivalent street in London's legal district). Two old legal chambers, Normanby Chambers (1883) and Stalbridge Chambers (1891), still stand. Turn right on to quiet Bank Place, containing the much-loved Mitre Tavern, a favourite meeting place for Melbourne lawyers and sporting men since the 1860s. Continue along Bank Place and then turn left into Collins Street.

❸ The block between Queen and Elizabeth streets, a blend of old and new architecture, has always been Melbourne's business district. Victorian exuberance survives in the ornate banking chamber of the 1887 ANZ Gothic Bank (iron columns and gilded decoration), the adjoining Great Hall or Cathedral Room of the first Stock Exchange of Melbourne, and the 1891 domed banking chamber of the former Commercial

Bank of Australia, hidden behind the modern granite facade of 333 Collins Street. The ANZ Banking Museum at 380 Collins Street tells the city's financial history.

Continue along Collins Street across the Elizabeth Street intersection to the historic shopping heart of the city, traditionally known as the 'Block'. The area's covered shopping arcades were modelled on those of London and Milan. Turn left into the hidden entrance to the grand Block Arcade, with its mosaic floor and 1907 ceiling murals. Walk through the arcade and turn right at Little Collins Street, glimpsing the glass-vaulted Royal Arcade. Continue down Little Collins Street, turn right into Howey Place and then left into the Capitol Arcade. When you reacy Swanston Street, turn right to return to Collins Street.

4 Between the Town Hall on your left and the end of Collins Street at the Spring Street intersection are three blocks of fine churches, theatres and shops. Despite its raucous beginnings, Melbourne had an intellectual and religious side, and the area around the Russell Street intersection was favoured by the Baptists, the Independents St. Michael's Uniting Church, 1886) and the Scots (Scots Church, 1873). Beyond the churches is the haute couture end of Collins Street. The Melbourne Club, on the left as you approach Spring Street, was founded by young squatters (sheep farmers) in 1839 and is still regarded as a bastion of the powerful Melbourne establishment. The Spring Street intersection is dominated by the monumental Old Treasury (Gold Treasury Museum, ▷ 142).

Turn left up Spring Street to the classical 19th-century Parliament House, home to Australia's first Commonwealth Parliament from 1901 to 1927 (free tours when the state Parliament is not sitting; tel 03 9651 8568). The Windsor

Hotel across the street is the only remaining example of Melbourne's once plentiful grand Victorian hotels. Continue past the majestic 1886 Princess Theatre and turn left down Little Bourke Street.

5 Off Little Bourke Street, you'll see the entrance to vibrant Chinatown, which developed around the boarding houses and stores established by the first immigrants from southern China in 1851, catering for their countrymen on their way to the goldfields (▷ 133). The area in and around Little Bourke and Lonsdale streets was notorious for its brothels and prostitutes.

Turn right at Punch Lane to Lonsdale Street. Number 32–34 Lonsdale Street is the site of the brothel where, it is rumoured, the gold-plated Mace of the Legislative Assembly, which mysteriously disappeared in 1891, was left by drunken parliamentarians. Turn left down Lonsdale Street to Exhibition Street, then right to Carlton Gardens across Victoria Street, leaving the grid of central Melbourne.

6 Pass through the shady Carlton Gardens to the glorious 1880 Royal Exhibition Building (▷ 146). Trees tower above the golden dome. Carlton Gardens were part of a belt of parkland around the city, created by Victoria's first governor, Charles LaTrobe, in the early 1850s. Across Nicholson Street from the Exhibition Building is the bluestone Regency Royal Terrace (1853–58).

The walk ends in the plaza between the Royal Exhibition Building and the modern Melbourne Museum.

WHEN TO GO
All year round. Dress for changeable weather and remember that Melbourne is prone to some very wet, windy winter days.

GUIDED TOURS
There is an excellent A$8 guide booklet to accompany the walk,

available from the Federation Square Visitor Centre and many tourist outlets and sights.

WHERE TO EAT
The heart of Melbourne has many opportunities for coffee, lunch or other refreshments. Three places are particularly in keeping with the Golden Mile theme:

The Mitre Tavern at 5 Bank Place nestles among high rises. This little yellow pub is ideal for a glass of beer or Australian wine.

Hopetoun Tea Rooms, at the entrance to the Block Arcade, 282 Collins Street, is a survivor of the days when women used to wear hats and gloves to take tea when coming to the city. Nearer the end of the trail, revive yourself at the elegant Windsor Hotel, 103–111 Spring Street, with a grand afternoon tea complete with scones, cakes and chocolate wonders.

PUBLIC TOILETS
Most major public buildings along the route have public toilets, all with disabled access.

Opposite *The Royal Exhibition Buildings*
Below *The entrance hall of Parliament House*

WHAT TO DO

BALLARAT
SOVEREIGN HILL
See page 133.

DAYLESFORD
THE CONVENT GALLERY
www.conventgallery.com.au
Dominating the town from its
perch on Wombat Hill, The Convent
Gallery is a former boarding school
and convent and now a showcase
for a community of artists and
craftworkers. It's a browsers'
delight—a complex of rooms that
take you from fashion accessories
to jewellery and antiques stores and
various galleries with a café and an
event space on the upper levels.
✉ Corner of Hill and Daly streets,
Daylesford, VIC 3460 ☎ 03 5348 3211

SWEET DECADENCE
www.sweetdecadence.com.au
The past winner of several tourism
awards, Sweet Decadence is
renowned for its handmade
chocolates, cakes and novelty
goods. The shop is in the pretty
town of Daylesford, northeast of
Ballarat. On request, staff will show
visitors how the chocolates are
made (weekdays only).
✉ 87 Vincent Street, Daylesford, VIC 3460
☎ 03 5348 3202 🕐 Daily 9.30–5 🚻

ECHUCA
MURRAY RIVER
PADDLESTEAMERS
Based at the historic wharf at
Echuca, this company offers daily
cruises at various times of the
day aboard its fleet of three
restored historic vessels. The
cruise aboard the PS *Emmylou*
is particularly recommended.
✉ 57 Murray Esplanade, Echuca, VIC 3564
☎ 03 5482 5244 🖐 Adult A$24.50, child
A$11

GEELONG
THE NATIONAL WOOL MUSEUM
www.geelongaustralia.com.au
Located in an 1872 woolstore in
central Geelong, the museum is
devoted to Australia's wool industry.
The shop has a range of handmade
woollen clothing such as sweaters,
coats, hats and scarves. There are
also pieces of pottery, glassware and
other souvenirs.
✉ 26 Moorabool Street, Geelong, VIC 3220
☎ 03 5272 4701 🕐 Mon–Fri 9.30–5,
Sat–Sun 1–5 🍽 The Black Sheep Café

HEPBURN SPRINGS
HEPBURN BATHHOUSE AND SPA
www.hepburnbathhouse.com
The oldest spa in the country
underwent a A$13 million refit in

2008, making it the most complete
and accomplished facility in
Australia. Treatments include organic
herbal baths, aromatic elixirs,
marine soaks, detox treatments,
body polishes, beauty treatments
and ear candling. It's also vast, with
several therapy pools and more than
30 treatment rooms. This is the
only spa that has mineral-enhanced
springs on tap.
✉ Mineral Springs Reserve Road, Hepburn
Springs, VIC 3461 ☎ 03 5321 6000
🖐 Entry to the Bathhouse starts from A$15,
treatments start from A$65.

MANSFIELD
WATSON'S MOUNTAIN
COUNTRY TRAIL RIDES
www.watsonstrailrides.com.au
Saddle up and explore the hills of
the high country around Mansfield.
Guided rides from one hour to a
full day.
✉ Three Chain Road, Mansfield, VIC 3724
☎ 03 5777 3552 🖐 From A$35 per person
for one hour

MELBOURNE
ABORIGINAL
GALLERIES OF AUSTRALIA
www.agamelbourne.com
One of Melbourne's finest galleries
of Aboriginal art, this establishment

specializes in paintings and other artworks by both 'collectable' and 'emerging' artists. In addition to the gallery, a warehouse showroom may be visited by appointment only.
✉ 35 Spring Street, Melbourne, VIC 3000 ☎ 03 9654 2516 🕐 Mon–Sat 10–6 🚊 Trams along Bourke Street 🚇 Parliament

ALICE'S BOOKSHOP
www.alices.com.au
This antiquarian and second-hand bookstore has 20,000 books in four ground-level rooms. The emphasis is on the arts, literature, humanities, travel, and ancient and medieval history. Alice's also provides a free search service for out-of-print books. The shop is in Carlton North, a short tram ride from the city.
✉ 629 Rathdowne Street, Carlton North, VIC 3054 ☎ 03 9347 4656 🕐 Daily 10.30–6 🚊 Trams 1, 22, 96

THE ARTS CENTRE
www.theartscentre.net.au
Under the iconic spire of Melbourne, the Arts Centre presents musicals, plays and concerts in a range of venues, including the 2,000-seat State Theatre and the 2,600-seat Hamer Concert Hall.
✉ 100 St. Kilda Road, Melbourne, VIC 3000 ☎ 03 9281 8000 🚊 Tram along St. Kilda Road 🍴

THE ASTOR THEATRE
www.astor-theatre.com
One of Melbourne's first cinemas, the Astor opened in 1935. It now shows classic movies.
✉ 1 Chapel Street, St. Kilda, VIC 3182 ☎ 03 9510 1414 🕐 Mon–Fri 6.30–11.30, Sat, Sun 1–11.30 🚊 Tram or bus to Chapel Street, Prahran 🍴 Snack bar 🍴

AUSKI
www.auski.com.au
This is the place to go if you're thinking about a trip to the Victorian ski resorts. Auski rents and sells a full range of equipment, including children's and adults' clothing and skis, snowboards, walking boots, toboggans, helmets and car tyre snow chains.

✉ 9 Hardware Lane, Melbourne, VIC 3000 ☎ 03 9670 1412 🕐 Mon–Thu 9.30–5, Sat 1–5, Sun (winter only) 11–5 🚊 Trams along Bourke Street

BALLOON SUNRISE
www.hotairballooning.com.au
Watch the sun rise over central Melbourne from a hot-air balloon. Breakfast is served after the hour-long flight.
✉ 2 Bell Street, Yarra Glen, VIC 3775 ☎ 03 1800 468 247 🕐 Depart at dawn; meeting time and place confirmed the day before 💳 Adult from A$345, child A$240

BENNETTS LANE JAZZ CLUB
www.bennettslane.com
Live local and international jazz acts perform at Bennetts Lane club every night.
✉ 25 Bennetts Lane (off Little Lonsdale Street), Melbourne, VIC 3000 ☎ 03 9663 2856 🕐 Daily from 8.30pm 🎫 Ticket prices vary

THE COMEDY CLUB
www.thecomedyclub.com.au
This club played a major role in creating Melbourne's reputation as Australia's comedy capital. The line-up changes regularly and includes both local and international stars.
✉ 188 Collins Street, Melbourne, VIC 3000 ☎ 03 9650 6668 🕐 Fri, Sat from 8.30pm (doors open 7pm) 💳 A$40, including dinner 🚌 Bus to Lygon Street or tram up Swanston Street, then a short walk 🍴🍴

CROWN CASINO
www.crowncasino.com.au
Besides gambling, there are bars and clubs and a variety of dining options here.
✉ 8 Whiteman Street, Southbank, VIC 3006 ☎ 03 9292 8888 🕐 Daily 24 hours

DAN MURPHY'S
www.danmurphys.com.au
Dan Murphy's is an enormous discount liquor store, with a wide range of Australian and international wines, beers and spirits. The store stocks everything from cheap wines to rare, collectable vintages. A great place to buy some of the best Australian wines.

✉ 273 Chapel Street, Prahran, VIC 3181 ☎ 03 9497 3388 🕐 Mon–Sat 9–8 (also Thu, Fri 8–9pm), Sun 10–6 🚊 Trams 6, 67 and 78 🚆 Prahran or Sandringham train from Flinders Street

DAVID JONES
www.davidjones.com.au
This is the main Melbourne city branch of the Australia-wide David Jones department stores. It stocks most major Australian and international brands, and is a little more sophisticated than its competitor Myer, located across Bourke Street Mall. There is an excellent food hall.
✉ 310 Bourke Street, Melbourne, VIC 3000 ☎ 03 9643 2222 🕐 Mon–Sat 9.30–6, Sun 10–6 (also Thu 6–7pm and Fri 6–9pm) 🚊 Trams along Bourke Street 🍴

DOCKLANDS AND NEW QUAY
www.docklands.com
Melbourne's new waterfront dining and shopping precinct includes cool bars, cafés, restaurants and galleries. Public artworks adorn the foreshore, events and festivals take place here, and boat tours of surrounding waterways depart from the marina area.
✉ Docklands, Melbourne, VIC 3000 ☎ 1300 663 008 🕐 Daily 10am–late 🚊 City Circle tram

THE ESPLANADE HOTEL
www.espy.com.au
A Melbourne icon, 'The Espy' is best known for its live bands. There's a great view over St. Kilda beach.
✉ 11 The Esplanade, St. Kilda, VIC 3182 ☎ 03 9534 0211 🕐 Daily until 1am 🚊 Tram to St. Kilda Beach 💳 Cover charge for some bands

FITZROY GARDENS
www.fitzroygardens.com
On the eastern fringe of the city centre, Fitzroy Gardens is a showpiece of green-fingered expertise, featuring a flower-filled conservatory, a 150-year-old avenue of magnificent elms, a miniature

Opposite *The well-stocked Tina's Deli in Queen Victoria Market*

Tudor village and a fairy tree. The gardens also include Cook's Cottage, the home James Cook's parents, relocated from England.

✉ Corner of Wellington Parade and Albert Street, East Melbourne, VIC 8002 🕐 Cook's Cottage: daily 9–5, conservatory: daily 7–5 🚋 Trams along Flinders Street

FLEMINGTON RACECOURSE
www.vrc.net.au
Home of the Melbourne Cup, Australia's premier horse race.

✉ 400 Epsom Road, Flemington, VIC 3031 ☎ 03 9371 7171 🕐 Two hours prior to first race 💰 Adult from A$9, depending on event 🚉 Flemington Racecourse 🚋 Northwest of the city 🍴 🛍 🍷

GASWORKS ARTS PARK
www.gasworks.org.au
Gasworks is run by an independent community arts group and includes a 240-seat theatre and a gallery.

✉ 21 Graham Street, Albert Park, VIC 3206 ☎ 03 8606 4200 🚋 3km (2 miles) south of Melbourne

GIN PALACE
www.ginpalace.com.au
This plush basement bar specializes in martinis.

✉ 10 Russell Place, Melbourne, VIC 3000 ☎ 03 9654 0533 🕐 Daily 4pm–3am

GPO
www.melbournesgpo.com
Melbourne's heritage-listed General Post Office building, covering an entire city block, has been transformed into a sophisticated fashion, food and general shopping precinct.

There are more than 60 stores in this beautifully renovated centre, including Australian and international designer labels.

✉ Cnr Elizabeth and Bourke streets, Melbourne, VIC 3000 ☎ 03 9663 0066 🕐 Mon–Thu, Sat 10–6, Fri 10–9, Sun 11–5 🚋 Trams along Bourke Street

HENRY BUCK'S
www.henrybucks.com.au
This menswear store has been in business for more than 110 years, mainly serving the needs

of middle-aged men. It sells the company's own brands as well as imported labels, and offers a full tailoring service. It is in the heart of Melbourne city.

✉ 320 Collins Street, Melbourne, VIC 3000 ☎ 03 8102 4700 🕐 Mon–Fri 9–5.30 (also Fri 5.30–7pm), Sat 9–5 🚋 Trams to Collins Street

HER MAJESTY'S THEATRE
www.hmt.com.au
Opened in 1886, 'The Maj' remains a popular venue for ballet, opera and musicals.

✉ 219 Exhibition Street, Melbourne, VIC 3000 ☎ 03 8643 3300 🚋 Tram from Bourke Street to Exhibition Street, then a short walk 🍷

HOTEL WINDSOR
www.thewindsor.com.au
The aristocrat of Melbourne's five-star elite, this swanky, Victorian-era hotel has been serving high tea since 1883. Served on three-tiered silver stands, the tea consists of freshly baked scones with jam and cream, pastries and finger sandwiches, with a glass of sparkling wine and tea or coffee.

✉ 111 Spring Street, Melbourne, VIC 3000 ☎ 03 9633 6000 🕐 Mon–Fri 2.30 💰 A$49 🚋 Trams along Bourke Street

THE JAM FACTORY
www.thejamfactory.com.au
Housed inside a converted factory in the swanky Chapel Street shopping precinct, this landmark building offers funky fashions, homewares, cafés and cinemas.

✉ 500 Chapel Street, South Yarra, VIC 3141 ☎ 03 9860 8500 🕐 Daily 9am–11pm 🚋 Trams along Chapel Street

THE LAUNDRY
www.thelaundrybar.com.au
DJs and bands play dance music at this informal venue. Dirty Laundry (Tuesday) is popular with the gay community.

✉ 50 Johnston Street, Fitzroy, VIC 3065 ☎ 03 9419 7111 🕐 Daily 3pm–3am 💰 Small cover charge some nights 🚋 Tram 96 (East Brunswick) or 112 (West Preston)

MALTHOUSE THEATRE
www.malthousetheatre.com.au
A short distance from the city, the Malthouse stages plays at the 512-seat Merlyn Theatre and the more intimate 196-seat Beckett Theatre.

✉ 113 Sturt Street, Southbank, VIC 3205 ☎ 03 9685 5111 🚋 Tram or bus to South Melbourne

THE MARKET
www.markethotel.com.au
Popular with gay clubbers, the Market has live shows and the latest DJs.

✉ 143 Commercial Road, South Yarra, VIC 3141 ☎ 03 9826 0933 🕐 Fri, Sat 10pm–late 🚋 Tram 72 💰 Non-members nightly A$5 before 12am, A$7–A$15 after 12am

MELBOURNE AQUARIUM
▷ 143.

MELBOURNE CRICKET GROUND (MCG)
www.mcg.org.au
Cricket (in summer) and Australian Rules football (in winter) are the major draws at Australia's biggest sports stadium (▷ 143).

✉ Jolimont Terrace, Jolimont, VIC 3002 ☎ Ticketmaster 1300 136 122, for ticket prices and details of events 🚋 Trams 48, 7 🚉 Jolimont, Richmond 🍴 🛍 🍷

MELBOURNE MUSEUM SHOP
www.museumvictoria.com.au
This two-level museum shop is a good place to buy reasonably priced and genuine Aboriginal items such as didgeridoos, boomerangs, shields, spears and pottery—all made in Victoria. The shop also sells a good selection of general souvenirs, children's toys and books.

✉ 11 Nicholson Street, Carlton, VIC 3053 ☎ 03 8341 7620 🕐 Daily 10.30–5 🚋 Tram 86 or 96 to Museum and Royal Exhibition Building stop, or City Circle Tram to Carlton Gardens 🛍

MELBOURNE SPORTS AND AQUATIC CENTRE
www.msac.com.au
This large sports venue has Olympic-size pools, a wave pool,

water slide, diving boards, and halls for everything from basketball to badminton, squash and yoga.

✉ Aughtie Drive, Albert Park, VIC 3206 ☎ 03 9926 1555 🕐 Swimming complex: Mon–Fri 5.30am–10pm, Sat, Sun 7am–8pm 🖐 Swimming: adult from A$6.75, child from A$4.95; Squash: from A$24.35 per hour; Basketball court: from A$38.60 🛒 🍴 🚊 Tram 112 🚉 Wright Street on light rail 96

MELBOURNE ZOO

▷ 144.

MYER

www.myer.com.au

Myer is a department store that began life in Melbourne in 1911, and became part of an Australia-wide retail group in the 1980s. The Melbourne store is particularly popular at Christmas when young children queue with their parents to see the Bourke Street Mall store's Yuletide window displays.

✉ 314 Bourke Street, Melbourne, VIC 3000 ☎ 03 9661 1111 🕐 Mon–Sat 9–6 also Thu 6–7pm and Fri 6–9pm), Sun 10–6 🚊 Trams along Bourke Street 🛒

THE PALMS AT CROWN

www.crownltd.com.au

A multi-layered auditorium with a classy cabaret style, where top performers entertain.

✉ Crown Casino, Southbank VIC 3006 ☎ 03 9292 5103 🕐 Daily 9pm–late 🖐 Various ticket prices

PELLEGRINI'S ESPRESSO BAR

A Melbourne institution, this narrow café has introduced generations of Melburnians to the pleasures of strong, Italian-style espresso. The prime positions are at the bar, with stool seating flanked by gold-backed mirrors.

✉ 66 Bourke Street, Melbourne, VIC 3000 ☎ 03 9662 1885 🕐 Daily 11am–11.30pm 🚌 Trams along Bourke Street

PRINCESS THEATRE

www.marrinertheatres.com.au

This beautiful Victorian theatre dating from 1886 seats more than 1,400. Large-scale musicals and plays are staged here.

✉ 163 Spring Street, Melbourne, VIC 3000 ☎ 03 9299 9800 🚊 Tram along Bourke Street 🚉 Parliament 🛒

PUFFING BILLY

www.puffingbilly.com.au

Take a ride on a steam train through 25km (15 miles) of rural scenery, including towering forests and fern gullies. There is also a lunch special and a night (wine and dine) special. Great for children.

✉ Old Monbulk Road, Belgrave, VIC 3160 ☎ 03 9754 6800 🕐 Daily 10.30–4

🖐 From A$10 (for a child, one-way, on a single section) to A$97 (for a family, round-trip, entire distance); extra for specials—booking essential 🚉 Belgrave

QUEEN VICTORIA MARKET

www.qvm.com.au

The Queen Victoria Market is the largest open-air market in the southern hemisphere, spread over 7ha (17 acres). There are about 1,000 traders, who sell everything from fruit and vegetables and local and imported gourmet foods, meat, fish and poultry, to hardware, clothing and authentic Australian objects and souvenirs.

✉ 513 Elizabeth Street, Melbourne, VIC 3000 ☎ 03 9320 5822 🕐 Tue, Thu 6–2, Fri 6–6, Sat 6–3, Sun 9–4 🚊 Any tram heading north along Elizabeth and William streets 🛒

ROD LAVER ARENA

www.mopt.com.au

Play on the courts used during the Australian Open. Coaching is also available.

✉ Batman Avenue, Melbourne, VIC 3000 ☎ 03 9286 1600 🕐 Tennis: Mon–Fri 7am–11pm, Sat, Sun 9–6 🚊 Tram 70 🚉 Jolimont, Richmond 🖐 Court hire from A$26 per hour 🛒

Below *Crown Oaks Day is an excuse to dress up at the Flemington Racecourse*

SOUTHGATE ARTS AND LEISURE PRECINCT
www.southgate-melbourne.com.au
Along with its many restaurants and cafés, the Southgate Precinct contains a good selection of shops, many of which sell Australian crafts, Aboriginal art and quality gifts and souvenirs. Suggestions include Potoroo Fine Australian Craft, Kirra Galleries and the Redrock Gallery.
✉ Southbank, Melbourne, VIC 3006 ☎ 03 9686 1000 ⏰ Shops generally daily 10–6 🚆 Flinders Street 🚊 96, 109, 112, City Circle

ST. KILDA ESPLANADE ARTS AND CRAFTS MARKET
www.stkildamarket.com
A row of colourful market umbrellas lining St. Kilda's Esplanade marks the site of the oldest arts and crafts market in Melbourne. Browse for a bargain among more than 150 stalls, which mainly show handmade furniture, jewellery and accessories, metalwork, leatherwork, musical instruments, clocks, homewares and candles.
✉ Upper Esplanade, St. Kilda, VIC 3182 ☎ 03 9209 6397 ⏰ Sun 10–5 🚊 Tram 16 or 96, bus 606

SIDNEY MYER MUSIC BOWL
www.theartscentre.net.au
This amphitheatre is tucked into the gardens of Kings Domain. It has state-of-the-art sound and lighting, and is used for free concerts in summer. Take a picnic and a rug and make an evening of it.
✉ Kings Domain, Linlithgow Avenue, Melbourne, VIC 3000 ☎ 03 9281 8000 🚊 Tram along St. Kilda Road

STRIKE BOWLING BAR
www.strikebowling.com.au
This 10-pin bowling alley has public and private lanes, and also a bar, lounge, pool tables, games and karaoke.
✉ 325 Chapel Street, Prahran, VIC 3181 ☎ 03 9573 9573 ⏰ Mon–Fri 12pm–late, Sat, Sun 10am–late 🚊 Trams 6, 78, 79 🚆 Prahran ✋ From A$12 per game 🍸

SCIENCEWORKS MUSEUM
▷ 148.

MORNINGTON PENINSULA
CAPE SCHANCK RESORT
www.racv.com.au/capeschanck
The Mornington Peninsula is famous for its golf courses, and this is a dazzling and challenging 18-holer, tailored by legendary US golf course architect Robert Trent Jones, Jr. Pitched high on a coastal headland with spectacular ocean views, runway-size greens, big open bunkers and fairways carved from native timber, the well drained championship course offers excellent play all year round.
✉ Trent Jones Drive, Cape Schanck, VIC 3939 ☎ 03 5950 8100 ✋ From A$45 midweek

RED HILL MARKET
This popular and well established market sells fresh farm produce, local wines and arts and crafts, in a convivial atmosphere.
✉ Red Hill Recreation Reserve, Arthur's Seat Road, Red Hill VIC 3937 ⏰ First Sat each month, Sep–May, 8–1

NAGAMBIE
SKYDIVE NAGAMBIE
www.skydivenagambie.com.au
Experience the thrill of sky-diving in a solo jump or a tandem jump with an experienced instructor. Nagambie is just a one-hour drive north of Melbourne.
✉ 1232 Kettels Road, Nagambie, VIC 3608 ☎ 1800 266 500, 03 5794 1466 ⏰ Daily by appointment ✋ From A$365 for tandem dive

PHILLIP ISLAND
PHILLIP ISLAND PENGUIN PARADE
www.penguins.org.au
Watch penguins emerge from the water at sunset and waddle across the beach to their burrows in the sand dunes (▷ 150).
✉ Summerland Beach, Phillip Island, VIC 3922 ☎ 03 5951 2800 ⏰ Daily from dusk ✋ Penguin parade and visitor centre: adult A$20.60, child A$10.30 (under 4 free), family A$51.50

RYE
THE DUNES GOLF LINKS
www.thedunes.com.au
One of the best public 18-hole courses in Victoria.
✉ Browns Road, Rye, VIC 3941 ☎ 03 5985 1334 ⏰ Daily dawn–dusk ✋ 9 holes: adult from A$40, juniors from A$20 🍽 🍸

SHEPHERDS FLAT
LAVANDULA
www.lavandula.com.au
Lavandula is a lavender farm that also includes gardens, a restaurant and farmyard animals. The shop carries a large range of home-grown lavender products, country-style goods, art and crafts, dried herbs and flowers.
✉ 350 Hepburn–Newstead Road, Shepherds Flat, VIC 3461 ☎ 03 5476 4393 ⏰ Sep–end May daily 10.30–5.30; Jun–end Aug Sat, Sun only 🍽 La Trattoria serves Swiss Italian cuisine

SORRENTO
POLPERRO DOLPHIN SWIMS
www.polperro.com.au
Watch or swim with bottlenose dolphins and seals in Port Phillip Bay.
✉ Sorrento Pier, Esplanade, Sorrento, VIC 3943 ☎ 03 5988 8437 ⏰ Oct–end Apr daily trips 8.30am and 1.30pm ✋ Dolphin watch: adult A$55, child A$35; dolphin swim: A$120

TORQUAY
ROXY
http://au/roxy.com
Torquay is the home of surfing in Victoria, and this surf shop sells Roxy brand clothes, swimwear, bodyboards and surfboards.
✉ Shop 5, Surf City Plaza, Torquay, VIC 3228 ☎ 03 5261 4768 ⏰ Daily 9–5.30

WESTCOAST SURF SCHOOL
www.westcoastsurfschool.com
Surfing tuition for all ages and abilities at Torquay, one of the country's best surfing locations.
✉ Voss's Car Park, Torquay, VIC 3228 ☎ 03 5261 2241 ⏰ Daily classes 10–12 in summer school holidays and Easter, or or demand ✋ Adult from A$55, child (under 16) from A$45

FESTIVALS AND EVENTS

JANUARY

AUSTRALIAN OPEN
www.ausopen.org
The Australian Open at Rod Laver Arena is one of the world's four Grand Slam tennis tournaments.

JANUARY OR FEBRUARY

CHINESE NEW YEAR FESTIVAL
www.visitmelbourne.com
Melbourne's Chinese community celebrates the Chinese New Year Festival in Little Bourke Street.

MARCH

AUSTRALIAN GRAND PRIX
www.grandprix.com.au
The Foster's Formula One Australian Grand Prix takes place on a street circuit at Albert Park, Melbourne.

PORT FAIRY FOLK FESTIVAL
www.portfairyfolkfestival.com
Port Fairy Folk Festival is the premier folk music event in Australia.

SUPERBIKE WORLD CHAMPIONSHIPS
www.phillipislandcircuit.com.au
The Superbike World Championships at Phillip Island Circuit is an international event, with many high-profile riders.

MELBOURNE INTERNATIONAL COMEDY FESTIVAL
www.comedyfestival.com.au
There are usually more than 200 different shows and over 2,000 performances at the Melbourne International Comedy Festival. It attracts performers and audiences from all around the world.

MARCH–APRIL

RIP CURL PRO
www.surfingaustralia.com
Each year the world's top-ranked surf riders carve up the waves at Bells Beach near Anglesea, southwest of Melbourne.

APRIL

MELBOURNE INTERNATIONAL FLOWER AND GARDEN SHOW
www.melbflowershow.com.au
The Melbourne International Flower and Garden Show at the Royal Exhibition Building has more than 300 exhibitors.

JULY–AUGUST

MELBOURNE INTERNATIONAL FILM FESTIVAL
www.melbournefilmfestival.com.au
The Melbourne International Film Festival presents work from filmmakers worldwide.

SEPTEMBER

ROYAL MELBOURNE SHOW
www.royalshow. com.au
The Royal Melbourne Show at Ascot Vale has animals and events, produce, arts and crafts, and live entertainment.

AFL GRAND FINAL
www.afl.com.au
AFL Grand Final fever reaches its pitch at the MCG.

SEPTEMBER–OCTOBER

MELBOURNE FRINGE FESTIVAL
www.melbournefringe.com.au
Celebrates the best arts fringe performers.

OCTOBER

MELBOURNE INTERNATIONAL ARTS FESTIVAL
www.melbournefestival.com.au
The Melbourne Festival has an outstanding reputation.

NOVEMBER

MELBOURNE CUP
www.vrc.net.au
The Melbourne Cup horse race is an extremely popular sporting and social event. It is run on the first Tuesday in November.

Left *Performers at the Melbourne Fringe Festival*

EATING

PRICES AND SYMBOLS

The restaurants are listed alphabetically (excluding Le, La and Les). The prices given are the average for a two-course lunch (L) and a three-course dinner (D) for one person, without drinks. The wine price is for the least expensive bottle.

For a key to the symbols, ▷ 2.

BALLARAT

THE BOATSHED RESTAURANT

www.ballarat.com/boatshed
Stop at this casual restaurant on the edge of Lake Wendouree for a quick bite or a sunset dinner. The international menu includes oysters, pasta, risottos and fish and chips.
✉ 27a Lake Wendouree Foreshore, Ballarat, VIC 3350 ☎ 03 5333 5533 🕐 Daily 7 am–late 🍴 Dishes A$20–A$30, D A$30–A$40, Wine A$20

L'ESPRESSO

www.ballarat.com/lespresso.htm
Italian-style café: home-made lunch favourites include an assortment of pastas, risottos and desserts. Extensive list of Australian wines.
✉ 417 Sturt Street, Ballarat, VIC 3350 ☎ 03 5333 1789 🕐 Daily 7am–6pm 🍴 L A$25, D A$45, Wine A$28

BEECHWORTH

THE BANK RESTAURANT

www.thebankrestaurant.com
Alfresco dining in the tree-lined, brick-paved courtyard is a feature in warmer weather, and accommodation is also available.
✉ 86 Ford Street, Beechworth, VIC 3747 ☎ 03 5728 2223 🕐 Daily 6.30–late, Sat, Sun 9.30–12 🍴 L A$26, D A$50, Wine A$21

BENDIGO

BAZZANI

www.bazzani-bendigo.com
The array of delights include stunning fresh food, gourmet treats, casual light lunches and regional wines, including wine from the Bazzani family label, Warrenmang.
✉ 2–4 Howard Place, Bendigo, VIC 3550 ☎ 03 5441 3777 🕐 Tue–Fri 12–3, 6–late, Sat 12–late, Sun 12–4 🍴 Set price lunch L A$25, D A$45, Wine from A$24

DAYLESFORD

LAKE HOUSE

www.lakehouse.com.au
The Lake House is one of Victoria's premier country hotels. The food has a French influence. Reservations are essential.
✉ King Street, Daylesford, VIC 3460 ☎ 03 5348 3329 🕐 Daily 8–11, 12–3, 7–9.30 🍴 L A$60, D A$75, Wine A$33

HEALESVILLE

HEALESVILLE HOTEL

www.healesvillehotel.com.au
There are light meals in the Harvest Bistro, and the more expensive restaurant serves Modern Australian food, including pasta from Healesville, local beef fillet or fresh salmon.
✉ 256 Maroondah Highway, Healesville, VIC 3777 ☎ 03 5962 4002 🕐 Daily 12–3, 6–9; bar meals 12–9 🍴 L A$50, D A$55; bar meals A$12–A$25, Wine A$27

MELBOURNE

ABLA

www.ablas.com.au
One of Melbourne's most popular restaurants—quality Lebanese cuisine and top value as well. Great for banquet-style get togethers—ask for the set price menu.
✉ 109 Elgin Street, Carlton, Melbourne, VIC 3053 ☎ 03 9347 0006 🕐 Thu, Fri 12–3, Mon–Sat 6–11 🍴 L A$33, D A$45 🚃 Tram along Swanston Street, from the city to Melbourne University and Lygon Street

Opposite *A kookaburra eyes up the menu at the Lake House in Daylesford*

BEAR BRASS
www.bearbrass.com.au
An international menu includes snacks such as Turkish bread and dips, pizza and meals of spiced chorizo sausages or grilled *saganaki* with dried prosciutto.
✉ Shop 3A, River Level, Southgate Complex, Southbank, VIC 3006 ☎ 03 9682 3799 🕐 Mon–Fri 8am–late, Sat, Sun 9am–late 🍴 B A$15, L A$25, D A$35, Wine A$24 🚋 Tram down Swanston Street to Princes Bridge, then boardwalk to Southgate

CAFÉ DI STASIO
www.distasio.com.au
The menu in this Italian restaurant includes saltimbocca, carpaccio and, of course, a range of pasta. Reservations advised.
✉ 31 Fitzroy Street, St. Kilda, Melbourne, VIC 3182 ☎ 03 9525 3999 🕐 Daily 12–3, 6–11 🍴 Set lunch A$35, D A$85, Wine A$33 🚋 Tram 16, 96

CECCONI'S CANTINA
This classy restaurant serves up pasta, risotto, ossobuco, rabbit and many other Italian classics. Don't miss the tiramisù for dessert. The wine list is long, but expensive. Reservations advised.
✉ 61 Flinders Lane, Southgate, Melbourne, VIC 3006 ☎ 03 9663 0222 🕐 Mon–Fri 12–3.30, Mon–Sat 6–10.30 🍴 L A$50, D A$65, Wine A$40 🚋 Tram along Flinders Street to Exhibition Street

ESPOSITO AT TOOFEY'S
Chef Maurice Esposito has drawn from his Italian heritage to create one of Melbourne's finest dining experiences in this city-fringe restaurant with a menu strong on seafood.
✉ 162 Elgin Street, Carlton, VIC 3053 ☎ 03 9347 9838 🕐 Mon–Fri 12–3, Mon–Sat 6–10 🍴 L A$55, D A$70, Wine A$32

FEDDISH BAR & GRILL
www.feddish.com.au
With three different dining areas and a large terrace, the Modern Australian menu here includes Asian and Italian dishes, as well as a good range of meat, chicken and vegetarian offerings.
✉ River Terrace, Federation Square, Melbourne, VIC 3000 ☎ 03 9654 5855 🕐 Tue–Thu 12–11pm, Fri, Sat 12pm–1am, Sun 12–11 🍴 L A$45, D A$55, Wine A$34

FRANCE-SOIR
www.france-soir.com.au
The menu is classic French bistro, offering everything from onion soup to *escargots*, to *steak frites* and *boeuf bourguignon*. Reservations are essential.
✉ 11 Toorak Road, South Yarra, Melbourne, VIC 3141 ☎ 03 9866 8569 🕐 Daily 12–3, 6–12 🍴 L A$50, D A$75, Wine A$27 🚋 Tram 8 from Flinders Street Station in the city to Toorak 🚉 From Flinders Street to South Yarra

GROSSI FLORENTINO
www.grossiflorentino.com.au
The grandest of Melbourne's formal restaurants, it is renowned for its exemplary Tuscan food. Favourites include suckling lamb, and their signature chocolate soufflé. The Florentino Grill is a stylish bistro, and the adjacent Cellar Bar serves inexpensive pasta. Reservations are essential for Florentino's Mural Room, the Wynn Room and the Grill.
✉ 80 Bourke Street, Melbourne, VIC 3000 ☎ 03 9662 1811 🕐 Florentino's: Mon–Sat 12–3, 6–11 🍴 Florentino's: L A$85, D A$125, set menu (eight courses plus coffee) A$195 per person, Wine A$38 🕐 The Grill: Mon–Sat 12–3, 6–11 🍴 The Grill: L A$60, D A$75 🕐 Cellar Bar: Mon–Sat 7.30am–1am 🍴 Cellar Bar: L A$25 🚋 Any tram up Bourke Street, including the 96 light-rail tram from St. Kilda, or free City Circle tram to Parliament House 🚉 Parliament

HOPETOUN TEA ROOMS
The Victorian tea rooms have refreshed shoppers for more than a century. Afternoon teas include savoury sandwiches and delicious cakes. More substantial light meals include pasta and pizzas.
✉ Shops 1 & 2 Block Arcade, 282 Collins Street, Melbourne, VIC 3000 ☎ 03 9650 2777 🕐 Mon–Thu 9–4.30, Fri 9–5.30, Sat 10–3.30 🍴 Light meals A$7–A$14 🚋 Tram up Bourke Street 🚉 Flinders Street

THE ITALIAN
www.theitalian.com.au
This sophisticated restaurant pays great attention to detail. The classic Italian menu offers delicious pastas, risottos, and innovative mains such as roast duck with grapes.
✉ 101 Collins Street, Melbourne, VIC 3000 ☎ 03 9654 9499 🕐 Mon–Fri 12–3.30, Mon–Sat 6–11 🍴 L A$40, D A$70, Wine A$33 🚋 48 or 70, to corner of Exhibition and Flinders streets

JACQUES REYMOND RESTAURANT
www.jacquesreymond.com.au
Jacques Reymond's excellent international flavours are achieved by a combination of the best ingredients and classic French techniques. There is a *dégustation* menu, and good vegetarian options.
✉ 78 Williams Road, Prahran, Melbourne, VIC 3181 ☎ 03 9525 2178 🕐 Thu, Fri 12–2, Tue–Sat 6.30–10 🍴 L A$48 (set price), D A$98, Wine A$45 🚉 Prahran then 1.5km (1-mile) walk

JIMMY WATSON'S WINE BAR & RESTAURANT
The place to go for local and imported wines (and share opened bottles). Sit and enjoy a glass of wine, eat a casual lunch, or enjoy a dinner of modern European fare.
✉ 333 Lygon Street, Carlton, Melbourne, VIC 3053 ☎ 03 9347 3985 🕐 Mon–Sat 12–2.30, Tue–Sat 6–9.30 🍴 L A$45, D A$55, Wine A$36 🚋 200 or 201 from Russell Street along Lygon Street. Tram along Swanston Street from the city to Melbourne University

JOE'S GARAGE
www.joesgarage.net.au
Bright, loud and hip, the menu, like the atmosphere, is casual and runs from breakfast through to late-night snacks. The crowds are often huge. Quick, noisy but enjoyable. Evening reservations accepted.
✉ 366 Brunswick Street, Fitzroy,

SPIRIT OF INDIA
www.spiritofindiamelbourne.com
This mid-range, friendly restaurant is popular with the locals. The menu has an extensive range of mains and entrées, including lamb, prawn and fish tandoori dishes. Be sure to try the hot lamb curry.
✉ 401–403 Clarendon Street, South Melbourne, VIC 3205 ☎ 03 9682 6696 🕒 Thu–Fri 12–2.30, daily 5.30–11 ✋ L, D A$26 🚊 Tram 112 to Park and Clarendon streets

STALACTITES
www.stalactites.com.au
The relaxed atmosphere, central location, delicious authentic Greek cuisine and reasonable prices will appeal to families holidaying near the city. Can be crowded in the early evening.
✉ 177–183 Lonsdale Street, Melbourne, VIC 3000 ☎ 03 9663 3316 🕒 Daily 24 hours ✋ L $A25, D A$35 🚊 Tram along Lonsdale Street to Russell Street

THE STOKEHOUSE
www.stokehouse.com.au
A casual drop-in café and bistro downstairs, with a more classy and expensive dining room upstairs, a favourite in showbiz circles. Reservations advised, especially for upstairs.
✉ 30 Jacka Boulevard, St. Kilda, Melbourne, VIC 3182 ☎ 03 9525 5555 🕒 Dining room: daily 12–2.30, 6–10. Café: Mon–Fri 12–late, Sat, Sun 11–late ✋ L A$55, D A$75, Wine A$30 🚊 St. Kilda light-rail tram 96 down Bourke Street from the city to the Esplanade near the pier and Acland Street

THY THY 1
This is one of the local Vietnamese community's favourite restaurants. A mixed clientele dine at the paper-covered tables. They are all here for the fresh, yet budget-cheap food. Busy, noisy, quick and fun. BYO.
✉ Level 1, 142 Victoria Street, Richmond, Melbourne, VIC 3121 ☎ 03 9429 1104 🕒 Daily 8am–10pm ✋ L A$15, D A$25 🚊 42 Mont Albert tram from Collins Street

---

Melbourne, VIC 3065 ☎ 03 9419 9944 🕒 Daily 7.30am–1am ✋ L A$25, D A$35, Wine A$24, BYO corkage A$2.50 per person 🚊 Light-rail tram 109 up Collins Street and along Brunswick Street; get off after Johnson Street stop

KRI KRI MEZETHOPOLEION
www.krikri.com.au
Diners at this casual but interesting little Greek restaurant can share small *mezze* dishes. Main dishes include *dolmades*, white beans in tomatoes, eggplant (aubergine) baked with feta and olives, and *saganaki*. Reserve ahead.
✉ 39–41 Little Bourke Street, Melbourne, VIC 3000 ☎ 03 9639 3444 🕒 Tue–Fri 12–3, Mon–Sat 5–11 ✋ L A$30, D A$40, Wine A$21 🚊 Any tram up Bourke Street to Exhibition Street

LEMONGRASS
www.lemongrassrestaurant.com.au
Not the cheapest Thai restaurant, Lemongrass has a menu based on ancient Siam recipes. Along with the standard curries, there are more unusual dishes, such as *poo ja* (stuffed blue swimmer crab) and a green papaya salad. Reserve ahead.
✉ 176 Lygon Street, Carlton, Melbourne, VIC 3053 ☎ 03 9662 2244 🕒 Mon–Fri 12–3, Mon–Sun 5.30–late ✋ L A$35, D A$53, Wine A$28 🚊 200 or 201 from Russell Street, City, along Lygon Street. Tram along Swanston Street from the city to Melbourne University, stop at Queensberry Street or Grattan Street

THE NUDEL BAR
A busy, lively eatery, with casual, counter seating downstairs and tables upstairs. Noodle dishes, pasta and soups are served. The wine list is limited but changes often.
✉ 76 Bourke Street, Melbourne, VIC 3000 ☎ 03 9662 9100 🕒 Mon–Sat 11am–10.30pm ✋ Dishes from A$15–A$28 🚊 Any tram up Bourke Street

THE OXFORD SCHOLAR HOTEL
This 1887 pub in the heart of the city has 14 beers on tap, a beer garden, pool tables, juke box and large TV screens for sports fans. Specials include fish or risotto dishes, and delicious home-made hamburgers and pies.
✉ 427 Swanston Street, Melbourne, VIC 3000 ☎ 03 9663 1619 🕒 Mon–Fri 10am–late ✋ L, D $24, Wine $18 🚊 Tram up Swanston Street to Latrobe Street 🚉 Melbourne Central Station (Swanston Street exit)

RICHMOND HILL CAFÉ AND LARDER
www.rhcl.com.au
Light meals are available all day at this casual, welcoming café and cheese shop. The Mediterranean food is excellent and wines are available by the glass.
✉ 48–50 Bridge Road, Richmond, Melbourne, VIC 3121 ☎ 03 9421 2808 🕒 Daily 8.30–5 ✋ Dishes A$19–A$30, Wine A$8 per glass 🚉 West Richmond 🚊 2km (1.5 miles) east from the city

VLADO'S

This is one of Melbourne's favourite restaurants and a temple for meat-lovers. The set four-course meal can include a mixed grill meat platter, various sizes of steak, finishing off with a filling dessert.

✉ 61 Bridge Road, Richmond, Melbourne, VIC 3121 ☎ 03 9428 5833 🕐 Mon–Fri 12–3.30, 6–11, Sat 6–11 🖐 Set menu A$84 (four courses and coffee), Wine A$29 🚊 Tram down Flinders Street and along Bridge Road

WALTER'S WINE BAR

www.walterswinebar.com.au

With one of the city's best wine cellars, in the Southgate complex next to The Arts Centre, this is a perfect place for a drink or snack before or after a show. It's a favourite haunt of actors, where late evening meals are served. The views of the Yarra River and the Melbourne skyline are stunning.

✉ Upper level 3, Shop 1, Southgate, Southbank, Melbourne, VIC 3006 ☎ 03 9690 9211 🕐 Daily 8am–late 🖐 L A$45, D A$65, Wine A$35 🚊 Any tram down Swanston Street to the Victorian Arts Centre stop 🚆 Flinders Street then walk across bridge to Southgate

MILAWA
THE EPICUREAN CENTRE

www.brown-brothers.com.au

At the Brown Brothers winery, the menu is strong on the best local ingredients, changing seasonally to reflect availability.

✉ Brown Brothers Vineyard, Bobinawarrah Road, Milawa, VIC 3678 ☎ 03 5720 5540 🕐 Daily 11–3 🖐 L A$60, Wine A$29 🚊 Northeast Victoria, 64km (40 miles) south from Rutherglen

MILDURA
STEFANO'S

www.stefano.com.au

A set-price, five-course meal at Stefano's uses only seasonal local produce for Italian-inspired recipes. The café/bakery sells sandwiches and pastries. Reservations are advised.

✉ Longtree Avenue, Mildura, VIC 3500 ☎ 03 5023 0511 🕐 Stefano's: Mon–Sat 7–late 🖐 Stefano's 5-course dinner A$85

🕐 Café/bakery daily 9–3 🚊 In the far northwest of Victoria, 400km (248 miles) east from Adelaide, 295km (183 miles) south from Broken Hill

MORNINGTON PENINSULA
MAX'S AT RED HILL ESTATE

www.redhillestate.com.au

The menu is a spectrum of international and Asian influences, using the best local produce, such as Flinders mussels poached in a Red Hill Estate Chardonnay cream sauce. Each meal is matched with glasses of Red Hill Estate wines. Reservations are advised.

✉ Red Hill Estate Winery, 53 Red Hill–Shoreham Road, Red Hill South, VIC 3937 ☎ 03 5931 0177 🕐 Daily 12–5, Fri, Sat 7–late (also Thu Nov–Easter) 🖐 L A$48, D A$65, Wine A$26

SORRENTO
THE BATHS

The menu, covering breakfast through to dinner, is Asian and Mediterranean, with generous portions and well-priced wines. There is a fish and chips outlet at the back. Reserve ahead.

✉ 3278 Point Nepean Road, Sorrento, VIC 3943 ☎ 03 5984 1500 🕐 Daily 9am–late 🖐 L A$45, D A$55, Wine A$26 🚊 39km (24 miles) southwest from Mornington, on the western tip of the Mornington Peninsula

PHILLIP ISLAND
HARRY'S ON THE ESPLANADE

www.harrysrestaurant.com.au

A European bistro specializing in fresh seasonal produce, seafood and prime meats. Also a patisserie that makes its own breads, pastries and ice cream, which are all on the bistro menu.

✉ 17 The Esplanade, Cowes, Phillip Island, VIC 3922 ☎ 03 5952 6226 🕐 Tue–Sun 12–3, 6–9 🖐 L A$40, D A$50, Wine A23

MADCOWES

Casual dining takes a gourmet turn at this sunny waterfront café, which takes its inspiration from the Asian and Middle Eastern cookbooks.

✉ 17 The Esplanade, Cowes, VIC 3922 ☎ 03 5952 2560 🕐 Mon–Fri 8–4, Sat, Sun 7–4 🖐 L A$25

QUEENSCLIFF
VUE GRAND HOTEL

www.vuegrand.com.au

The imposing 1881 Vue Grand Hotel has a grand dining room where you can enjoy excellent French food accompanied by Bellarine Peninsula wines. This is a restaurant for a special occasion.

✉ 46 Hesse Street, Queenscliff, VIC 3225 ☎ 03 5258 1544 🕐 Wed–Sun 6–10.30 🖐 L A$45, D A$75, Wine A$32

WARRNAMBOOL
PIPPIES BY THE BAY

www.pippiesbythebay.com.au

Open for breakfast, lunch and dinner, this restaurant serves imaginative Modern Australian cuisine with Italian influences. The seafood is recommended; seasonal ingredients are used.

✉ Flagstaff Hill, 23 Merri Street, Warrnambool, VIC 3280 ☎ 03 5561 2188 🕐 Daily 10am–late 🖐 L A$40, D A$60, Wine A$32

YARRA VALLEY
LOCALE RESTAURANT

www.debortoli.com.au

Part of the De Bortoli Yarra Valley vineyard and winery complex, this restaurant concentrates on northern Italian cuisine, made with fresh regional ingredients. On Sundays try the five-course 'Italian Family Feast' lunch. Reservations are recommended.

✉ De Bortoli Winery, 58 Pinnacle Lane, Dixons Creek, VIC 3775 ☎ 03 5965 2271 🕐 Thu–Mon 12–3, Sat from 7pm 🖐 L A$45, A$60 for the Italian Family Feast, D A$65, Wine A$25

YERING STATION RESTAURANT

Yering Station's wine bar and restaurant is in an elegant sandstone and glass building. The menu changes seasonally, with many of the fresh ingredients sourced locally; the cuisine is Modern Australian with Asian and French touches. Yering Station wines are available.

✉ 38 Melba Highway, Yering, VIC 3775 ☎ 03 9730 1107 🕐 Daily 10–5 🖐 L A$45, Wine A$24 🚊 3km (2 miles) south from Yarra Glen in the Yarra Valley

STAYING

PRICES AND SYMBOLS

Prices are for a double room for one night including breakfast, unless otherwise stated. All the hotels listed accept credit cards, unless otherwise stated. Note that rates can vary widely throughout the year.

For a key to the symbols, ▷ 2.

BALLARAT
THE ANSONIA

www.theansonianlydiard.com.au
This boutique hotel has 20 guest suites, ranging from studios to suites, family rooms and an apartment. The restaurant serves breakfast, lunch and dinner.
✉ 32 Lydiard Street South, Ballarat, VIC 3350 ☎ 03 5332 4678 ⊕ All year
✋ A$165–A$275 excluding breakfast
ⓘ 20 🚉 Ballarat

DAYLESFORD
THE LAKE HOUSE

www.lakehouse.com.au
This lakeside hotel is famous as a food destination, where owners

Alla and Allan Wolf-Tasker continue to refine and redefine the cuisine of Victoria's spa region with a menu that revels in the fresh local produce, much of it sourced from small producers. Rooms come in several different styles and the best are the vast and well-tailored Waterfront Suites.
✉ King Street, Daylesford, VIC 3460
☎ 03 5348 3329 ⊕ All year
✋ A$500–A$740 ⓘ 33

GREAT OCEAN ROAD
CUMBERLAND LORNE RESORT

www.cumberland.com.au
These self-contained, comfortable apartments have either one or two bedrooms, a spa bath, private balcony, kitchen and laundry. Restaurant and bar; guest facilities include an indoor pool, tennis courts, gym and games room.
✉ 150 Mountjoy Parade, Lorne, VIC 3232
☎ 03 5289 2400, 1800 037 010 ⊕ All year ✋ A$265–A$430 excluding breakfast
ⓘ 99 🅢 🏊 Indoor 🌀

MELBOURNE
THE COMO MELBOURNE

www.mirvachotels.com
In luxurious surroundings there are one- and two-bedroom suites, penthouses and studios. Facilities include a gymnasium, covered swimming pool, sun deck, and a bar. The Brasserie serves breakfast.
✉ 630 Chapel Street, South Yarra, VIC 3141 ☎ 03 9825 2222, 1800 033 400
⊕ All year ✋ A$315–A$1,150 ⓘ 107
🅢 🏊 Indoor heated 🌀 🚌 Any tram down Toorak Road to South Yarra
🚉 South Yarra then tram 🚌 Along Alexandra Avenue on south side of Yarra River, right at Chapel Street

GEORGIAN COURT

www.georgiancourt.com.au
An inexpensive bed-and-breakfast with single, double, triple and family rooms; some share bathrooms.
✉ 21–25 George Street, East Melbourne, VIC 3002 ☎ 03 9419 6353 ⊕ All year
✋ A$120–A$160 ⓘ 12 🅢 🚌 Bus 246 down Hoddle Street

Opposite *Rooms at The Queenscliff Hotel have historic charm*

HILTON ON THE PARK
www.melbourne.hilton.com
All the large bedrooms have private bathrooms. There is an excellent restaurant, a fully equipped day spa with treatment rooms, a wedding chapel, an Aussie pub and a gaming room.
✉ 192 Wellington Parade, East Melbourne, VIC 3002 ☎ 03 9419 2000 🌐 All year ✋ A$245–A$405 ⓘ 404 🏊 Outdoor heated 🔗 🔧 🚃 Trams 48 or 75 from Flinders Street 🚉 Jolimont

THE LYALL
www.thelyall.com
Small, serene and friendly, this urbane refuge is favoured by the famous. Rooms come in several configurations and the muted olive and yellow accents evoke a modern oriental design. The Lyall is strong on the homely touches, and most suites have a kitchen and clothes washer/dryer and ironing board.
✉ 14 Murphy Street, South Yarra, VIC 3141 ☎ 03 9868 8222 🌐 All year ✋ A$425–A$845 ⓘ 40

MAGNOLIA COURT BOUTIQUE HOTEL
www.magnolia-court.com.au
A family-run boutique hotel with its own breakfast café. Rooms range from a luxury self-contained apartment to compact units.
✉ 101 Powlett Street, East Melbourne, VIC 3002 ☎ 03 9419 4222 🌐 All year ✋ A$160–A$300 ⓘ 27 🔗 🚃 Trams 48 or 75 from Flinders Street 🚉 Jolimont

THE MANSION HOTEL AT WERRIBEE PARK
www.mansionhotel.com.au
The hotel has contemporary guest rooms and suites with their own bathrooms. Facilities include a fitness centre and spa, beauty treatments, gymnasium, tennis courts, library, snooker room and Joseph's Restaurant.
✉ K Road, Werribee, VIC 3030 ☎ 03 731 4000 🌐 All year ✋ A$239–A$339 excluding breakfast ⓘ 92 🏊 Indoor 🔧

🚗 30km (19 miles) southwest from city on Princes Freeway over Westgate Bridge to Werribee Park

ROBINSONS IN THE CITY
www.robinsonsinthecity.com.au
The only B&B accommodation in central Melbourne. All the rooms have bathrooms. The home-cooked breakfast is a special treat.
✉ 405 Spencer Street, Melbourne, VIC 3003 ☎ 03 9329 2552 🌐 All year; reception 5.30am–late ✋ A$155–A$240 ⓘ 6 🔗 Most rooms 🚃 City Circle tram to cnr Latrobe and Spencer streets

THE SEBEL MELBOURNE
www.mirvachotels.com.au
The hotel has spacious studios and self-contained suites, the latter with living and dining areas, business desks, kitchenette and laundry. The loft suites have spa baths. Also try the Treasury Restaurant.
✉ 394 Collins Street, Melbourne, VIC 3000 ☎ 03 9211 6600, 1800 500 778 🌐 All year ✋ A$240–A$615 ⓘ 115 🔗 🚃 Any tram along Collins Street

THE HOTEL WINDSOR
www.thehotelwindsor.com.au
Built in 1883, and one of the Oberoi chain of hotels, it combines Victorian opulence with modern comforts and facilities. The restaurant and cocktail bar, One Eleven Spring Street, is famous for its traditional afternoon teas. Particularly splendid is the Grand Ballroom where special functions are held.
✉ 111 Spring Street, Melbourne, VIC 3000 ☎ 03 9633 6000, 1800 033 100 🌐 All year ✋ A$385–A$2,250; cheaper packages available ⓘ 180 🔗 🚃 City Circle tram

MORNINGTON PENINSULA
CAPE SCHANCK RESORT
www.racv.com.au/capeschanck
The resort's Ocean View Suites have a cozy, contemporary decor and they're a bargain, especially the two- and three-bedroom villas. This is a golf resort and the 18-hole course designed by US golf course architect Robert Trent Jones, Jr. is challenging and exhilarating.

✉ Trent Jones Drive, Cape Schanck, VIC 3939 ☎ 03 5950 8000 🌐 All year ✋ A$200–A$350 ⓘ 63

MILDURA
QUALITY HOTEL MILDURA GRAND
www.qualityhotelmilduragrand.com.au
Rooms to suit all budgets and tastes, from presidential suites to older, renovated rooms (all with private bathroom). Facilities include Stefano's restaurant (▷ 165), gymnasium, spa and sauna.
✉ Seventh Street, Mildura, VIC 3500 ☎ 03 5023 0511, 1800 034 228 🌐 All year ✋ A$110–A$400 ⓘ 102 🔗 🔧 🏊 Heated outdoor

POREPUNKAH
ALPINE PARK COTTAGES
www.alpineparkcottages.com.au
These fully self-contained cottages, set in beautiful parklands along the Ovens River, are at the foot of Mt Buffalo. They are ideal for fishing, swimming, canoeing or just relaxing. Only 45 minutes to the ski fields in winter.
✉ Great Alpine Road, Porepunkah, VIC 3740 ☎ 03 5756 2334 🌐 All year ✋ A$110–A$140 ⓘ 6 cottages 🚉 🚉 Train to Wangaratta, then bus to Alpine Park 🚌 Turn off from the Hume Highway at Wangaratta for Great Alpine Road

QUEENSCLIFF
THE QUEENSCLIFF HOTEL
www.queenscliffhotel.com.au
Built in 1887 for wealthy Victorian society, the hotel has retained its period feel. There are several sitting rooms with high ceilings, three dining areas and a bar. The bedrooms are small but most rooms look over the parkland facing on to Port Phillip Bay. The conservatory dining area is formal, while the Courtyard Restaurant is more casual.
✉ 16 Gellibrand Street, Queenscliff, VIC 3225 ☎ 03 5258 1066 🌐 All year ✋ A$195–A$240 ⓘ 18 🚌 Regular buses from Geelong 🚗 31km (19 miles) southeast from Geelong on Bellarine Highway (B110)

QUEENSLAND

Big, bold, brash and beautiful, Queensland is the tropical state, home to palm-fringed coral islands, sugar cane and mango plantations, crocodile-infested rivers and primeval rainforests where flowering plants first appeared on the planet. Together with Western Australia, Queensland is also one of the engine rooms of the Australian economy, the source of the mining boom that is feeding the blast furnaces and the power stations of China, and which drives Australia's prosperity into the 21st century.

The capital, Brisbane, is a thrusting, go-ahead city with a population approaching two million. It's essentially a modern city with a character that will be familiar to most visitors from Europe and North America. Most visitors come to Queensland for its coastal pleasures. To the south of Brisbane is the Gold Coast, a major holiday zone, where high-rise condominium towers overshadow the beach. North of Brisbane is the Sunshine Coast, melding glorious beaches with resorts, boutiques and smart cafés in a cocktail that attracts many Australians in search of a glamorous holiday. To the west of both these regions is a lush, undulating hinterland of rainforests, tropical fruit plantations, national parks and quirky country towns.

Most visitors from overseas come to Queensland for a single reason, the Great Barrier Reef, which stretches for more than 2,000km (1,240 miles) along the Queensland coast, the world's largest coral reef system. This is one of nature's most dazzling creations. The moment you first put on a snorkel and face mask, plunge into the water and lie suspended on the surface as fish swarm around, you're in a kaleidoscope of pin stripes, polka dots, rainbows and neon colours that you'll never forget. Access is easy via any of a number of Queensland coastal towns and islands, and tourism operators offer a huge array of underwater experiences.

ATHERTON TABLELAND

www.athertontableland.com

A refreshing change from busy Cairns, this upland region, lying between the Bellenden Ker Range and the Great Dividing Range, is cooler and much less humid than the coast. Atherton is the main town. The fertile soils are the result of volcanic activity, which also gave the Tableland its wealth of natural attractions, including the crater lakes Eacham and Barrine near Yungaburra, Mount Hypipamee Crater, hundreds of waterfalls, and the rainforests of the Wet Tropics World Heritage Area.

In the north, Kuranda bustles with a large daily market (9–5). Barron Gorge National Park adjoins the town; the Barron River is impressive after wet-season rain. The information office at Malanda explains the region's volcanic past. Stop in the township for crafts and a drink at the classic old wooden pub. Malanda also has Australia's only tropical dairy, the Malanda Dairy Centre (daily 9–4; tel 07 4095 234). The Malanda Falls trail is a short rainforest walk, and the Millaa Millaa waterfall circuit from Malanda takes you past three waterfalls in rainforests. The historic village of Yungaburra has a monthly market (fourth Saturday of the month 7–1), restaurants and craft shops. Watch out for the Curtain Fig tree, near Yungaburra, which has a huge drape of aerial roots.

🚩 348 T4 🚹 Kuranda Information Centre, Kennedy Highway, Kuranda, QLD 4872 ☎ 07 4093 9311 🚹 Malanda Falls Visitor Centre, Atherton Road, Malanda, QLD 4885 ☎ 07 4096 6957 🚹 Cairns. Kuranda Scenic Railway departs Cairns daily, tel 07 4036 9333. Skyrail cableway from Smithfield to Kuranda, tel 07 4038 1555

BRISBANE
▷ 172–176.

BUNYA MOUNTAINS NATIONAL PARK

www.epa.gov.au

This remote park protects the world's last major stand of bunya pines. All routes to the mountains are steep; caravans and trailers are not recommended. The mountains were formed over 30 million years ago, and the various soils support many types of rainforest, the densest dominated by bunya pines. There are 40km (25 miles) of trails; a good starting point is the Danabah picnic ground. The most popular route is the Scenic circuit track, which features a huge strangler fig (the Festoon), Tim Shea Falls and the Pine Gorge Lookout.

🚩 353 W9 🚹 Bunya Mountains National Park Information Centre, 57 Bunya Avenue, Bunya, QLD 4055 ☎ 07 4668 3127 🕐 Daily 8–4; Park daily 24 hours 🖐 Free 🍴 🍽 🏛

CAIRNS
▷ 177–178.

CAPE YORK PENINSULA

www.naturespowerhouse..com.au

The huge expanse of wilderness that occupies the northern point of Australia requires weeks to see. But a day's drive (via the inland route) from Cairns to Cooktown will take you through the southern part, an adventure in itself. Much of the journey to Cooktown is through sparse woodlands with termite mounds and dry creeks. In some places this changes to rainforest and coastal wetlands. A self-drive 4WD vehicle tour starts from Cairns or Mareeba and proceeds via Mount Molloy, Lakeland and Black Mountain to Cooktown. Take a side trip from Lakeland to Laura to visit the Split Rock Gallery with its Aboriginal rock art. Farther on, the Lakefield National Park has broad flood plains where waterholes attract prolific bird life.

Cooktown retains many of its late 19th-century buildings, when it was the coastal port for the Palmer River goldfields. The James Cook Historical Museum has relics from Cook's *Endeavour*, which was beached near here in 1770 (Mon–Sat 10–4). Chillagoe, inland from Cairns, is renowned for the nearby limestone outcrops and the extensive cave systems protected within Chillagoe-Mungana Caves National Park.

Above *Carnarvon National Park is within the Great Dividing Range*
Opposite *Millaa Millaa Falls are in the Atherton Tableland*

🚩 343 R2 🚹 Nature's Powerhouse, Botanic Gardens, Cooktown, QLD 4871 ☎ 07 4069 6004 🕐 Daily 9–5

CARNARVON NATIONAL PARK

www.carnarvongorge.com

Carnarvon Gorge is one of a series of inaccessible gorges that make up the spectacular Carnarvon National Park. Because of its isolation, the place is not crowded and it's best to visit during the cooler months from April to the end of October. Among the impressive features of the sandstone gorge are the Moss Garden, a hollow filled with tree ferns, and the Amphitheatre, where two fault lines have formed a giant cavern. There is also a rock art gallery, which has one of Queensland's finest displays of Aboriginal rock art.

🚩 350 V8 🚹 Visitor Centre, Carnarvon National Park, Carnarvon Gorge ☎ 07 4984 4505 🕐 Daily 8–5; Park daily 24 hours 🖐 Free 🍽 🏛

BRISBANE

INFORMATION

www.visitbrisbane.com.au

🛈 Queen Street Mall Information Centre, Queen Street Mall ☎ 07 3006 6290 🕓 Mon–Fri 9–5.30, Sat 9–5, Sun 9.30–4.30

INTRODUCTION

With its leisurely subtropical ambience, spacious botanic gardens and bustling city centre, Brisbane is regularly voted as one of the world's most liveable cities. The city, founded along the banks of the winding Brisbane River in 1824, when a penal colony was established on nearby Moreton Island, is now Australia's third-largest. Be sure to visit Mount Coot-tha to get your bearings before visiting Brisbane's main attractions. The central districts, such as Paddington and Milton, with their distinctive timber buildings, offer fabulous specialty shopping, great old pubs, and excellent restaurants, while multicultural Fortitude Valley is great for dining and nightlife. Later you can relax on one of the River City Cruises or CityCat Ferries. A daily ticket will let you ride the ferries, buses and trains all day for a set price according to zone.

WHAT TO SEE

BRISBANE BOTANIC GARDENS—MOUNT COOT-THA

www.brisbane.qld.gov.au

At the foot of Mount Coot-tha, 8km (5 miles) west of the city, this subtropical botanic garden covers 52ha (128 acres) and is home to 25,000 plants. Themed sections include a scented garden and an arid zone, while cascades and waterfalls weave through rainforest terraces. Make sure that you visit the Tropical Dome, a geodesic-domed greenhouse containing an impressive range of tropical plants. The Japanese Garden and the Bonsai House are both excellent. Also within the gardens is the Cosmic Skydome and Planetarium, where images of the southern hemisphere's night sky are projected on to a large domed ceiling.

✚ Off map 175 A1 ✉ Western Freeway Route 5, Toowong, QLD 4066 ☎ 07 3403 2531 (Mon–Fri 8–4.30) 🕓 Gardens: 5 Apr–end Aug daily 8–5.30. Tropical Dome: daily 9.30–4. Bonsai House: Mon–Fri 10–12, 1–3, Sat, Sun 10–3. Planetarium: Tue–Sun 11.30–2 👋 Free 🚌 471 from Adelaide Street 🚹 🏛

CITY BOTANIC GARDENS

www.brisbane.qld.gov.au

One of Brisbane's most popular free attractions, the City Botanic Gardens are among the loveliest parks in the state capital. The area was first cleared by

Above *Brisbane's cityscape is reflected in the waters of the Brisbane River*

onvict workers in 1828 to grow crops for the infant town of Brisbane. The first
f the present gardens was created in 1855 for experimental plantings used to
evelop colonial agriculture.

⊞ 175 C2 ✉ Alice Street, Brisbane, QLD 4000 ☎ 07 3403 0666 🕓 Daily 24 hours ✋ Free
🚌 City Sights bus, alight at QUT stop ▢

CUSTOMS HOUSE

www.customshouse.com.au

he Customs House is the home of the Stuartholme Behan Collection of
ustralian Art. Dr. Norman Behan's collection was assembled over 40 years
nd comprises more than 100 works dating back to 1788. Prominent Australian
rtists represented include Impressionists Tom Roberts, George Lambert,
rederick McCubbin, Rupert Bunny and Arthur Streeton. The domed Victorian
uilding was opened in 1889 in what was a bustling waterfront area. It served as
he city's Customs House for almost a century before the port moved closer to
he mouth of the Brisbane River.

⊞ 175 C1 ✉ 399 Queen Street, Brisbane, QLD 4000 ☎ 07 3365 8999 🕓 Daily 10–4; free
uided tours Sun 10–4 ✋ Free 🚌 City Sights bus, alight Telstra House ⛴ CityCat stop at the
iverside Centre 🍴 🏛

FORTITUDE VALLEY

www.brisbanetourism.com.au

nown locally as 'The Valley', this is Brisbane's liveliest and most multicultural
uburb. Some of Brisbane's best nightspots and pubs are here, and at night
he Valley is a popular place for entertainment and ethnic dining. Brunswick
treet is the Valley's main thoroughfare, a 10-minute walk north of the Queen
treet Mall. It is lined with bars, cafés, restaurants, cinemas and galleries. The
cWhirters Building, a graceful old emporium, continues as an indoor market.
earby Chinatown Mall is where you'll find some of the city's best Asian
uisine. The park has playgrounds, flowerbeds, and a theatre and performance
pace, the Powerhouse.

⊞ Off map 175 C1 ℹ Queen Street Mall ☎ 07 3229 5918 🚉 Brunswick Street

ONE PINE KOALA SANCTUARY

www.koala.net

f you want to hold a koala, feed kangaroos, emus and lorikeets, and learn about
ther native fauna, this is the place. It also shelters wombats in their hollow log
omes, Tasmanian devils and the flightless cassowary. Enjoy the sanctuary's
0ha (50 acres) alongside the Brisbane River.

⊞ Off map 175 A1 ✉ Jesmond Road, Fig Tree Pocket, QLD 4069 ☎ 07 3378 1366 🕓 Daily
30–5 ✋ Adult A$28, child A$19, family A$65 🚌 445, 430 ⛴ Mirimar boat cruise departs
orth Quay; tel 07 3221 0300 ▢ 🏛

MORETON ISLAND

www.epa.qld.gov.au and www.tangalooma.com

opular with day trippers from Brisbane, Moreton Island is a coastal wilderness
xperience within easy reach of the city. The 19,000ha (46,930-acre) island is
irtually all national park. Flora include eucalypts, banksias and heathland, while
reshwater lakes and wetlands support more than 180 bird species. Whales
nigrate along the coast between July and late October. The scenery is stunning
nd there are long, empty beaches. Access is by a 75-minute ferry trip. The only
neans of travel on the island is by all-terrain vehicle. Permits for island access
nd camping are available from ferry operators and national park officers. You can
and-feed dolphins at the Tangalooma Wild Dolphin Resort.

⊞ 353 X9 ℹ Moreton Island Recreation Area, Tangalooma, QLD 4025 ☎ 07 3408 2710
🚤 From Scarborough: Combie Trader Ferry, tel 07 3203 6399. From Holt St. Wharf, Brisbane:
angalooma Wild Dolphin Resort, tel 07 3268 6333

TIPS

» Summer can be hot and humid, so
arrive early at the Sunday Riverside
Markets.

-» City Sights buses, which make a circuit
every 45 minutes, are convenient for
getting to 19 of Brisbane's attractions.

» Take a trip to Morton Island to
hand-feed the bottlenose dolphins at
Tangalooma Resort.

Below *Chinatown in Fortitude Valley has
the city's best Asian cuisine*

Above *Newstead House is the city's oldest-surviving domestic dweling*
Below *Parliament House was inspired by Victorian Renaissance architecture*

NEWSTEAD HOUSE

www.newsteadhouse.com.au

Newstead House is a colonial, Georgian building on the banks of Breakfast Creek and the Brisbane River. It was built by Scotsman Patrick Leslie in 1846 and is now the city's oldest-surviving domestic dwelling. The two-storey house-museum comes complete with fine late Victorian fittings and period furniture. There are regular Sunday concerts and traditional cream teas and theme days.

✚ Off map 175 C1 ✉ Newstead Park, Breakfast Creek Road, QLD 4010 ☎ 07 3216 1846 🕓 Mon–Fri 10–4, Sun 2–5 💷 Adult A$4, child A$2 🚌 300

NORTH STRADBROKE ISLAND

www.stradboketourism.com

'Straddie', as the locals call it, is on Moreton Bay 30km (19 miles) to the east of Brisbane. The island is a one-hour ferry ride from suburban Cleveland—the effort is rewarded by stunning coastal and bushland scenery. Activities include surfing, fishing and horseback riding, or you can take the one-hour Goompi Trail from Dunwich with a local Aboriginal guide to learn about the local flora and fauna. The North Gorge trail leads around the headland and past the Blowhole for near-guaranteed sightings of dolphins and manta rays in the waters below, especially in the summer months.

Accommodation on the island is mostly based around Point Lookout. The settlement of Dunwich was a convict out-station, Catholic mission, quarantine station and benevolent institution during the 19th century.

✚ 353 X10 ℹ Stradbroke Island Visitor Centre, 21 Cummings Parade, Point Lookout ☎ 07 3415 3044 ⛴ Cleveland to Dunwich daily every hour 5.30am–8.30pm. Booking essential: Stradbroke Ferries, tel 07 3286 2666

PARLIAMENT HOUSE

www.parliament.qld.gov.au

Completed in 1868, when Queensland was a fledgling colony, Parliament House is an elegant Victorian Renaissance building—a fine example of colonial architecture. There are free tours on weekdays unless Parliament is sitting, when visitors can watch proceedings from the public gallery. Many of the materials in the interior, including stained glass and ornamental fittings, were imported from England.

✚ 175 B2 ✉ William Street, Brisbane, QLD 4000 ☎ 07 3406 7111 🕓 Guided tours Mon–F 9–4, Sat, Sun 10–2 💷 Free 🚌 City Sights bus, alight at QUT stop 🍴 🎫

QUEENSLAND ART GALLERY

www.qag.qld.gov.au

The Queensland Art Gallery is part of the Queensland Cultural Precinct, just south of Victoria Bridge. The excellent collection covers Australian art from colonial times to the present, and includes painting, sculpture, prints, drawings, photographs, decorative arts and crafts, and Aboriginal art spanning the last 130 years.

✚ 175 A2 ✉ Melbourne Street (south end of the Victoria Bridge), South Brisbane, QLD 4000 ☎ 07 3840 7303 🕓 Mon–Fri 10–5, Sat, Sun 9–5 💷 Free. Charge for exhibitions 🚌 The Cultural Centre Busway is outside the gallery, with regular buses from central Brisbane 🚉 South Brisbane 🎫 🎫

QUEENSLAND MARITIME MUSEUM

www.maritimemuseum.com.au

The museum, at the southern end of South Bank Parklands, recalls the state's maritime history through models and displays of sailing, merchant and early cargo ships, modern vessels and marine memorabilia. The site also features dry docks dating from 1881. Among the historic boats is *Happy II*, a small

BRISBANE

Hargrave Park

PETRIE TERRACE

Roma Street Parkland

BRISBANE TRANSIT CENTRE (ROMA ST)

Brisbane Botanic Gardens

UPR ROMA ST

CORONATION DRIVE

Lone Pine Koala Sanctuary

WILLIAM JOLLY BR

MERIVALE BRIDGE

QEII Park

Queensland Museum & Art Gallery

Casino

VICTORIA BRIDGE

Queensland Performing Arts Centre

South Brisbane

South Bank Parklands

SOUTH BRISBANE

Musgrave Park

Queensland Maritime Museum

Vulture Street

HIGHGATE HILL

Fortitude Valley, Newstead House

St John's Cathedral

Customs House

Riverside Centre

City Hall

St Stephen's Cathedral

CT White Park

KANGAROO POINT

City Botanic Gardens

Queens Gardens

Parliament House

CAPTAIN COOK BR

RIVERSIDE EXPRESSWAY

Gardens Point

South Brisbane Reach

Brisbane River

The cliffs Boardwalk

STORY BRIDGE

BRADFIELD HIGHWAY

Capt John Burke Park

Kangaroo Point

Holman St

Wharf St

Baildon St

Thornton St

Ferry St

Cairns Street

SHAPSTON AVE

Pearson St

Thomas St

Street

Sinclair St

Raymond Park

Baines St

Bromley St

Toohey St

Princess St

Mark Lane

Linton St

Brisbane Cricket Ground

250 m
250 yds

sailing boat that in the 1980s voyaged from the US, through the Panama Canal and across the Pacific to the north coast of New South Wales. The coal-fired tug *SS Forceful*, built in 1925, cruises the Brisbane River and Moreton Bay.

☩ 175 B3 ✉ Sidon Street, South Brisbane, QLD 4000 ☎ 07 3844 5361 ⏱ Daily 9.30–4.30 ✋ Adult A$7, child A$3.50 🚌 The Cultural Centre Busway is 500m (545 yards) northwest, outside the Queensland Art Gallery 🚉 South Bank, 250m (272 yards) west 🚲

QUEENSLAND MUSEUM

www.qm.qld.gov.au

As its name suggests, the museum gives an introduction to Queensland's natural and cultural history. Spread over four levels, the range of exhibits takes in a Dinosaur Garden, a hands-on science centre, Aboriginal objects as art, pioneer women in the outback, endangered species, and the story of the local whales, including the complete skeleton of a humpback whale. The museum is next to the Queensland Art Gallery.

☩ 175 A2 ✉ Melbourne Street (south end of Victoria Bridge), South Brisbane, QLD 4000 ☎ 07 3840 7555 ⏱ Daily 9.30–5 ✋ Free. Charge for special exhibitions 🚌 The Cultural Centre Busway is outside the nearby Queensland Art Gallery 🚉 South Brisbane 🚲

ROMA STREET PARKLAND

www.romastreetparkland.com

The 16ha (40-acre) Roma Street Parkland is the world's largest subtropical garden in a central city area, with more than 100,000 shrubs, 1,200 mature trees and 350 palms. The Forest Walk features rainforests, palm groves and open forests via a pathway system and boardwalk over cascading waterways and rocky outcrops. A lookout gives views towards the city skyline. Free guided walks depart from The Hub in the middle of the Parkland (Thu–Sun; bookings tel 07 3006 4531/4545). There are also playgrounds for children.

✚ 175 A1 ✉ 1 Parkland Boulevard, Brisbane, QLD 4000 ☎ 07 3006 4545 ⏰ Daily 24 hours. Spectacle Garden 6.30am–7pm 🖐 Free 🚉 Roma Street 🍽 Café Tomoko 🎭 Activity Centre

SOUTH BANK PARKLANDS

www.visitsouthbank.com

South Bank is the city's major recreation precinct. Street entertainers, pubs and a varied events schedule ensure that the area is a popular place for Brisbanites. South Bank Lifestyle Markets are open on Friday evenings (5–10) and on Saturday (11–5) and Sunday (9–5). The nearby Brisbane Convention and Exhibition Centre hosts special events and exhibitions. South Bank Beach is a man-made shore overlooking the Brisbane River and the central city area, comprising a crystal-clear lagoon with clean, white sand beaches, palm trees, rocky creeks and shady shallows with subtropical vegetation. South Bank is easily reached from Queen Street Mall via the Victoria Bridge (300m/327 yards) or from the City Botanic Gardens (500m/545 yards) via the Goodwill Bridge, a pedestrian and bicycle bridge.

Other outdoor attactions at South Bank include the Suncorp Piazza, a large covered space at the heart of the South Bank. It is a venue for a range of entertainments, ranging from concerts to sporting events. The Energex Brisbane Arbour is a stunning arbour that winds for more than 1km (0.6 mile) through the parklands at South Bank, connecting all the main sights.

South Bank is also known for its markets. Little Stanley Street and the Energex Arbour are busy with art and craft markets every Friday, Saturday and Sunday, and are a great place to browse for a craft souvenir. Street performers add to the fun, and the street itself is a Brisbane eating spot. On the first and third Saturday of the month the morning farmers' and seafood markets have fresh local produce; you'll find them at the Cultural Forecourt near the QPAC.

✚ 175 B2 ℹ Visitor Information Centre, Stanley Street Plaza, South Bank ☎ 07 3867 2051 ⏰ Daily 9–5 🚌 Busway stations in Melbourne Street (Cultural Centre Station) and cnr Colchester and Tribune streets (South Bank Busway Station). Brisbane City buses stop at several locations around South Bank 🚉 Vulture Street and South Brisbane 🚢 CityCat terminal outside the riverside restaurants on the Clem Jones Promenade.

QUEENSLAND PERFORMING ARTS CENTRE

www.qpac.com.au

The Queensland Performing Arts Centre (QPAC) is home to Brisbane's key cultural institutions, including the Queensland Theatre Company, Queensland Opera and the Queensland Symphony Orchestra. Opera, concert and theatre lovers should check the website or local papers for details of current performances at the Optus Playhouse (850 seats), Lyric Theatre (2,000 seats), Concert Hall (1,800 seats) and Cremorne Theatre (312 seats). The Queensland Performing Arts Museum at the QPAC presents small exhibitions of theatre memorabilia and theatre design in the Tony Gould Gallery.

✚ 175 A2 ✉ South Bank ☎ 13 62 46 ❓ The Visitor Centre at South Bank ☎ 07 3867 2051) can book tickets, and provides wheelchair hire 🚌 Busway stations in Melbourne Street (Cultural Centre Station) and cnr Colchester and Tribune streets (South Bank Busway Station). Brisbane City buses stop at several locations around South Bank 🚉 Vulture Street and South Brisbane 🚢 CityCat terminal

CAIRNS AND THE TROPICAL NORTH

INTRODUCTION

Queensland's tropical capital is a stepping stone to the Wet Tropics of Queensland and Great Barrier Reef World Heritage areas. Cairns is Queensland's most cosmopolitan city north of Brisbane. The area around the city is best explored with a rental car but there are hundreds of day tours to choose from: boat trips to the reef and coach tours up the coast and into the hinterland.

In the 19th century Cairns was renowned for its wild frontier style. Port Douglas was then the region's main town, serving the Palmerston goldfields. In the 1880s tin was discovered on the Atherton Tableland and Cairns grew in importance. Sugar and timber dominated the local economy during the 20th century, until tourism entered the scene in the 1970s.

WHAT TO SEE

CAIRNS

An initial walk along the Esplanade, where there's all manner of shopping, entertainment and dining options, will get you in the holiday mood. The stunning swimming lagoon in front of Fogarty Park is the best place for a year-round dip. Cairns central shopping mall, in McLeod Street, has more than 100 specialty shops, food courts and a cinema. Other attractions include a casino, the Pier Marketplace and a busy nightlife. The city also has a splendid botanical garden and a historical museum. The Cairns Regional Art Gallery is on the corner of Shields and Abbott streets (Mon–Sat 10–5, Sun 1–5).

For many visitors the city is a fun starter for journeys along the coast, inland or farther north. There are numerous boat tours available out to the Great Barrier Reef, usually all-day trips; and a sedate view of the rainforests

INFORMATION

www.cairnsgreatbarrierreef.org.au
✚ 348 T4 ⓘ Tourism Tropical North Queensland Visitor Information Centre, 51 The Esplanade, Cairns, QLD 4870 ☎ 07 4051 3588 ⓒ Daily 9–5 ▣ Cairns

DAINTREE DISCOVERY CENTRE

www.daintree-rec.com.au
✉ Cnr Cape Tribulation and Tulip Oak roads, Cow Bay, QLD 4873 ☎ 07 4098 9171 ⓒ Daily 8.30–5 ▣ Adult A$28, child A$14

KURANDA SCENIC RAILWAY

www.ksr.com.au
✉ Cairns Railway Station, Cairns, QLD 4870 ☎ 07 4036 9333 ⓒ Departs daily 8.30 and 9.30am. Returns daily 2 and 3.30pm ▣ Adult A$41 one way, A$61 round trip; child A$21 one way, A$31 round trip

Above *The view across the Esplanade Lagoon at dusk*

SKYRAIL

www.skyrail.com.au

✉ Smithfield, QLD 4878 ☎ 07 4038 1555 🕐 Daily 8.15–3.45 💵 Adult A$41 one way, A$59 round trip; child A$20.50 one way, A$29.50 round trip

TJAPUKAI ABORIGINAL CULTURAL PARK

www.tjapukai.com.au

✉ Smithfield, QLD 4878 ☎ 07 4042 9999 🕐 Daily 9–5 and 7–10pm 💵 Adult A$33, child A$16.50, evening show adult A$90, child $46.50 🚌 13km (8 miles) north of Cairns on the Captain Cook Highway

TIPS

» The tourist high season is the cooler and drier winter months, from April to the end of October.

» It may be a good idea to avoid the tropical north's wet season, which runs from December to the end of March. Heavy rain and flooding make access to some areas chancy; destructive cyclones may also occur at this time. Temperatures can be in the mid-30s°C (mid-90s°F) and the humidity approaches 100 per cent.

Below *The Great Barrier Reef stretches some 2,000km (1,240 miles)*

from Skyrail. Also nearby are adventure activities such as bungee jumping, white-water rafting, scuba diving, ballooning and parasailing. Those who find the summer humidity of the coast too stifling head for the Atherton Tableland (▷ 171) where visitors can explore the rainforest and discover scenic waterfalls, with temperatures that can be several degrees cooler.

GREAT BARRIER REEF MARINE PARK

Away from dry land, the Great Barrier Reef Marine Park is renowned as the world's largest system of coral reefs (▷ 182–184). It extends over 2,000km (1,240 miles) from the Torres Strait north of the Cape York Peninsula to just south of the Tropic of Capricorn near Fraser Island, and is made up of about 2,800 individual reefs, coral cays and atolls, and hundreds of continental islands. A huge variety of soft and hard corals growing in warm, shallow waters form a thin, living veneer.

Hundreds of coral cays and continental islands lie off the North Queensland coast and many of these can be visited. Lizard Island, 80km (50 miles) north of Cooktown, best accessed by air, is a base for deep-sea game fishing and scuba diving. Fitzroy Island, 26km (16 miles) east of Cairns, with a rainforest and a clam and pearl oyster hatchery, has a resort with varied accommodation. Forty-five minutes by boat offshore from Cairns, Green Island is a 15ha (37-acre) national park coral cay with a superb underwater observatory and aquarium.

RAINFORESTS

The Wet Tropics World Heritage Area encompasses nearly all the tropical rainforest in Australia and is regarded as one of the world's most significant ecosystems. Tropical rainforests have a diverse array of flora and fauna. Australia's Wet Tropics stretch from Black Mountain, south of Cooktown, to just south of Townsville, with Cairns roughly central. The mountain ranges have fast-flowing streams and waterfalls; in places, the tropical rainforest runs down to the sea.

NORTH TO CAPE TRIBULATION

The drive from Cairns to Cape Tribulation is one of the world's great scenic drives, with rainforests, fields of waving sugar cane and long sandy beaches. Just 11km (7 miles) north of Cairns, at Smithfield, is the lowland terminus of Skyrail, the aerial cableway that runs over the rainforest canopy via a series of pylons to the mountain village of Kuranda. Here you will find a large daily market (9–5) and a number of interesting craft shops.

There are two stations along the way: Red Peak, which has a forest walkway, and Barron Falls, with an interpretative unit and a lookout. An alternative is to take the popular 34km (21-mile) scenic Cairns–Kuranda rail journey on one of the legs of your trip. The indigenous experience at the Tjapukai Aboriginal Cultural Park at Smithfield includes didgeridoo performances, fire-making demonstrations, bush food displays and boomerang throwing. Visitors are encouraged to try their hand at a variety of bushcrafts.

Farther north is a series of beaches; the best is at Palm Cove, a 20-minute drive north of Cairns. A 1-hour drive north of Cairns is the stylish coastal resort town of Port Douglas (▷ 185). The sugar-milling town of Mossman, 75km (46 miles) north of Cairns, is set amid fields of sugar cane. Nearby is picturesque Mossman Gorge, which has picnic facilities. After crossing the Daintree River by car ferry, on the way to Cape Tribulation, there are a number of walks giving spectacular views over the rainforest out to sea. Although Cape Tribulation is accessible by ordinary vehicles in most weather conditions, the road past this point to Bloomfield is for 4WD vehicles only.

The bird life in these areas is prolific and over half of Australia's bird species are found here; these include the rare cassowary (▷ 24).

CHARTERS TOWERS

www.charterstowers.qld.gov.au
This former gold-mining town,
once the financial hub of north
Queensland, has some of the
grandest historic buildings in
rural Queensland. A day trip from
Townsville, Charters Towers is a
classic example of an outback town.
It was built during the gold boom of
the late 19th century. By the end of
1872 some 3,000 people inhabited
the new goldfield. Some miners
left soon after for the Palmer River
discoveries to the north, but others
remained, seeking the gold in the
deep veins underground. By 1899
gold production was at its peak and
the city had developed streets. The
wealthy built fine homes, impressive
public buildings were erected,
and 65 hotels quenched the thirst
of the miners. After 1945 mining
declined, but modern methods are
bringing new life to the old mines.
For a walking tour, start at the 19th-
century Stock Exchange Arcade in
Mosman Street, next to the tourist
office. The Assay Room and Mining
Museum (tel 07 4761 5533, daily
9–5) is at the end of the arcade. The
Zara Clark Museum (tel 07 4787
4161; daily 10–3) has a collection of
old farming gear, domestic wares
and period clothing. Ay Ot Lookout
house, on the corner of Hodgkinson
and High streets, is a mining
magnate's mansion (Mon–Fri 8–3).
✚ 349 T6 🛈 Charters Towers Visitor
Information Centre, 74 Mosman Street,
Charters Towers, QLD 4820 ☎ 07 4761
5533 🕐 Daily 9–5 🚉

FRASER ISLAND
▷ 180.

GOLD COAST
▷ 181.

GREAT BARRIER REEF
▷ 182–184.

HERON ISLAND
www.heronisland.com
Heron Island is a tiny, 16ha (40-acre)
vegetated coral cay, part of the
Capricorn-Bunker group of reefs.

The corals and marine life are among
the best in the world. The island is
also home to a variety of bird life,
including black noddies, mutton birds
and reef herons during the nesting
season. Sea turtles come ashore
(Nov–end Jan) to lay their eggs in the
warm sand. Island activities include
diving, snorkelling and birding.
✚ 351 W7 🛈 Heron Island Resort ☎ 03
9413 6288 🚉 Gladstone

HINCHINBROOK ISLAND

www.hinchinbrooklodge.com.au
www.hinchinbrookferries.com.au
Covering 393sq km (152sq miles),
this is Australia's largest island
national park. This stunning
wilderness has mangrove wetlands,
eucalypts, long white beaches and
rainforests. The granite outcrop
of Mount Bowen rises 1,121m
(3,677ft) in the centre. Visitors
come for the bushwalking, fishing,
snorkelling, swimming and birding.
Insect repellent, sunscreen, water
and a good hat are essential.
Keen hikers undertake the 32km
(20-mile), four-day wilderness trek
along the Thorsborne Trail. The only
accommodation is the Hinchinbrook
Island Wilderness Lodge and
Resort. Boats leave Cardwell daily.
Camping is by permit only; contact
the Queensland National Parks and
Wildlife Service (tel 07 4066 8601).
✚ 349 T5 🛈 Hinchinbrook Island
Wilderness Lodge and Resort, Cape
Richards, Hinchinbrook Island, QLD
4849 ☎ 07 4066 8270 🚉 Cardwell
🖥 Hinchinbrook Island Ferries, tel 07
4066 8585

LAMINGTON NATIONAL PARK

www.verygc.com
Spectacular rainforests blend with
classic mountain scenery, steep
valleys, sheer gorges, tumbling
waterfalls and rocky creeks in
Lamington National Park. The park
is a great natural destination within
easy reach of Brisbane and the Gold
Coast; it has more than 160km
(99 miles) of trails, both long and
short, to suit all hikers. Serious
hikers should pack appropriate gear
and try some of the longer trails.

A well-known trek involves a visit
to the site of the famous Stinson
plane wreck and rescue in 1937.
Alternatively, well-formed trails
lead to the majority of the park's
features, from palm-filled valleys
with waterfalls and streams, to
misty mountaintops (1,100m/3,608ft)
in cool temperate rainforests,
dominated by Antarctic beech trees.
　The bird life in the park includes
the satin and regent bowerbirds,
which build distinctive ground
bowers for courting and nesting.
Lorikeets, crimson rosellas and other
parrots will feed from your hand
in the cleared areas around visitor
offices, while tame pademelons—a
variety of small wallaby—feed on
grass along the edge of the forest in
the evenings. There is an excellent
treetop canopy walk at the O'Reilly's
accommodation. In the evenings,
visitors can gather around a log fire
after a hearty dinner, take a guided
walk to see the glow worms, spotlit
pademelons, possums and gliders,
and view a rainforest audio-visual
presentation of the district's flora
and fauna.
✚ 353 X10 🛈 Gold Coast Tourism Bureau,
Cavill Avenue, Surfers Paradise, QLD 4217
☎ 07 5538 4419 🕐 Mon–Fri 8.30–5.30,
Sat 9–5.30, Sun 9–4.30 🛈 O'Reilly's
Rainforest Guesthouse, Lamington National
Park Road, via Canungra, QLD 4275
☎ 07 5544 0644, www.oreillys.com.au
🚉 Services from Brisbane to the
Gold Coast

*Below A crimson rosella eats seed from a
visitor's hand at Lamington National Park*

Above *A humpback whale breaches near Hervey Bay*

INFORMATION

www.seefraserisland.com.au

✚ 351 W8/X8 ℹ Fraser Island National Park Office, Eurong, Fraser Island, QLD 4581 ☎ 07 4127 9128 🕐 Mon–Fri 9–5, Sat 9.30–12.30 ❓ The Fraser Island Company, tel 1800 063 933; Fraser Island Adventure Tours, tel 07 5444 6957. Safari 4WD Hire, Hervey Bay, tel 07 4124 4244 🚢 Hervey Bay to Moon Point, tel 07 4194 9222; River Heads to Kingfisher Bay Resort, tel 1800 072 555; Rainbow Beach to Hook Point, tel 07 5486 3154

FRASER ISLAND AND HERVEY BAY

Tall rainforest, huge sand dunes and crystal-clear lakes are all on Fraser Island, the world's largest sand island.

HERVEY BAY

Hervey Bay is the main departure point to the Fraser Island World Heritage Area, and one of the world's best places to observe humpback whales. From August to the end of October, groups of them rest in the calm, relatively shallow waters off the coast.

FRASER ISLAND

The island stretches 123km (76 miles) from north to south, has an average width of 14km (9 miles) and was inhabited by Aboriginal people for thousands of years. In more recent times, timber cutters, sand miners and fishermen had the island to themselves, but after protests the logging and sand mining were halted and the island is now World Heritage-listed.

Fraser Island is a popular beach-fishing destination, and camping is permitted on the fore dunes. Tours of the island include a drive through the heaths and rainforests, and along the eastern beaches. The remarkable freshwater lakes are more popular as swimming spots than the dangerous eastern surf beaches. Inland there is a cool walk among the giant hoop pines of the Yidney Scrub, the last of the island's virgin rainforests.

GOLD COAST

The Gold Coast spreads from Coolangatta, near the New South Wales border, 70km (43 miles) north to Beenleigh. Visitors from around the world soak up the sun, visit theme parks, party at nightspots, shop at malls and specialty shops, and dine at some of the state's best eateries.

SURFERS PARADISE

A one-hour drive south of Brisbane, 'Surfers' has surf beaches, excellent shopping and dining, and plenty of evening fun. The action is focused around the area bounded by Cavill Avenue, the Esplanade and the Gold Coast Highway.

BURLEIGH HEADS

About 10km (6 miles) south of Surfers, Burleigh Heads is one of Australia's top surfing locations, known for its fast and deep barrel rides. A walking trail runs around the rocky headland and part of the tiny Burleigh Heads National Park.

COOLANGATTA

The laid-back holiday town of Coolangatta, on the New South Wales border, combines old-fashioned charm with modern amenities. Its broad, long beaches are uncrowded and surfers mingle with holidaying families.

CURRUMBIN WILDLIFE SANCTUARY

Northwest of Coolangatta this sanctuary has the world's largest collection of Australian animals (daily 8–5). You can feed wild lorikeets and get close to koalas, kangaroos, emus and other wildlife. Aboriginal dancers perform daily.

THEME PARKS

Sea World (daily 10–5) has entertaining rides and attractions. A dolphin show, the Water Ski Spectacular, the Corkscrew Rollercoaster, Cartoon World, a 3-D pirate movie and an aquarium will fill the day. Head for Dreamworld (daily 10–5), if you enjoy scary rides. Go behind the scenes to learn all about movie-making at Warner Bros. Movie World (daily 10–5). Wet'n'Wild Water World (▷ 200) is a water-themed fun park.

INFORMATION

www.verygc.com

➕ 353 X10 🛈 Gold Coast Tourism Bureau, Cavill Avenue, Surfers Paradise, QLD 4217 ☎ 1300 309 400 🕐 Mon–Fri 8.30–5.30, Sat 9–5.30, Sun 9–4.30

🚆 Services from Brisbane (timetables: tel 13 12 30)

TIP

» Avoid mid-November to mid-December when school groups invade the place for 'Schoolies Week'.

Above *Highrises above the sands at Surfers Paradise*

GREAT BARRIER REEF

INFORMATION

www.reefhq.com.au
www.gbrmpa.gov.au
➕ 348 T3–351 X8 ✉ Reef HQ
Aquarium, 2–68 Flinders Street, PO Box
1379, Townsville, QLD 4810 ☎ 07 4750
0800 🕒 Daily 9.30–5 💲 Adult A$24.75,
child A$12.10, family A$62.10

INTRODUCTION

The world's largest coral reef system is made up of some 2,800 individual reefs, coral cays and atolls, and hundreds of continental islands, stretching over 2,000km (1,240 miles) from Torres Strait, north of Cape York, down to Lady Elliot Island, just south of the Tropic of Capricorn.

Nothing prepares you for the profusion of marine life encountered on a snorkel or dive in the protected waters of the Great Barrier Reef Marine Park, the largest marine reserve in the world. This finely balanced environment includes hundreds of species of corals, thousands of different molluscs, sponges, worms, crustaceans and echinoderms, and more than a thousand species of fish.

Reef invertebrates and fish have adapted to make the most of their environment, such as the parrot fish that uses its beak-like teeth to scrape algal food from the hard underlying calcareous layer of the reef. The reef is also home to green and loggerhead turtles, sharks, manta rays and one of the largest dugong (sea cow) populations in the world. In winter (July–end September) humpback whales gather in the warm waters around the Whitsunday Islands (▷ 191) on their annual migration to and from Antarctica.

Numerous tour operators run cruises to the continental islands, reefs and cays from coastal locations, including Bundaberg, Gladstone, Rockhampton, Airlie Beach, Townsville, Mission Beach, Cairns and Port Douglas. And many of the continental islands, such as those in the Whitsundays, have fringing reefs that are easily accessible. As part of a trip to the reef, you may be offered a glass-bottomed boat tour, a ride in a semi-submersible or a snorkel above the coral. Most people who visit the Great Barrier Reef on a boat tour have a go at snorkelling.

WHAT IS CORAL?

Coral is the stony skeleton produced by various polyps—small colonial marine animals—which builds up to form reefs. The complex food chain begins with the free-floating plankton, the small, mostly microscopic plants and animals that inhabit the sunlit layer of the ocean. These are devoured by small fish and reef invertebrates, which are in turn eaten by larger predators. At full moon in late spring or early summer there is a spectacular nighttime display of coral spawning, when masses of coral eggs and sperm are simultaneously released.

Above *The reef appears brighter when diving with lights at night*

WHAT TO SEE

BUNDABERG

Some of the best shore diving in Queensland is in Bundaberg's Woongarra Marine Park, with soft and hard corals, urchins, rays, sea snakes, and more than 50 fish species. Lady Musgrave Island Dive Tours offers diving, snorkelling and fishing at various reefs (www.divemusgrave.com.au). A vegetated coral cay, Lady Elliot Island, is the southernmost Great Barrier Reef island. From November to the end of January loggerhead turtles come ashore to lay their eggs. Air transportation from Bundaberg or Hervey Bay is the best way to arrive, since the island has a small airstrip. The Lady Elliot Island Resort provides several standards of accommodation and conducts diving certificate courses (www.ladyelliot.com.au). The uninhabited Lady Musgrave Island is a tiny coral cay covered in rare pisonia forest, about 100km (62 miles) northeast of Bundaberg. Camping is permitted in several locations, but there are day-trip cruises from both Bundaberg and The Town of 1770. The island's 1,200ha (3,000-acre) navigable lagoon is a good calm spot for beginner divers and snorkellers. For those averse to getting wet, semi-submersible and glass-bottomed boats take visitors over coral reefs. Lady Musgrave Great Barrier Reef Cruises is based at Agnes Water (tel 1800 072 110).

➕ 351 W8

HERON ISLAND

Two hours by fast boat from the city of Gladstone, Heron Island (▷ 179) is a 16ha (40-acre) vegetated coral cay, part of the Capricorn-Bunker Group. From November to the end of January, sea turtles come ashore to lay their eggs. Island activities include some of Australia's best snorkelling, scuba diving and reef walks. Offshore, Heron Bommie is renowned for its rays and eels, and also Spanish dancers—very pretty shell-less marine molluscs that float in the water and look like Spanish dancers. Heron is one of the very few island resorts situated on the Great Barrier Reef (tel 1300 233 432).

➕ 351 W7

GREAT KEPPEL ISLAND

Great Keppel Island (▷ 188) is surrounded by the clear Coral Sea. About 18km (11 miles) of beautiful sandy beaches surround the island, and snorkelling and diving can be enjoyed on the fringing reefs off Monkey Beach. The island is just 30 minutes by fast cruise boats from Rosslyn Bay Harbour, near Rockhampton (▷ 188).

➕ 351 V7

AIRLIE BEACH AND THE WHITSUNDAYS

This coastal town is usually crowded with visitors, particularly backpackers, from all around the world. Boats leave from the busy marina and neighbouring Shute Harbour to the Great Barrier Reef, the Whitsunday Islands and other popular destinations. There are countless dive sites, both among the islands and on the outer Great Barrier Reef, 90 minutes away, including Bait Reef, known for its cascading drop-offs. Snorkellers will find plenty of coral and marine life around many island shores.

There are several ways to explore the 74 Whitsunday Islands (▷ 191). Airlie Beach and some of the larger islands such as Hamilton Island make a good base for sailing and reef trips. You can get to the islands on your own by ferry, or join one of the many organized day trips. Bareboat rental would suit those who want a full-on sailing experience, while crewed charters are fun for those prepared to bunk down with a crowd. Fanta Sea Cruises runs a day trip to Whitehaven Beach, where you can snorkel and view the coral from a large semi-submersible; tel 07 4967 5455; day trip costs: adult A$145, child A$60.

➕ 349 U6

TIPS

» Day trips out to islands or the reef usually depart early—often from 8am—so check timetables in advance.
» Experienced divers with a scuba diving ticket can dive to depths where marine creatures dwell in gullies and caves. Otherwise for an extra charge some operators offer an introductory dive, which is a diving experience for those without suitable qualifications.
» Most boat tours travel to the outer reef, the platform and ribbon reefs that lie an average of 65km (40 miles) off the coast. These trips take from 60 to 90 minutes by fast catamaran and travel conditions are dependent on the weather. If you suffer from seasickness, remember to take appropriate medication before a voyage. For those not keen on a long boat trip, explore one of the fringing reefs around the continental islands that lie closer to the mainland.
» An important factor is water clarity—wait until you arrive at your destination and see what the weather and water is like before booking a tour.

Below *Airlie Beach makes an excellent base for those who want to explore the Whitsundays*

TOWNSVILLE

Reef HQ on Flinders Street East, Townsville, is the best place in Australia to learn about marine life on the Great Barrier Reef (daily 9.30–5). There are interactive exhibits, and the main tank includes a replica of one of the world's top wrecks, the SS *Yongala*, which forms a backdrop to sharks, rays and reef fish. The SS *Yongala* itself, sunk by a cyclone in 1911, lies in the Coral Sea off Townsville. Large schools of trevally, kingfish and barracuda circle the wreck, while giant Queensland grouper live under the bow, turtles graze on the hull, and hard and soft corals have settled on the decks. Pro Dive runs a day trip (tel 07 4721 1760) to the *Yongala*. Orpheus Island is a 1,300ha (3,211-acre) continental island 70km (43 miles) northwest of Townsville. Bordered by sheltered bays and deserted sandy beaches, the island is covered in coastal forests and is rich in bird life. Snorkellers and divers can explore the fringing coral reefs. Orpheus Island Resort, closed to day trippers, nestles in a protected bay on the west side of the island and caters for up to 42 guests; access to the resort is by seaplane from Townsville (tel 07 4777 7377).
✚ 349 T5

DUNK ISLAND

The resort on rainforested Dunk Island, a 15-minute ferry ride from Mission Beach (▷ 185), provides many water- and land-based activities. Quick Cat Cruises runs round-trip cruises daily from Clump Point Jetty, including use of snorkelling gear (tel 07 4068 7289; adult A$56, child A$28).
✚ 349 T5

CAIRNS

Cairns is an embarkation point (▷ 177) for cruises to many parts of the Great Barrier Reef, whether for day trips or longer vacations. Sunlover Cruises runs an outer reef day trip in a catamaran, departing Trinity Wharf, which stops at Fitzroy Island National Park for a one-hour guided rainforest walk before arriving at Moore Reef. A guided snorkel safari is included (Sunlover Cruises, tel 07 1800 810 512; adult A$180, child A$65). Great Adventures also runs a catamaran from Reef Fleet Wharf, to a three-level pontoon on the outer reef. The pontoon has a children's swimming area, a semi-submersible and an underwater observatory (Great Adventures, tel 07 4044 9944; one day adult A$186, child A$93;).

Fitzroy Island National Park, 26km (16 miles) east of Cairns, has a well-established rainforest, and a clam and pearl oyster hatchery. Fitzroy Island Resort has accommodation (tel 07 4051 9588).

Farther north but the same distance from Cairns, Green Island National Park is a 15ha (37-acre) coral cay with a superb underwater observatory. The exclusive Green Island Resort, limited to 90 guests, has been designed for low impact on its ecologically sensitive surroundings. At this popular day-trip destination, you can snorkel off the island's beach and ride in a glass-bottomed boat. A walk around the island takes about 20 minutes (Green Island Resort, tel 07 1800 673 366).

Lizard Island National Park, 245km (152 miles) north of Cairns, is Australia's northernmost island resort. The island is a base for deep-sea game fishing and scuba diving; snorkel above 150-year-old giant clams or, at the famous Cod Hole, dive to hand-feed a school of giant potato cod. Lizard Island Resort is a one-hour flight north from Cairns (tel 1300 233 432). Great Adventures, Quicksilver (below) and Sunlover all offer helicopter flights over the reef from pontoons.
✚ 348 T4

PORT DOUGLAS
▷ 185..

Above *An aerial view of Heart Reef*
Below *Take a snorkelling tour along the Great Barrier Reef*

MACKAY AND EUNGELLA NATIONAL PARK

www.mackayregion.com

The port and solid regional city of Mackay is a good base for excursions to the Great Barrier Reef (▷ 182–184), the Eungella Range National Park to the north, and the stunning coastal Cape Hillsborough National Park. Or you can just relax on one of the many local beaches. The Broken River Picnic ground in Eungella National Park has a viewing platform where platypus come to the surface in the early mornings and evenings. The city has some of the finest beaches of the mid-Queensland coast, while boat-operators offer easy access to the islands at the southern end of the Whitsundays. This thriving sugar-growing district produces one-third of the nation's crop, and you can watch the sugar-making process on a sugar mill tour (Jun–end Nov).

Finch Hatton Gorge, the valley entrance to Eungella National Park, 66km (41 miles) west of Mackay, has a series of walks that wind their way up from the rocky creeks to superb vantage points over tumbling waterfalls. Farther up the valley you come to the rainforest-draped upper reaches of the park.

Various trails, many with identified plant species, make exploration of the rainforests easy. Just 47km (29 miles) north of Mackay, Cape Hillsborough National Park also offers a rainforest walk, with explanations of the Aboriginal uses of plants. Some 150 or so bird species are found here. Look also for the tropical butterflies, wallabies, brush turkeys and possums, which congregate around the picnic grounds.

➕ 350 U6 ℹ️ Visitor Information Centre, 320 Nebo Road, Mackay, QLD 4740 ☎ 1300 130 001 🕐 Mon–Fri 8.30–5, Sat–Sun 9–4 🚆 Mackay

MISSION BEACH AND DUNK ISLAND

www.missionbeachtourism.com.au
www.dunk-island.com

Some of Australia's prettiest coastal scenery is around Mission Beach, 140km (87 miles) south of Cairns. The coastal villages of Clump Point and Bingal Bay to the north, Wongaling Beach, South Mission Beach and Mission Beach itself offer white, sandy beaches, coastal wetlands and rainforests that reach down to the sea. This is one of the few places in Australia where you can see the elusive flightless cassowary (▷ 24). The lookout on Bicton Hill offers views over outlying islands, while the Ulysses Link Walk winds along the Mission Beach foreshore.

Dunk Island is a 15-minute ferry ride from Mission Beach; the largest of the Family Islands, it was popularized by the author and naturalist Edmund J. Banfield, an island resident from 1897 until his death in 1923. Much of the island fits the popular image of a tropical island: swaying palms, great beaches, and grassy knolls offering fine vantage points. Camping on Dunk Island is possible and the resort (tel 1300 134 044) has excellent accommodation with the option of many activities. There are superb coastal views from the summit of Mount Kootaloo (271m/889ft) on Dunk Island.

➕ 349 T5 ℹ️ Mission Beach Information Centre, Porters Promenade, Mission Beach, QLD 4852 ☎ 07 4068 7099 🕐 Mon–Sat 9–4.45, Sun 10–4 🚆 Tully

NOOSA AND EUMUNDI
▷ 186.

OUTBACK QUEENSLAND
▷ 187.

PORT DOUGLAS

www.pddt.com.au

The road from Cairns, 70km (43 miles) north to Port Douglas, and on to Cape Tribulation, is a great scenic drive, with coastal ranges, sugar cane fields and impressive panoramas (see Cairns, ▷ 177–178). Port Douglas is a laid-back waterfront town with a tropical feel, though for the more adventurous there is diving, paragliding, horseback riding and bicycle tours. Port Douglas was the gateway to the Hodgkinson River goldfields in the 19th century, a role later usurped by Cairns. There are excellent restaurants and accommodation. Reef tours depart from the town wharf. The lookout on Flagstaff Hill overlooks Four Mile Beach and the Low Isles. The town's main street has good shopping and trendy eateries. Marina Mirage is an exclusive shopping complex. There may be more chance of a bargain at the Sunday Markets, where crafts, clothing and tropical produce are sold. The nearby Rainforest Habitat Wildlife Sanctuary on Port Douglas Road (tel 07 4099 3235) is a recreated natural environment housing more than 180 species of tropical birds and animals such as koalas, kangaroos and crocodiles (daily 8–5; adult A$30, child A$15).

➕ 348 T4 ℹ️ Port Douglas Daintree Tourism, 23 Macrossan Street, Port Douglas, QLD 4871 ☎ 07 4099 5599 🕐 Mon–Fri 9–5 🚆 Port Douglas

Below *Keep a lookout for wildlife in Cape Hillsborough National Park near Mackay*

INFORMATION

www.visitnoosa.com.au

➕ 353 X8/X9 ℹ️ Visitor Information Centre, Hastings Street, Noosa Heads, QLD 4567 ☎ 07 5430 5000 🕐 Daily 9–5 🚉 Nambour or Cooroy

TIP

» Noosa's main beach is not always flush with sand—nearby Sunshine Beach is good for swimming and surfing, as are the southern beaches of Sunrise, Marcus and Peregian.

NOOSA AND EUMUNDI

The Lifestyle Capital of Australia? Noosa's Hastings Street stores have all the best brands while the quality of the Noosa district restaurants rivals that of eateries in Sydney and Melbourne. But in recent years Noosa has become a victim of its own popularity and, like other parts of the Sunshine Coast (▷ 189) the town can be crowded during the holiday seasons of Easter and Christmas. There are three main beaches: Noosa Main Beach (a sheltered bay), Alexandria Bay (a clothes-optional surf beach) and Sunshine Beach (one of the Sunshine Coast's best surfing beaches).

NOOSA NATIONAL PARK

A mixture of coastal heath, eucalypt forests and rainforest, Noosa National Park is only a leisurely 10-minute walk from Hastings Street. A good interpretative unit at the entrance to the park has information on the trails. The excellent coastal trail passes beautiful beaches before leading to the promontory of Noosa Heads, which has sweeping views out to sea and over pristine Alexandria Bay. Only minutes from Noosa, the seaside village of Sunshine Beach lies on the southern edge of Noosa National Park. Head for Duke Street, near the beach, for restaurants with ocean views.

BOATING OPPORTUNITIES

Noosa is on the Noosa River, one of Queensland's cleanest waterways. There are more than 40km (25 miles) of navigable water: Rent a boat or take a day cruise through Lake Cooroibah and Lake Cootharaba to the Everglades, a stretch of the river lined with mangroves and featuring bird life. Along the Noosa River, between Tewantin and Noosa Heads, is the suburb of Noosaville. Gympie Terrace has a long park on its riverside, while the other side is lined with shops, cafés and restaurants. The Noosa Regional Gallery, in the service town of Tewantin, exhibits local, national and international art, and local crafts.

THE HINTERLAND

Eumundi, a 20-minute drive southwest of Noosa, has been revitalized as the home of one of Australia's best art and crafts markets. The town comes alive on Saturday mornings (7–1) when more than 400 stalls fill out Main Street and the side streets around with art, crafts, clothing and produce; there is also music and street theatre. There is a market on Wednesday (8–1) with about 250 stalls. Eumundi is worth a visit outside market days for its many art and craft shops and its range of cafés and food outlets.

Below *Hastings Street at Noosa has a Mediterranean feel*

OUTBACK QUEENSLAND

Queensland's enormous outback is a holiday destination with a difference and is well worth the diversion from the coastal regions. The region is bisected by the Landsborough (or Matilda) Highway running from Karumba on the Gulf of Carpentaria in the north almost to the New South Wales border. When planning a trip, air travel may be necessary if your time is limited. Much of the outback is arid, with broad areas used only for grazing.

THE NORTH

In the far northwest, Lawn Hill National Park has permanent spring waters, and the moisture allows rainforest vegetation and bird life to flourish along the gorge. Two Aboriginal rock art sites are accessible on part of the 20km (12 miles) of trails.

Set among the ochre-red Selwyn Ranges, the city of Mount Isa is dominated by the world's largest silver, lead and zinc mine. Mining is the key experience at the Outback at Isa Centre (daily 9–5), which features the Riversleigh Fossil Centre and Hard Times Mine.

About 118km (73 miles) east of Mount Isa, Cloncurry is a lively frontier mining town. It holds the record as Australia's hottest town, with a temperature of 53°C (127.4°F) in 1887. The John Flynn Place Museum and Art Gallery (Mon–Fri 8–4.30, Sat, Sun 9–3) is a tribute to the founders of the Flying Doctor Service.

AROUND THE TROPIC OF CAPRICORN

Walk the streets of Winton and check out the old pubs and the open-air Royal Theatre. The Waltzing Matilda Centre (Mon–Fri 9–5, Sat–Sun, 9–3) explores Australia's national song. Lark Quarry Conservation Park (tours daily 10, 12, and 2), 115km (71 miles) southwest, protects dinosaur footprints preserved in rock.

Longreach, Queensland's most prosperous central western town, sits beside the Thomson River. There is a wide, tree-lined main street, and the Australian Stockman's Hall of Fame and Outback Heritage Centre (daily 9–5) is a major outback attraction.

FARTHER SOUTH

Charleville lies at the heart of a rich pastoral and opal-mining district, while Roma has many grand historic buildings. Birdsville is a tiny settlement in the state's far south, on the edge of the Simpson Desert. Travelling the 500km (310-mile) Birdsville Track, from here to central South Australia, is one of the great Australian motoring adventures, best attempted in the cooler months.

INFORMATION

www.outbackatisa.com.au

✚ 343 Q6 🛈 Birdsville, Information Centre, Billabong Blvd, Birdsville, QLD 4482 ☎ 07 4656 3300 ⊙ Apr–end Oct daily 8.30–4..30; Nov–end Mar Mon–Fri 8.30–4.30 🛈 Longreach Visitor Information Centre, Eagle Street, Longreach, QLD 4730 ☎ 07 4658 4150 ⊙ Daily 9–5 🚆 Longreach (from Brisbane via Rockhampton) 🛈 Mount Isa Visitor Centre, 19 Marian Street, Mount Isa, QLD 4825 ☎ 07 4749 1555 ⊙ Daily 8.30–5 🚆 Mount Isa (from Townsville)

TIPS

» Avoid driving between dusk and dawn; watch for animals.

» Slow down and move off the road for oncoming road trains.

» Leave all gates as you find them; watch your fuel levels; keep your vehicle well maintained; carry plenty of spare water and a first-aid kit.

» If your vehicle breaks down, stay with it until help arrives.

Above *Hot dry landscape near Mount Isa*

INFORMATION
www.freedomfastcats.com
➕ 351 V7 🚹 Rockhampton
Tourist Information Centre, Quay
Street, Rockhampton, QLD 4700
☎ 07 4922 5339 ⊕ Daily 9–5
www.capricorntourism.com.au
🚹 Rockhampton 🚢 Freedom Fast Cats,
Keppel Bay Marina, Rosslyn Bay, QLD
4703 ☎ 07 4933 6888

TIP

» Check with lifeguards before swimming
in case of 'stingers'—box jellyfish—
which can be deadly.

ROCKHAMPTON AND CAPRICORN REGION

Central Queensland's Capricorn Region contrasts popular coastal attractions—
resorts, Great Keppel Island, a historic gold-mining town and gem fields—with
a more peaceful rural life inland.

WHAT TO SEE

ROCKHAMPTON

Billed as the beef capital of Australia because of the surrounding cattle grazing,
Rockhampton stretches out along the banks of the Fitzroy River, 40km
(25 miles) from the sea. A walk around central Rockhampton will pass many
buildings dating back to the late 19th century. Include the Rockhampton Art
Gallery (Tue–Fri 10–4, Sat, Sun 11–4) as part of a tour. On the south side of
the river, the Botanic Gardens are fine tropical gardens; there is a lagoon, a
large collection of palms, an orchid and fern house and a Japanese garden.
Mount Archer Environmental Park (daily 24 hours) has a lookout over the city
and surrounding areas, and has picnic and hiking options. The Dreamtime
Aboriginal Cultural Centre (Mon–Fri 10–3.30), in 12ha (30 acres) of natural
bushland, is 6km (4 miles) north of the city on the Bruce Highway. There is
a traditional dance performance, didgeridoo music, a Native Plant Tour, and a
boomerang display after which you can test your own skill.

GREAT KEPPEL ISLAND

Northeast of Rockhampton, the resort of Yeppoon has beautiful beaches
washed by the warm, clear waters of the Coral Sea. Rosslyn Bay Harbour, 6km
(4 miles) from Yeppoon, is the departure point for the 30-minute ferry to Great
Keppel Island, a continental island in the Great Barrier Reef Marine Park. Glass-
bottomed cruises also depart from Rosslyn Bay Harbour (daily 9.15) for views of
the coral reef that surrounds Great Keppel Island. The island itself, covering
14sq km (5.5sq miles), has accommodation ranging from budget to a smart
resort. Attractions include 17 white sand beaches, snorkelling and diving, and
plenty of hiking options across the bushland interior.

MOUNT MORGAN

A 30-minute drive southwest of Rockhampton will bring you to the former
gold- and copper-mining town of Mount Morgan, which once serviced one of
Australia's richest mines. Huge mounds of mine tailings and a mining museum
evoke a past way of life.

Above *Long Beach is one of the beaches
on Great Keppel Island*

SUNSHINE COAST

The coast's 60km (37 miles) of beaches, an hour's drive north of Brisbane and set against the backdrop of the Blackall Range, are among Australia's best.

The Sunshine Coast stretches from just north of Brisbane to the resort town of Noosa (▷ 186). With average winter temperatures around 25°C (77°F), and little of the summer humidity prevalent in the tropical north of the state, the Sunshine Coast has close to perfect weather. The region attracts artisans who sell their crafts in shops and the weekend markets. Eumundi Markets (▷ 186) are the best, but Maleny also has a highly regarded craft market. The dominant feature of the Sunshine Coast is the Glass House Mountains, 30km (19 miles) southwest of Caloundra, a dramatic group of 13 volcanic plugs.

THE COAST

Caloundra has excellent surf beaches, top fishing spots and great windsurfing locations. The town is quieter and less developed than Noosa, and this adds to its appeal. Just north of the Caloundra turnoff on the northern expressway, Aussie World (daily 9–5) is a fun outing for families. There are theme rides, an Aboriginal Cultural Centre, camel rides and craft outlets. Inland from Caloundra, 4km (2.5 miles) south of Landsborough, the 20ha (49-acre) Australia Zoo houses more than 550 animals, including reptiles, fishes, birds, otters and the world's oldest captive giant tortoise (daily 9–4.30). The biggest attraction is the crocodile show, which sometimes features wildlife TV star Bindi Irwin. Maroochydore and Alexandra Headland lie at the heart of the Sunshine Coast: They have great surf beaches, and the parkland along the Maroochy River is ideal for picnics. The calm river is good for boating and fishing. The Wharf, a boardwalk village on the Mooloolah River, is a shopping and eating complex that includes the Underwater World aquarium (daily 9–5).

THE HINTERLAND

For a change from the beach culture, the mountain towns of Maleny, Montville, Mapleton and Flaxton, high in the Blackall Range, are popular. The former dairying town of Maleny, 84km (52 miles) south of Noosa, is known for its cafés and restaurants, and its art and craft galleries. Nearby Mary Cairncross Scenic Reserve has rainforest walks and magnificent views of the Glass House Mountains.

Mapleton, on the most northerly point of the Blackall Range, has great views of the surrounding country. Nearby Flaxton has more galleries and craft shops, and is close to Kondalilla National Park. Montville is popular with weekend visitors who enjoy the mountain scenery and potteries, galleries and cafés. The Big Pineapple (daily 9–5), 7km (4 miles) south of Nambour, is a pineapple plantation with train rides, a macadamia orchard, a boat ride and shops. The Ginger Factory in Yandina has ginger products, food and rides (daily 9–5).

INFORMATION

www.maroochytourism.com.au
www.caloundratourism.com.au
✚ 353 X9 ⓘ Caloundra Tourist Information Centre, 7 Caloundra Road, Caloundra, QLD 4551 ☎ 1800 700 899 ◷ Daily 9–5
ⓘ Maroochydore Tourist Information Centre, Cnr Sixth Avenue and Melrose Parade, Maroochydore, QLD 4558 ☎ 07 5459 9050 ◷ Mon–Fri 9–5, Sat 9–4
🚃 Nambour

TIPS

» Public transportation is limited—a rented car is the best option.
» Parts around Maroochydore are over-developed—Noosa (▷ 186) in the north is the most scenic.
» During school holidays accommodation on the Sunshine Coast is stretched to the limit, so book ahead.

Below *Aerial view of Point Cartwright and Mooloolaba on the Sunshine Coast*

ROCKHAMPTON AND CAPRICORN REGION

▷ 188.

SUNSHINE COAST

▷ 189.

TOWNSVILLE AND MAGNETIC ISLAND

www.townsvilleholidays.info

The tropical city of Townsville is a good base for exploring the Great Barrier Reef, the outback, national parks and rainforests, and nearby Magnetic Island. Set around the craggy lookout of Castle Hill, the university city is north Queensland's largest regional complex, where many grand old buildings hold their place among more recent additions. The Strand is a popular waterfront precinct with a protected swimming enclosure. On Sundays the Flinders Mall hosts an art and crafts market.

Overlooking Ross Creek, the Museum of Tropical Queensland on Flinders Street East includes finds from the wreck of HMS *Pandora*, the ship sent to capture the mutineers of HMAV *Bounty* in 1790–91 (daily 9.30–5). Next door, the Reef HQ, allied to the Great Barrier Reef Marine Park, presents the world's largest coral reef aquarium (daily 9.30–5).

Magnetic Island is 20 minutes by catamaran ferry from Townsville, or 60 minutes by car ferry. Land- and water-based activity trips are popular on the island in almost year-round sunshine. With a good bus service and rental 'Mokes' as transport, it's easy to reach the many bays with their sandy beaches bounded by granite headlands. Walks are best in the cool of the morning or evening when it is often possible to see koalas in the wild in the island's large national park. Tours to the Great Barrier Reef (▷ 182–184) depart from the island daily.

🚌 349 T5 🛈 Bruce Highway, Townsville, QLD 4810 ☎ 07 4778 3555 🛈 Flinders Mall, Townsville, QLD 4810 ☎ 07 4721 3660 🚂 Townsville 🛳 Magnetic Island: Sunferries tel 07 4726 0800; www.sunferries.com.au

TOOWOOMBA AND THE DARLING DOWNS

www.toowoomba.com

The land west of the Great Dividing Range on the rolling plains of the Darling Downs is a great introduction to rural Australia. The fertile Darling Downs were first settled in the 1840s, and the black volcanic soils now produce 90 per cent of the state's wheat and half of its maize (corn). The region is also a major producer of sheep, cattle and dairy products.

The garden city of Toowoomba is known for its 19th-century buildings and botanic gardens, and is the perfect base for exploring the Downs. There is a craft market on the third Sunday of each month, while tree-lined Margaret Street has restaurants, cafés and antiques shops. The Cobb & Co. Museum on Lindsay Street (daily 10–4) has Australia's largest collection of horse-drawn vehicles.

Near the eastern Downs town of Oakey, 55km (34 miles) west of Toowoomba, the Jondaryan Woolshed is a working museum of 19th-century rural life (daily 10–4). The Museum of Australian Army Flying at Oakey has a top collection of military aircraft and memorabilia (daily 10–4).

The Granite Belt, around the town of Stanthorpe, in the south, is the heart of Queensland's expanding wine industry. Most vineyards open at weekends for tastings, and there are plenty of roadside stalls where you can buy fresh fruit and vegetables in season. The Stanthorpe Heritage Museum (Wed–Fri 10–4, Sat 1–4, Sun 9–1) has local memorabilia as well as the town's old timber jail, from 1876. The Girraween National Park, 26km (16 miles) south of Stanthorpe, is renowned for its spring wild flowers, huge granite boulders, scenic trails, grey kangaroos and excellent camping ground (daily 8–6; free).

🚌 353 V10/W10 🛈 Toowoomba Visitor Information Centre, cnr James and Kitchener streets, Toowoomba, QLD 4352 ☎ 07 4639 3797 🕔 Daily 9–5

UNDARA VOLCANIC NATIONAL PARK

www.undara.com.au
www.savannah-guides.com.au

The name 'Undara' comes from an Aboriginal word meaning 'a long way' referring to the world's longest-known lava flow, which extends some 160km (100 miles). Undara is located 275km (170 miles) inland from Cairns. The remote national park is a temperate and unusual outback destination, set on the eastern edge of the rugged Gulf Savannah, part of a tropical landscape of grass and scattered trees that stretches across northern Australia. With minimal humidity, the pleasant climate has warm days and cool evenings.

But the park's big attraction is its unique tubular caves, remnants of a shield volcano that erupted 190,000 years ago. Over time, sections of the caves have collapsed, and indigenous rainforest animals and plants have evolved in these fallen cavities. All tours are run from the Undara Experience camp, where the Undara Lava Lodge can provide accommodation in tents or restored train carriages (cars), or a place to camp if you bring your own gear. The various lava tube tours visit different sections of the tubes and last from two hours to a full day. Openings allow easy access for visitors, who can see the unusual rock formations and how the lava flow dramatically changed course. There is also a separate Aboriginal Culture tour. Lunch is included on some tours, and all outings feature morning or afternoon tea.

At night, campfire activities are organized with attractions such as bush poetry, singalongs and night walks. Be sure to rise early for the hearty camp kitchen bush breakfasts, which make for a great start to the day's activities. During the hot, summer months, Undara operates on reduced staff, so it is best to phone in advance for details.

🚌 348 S5 🛈 Undara Experience, Lava Lodge, Mount Surprise, QLD 4871 ☎ 07 4097 1900 🚂 Cairns

WHITSUNDAY ISLANDS

Whatever your nautical skills, rent a yacht, join a crew, or just board an excursion to discover the sheltered turquoise waters and reefs of the Whitsunday Islands.

The Whitsundays consist of 74 continental islands—many fringed by reefs. Cruises and ferries depart from Airlie Beach and neighbouring Shute Harbour; you can also charter yachts—with or without crew—at these ports. Southeast of Airlie Beach, mangrove bays along the coastline of the Conway National Park shelter amazing fish life, while estuaries are home to crocodiles. Inland, rainforests shroud the ranges and valleys. The islands themselves attract snorkellers and divers, who can swim with manta rays, dolphins, green turtles and hundreds of species of tropical fish. Humpback whales pass nearby (Jul–end Sep).

HIGHLIGHTS

Only 5km (3 miles) from Shute Harbour, Daydream Island is popular with day visitors. A 20-minute hike over the steep, rocky centre of the island brings you to the beach.

The most developed island of the group, Hamilton Island has an airport, shops, bank, school, marina and a hotel resort with a variety of accommodation from self-catering apartments to five-star hotels.

Hayman Island is the northernmost Whitsunday, 25km (15.5 miles) from Shute Harbour and is closest to the Great Barrier Reef. This 400ha (988-acre) island, its tallest peak at 250m (820ft), is covered in eucalypt and hoop pine vegetation and has prolific bird life. Its luxury resort provides dive courses, and there are regular trips to the reef on the resort's own vessel, the *Reef Goddess*.

Only basic, budget accommodation is available on Hook Island, 20km (12.5 miles) northeast of Shute Harbour, but there are the usual diving, snorkelling and reef trips.

Mostly national park, Lindeman Island is one of the most southerly of the Whitsundays, with over 20km (12.5 miles) of trails, and many secluded bays and beaches.

At 109sq km (42sq miles), Whitsunday Island is the largest of the group. Many tour vessels stop at Whitehaven Beach, where there is a stunning 6km (3.7-mile) stretch of sand. Snorkellers can explore the coral off the southern end of the beach.

INFORMATION

www.whitsundaytourims.com

➕ 349 U6 🛈 Airlie Beach Tourist Information Centre, 277 Shute Harbour Road, Airlie Beach, QLD 4802 ☎ 07 4946 6665 🚢 From Shute Harbour

TIP

» The best way to see the islands is from the deck of a sailing vessel.

Above *South Molle Island is one of the many islands in the Whitsunday archipelago*

OLD BRISBANE AND
THE BOTANIC GARDENS

The walk explores the historic core of Brisbane, now hemmed in by the modern city (▷ 172–176). Fine colonial buildings reflect the city's origins as a penal settlement and its later development as capital of the colony of Queensland.

THE WALK

Distance: 3km (2 miles)
Allow: Half a day
Start at: Anzac Square; see map ▷ 175, B1
End at: City Hall
How to get there: Anzac Square is opposite Central Station

★ Walk to Anzac Square, between Ann and Adelaide streets, and make your way to the square's focus, the Shrine of Remembrance.

❶ The sandstone Shrine of Remembrance was erected in 1930 as a memorial to the 60,000 Australian soldiers who died during World War I. A Classical Doric colonnade surrounds an eternal flame. A number of distinctively shaped bottle trees, manicured lawns, and gardens and memorial sculptures add to the charm of the square.

Cross Adelaide Street and walk through Post Office Square to the General Post Office in Queen Street. Pass through the arcade beside the post office to Elizabeth Street and cross the street to the St. Stephen's Church complex, dominated by St. Stephen's Cathedral.

❷ Neo-Gothic in design, St. Stephen's Cathedral was begun in 1863 and completed in 1874. Constructed of porphyry stone, the main facade has twin spires and stained-glass windows.

Return to Elizabeth Street and go right, turn right again on to Eagle Street and make your way to the riverside walkway at the Eagle Street Pier. Walk south to the Edward Street gates of the City Botanic Gardens.

❸ City Botanic Gardens is Brisbane's loveliest park, a gently undulating landscape spread with plantings of native and exotic species (▷ 172).

The gardens front the Brisbane River, and you can walk down through the park to the foreshore. Look also for the avenue of bunya pines and the shady palm forest. The City Gardens Café on Alice Street is a good place for a break.

Follow the sign from the café southwest across Alice Street to the Old Government House.

❹ Old Government House is a grand neoclassical building built in 1862 as the colonial governor's residence, a role it served until 1910. The house is now occupied by the Queensland University of Technology.

Walk a short distance back along Alice Street to the heart of the city and Parliament House.

❺ The main part of the Victorian Renaissance-style Parliament House was built in 1868 (▷ 104). Note how the building's verandahs provide the interior with some shade from the sun.

Nearby, in George Street, is the ornate Victorian exterior of the Queensland Club. Nearly opposite is The Mansions, a striking group of 1890s terrace (row) houses in red brick and pale limestone, now housing shops and restaurants.

Walk along George Street and go left through Queens Gardens to William Street. Cross the street to the Commissariat Stores.

❻ Convict workers constructed the Commissariat Stores in 1829 (Tue–Sat 10–4). Originally only two floors high, the third floor was added in 1913.

The Commissariat Stores was a government warehouse, storing goods brought from ships anchored in the nearby river. It now houses the museum and library of the Royal Historical Society of Queensland.

Return through the gardens to George Street and go left across the intersection with Queen Street to the former Treasury Building.

❼ Now refurbished as the Treasury Casino, this grand Italianate structure was completed in 1889. As with Parliament House, its verandas cool internal rooms. The interior retains many original features. Except for the inner walls of the arcade, the building is faced with dressed sandstone. Each phase of construction used sandstone from a different source, and there is a discernable difference between the Elizabeth Street frontage and those on Queen and

George streets, which were the last to be completed.

Opposite the Treasury Casino, walk down Queen Street Mall and cross the Albert Street intersection to the Regent Theatre.

❽ The exuberant exterior of the Regent Theatre, which dates from 1928, has been described as Spanish Perpendicular–Gothic Rococo. The Queen Street entrance leads past a booking hall, café and foyer to a monumental stairway. Originally designed to host live entertainment and films, the theatre is now exclusively a cinema.

Retrace your steps to Queen Street Mall, then turn right on to Albert Street to Brisbane City Hall.

❾ Facing King George Square and bounded by Adelaide and Ann streets, City Hall is an impressive neoclassical structure dating from 1930. City Hall is closed from 2010 for approximately three years to undergo extensive restoration..

WHEN TO GO
All year round.

WHERE TO EAT
There are numerous good refreshment outlets along the route.
Popular and well known is Jimmy's on the Mall in Queen Street Mall, selling light meals and drinks around the clock. City Gardens Café in Alice Street serves breakfast, lunch and afternoon tea. Or you can stock up for a picnic lunch in the Botanic Gardens.

PLACES TO VISIT
Customs House, Queen Street, ▷ 173.

Below *City Hall sits on King George Square in central Brisbane*

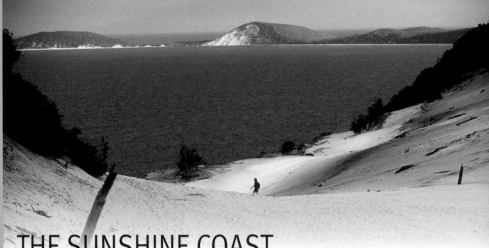

THE SUNSHINE COAST
AND ITS HINTERLAND

The drive heads into the hills behind the Sunshine Coast (▷ 189), just north of Brisbane, and ends at the coastal resort of Noosa Heads. It offers a mix of mountain and coastal scenery, long sandy beaches, pretty mountain towns, broad sugar cane fields and pristine national parks.

THE DRIVE
Distance: 290km (180 miles)
Allow: 1–2 days
Start at: Brisbane
End at: Brisbane

This trip can be done in a day but an overnight stop around Noosa Heads will allow you to see more.

★ From Brisbane take the Bruce Highway (Metroad 3, National Highway 1) north, and after 57km (35 miles) turn left on to the Glass House Mountains Tourist Drive. Drive through the town of Glass House Mountains and follow the signs to Australia Zoo.

❶ Australia Zoo, made famous by naturalist Steve Irwin (1962–2006), has hundreds of native and other animals on display (▷ 189).

Continue for 3km (2 miles) to Landsborough and turn left on to

the Blackall Range Road to Maleny. After 12km (7 miles) turn left into Mary Cairncross Scenic Reserve.

❷ From the reserve a short track threads for 1.7km (1 mile) through subtropical rainforest. From the parking area there are fine views of the peaks of the impressive Glass House Mountains.

Drive on for 5km (3 miles) to Maleny.

❸ The craft shops and cafés of Maleny provide a day-trip escape from the summer heat of the coast.

Head 5km (3 miles) back on the road to Landsborough and take a left turn for the 12km (7-mile) mountain ridge drive to Montville. Continue north for 4km (2.5 miles) and turn left to Kondalilla National Park.

❹ Kondalilla National Park, running down the western slopes of the

Blackall Range, encloses a remnant of the region's once-extensive rainforests, much of which were cleared in the late 19th and early 20th centuries. The moderate Kondalilla Falls 2.7km (1.7-mile) circuit walk passes through rainforest and crosses a creek suitable for swimming.

Drive north for 4km (2.5 miles) to the village of Mapleton.

❺ Attractive Mapleton has excellent views over the coastal plain to the Pacific Ocean. About 4km (2.5 miles) west of here is the turnoff to the small Mapleton Falls National Park. The easy Wompoo Circuit walking track winds for 1.3km (0.8 miles) through rainforest.

From Mapleton, take the road to Nambour and after 14km (9 miles) turn on to the Bruce Highway to Yandina, 8km (5 miles) north. In

Opposite *The beach near Noosa Heads*

Yandina follow signs to the Buderim
Ginger Factory.

6 The region's rich volcanic soils,
high rainfall and warm climate
are ideal for growing ginger. Visit
Yandina's ginger factory for its large
selection of ginger products.

Travel north on the Bruce Highway
for 16km (10 miles) to Eumundi.

7 Eumundi was once the heart
of dairy and timber industries.
Nowadays its economy relies largely
on the busy markets that are held on
Wednesday and Saturday (▷ 186).

Take the Eumundi–Noosa Road to
Noosa Heads, about 25km (15.5
miles). You pass through agricultural
districts before reaching the Noosa
River and and then the town itself.

8 Noosa, surrounded by Noosa
National Park, is the busy and stylish
heart of the Sunshine Coast.

Take the coast road from Noosa
south to Coolum Beach, a distance
of 22km (14 miles), via the coastal
villages of Sunshine Beach, Marcus
Beach and Peregian Beach. At
Coolum Beach, take the road west
to Yandina for 15km (9 miles), past
fields of sugar cane, to rejoin the
Bruce Highway for the return drive
of 107km (66 miles) to Brisbane.

WHEN TO GO
From April to October there are fine
days and cool nights. December and
January are hot and crowded.

WHERE TO EAT
Montville: Monkey Business Café,
184 Main Street, is a popular, family-
run café (daily 9–9).
   Noosa Heads: Sails Beach Café
& Bar, 75 Hastings Street, has great
coffee, nice sweet things and ocean
views (daily 8–10).

PLACES TO VISIT
Brisbane, ▷ 172–176.

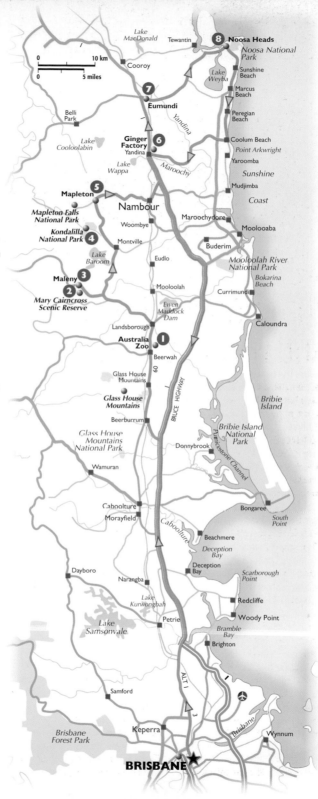

THROUGH THE ATHERTON TABLELAND

Explore the heart of the southern Atherton Tableland (▷ 171), its lush rainforests, crater lakes, farmlands and pretty country towns, all set between the Bellenden Ker/Bartle Frere Mountain Ranges and the Great Dividing Range.

THE DRIVE
Distance: 325km (202 miles)
Allow: 2 days
Start at: Cairns
End at: Cairns

★ Drive south from Cairns along the Bruce Highway (National Highway 1) for 24km (15 miles) to Gordonvale. Look for the Atherton Tableland sign and turn right on to the Gillies Highway, which winds up the range (the hairpin bends can be slippery when wet). There are a couple of stopping points with views down the range. After 31km (19 miles) turn right from the highway for the signposted Cathedral Fig, a 6km (4-mile) drive along a narrow road, 1.5km (1 mile) of which is unsealed.

❶ A 100m (109-yard) walk from the parking area leads through rainforest to the 500-year-old Cathedral Fig tree, within the Wet Tropics World Heritage Site. As high as a 12-floor building and with a girth of 43m

(141ft), the tree shelters birds, reptiles, tree kangaroos, sugar gliders and possums.

Backtrack to the Gillies Highway, and turn right on to it. After about 4km (2.5 miles), turn left into the Lake Barrine parking of the Crater Lakes National Park.

❷ Lake Barrine is a lake formed by the volcanic activity that moulded much of the Atherton region. It is surrounded by high-altitude tropical rainforest. An easy 5km (3-mile) walking track circles the lake, or take a 40-minute guided boat trip. There are tea rooms by the lake.

Continue on the highway southwest and after about 10km (6 miles) turn right to the town of Yungaburra.

❸ Yungaburra was once the hub of a thriving timber-felling area, and retains many early 20th-century buildings, some of which now

house craft shops. One of north Queensland's best country markets is held on the fourth Saturday of each month. A track leads from the town to the Curtain Fig tree, a tall strangler fig that has grown a spectacular curtain of aerial roots.

Yungaburra is a good place to break the drive and stay overnight. On day two, head south for 17km (11 miles) through mainly dairy country to the town of Malanda.

❹ Malanda is still very much an agricultural town, producing milk for most of north Queensland. Among its buildings is the Lake Eacham Hotel; built in 1911. The Malanda Dairy Centre, in James Street, has a museum on the local food and dairy industry (Tue–Sat 9–4, closed Sun and Mon). Just outside the town, on the road to Atherton, is Malanda Falls Environmental Park, where the falls drop into the town's swimming pool. Nearby is a rainforest walking

Opposite *The Atherton Tablelands stretch between Cairns and Innisfail*

track. The Malanda Falls Visitor Centre explains the Tableland's volcanic origins.

Travel the scenic rural road for 24km (15 miles) south to Millaa Millaa. Just east of the town, take Scenic Route 9 through lush pastures to Millaa Millaa Falls.

5 The Millaa Millaa Falls drops gracefully on to rocks, forming a beautiful curtain of water as it does so. You can stay and swim in a rock pool here, or drive a few kilometres farther east to visit Zillie Falls and, farther still, Ellinjaa Falls.

Back on the main road, drive southeast for 6km (4 miles) and look for the sign on the left for the turn-off to Mungalli Creek Dairy, 3km (2 miles) from the highway.

6 Mungalli Creek Dairy has north Queensland's only boutique farmhouse cheese shop (daily 10–4). Taste the cheese and yogurt products made on the premises, or buy something to eat or drink at the dairy's tea room.

Rejoin the main road, now the Palmerston Highway, and drive 17km (11 miles) southeast to the small parking area just off the highway that indicates the start of the Vallicher and Tchupala Falls walks.

7 Choose the track to Tchupala Falls, the more scenic of the two walks. You pass through a short section of rainforest to reach a lookout with a view over the falls. A gentle ribbon of water at dry times of the year, Tchupala Falls becomes a torrent in the wet season. Climbing a series of steep steps brings views of the gorge and Henrietta Creek.

Continue east on the Palmerston Highway in the direction of Innisfail. After 31km (19 miles) pass the turn off for Innisfail and keep driving

north along what is now the Bruce Highway. After 17km (11 miles) turn left to Josephine Falls, 8km (5 miles) from the highway.

8 After parking, walk 800m (872 yards) through rainforest to the base of Josephine Falls, which is fed by rains falling on Mount Bartle Frere, the highest mountain in Queensland, which rises above you.

Rejoin the Bruce Highway and drive north for 16km (10 miles). Some 7km (4 miles) after the town of Babinda, turn off to Babinda Boulders.

9 Babinda Boulders is a popular swimming and picnic spot. The boulder-strewn watercourse has some good pools for summer swimming. Caution: It is dangerous to swim here after heavy rain. On the Wonga Track Rain Forest Circuit, you cross the creek on a suspension bridge and do an easy 850m (926-yard) round trip.

Go back to the highway, and head north for Cairns, which is about 60km (37 miles) away through

arable land flanked by often mist-covered mountains.

WHEN TO GO
Most times of the year. December to March are the hottest, wettest but least crowded months; from April to the end of October there are fine, sunny days and cool nights.

WHERE TO EAT
Lake Barrine: Lake Edge Teahouse is a popular, family-run café (daily 9–5).
  Yungaburra: Flynns Café has good coffee and light gourmet lunches (Tue–Sat 9–5).
  Malanda: Malanda Dairy Centre and Café (daily 9.30–4.30) uses fresh local ingredients.
  Mungalli Creek Dairy: morning and afternoon teas and snacks (daily 10–4).

PLACES TO VISIT
Atherton Tableland and Kuranda, ▷ 171.
Cairns, ▷ 177.
Hinchinbrook Island, ▷ 179.
Mission Beach and Dunk Island, ▷ 185.
Undara Volcanic National Park, ▷ 190.

WHAT TO DO

AIRLIE BEACH

PRO SAIL
www.prosail.com.au
Let an experienced crew take you on a three-day maxi cruise among the sun-drenched Whitsunday Islands (▷ 191).
✉ 251 Shute Harbour Road, Airlie Beach, QLD 4802 ☎ 07 4946 7533 🕐 Depart daily 🖐 From A$399 per person for two nights, two days

BEERWAH

AUSTRALIA ZOO
www.australiazoo.com.au
Australia Zoo is home to hundreds of native and exotic animals, including koalas, wallabies, snakes, alligators and crocodiles.
✉ Steve Irwin Way, Beerwah, QLD 4519 ☎ 07 5436 2000 🕐 Daily 9–4.30 🚌 Buses available 🚉 Beerwah; free pick-up can be arranged 🖐 Adult A$55, child A$33, family A$164 🍴

BRISBANE

BRISBANE ARTS THEATRE
www.artstheatre.com.au
The 'Arts' is a venue popular with locals and visitors, who come for comedy, theatre and musicals.
✉ 210 Petrie Terrace, Brisbane, QLD 4000 ☎ 07 3369 2344 (Mon–Fri 11–2) 🚉 Roma Street 🍸

BRISBANE ENTERTAINMENT CENTRE
www.brisent.com.au
International stars draw the crowds to this venue, 16km (10 miles) north of the city.
✉ Melaleuca Drive, Boondall, QLD 4034 ☎ 07 3265 8111 🚌 Boondall (Brisbane city council buses) 🚉 Boondall 🍴 ◻

EMPIRE HOTEL NIGHTCLUB
A smart cocktail bar and nightclub with local and international DJs.
✉ 339 Brunswick Street, Fortitude Valley, QLD 4006 ☎ 07 3852 1216 🕐 Cocktail bar: Mon–Sat 5pm–5am, Sun 5pm–3am; Nightclub: Mon–Thu 10pm–5am, Fri, Sat 9pm–5am, Sun 9pm–3am 🚉 Fortitude Valley 🖐 Entrance fee A$10 after 10

GOLDEN CIRCLE LIVE!
www.livegoldencircle.com.au
Tour one of Australia's largest fruit and vegetable processing facilities, have lunch at the Circle Café, and shop for bargains in the factory outlet.
✉ 260 Earnshaw Road, Northgate, QLD 4013 ☎ 07 3266 0678 🕐 Daily 9–1.30 🖐 Adults A$12, child A$7 🚉 Binda

HOTEL WICKHAM
www.thewickham.com.au
This gay and lesbian pub has a gaming room, drag shows and DJs every night.
✉ 308 Wickham Street, Fortitude Valley, QLD 4006 ☎ 07 3852 1301 🕐 Gaming room: from 9am; Hotel: Sun, Mon 12pm–12am, Tue–Thu 12pm–2am, Fri, Sat 12pm–5am 🚉 Fortitude Valley

JAZZ CLUB
www.brisbanejazzclub.com.au
Local and international jazz musicians play in a venue that overlooks the Brisbane River.
✉ 1 Annie Street, Kangaroo Point, QLD 4169 ☎ 07 3391 2006 🕐 Sat 4.30–11.30pm, Sun varies from week to week ⛴ Ferry from Eagle Street 🖐 Members from A$8, visitors from A$10

LIFESTYLE MARKETS
www.southbankmarket.com.au
This open-air market features more than 130 stalls selling local produce and crafts—hats, jewellery, clothing, pottery, woodcraft and homewares—all home-made.
✉ Stanley Street Plaza, South Bank Parklands, Brisbane, QLD 4101 ☎ 07 3867 2051 🕐 Fri 5–10pm, Sat 10–5, Sun 9–5 🚉 South Bank

LONE PINE KOALA SANCTUARY
www.koala.net
This celebrated zoo has a breeding

population of more than 130 koalas.
Unlike in other states of Australian,
in Queensland you can cuddle, feed
or just watch the koalas. There are
other native animals on display,
including kangaroos and wallabies.
✉ Jesmond Road, Fig Tree Pocket,
Brisbane, QLD 4069 ☎ 07 3378 1366
🕐 Daily 8.30–5 🚌 430, hourly from
Myer Centre, Queen Street Mall, Brisbane
🚢 Mirimar Cruises from city (Adult A$28,
child A$19, family A$65) ☕

PADDINGTON ANTIQUE CENTRE
www.southbankmarket.com.au
Occupying a former theatre built in
1929, Paddington Antique Centre
has around 60 dealers. There are
other antiques shops nearby.
✉ 167 LaTrobe Terrace, Paddington, QLD
4064 ☎ 07 3369 8088 🕐 Daily 10–5
🚌 Paddington (stop 11)

QUEENSLAND PERFORMING ARTS CENTRE
www.qpac.com.au
Theatre, dance, opera, musicals,
plays and classical music concerts
are performed at this modern
arts venue.
✉ Cnr Grey and Melbourne streets, South
Bank, QLD 4101 ☎ qtix 13 62 46 🚌 South
Bank 🚉 South Bank 🍴 ☕ 🍷

QUILPIE OPALS
www.quilpieopals.com.au
One of Queensland's best-known
opal retailers, Quilpie Opals sells
many varieties of opal and settings.
Stones can be bought individually
or in jewellery pieces and come with
certificate of authenticity.
✉ 266 George Street, Brisbane,
QLD 4000 ☎ 07 3221 7369 🕐 Mon–Fri
9–6, Sat 9–4, Sun 10.30–3.30 🚌 Queen
Street 🚉 Queen Street Mall

SUNCORP STADIUM
www.broncos.com.au
Watch Brisbane's rugby league
team, the Broncos, on their home
ground.
✉ Milton, Brisbane, QLD 4000 ☎ Ticketek
13 28 49 🕐 Check with Broncos 🚉 Milton
🖐 Adult from A$29, child from A$14.50

TREASURY CASINO
www.conradtreasury.com.au
Brisbane's casino has bars, live
entertainment and restaurants.
✉ Queen Street Mall, Brisbane, QLD
4000 ☎ 07 3306 8888 🕐 Daily 24 hours
🚌 Queen Street 🚉 Queen Street Mall

THE ZOO
www.thezoo.com.au
Local and international cabaret,
comedy acts and bands.
✉ 711 Ann Street, Fortitude Valley, QLD
4006 ☎ 07 3854 1381 🕐 Thu–Sat
8pm–2am, occasionally Sun 8pm–12am
🚉 Fortitude Valley 🖐 Depends on the act

BUNDABERG
BUNDY KEGS
www.schmeider.bizland.com
Schmeider's Cooperage houses
one of the largest selections of
woodwork in Australia. Spinners,
weavers, glass-blowers, jewellers,
potters and leatherworkers also
display and sell their products here.
✉ 3–7 Alexandra Street, East Bundaberg,
QLD 4670 ☎ 07 4151 8233 🕐 Mon–Fri
9–5, Sat 9–3 🚉 Bundaberg ☕

CAIRNS
A. J. HACKETT BUNGY TOWER
www.ajhackett.com.au
Bungee jump from a 50m (164ft)
tower amid rainforest 15km
(9 miles) north of Cairns; minimum
age is 10.
✉ MacGregor Road, Smithfield, QLD 4870
☎ 1800 622 888 🕐 Daily 10–5 🚌 Pick-
up service at 9, 11, 1 and 3 (call to reserve)
🖐 From A$125

CAIRNS NIGHT MARKETS
www.nightmarkets.com.au
The Night Markets off the Esplanade
are some of the most popular. They
sell a wide range of manufactured
and handmade items, including
clothing, toys, gifts, jewellery, opals
and paintings.
✉ 71–75 The Esplanade, Cairns, QLD 4870
☎ 07 4051 7666 🕐 Daily 5–11

GEO PICKERS CAMPING AND CANVAS
This shop sells and rents camping
goods and specialist equipment,

including tents, cooking utensils,
maps, clothing, mosquito hats
and repellents.
✉ Shop 270 Mulgrave Road, Cairns, QLD
4870 ☎ 07 4051 1944 🕐 Mon–Fri 8.30–5,
Sat 8.30–1

PARADISE PALMS GOLF COURSE
www.paradisepalms.com.au
A demanding 18-hole course only
20 minutes north of Cairns.
✉ Paradise Palms Drive, Clifton Beach,
QLD 4879 ☎ 07 4059 9900 🕐 Tee times
6.30–3.40 🖐 A$120, including motorized
cart and clubhouse facilities 🍴 🍷
🚗 23km (14 miles) north from Cairns

PRO DIVE CAIRNS
www.prodive-cairns.com.au
Pro Dive, in the heart of Cairns, offers
tuition for beginners and advice and
dive trips for the experienced. The
shop sells dive gear, wetsuits, stinger
bodysuits, snorkelling equipment and
souvenirs.
✉ 116 Spence Street, Cairns, QLD 4870
☎ 07 4031 5255 🕐 Daily 8.30am–9pm

REEF CASINO
www.reefcasino.com.au
A full range of gaming tables, bars
and clubs.
✉ 35–41 Wharf Street, Cairns 4870 ☎ 07
4030 8888 🕐 Sun–Thu 9am–3am, Fri, Sat
9am–5am

REEF MAGIC CRUISES
www.reefmagiccruises.com
The catamaran *Reef Magic* will
take you to the outer Great Barrier
Reef (▷ 182–184) for five hours for
snorkelling or scuba-diving. Basic
scuba lessons are provided.
✉ 1 Spence Street, Cairns, QLD 4870
☎ 07 4031 1588 🕐 Tours depart daily
at 9am 🖐 Adult from A$175, child A$90,
family A$440

R'N'R WHITE-WATER RAFTING
www.raft.com.au
Brave the rapids of the Tully River
on a full-day trip. Rafters must be
13 or over.
✉ 278 Hartley Street, Cairns, QLD 4870
☎ 07 4041 9444 🕐 Tully River tours daily
🖐 From A$150, from Mission Beach, or
Cairns (A$10 extra). Lunch included.

TJAPUKAI ABORIGINAL CULTURAL PARK
www.tjapukai.com.au
At one of Cairns's most popular tourist attractions, the store sells Aboriginal artworks and materials from Far North Queensland. Items include paintings, pottery, clapsticks, handcrafted emu eggs, didgeridoos and boomerangs.
✉ Kamerunga Road, Smithfield, QLD 4878 ☎ 07 4042 9900 ⏰ Shop: daily 9–5, 7–10; Park: daily 9–5 🅿

THE WOOLSHED
www.thewoolshed.com.au
A raucous backpackers' haunt with Top 40 hits and classics.
✉ City Place, Cairns, QLD 4870 ☎ 07 4031 6304 ⏰ Sun–Thu 6pm–3am, Fri, Sat 6pm–5am ✋ A$6 after 10pm

EUMUNDI
EUMUNDI MARKETS
www.eumundimarket.com.au
Every Saturday and Wednesday the small town of Eumundi, in the Sunshine Coast hinterland, comes alive with more than 300 stalls selling everything from freshly grown produce to home-made crafts. Saturday's is the main market. It pays to get there early.
✉ Main Street, Eumundi, QLD 4562 ⏰ Sat 6.30am–2pm, Wed 8–1.30

FRASER ISLAND
THE FRASER ISLAND COMPANY
www.fraserislandco.com.au
Join your guide aboard a 4WD bus to explore Fraser Island (▷ 180).
☎ 07 4125 3933, 1800 063 933 ⏰ Depart daily at 8.30am ✋ Adult A$199, child A$145

FRASER ISLAND DISCOVERY
Travelling aboard 4WD vehicles, passengers make a one-day tour of the natural wonders of Fraser Island.
✉ 11 Bartlett Street, Noosaville, QLD 4566 ☎ 07 5449 0393 ⏰ Daily at 8am ✋ Adult from A$155, child from A$105

GOLD COAST
ART AND CRAFT MARKETS
www.artandcraft.com.au
More than 200 outdoor stalls display a wide variety of locally handmade products, ideal for souvenirs and gifts. The markets are set up on the beachfront on the first and third Sunday of the month at Broadbeach, the second Sunday at Coolangatta and the last Sunday at Burleigh.
✉ Broadbeach, Coolangatta and Burleigh beaches ☎ 07 5533 8202 ⏰ 8–2.30

GOLD COAST ARTS CENTRE
www.gcac.com.au
Here you will find two cinemas, a theatre and comedy club.
✉ 135 Bundall Road, Surfers Paradise, QLD 4217 ☎ 07 5581 6500 ⏰ Café open daily from 11am 🍴 ☕

JUPITERS CASINO
www.conrad.com.au
The casino has several bars, nightly live entertainment and a number of restaurant options.
✉ Broadbeach Island, Gold Coast, QLD 4218 ☎ 07 5592 8100 ⏰ Daily 24 hours 🚌 Broadbeach Island

MELBA'S ON THE PARK
www.melbas.com.au
Restaurant and cocktail bar. Late-night menu. Dine in or takeaway.
✉ 46 Cavill Avenue, Surfers Paradise, QLD 4217 ☎ 07 5538 7411 ⏰ Daily 7.30am–11pm ✋ Varies

PALM MEADOWS
www.palmmeadows.com.au
An 18-hole tournament golf course designed by the Australian golfer Greg Norman.
✉ Palm Meadows Drive, Carrara, QLD 4211 ☎ 1800 651 117 ⏰ Tee times between 7 and 9 and all afternoon ✋ A$115 per player, A$65 per junior playing with adult, including motorized cart 🍴 🅿

WALKIN' ON WATER SURF SCHOOL
www.walkinonwater.com
This popular surfing school runs classes on the beaches of Rainbow Bay, Greenmount and Coolangatta. Classes are small, with a maximum of eight surfers to each coach. The surrounding area is exceptionally beautiful, and whales and dolphins are often seen nearby.

✉ Greenmount Beach, near Coolangatta ☎ 07 5534 1886 ⏰ Daily from about 6am (summer) 🚌 Surfside Bus Lines, alight at Twin Towns Services Club ✋ From A$40 for a two-hour group lesson, A$120 personal lesson, equipment included

DREAMWORLD
www.dreamworld.com.au
▷ 181.
✉ Dreamworld Parkway, Coomera, QLD 4209 ☎ 07 5588 1111 ⏰ Daily 10–5 🚌 Brisbane–Gold Coast buses stop here. Shuttle services from major Surfers Paradise hotels 🚆 Coomera then bus ✋ Adult A$75, child A$49 🍴 🅿

SEA WORLD
www.seaworld.com.au
▷ 181.
✉ Sea World Drive, The Spit, Main Beach, Gold Coast, QLD 4217 ☎ 07 5588 2222 ⏰ Daily 10–5 🚌 The Spit ✋ Adult A$75, child A$49 🍴 🅿

WARNER BROS. MOVIE WORLD
www.movieworld.com.au
▷ 181.
✉ Oxenford, Gold Coast, QLD 4210 ☎ 07 5573 8485 ⏰ Daily 10–5 🚌 Surfside Bus Lines shuttle, tel 13 12 30 🚆 Helensvale then bus ✋ Adult A$70, child A$46. Superpass (entry to Movie World, Wet'n'Wild and Sea World, with a return visit to the park of your choice): adult A$130, child A$110 🍴 🅿

WET'N'WILD WATER WORLD
www.wetnwild.com.au
▷ 181.
✉ Pacific Motorway, Oxenford, QLD 4210 ☎ 07 5573 2255 ⏰ Nov–end Feb daily 10–5 (also 5–9pm Dec 27–Jan 26); Mar, Apr, Sep, Oct 10–4.30; May–end Aug 10–4 🚆 Helensvale then bus ✋ Adult A$42, child A$33 🍴

HERVEY BAY
HERVEY BAY WHALE WATCH
www.herveybaywhalewatch.com.au
Half-day cruises on a catamaran to see humpback whales as they swim past on their annual migration.
✉ Hervey Bay, QLD 4655 ☎ 1800 671 977 ⏰ Departs daily at 7am and 1pm, late Jul–early Nov ✋ Adult A$110, child A$60

KURANDA

KURANDA MARKETS

www.kurandamarkets.com.au

A tropical North Queensland institution, these breezy, relaxed markets near Cairns have high quality handmade goods and artworks for sale. Items can be packed ready for transport overseas. There are also several shops open later in the day.

✉ Rob Veivers Drive, Kuranda, QLD 4872 ☎ 07 4093 8060 🕒 Daily 9–3
🚉 Kuranda

PORT DOUGLAS

ANZAC PARK MARKET

The emphasis at this popular market is on handmade goods, including jewellery, clothing, crafts, pottery and painting. There are several good food stalls.

✉ Anzac Park, Wharf Street, Port Douglas, QLD 4871 🕒 Sun 8–1.30

QUICKSILVER CONNECTIONS

www.quicksilver-cruises.com

A catamaran whisks you to the outer Barrier Reef for diving or snorkelling. You can also view the reef from an underwater observatory.

✉ Marina Mirage, Port Douglas, QLD 4871 ☎ 07 4087 2100 🕒 Depart 9.30am, return 4.30pm (hotel pick-up from Cairns to Mossman) 💺 Adult from A$197, child A$99

SUNSHINE COAST

ROLLING ROCK NIGHTCLUB/ NEW YORK BAR

www.rollingrock.com.au

Dance to DJs and live bands, or relax in the cocktail bar.

✉ Bay Village, Hastings Street, Noosa Heads, QLD 4567 ☎ 07 5447 2255
🕒 Daily from 8pm

THE SPA

www.coolum.regency.hyatt.com

The Spa, part of the Hyatt Regency resort at Coolum, has more than 100 treatments, including massages, facials and reflexology.

✉ Warran Road, Coolum Beach, QLD 4573 ☎ 07 5446 1234 🕒 Daily 6.30am–7pm
💺 From A$125 for a one-hour massage
🍴 🅿

FESTIVALS AND EVENTS

MARCH

QUIKSILVER PRO

For two weeks from early March, the world's best surfers compete at Burleigh Heads on the Gold Coast in the Quiksilver Pro.

APRIL–JULY

QUEENSLAND WINTER RACING CARNIVAL

www.racingqueensland.com.au

Australia's top horses and jockeys compete in the Queensland Winter Racing Carnival.

MAY

CAXTON STREET SEAFOOD AND WINE FESTIVAL

www.caxtonstseafoodandwinefestival.com

This one-day celebration brings out the very finest of Queensland's produce, with the city's top chefs on hand to display their talents.

JULY

GOLD COAST MARATHON

www.goldcoastmarathon.com.au

The Gold Coast Marathon on the first Sunday in July attracts competitors from all over the world for a full or half-marathon or 10km (6-mile) run, as well as walking and wheelchair races.

CAIRNS SHOW

www.cairnsshow.com.au

At the Cairns Show at Cairns Showgrounds you'll see animals, equestrian events, horticulture, live entertainment and sideshows.

QUEENSLAND MUSIC FESTIVAL

www.qmf.org.au

The Queensland Music Festival, held in odd-numbered years, presents fine performers from Australia and around the world. The festival lasts for two weeks and takes place in odd-numbered years. Performances are held in various towns and cities.

AUGUST

ROYAL QUEENSLAND SHOW

www.ekka.com.au

The Royal Queensland Show is the state's main agricultural show, and is held annually at the RNA Exhibition Grounds, Bowen Hills, Brisbane. Events over the 10 days include animal judging, exhibits, demonstrations, arena events and sideshows.

HAMILTON ISLAND RACE WEEK

www.hamiltonislandraceweek.com.au

Yachtsmen and women from all over the world compete in this eight-day event held in the Whitsunday Islands.

MOUNT ISA RODEO

www.isarodeo.com.au

The Mount Isa Rodeo is the biggest event on Australia's rodeo calendar.

SEPTEMBER

BIRDSVILLE RACES

www.birdsvilleraces.com

Horses race on a dirt track at the Birdsville Races, an outback institution held on the first Saturday in September.

BRISBANE FESTIVAL

www.brisbanefestival.com.au

The Brisbane Festival is a three-week international festival of dance, drama, music and the visual arts. Expect to see world premieres.

NOOSA JAZZ FESTIVAL

www.noosajazz.com.au

The Noosa Jazz Festival at Noosa Heads features more than 150 Australian and international jazz performers.

OCTOBER

GOLD COAST INDY 300

www.indy.com.au

In the Indy 300, the world's leading Indy car drivers race around a street circuit on the Gold Coast in late October.

PRICES AND SYMBOLS

The restaurants are listed alphabetically (excluding Le, La and Les). The prices given are the average for a two-course lunch (L) and a three-course dinner (D) for one person, without drinks. The wine price is for the least expensive bottle.

For a key to the symbols, ▷ 2.

BRISBANE

ANISE

Reputed to be Australia's best wine bar, it seats only 20 people, so it's often crowded. Regional French food is served; vegetarian options available; and a superb range of wines from Australia and Europe.
✉ 697 Brunswick Street, New Farm, Brisbane, QLD 4005 ☎ 07 3358 1558 🕓 Thu–Sat 12pm–1am, Sun–Wed 5pm–12am 🖐 L A$46, D A$60, Wine A$29 🚌 190, 193, 191

CHA CHA CHAR WINE BAR AND GRILL

Smartly tailored with a clean-cut, nautical look, this waterfront bistro serves some of Brisbane's finest steaks, with Mediterranean and Asian accents on the modern Australia menu. Reserve ahead.
✉ Shop 5, Eagle Street Pier, Eagle Street, Brisbane, QLD 4000 ☎ 07 3211 9944

🕓 Mon–Fri 12–2.30, Mon–Sun 6–9 🖐 L A$55, D A$65, Wine A$30 🚢 Inner city ferry to Eagle Street Pier

CITY GARDENS CAFÉ

www.gardencafes.info
Hearty breakfasts are served at this café, as well as modern-style lunches and Devonshire teas. Reserve ahead.
✉ City Gardens Alice Street, Botanical Gardens, Brisbane, QLD 4000 ☎ 07 3229 1554 🕓 Daily 8–4 🖐 L A$35, Wine A$26 🚌 City Loop

E'CCO BISTRO

www.eccobistro.com
Owner/chef Philip Johnson has long been the pacesetter for bistro dining in Brisbane, and he continues to refine his cuisine with the focus on fresh, seasonal ingredients, a stylish infusion of Mediterranean influences and skilful execution. To ensure you get a table, reserve ahead.
✉ 100 Boundary Street, Brisbane, QLD 4000 ☎ 07 3831 8344 🕓 Tue–Fri 12–2.30, 6–9, Sat 6–9 🖐 L A$63, D A$80, Wine A$40

ERA BISTRO

www.erabistro.com.au
Modern Australian cuisine using the best seasonal produce. Check out

the à la carte menu; plus there are panninis and salads for lunch, and breakfasts feature hearty favourites like fried eggs.
✉ 102 Melbourne Street, Brisbane, QLD 4000 ☎ 07 3255 2833 🕓 Mon–Sat 7am–9pm, Sun 7am–3pm 🖐 B A$20, L A$40, D A$65, Wine A$32

IL CENTRO

Alsace-born chef Romain Bapst brings fresh creativity and energy to the classic Italian cookbook and delivers sophisticated European food that draws the crowds to this large and boisterous riverside fine diner. Crab lasagne is a signature dish. Reserve ahead.
✉ Eagle Street Pier, Eagle Street, Brisbane, QLD 4000 ☎ 07 3221 6090 🕓 Sun–Fri 12–3, daily 6–10 🖐 L A$50, D A$70, Wine A$34 🚢 CityCat to Eagle Street Pier

JIMMY'S ON THE MALL

Ideal for a light meal or a coffee break, menu changes regularly, but might include Tasmanian oysters, king prawns and Moreton Bay bugs with lemon dill and Riesling saffron cream, and wok-tossed vegetables. Wines available by the glass.
✉ Queen Street Mall, Brisbane, QLD 4000 ☎ 07 3229 9999 🕓 Daily, 24 hours 🖐 L A$38, D A$50, Wine A$27

MONDO ORGANICS
www.mondo-organics.com.au

Brisbane's finest organic restaurant brings passion and creativity to the table with the finest, freshest local produce, much of it sourced from small producers. The restaurant also has an outstanding choice of gluten- and dairy-free options.

✉ 166 Hardgrave Road, West End, Brisbane, QLD 4101 ☎ 07 3844 1132 🕐 Tue 6pm–late, Wed–Fri 12pm–3, 6pm–late, Sat 8.30am–2.30pm, 6pm–late 🖐 L A$501, D A$65, Wine A$38 🚌 190, 194 from Adelaide Street stand 47

SIANA
Asian-inspired food is the forté of this breezy riverfront bar/bistro that attracts the style brigade, who come to graze over cocktails as well as to sit down and unfurl a white napkin. The all-embracing Asian menu features selections from the tandoori oven as well as the wok.

✉ Upper Plaza, Level 1, 71 Eagle Street, Brisbane, QLD 4000 ☎ 07 3221 3887 🕐 Mon–Fri 12pm–3pm, 6–10, Sat 5–10 🖐 L A$40, D A$55, Wine A$32

SUMMIT RESTAURANT
www.brisbanelookout.com

A great place to go for Sunday brunch. The view is the star attraction, yet the food offers stiff competition, especially the excellent seafood dishes. Reserve ahead.

✉ Sir Samuel Griffith Drive, Mount Coot-tha Lookout, Brisbane, QLD 4066 ☎ 07 3369 9922 🕐 Daily 12–2.30, 6–9, Sun brunch from 8am 🖐 L A$43, D A$70, Wine A$33 🚌 471 from Adelaide Street stand 45 🚗 8km (5 miles) west from Brisbane via Milton Road (State Route 32)

BURLEIGH HEADS
MERMAIDS CAFÉ AND BAR
In a prime position overlooking a surfing hotspot, the specialty of this glassy restaurant is Mediterranean/Asian fusion food that revels in piquant flavours applied to local seafood dishes and salads in particular. A great choice for breakfast. Reserve ahead for Friday,

Saturday and Sunday breakfast.

✉ Burleigh Beach Pavilion, 43 Goodwin Terrace, Burleigh Heads, QLD 4220 ☎ 07 5520 1177 🕐 Daily 7am–3pm, Thu–Sun 5.30–10 🖐 L A$40, D A$55, Wine A$29

CAIRNS
OCHRE RESTAURANT
www.ochrerestaurant.com.au

This restaurant takes the taste buds into the culinary outback with a menu that makes extensive use of native foods such as kangaroo, crocodile, Kakadu plums and riberries. The restaurant also offers gluten-free, vegetarian and tasting menus. Reserve ahead.

✉ 43 Shields Street, Cairns, QLD 4870 ☎ 07 4051 0100 🕐 Mon–Fri 12–3, 6–10, Sat, Sun 6–10 🖐 L A$48, D A$65, Wine A$33

PERROTTA'S AT THE GALLERY
Spilling from the front of a colonial-era building, this popular, casual restaurant has a comfort-food menu that works hard all day, from the breakfast pancakes to the lamb shanks at dinnertime. Dinner reservations advised.

✉ Cairns Regional Art Gallery, cnr Shields and Abbott streets, Cairns, QLD 4870 ☎ 07 4031 5899 🕐 Daily 7.30am–late 🖐 L A$45, D A$55, Wine A$28

SUSHI TRAIN
Right in the Cairns Central shopping centre, this popular eatery serves sushi and other Japanese snack foods, priced by plate colour, from a conveyor belt.

✉ 144 Cairns Central, Cairns, QLD 4870 ☎ 07 4031 5444 🕐 Mon–Fri 10–9, Sat, Sun 10–4 🖐 L A$15, D A$25

MAIN BEACH
FELLINI
www.fellini.com.au

Crafted by the legendary Percuoco family, virtual royalty in Australian gastronomic circles, the classics of the Italian kitchen are served with proper panache at this plush restaurant with panoramic views across the Gold Coast Broadwater. Reserve ahead.

✉ Waterfront Level 1, Marina Mirage,

Seaworld Drive, Main Beach, QLD 4217 ☎ 07 5531 0300 🕐 Daily 12–3, 6.30–late 🖐 L A$65, D A$80, Wine A$28

MISSION BEACH
SCOTTY'S BAR AND GRILL
Excellent value for money. Among the dishes are New Zealand oysters, and barramundi grilled with stir-fried vegetables and Anita's tropical sauce. Vegetarian options and meals for children are available.

✉ 167 Reid Road, Mission Beach, QLD 4850 ☎ 07 4068 8870 🕐 Daily 5pm–late 🖐 D A$42, Wine A$19

NOOSA
HARBOUR MASTER
Great value and tasty Modern Australian cuisine, especially the daily lunch specials. Riverside location is perfect for sunny days.

✉ Noosa Marina, Noosaville, QLD 4566 ☎ 07 5474 1100 🕐 Daily 7am–late 🖐 B A$20, L A$35, D A$50, Wine A$27 ⛴ Noosa River Ferry stops outside

PORT DOUGLAS
MANGO JAM
www.mangojam.com.au

This no-frills diner dishes out the crowd pleasers, with a range of pizzas, salads, pasta dishes, noodles and burgers, in generous servings. The wine list is Australian.

✉ 24 Macrossan Street, Port Douglas, QLD 4871 ☎ 07 4099 4611 🕐 Daily 7.30–late 🖐 L A$30, D A$45, Wine A$20

YANDINA
SPIRIT HOUSE
www.spirithouse.com.au

Set in Asian-inspired gardens complete with stream and duck pond, the restaurant prepares Thai–West fusion dishes. Plate swapping is encouraged on a menu that features mild and hot curries with imaginative combinations of scallops, soft-shell crab, pork belly and duck. There is a good Australian wine list. Reserve ahead.

✉ 20 Ninderry Road, Yandina, QLD 4561 ☎ 07 5446 8994 🕐 Daily 12–2.30, Wed–Sat 6–9 🖐 L A$52, D A$70, Wine A$31 🚗 10km (6 miles) south from Eumundi

STAYING

PRICES AND SYMBOLS

Prices are for a double room for one night including breakfast, unless otherwise stated. All the hotels listed accept credit cards, unless otherwise stated. Note that rates can vary widely throughout the year.

For a key to the symbols, ▷ 2.

AIRLIE BEACH
CORAL SEA RESORT

www.coralsearesort.com
This is the only waterfront resort on the Whitsunday coast, a short walk from Airlie Beach. It has suites, two-bedroom apartments, family units and one-, two- and three-bedroom luxury penthouses. Two restaurants, and watersports.
✉ 25 Oceanview Avenue, Airlie Beach, QLD 4802 ☎ 07 4946 6458 🕐 All year
✋ A$235–A$420 excluding breakfast;

apartments A$340–A$595 ① 77
🔄 ⛱ Outdoor 🚗 26km (16 miles) northeast from Proserpine off Bruce Highway

ATHERTON TABLELAND
ROSE GUMS WILDERNESS RETREAT

www.rosegums.com.au
Nine luxury treehouses set in a wildlife sanctuary; each is self-contained, with a fully equipped kitchen and spa bath. Sizes range from studios to two-bedroom treehouses sleeping up to six, and each has a wood-burning stove.
✉ Land Road, Butchers Creek, QLD 4872 ☎ 07 4096 8360 🕐 All year
✋ A$275–A$315 (family chalets: extra persons A$25) 🚗 82km (51 miles) southwest from Cairns, 15km (9 miles) east from Malanda, 18km (11 miles) southeast from Yungaburra

BRISBANE
THE MARQUE HOTEL

www.marquehotels.com
The rooms include deluxe, spa and executive suites with all the usual facilities.
✉ 103 George Street, Brisbane, QLD 4000 ☎ 07 3221 6044 🕐 All year
✋ A$129–A$209 excluding breakfast
① 99 🔄 ⛱ Outdoor 🚌 Brisbane Loop

METRO INN TOWER MILL BRISBANE

www.metroinns.com.au
Each room has a balcony; and all are well equipped. There is a rooftop restaurant.
✉ 239 Wickham Terrace, Brisbane, QLD 4000 ☎ 07 3832 1421 🕐 All year
✋ A$125–A$325 (family room) excluding breakfast ① 80 🔄 🚇 Roma Street, Central

RENDEZVOUS HOTEL
www.rendezvoushotels.com
Rooms and one- or two-bedroom apartments, the latter with living/ dining areas and kitchens.
✉ 255 Ann Street, Brisbane, QLD 4000 ☎ 07 3001 9888 All year
A$205–A$412 excluding breakfast 138 Opposite Central Station

RYDGES SOUTH BANK
www.rydges.com
This hotel is in the heart of the South Bank Parklands.
✉ Cnr Grey and Glenelg streets, South Bank, Brisbane, QLD 4101 ☎ 07 3364 0800 All year A$189–A$379 excluding breakfast 305 Buses to Exhibition Centre or South Brisbane bus station South Brisbane

CAIRNS
LILYBANK B & B
www.lilybank.com.au
Every room has a private bathroom and there is a saltwater pool.
✉ 75 Kamerunga Road, Stratford, Cairns, QLD 4870 ☎ 07 4055 1123 All year A$99–A$121 5 Outdoor 10 mins from Cairns

THE MANTRA ESPLANADE
www.mantraesplanadecairns.com.au
The one- and two-bedroom units include kitchens. Facilities include a pool, fitness room, sauna, spa and health club.
✉ 53–57 The Esplanade, Cairns, QLD 4870 ☎ 07 4046 4141 All year A$165–A$495 excluding breakfast 123 Outdoor 500m (545 yards) from bus terminal 1km (0.6 mile) from Cairns station

CAPE TRIBULATION
CAPE TRIB BEACH HOUSE
www.capetribbeach.com.au
The resort has a variety of wooden cabins—either bunkhouses or rooms (some with private bathrooms); no TV, phone or radio. There is a separate shared kitchen.
✉ Rykers Road, Cape Tribulation, QLD 4873 ☎ 07 4098 0030 All year A$89– A$199 excluding breakfast

Most rooms Outdoor Follow Captain Cook Highway north from Cairns for 100km (62 miles), through Mossman, and cross Daintree River by cable ferry. Cape Trib Beach House is 38km (24 miles) north

HAYMAN ISLAND
HAYMAN ISLAND RESORT
www.hayman.com.au
The perfect high-life retreat with all the panache that a glossy resort brings to purposeful pleasure. Impressive natural credentials are given the full-gloss treatment with waterfalls, reflecting ponds, sculpted gardens and titanic pools.
✉ Great Barrier Reef, QLD 4801 ☎ 07 4940 1838, 1800 075 175 All year A$295–A$1,450 212 Outdoor pools Boat transfer from Hamilton Island (Airport)

HERVEY BAY
KINGFISHER BAY
www.kingfisherbay.com
The self-contained villas have two or three bedrooms, and some have spa baths. There are three restaurants, four bars, and a coffee shop and café.
✉ Kingfisher Bay Resort & Village, PMB 1, Urangan, Hervey Bay, QLD 4655 ☎ 07 4120 3333, 1800 072 555 All year Rooms A$220 excluding breakfast Villa A$185–A$350 152 rooms, 110 villas Four outdoor pools (one heated)

MOSSMAN
SILKY OAKS LODGE
www.silkyoakslodge.com.au
Buried in tropical rainforest on the banks of the Mossman River, these stylish bungalows blend unbuttoned living and screaming colours, buffed with a few stylish details in the food and recreation department. There's a spa by the river, canoes for paddling and bikes for lazy rides through the cane fields.
✉ Finlayvale Road, Mossman, QLD 4873 ☎ 07 4098 1666 All year A$598–A$798

NOOSA
FRENCH QUARTER RESORT
www.frenchquarternoosa.com.au
Most suites overlook the central pools and spa and all have a spa bath. They have cooking and laundry facilities. Also Lorenza's restaurant and bar.
✉ 62 Hastings Street, Noosa, QLD 4567 ☎ 07 5430 7100 All year A$220–A$625 119 Outdoor

PALM COVE
THE SEBEL REEF HOUSE & SPA
www.reefhouse.com.au
Small, elegant and relaxed, this white-on-white sanctuary on the beach just north of Cairns revels in the Queensland colonial style with lots of cool cane, big balconies and swooning greenery.
✉ 99 Williams Esplanade, Palm Cove, QLD 4879 ☎ 07 4055 3633 All year A$169–A$439 69

PORT DOUGLAS
RYDGES REEF RESORT
www.rydges.com
Accommodation ranges from hotel rooms and suites to self-contained villas. The activity centre includes a gymnasium, pool, tennis courts, and pitch and putt golf. There are several restaurants.
✉ Port Douglas Road, Port Douglas, QLD 4871 ☎ 07 4099 8900 All year Rooms A$225–A$280 excluding breakfast. Villas (three-bed) A$350 282 rooms, 180 villas Five outdoor Shuttle bus to Port Douglas. Airport pick-up transfer available: adult A$28, child A$14 73km (45 miles) northwest from Cairns

SURFERS PARADISE
COURTYARD SURFERS PARADISE RESORT
www.marriott.com
Large resort; rooms have private balconies; a penthouse has an outdoor spa. Facilities include gymnasium, spa and tennis court.
✉ Cnr Gold Coast Highway and Hanlan Street, Paradise Centre, Surfers Paradise, QLD 4217 ☎ 07 5579 3499 All year A$305–A$350 excluding breakfast 404 Outdoor pool 25km (15 miles) north from Coolangatta Airport along Gold Coast Highway to Cavill Avenue, Surfers Paradise; turn right on to southbound Gold Coast Highway to Hanlan Street

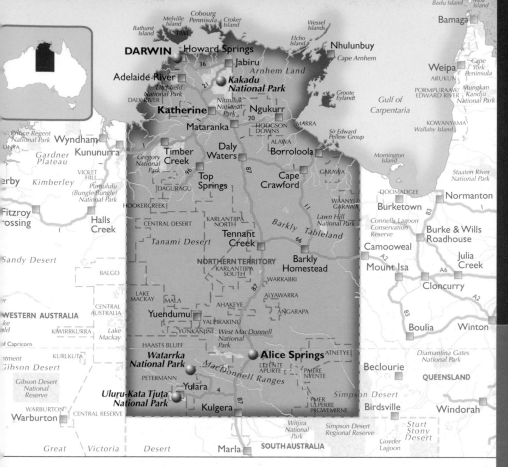

NORTHERN TERRITORY

Often called Australia's last frontier, the Northern Territory is the most sparsely populated part of Australia. The capital, Darwin, is essentially a whistle stop, a gateway to the territory's rugged natural splendours.

The Northern Territory has two distinct faces. In the coastal north is a tropical wetland that is deluged by huge rains that fall in the wet season between December and March. This tropical downpour powers a fertile ecosystem that is seen at its best in the palm-fringed creeks, rock gorges and paperbark wetlands of Kakadu, Australia's largest national park, and is home to spectacular concentrations of bird and reptile life, including many large and fearsome saltwater crocodiles.

Farther south the landscape becomes parched and harsh, until it encounters the deserts of the Red Centre. Here aeons of scorching sun have sculpted an ancient, scarred landscape where the cattle stations are measured in square miles and where the land, sky and even the silence exert an almost mystical force. At the heart of the Red Centre, Alice Springs is the gateway to the attractions of the region, which include Uluru, a national icon, also known as Ayers Rock.

Due to its relative isolation from the European centres of population along the east coast, the Northern Territory has the most intact Aboriginal culture of any state. There is nowhere better to see examples of the rock art that dates back more than 50,000 years and ends only when Australia's Aboriginal people were evicted from the ancestral lands during the period of European settlement—the world's longest tradition of creative expression.

The Northern Territory also has an emerging Aboriginal tourism industry that uses Aboriginal Australians to tell stories of the Dreamtime, introduce visitors to the savoury pleasures of witchetty grubs or decipher rock art paintings. For the traveller, journeying through the country with people who have absorbed it through the bare soles of their feet brings another dimension to the experience.

ADELAIDE RIVER QUEEN

www.jumpingcrocodilecruises.com.au
During the 90-minute cruise on the *Adelaide River Queen,* you'll be entertained by saltwater crocodiles that jump out of the murky river for a meal. The river bird life is less voracious and includes magpie geese, brolgas, dollar birds and hawks. Kingfishers and corellas gather in large flocks on the floodplains and it is not uncommon to see wild pigs and buffalo.

✚ 342 K2 ✉ Adelaide River Bridge, Arnhem Highway, via Humpty Doo; 64km (40 miles) southeast of Darwin ☎ 08 8988 7144, 1800 888 542 🕐 Cruises: daily 9am, 11am, 1pm, 3pm 🖐 Adult A$30, child A$20 🚌 Daily shuttle from Darwin (bookings 08 8924 1111) 🍴 🎁

ALICE SPRINGS

▷ 210.

AYERS ROCK (ULURU)

▷ 215–218.

BATHURST AND MELVILLE ISLANDS

www.aussieadventures.com.au
Also known as the Tiwi Islands, Bathurst and Melville are popular one- or two-day trips 80km (50 miles) north from Darwin across the Beagle Gulf. Both islands are thickly forested with eucalypt, woolly-butt and paperbark, and there are open marshlands and wetlands. Among the wildlife are wallabies, possums, reptiles and many kinds of birds. The sandy beaches accommodate nesting turtles, while the waters are home to stingrays, sharks, manta rays and saltwater crocodiles. Mangroves provide a habitat for mud crabs and many fish varieties. The Tiwi people have traditionally painted their bodies in preparation for ceremonies. Dancing is a part of everyday life on the islands, again particularly for ceremonial events.

🔲 341 K1 ℹ️ Visitors to the islands must obtain permits from the Tiwi Island Land

opposite A view of Alice Springs from Anzac Hill
right A saltwater crocodile leaps out of the water at Crocodylus Park

Council ☎ 08 8981 4891 ❓ Tiwi Tours run one- or two-day tours (meals and camping accommodation included), tel 1300 721 1365

CROCODYLUS PARK

www.crocodyluspark.com
The wildlife park, a 15-minute drive east of Darwin, cares for lions and tigers, iguanas, cassowaries, dingoes and wallabies—as well as hundreds of saltwater crocodiles, the largest living relics of the dinosaur age. Bellair's Lagoon is home to more than 70 crocodiles. Twenty pens house breeding pairs of crocodiles, which can be seen from an overhead walkway.

✚ 341 K2 ✉ 815 McMillans Road, Berrimah, NT 0828, 10km (6 miles) east from Darwin on National Highway 1 ☎ 08 8922 4500 🕐 Daily 9–5. Feeding times 10, 12, 2 and 3.30 🖐 Adult A$30, child A$15, family A$80 🚌 5 from Darwin 🍴 🎁

DARWIN

▷ 211.

KAKADU NATIONAL PARK

▷ 212–213.

KATHERINE

www.visitkatherine.com.au
Katherine is a popular town about 300km (186 miles) from Darwin and 640km (397 miles) from Alice Springs. The Jawoyn people once lived along the Katherine River. The town developed after a telegraph station was established

in the 1870s and subsequently Katherine became the focus of a grazing economy. The photographs and objects at the Katherine Museum (daily 9–4) on Gorge Road relate to the history of the region.

Katherine Hot Springs are approximately 3km (2 miles) southwest along the Victoria Highway, near the Katherine River. Springvale Homestead, 8km (5 miles) southwest of Katherine on Shadforth Road, dates from 1878 and is the oldest surviving homestead in the Northern Territory (daily 9–5; free tour at 3). The Cutta Cutta Caves are 27km (17 miles) south of Katherine off the Stuart Highway (guided tours in the dry season daily at 9, 10, 11, 1, 2 and 3; adult A$14, child A$7). These spectacular limestone caves are a habitat for rare species of bat.

North of Katherine lies Nitmiluk (Katherine Gorge) National Park (daily 7–6). A good way to see the park is by a boat tour of one of the five accessible gorges. If you don't have time to do this, though, the 3,000sq km (1,170sq mile) park has more than 100km (62 miles) of trails, with walks from one hour to five days. You can see ancient Aboriginal rock art, and among the wildlife are freshwater crocodiles, rare crimson and double-barred finches, giant fruit bats and wallabies. Entry to the park is free.

✚ 342 L3 ℹ️ Katherine Visitor Information Centre, cnr Lindsay Street and Katherine Terrace, Katherine, NT 0852 ☎ 08 8972 2650

INFORMATION

www.centralaustraliantourism.com
⊞ 342 M8 ℹ Central Australian
Tourism Industry Association, 60 Gregory
Terrace, Alice Springs, NT 0870 ☎ 08
8952 5800, 1800 645 199 🕐 Mon–Fri
8.30–5.30, Sat–Sun 9–4 🚂 Ghan train
from Sydney, Melbourne, Adelaide or
Darwin; vehicles can be transported

TIP

» Reserve your accommodation ahead as
the Alice is very popular.

ALICE SPRINGS

This is the main base for a tour of Australia's Red Centre—truly hot, but there's
much to see and do.

Set between the East and West MacDonnell Ranges, the Alice Springs area
is the home of the Arrernte Aboriginal people. The town was named after a
waterhole that enabled European expansion and control of central Australia
in the late 19th century. Following the footsteps of explorer John McDouall
Stuart, the construction of the telegraph line from Adelaide to Darwin was
completed in 1872, which made it viable for pastoralists to take up leases in
the area. Discovery of gold 100km (62 miles) east of the Alice in 1887 led to a
population boom. The settlement was first known as Stuart and the telegraph
station was Alice Springs. The latter became a reference for the town in 1933
to avoid confusion.

ALICE SPRINGS

On the Todd River (usually dry), the Alice lies almost in the geographical middle
of the continent, 1,500km (930 miles) from the nearest state capital. But remote
as it is, the town offers enough facilities to qualify as a holiday spot. Have dinner,
take in a show and perhaps wander into Lasseters Casino, next to the top hotel,
the Rydges Plaza. There's a good choice of quality restaurants. Outdoor pursuits
include rock climbing, bicycling, bushwalking, horseback and camel riding and
off-road driving.

More than 100 domestic flights arrive each week with visitors who take
tours to Uluru-Kata Tjuta National Park (▷ 215–218) and Watarrka National Park
and Kings Canyon (▷ 219).

ALICE SPRINGS DESERT PARK

www.alicespringsdesertpark.com.au
At this parcel of Australia's arid zone just west of the Alice, a 1.5km (1-mile) trail
leads through three recreated desert habitats—Sand Country, Woodland and
Desert Rivers—with native animals and plants.
✉ Larapinta Drive, PO Box 1120, Alice Springs, NT 0871 ☎ 08 8951 8788 🕐 Daily 7.30–6
✋ Adult A$20, child A$10

TENNANT CREEK

The classic outback town of Tennant Creek is 530km (329 miles) north of Alice
Springs on the Stuart Highway (Information Centre, tel 08 8962 1281). This
former gold-mining town is best known for the Devils Marbles Conservation
Reserve, a landscape of precariously balanced boulders 90km (56 miles) south
on the Stuart Highway.

Below *The Devils Marbles are about
530km (329 miles) north of Alice Springs*

DARWIN

Darwin's distance from other cities and its frontier history have given it a distinct character—part Asian, part Australian.

Largely destroyed by Japanese bombing in 1942 and Cyclone Tracy in 1974, Darwin today is a prosperous city with a youthful population. There is a large Aboriginal community, as well as a strong Asian presence from its pearling and gold-mining days.

DARWIN BOTANIC GARDENS
The 42ha (104-acre) gardens are a tropical world of palms, orchids, rainforest species, bottle trees and mangroves. Features include a rainforest gully, a wetland and a mangrove boardwalk.
✉ Gardens Road, The Gardens, NT 0820 🕐 Daily 7–7 ✋ Free

DARWIN MILITARY MUSEUM AND RESERVE
The museum displays war memorabilia and objects, photographs and a video showing the bombing of Darwin. The 4ha (10-acre) tropical grounds are home to wallabies and a remnant monsoon rainforest.
✉ 5434 Alec Fong Lim Drive, East Point, NT 0820 ☎ 08 8981 9702 🕐 Daily 9.30–5 ✋ Adult A$12, child A$5

FANNIE BAY GAOL MUSEUM
Darwin's notorious penal institution operated from 1883 to 1979. The starkness of prison life and the old gallows are still evident.
✉ East Point Road, Fannie Bay, NT 0820 ☎ 08 8999 8290 🕐 Daily 10–5 ✋ Free

INDO-PACIFIC MARINE EXHIBITION
Live coral, fish and tanks containing complete ecosystems are on display. The sealife includes box jellyfish, sea horses and stonefish.
✉ Stokes Hills Wharf, Darwin, NT 0820 ☎ 08 8981 1294 🕐 Apr–Oct daily 10–5; Nov–Mar Mon–Fri 9–1, Sat–Sun 10–5 ✋ Adult A$18, child A$8

MUSEUM AND ART GALLERY OF THE NORTHERN TERRITORY
This major cultural institution covers art and crafts, natural history, Aboriginal culture, archaeology and history. The Cyclone Tracy Gallery recalls Christmas Day in 1974, when the cyclone devastated the city.
✉ Conacher Street, Fannie Bay, NT 0820 ☎ 08 8999 8264 🕐 Mon–Fri 9–5, Sat–Sun 10–5 ✋ Free

INFORMATION
www.tourismtopend.com.au
✚ 341 K2 ℹ Tourism Top End Visitor Information, 6 Bennett Street, Darwin, NT 0800 ☎ 08 08 8980 6000 🕐 Daily 8.30–5.30

TIP
» The wet season (Nov–end Apr) can cause flooding on the roads. Temperatures can be in the mid-30s°C (mid-90s°F) with humidity nearing 100 per cent. For current road conditions, tel 1800 246 199.

Above *Few of Darwins buildings were built before Cyclone Tracy in 1974*

KAKADU NATIONAL PARK

INFORMATION

www.environment.gov.au/parks/kakadu
✚ 342 L2 ℹ Bowali Visitor Centre, Jabiru, NT 0886 ☎ 08 8938 1121
🕐 Daily 8–5 ℹ Tourism Top End Visitor Information Centre, 6 Bennett Street, Darwin, NT 0800 ☎ 08 8980 6000
🕐 Daily 8.30–5.30 ✋ National Park entry is free 🚌 AAT Kings 08 8923 6555
💻 🏛

INTRODUCTION

Wetlands teeming with wildlife, sheer rock cliffs, monsoon forests and ancient Aboriginal rock art put Kadadu firmly in the league of Australia's finest national parks.

Although the park is most accessible in the dry season (May to the end of September), it is actually at its most impressive in the wet season (November to the end of April), when evening storms create huge floodplains teeming with tens of thousands of waterbirds. At Jim Jim, Gunlom and Twin Falls, water tumbles from the 200m (656ft) sandstone escarpments. The dry season is the best time to get around and the humidity is lower. There is accommodation at Jabiru, Cooinda (near Yellow Water) and South Alligator, and plenty of camping grounds.

A 19,000sq km (7,410sq mile) World Heritage Site, Kakadu has been home to Aboriginal people for more than 50,000 years. Cave paintings, rock carvings and archaeological sites tell the story of their beliefs, skills and culture. More than 5,000 sites have been catalogued, including the remarkable rock art galleries at Ubirr and Nourlangie Rock. Many paintings depict everyday scenes, with images of fish, birds, animals and Dreamtime creation legends. There are well-marked walking tracks leading to some of the more famous sites.

The landscape is a rare complex of interlinked ecosystems—tidal flats, floodplains, lowlands and plateaux—habitats for rare or endemic plants and animals. Mammals include species of kangaroo, wallaby and flying foxes.

Above *Sunrise at Yellow Water*

WHAT TO SEE

SOUTH ALLIGATOR AREA

The Arnhem Highway crosses the South Alligator River about 40km (25 miles) past the northern park entrance. From Kakadu Resort, just before the river, the 3.5km (2-mile) Gungarre walk goes through monsoon forest and woodlands along the edge of Nggardabal Billabong. The Mamukala Wetlands, 7km (4.5 miles) east of the South Alligator River bridge, are accessed by a 3km (2-mile) walk.

JABIRU AREA

Jabiru, the service town for the Ranger Uranium Mine, is at the northeast edge of the park. Book tours at the travel office. The Bowali Visitor Centre is 5km (3 miles) west of Jabiru. The Marrawuddi Gallery sells Aboriginal arts and crafts and there is a café. A 2km (1.2-mile) woodland trail leads to the Gagudju Crocodile Hotel.

EAST ALLIGATOR AREA

The rock art at Ubirr is the main attraction here. Near the end of the Arnhem Highway, a sealed road branches 34km (21 miles) north to Border Store/ Manbiyarra and the Ubirr Rock Art Site (Apr–end Nov daily 8.30–dusk; Dec– end Mar 2–dusk). A 1km (0.6-mile) trail (mostly accessible by wheelchair) leads past several galleries, and the 250m (820ft) climb to the lookout is rewarded with panoramas over the Narbab floodplain and rocky terrain. Around Border Store are walks through rainforest, riverside vegetation and sandstone country.

NOURLANGIE AREA

The Kakadu Highway leads southwest from Jabiru. A sealed road to Nourlangie Rock branches off 21km (13 miles) from the Bowali Visitor Centre. The rock is best viewed from the Gunwarddehardde Lookout and is spectacular near sunset. A 1.5km (1-mile) walk passes an Aboriginal shelter and rock art sites. The 3.5km (2-mile) Bubba Trail runs from the Muirella Park camping ground and passes through wetland waterbird habitats.

JIM JIM AND TWIN FALLS

About 39km (24 miles) from the Bowali Visitor Centre, a vehicle track leads south to the Jim Jim Falls—a 60km (37-mile), two-hour drive. The falls are at their spectacular best after the wet season. The rock pool, with its white sandy beach, can be accessed by 4WD only from June to the end of November. Surrounded by dense forest, nearby Twin Falls, with its sandy beaches, is open from May to the end of November.

YELLOW WATER AREA

The Warradjan Aboriginal Cultural Centre (daily 9–5), 55km (34 miles) southwest of the Bowali Visitor Centre, provides an introduction to Aboriginal life in Kakadu. The art and craft shop has an excellent range of products. A boat tour on South Alligator floodplain, with its prolific bird life and dramatic wetland scenery, is not to be missed. Crocodile sightings are common. Scenic flights operate from Cooinda airstrip.

MARY RIVER AREA

About 45km (28 miles) southwest from Yellow Water along the Kakadu Highway, a track suitable only for 4WD vehicles leads to the Maguk Plunge Pool 12km (7 miles) away. This is a popular destination in summer. A 2km (1.2-mile) partly raised boardwalk follows a creek bed to the natural rock pool fed by a waterfall. This southern section of the park has a number of walks and two camping grounds.

TIPS

» Detailed maps and brochures are available from Bowali Visitor Centre, near Jabiru, and the entrance stations on the Arnhem and Kakadu highways.

» You can see much of the park in a conventional vehicle, but some areas are accessible only to 4WD vehicles. Whatever you are driving, make sure the vehicle is roadworthy and you have adequate supplies of fuel.

» The wet season is from November to the end of April and roads can flood. Some park roads are closed for six months from the start of the wet season. For road conditions, tel 1800 246 199.

Below The Kakadu escarpment towers over the flood plains

LITCHFIELD NATIONAL PARK

www.travelnt.com

Litchfield, 100km (62 miles) south of Darwin, is a popular place at weekends for picnics and swimming. The famous waterfalls cascade off the Tabletop Range plateau; the larger ones are fed by springs that flow all year round, but all are particularly impressive during the wet season. Waterfalls, rainforest and dramatic sandstone formations make this national park popular with locals.

There are several popular and easily accessible sites to see within the park. The double Florence Falls waterfall cascades into a swimming hole surrounded by monsoon forest. There are panoramic views from the escarpment, a short walk from the parking area, and a steep trail with stairs leads to the swimming pool. You can also swim in nearby Buley Rockhole, a series of waterfalls and rockholes.

About 10km (6 miles) off the main road down a 4WD track is an area known as the Lost City, where strange block and pillar sandstone formations resemble buildings, people and animals.

Tolmer Falls is one of the most dramatic waterfalls in the park, it has viewing platforms and some good walking tracks. Caves at the base of the falls house colonies of rare ghost bats and orange horseshoe bats.

Wangi Falls waterfalls and swimming hole are the most popular attractions in the national park. A 3km (2-mile) trail goes through monsoon rainforest to the top of the falls. There is a large picnic area and kiosk. Note that the swimming hole may be closed after heavy rain.

✚ 341 K2 🛈 Tourism Top End Visitor Information Centre, 6 Bennett Street, Darwin, NT 0800 ☎ 08 8980 6000 ❓ Odyssey Safaris (1300 661 229) run a two-day Hidden Secrets Safari

MACDONNELL RANGES AND STANDLEY CHASM

www.centralaustraliantourism.com

The magnificent gorges and rocky ridges of the MacDonnell Ranges have inspired artists for decades. The scenery has a dynamic character that changes with the rising and setting of the sun. Simpsons Gap, with a rare, permanent waterhole, is a good introduction to the landscape, only 18km (11 miles) from Alice Springs (daily 8–8). The walk to Cassia Hill gives commanding views of the MacDonnell Ranges. A good time to visit is late afternoon or early morning, when the black-footed rock wallabies are more active.

Farther west, Standley Chasm is a spectacular narrow gap in the MacDonnell Ranges, 50km (31 miles) from Alice Springs (daily 8–6, last entry 5; adult A$8, child A$6.50). At noon the sun hits the chasm floor and ignites its sheer quartzite walls, which for a few brief moments light up fiery orange. The rest of the day it is cool and shady but still impressive, surrounded by cycads, ferns and river gums. The pretty 1km (0.6-mile) trail from the parking area and kiosk to the chasm follows Angkerle Creek. A café, built into the side of the hill, provides cold drinks and refreshments.

To the west along the Namatjira Drive, the picturesque waterholes at Ellery Creek Big Hole—89km (55 miles) from Alice Springs—Ormiston Gorge and Glen Helen Gorge are perfect for a dip. Also in this area are the Ochre Pits, which the Aboriginal people once quarried. Ochre was traditionally a valuable material used for cave paintings and ceremonial body decorations.

✚ 342 L8/M8 🛈 Central Australian Tourism Industry Association, 60 Gregory Terrace, Alice Springs, NT 0870 ☎ 08 8952 5800

TERRITORY WILDLIFE PARK

www.territorywildlifepark.com.au

The park, set in 400ha (988 acres), is an excellent introduction to the wildlife of the Northern Territory. More than 6km (3.5 miles) of trails weave through managed habitats, past a huge aviary, a lagoon teeming with waterbirds, and open fields of kangaroos and wallabies. An entire Top End river system has been recreated in an aquarium and the nocturnal house has rare native species. A free shuttle train links major exhibits.

✚ 341 K2 ✉ Cox Peninsula Road, Berry Springs, NT 0837 ☎ 08 8988 7200 🕐 Daily 8.30–6 💲 Adult A$20, child A$10 🚌 Daily service to and from the outer Darwin region; bookings essential, tel 08 8948 7200 📱 🏧

TJUWALIYN (DOUGLAS) HOT SPRINGS PARK

www.nt.gov.au

An easy day trip from Darwin, the park encloses a section of the Douglas River where thermal pools create an oasis in the dry woodland. The waters attract wildlife such as bandicoots, frill-necked lizards (below) and flying foxes. The most comfortable time to visit is in the dry season; heavy rains in the wet season can cut off roads. Swimming is banned in the main hot springs—make for the cooler pools up- and downstream.

✚ 342 L2 ✉ Off Oolloo Road from Stuart Highway ☎ 08 8976 0282 💲 Free. Camping: adult A$6.60, child A$3.30 🚌 200km (124 miles) south of Darwin

Below *A frill-neck lizard warns off predators*

INTRODUCTION

There are some world wonders that are simply breathtaking—Uluru (Ayers Rock) is one of them.

Uluru and Kata Tjuta are the ancient Aboriginal names for Ayers Rock and The Olgas. These geological wonders continue to be known by both their Aboriginal and English names. Uluru is one of the world's greatest natural attractions, a giant red monolith rising from the semi-arid plains in the middle of Australia's outback. Kata Tjuta is equally remarkable, 36 enormous domes about 50km (31 miles) west of Uluru. Both outcrops are sedimentary rocks. At sunset, Uluru and Kata Tjuta change from bright red to orange to lilac in a matter of minutes; at sunrise they are equally dramatic. Both landforms have great spiritual and cultural significance to Anangu (Traditional Owners).

The Uluru-Kata Tjuta National Park is a UNESCO World Heritage Site, covering 1,325sq km (517sq miles). The park is listed for both its natural and cultural significance. Uluru measures 9.4km (6 miles) around the base and is 340m (1,115ft) high. The domes of Kata Tjuta rise up to 546m (1,791ft). There is excellent accommodation at Ayers Rock Resort, from camping grounds to five-star hotels, and also shops, a post office, a bank and a supermarket.

AN ANCIENT LAND

The region is culturally significant to the local Pitjantjatjara and Yankuntyjatjara Aboriginal people, collectively known as the Anangu. Anangu believe their ancestors have lived here since time began; archaeological evidence suggests the area has been occupied for 10,000 years.

TJUKURPA, ABORIGINAL LAW

Tjukurpa was laid down at the Creation and it still defines and guides the daily lives of Anangu people. For them it clarifies the nature of the earth's creation and the relationship between people, plants, animals and landscapes. It also explains rules for social structure, living together and caring for each other and

INFORMATION

www.environment.gov.au/parks/uluru

✚ 346 K9 🅸 Uluru-Kata Tjuta Cultural Centre, National Park Headquarters, Yulara, NT 0872, 1km (0.6 mile) from Uluru on the road from Ayers Rock Resort
☎ 08 8956 3138 ◷ Daily 7–6 🖐 Free

Uluru-Kata Tjuta National Park
www.environment.gov.au/parks/uluru
☎ 08 8956 2299 ◷ One hour before dawn to one hour after dusk (5–6.30am and 7.30–9pm) 🖐 Three-day visit or part thereof: adult A$25, under 16s free 🅸 The Visitors Centre, Yulara Drive, Yulara, NT 872 ☎ 08 8957 7377
◷ Daily 8.30–7.30

Above Uluru glows a deep red at the sun sets over the area

TIPS

» Try to stay for at least two nights.

» If you are walking independently, do so early in the morning as temperatures soar later on.

» At Ayers Rock Resort (▷ 229), each hotel and campground has its own swimming pool. Campers may use only their own pool and the Sails in the Desert pool is strictly for Sails guests, but otherwise hotel guests are able to cross-use facilities.

» Climbing Uluru is against Anangu spiritual beliefs, but is not prohibited. Anangu prefer that you respect their culture by not climbing the rock. Moreover, the climb is dangerous for the unfit and for people with health conditions, especially during the hotter months. The Uluru Climb and the Kata Tjuta Valley of the Winds walk are closed if temperatures are predicted to exceed 36°C (97°F), usually from 8am and 11am respectively.

» Both Uluru and Kata Tjuta are stunning to photograph from various angles and especially at dawn or dusk. Some sections are restricted and cannot be photographed.

Below *Camel tours are available at Ayers Rock Resort*

the land. There's a story to be told in each of the many nooks and crannies in the rock surfaces, as well as in the ancient rock paintings.

Tjukurpa also determines sacred places, which are often associated with important Aboriginal ancestors. The creation story of the Kuniya Python Woman explains the scars on Uluru and the ripples in the nearby Mutitjulu Waterhole. It is the religious duty of Anangu, as traditional custodians of Uluru and Kata Tjuta, to protect certain sites in the area. In the National Park sacred sites are further protected by law. Visitors are encouraged to join the many walks and tours led by Anangu, who have a wide knowledge of the environment, plantlife and wildlife, and survival in the landscape. They prefer visitors to refrain from climbing the rock, though it is permitted.

THE FIRST EUROPEANS

The area has been known to white immigrants only since 1872, when Ernest Giles came across Kata Tjuta. He named it Mount Ferdinand after the botanist Baron von Mueller, who in turn renamed it Mount Olga after Queen Olga of Württemberg. In 1873 William Gosse led a party that discovered and named Mount Connor, a 863m (2,830ft) tabletop mountain, which is often mistaken for Uluru by those driving west along the Lasseter Highway. Farther west Gosse spotted a hill and accordingly stated: 'The hill, as I drew closer, presented a most unusual appearance with the upper portion being covered with holes or caves. When I got clear of the sandhills and was only two miles distant, and the hill for the first time coming fairly into view, what was my astonishment to find was one immense rock rising abruptly from the plain. I have named this Ayers Rock after Sir Henry Ayers, the premier of South Australia.' (The Aboriginal name for the rock, Uluru, has no English translation.)

With the increasing number of European visitors and settlers, conflict arose between the foreign and native cultures. In the early 1900s grazing stock and drought impinged on Anangus' food and hunting. The government set aside land (reserves) for Anangu, who regarded these areas as temporary refuges. Government officials hoped that in time Anangu would 'fit in' to white society; instead they continued their traditional lifestyle.

TOURISM

Tourism developed in the 1950s with the construction of motels and an airstrip. During the early 1970s Yulara Resort (now Ayers Rock Resort) tourist village was built just outside the national park about 20km (12 miles) from Uluru and 50km (31 miles) from Kata Tjuta. This replaced the earlier accommodation that had been built too close to Uluru and had impacted negatively on the

environment. By 1973 the Aboriginal people had become involved in managing the park and in 1979 the federal government finally recognized their traditional ownership of the area.

In October 1985 Anangu were granted freehold title to the National Park, which was then leased back to the government's Parks Australia for 99 years. It is now one of Australia's most popular national parks.

TOURS

There are a number of great ways to see the Uluru-Kata Tjuta National Park. Harley-Davidson tours and fixed-wing and helicopter flights are all enjoyable, but the best way to appreciate it is on foot. Paths are marked and several walks can be taken independently; a self-guiding walks brochure is available from the Cultural Centre close to Uluru. Other walks are enhanced by having an Anangu guide, who will help you to appreciate the Aboriginal influence on the landscape.

SELF-GUIDED WALKS

ULURU: BASE *9.4KM (6 MILES) 3–4 HOURS*
The longest defined walk goes around the circumference of Uluru. You can start at either the Mutitjulu or Mala parking areas. This walk soaks up the atmosphere of the cave paintings and various rock features. Be aware that there are a number of sacred Aboriginal sites that cannot be entered or photographed, but these are clearly marked.

ULURU: MALA *2KM (1.2 MILES) 1.5 HOURS*
This track begins at the base of the Uluru Climb parking area and is wheelchair accessible. A Ranger at the Mala Walk sign explains the local Aboriginal perceptions of Uluru and how Anangu and the rangers look after the park together.

ULURU: MUTITJULU *1KM (0.6 MILES) 45 MINUTES*
The walk follows the track from the Mutitjulu parking area to a special waterhole that is home to Wanampi, an ancestral watersnake.

KATA TJUTA: VALLEY OF THE WINDS *7.5KM (4.5 MILES) 3 HOURS*
This is a magnificent, reasonably flat walk and is highly recommended. Two lookout points provide excellent views of the spectacular landscape.

KATA TJUTA: WALPA GORGE *2.5KM (1.5 MILES) 1 HOUR*
The walk takes you to the end of the gorge and, as the track rises gently, there are great views of the surrounding countryside.

SOUNDS OF SILENCE

Another unforgettable experience is the Sounds of Silence dinner in the desert (▷ 226). Watch the sun set over both Kata Tjuta and Uluru while sipping champagne. A didgeridoo plays in the background, a gourmet buffet of Australian delicacies is served and an astronomer explains the stars.

Above *The domed summits of Kata Tjuta*

GUIDED TOURS

ANANGU TOURS

www.ananguwaai.com.au

Anangu Tours was established by the Aboriginal owners of Uluru and Kata Tjuta to provide tours with an Aboriginal guide. Bookings can be made at the Anangu Tours desk within the Touring Information Centre at Ayers Rock Resort (▷ 229), at hotel receptions throughout the Ayers Rock Resort, or through a travel agent. Tours do not include park entry fees unless specified.

☎ 08 8950 3030

ABORIGINAL ULURU TOUR *2KM (1.2 MILES) 5 HOURS*

This morning tour takes in sunrise at Uluru and a short walk along its base. To complete a morning you can join the Liru Walk afterwards (adult A$139, child A$93).

LIRU WALK *2KM (1.2 MILES) 2 HOURS*

An excellent morning walk from the Cultural Centre through mulga scrub to the base of Uluru. Learn about the area's plants, wildlife and indigenous bush tucker (food) (adult A$69, child A$35).

KUNIYA WALK *1.5KM (1 MILE) 2 HOURS*

From the Cultural Centre a guide takes you on an afternoon walk to the Mutitjulu Waterhole on the east side of Uluru; on the way you learn about Aboriginal creation stories associated with Uluru and how to prepare bush tucker (adult A$69, child A$35).

KUNIYA SUNSET TOUR *1.5KM (1 MILE) 4.5 HOURS*

This tour is based on the Kuniya Walk and ends with sunset at Uluru. It includes collection from your accommodation (adult A$116, child A$75).

ULURU-KATA TJUTA NATIONAL PASS

To experience sunrise and sunset, join the Aboriginal Uluru Tour in the morning and visit Kata Tjuta in the afternoon. Includes National Park entry fee (adult A$229, child A$155).

ANANGU CULTURE PASS

Do both the Aboriginal Uluru Tour at sunrise and the Kuniya Sunset Tour and get a 10 per cent discount (adult A$229, child A$155).

KUNIYA AND MORNING OLGAS PASS

This Pass includes a morning tour of the Valley of the Winds in Kata Tjuta and the Kuniya Sunset Tour (adult A$199, child A$125).

Left *Sturt's Desert Pea growing in the desert sand*
Right *A magical setting for dinner: the Sounds of Silence restaurant at the Ayers Rock Resort*

WATARRKA NATIONAL PARK

The spectacular sandstone walls of Kings Canyon are among the biggest attractions in the Red Centre.

Watarrka National Park is 330km (205 miles) southwest of Alice Springs ▷ 210). Two routes lead from the Stuart Highway. At Henbury, 133km 82 miles) south of the Alice, the unsealed Ernest Giles Road branches west or 107km (66 miles) to join the sealed Luritja Road that leads to Watarrka. This oute passes the Henbury Meteorites Conservation Reserve, where 12 craters were formed approximately 4,700 years ago when fragments of a meteor hit he surface.

Overall, Kings Canyon is part of the rugged George Gill Range, where moist gorges provide a refuge for plants and animals within the surrounding desert. Although the park is accessible year round, April to the end of September are he coolest months. Accommodation and camping facilities are available at he Kings Canyon Resort (tel 08 8956 7442), near to Kings Canyon, or at Kings Creek Station at the southern entrance (tel 08 8956 7474).

CANYON WALK

This 6km (3.5-mile) walk goes from the parking area to and around the rim of Kings Canyon and back by Kestral Falls (four hours). Blue trail markers show the way, which has steps and boardwalks. Cool off in the palm-fringed pools of the Garden of Eden waterholes (Sep–end May)—very welcome. Walkers must be it and healthy. In case of difficulties there are four emergency radio call boxes along the way and a first-aid box at the top.

KINGS CREEK WALK

This is a less strenuous walk than the Canyon, a 2.5km (1.5-mile) circuit at the outheast entrance to the park (one hour). About half of the walk is wheelchair accessible, otherwise strong footwear is required. Orange trail markers show he way.

INFORMATION

www.centralaustraliantourism.com
✚ 342 K8 🛈 Central Australian Tourism Industry Association, 60 Gregory Terrace, Alice Springs, N I 08/0 ☎ 08 8952 5800 🚌 Tours to Kings Canyon and Uluru 🚗 Kings Canyon 🏨 Kings Canyon

TIP

» The climate can be very hot and dry—visitors should follow park safety regulations and carry enough water, wear a hat, and use sunscreen and insect repellent.

Above *April to September is the best time of the year to attempt the Canyon Walk*

DARWIN TO LITCHFIELD NATIONAL PARK

The wide open spaces of the Top End encompass a diversity of attractions, including a crocodile farm, a wildlife park, two nature reserves and—the drive's highlight—a superb national park with spectacular waterfalls (▷ 214).

THE DRIVE
Distance: 280km (174 miles)
Allow: Full day
Start at: Darwin
End at: Darwin

★ From central Darwin take the Stuart Highway (National Highway 1) out of the city to the south. After about 25km (15.5 miles), turn left for the 10km (6-mile) drive to Howard Springs Nature Park.

❶ Howard Springs Nature Park contains about 1,000ha (2,470 acres) of monsoon rainforest and eucalypt woodland. Its main attractions are a spring-fed swimming pool and shaded picnic and barbecue areas nearby. Fish, including barramundi—

the Top End's best eating fish, can often be seen from the weir, and wallabies are attracted to the picnic areas. The park can be crowded on weekends during the dry season when Darwin people flock to the park to cool off.

Return to the Stuart Highway and continue south for 10km (6 miles) then turn onto the Arnhem Highway. Continue for 25km (16 miles) and turn left for 6km (4 miles) to Fogg Dam Conservation Reserve.

❷ This wetland on the lower Adelaide River is one of the best places to see the territory's wildlife in natural surroundings. From the end of the wet season in about

March, large flocks of wading birds gather here, as well as freshwater and saltwater crocodiles and a number of other reptile, amphibian and mammal species. The conservation reserve has a number of walking tracks, boardwalks and observation platforms as well as shaded areas. The best time to visit is early morning and evening.

Return to the Stuart Highway and turn left. Continue south for 12km (7 miles) and turn right toward Berry Springs. After about another 10km (6 miles), turn right to Berry Springs Nature Park.

❸ Berry Springs Nature Park is set around the spring-fed pools

of the surrounding wild country, strange-looking termite mounds, and arresting sandstone rock formations.

Most of the major sights are close to the sealed road that runs through the park. The so-called magnetic termite mounds are 17km (10.5 miles) from the park entrance. The termite mounds are actually not 'magnetic' at all, rather the termites build them to take advantage of the most beneficial alignment with the sun's rays.

Return to Darwin via Batchelor and the Stuart Highway.

WHEN TO GO
Most times of the year. December to the end of March are the hottest and wettest—but least crowded— months; April to October, the dry months, are busier.

WHERE TO EAT
Territory Wildlife Park: Light refreshments and full meals from a self-service buffet (daily 8.30–4).

PLACES TO VISIT
Darwin, ▷ 211.

Opposite *Wangi Falls*
Below *A big saltie looks menacing*

of Berry Creek. A short walking circuit, starting from the picnic area, takes you through typical Top End monsoon rainforest, which features palms and ferns, and dry eucalypt woodland. An interpretative display board provides information about the park's flora and fauna, as well as its history.

It is just a short drive to the adjoining Territory Wildlife Park (▷ 214), an open-air zoo set in 400ha (988 acres) of bushland. The park is an excellent introduction to the wildlife of the Northern Territory, both native and feral, in natural settings. The larger animals include water buffalo, banteng (a type of Asian ox), pigs, deer, wallabies and emus.

Other attractions include a walk-through aviary, an aquarium, the Monsoon Forest Walk and a lagoon teeming with birds. A free shuttle train links major exhibits, a major benefit in hot and humid conditions.

Return to the Stuart Highway and continue south for 39km (24 miles) then turn right to Batchelor, 14km (9 miles) west of the highway.

④ Stretch your legs at Batchelor, a town built in the 1950s to house workers on the nearby Rum Jungle uranium mine (now abandoned). Wallabies are often seen grazing on the residents' lawns. The 3m (10ft) high castle in the main street is a replica of one near the builder's home in Germany.

Drive on for another 21km (13 miles) through flat country dotted with termite mounds to Litchfield National Park.

⑤ The prime attractions at this 146sq km (57sq mile) national park are the four main waterfalls, each with a refreshing swimming hole (▷ 214). Florence Falls and Buley Rockhole 23km (14 miles); the Lost City 28km (17 miles), down a 4WD track; Tolmer Falls 40km (25 miles); Tjaynera (Sandy Creek) Falls 45km (28 miles), down a 4WD track; and Wangi Falls 52km (32 miles). A large picnic area and kiosk are located at Wangi Falls, the park's most popular spot. Swimming holes are often closed after heavy rain because of dangerous currents. There are also walking tracks, superb views

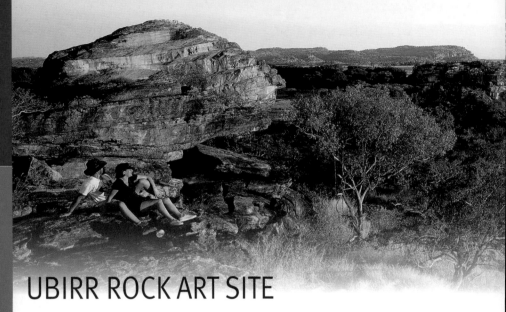

UBIRR ROCK ART SITE

At the northern border of Kakadu National Park (▷ 212–213), Ubirr Rock has some of the oldest rock art in the world. The short walk stops at three 'galleries' and a vantage point for a Kakadu panorama.

THE WALK
Distance: 1km (0.6 miles)
Allow: 2 hours
Start at: Ubirr parking area
End at: Ubirr parking area
How to get there: Ubirr Rock is 36km (22 miles) north of Jabiru, in Kakadu National Park, and 283km (175 miles) east of Darwin

★ There are three main galleries of Aboriginal rock art: the Main Gallery, the Namarrgarn Sisters and the Rainbow Serpent. At the start of the track, take the right branch and walk for 300m (327 yards) past the Mabuyu Gallery to the Main Art Gallery. The rangers ask that you follow signs, keep to defined walking paths and do not touch the painted rock surfaces. The Main

Gallery and Rainbow Serpent Gallery have wheelchair access.

❶ Aboriginal people have occupied northern Australia for at least 50,000 years, and probably for much longer. The rock shelters and overhangs of Ubirr, like the Main Gallery, were lived in until recent times, and the Aborigines took advantage of the abundant food supplies in the East Alligator area. They caught game such as catfish, mullet and long-necked turtles in nearby watercourses, and depicted these and other foods on the rocks before you.

Rock art here, as elsewhere at Ubirr, is mainly in the X-ray style. This

shows the internal organs of animals and humans as well as the figure's outward appearance. The Ubirr images date from between 300 and 1,500 years ago, and some have been repainted over the years. More recent paintings show Europeans who came to hunt water buffalo in the 1880s—one white man is shown with a pipe in his mouth and hands on hips. High up on the ceiling of the overhang are red and yellow sorcery images said by Aborigines to have been painted by beings called Mimi spirits. Near the Main Gallery is a red-ochre painting of a thylacine (Tasmanian tiger), a species that became extinct on the Australian mainland about 2,000 to 3,000 years ago.

Opposite *Late afternoon light on Ubirr Rock*

Take the path up the rock face past the Crosshatching Gallery to the Namarrgarn Sisters site.

❷ In this gallery the Namarrgarn Sisters are depicted pulling string apart.

In an Aboriginal myth the Namarrgarn Sisters throw down pieces of string from their home in the stars, attach the string to humans' internal organs, and bring sickness to those people when they make their way down the string.

Walk up the 250m (272-yard) track along the rock face to the Nadab Lookout.

❸ Nadab Lookout gives amazing vistas over Cahills Plain (Nardab), the Cannon Hill outliers (Garrkanj and Nawurrkbil) to the north, and the East Alligator River and floodplain. Visit in late afternoon for beautiful sunsets over the wetlands. The river, outlined by a fringe of trees to the northeast, marks the boundary between Kakadu and the Aboriginal-owned Arnhem Land.

Until the late 1980s water buffalo, introduced from Asia, grazed on the plains, doing terrible damage to the landscape. Since their removal the natural vegetation is returning. In the evenings short-eared rock wallabies frequent the rocks around the art sites; some may be spotted resting during the day.

Retrace your steps and take the return section of the circular path, and detour on to the boardwalk that runs past the Rainbow Serpent art site.

❹ This gallery has a painting of a Rainbow Serpent on a cliff wall above a site that has traces of many generations. In traditional Aboriginal beliefs the Rainbow Serpent is the ancestor that created people and the world in which they live.

Stories about the Rainbow Serpent vary from place to place, but to Kakadu Aborigines the Serpent is a powerful female, ever present, and usually resting in quiet waterways unless disturbed. They believe that when the Serpent passed through Ubirr she painted her image on the rock as a reminder of her presence.

Follow the trail back to the parking area.

WHEN TO GO
April to the end of October. Ubirr is open Apr–end Nov daily 8.30–dusk; Dec–end Mar 2–dusk. Entry free.

There are ranger talks at the Main Gallery May to the end of September at 9.30, 12pm and 4; the Namarrgarn Sisters at 10.30 and 5.30; and the Rainbow Serpent at 11.30 and 4.

Although the roads to Ubirr are sealed, they can be inundated during the wet season. If in doubt, check local road conditions at Bowali Visitor Centre, Jabiru (daily 8–5; tel 08 8938 1121).

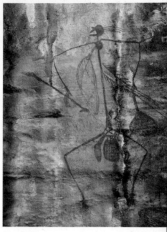

Above *There are several rock art galleries around Ubirr Rock, some probably dating from 1,500 years ago*

WHERE TO EAT
The closest refreshment stop is Border Store Manbiyarra, 3km (2 miles) south of Ubirr, where snacks, lunch, and morning and afternoon teas are served (daily 8.30–5.30).

PLACES TO VISIT
Kakadu National Park, ▷ 212–213.

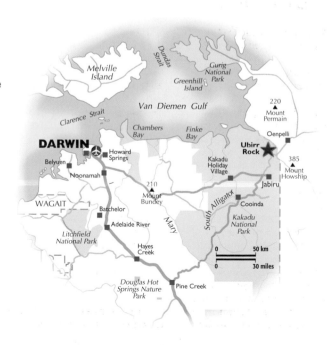

WHAT TO DO

ALICE SPRINGS

ALICE SPRINGS SOUVENIRS
Australian brand clothing such as R. M. Williams and Akubra, as well as Aboriginal art and crafts, boomerangs, didgeridoos and souvenirs. Purchases can be shipped overseas.
✉ 64 Todd Mall, Alice Springs, NT 0870 ☎ 08 8953 0222 ⏰ Mon–Fri 9–8, Sat 10–3, Sun 9–4

GALLERY GONDWANA
www.gallerygondwana.com.au
Contemporary works of non-Aboriginal and Aboriginal artists, the latter including those from Central Australia, Cape York, the Tiwi Islands and Arnhem Land. Purchases can be shipped overseas.
✉ 43 Todd Mall, Alice Springs, NT 0870 ☎ 08 8953 1577 ⏰ Mon–Fri 9.30–6, Sat 10–5

LEAPING LIZARDS GALLERY
www.leapinglizardsgallery.com.au
Australian-made fine art and crafts, and goods made in Alice Springs, ranging from wood, glass and pottery to jewellery and children's clothes.
✉ Shop 5, Reg Harris Lane, Todd Mall, Alice Springs, NT 0870 ☎ 08 8952 5021 ⏰ Mon–Fri 9–5.30, Sat 9–2

THE SOUNDS OF STARLIGHT THEATRE
www.soundsofstarlight.com
The Sounds of Starlight show combines live music and lighting effects to evoke Central Australia's unique landscape.
✉ 40 Todd Mall, Alice Springs, NT 0870 ☎ 08 8953 0826 ⏰ Apr–Nov Tue, Fri, Sat 8pm–9.30pm (doors open 7.30) ✋ Adult A$30, family A$90

BOJANGLES SALOON
www.bossaloon.com.au
Old photos, pioneers' belongings and motorcycles decorate the interior of this lively bar.
✉ 80 Todd Street, Alice Springs, NT 0870 ☎ 08 8952 2873 ⏰ Daily 11.30am–2 or 3am

SUKRA/LASSETERS HOTEL CASINO
www.lassetershotelcasino.com.au
This restaurant offers Asian fusion dining in a contemporary atmosphere.
✉ 93 Barrett Drive, Alice Springs, NT 0870 ☎ 08 8950 7740 ⏰ Daily 6–10

OUTBACK BALLOONING
www.outbackballooning.com.au
The 30-minute breakfast flights over bushland are a great way to see emus and kangaroos.
✉ Kennett Court, Alice Springs, NT 0870 ☎ 08 8952 8723 ⏰ All year ✋ Adult from A$275, child A$220 for 30-minute flight (includes transfers and champagne breakfast)

OUTBACK QUAD ADVENTURES
www.outbackquadadventures.com.au
Bounce around Undoolya cattle station on a quad bike. No experience necessary.
✉ Undoolya Station, 17km (10 miles) east of Alice ☎ 08 8953 0697 ⏰ All year ✋ From A$120 per person for two hours (includes transfers from Alice)

PYNDAN CAMEL TRACKS
www.cameltracks.com
Guided camel treks from one hour to half day to overnight safaris.
✉ PO Box 1939, Alice Springs, NT 0871 ☎ 0416 170 164 ⏰ One hour rides at 12, 2.30 and sunset ✋ Adult A$45, child A$25

DARWIN

MICK'S WHIPS
www.mickswhips.com.au
Mick's Whips, an hour by road from Darwin, makes kangaroo and crocodile leather goods such as belts, boots, hats, whips and

Opposite *Ballooning near Alice Springs*

wallets. The goods are also available at the Mindil Beach markets.

✉ 555 Parkin Road, Darwin River, NT 0837
☎ 08 8988 6400 🕐 Daily from 8am

MINDIL BEACH SUNSET MARKETS

www.mindilbeachsunsetmarkets.com.au
The bustling markets display the wares of more than 200 local craftspeople. There are also food stalls. The Thursday night markets are bigger than the Sunday markets.
✉ Mindil Beach, off Gilruth Avenue, Darwin, NT 0800 ☎ 08 8981 3454
🕐 May–end Oct Thu 5–10pm, Sun 4–9pm

DECKCHAIR CINEMA

www.deckchaircinema.com
Watch a movie from a deckchair at this outdoor cinema. Bring a picnic dinner; alcohol is available on site.
✉ Wharf Precinct, Darwin, NT 0800 ☎ 08 8981 0700 🕐 Apr–mid-Nov daily 🎟 Adult A$13, child A$6

DISCOVERY AND LOST ARC

www.discoverynightclub.com.au
Discovery is the largest dance club in the Northern Territory with live shows, fashion events and a park-like atmosphere. Lost Arc is a dance venue.
✉ 89 Mitchell Street, Darwin, NT 0800
☎ 08 8942 3300 🕐 Discovery: 9pm–4am, four nights a week; Lost Ark: daily 8pm–4am
🎟 Discovery: Fri, Sat A$20

DARWIN TURF CLUB

www.darwinturfclub.com.au
About 40 race meetings a year: The highlight is the Darwin Cup Carnival (Jul, Aug).
✉ Dickwood Drive, Fannie Bay, NT 0820
☎ 08 8941 1566 🕐 See race schedule
🎟 From A$15 on non-major race days; child under 18 free when accompanied by an adult
🚻 🅿

DARWIN DIVE CENTRE

www.darwindivecentre.com.au
Scuba-diving tours.
✉ Cullen Bay Marina, Darwin Harbour, NT 0800 ☎ 08 8981 3049 🕐 All year
🎟 From A$120 per person for half-day dive

JULY

ALICE SPRINGS SHOW

The Alice Springs Show, at Blatherskite Park Showground, is a traditional agricultural and horticultural show which also includes sideshows and arts and crafts displays.

CAMEL CUP CARNIVAL

www.camelcup.com.au
Watch camel races at the Camel Cup Carnival at Alice Springs in mid-July.

ROYAL DARWIN SHOW

www.darwinshow.com.au
The Royal Darwin Show, at Darwin Showgrounds in late July, is an agricultural show with displays of arts, crafts, commerce and industry, cattle and small livestock, an animal nursery, sideshows and food stalls.

JULY/AUGUST

DARWIN CUP CARNIVAL

www.darwinturfclub.org.au
The Darwin Cup Carnival begins

HUMPTY DOO

THE DIDGERIDOO HUT

www.didgeridoohut.com.au
Visitors to the Didgeridoo Hut, on a 10ha (25-acre) emu farm, can see Aboriginal artists at work and discuss their culture with them.
✉ 1 Arnhem Highway, Humpty Doo, NT 0836 ☎ 08 8988 4457 🕐 Daily 9–7
🚗 30km (19 miles) southeast from Darwin

KATHERINE

NITMILUK TOURS

www.nitmiluktours.com.au
A canoe is the best way to see Katherine Gorge (▷ 209). Half-day, full-day or overnight tours.
✉ Nitmiluk Visitor Centre, Nitmiluk (Katherine Gorge) National Park, Katherine, NT 0850 ☎ 08 8972 1253 🕐 Canoe hire: Apr–end Nov 🎟 Single canoe: half-day from A$42, full day A$54; Double canoe: half-day A$63, full day A$80

in late July and reaches its climax in August with the Darwin Cup horse race at Fannie Bay Racecourse, Darwin.

AUGUST

FESTIVAL OF DARWIN

www.darwinfestival.org.au
The Festival of Darwin, held in the city in mid- to late August, celebrates the visual and performing arts.

DARWIN FRINGE FESTIVAL

www.darwinfringe.com.au
The Darwin Fringe Festival showcases visual arts, film, comedy, drama, dance, poetry and music.

SEPTEMBER

HENLEY-ON-TODD REGATTA

www.henleyontodd.com.au
The Henley-on-Todd Regatta at Alice Springs is a boat race with a difference: Crews use foot power to propel bottomless 'boats' along the dry bed of the Todd River.

ULURU (AYERS ROCK)

WALKATJARA ART

www.walkatjara.com.au
This gallery is owned and operated by artists from the local Mutijulu Aboriginal community, who sell ceramic vases and plates, paintings, and T-shirts featuring local designs.
✉ Uluru-Kata Tjuta Cultural Centre, Uluru-Kata Tjuta National Park, NT 0872 ☎ 08 8956 2537 🕐 Daily 8.30–5.30

PROFESSIONAL HELICOPTER SERVICES

www.phs.com.au
Fly above Uluru, Kata Tjuta and Kings Canyon (▷ 215–219) in a helicopter.
✉ Tourist Information Centre, Ayers Rock Resort, NT 0872 ☎ 08 8956 2003
🎟 From A$120 for 12- to 15-minute flight around Uluru; from A$230 for 30-minute flight over Uluru and Kata Tjuta

PRICES AND SYMBOLS

The restaurants are listed alphabetically (excluding Le, La and Les). The prices given are the average for a two-course lunch (L) and a three-course dinner (D) for one person, without drinks. The wine price is for the least expensive bottle.

For a key to the symbols, ▷ 2.

ADELAIDE RIVER
ADELAIDE RIVER INN

Simple, traditional food in hearty servings and not too many frills is the standard fare at this friendly pub/ restaurant, which sells alcohol. This is also the home of the late Charlie the Buffalo, made famous through his appearance in the *Crocodile Dundee* movie.

✉ 106 Stuart Highway, Adelaide River, NT ☎ 0846 08 8976 7047 ✦ Daily 7am–8.30pm ✋ L A$30, D A$40

ALICE SPRINGS
BLUEGRASS RESTAURANT

www.bluegrassrestaurant.com.au
A changing blackboard menu: vegetarian dishes, Indian curries, pasta, rib-eye steaks and pork; seafood antipasto platter; red wine-glazed kangaroo.

✉ Cnr Stott Terrace and Todd Street, Alice Springs, NT 0870 ☎ 08 8955 5188

✦ Wed–Mon 6–late. Closed 25 Dec–14 Jan ✋ D A$58, Wine A$26

HANUMAN RESTAURANT

www.hanuman.com.au
Authentic Thai dishes prepared with fresh seafood, vegetables and herbs, including grilled Hanuman oysters, with lemongrass sauce and basil; also chicken, beef and pork dishes.

✉ 82 Barrett Street, Alice Springs, NT 0870 ☎ 08 8953 7188 ✦ Mon–Fri 12–2, Mon–Sun 6–10.30 ✋ L A$45, D A$55, Wine A$35

OSCARS CAFÉ AND RESTAURANT

Mediterranean dishes with Portuguese and Spanish influences, and fresh fish, including barramundi.

✉ Shop 1, Cinema Complex, 86 Todd Mall, Alice Springs, NT 0870 ☎ 08 8953 0930 ✦ Daily 11.30–late (and Sat, Sun 7am–9am) ✋ L A$35, D A$48, Wine A$26

OVERLANDERS STEAK HOUSE

www.overlanders.com.au
Prime steak dishes, and the house specialty—all-you-can-eat of soup, damper (a rough bread), tastings of kangaroo, emu, camel, crocodile, and rump steak.

✉ 72 Hartley Street, Alice Springs, NT 0870 ☎ 08 8952 2159 ✦ Daily 6pm–late ✋ L A$40, D A$60, Wine $27

RED OCHRE GRILL

www.redochrealice.com.au
This is one of the leaders of the crusade to bring the flavours of wild Australia to the table with a menu that features traditional native fruits, berries, game meats and seafood.

✉ Todd Mall, Alice Springs, NT 0870 ☎ 08 8952 9614 ✦ Daily 6.30am–9.30pm ✋ L A$45, D A$58, Wine A$35

AYERS ROCK RESORT
KUNIYA RESTAURANT

www.voyages.com.au
Traditional and contemporary: roast kumera and mud crab pancake on a bed of spinach with horseradish aioli; kangaroo and lemon myrtle; chocolate mousse with a toffee tier.

✉ Sails in the Desert Hotel, Ayers Rock Resort, NT 0872 ☎ 08 8957 7888 ✦ Daily 7pm–9.30pm ✋ D A$60, Wine A$37

SOUNDS OF SILENCE/YULARA

www.voyages.com.au
A coach takes you to a desert dune area in the Uluru-Kata Tjuta National Park, where champagne is served as the sun sets. The barbecue buffet uses local meats—camel, kangaroo or emu; often crocodile and buffalo. Barramundi for fish-lovers; vegetarian options. It is advisable to reserve in advance.

Opposite *Kuniya Restaurant at Ayers Rock Resort*

✉ Nr Ayers Rock Resort, NT 0872 ☎ 08 8957 7888 ⏰ Every night, unless prevented by weather ✋ All inclusive A$155 per person

BERRY SPRINGS
TERRITORY WILDLIFE PARK
www.territorywildlifepark.com.au
At the self-service park café-bistro, dishes include beef curries, roast beef and vegetables, and salads. Children's meals are provided, as are some vegetarian dishes.
✉ Cox Peninsula Road, Berry Springs, NT 0837 ☎ 08 8988 6574 ⏰ Daily 8.30–5.30 ✋ L A$20, Wine A$20 🚌 Darwin Day Tours (tel 08 8924 1111)

DALY WATERS
DALY WATERS PUB
www.dalywaterspub.com
The food is simple but chances are you're ready for a meal anyway by the time you get to Daly Waters, and the character, the decor and the clientele of this eccentric pub/diner provide plenty of distractions.
✉ Stuart Highway, Daly Waters, NT 0852 ☎ 08 8975 9927 ⏰ Daily 8am–11pm ✋ L A$40, D A$45

DARWIN
BOARDWALK CAFE
www.boardwalkcafe.com.au
On the Darwin waterfront at swanky Cullen Bay, this inside/outside bistro offers excellent value for money. Portions are generous and much of the seafood-inspired menu comes fresh from the wharf to the kitchen.
✉ 56 Marina Boulevard, Larrakeyah, NT ☎ 0820 08 8981 0200 ⏰ Mon–Sat 9am–10pm ✋ L A$25, D A$35

CHAR RESTAURANT
www.charadmiralty.com.au
Set in the historic old Admiralty House, in lush gardens, Char's steak and seafood dishes feature top cuts and the latest catch.
✉ Cnr The Esplanade and Knuckey Street, Darwin, NT 0800 ☎ 08 8981 4544 ⏰ Daily 6–11pm, Mon–Fri 12–3 ✋ L A$40, D A$65, Wine A$28

CHARLIES RESTAURANT
The owners have been dishing up pasta, Italian seafood, and pizzas in Darwin for more than 40 years.
✉ 29 Knuckey Street, Darwin, NT 0800 ☎ 08 8981 3298 ⏰ Mon–Sat 12–2.30, 6–10 ✋ L A$25, D A$45, Wine A$18

CORNUCOPIA MUSEUM CAFÉ
www.cornucopiadarwin.com.au
The cuisine is Modern Australian, with raw energy salad, Greek salad with marinated octopus or vegetarian curry. Reserve ahead for Fridays and Saturdays.
✉ Conacher Street, Bullocky Point, Fannie Bay, NT 0820 ☎ 08 8981 1002 ⏰ Daily 9–5 (no meals after 3.30) ✋ L A$45, Wine A$25

CRUSTACEANS ON THE WHARF
Seafood specials; Taste of the Orient seafood platter; crocodile and kangaroo dishes. Children's meals available by request; vegetarians not well catered for. Reserve ahead.
✉ Darwin Wharf Precinct, Darwin, NT 0800 ☎ 08 8981 8658 ⏰ Dinner Mon–Sat 6.30–late ✋ D A$55, Wine A$22

THE DECK BAR
www.thedeckbar.com.au
At the bustling heart of Mitchell Street, this shady, sprawling café/bar has a buzzy atmosphere and a Mediterranean-style menu that makes it a popular choice for outdoor eating at all times of day.
✉ 22 Mitchell Street, Darwin, NT 0800 ☎ 08 8942 3001 ⏰ Daily 12–2.30, 6–10 ✋ L A$40, D A$55

HANUMAN
www.hanuman.com.au
This is one of Darwin's best restaurants. Nonya and Thai dishes are on the menu, and there is a Tandoori oven. Vegetarian options. Reservation essential.
✉ 28 Mitchell Street, Darwin, NT 0800 ☎ 08 8941 3500 ⏰ Mon–Fri 12–2.30, 6.30–8, Sat, Sun 6–9 ✋ L A$45 (set special A$27.50 per head), D A$58, Wine A$26

PEE WEES BEACHFRONT CAFÉ
www.peewees.com.au
The cuisine here is Australian Creole.

Reserve ahead.
✉ Alec Fong Lim Drive, East Point, NT 0820 ☎ 08 8981 6868 ⏰ Daily 5–10 ✋ D A$75, Wine A$36 🚗 4km (2.5 miles) north from central Darwin

THE ROMA BAR
www.romabar.com.au
The menu at this casual bistro-style café/restaurant reflects Darwin's proximity to Asia, but also its affection for the big Aussie breakfast, burgers and comfort-style dining. The restaurant has been a fixture on the Darwin food scene since the 1970s.
✉ 9–11 Cavenagh Street, Darwin, NT 0800 ☎ 08 8981 6729 ⏰ Mon–Fri 7–4, Sat–Sun 8–2 ✋ B A$15, L A$25

TASTY HOUSE
This casual Chinese diner has a big and satisfying menu with all the crowd pleasers from the oriental kitchen. It's popular with the local Chinese community for its *yum cha* (dim sum) lunches.
✉ Shop 9, Anthony Plaza, Smith Street Mall, Darwin NT 0800 ☎ 08 8981 2269 ⏰ Mon–Fri 11.30–3, Tue–Sat 6–11 ✋ L A$25, D A$30

JIM JIM
THE MIMI RESTAURANT AND BARRA BAR AND BISTRO
www.gagudjulodgecooinda.com.au
Australian bush cuisine with local delicacies such as kangaroo, barramundi, emu and crocodile.
✉ Gagudju Lodge Cooinda, Kakadu Highway, Jim Jim, NT 0886 ☎ 08 8979 0145 ⏰ Daily 12–9 ✋ L A$40, D A$50, Wine A$21 🚗 296km (184 miles) east from Darwin via the Arnhem Highway, 49km (30 miles) southwest from Jabiru, near Yellow Water recreation area in Kakadu National Park

KATHERINE
RJ'S
Northern Territory specialist dishes such as buffalo fillet, along with Thai dishes. Vegetarian dishes available, as is a children's menu.
✉ 3 Giles Street, Katherine, NT 0851 ☎ 08 8972 1622 ⏰ Mon–Sat 6.30–9 ✋ D A$55, Wine A$22

PRICES AND SYMBOLS

Prices are for a double room for one night including breakfast, unless otherwise stated. All the hotels listed accept credit cards, unless otherwise stated. Note that rates can vary widely throughout the year.

For a key to the symbols, ▷ 2.

ALICE SPRINGS

ALICE MOTOR INN

www.alicemotorinn.com.au
This family-operated motel offers simple accommodation at an excellent price. The pool is large and set in gardens, the location is quiet yet within walking distance of the city centre and the price includes wireless internet as well as breakfast.
✉ 27 Undoolya Road, Alice Springs, NT 0870 ☎ 08 8952 2322 🕙 All year ✋ A$90 🛈 20 🚗 0.5km (0.3 mile) from city centre

AURORA ALICE SPRINGS

www.auroraresorts.com.au
At the town centre of Alice Springs, this hotel was extensively renovated in early 2010. Rooms are spacious although the pool is small, and the staff is friendly and helpful. Family suites are often available at discounted rates.

✉ 11 Leichhardt Terrace, Alice Springs, NT 0870 ☎ 08 8952 7829 🕙 All year ✋ A$100–A$300 🛈 109

CROWNE PLAZA HOTEL ALICE SPRINGS

www.crowneplaza.com
Set against the backdrop of the MacDonnell Ranges, this sprawling, low-rise complex is the best of the town's resort-style accommodation. Guest rooms are pleasant but characterless. The hotel has a comprehensive array of restaurants, facilities and sports facilities.
✉ 82 Barratt Drive, Alice Springs, NT 0870 ☎ 08 8950 8000 🕙 All year ✋ A$139–A$469 🛈 236 🚗 2km (1.25 miles) from town centre

NTHABA COTTAGE B&B

www.nthabacottage.com.au
Large garden, close to town and golf club.
✉ 83 Cromwell Drive, Alice Springs, NT 0870 ☎ 08 8952 9003 🕙 All year ✋ A$145–A$200 🛈 2

BULLO RIVER

BULLO RIVER STATION

www.bulloriver.com
This huge outback cattle station measures some 200,000ha (494,000 acres) of grassy savannah and is

home to 8,000 cattle. There are also wild buffalo, crocodiles galore, rivers full of thrashing barramundi, boab trees, swimming holes and palm-lined gorges. Days are spent exploring, either by 4WD or helicopter.

Guests are accommodated in a purpose-built annexe within the ring of green lawns that surrounds the homestead. The property was the setting for best-selling author Sara Henderson's book, *From Strength to Strength*, and is now owned and operated by her daughter.
✉ PMB 94, Katherine, NT 0851 ☎ 08 9168 7375 🕙 Mar–Oct 🛈 12 ✋ A$800 per person per day all inclusive 🚗 Located near the WA border, 200km (124 miles) from Kununurra

DALY WATERS

DALY WATERS PUB

www.dalywaterspub.com
This historic pub offers basic accommodation in motel rooms, en-suite rooms and cabins. All are simple but clean, and all have air conditioning. Motel rooms share a bathroom, en-suite rooms offer slightly greater comfort, while

Above *Crowne Plaza Darwin*
Opposite *Gagudju Crocodile Holiday Inn*

the cabins are more private.
 Stuart Highway, Daly Waters, NT 0852
☎ 08 8975 9927 🕲 All year ⓘ 15
✋ A$50–A$95

DARWIN

CROWNE PLAZA DARWIN
www.crowneplaza.com.au
The spacious rooms have all the expected facilities, plus there is a spa, and an outdoor pool.
✉ 32 Mitchell Street, Darwin, NT 0801 ☎ 08 8982 0000 🕲 All year
✋ A$208–A$326 excluding breakfast
ⓘ 233 🕲 ☲ Outdoor

HOLIDAY INN ESPLANADE
www.ihghotels.com
Modern hotel with a swimming pool, spa bath, and sun terrace with pool bar.
✉ The Esplanade, Darwin, NT 0801 ☎ 08 8980 0800 🕲 All year ✋ A$196–A$352
ⓘ 197 ☲ Outdoor pool 📺 🕲

MANTRA PANDANAS
www.mghotels.com.au
Located right at the heart of downtown Darwin, this is the city's largest hotel. The property has a choice of studio or one- and two-bedroom apartment-style accommodation. Rooms and decor are comfortable but slightly bland, but offer good value.

✉ 43 Knuckey Street, Darwin, NT 0814 ☎ 1300 987 603 🕲 All year
✋ A$130–A$380 ⓘ 336

SKYCITY DARWIN
www.skycitydarwin.com.au
The pick of luxury accommodation in Darwin, this is the residential component of the city's casino complex. The beachside resort is surrounded by a vast area of gardens. Rooms are plush and international in style, although service can be patchy and not up to the five-star standards to which the hotel aspires.
✉ Gilruth Avenue, Mindil Beach, Darwin, NT 0814 ☎ 08 8943 8888 🕲 All year
ⓘ 117 ✋ A$170–A$770

JABIRU

GAGUDJU CROCODILE HOLIDAY INN
www.gagudju-dreaming.com
Facilities include fridge, hairdryer, movies, minibar, phone and TV. There are the Escarpment Restaurant and Escarpment Bar.
✉ 1 Flinders Street, Jabiru, NT 0886 ☎ 08 8979 9000 🕲 All year
✋ A$205–A$323 excluding breakfast
ⓘ 110 🕲 ☲ Outdoor 🚌 Shuttle bus from Darwin 🚗 8km (5 miles) south from Jabiru Airport, 270km (167 miles) east from Darwin Airport

KAKADU NATIONAL PARK

GAGUDJU LODGE COOINDA
www.gagudjulodgecooinda.com.au
Located close to Yellow Waters Lagoon, this lodge offers simple bungalow-style accommodation. Rooms can sleep up to four people. It's a good choice if you are booking onto an early-morning or late-evening wildlife cruise.
✉ Kakadu National Park, Kakadu Highway, Jim Jim, NT 0886 ☎ 08 8979 0145 🕲 All year ⓘ 48 ✋ A$120–A$245

KATHERINE

ALL SEASONS KATHERINE
This motel/inn has tennis courts and a pool. The large self-catering family units have a kitchenette.
✉ Stuart Highway, Katherine, NT 0850 ☎ 08 8972 1744 🕲 All year
✋ A$112–A$165 excluding breakfast
🕲 ☲ Outdoor 🚗 4km (2.5 miles) south from Katherine on Stuart Highway

YULARA

AYERS ROCK RESORT
www.voyages.com.au
The only base for exploring Uluru-Kata Tjuta National Park. Wide range of accommodation.
✉ Yulara Drive, Yulara, NT 0872 ☎ 1300 134 044 🕲 All year ✋ From A$250
🕲 ☲ 🚗 20km (12 miles) from Uluru, 53km (33 miles) from Kata Tjuta

SOUTH AUSTRALIA

As every Australian schoolchild learns, South Australia is the driest state in the world's driest inhabited continent, and South Australians have an almost sacred regard for water. Adelaide, the state capital, is a spacious, gracious city with many fine buildings, a taste for the good things in life and a lively festival calendar. Adelaide subtitles itself 'City of Churches', and although the city has its fair share of modern buildings, the name still applies.

On Adelaide's northeastern doorstep, the Barossa Valley is one of the most distinguished wine-growing areas in Australia, and the most attractive. The hard-working, God-fearing Silesian immigrants who settled the valley in the 1800s imported their own traditions that can be plainly seen in the solid bluestone architecture, the slender spires of the Lutheran churches and in the Barossa's culinary traditions.

South of Adelaide, Kangaroo Island is one of the best places to get a taste of Australia in its raw state. Its very separateness has insulated it against rabbits and foxes, and the whole island resonates with the sights and sounds of wild Australia. There are platypus in the creeks, koalas in the manna gums, fur seals wallowing on the beaches, ospreys on the clifftops, a howling breeze that sprints all the way from Antarctica and a relaxed crew of locals who firmly believe that they live in paradise. Spend a few days and you'll probably agree.

Few visitors will find any reason to venture far into the northern reaches of South Australia, although the state has one of Australia's finest outback national parks in the Flinders Ranges, and something unique in Coober Pedy, the opal mining town where much of the population lives underground.

ADELAIDE

INTRODUCTION

The central area is a compact, walkable square mile, and most of the attractions are gathered here. Formerly referred to as the 'City of Churches', Adelaide's sleepy reputation is far from accurate today—there are more wining and dining options per head, for example, than any other state capital city, and Adelaide is well known for its arts and entertainment scene.

Many of the major attractions are located on North Terrace—including the South Australian Museum, Art Gallery of SA and Botanic Garden. The main shopping area is around Rundle Mall, and nearby Rundle Street offers some of the city's best eating. Across the river, highlights include the Adelaide Oval and the shops, cafés and pubs of North Adelaide, and the beaches are worth a visit too.

Adelaide takes great pride in its 'convict-less' heritage—it was the only state capital founded exclusively by free settlers. The first official migrants arrived in 1836, when HMS *Buffalo* docked at Glenelg, and the city was planned by Colonel William Light, whose statue stands on Montefiore Hill. His simple grid layout, wide streets, attractive terraces and spacious parks are still admired and there is a British feel to Adelaide's buildings and social accents. The population today is just over one million.

ADELAIDE BOTANIC GARDEN

www.botanicgardens.sa.gov.au

The botanic garden, just northeast of the city, is remarkable for its huge Moreton Bay fig trees. The conservatory, with the largest single span in the southern hemisphere, houses tropical rainforest plants. Trails lead from here to the Palm House, Museum of Economic Botany and a lakeside restaurant. October is the best month for the Italianate Garden, the Wisteria Arbours and the Rose Garden.

234 C1 🖾 North Terrace (east end), Adelaide, SA 5000 ☎ 08 8222 9311 🕙 Mon–Fri from 7.15, Sat, Sun from 9 (closes 5.30–7 depending on time of year) 🖐 Free. Conservatory: adult A$4.50, child A$2.50 🚌 Free 99C City Loop bus 🚉 Adelaide, 1km (0.6 mile) west from North Terrace entrance 🍴 🖵 🏛

INFORMATION

www.southaustralia.com

🛈 South Australian Visitor and Travel Centre, 18 King William Street, Adelaide, SA 5000 ☎ 1300 655 276, 08 8303 2220 🕙 Mon–Fri 8.30–5, Sat, Sun 9–2

Opposite *Approaching the Adelaide Festival Centre*
Above *The Lipson Tea Room in Port Adelaide provides a welcome break*

TIPS

» The Free 99C City Loop bus service and the free tram service between South Terrace and North Terrace allow passengers to hop on and off at various stops.

» Good-value day and multipass transportation tickets are available from the Passenger Transport Information Centre (corner King William and Currie streets).

» Port Adelaide is well worth a visit—in addition to the Maritime and Railway museums, there are Sunday markets, dolphin cruises and historic buildings.

ADELAIDE FESTIVAL CENTRE

www.afct.org.au

Surrounded by Elder Park, on the south bank of the River Torrens, the Centre provides a world-class theatre and concert hall for top international and local performers. It is the main venue for the popular Adelaide Festival, held from February to the end of March in even-numbered years. WOMADelaide (World of Music and Dance), an outdoor world music festival, is held in February or March annually at nearby Botanic Garden.

🚩 234 B2 ✉ King William Road, Adelaide, SA 5000 ☎ 08 8216 8600 🕐 Varies according to performances 🎫 Bookings via BASS: www.bass.net.au; local call 13 12 46 (Mon–Sat 9–8). Current performances are listed in the *Advertiser* 🚌 Many bus routes stop outside the Centre or nearby on North Terrace 🚆 Adelaide 🍴 🎁

ADELAIDE ZOO

www.adelaidezoo.com.au

You know you are close to the zoo when you hear the hoots of siamang gibbons. The usual way in is from Frome Road, but another way to arrive is via the Popeye ferry along the river from Lake Torrens. Although the zoo is small, it

has more than 1,400 mammals, reptiles and fish, as well as one of the world's largest collections of birds. It also cares for many endangered species, such as the yellow-footed rock wallaby. Other natives include koalas, Tasmanian devils, hairy-nosed wombats and the world's most venomous snake, the inland taipan. Non native species include sun bears and the endangered Malayan tapir in the South-East Asian Rainforest area. This is the only zoo in Australia with giant pandas.

🔢 234 C1 ✉ Frome Road, Adelaide, SA 5000 ☎ 08 8267 3255 🕐 Daily 9.30–5 ✋ Adult A$26, child A$15 🚌 272, 273. The Adelaide Explorer, departing King William Street outside the SA Tourism Commission, stops at the zoo 🚊 Adelaide, 1km (0.6 mile) southwest on North Terrace 🖥 🏛 One of the best Australian souvenir shops in Adelaide

CARRICK HILL
www.carrickhill.sa.gov.au
This Elizabethan-style mansion is set in 40ha (99 acres) 6.5km (4 miles) south of Adelaide. It was built in the 1930s for Sir Edward Hayward, and is one of the few residences of this period with interior and grounds unchanged. The magnificent gardens combine the best of English flora and native Australian bushland.

🔢 Off map 234 C3 ✉ 46 Carrick Hill Drive, Springfield, SA 5062 ☎ 08 8433 1700 🕐 Wed–Sun 10–4.30; tours 11.30, 2.30 ✋ Adult A$10.50, family A$24, under 5s free 🚌 171C from King William Street, Sun; 171 stops outside Mercedes College, Springfield, then long walk via Carrick Hill Drive 🖥 🏛

CENTRAL MARKET
www.adelaidecentralmarket.com.au
The famous Adelaide Central Market is a bustling, multicultural food market in the heart of the city. The covered market is a blend of more than 40 ethnic cultures, where you can buy delicious fresh produce and gourmet foods. Lucia's Pizza & Spaghetti Bar is a popular meeting place.

Gouger Street, on the south side, is a dining precinct popular for its seafood restaurants; some may look a bit basic, but they serve Australia's best whiting and crayfish (lobster).

🔢 234 A3 📍 Central Market Precinct, Grote and Gouger streets, off Victoria Square, Adelaide, SA 5000 ☎ 08 8203 7494 🕐 Tue 7–5.30, Wed, Thu 9–5.30, Fri 7–9, Sat 7–3 ✋ Free 🚌 Free Bee Line bus 99B to Victoria Square from train station 🖥

CHARLES STURT MUSEUM
Born in India and educated in London, Captain Charles Sturt, a professional soldier who guarded convicts dispatched to New South Wales, was one of Australia's most courageous explorers. He discovered the course of the Macquarie, Murrumbidgee and Darling rivers, and made forays into South Australia's interior in search of an inland sea (but found the outback Cooper Creek instead). His large brick villa, built in 1840, contains period furniture and stands 10km (6 miles) west of Adelaide in a splendid garden with views to Mount Lofty.

🔢 Off map 234 A2 ✉ Jetty Street, Grange, SA 5022 ☎ 08 8356 8185 🕐 Sun and public holidays 2–5; times liable to change, phone first ✋ Adult A$5, child A$3 🚌 113 from Grenfell Street, Adelaide, then walk east along Jetty Street 🚊 East Grange, then walk south along the paved footpath 🏛

GLENELG
www.glenelgsa.com.au
Only 10km (6 miles) southwest of Adelaide on Gulf St. Vincent, Glenelg is the most popular of the long sandy beaches near the city. The vintage City to Bay tram stops directly opposite the beach and is a good excuse to leave your vehicle behind. The attractions here include alfresco dining, outdoor festivals

Above *Funi the panda is a prized resident at Adelaide Zoo*
Below *Glenelg's long sandy beaches make it a popular residential area*

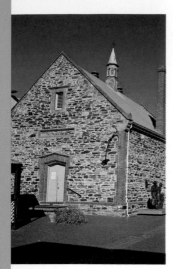

Above *The Migration Museum takes you back to early settlers' days*
Below *There's a long stretch of beautiful Victorian buildings along North Terrace*

and entertainment, beachfront lawns and, of course, the warm, clear blue water. The Victorian Town Hall dominates Moseley Square and from here the main street, Jetty Road, is packed with cinemas, shops and cafés, alongside the neo-Gothic St. Andrew's Church and fine Victorian mansions.

In 1836, Glenelg became the site of the first mainland settlement in South Australia. Captain John Hindmarsh, the first governor, landed on the beach on 28 December and proclaimed South Australia a province. Thus Proclamation Day is celebrated as a public holiday in South Australia only, and every year at the Old Gum Tree in McFarlane Street, the site of the proclamation, a full costume re-enactment is held. At the mouth of the Patawalonga Haven is a splendid replica of HMS *Buffalo*, one of the ships that carried the early settlers from England. It is now a seafood restaurant.

✚ Off map 234 A3 🛈 Glenelg Visitor Information Centre, Foreshore, Glenelg, SA 5045 ☎ 08 8294 5833 🚊 Tram (City to Bay; journey time 30 min) leaves about every 15 min from Victoria Square, Adelaide, to Moseley Square, Glenelg

MIGRATION MUSEUM

www.history.sa.gov.au/migration

The first of its type in Australia, the Migration Museum chronicles the histories of millions of immigrants. The building was once the Destitute Asylum, where many unfortunates found themselves, in particular women who had given birth to unwanted, illegitimate children of miners in Victoria's gold-rush days. The museum has exhibitions on the various traditions brought here by people of 100 different nationalities.

The commemorative tiles in Settlement Square outside the museum record peoples around the world who fled persecution. The Aboriginal Kaurna people are also remembered.

✚ 234 B2 ✉ 82 Kintore Avenue, Adelaide, SA 5000 ☎ 08 8207 7570 🕐 Mon–Fri 10–5, Sat, Sun 1–5 ✋ Free (donations welcome). Guided tours: adult A$10, child A$4 🚌 Free 99C City Loop and many other routes 🚉 Adelaide 🖥 🏛

NATIONAL RAILWAY MUSEUM

www.natrailmuseum.org.au

Although this is one of several museums in Port Adelaide, a serious train buff could easily spend a day here. It has one of the most comprehensive indoor collections of heritage locomotives, passenger carriages (cars), freight vehicles and rail memorabilia in Australia. Younger enthusiasts can enjoy the Friends of Thomas the Tank Engine event over nine days in July, when a small-scale replica of the children's book character is the star.

✚ Off map 234 A2 ✉ Lipson Street, Port Adelaide, SA 5015 ☎ 08 8341 1690 🕐 Daily 10–5 ✋ Adult A$12, child A$5, under 5s free 🚌 118, 118N stop at Commercial Road; Lipson Street is a block to the east 🚉 Port Adelaide Station, from Adelaide Station 🖥 🏛

NORTH TERRACE

www.southaustralia.com

When designing Adelaide's grid plan in 1836, Colonel William Light, chose North Terrace as the area of state government, culture, commerce, education, medicine and the arts, a role it continues to fulfil. At the west end by the university campus, the Lion Art Centre houses the Mercury art-house cinema and behind it is the JamFactory, with contemporary crafts and design. Beyond the central train station, the Sky City Casino occupies the original historic train building. Next door is Parliament House. Across the King William Street intersection are the gates of Government House, bordered by Prince Henry Gardens, with a Boer War memorial in front. The State Library, on the corner of North Terrace and Kintore Avenue, contains the Bradman Collection, an assemblage of memorabilia relating to the great cricketer Sir Donald Bradman (Mon–Fri 9.30–5, Sat, Sun 12–5).

Farther east are the South Australian Museum (▷ 238) and the Art Gallery of SA. The gallery (daily 10–5) has a comprehensive collection, with the emphasis on paintings by colonial and contemporary Australian artists. There is also a significant collection of Rodin sculptures.

On the south side, beyond the Frome Road intersection, is Ayers House, the Regency mansion of former state premier Henry Ayers, after whom Ayers Rock (▷ 215–218) was named.

✚ 234 B2 🚹 18 King William Street, Adelaide, SA 5000 ☎ 08 8303 2220 🚌 Free 99C City Loop stops along North Terrace 🚆 Adelaide

OLD ADELAIDE GAOL

www.adelaidegaol.org.au

In 1873, Elizabeth Woolcock was the only woman to be executed for murder in South Australia, and she was one of a total of 49 people hanged within the walls of Adelaide Gaol. The building dates from 1841 and it is one of the oldest surviving colonial public buildings in Adelaide, still functioning as a prison until 1988.

✚ Off map 234 A2 ✉ 18 Gaol Road, Thebarton, SA 5031 ☎ 08 8231 4062 🕐 Sun–Fri 11–3.30. Tours Sun 11, 12 and 1 ✋ Adult A\$10, child A\$6 🚌 151–155 stop on intersection of Port Road and Gaol Road 🏛

SOUTH AUSTRALIAN MARITIME MUSEUM

www.history.sa.gov.au/maritime/maritime.htm

The Maritime Museum, close to the lighthouse, is a berth for some of the world's greatest maritime stories. The main gallery occupies the former 1850 bond stores and contains a replica of a sailing ketch. Displays illustrate the conditions under which European migrants sailed to South Australia. There is also a floating collection that includes the 1949 *Yelta*, the state's last working steam tug, and the 1942 military launch *Archie Badenoch*.

There is a magnificent view of the Adelaide plains and the Mount Lofty Ranges from the top of the lighthouse.

✚ Off map 234 A2 ✉ 126 Lipson Street, Port Adelaide, SA 5015; 14km (9 miles) northwest of city ☎ 08 8207 6255 🕐 Daily 10–5 ✋ Adult A\$8.50, child A\$3.50, under 5s free 🚌 118, 118N from North Terrace terminate at Commercial Road 🚆 Port Adelaide from Adelaide Station 💻 🏛

Left *The Onkaparinga River flows into Gulf St. Vincent south of Adelaide*
Below *Port Adelaide's lighthouse*

Above *The South Australian Museum is one of the Victorian buildings on North Terrace*
Below *A rare pink-footed rock wallaby at Cleland Wildlife Park*

SOUTH AUSTRALIAN MUSEUM

www.samuseum.sa.gov.au

This grand 19th-century building has four floors of exhibition space. The Australian Aboriginal Cultures Gallery is the largest of its kind, exploring the indigenous people through hands-on displays and more than 3,000 items. Other galleries describe mammals from around the world, marine wildlife, fossils and minerals.

A gallery is devoted to the Antarctic explorer Sir Douglas Mawson (1882–1958), exhibiting his sled, an ice wall and Antarctic rock.

234 B2 ✉ North Terrace, Adelaide, SA 5000 ☎ 08 8207 7500 🕐 Daily 10–5 ✋ Free 🚌 Free 99C City Loop and many other routes 🚊 Adelaide 🖥 🏛

TANDANYA – NATIONAL ABORIGINAL CULTURAL INSTITUTE

www.tandanya.com.au

Paint a boomerang, learn how to play a didgeridoo or do the Kangaroo Dance—these are just some of the fun ways to discover indigenous culture. Forming the first major Australian Aboriginal cultural facility, the galleries here feature art, crafts and music, and a glimpse of the hunter-gatherer lifestyles and traditions of more than 85 communities.

234 C2 ✉ 253 Grenfell Street, Adelaide, SA 5000 ☎ 08 8224 3200 🕐 Mon–Fri 10–5, Sat, Sun 11–4 ✋ Adult A$5, child A$3 🚌 Free 99C City Loop 🚊 Adelaide 🖥 🏛

ADELAIDE HILLS

www.visitadelaidehills.com.au

The Mount Lofty Ranges and Adelaide Hills form a crescent of pretty towns, natural bushland, vineyards and gardens around the city. The Adelaide Hills is one of few regions in Australia with four distinct seasons. Temperatures here are about 2–4°C (3.5–7°F) cooler than in Adelaide city, so it's popular in summer. The Hills begin just 10km (6 miles) southeast of Adelaide, and much of their early colonization was by Prussians and Silesians fleeing religious persecution in the 19th century; their influence is still obvious in the region. Hahndorf is a pretty town, with several German-style restaurants and cake shops.

MOUNT LOFTY

Mount Lofty (720m/2,361ft) is a physical gateway to the Hills. Close to the summit is Cleland Conservation Park and Wildlife Park (daily 9.30–5), full of friendly marsupials. Farther north, Norton Summit lies amid fruit orchards, rocky gullies and vineyards.

TORRENS VALLEY

Quiet country roads and native wildlife in typical Australian bushland characterize the Torrens Valley. The winding drive from Adelaide along the gorge is spectacular. At dawn and dusk, kangaroos and emus graze near Chain of Ponds, against splendid backdrops of giant reservoirs and towering pine trees. The National Motor Museum at Birdwood is a must for vintage car enthusiasts (daily 10–5), but you should also visit some wineries.

ONKAPARINGA VALLEY

The town of Hahndorf, in the Onkaparinga Valley southeast of Adelaide, was settled in 1839 by German immigrants and is the former home of landscape artist Sir Hans Heysen (1877–1968); the homestead, The Cedars, is dedicated to his work (Tue–Sun 10–4). Lenswood, in the heart of the valley, has some of the Hills' most beautiful vineyards, orchards and farmland.

346 P14 ℹ Adelaide Hills Visitor Centre, 41 Main Street, Hahndorf, SA 5245 ☎ 1800 353 323, 08 8388 1185 🕐 Mon–Fri 9–5, Sat, Sun 10–4 ℹ Mount Lofty Summit Information Centre, Mount Lofty Summit Road, Crafers, SA 5152 ☎ 08 8370 1054 🕐 Daily 9–5

BAROSSA VALLEY

Australia's best-known wine region is only a one-hour drive, 68km (42 miles) north of Adelaide. There are more than 60 cellar door wineries, plus fine restaurants and accommodation in cottages, farmhouses and stately homes. Add heritage towns and villages spread among the undulating hills and valleys, and it's a classic area for touring.

South Australia was a free settlement, only proclaimed in 1836, and in 1840 the English settled in Angaston and Lyndoch. Dissidents from Germany made their way to the Barossa Valley soon after, and a Germanic accent reflected in the architecture and the traditional skills of smoking meats, preserving fruits and making cheeses. The English and German settlers were responsible for the development of a commercial wine industry, which grew rapidly from the 1880s. Today, more than 6 million litres (1.3 million gallons) of quality wine are exported each year.

Barossa is now a regional food brand and there is a Farmers' Market in Angaston on Saturday morning (7.30–11.30). Music also plays a role in the area's charm and atmosphere, with brass band and jazz festivals. The Barossa International Festival of Music is held each October and the Jazz Weekend every August.

The Barossa Reservoir, west of Lyndoch, is noted for its Whispering Wall, a dam begun in 1899. Then the highest dam in Australia, its innovative curving wall proved an influential design. It's equally famous for its acoustic properties as ordinary speech travels across the parabolic surface.

WINERIES

The wineries vary dramatically in size and attractiveness, but many have kept their original buildings, like the Rockford Winery in Tanunda and the Saltram Wine Estate in Angaston. Chateau Tanunda has been restored to its former glory with a croquet lawn and attractive gardens. The Jacobs Creek Visitor Centre offers historical information, tastings of Orlando wines and a good restaurant in a superb setting on Jacobs Creek. Peter Lehmann Wines, Wolf Blass and Penfolds are also well known outside Australia and so attract visitors. But don't forget the smaller wineries, directions to which are available at the Barossa Wine and Visitor Centre in Tanunda.

You can walk off the after-effects of too much good food and wine along many walking trails. There are marked walks in the Barossa Goldfields and six trails in the Para Wirra, around Mengler Hill and the Sculpture Park. Maps are available from the visitor office in Tanunda.

INFORMATION

www.barossa.com

✚ 347 P19 ℹ Barossa Visitor Information Centre, 66–68 Murray Street, Tanunda, SA 5352 ☎ 08 8563 0600, 1300 852 982 ◷ Mon–Fri 9–5, Sat, Sun 10–4

TIPS

» Because the Barossa towns, villages and wineries are spread across an area measuring 25km by 10km (15miles by 6 miles), a car is the best way to visit. Otherwise join a tour or rent a bicycle and ride through the backroads.

» Check major festival dates, when accommodation can be difficult to find unless reserved well in advance.

Above *The Barossa Valley is well known for its cabernet grapes*

Above *Camping in the Heysen Range in the Flinders Ranges National Park*

COOBER PEDY

www.cooberpedy.sa.gov.au

Coober Pedy is the world's opal capital, disgorging most of the global output of this fiery semi-precious stone. Craters, shafts and waste heaps mark the frontier landscape, where homes are gouged from bare hillsides, originally by pioneer miners escaping the searing summer heat and cold nights (March to the end of November is the best time to visit). You can stay at the world's only international-standard underground hotel or a subterranean bed-and-breakfast; there are even underground churches.

The Umoona Opal Mine and Museum (daily 9–7, tours at 10, 12, 2 and 4) explores the local geology and Aboriginal Dreamtime. Some 4WD tours include a 70km (43-mile) round trip along part of the Dog Fence—5,500km (3,410 miles) of barbed wire that protects sheep from dingoes. Another tour you might want to take is Martin's night star-gazing tour, which goes into the desert for fabulous views of the night sky (tel 08 8672 5223).

✚ 346 M10 ℹ️ Coober Pedy Visitor Centre, Hutchison Street, Coober Pedy, SA 5721 ☎ 1800 637 076 🕐 Mon–Fri 8.30–5, Sat–Sun 10–1 ✈️ Coober Pedy; daily flights from Adelaide

COONAWARRA

www.wattlerange.sa.gov.au

Coonawarra, inland from the Limestone Coast, is best known for its excellent red wines. The first winery was established in 1890, and later became Wynns Coonawarra Estate. The John Riddoch Centre (also housing the Visitor Information Centre) is where to learn about the region's agricultural history.

Penola, south of Coonawarra, is the home of Mother Mary Mackillop, founder of the Order of St. Joseph and Australia's only saint.

✚ 347 Q15 ℹ️ Penola/Coonawarra Visitor Centre, 27 Arthur Street, Penola, SA 5277 ☎ 08 8737 2855 🕐 Mon–Fri 9–5, Sat, Sun 10–4

COORONG NATIONAL PARK

www.environment.sa.gov.au/parks

Visitors flock to this 50,000ha (123,500-acre) south coast park to observe the 238 bird species, which have migrated from as far as Siberia, and to enjoy 130km (81 miles) of wetlands, lagoons and dunes. By walking for a day, into the boat-accessible parts of the Coorong, a genuine wilderness experience is possible, although accommodation and caravan (trailer) parks are within striking distance. There is surf fishing on the beach or by boat or jetty at Long Point and Jacks Point; and fishing at Lake Albert, Meningie.

✚ 347 Q14 ✉️ National Parks and Wildlife SA, Coorong District Office, 34 Princes Highway, Meningie, SA 5264 ☎ 08 8575 1200 🕐 Office times vary according to rangers' activities (call first). Camping permits are available from this office, or roadhouses and information units in the region 🏕️ Camping permits (per night) A$5 per vehicle or boat, A$3 per hiker or bicycle rider 🚌 Premier Stateliner daily service from Adelaide to Meningie, Kingston and Mount Gambier

EYRE PENINSULA

www.visitportlincoln.net

From the eastern steelworks city of Whyalla on Spencer Gulf to Ceduna on the Great Australian Bight, 1,000km (620 miles) of peninsula coastline produces more than

60 per cent of the nation's seafood. Port Lincoln, at the southern point, is the world's tuna capital, with Tunarama (January: six days around the Australia Day weekend) the only festival dedicated to the big fish. The world's largest oysters are farmed along the coast between Coffin Bay and Ceduna; the molluscs are celebrated at Ceduna's October Oysterfest. There is a maritime museum and theatre at Whyalla, while Port Lincoln has many museums. Coffin Bay National Park is great for fishing, watersports, walking and wildlife.

✚ 346 N13 ℹ️ Port Lincoln Visitor Information Centre, 3 Adelaide Place, SA 5606, ☎ 08 8683 3544 🕐 Daily 9–5

FLEURIEU PENINSULA

www.mclarenvale.info

The Fleurieu Peninsula is a holiday playground of craft markets and country music, art and jazz festivals. There are 60 wineries for tasting and dining. Victor Harbor is the main resort town, where you can whale-watch from June to the end of September or take a horse-drawn tram to Granite Island and see nesting penguins. Strathalbyn, inland, is good for browsing antiques and craft stores.

The peninsula is fringed with beaches, while the interior has several national and conservation parks, which are ideal for bird- and wildlife-spotting, watersports or walking. Cape Jervis is the ferry point for Kangaroo Island (▷ 241).

The Cockle Train steams between Goolwa and Victor Harbor at Easter, Sundays and school holidays.

✚ 346 P14 ℹ️ McLaren Vale and Fleurieu Visitor Centre, Main Road, McLaren Vale, SA 5171 ☎ 08 8323 9944 🕐 Mon–Fri 9–5, Sat, Sun 10–5

FLINDERS RANGES

www.flindersoutback.com

www.environment.sa.gov.au/parks

Moody, awesome and the spiritual home of the Adnyamathanha people, the Flinders Ranges extend from Peterborough to the untamed Gammon Ranges. The ranges take in five national and four conservation parks, and offer challenging walking trails, including the 1,200km (744-mile) Heysen Trail from Cape Jervis on the Fleurieu Peninsula (▷ 240) to Parachilna.

The Ranges' landmark is Wilpena Pound, a crater-like bowl rimmed with mountain peaks. Non-adventurers may opt for a flight over the area. Farther north, the settlement of Blinman has a number of art and craft galleries.

The Ranges' capital is Quorn, a three-hour drive from Adelaide. Its Pichi Richi tourist railway to Port Augusta (Mar–end Nov) attracts rail enthusiasts, as do Peterborough's return Steamtown weekend winter journeys to Eurelia or Ororoo.

Outside the towns this is a wild, often forbidding country, much of it accessible only by 4WD vehicles; various operators conduct tours. Northeast of Quorn, the central part of the Ranges lies largely within the 95,000ha (234,650-acre) Flinders Ranges National Park. Besides its rich natural and cultural heritage, the park is a challenge for lovers of outdoor activities (entry and camping fees apply; tel 08 8648 0048).

The Flinders Ranges are known for their night skies and you can see the amazing spectacle on Arkaroola Wilderness Sanctuary's Ridgetop 4WD tour and stargazing at its astronomical observatory (tel 08 8648 4848).

✚ 347 P12 ℹ️ Flinders Ranges Visitor Information Centre, 3 Seventh Street, Quorn, SA 5433 ☎ 08 8648 6419 🕐 Daily 9–5

KANGAROO ISLAND

Visitors travel from around the world to experience the natural heritage of Kangaroo Island, Australia's third-largest island. A 45-minute ferry ride across the Backstairs Passage separates Kangaroo Island from Cape Jervis on the Fleurieu Peninsula (▷ 240). About 155km (96 miles) long and up to 60km (37 miles) wide, with 450km (279 miles) of spectacular cliff coastline and gentle beaches, the

island is too big to circumnavigate in a day. The coastline includes wonders such as Remarkable Rocks, Admiral's Arch and Kelly Hill Caves. There are 21 national and conservation parks, interspersed with pastoral land and thick scrub. Prepare for your visit to Kangaroo Island well, remember that distances are very long and visitors in self-contained accommodation away from the main settlements should ensure they have adequate water, food and fuel.

Discovered by the explorer Matthew Flinders in 1802, Kangaroo Island was settled at American River by renegade American sealers in 1803, later to become South Australia's first capital at Reeves Point, near Kingscote. Lack of water meant re-establishment of the capital to Adelaide in 1836.

Some 850 native plant species thrive here and wildlife includes a colony of sea lions on pristine Seal Bay. There are kangaroos (of course), Tammar wallabies, emus, Cape Barren geese, platypuses

and koalas at Flinders Chase, the largest of the conservation parks. Fairy penguins (also known as little penguins) parade at dusk at northern Penneshaw and at Kingscote.

Other ways to spend time include visiting museums, fishing, diving around 50 shipwrecks, sailing, surfing, bushwalking, bicycling, or watching for rare glossy black cockatoos and the 256 other bird species. Make sure you try the Ligurian-style honey, cheeses, corn-fed chicken, crayfish (lobster) and local wine. You can also get close to the wildlife: you can watch pelican feeding (daily 5pm) and penguin walks at KI Penguin Centre in Kingscote (tel 08 8553 3112).
✚ 346 N14 ℹ️ Gateway Visitor Information Centre, Howard Drive, Penneshaw (near Sealink ferry terminal), SA 5222 ☎ 08 8202 8686 🕐 Mon–Fri 9–5, Sat, Sun 10–4 🚢 Sealink ferries make four crossings daily from Cape Jervis to Penneshaw, more in peak seasons, tel 08 8553 1185 and 13 13 01; www.sealink.com.au ❓ Sealink organizes coach travel from Adelaide to Cape Jervis

Below *The Remarkable Rocks are a huge natural sculpture*

KAPUNDA

www.kapundatourism.com.au

Kapunda, and South Australia's fledgling 19th-century economy, were built on the wealth of the copper mines. The southern approach is dominated by Map Kernow (Son of Cornwall), an 8m (26ft) bronze statue that commemorates the Cornish miners who worked the early mines. The copper seams had become exhausted or were flooded by the end of the 19th century and the township then became a base for cattle ranching.

The 10km (6-mile) Kapunda Heritage Trail passes old mine areas, tunnels, open cuts and cottages; the landmark Kapunda Chimney is here. Many Victorian buildings in the south end of town are adorned with magnificent metal openwork. Kapunda Museum (daily 1–4; adult A$5, child A$2) contains historical town objects.

✚ 347 P13 ℹ Kapunda Visitor Information Centre, corner Main and Hill streets, Kapunda, SA 5373 ☎ 08 8566 2902

MOUNT GAMBIER

www.mountgambiertourism.com.au

The town of Mount Gambier lies on the slopes of an extinct volcano. The water-filled crater, known as the Blue Lake, is normally crystal clear with the water that has filtered through limestone beneath the city. But each November the lake changes from a subdued winter blue to brilliant turquoise, and then back again in March.

A 3.5km (2-mile) trail follows the rim of the Blue Lake. In the town itself, its strong café society imbued with country charm, historic buildings, antiques stores, shopping malls, museums, galleries, cinemas and heritage pubs provides the entertainment. There are also tours of limestone caves that run under the town's streets.

✚ 347 Q15 ℹ Lady Nelson Visitor and Discovery Centre, Jubilee Highway East, Mount Gambier, SA 5290 ☎ 08 8724 9750; ✪ Daily 9–5

MURRAY BRIDGE

www.murraylands.info
www.riverland.info

The mighty Murray is one of the world's great rivers. The South Australian course is divided into two regions, the lower Murraylands and the upper Riverland, where Waikerie is Australia's gliding capital. Carving through sandstone cliffs dotted with red gum trees, the river is a sanctuary for wildlife, as well as offering houseboat cruises, fishing and water-skiing. Where paddle-steamers once carried wool, tea and gold bullion to towns from Tailem Bend to Echuca in central Victoria, they now carry holidaymakers. The giant *Murray Princess* paddle-wheeler offers two- to seven-night cabin cruises from Mannum, upstream from Murray Bridge, and Tailem Bend, while the *Proud Mary* runs from Murray Bridge.

There is a scenic drive around Monarto Zoo on the way to Murray Bridge; Ruston's rose garden at Renmark.

✚ 347 P14 ℹ Murray Bridge Visitor Information and Tourist Centre, 3 South Terrace, Murray Bridge, SA 5253 ☎ 08 8539 1142 ✪ Mon–Fri 8.30–5.30, Sat, Sun 10–4

OUTBACK SOUTH AUSTRALIA

▷ 243.

ROBE

www.robe.com.au

October to the end of April is really the best time to visit Robe, when the crayfish (lobster) are in season.

This popular, pretty waterfront holiday spot on Guichen Bay is known for its seafood, best accompanied by a wine from Coonawarra or a local winery. Robe was where miners disembarked in the mid-1800s on their way to the Victorian goldfields. A heritage walk through the town takes in Victorian buildings and the ruins of the 1861 Old Gaol.

The bay is suitable for sailing and swimming, and there are plenty of opportunities for fishing and diving along the coast.

Above *Mining chimneys are a common sight around Kapunda*

✚ 347 Q15 ℹ Robe Visitor Information Centre, Mundy Terrace, Robe, SA 5276 ☎ 08 8768 2465

YORKE PENINSULA

www.yorkepeninsula.com.au

You are never more than 25km (16 miles) from the sea on the Yorke Peninsula. Inland the peninsula is the granary of South Australia, while the coast is a fishing paradise. Many of the small waterfront towns have jetties for those without boats. Among the coastal towns, Ardrossan is known for its soaring cliffs, local history museum and the shipwreck of the *Zanoni*—one of Australia's best diving challenges. Little Cornwall comprises the 'copper triangle' towns of Moonta, Wallaroo and inland Kadina. This was once a rich copper-mining region that attracted Cornish miners in the 19th century. These towns host the world's largest Cornish festival, Kernewek Lowender, in May during odd-numbered years. Innes National Park is a haven for bushwalking, camping, diving and surfing.

✚ 346 P13 ℹ The Farm Shed Museum and Tourism Centre, 50 Moonta Road, Kadina, SA 5554 ☎ 1800 654 991 ✪ Mon–Fri 9–5, Sat, Sun 10–3.30

OUTBACK SOUTH AUSTRALIA

Go to the outback to agree with explorer Charles Sturt, who said in 1845 of its harsh, brilliant, unyielding splendour that it had 'no parallel on earth's surface'.

The South Australian outback is a vast backyard in the driest state in the second-driest continent, and remains one of the world's great adventure challenges. It was first explored in 1839, and later by the ill-fated Burke and Wills (▷ 29), who perished by Cooper Creek. Memorials to them both are near Innamincka. The main north–south road is the 3,245km (2,012-mile) sealed Stuart Highway, which can be left for forays into the eastern outback. Locals will helpfully direct people from point A to B, but be aware of the distances and dangers.

South Australia's outback is a landscape of stony red desert and boulder-strewn plains, pockets of saltbush and scrub, blinding-white salt lakes, rocky eruptions and endless star-filled night skies.

Heading northwest to the Great Victoria Desert, key towns along the Stuart Highway are Port Augusta, Woomera, Glendambo, Coober Pedy (▷ 240) and Marla. From Marla, if you don't want to continue to Alice Springs (▷ 210), turn southeast to Oodnadatta, William Creek, Lyndhurst and Leigh Creek back to Port Augusta.

WOOMERA

Woomera has the southern hemisphere's only rocket-launching range. To the north, modern Roxby Downs serves Olympic Dam, the world's biggest copper-uranium complex, with mine tours. Andamooka is another mineral town, which has yielded the world's biggest opal.

WILLIAM CREEK

This town adjoins the world's largest cattle station, Anna Creek. It's a gateway to Lake Eyre North (4WD only), which has filled, or partially filled, only four times since its discovery (last time in 2000, attracting prolific bird life).

MARREE

The road southeast to Marree follows the Oodnadatta Track and passes Lake Eyre South. Marree itself has a mosque, founded by Afghan cameleers who took supplies to remote settlements and returned with wool. The Birdsville Track heads north to Birdsville through the Stony Desert. Farther south, you can tour the coal mines at Leigh Creek.

INFORMATION

www.wadlatasa.gov.au
www.flindersoutback.com
➕ 346 N11 ℹ Wadlata Outback Centre (includes tourist information), 41 Flinders Terrace, Port Augusta, SA 5700 ☎ 08 8641 9193 ⊘ Mon–Fri 9–5.30, Sat, Sun 10–4

TIPS

» Unless you're on an organized tour, inform friends of your travel plans. If you deviate from a major town or road, inform police of your schedule and destination.
» Carry good maps (many roads are not signposted) and extra water, food, fuel and a spare fan belt
» If you break down, do not leave your vehicle. Lie under it for shade until you are found.
» Always check road conditions ahead—in or just after rain it's easy to get stuck in mud.

Above *The Breakaways are near Coober Pedy*

WALK

ADELAIDE: FROM NORTH TERRACE TO THE CENTRAL MARKET

Adelaide's compact central area is easy to explore on foot (▷ 234–239). The walk takes in the string of grand public buildings along North Terrace, the city's most attractive boulevard, the retail district of Rundle Mall, and the beautiful Botanic Gardens.

THE WALK

Distance: 5–6km (3–4 miles)
Allow: Half a day
Start: Adelaide Festival Centre; see map ▷ 234, B2
End: Victoria Square or Central Market
How to get there: Adelaide Station is near Festival Centre, on North Terrace

Note: Central Market, where the walk ends, is open on Tuesday, Thursday, Friday and Saturday. On non-market days finish your walk at Victoria Square.

★ At the Adelaide Festival Centre in King William Road (▷ 234), face away from the park and the River Torrens and take the walkway to North Terrace. When you reach the Adelaide SkyCity Casino, turn left and stay on the north side of North Terrace. Walk past Parliament House. As you cross King William Road, Government House (the governor's residence) is just visible

on your left behind its high garden wall. Continue along North Terrace until you come to the State Library of South Australia.

❶ Three of the state's main cultural institutions line up side by side on North Terrace, making an impressive row of grand Victorian architecture. First is the State Library of South Australia, then the Art Gallery of South Australia, and finally the South Australian Museum (▷ 238).

Diagonally opposite, near the Botanic Hotel, is Ayers House.

❷ Ayers House (Tue–Fri 10–4, Sat, Sun 1–4), built in 1846 of local bluestone, is a single-floor mansion that was once the home of Sir Henry Ayers, one of South Australia's early premiers. Owned by the National Trust, it houses a restaurant and museum of Adelaide (A\$8 adult, A\$4 child).

From Ayers House, cross over North Terrace again to the Royal Adelaide Hospital, then continue on the original eastward direction until you reach the main gate of the Botanic Garden.

❸ It's worth taking some time to explore the beautifully landscaped Botanic Garden (▷ 233). One option is to walk straight ahead from the main gate and bear left at an intersection to visit the Palm House, a striking 1875 glasshouse that contains a collection of plants from Madagascar. You can then stroll to the middle of the gardens, past the Main Lake (where there is a restaurant and kiosk) to the Bicentennial Conservatory, with its rainforest plants. Nearby is the International Rose Garden.

Make your way through the gardens to the National Wine Centre of Australia, which faces Botanic Road.

❹ The National Wine Centre (Mon–Fri 9–5, Sat, Sun 10–5) has an interactive wine industry showcase, a café and shop. You can taste and buy wines, and learn about wine-making.

Walk back to the main gate of the Botanic Garden and on to North Terrace again. Almost diagonally opposite is East Terrace, with Rundle Park on the left and a hotel on the right. Walk south along East Terrace for one block with the park on your left and turn right on to Rundle Street with the park behind you.

❺ This is the East End of Rundle Street, one of Adelaide's main wining and dining precincts. Many of the cafés and restaurants that line the street have alfresco dining areas that make the most of Adelaide's sunny weather. This is a lively and popular place until well after dark.

Continue along Rundle Street for 400m (436 yards) to King William Street through the pedestrian precinct of Rundle Mall.

❻ Rundle Mall is the retail hub of Adelaide. There are shopping complexes and department stores, including the Myer Centre and Adelaide Central Plaza, and flower stalls, restaurants, street musicians and boutiques. Among the shopping arcades running off the mall is the ornate Adelaide Arcade, a good example of high Victoriana.

Walk up the mall to where it finishes at King William Street. Turn left on to King William Street and walk three blocks past Grenfell, Pirie and Flinders streets to Victoria Square.

❼ Adelaide's founder, Colonel William Light, planned Victoria Square as the city's official centre. In the middle, a fountain celebrates the rivers that supply Adelaide's water, and a statue commemorates the British queen after whom the square was named. Facing Victoria Square are the Glenelg tram terminus, the Supreme Court, the Cathedral of St. Francis Xavier and the Hilton Hotel.

If you are walking on Tuesday to Saturday, continue to Central Market by crossing over to the Hilton Hotel and walking west for a block along Grote Street.

❽ Fruit, vegetables, small goods, cheeses, meats and seafood are among the produce for sale at the Central Market (▷ 235). Stop at one of the cafés or food stalls.

To return to the start point at the Adelaide Festival Centre, walk back to Victoria Square and north along King William Street, passing the Town Hall on your right. Continue for about 0.6km (0.3 mile) until you reach North Terrace and cross into King William Road. The Festival Centre is on your left.

WHEN TO GO
All year round.

WHERE TO EAT
Ayers House, the Botanic Garden and the National Wine Centre, all of which are along the route, all have restaurants.

Rundle Street offers many excellent cafés and restaurants. On market days you can get food and refreshments at the Central Market.

PLACES TO VISIT
Migration Museum, ▷ 236.
Tandanya, ▷ 238.

Opposite View from the Torrens River to Adelaide's central business district
Left Sunset over the Palm House in the Botanic Gardens
Below Victoria Square's fountain

THE BAROSSA VALLEY: FROM WILLIAMSTOWN TO SPRINGTON

The Barossa Valley is Australia's best-known wine region (▷ 239). There are many other attractions apart from wine, however—historic towns, a unique German influence, good food and unspoiled rural scenery.

THE DRIVE
Distance: 50–90km (31–56 miles)
Allow: 1 day
Start at: Adelaide
End at: Adelaide

★ From central Adelaide proceed east along North Terrace with the Botanic Garden on your left. Cross Dequetteville Terrace and continue to Payneham Road (A11). Branch left along Lower North East Road and after 1km (0.6 mile) take Gorge Road (B31) on the right. Continue on Gorge Road through Athelstone and alongside the River Torrens (B31) to Chain of Ponds. Turn right on to the B10. After Gumeracha, go north on Forreston Road and join the B34 to Williamstown. From here, drive north a short distance on the B31, then turn left on to Yettie Road to the Barossa Reservoir and Whispering Wall.

❶ The wall of the Reservoir is known as the Whispering Wall because of its acoustic properties. The curve of the wall is such that a person standing at one end can hear a whisper spoken at the other end, 140m (153 yards) away.

Off Williamstown Road are the Barossa Goldfields, scene of a gold rush in the 1860s. Walking tracks lead past the old workings.

Return to the B31 and head north to Lyndoch.

❷ Lyndoch bills itself as the gateway to the Barossa Valley because of the numerous wineries in the immediate area. The largest is Chateau Yaldara, 5km (3 miles) northwest of Lyndoch.

An alternative bouquet is the Lyndoch Lavender Farm, 7km (4.5 miles) southeast of town off the B31. Stroll through 2.5ha (6 acres) of lavender, or sample some of the herb products (Sep–end Feb daily 10–4.30; Mar–end Aug Mon, Fri 10–4.30).

From Lyndoch take the Barossa Valley Way (B19) to Tanunda. As you approach Tanunda, turn right on to Bethany Road to the small town of Bethany.

3 Bethany was the first German settlement in the valley in 1842. The layout—long strips of farmland stretching out behind the cottages—is in the traditional Hufendorf style brought here by the settlers. Historic buildings include the 1851 Herberge Christi Church, and the Landhaus, a mud-and-stone house built in the 1840s and now a restaurant. Bethany Wines, on Bethany Road, is a long-established and picturesque family-owned winery. A few kilometres southeast of the winery, on Mengler Hill Road, is Mengler Hill Lookout, which has a magnificent view of the vineyards.

From Bethany, go back to the Barossa Valley Way for the short drive to Tanunda.

4 Tanunda, on the banks of the North Para River, preserves much of its German heritage, including three Lutheran churches and the marketplace, the Ziegenmarkt (Goat Market). Shops sell German breads, sausages and pastries. The main wineries in the area are Chateau Tanunda, Richmond Grove, Peter Lehmann Wines, Rockford Wines, Kaiser Stuhl and Basedow. For more information visit the Barossa Wine and Visitor Centre in Murray Street Mon–Fri 9–5, Sat, Sun 10–4).

From Tanunda continue on the Barossa Valley Way to Nuriootpa, at the northern end of the valley.

5 Nuriootpa is the commercial heart of the Barossa. Wineries straddle the train line. Along the banks of the North Para River are public parks, a swimming pool and shaded picnic spots. The Penfolds Winery is at the northern end of town on Tanunda Road.

Go back 1km (0.6 mile) along the Barossa Valley Way, then turn left to Angaston (B10), about 7km (4.5 miles) from the turnoff.

6 Angaston is an attractive rural settlement among the rolling

Barossa Ranges. Walk down the tree-lined main street to savour art and craft shops, galleries, tea rooms and restaurants. Schulz Butchers sell excellent German *mettwursts*. The Angas Park Fruit Company, also in the main street, sells locally grown and processed dried fruit, as well as nuts. Wineries nearby are Saltram, Yalumba and Henschke Cellars. Some 5km (3 miles) southeast of town on the Eden Valley Road is Collingrove Homestead, a country house dating from the 1850s. It is open to the public (Mon–Fri 1–4.30, Sat, Sun 12–4.30; guided tours only Mon–Fri 1.30, 2.30, 3.30; Sat, Sun 12.30, 1.30, 2.30, 3.30), and has a restaurant and accommodation.

From Angaston, head south along the B10 through the Eden Valley with its gum-studded pastures and rocky hilltops. Springton is about 20km (12 miles) south of Angaston.

7 Springton's main drawcard is the Herbig Family Tree. This huge, old, hollow gum tree was once home to

a German pioneer, Johann Herbig, his wife and two children, for five years from 1855.

Continue on the B10 via Mount Pleasant and Birdwood to Chain of Ponds, where you fork left on to the B31 for the return drive to Adelaide.

Opposite *Bringing in the harvest*
Below *The Herbig Family Tree at Springton was once home to a pioneering family*

WHAT TO DO

ADELAIDE

AAMI STADIUM

This is South Australia's main Australian Rules football ground. Visiting sides from interstate take on one of the local teams, Port Adelaide or Adelaide.

✉ West Lakes Boulevard City, West Lakes, SA 5021 ☎ 08 8268 2088 🕒 Season Apr–end Sep 🎫 From A$25 🚌 10km (6 miles) northwest from Adelaide

ADELAIDE AQUATIC CENTRE

www.cityofadelaide.com.au
Enjoy swimming pools, a diving pool, gymnasium, sauna, and spa and steam rooms.

✉ Jeffcott Road, North Adelaide, SA 5006 ☎ 08 8344 4411 🕒 Mon–Sat 5am–10pm, Sun 7am–8pm 🚌 231, 233, 235, 237 🎫 Adult A$6.80, child A$5.20, family from A$17.20

ADELAIDE CENTRAL MARKET

www.centralmarkettour.com.au
The people of Adelaide have been shopping for fruit and vegetables at the Central Market for more than 135 years. Cheeses and preserved meats are also available. Surrounding the produce market are arcades with specialist stores that sell a variety of goods, including souvenirs, books and craftworks. The market has a lively, bustling atmosphere, especially on Saturday mornings.

✉ Grote Street, Adelaide, SA 5000 ☎ 08 8203 7494 🕒 Tue 7–5.30, Wed, Thu 9–5.30, Fri 7am–9pm, Sat 7–3 🚌 City Loop. Close to Central Bus Station 🍴

ADELAIDE ENTERTAINMENT CENTRE

www.theaec.net
The Centre hosts large-scale events, such as pop concerts by star names, touring international circus troupes and dance spectaculars.

✉ Port Road, Hindmarsh, SA 5007 ☎ 08 8208 2222 🚆 Bowden from Adelaide station 🍴 🍷

ADELAIDE FESTIVAL CENTRE

www.afct.org.au
The Festival Centre is Adelaide's main venue for drama, dance, classical music and opera. It hosts various festivals including a cabaret festival and a guitar festival.

✉ King William Road, Adelaide, SA 5000 ☎ 08 8216 8600 🚌 City Loop to intersection of North Terrace and King William Road 🚆 Adelaide 🍴 🍷

ADELAIDE OVAL TOURS

www.cricketsa.com.au
Sports fans will enjoy this fascinating two-hour tour of the Adelaide Oval, one of the world's most picturesque cricket grounds. The tour takes in the heritage-listed manual scoreboard, stands, media areas, dressing rooms and the Adelaide Oval Museum.

✉ SA Cricket Ground, North Adelaide, SA 5006 ☎ 08 8300 3800 🕒 Tours Mon–Fri 10am (except public holidays and match days) 🎫 $10 adult, $5 child 🚌 204, 235–237

ELECTRIC LIGHT HOTEL

www.electriclighthotel.com
A happening pub with free entry and an adjoining music venue that attracts a diverse range of top Australian artists.

✉ 235 Grenfell Street, Adelaide, SA 5000

Opposite *Adelaide's Central Market is open Tuesday to Saturday*

☎ 08 8232 2666 🕐 Tue–Fri 11am–3am, Sat, Sun 5pm–3am 🖐 Cover charge varies 🚌 City Loop

HEAVEN NIGHTCLUB
www.heaven.com.au
Retro, trance, R & B and contemporary rock are among the musical flavours you can savour in Heaven. The website lists upcoming performances and costs.
✉ 1 North Terrace, Adelaide, SA 5000 ☎ 08 8216 5200 🕐 Wed 8pm–5am, Thu 9pm–5am, Sat 9pm–6am 🖐 See website 🚌 Central Bus Station in Grote Street

JAMFACTORY CONTEMPORARY CRAFT AND DESIGN
www.jamfactory.com.au
A retail shop, part of the JamFactory Contemporary Craft and Design complex, sells high-quality work from the JamFactory studios dealing in ceramics, hot glass, metal design and contemporary furniture. You can also buy leather goods. Packaging and shipping assistance to your home country is provided.
✉ 19 Morphett Street, Adelaide, SA 5000 ☎ 08 8410 0727 🕐 Mon–Sat 10–5, Sat 10–5, Sun 1–5 🚌 City Loop to cnr Morphett and Grote streets. Central Bus Station nearby

JIVE
www.jivevenue.com
A popular live music venue with everything from pop to punk in comfortable surroundings. Comedy and the fun 'theatre sports' game are also on offer.
✉ 181 Hindley Street, Adelaide, SA 5000 ☎ 08 8211 6683 🕐 Daily, early afternoon until late 🖐 From A\$15 🚌 City Loop (99C)

KING WILLIAM ROAD
www.kingwilliamroad.com.au
Just five minutes south of the city centre, leafy King William Road is Adelaide's most attractive shopping precinct. Stylish boutiques sell men's and women's designer

fashions, footwear and accessories, children's clothes, homewares and gifts, and there are also many cafés and restaurants.
✉ Hyde Park, Adelaide, SA 5061 🕐 Mon–Wed, Fri, Sat 9–5, Thu 9–9, Sun 9–5 (some shops only) 🚌 203 from city centre

THE LION HOTEL
www.thelionhotel.com
In one of North Adelaide's trendiest streets, this pub offers great bars, a bistro and stylish restaurant, as well as Thursday evening DJs and live entertainment every other night.
✉ 161 Melbourne Street, North Adelaide, SA 5006 ☎ 08 8367 0222 🕐 Daily, entertainment generally from 9pm 🖐 Free 🚌 204, 272, 273

MARS BAR
www.themarsbar.com.au
Everyone, gay or straight, is welcome at this gay and lesbian venue. Dance shows on Friday and Saturday nights.
✉ 120 Gouger Street, Adelaide, SA 5000 ☎ 08 8231 9639 🕐 Wed–Sun 9pm–5am 🖐 Wed–Thu, Sun free, Fri, Sat A\$8, including show 🚌 Central Bus Station in Grote Street, or taxi (approx A\$7) from city

MISS GLADYS SYM CHOON
www.missgladyssymchoon.com.au
An Adelaide institution, this shop sells men's and women's clothing and footwear. The shop stocks both its own in-house-designed funky and hip labels, which it sells around Australia and exports to New Zealand, and the collections of some of Australia's best-known young fashion designers.
✉ 235A Rundle Street, Adelaide, SA 5000 ☎ 08 8223 1500 🕐 Mon, Wed, Thu 10–6.30, Sat 10–10, Sun 11–6 🚌 City Loop to cnr Rundle Street and East Terrace

NATIONAL WINE CENTRE
www.wineaustralia.com.au
The National Wine Centre of Australia adjoins the Botanic Garden. The Centre's store sells Australian wines and wine-related merchandise, such as glassware, books and corkscrews.
✉ Cnr Botanic and Hackney roads,

Adelaide, SA 5000 ☎ 08 8303 3355 🕐 Mon–Fri 9–5, Sat, Sun 10–5 🚌 City Loop to cnr North and East terraces then 500m (545-yard) walk. Buses from Adelaide station 🚌

OLYMPIC OPAL GEM MINE
www.olympicopal.com.au
A re-created opal mine with walk-through tunnels gives an idea of what opals look like in nature. Besides opal jewellery, you can buy pearl jewellery, hand-blown glass, pottery and Aboriginal art and crafts.
✉ 5 Rundle Mall, Adelaide, SA 5000 ☎ 08 8211 7440 🕐 Mon–Fri 9.30–5.30 (also Fri 5.30–9pm), Sat 9.30–5, Sun 11–5 🚌 City Loop to intersection of North Terrace and King William Street, then short walk

OPAL FIELD GEMS MINE AND MUSEUM
The star attraction at this opal shop is the world's largest opal specimen. The basement features a realistic recreation of an outback opal mine.
✉ 33 King William Street, Adelaide, SA 5000 ☎ 08 8212 5300 🕐 Mon–Thu 9–6 Fri 9–7.30, Sat 9–5, Sun 10–5 🚌 City Loop

SUGAR
www.sugarclub.com.au
This classy club in the heart of town has a gallery, café, pool hall, DJ-record store, and DJs every night in the dance club.
✉ Level 1, 274 Rundle Street, Adelaide, SA 5000 ☎ 08 8223 6160 🕐 Daily 9pm–late 🖐 From A\$10

SKYCITY ADELAIDE
www.skycityadelaide.com.au
This casino has the usual gambling attractions plus bars, restaurants, cafés and live entertainment.
✉ North Terrace, Adelaide, SA 5000 ☎ 08 8212 2811 🕐 Daily 10am–4am (also Fri, Sat 4–6am) 🚌 City Loop 🚆 Adelaide

SWIM WITH THE DOLPHINS
www.dolphinboat.com.au
Watch or swim with dolphins on a boat trip from Glenelg.
✉ Holdfast Shores Marina, Glenelg, SA 5045 ☎ 0412 811 838 🕐 Cruises depart daily

8am 🚋 Trams to Glenelg 🖐 Watching:
adult A$58, child A$48; Swimming: adult
A$98, child (over 8) A$88

TANDANYA–NATIONAL ABORIGINAL CULTURAL INSTITUTE

www.tandanya.com.au
The Institute displays contemporary
and traditional Aboriginal artworks.
Some of the works are for sale
in the gift shop, which also has a
range of authentic crafts. There is a
resident artist (daily 1–4). Entry to
the shop is free but there is a fee to
enter the Institute (▷ 238).
✉ 253 Grenfell Street, Adelaide, SA 5000
☎ 08 8224 3200 🕒 Daily 10–5 🚌 City
Loop to Hindmarsh Square 🖐 Adult A$5,
child A$3; includes 12pm performance
Tue–Sun

THEBARTON THEATRE

www.thebartontheatre.com.au
A venue for local and international
music concerts.

✉ 112 Henley Beach Road, Torrensville,
SA 5031 ☎ 08 8443 5255 🚌 Torrensville
🚌 2km (1.5 miles) east from West Terrace,
Adelaide

THE VINES GOLF CLUB OF REYNELLA

www.vinesofreynella.com
This 18-hole course is set on a
former vineyard and surrounded by
native bush.
✉ Cnr Reynell Road and Mark Street,
Happy Valley, SA 5159 ☎ 08 8381 1822
🕒 Dawn–dusk; closed to the public Tue
morning, Wed, Sat, and Sun before 11
🖐 A$40 for 18 holes 🚌 18km (11 miles)
south from Adelaide

BAROSSA VALLEY

THE BAROSSA SMALL WINEMAKERS CENTRE

www.chateautanunda.com/wine/
smallwine.php
The Winemakers Centre is a
showcase for the numerous Barossa
Valley's small-scale wineries. The

Centre is in the cellar-door sales area
at historic Chateau Tanunda. More
than 50 different wines from about
20 boutique wineries are available
for sale, mostly handmade vintages
produced in very small quantities.
✉ Basedow Road, Tanunda, SA 5352
☎ 08 8563 3888 🕒 Daily 10–5 🚌 See
drive tour from Adelaide to the Barossa
Valley, ▷ 246–247

COOBER PEDY

THE OPAL CAVE

In the opal-mining outback town of
Coober Pedy (▷ 240), this shop sells
opals in rough and finished state.
A range of handcrafted jewellery is
also available, and goods come with
a certificate of authenticity. This is
a good place to learn how opals are
mined and about life generally in
Coober Pedy.
✉ Hutchison Street, Coober Pedy, SA 5723
☎ 08 8672 5028 🕒 Daily 8–6 🚌 540km
(335 miles) northwest from Port Augusta via
Stuart Highway (A87)

FLEURIEU PENINSULA

ADELAIDE ADVENTURE CHARTER

Qualified divers can join a tour to explore the HMAS *Hobart*, a specially prepared dive site.

✉ 4/1048 Grand Junction Road, Holden Hill, SA 5088 ☎ 08 8263 3337

KANGAROO ISLAND

KANGAROO ISLAND GALLERY

The gallery shows the work of Kangaroo Island's artists and craftspeople. Items for sale include paintings, pottery, handknits, patchwork, jewellery, handmade paper, stained glass and photographs.

✉ 1 Murray Street, Kingscote, SA 5223 ☎ 08 8553 2868 ◷ Daily 10–5

SEAL BAY CONSERVATION PARK

www.environment.sa.gov.au/parks

The park is home to more than 600 sea lions, which you can see on a boardwalk tour. For a closer view join the 45-minute ranger-guided tour of the beach.

✉ Kangaroo Island ☎ 08 8559 4207 ◷ Seal Bay Conservation Park: daily 9–5. Guided tours of Seal Bay beach 9–4.15. During South Australian summer school holidays park open until 7.45 and the last tour is at 7pm ✋ Boardwalk tours: adult A$12.50, child A$8, family A$35; Beach tours: adult A$27.50, child A$16.50, family A$75 ⛴ Cape Jervis ferry to Kangaroo Island, 106km (66 miles) south of Adelaide; Seal Bay is on the south of the island

MOUNT LOFTY

CLELAND WILDLIFE PARK

www.environment.sa.gov.au/parks

Get close to native animals at this wildlife park just 20 minutes from Adelaide. You'll see Tasmanian devils, tawny frogmouths and dingos, as well as koalas and emus.

✉ Summit Road, Mount Lofty, SA 5152 ☎ 08 8339 2444 ◷ Daily 9.30–5 ✋ Adult A$16, child A$9.50, family A$43.50 🚌 164F (Mon–Fri) or 165 (Sat, Sun) park-and-ride bus from the city and link with 823 service (four services a day) 🅿

Opposite *Stylish boutiques along King William Road*

Right *Adelaide has several annual festivals*

FESTIVALS AND EVENTS

FEBRUARY–MARCH

WOMADELAIDE

www.womadelaide.com.au

WOMADelaide is a major world music, art and dance festival in Adelaide's Botanic Park held over three days each year.

ADELAIDE FESTIVAL OF ARTS

www.adelaidefestival.org.au

The Adelaide Festival of Arts, held in even-numbered years, includes music, theatre, dance, visual art, free outdoor events, locally made films, food and music, an architecture programme, Adelaide Writers' Week, masterclasses and late-night venues.

ADELAIDE FRINGE FESTIVAL

www.adelaidefringe.com.au

The Adelaide Fringe Festival is held at the same time as the Adelaide Festival (above). It stages what's new across all forms of the independent arts.

MARCH–APRIL

CLIPSAL 500

www.clipsal500.com.au

The Clipsal 500, South Australia's V8 Supercar event, is held on a circuit that winds through Adelaide's streets.

NOVEMBER

ADELAIDE INTERNATIONAL HORSE TRIALS

www.australian3de.com.au

The Adelaide International Horse Trials is an annual event that attracts top Australian and international riders. Spectators enjoy three days of dressage, show jumping and cross-country competitions.

CREDIT UNION CHRISTMAS PAGEANT

www.cupageant.com.au

The Credit Union Christmas Pageant has been an Adelaide tradition since 1933. Join the thousands who line the route to watch a parade of festive and fairy-tale floats, marching bands and costumed characters.

EATING

PRICES AND SYMBOLS

The restaurants are listed alphabetically (excluding Le, La and Les). The prices given are the average for a two-course lunch (L) and a three-course dinner (D) for one person, without drinks. The wine price is for the least expensive bottle.

For a key to the symbols, ▷ 2.

ADELAIDE

CENTRAL MARKET FOOD COURTS AND CAFÉS

www.adelaide.sa.gov.au/centralmarket
For cheap varied food, mainly Asian and some Mediterranean, head for the central market. At Market Plaza and the International Food Plaza it's mainly Chinese, Thai, Malay and Vietnamese specials. Breakfast at Kelly's Kitchen, 38 Gouger Street (daily 7–3; tel 08 8231 2049).
✉ Gouger Street, Adelaide, SA 5000 ☎ 08 8203 7494 ⊙ Mon–Thu 7–5.30, Fri 7–9, Sat 7–4; Sun 11–2 for *yum cha*. Closed public holidays ✋ Stall meal A$16, Wine from A$5 per glass

CHLOE'S RESTAURANT

www.chloes.com.au
The largest wine list in Australia, plus Modern Australian and French menus that change seasonally. Host Nick Papazahariakis' cuisine also includes dishes with Mediterranean and Asian influences. Greek he may be, but you won't find moussaka on his menu.
✉ 36 College Road, Kent Town, Adelaide, SA 5067 ☎ 08 8362 2574 ⊙ Mon–Fri 12–3, Mon–Sat 6–9 ✋ L A$65, D A$90, Wine A$32 🚌 2km (1.5 miles) northeast from central Adelaide

CITRUS

www.citrus.net.au
At this modern Australian restaurant, dishes include risottos, daily pasta specials, and fish and meat dishes. Famous for its breakfasts; serves alcohol and BYO.
✉ 199 Hutt Street, Adelaide, SA 5000 ☎ 08 8224 0100 ⊙ Mon–Sat 7–2.30 and 6–late, Sun 7–5 ✋ L A$40, D A$55, Wine A$30

MAGILL ESTATE RESTAURANT

www.penfolds.com.au
The Modern Australian cuisine on offer here is pricey, and features seafood and meat such as roasted quail, grilled Angus beef and local venison. Vegetarian options are available, as well as more than 20 vintages of the Penfolds Grange wine. Reservations are essential.
✉ 78 Penfold Road, Magill, SA 5072 ☎ 08 8301 5551 ⊙ Tue–Sat from 6.30pm ✋ D A$90; Wine A$45 ✚ 7.5km (5 miles) (a 15-minute drive) east of cental Adelaide

SPARROW KITCHEN AND BAR

www.sparrowkitchenandbar.com.au
The menu at this handsome bar/ brasserie takes its inspiration from the cuisines of Spain and Italy.
✉ 10 O'Connell Street, North Adelaide, SA 5006 ☎ 08 8267 2444 ⊙ Mon–Fri 11.30am–11pm, Sat, Sun 8am–1am ✋ L A$35, D A$50, Wine A$38

THE SUMMIT

Enjoy wonderful views over the city from this restaurant along with Modern Australian dishes made with fresh ingredients. There's a good selection of wines from the region.
✉ Summit Road, Mount Lofty, via Crafers, SA 5152 ☎ 08 8339 2600 ⊙ Daily 12–3, Wed–Sun 6–10 ✋ L A$50, D A$70, Wine A$26 🚌 19km (12 miles) southeast from Adelaide via Princes Highway (A1/M1)

WINDY POINT RESTAURANTS

www.windypoint.com.au
High on a viewpoint overlooking the city, there are two restaurants here. The restaurant serves Australian cuisine influenced particularly by Japan and Malaysia. The more casual Windy Point Café specializes in Mediterranean dishes.

Belair Road, Belair, Adelaide, SA 5052
☎ 08 8278 8255 ⊙ Restaurant: Mon–Sat
6–late; last orders 9.30 🍴 D A$60, Wine
A$35 ⊙ Windy Point Café: Mon–Sat 6–11
🍴 D A$50, Wine A$37 🚗 9km (5.5 miles)
south from Adelaide via Pulteney Street

YING CHOW

Popular and affordable, the authentic
Chinese cuisine includes a good
selection of vegetarian dishes and
an outdoor dining area.
✉ 114 Gouger Street, Adelaide, SA 5000
☎ 08 8221 7998 ⊙ Daily 11am–10pm
🍴 L A$20, D A$30, Wine from A$15

ADELAIDE HILLS

BRIDGEWATER MILL

www.bridgewatermill.com.au
At Petaluma winery's restaurant,
chef Le Tu Thai is a Francophile with
an intuition for blending the flavour
and textures of Asia and Europe.
✉ Mount Barker Road, Bridgewater, SA
5155 ☎ 08 8339 3422 ⊙ Thu–Mon
12–2.30. Wine tastings daily 10–5
🍴 L A$75, Wine A$36 🚗 23km (14.miles)
southeast from Adelaide along Princes
Highway and Eastern Freeway (A1/M1) to
Bridgewater exit

BAROSSA VALLEY

APPELLATION

www.appellation.com.au
An elegant dining experience among
vineyards with Modern Australian
dishes such as smoked duck breast
and liver parfait, and grilled fillet of
Angus beef.
✉ Peppers The Louise, Seppeltsfield Road,
Marananga, SA 5355 ☎ 08 8562 4144
⊙ Daily 7pm–late 🍴 D A$105, Wine
A$37

VINTNERS BAR AND GRILL

www.vintners.com.au
Dishes focus on local Barossa
produce, combining Australian with
Asian and Mediterranean influences.
The menu changes seasonally.
Reserve ahead.
✉ Nuriootpa Road, Angaston, SA 5353
☎ 08 8564 2488 ⊙ Daily from 12,
Mon–Sat from 6.30pm 🍴 L & D A$65,
Wine A$35 🚗 5km (3 miles) east from
Nuriootpa on road to Angaston, near
junction with Stockwell Road

CLARE

THORN PARK BY THE VINES

www.thornpark.com.au
This luxurious and welcoming bed
and breakfast combines fine dining
with excellent accommodation with
bush and vineyard views. Hosts
David Hay and Michael Speers serve
breakfast and dinner (for house
guests only) from their kitchen.
✉ Quarry Road, Sevenhill, Clare, SA 5453
☎ 08 8843 4304 ⊙ All year 🍴 A$380
(B & B) 🛏 2

COOBER PEDY

UMBERTO'S RESTAURANT

www.desertcave.com.au
Umberto's provides silver-service
Italian, Asian and Australian
variations on outback produce.
✉ Hutchison Street, Coober Pedy, SA 5723
☎ 1800 088 521 or 08 8672 5688 ⊙ Daily
6–late, last orders 9 🍴 D A$60, Wine A$29

COONAWARRA

THE POPLARS AT CHARDONNAY LODGE

www.chardonnaylodge.com.au
This country lodge/motel is on the
doorstep of Australia's most-famed
region for red wine production. The
cuisine is local, with Mediterranean
influences, and about 100 fine
Coonawarra wines are available. A
coffee shop is open all day.
✉ Riddoch Highway, Coonawarra, SA 5263
☎ 08 8736 3309 ⊙ All year. Restaurant
daily 6–8.30 🍴 D A$55, Wine A$29. Rooms
from A$155; includes Continental breakfast
🛏 38 ⊙ 🏊 🚗 8km (5 miles) north
from Penola

EYRE PENINSULA

WHYALLA FORESHORE MOTOR INN

www.whyallaforeshore.com.au
Seafood features strongly, including
salmon, kingfish and locally farmed
Murray cod. Oysters are served in
six different ways.
✉ Watson Terrace, Whyalla, SA 5600
☎ 08 8645 8877 ⊙ Mon–Fri 12–2, 6.30
onwards, Sat 6.30–late 🍴 L A$25, D A$60,
Wine $25. Rooms from A$120, excluding
breakfast 🛏 40; 1 self-catering apartment
🏊 🚗 From Highway 1 through town to
the foreshore

FLINDERS RANGES

PRAIRIE HOTEL, PARACHILNA

www.prairiehotel.com.au
Feast on kangaroo burgers, wallaby
and emu pâté at this laid-back,
colonial homestead.
✉ Cnr High Street and West Terrace,
Parachilna, SA 5730 ☎ 08 8648 4844
⊙ Daily. Food served 8am–9pm; restaurant
menu served 12–3, 6–9 🍴 L A$35,
D A$45, Wine A$22. Hotel and cabins
A$130–A$230; backpackers A$35 single
🛏 12; 100 backpackers in separate units
🏊 🚗 194km (120 miles) northeast from
Port Augusta, on the B83 road

KANGAROO ISLAND

AURORA OZONE HOTEL

www.ozonehotel.com
The bistro has a wide range of
starters and mains, based on
fresh island produce and fish,
with Asian dishes and gluten-free
and vegetarian menus. Wines are
mainly from Kangaroo Island. Order
dinner in advance.
✉ The Foreshore, Kingscote, Kangaroo
Island, SA 5223 ☎ 08 8553 2011 ⊙ Daily
7–9, 12–2, 6–8.30 (dinner to order)
🍴 L A$30, D A$45, Wine A$32. Rooms
from A$125 🛏 63

RIVERLAND

BANROCK STATION WINE AND WETLAND CENTRE

www.banrockstation.com.au
At Australia's biggest wine
ecotourism venue, the vista
includes the start of a 7km
(4.5-mile) boardwalk trail winding
through trees and bush, which
has been rejuvenated for wildlife
conservation. The food is light and
innovative and features Australian
native ingredients. Kangaroo, bush
tomato, wattleseed and quandong
feature as well as lamb and beef
dishes. Grazing, tasting plates
(such as smoked kangaroo
prosciutto with pepperleaf sauce)
are also served.
✉ Holmes Road, Kingston-on-Murray,
SA 5331 ☎ 08 8583 0299 ⊙ Daily 10–5
🍴 L A$20–A$30, Wine A$28 🚗 220km
(137 miles) northeast from Adelaide on the
Sturt Highway, 32km (20 miles) east from
Waikerie near Kingston-on-Murray

STAYING

PRICES AND SYMBOLS

Prices are the lowest and highest for a double room for one night. Breakfast is included unless noted otherwise. All the hotels listed accept credit cards unless otherwise stated. Note that rates vary widely throughout the year.

For a key to the symbols, ▷ 2.

ADELAIDE
ADABCO BOUTIQUE HOTEL

www.adabcohotel.com.au
At the centre of Adelaide's business district, this small and friendly hotel offers modern accommodation with character in historic surroundings.
✉ 223 Wakefield Street, Adelaide, SA 5000 ☎ 08 8100 7500 ◑ All year
♨ A$130–A$250 ❶ 17

HOTEL GRAND CHANCELLOR ADELAIDE ON HINDLEY

www.ghihotels.com
Standard rooms plus 40 suites. Heated outdoor pool, gymnasium, spa and sauna; restaurant and bar.
✉ 65 Hindley Streeet, Adelaide, SA 5000 ☎ 08 8231 5552 ◑ All year
♨ A$145–A$450 excluding breakfast
❶ 180 ◔ ⛱ Outdoor heated 🏧 🚌 On the northwest side of the city centre, close to North Terrace

STAMFORD PLAZA ADELAIDE

www.stamford.com.au
In a prime position close to most of Adelaide's cultural and historic attractions, this hotel offers international style rooms and a long list of facilities. The service is fast, efficient and friendly.
✉ 150 North Terrace, Adelaide SA 5000 ☎ 02 8461 1111 ◑ All year
♨ A$145–A$395 ❶ 334 ◔ ⛱ 🏧

BAIRD BAY
BAIRD BAY OCEAN ECO APARTMENTS

www.bairdbay.com
Bold and dramatic, these two handsome lodges are a stark contrast to the fishermen's cottages on the edge of the bay.

Built from rammed earth, the lodges are palatial, and equipped to high standards in a clean-cut, contemporary style. The headline event here is swimming with the sea lions off Jones Island, one off the few places in the world where visitors can swim with these playful mammals. The fishing is sensational most of the year, and the peace and tranquillity rate five stars.
✉ Lot 217 Government Road, Baird Bay, SA 5671 ☎ 08 8626 5017 ◑ All year
♨ A$130–A$180 ❶ 2 lodges 🚌 330km (200 miles) northwest of Adelaide

BAROSSA VALLEY
BELLE COTTAGES

www.bellescapes.com
Fifteen self-catering heritage properties. Some have spas.
✉ Box 481, Lyndoch, SA 5351 ☎ 08 8524 4825 ◑ All year ♨ A$190–A$220 including breakfast ❶ 5 self-catering properties ◔ 🚌 58km (36 miles) northeast from Adelaide along Main North Road, through Gawler to Lyndoch Highway.

Opposite *The Fire Engine Suite, part of the North Adelaide Heritage Group*

THE LODGE COUNTRY HOUSE

www.thelodgecountryhouse.com.au
This rambling bluestone homestead offers patrician accommodation with great character and style. The grounds are delightful and dinners are served with all the pomp and circumstance that the surroundings demand—but also a great sense of fun.

✉ Seppeltsfield Road, Seppeltsfield, SA 5355 ☎ 08 8562 8277 🕙 All year ✋ A$380–A$420 ⓘ 4 🚗 About an hour's drive from Adelaide

NORTH ADELAIDE HERITAGE GROUP

www.adelaideheritage.com
A selection of 21 renovated self-contained properties within 2km (1.2 miles) of Adelaide.

✉ Office at 109 Glen Osmond Road, Eastwood, SA 5063 ☎ 08 8272 1355 🕙 All year ✋ From A$214 (excluding breakfast) to A$420 (including breakfast) ⓘ 21 premises 🚗 Locations revealed when booking confirmed

OAKS PLAZA PIER APARTMENT HOTEL & SUITES

www.oakshotelsresorts.com
One- and two-bedroom apartments, restaurants, café, gym, sauna, spa, indoor heated pool.

✉ 16 Holdfast Promenade, Glenelg, SA 5045 ☎ 08 8350 6688 🕙 All year ✋ A$137–A$164 💲 🏊 Indoor 🍸 🚋 Tram from Victoria Square to Jetty Road 🚗 From the southwest end of West Terrace follow Anzac Highway to Holdfast Promenade

CLARE VALLEY
THORN PARK BY THE VINES

www.thornpark.com.au
Looking across native bushland and vineyards, this intimate country retreat offers outstanding accommodation with a collection of artworks assembled by its charismatic owners. This is a well-known food destination with an excellent reputation. Guests are advised to book in for dinner.

Above *Late afternoon outside the Prairie Hotel in Parachilna*

✉ Quarry Road, Sevenhill via Clare, SA 5453 ☎ 08 8843 4304 🕙 All year ✋ A$195–A$225 ⓘ 2

FLINDERS RANGES
WILPENA POUND RESORT

www.wilpenapound.com.au
The closest accommodation to Wilpena Pound, this complex offers a range of self-contained units, caravan (trailer) and camping park. There is a restaurant and bar, plus a shop, vehicle fuel, an ATM and an internet kiosk.

✉ Wilpena Road, via Hawker, SA 5434 ☎ 08 8648 0004 🕙 All year ✋ Self-contained unit A$195–A$220; tent/caravan pitch A$26 plus A$7.50 parking fee ⓘ 60 self-contained units, 400 tent and caravan pitches

KANGAROO ISLAND
STRANRAER HOMESTEAD

www.stranraer.com.au
Rising from the rippling sheep pastures at the centre of Kangaroo Island, this bed and breakfast brings character, sophistication, wonderful food and fine surroundings to the wild majesty of the island experience. The homestead is decorated and furnished with antique furnishings and a sumptuous, Victorian-inspired decor. Beyond the limestone garden wall, the sheep pastures dip gently

toward two vast, shallow lagoons that are a favourite roosting ground for the island's water birds. Dinners are optional, but most guests choose to dine in, and Lyn Wheaton's cooking gives reason enough.

✉ Barretts Road and Wheatons Road, Kingscote, Kangaroo Island SA 5223 ☎ 08 8553 8235 🕙 All year ✋ A$195–A$235 ⓘ 4

PARACHILNA
PRAIRIE HOTEL

www.prairiehotel.com.au
A five-hour drive north of Adelaide, on the parched plains that gutter the western flanks of the Flinders Ranges, the Prairie Hotel at Parachilna is a chunk of Australia straight out of outback mythology.

Heritage Rooms are neat and spacious, with en-suite bathrooms. Newer and larger, the deluxe rooms in the modern wing are sunk waist-deep into the ground to take advantage of natural insulation. At the heart of the historic stone and corrugated iron hotel is a restaurant with unique decor and a cutting sense of humour that even extends to the menu.

✉ Corner High Street and West Terrace, Parachilna, SA 5730 ☎ 08 8648 4844 🕙 All year ✋ A$175–A$275 🚗 450km (280 miles) north of Adelaide ⓘ 26

WESTERN AUSTRALIA

Western Australia is virtually another world for most Australians, so remote is it from the other Australian states. Perth, the state capital, is closer to Bali than it is to Sydney or Melbourne. It is also the largest of all the Australian states, almost four times the size of Texas, yet home to just two million people. This is also Australia's current boom state, richly endowed with mineral wealth that is dug out and loaded onto a never-ending succession of ships heading for China.

Perth is a glorious city built on the banks of the Swan River, spacious, cosmopolitan and well supplied with parks. Deep in the south of the state is Margaret River, a luscious region with an extravagantly beautiful coastline, and the source of some of Australia's finest wines.

Close to the northwest corner of the continent, the town of Broome has a swashbuckling history, blood-red earth, and 8m (26 feet) tides that leave its spectacular apron of sand, Cable Beach, high and dry. Its population is an amiable mix of indigenous Australians and the descendants of the pearl divers who were imported from the Philippines, Malaya and Japan, each of which has contributed their food, architecture and genes to the fabric of modern Broome.

Broome is the western gateway to the Kimberley region, a wild, arid plateau twice the size of the United Kingdom with a population of barely 30,000 that is crossed by only a single road, where the coastline is almost totally inaccessible except from the sea, where the cattle stations are measured by the million acres, where the trees come from Africa and the climate from the furnace. Remote, intense, desiccated, surreal in its beauty, the reality of the Kimberley leaves words panting in its wake.

ALBANY

www.albanytourist.com.au

Established in 1826, Albany is WA's oldest colonial town, built around the picturesque harbour between the viewpoints of Mount Melville and Mount Clarence. Albany's heritage sights include the 1851 Old Gaol (daily 10–4.15); the WA Museum, a former convict store dating back to the 1850s (daily 10–5); and the 1893 Princess Royal Fortress (daily 9–5). Try a wine from the nearby Mount Barker region with your lunch. The coastal scenery is some of the most spectacular in Australia, and there are whale-watching tours from July to the end of October. The Torndirrup National Park peninsula is pounded by the Southern Ocean.

✚ 344 C13 ℹ️ Old Railway Station, Proudlove Parade, Albany, WA 6330 ☎ 08 9841 9290

AUGUSTA

www.margaretriverwa.com

Augusta is sheltered by Cape Leeuwin, the point where the Indian and Southern oceans meet. The small waterfront resort is known for its water activities and attractive coastline, but accommodation is limited; many people visit on a day trip. From June to the end of December whales can be seen from the viewpoint of the 1896 Cape Leeuwin Lighthouse (daily 8.45–5). From the cape the Leeuwin-Naturaliste National Park extends 120km (74 miles) north along the coast; Jewel Cave, in the park 10km (6 miles) northwest of the town, is massive, with amazing stalactites (daily 9.30–3.30).

✚ 344 B13 ℹ️ Augusta Visitor Centre, 70 Blackwood Avenue, Augusta, WA 6290 ☎ 08 9750 5911

BROOME

www.broomevisitorcentre.com.au

The climate and wonderful Cable Beach form an oasis among the Indian Ocean, the Great Sandy Desert and the Kimberley, one of Australia's great wilderness areas.

Pearlers first arrived in the 1870s and by 1910 Broome had become the pearl capital of the world, producing around 80 per cent of the world's pearl shell. The first divers were Aboriginal people, followed by divers from Asia and the Pacific. The Japanese Cemetery in Port Drive has the graves of more than 900 Japanese divers who died in Broome. Restored pearl luggers in the heart of Broome show how divers worked in the 19th and 20th centuries. After a downturn in demand during the 20th century, the pearl industry is back in full swing, although the pearls are now cultivated. Willie Creek Pearl Farm, 38km (24 miles) north of Broome, demonstrates how pearls are produced (tour bookings 08 9192 0000).

Broome is a small town lying at the northern end of the mangrove-filled shores of Roebuck Bay. Shopping areas include the Chinatown and several pearl outlets. Chinatown was originally a collection of eateries and pearl sheds, but its architecture now ranges from small traditional wooden buildings to modern shopping complexes. The 1916 Sun Pictures movie theatre is believed to be the world's oldest open-air cinema.

Broome is perhaps best known for Cable Beach, 22km (14 miles) of white sand north of the town. Watching a beach sunset is a must, whether on a camel ride or idling on the sands. Beware of swimming in the sea from November to the end of May, box jellyfish can be a problem—their sting is incredibly painful and can be fatal.

If you visit the town at the time of the full moon, watch out for The Staircase to the Moon, which is caused by a full moon rising over the exposed mudflats of Roebuck Bay at very low tides, creating an illusion of a staircase reaching to the moon. It occurs from March to the end of October for three nights every month. Town Beach and the Mangrove Hotel are good viewpoints.

✚ 340 F5 ℹ️ Broome Visitor Centre, 1 Hamersley Street, PO Box 352, Broome, WA 6725 ☎ 08 9192 2222 🕐 Mon–Fri 8–5, Sat–Sun 8.30–4 🚌 Service between Broome and Cable Beach

Opposite *A camel trek across Cable Beach near Broome is an unforgettable experience*
Below *Coastal scenery at Two Peoples Bay Reserve near Albany*

BUNBURY
www.visitbunbury.com.au
Western Australia's second-largest city is the gateway to the south-west of the state. Occupying a peninsula, Bunbury has great, often deserted, beaches. Victoria Street is a refreshment stop after a visit to the large regional art gallery or the historic churches. There are more than 70 species of water birds at the Big Swamp Reserve and Boardwalk, 1.5km (1 mile) south.

There is an opportunity to swim with dolphins or join a dolphin boat tour in Koombana Bay via the Dolphin Discovery Centre (Sep–end May daily 8–5; Jun–end Aug daily 9–3).

✚ 344 B13 ℹ Bunbury Visitor Information Centre, Old Railway Station, Carmody Place, Bunbury, WA 6230 ☎ 08 9792 7205 🚆 Bunbury

DENMARK
www.denmarkvisitorcentre.com.au
Denmark's natural beauty and the warm climate are good reasons to break a tour along WA's south coast. The town spreads along the western bank of the lower Denmark River and Wilsons Inlet and is popular with artists and city folk seeking a less stressful lifestyle. Since being settled in 1895 as a timber town, Denmark has supported fishing, potato and fruit growing, dairy farming, and now wineries and tourism.

The Treetop Walk in the Valley of the Giants is a 600m (1,968ft) walkway, 40m (131ft) above ground in the tree canopy, with fantastic views. The Valley is 45km (28 miles) west from Denmark near the town of Walpole.

✚ 344 C13 ℹ Denmark Visitor Centre, 73 South Coast Highway, Denmark, WA 6333 ☎ 08 9848 2055

ESPERANCE
www.visitesperance.com
Esperance, on Esperance Bay, is a small town mainly popular for its coastal scenery, wildlife and pristine, quiet beaches. Remote from the main tourist routes, the place is a relaxing stop, even during the summer months. The coastal scenery ranges from massive granite outcrops to small bays, and there are four national parks in the region. There are cruises available around the Recherche Archipelago of more than 100 offshore islands, for close views of the wildlife.

✚ 344 F13 ℹ Esperance Visitor Centre, Historical Museum Village, Dempster Street, Esperance, WA 6450 ☎ 08 9083 1555

EXMOUTH
www.exmouthwa.com.au
Exmouth was established only in 1967 and is fairly small. If not worth a visit in its own right—it was much rebuilt after a cyclone in 1999—Exmouth is the best base for exploring Cape Range National Park, Ningaloo Reef and the surrounding region. Cape Range National Park is 40km (25 miles) from Exmouth going north around the North West Cape to Yardie Road. The 50,581ha (124,935-acre) park has limestone ranges, deep canyons and 50km (31 miles) of beaches. Yardie Creek Gorge is particularly impressive, with deep blue waters and coloured rock strata.

The same access route leads to Ningaloo Reef, the backbone of Ningaloo Marine Park, which stretches for 260km (161 miles) from Bundegi Reef in the Exmouth Gulf around the North West Cape to Coral Bay. The reef extends about 18.5km (11.5 miles) into the Indian Ocean and is rich in fauna. It is only about 100m (328ft) offshore at its nearest point and less than 7km (4.5 miles) at its farthest. From mid-March to the end of June the reef is visited by the world's biggest species of fish, the whale shark. Boat tours leave from Coral Bay and Exmouth.

✚ 344 B7 ℹ Exmouth Visitors Centre, Murat Road, Exmouth, WA 6707 ☎ 08 9949 1176 🚌 Buses from Exmouth to Turquoise Bay daily during high season

FREMANTLE
▷ 262–263.

KALBARRI NATIONAL PARK
www.kalbarri.com
Kalbarri National Park covers 183,000ha (452,010 acres) and has two distinct features: the river gorges inland, with the coastal cliffs together with the rolling sandplains. The cliffs are near Kalbarri and rise more than 100m (328ft) above the Indian Ocean. The red and white banded gorges are around 40km (25 miles) from the town and were formed by the Murchison River; there are great views from the Loop and the Z Bend. The park has about 1,000 species of wild flowers—in spring (after July) the heathlands are spectacular.

Below *If you can cope with heights, the Treetop Walk near Denmark is exhilarating*

📍 344 B10 ℹ️ Kalbarri Visitors Centre, Grey Road, Kalbarri ☎ 08 9937 1104 ✉️ National Park Office, Kalbarri/Ajana Road, PO Box 37, Kalbarri, WA 6536 ☎ 08 9937 1140 ✋ Day passes: A$10 per vehicle, A$5 per motorcycle, A$3 per bus passenger. No camping in the park 🚌 Kalbarri

KALGOORLIE-BOULDER
www.kalgoorlietourism.com
Kalgoorlie-Boulder has been a goldfield town for more than a century. The operating Super Pit open-cut gold mine in Boulder is 290m (951ft) deep, 1.6km (1 mile) wide and 4km (2.5 miles) long. Since gold was first discovered in 1893, Kalgoorlie ore deposits have produced over 35 million ounces of gold. Lying 5km (3 miles) apart, Kalgoorlie and Boulder operated as separate towns until the 1980s, when they amalgamated. The wide streets survive from the time when Afghan camel drivers needed large areas to turn their mounts around. The town's museums have a general appeal and some are of specialist interest. The Australian Prospectors and Miners Hall of Fame highlights Australia's mining industry. Try gold panning or join an underground tour (daily 9–4.30).
📍 344 E11 ℹ️ Kalgoorlie-Boulder Tourist Centre, 316 Hannan Street, Kalgoorlie, WA 6430 ☎ 08 9021 1966 🚌 Kalgoorlie; Prospector train daily from Perth and back; Indian Pacific stops at Kalgoorlie four times a week

KARIJINI NATIONAL PARK
www.westernaustralia.com
Karijini is a truly spectacular park, well worth the long journey. The 627,442ha (1.5 million-acre) national park protects some of Australia's most impressive gorge scenery, and many of the finest sights are easily accessible. Set just north of the Tropic of Capricorn, the Pilbara region climate is tropical semi-desert. Late autumn, winter and early spring are best; winter days are warm and clear, but nights are cold and sometimes frosty. In the cooler months the land is covered

with yellow-flowering cassias and wattles, northern bluebells and purple mulla-mullas. After rain, many plants bloom profusely. Walking tracks take in the gorges and fern-filled pools and waterfalls.
📍 340 D7 ℹ️ Visitor Centre, Banyjima Drive, Karijini National Park ☎ 08 9189 8121 🕐 Visitor Centre daily 9–4 ✋ Day passes: A$12 per vehicle, A$6 per motorcycle, A$5 per bus passenger. Camping fees: adult A$7 per night, child (5–16) A$4 per night 📷

THE KIMBERLEY
www.kimberleytourism.com
The remote Kimberley region covers the far northern part of Western Australia, bordered by Northern Territory, the Great Sandy Desert, the Indian Ocean and the Timor Sea. This is true outback: rugged ranges, gorges, arid desert and vast open plains. Heading east from Broome (▷ 259), two routes lead to the inland town of Kununurra near the Northern Territory border. The longer, easier route is along the Great Northern Highway. At Fitzroy Crossing, boat tours venture up the large gorge of Geikie Gorge National Park, where the Fitzroy River cuts through the Geikie Range. Northeast of Halls Creek, the Bungle Bungles in the Purnululu National Park—a World Heritage Site—are among the world's most unusual geological formations. Thousands of beehive-shaped sandstone hills rise up out of the plain, striped in red, orange and black bands. Access to the park from the highway is by a 55km (34-mile) 4WD track. The Gibb River Road from Derby is a dirt track best suited to a 4WD, but which passes stunning scenery. At Windjana Gorge National Park the gorge itself encompasses a section of the Lennard River; the area is rich in birds and freshwater crocodiles. Seasonal rains from December to April can close sealed roads for hours or even days; unsealed roads are likely to be closed for all of the wet season.
📍 341 H4 ℹ️ Derby Visitor Centre, 2 Clarendon Street, PO Box 48, Derby, WA

Above *You'll need a 4WD to get to the Bungle Bungles in Purnululu National Park*

6728 ☎ 08 9191 1426 ℹ️ Kununurra Visitor Centre, East Kimberley Tourism House, Coolibah Drive, PO Box 446, Kununurra, WA 6743 ☎ 08 9168 1177 ❓ There are tourist offices also at Broome, Fitzroy Crossing, Halls Creek and Wyndham

MARGARET RIVER
▷ 264–265.

MILLSTREAM-CHICHESTER NATIONAL PARK
www.dec.wa.gov.au
The 200,000ha (494,000-acre) park is an oasis in the heart of dusty and spinifex-covered desert hills in the Pilbara region. Freshwater pools support water lilies and paperbark, and palm trees surround the deep Chinderwarriner Pool on the Fortescue River; there is also a large wetland area. The Millstream Homestead Visitor Centre is dedicated to the Yinjibarndi people, early settlers and the environment. Python Pool is a permanent freshwater pool at the base of the Chichester Range escarpment.
📍 340 C6 ℹ️ Millstream Homestead Visitor Centre ☎ 08 9184 5144 ✋ Day passes: A$11 per vehicle, A$5 per motorcycle, A$5 per bus passenger. Camping: adult A$7 per night, child (5–16) A$4 per night 🚗 75km (46.5 miles) from Roebourne; access by 50km (31-mile) unsealed road from the North West Coastal Highway

FREMANTLE

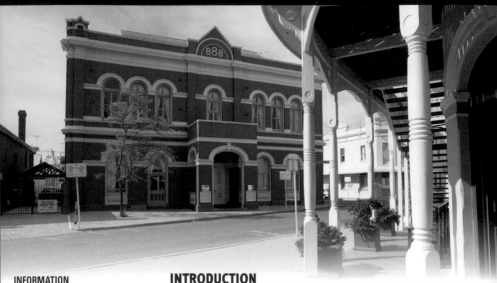

INFORMATION

www.fremantlewa.com.au

344 B12 Fremantle Visitors Centre, Town Hall, Kings Square, Fremantle, WA 6160 08 9431 7878 Mon–Fri 9–5, Sat 10–3, Sun 11.30–2.30 Fremantle

INTRODUCTION

Fremantle is a thriving cosmopolitan maritime community dominated by restaurants, great historical buildings, markets and galleries. The town is also an enjoyable place to spend the day for its mixture of historic buildings and shops. It is 19km (12 miles) southwest of Perth on the mouth of the Swan River, which flows out through Fremantle Harbour into the Indian Ocean. A number of attractions are along the harbour and the ocean. On the harbour side is the overseas passenger terminal and the Western Australia Maritime Museum. On the ocean side is Fishing Boat Harbour, which shelters Fremantle's 500-strong fishing fleet and is a great venue for a seafood or fish-and-chip lunch or dinner. Fremantle is also renowned for its alfresco cafés, many of which are on the cappuccino strip of South Terrace and are popular with locals and visitors alike.

Aborigines were the first inhabitants of the Fremantle area. On 1 June 1829, 68 settlers established the Swan River Colony, the first European settlement in Australia to consist entirely of freemen. They eventually decided to accept convicts in order to provide cheap labour for the colony. From the 1850s a number of substantial buildings began to appear, most notably the convict prison. Fremantle was declared a city in 1929, but it was still regarded as a sleepy port. Then in 1983, after the yacht *Australia II* won the Americas Cup, it underwent a major facelift. Although the cup was lost in 1987, when the races were held off Fremantle, the party atmosphere and restored Victorian buildings remain.

WHAT TO SEE

VICTORIAN PAST

The main streets of Fremantle retain numerous restored Victorian buildings, many of which are classified by the National Trust. Most popular among the heritage sights is Fremantle Prison on The Terrace (daily 10–5; adult A$18, child A$9.50). It was built by convicts between 1850 and 1855 in limestone quarried on the site. After the end of transportation in 1868 the convict population declined and in 1886 it became a state prison, for men and women. Since then military prisoners, enemy aliens and prisoners of war have been held here. The prison closed in 1991.

Above *Fremantle has a selection of historic buildings*

The Round House on Arthur Head is Western Australia's oldest building, constructed in 1830 as a jail. Despite the name the simple Georgian structure is 12-sided and the cells are arranged around a central courtyard (daily 10.30–3.30).

For city life in late 19th-century Fremantle, try the Samson House Museum on Ellen Street (Sun 1.15–5). This was the home of the prominent Samson family and many period features survive.

For a lighter take on Victorian Fremantle, visit the 1897 Fremantle Markets on the corner of Henderson Street and South Terrace (Fri 10–8, Sat–Mon 10–6). More than 170 stalls sell fresh and cooked food, art, crafts, clothing, antiques and just about anything else. Worth a visit for the ethnic colour and street performers alone.

WESTERN AUSTRALIAN MARITIME MUSEUM
www.museum.wa.gov.au/maritime

The Maritime Museum, on the edge of Fremantle Harbour, is part of a historical maritime precinct that includes the convict-built Shipwreck Galleries on Cliff Street and the 1969 submarine HMAS *Ovens* (both daily 9.30–5). The Shipwreck Galleries contain Australia's earliest Dutch shipwrecks, the remains and objects of the 1629 Dutch East India Company ship *Batavia* (Australia's second-oldest surviving wreck) and tales of travel, trade, mutiny and murder.

HMAS *Ovens* is on a World War II slipway next to the Maritime Museum and depicts the arduous and cramped conditions of submariner life in the late 20th century (adult A$8, child A$3).

Opened in 2002, the Maritime Museum also shelters the Americas Cup-winning yacht *Australia II* and the yacht Jon Sanders used for his record-setting triple solo circumnavigation of the world in the 1980s. Boats range from the historic to the latest in sailing technology. Themed exhibits, some interactive, cover the maritime developments of the Swan River and Fremantle, naval defence, trade, fishing and the movements of people and goods and cultures throughout the Indian Ocean region. The museum also highlights the maritime traditions and cultures of Aboriginal people.

✉ Victoria Quay, WA 6160 ☎ 08 9431 8334 🕓 Daily 10.30–5 ✋ Adult A$10, child ,5–15) A$3

TIPS
» The Fremantle Tram provides a range of great tours around the city.
» The Fremantle CAT bus is a free, quick and easy way to get about.
» The city gets very crowded at weekends, when there is the most action.

Below *The Round House was Australia's first prison*

MARGARET RIVER .

INFORMATION

www.margaretriver.com

344 B13 ℹ Margaret River Visitor Centre, 100 Bussell Highway, Margaret River, WA 6285 ☎ 08 9780 5911

🕐 Daily 9–5

INTRODUCTION

The small town of Margaret River is midway between Cape Naturaliste in the north and Cape Leeuwin to the south. The Margaret River flows through the town, 10km (6 miles) east from the estuary to the Indian Ocean; walking and bicycling tracks are marked along the banks of the river and through the town. The river, combined with parkland, art and craft galleries and a number of excellent restaurants, many of which are attached to wineries, add to the town's relaxed appeal. The Margaret River region has more than 70 wineries, mainly concentrated between the Bussell Highway and the more scenic Caves Road, which runs from Dunsborough on Geographe Bay in the north to Karridale in the south (▷ 274–275). Apart from wine, a number of local producers cater for gourmet tastes. These include Berry Farm, specializing in fruits, the Fonti Farm and Margaret River Dairy Company, which makes fine cheeses (including ricotta and the flagship brie) and yoghurt, and the Margaret River Chocolate Company.

Settlement in the area dates from the 1850s and there was timber felling from the 1870s. The town largely developed from the Group Settlement Scheme in the early 1920s, an attempt to expand agricultural land in the southwest of the state. The scheme attracted migrants from Britain where there was high unemployment after World War I, but was hindered by poor planning. The wine industry dates only to the 1960s: There were experimental plantings of grapes in 1966, and in the following year the first winery, Vasse Felix, was established.

WHAT TO SEE

WINE STOP

Wine enthusiasts should start a visit at the Margaret River Wine Tourism Showroom in the Margaret River Visitor Centre. Find out about all the wineries in the region and decide which to visit; several offer wine appreciation classes, which are great fun.

LEEUWIN-NATURALISTE NATIONAL PARK

Above *Margaret River flows through the sand dunes to the ocean*

Windswept granite headlands and weathered sea cliffs, such as Canal Rocks and Sugarloaf Rock, characterize the coastal national park, which stretches 120km (74 miles) from Bunker Bay and Cape Naturaliste in the north to Augusta in the south. Walking trails, caving, camping and watersports are among the ways to enjoy the park. Most access roads in the area are sealed; gravel roads are usually suitable for two-wheel drive vehicles. From June to the end of December whales are visible off the coast. The hilly Boranup Forest, between Margaret River and Augusta, is home to the impressive karri tree, the farthest point west that it grows; the karris stand up to 60m (197ft) high. Boranup Lookout, off the Caves Road, looks across the forest to Hamelin Bay.

WAVES

Surfers from all around the world flock to the beaches of the Margaret River coastline, and the Caves Road connects the most popular beaches. For surfing (or watching) try Yallingup, 43km (27 miles) north of Margaret River; Ellensbrook, 14km (8.5 miles) northwest; or Redgate, 15km (9.5 miles) southwest. Safe swimming beaches include Cowaramup Bay, 19km (12 miles) northwest of Margaret River; Gnarabup, 12km (7.5 miles) west; and Hamelin Bay, 42km (26 miles) south.

CAVES

Some of Western Australia's best-known caves lie between Margaret River and Augusta (▷ 259), 45km (28 miles) to the south. They occur within the Leeuwin-Naturaliste Ridge, which is composed of granite, limestone and dunes; the caves are formed in the softer, more soluble limestone strata. Several caves are open to the public. Calgardup Cave and Giants Cave are a short distance south of Margaret River: Calgardup's shallow mirror lake multiplies the stalactites above (daily 9–4.15); the Giants Cave, going down 86m (282ft), is one of the deepest (daily 9.30–3.30 in school holidays and public holidays). Farther south are Mammoth Cave, with fossils (daily 9–5, last entry 4); Lake Cave (daily 9.30–3.30); and Jewel Cave, with one of the longest stalactites found in any tourist cave (see Augusta, ▷ 259).

On its own to the north at Yallingup, Ngilgi Cave, with stalactite and stalagmite formations (daily 9.30–4.30, also until 5 or 6 in school holidays), is associated with the Aboriginal legend of Ngilgi (a good spirit) and Wolgine (an evil spirit). Although torches and helmets are often provided, you should wear strong shoes or boots.

TIPS

» To get the best out of the Margaret River region you need a car—many of the attractions are some distance from the main towns.

» Margaret River gets very busy at weekends during the high season and public holidays; midweek is the best time to visit, otherwise ensure you reserve accommodation.

» If you are planning to drive and try wine, then designate a non-drinking driver—the police are strict about drink-driving.

Left *Lake Cave is just one of the many caverns south of the town*
Below *Several of the wineries have excellent restaurants*

PERTH

INFORMATION

www.wavisitorcentre.com

🛈 Western Australia Visitors Centre, Forrest Place, Perth WA 6000 ☎ 08 9483 1111 🕓 Mon–Thu 8.30–6, Fri 8.30–7, Sat 9.30–4.30, Sun 11–4.30

✈ Airport

Perth International Airport, 20km (12.5 miles) east of the city.

🚆 Train station

Perth Railway Station is in the city centre (Wellington Street)

INTRODUCTION

One of the world's most isolated cities, Perth moves at a pace that feeds off Western Australia's mineral and agricultural wealth. A modern, compact metropolis, with some fine colonial architecture, the city is nicely situated on a bend of the meandering Swan River. Getting around is easy with bus and rail services connecting major attractions. The city lends itself to self-guiding walking tours, while the popular Kings Park is perfect for bicycling. The shopping precinct centres on Hay Street and Murray Street malls and the arcades connecting them. Be sure to take a boat trip to nearby Rottnest Island to check out secluded beaches and bays and sight the distinctive native quokkas. And long, sandy beaches run along the coast north of the city, aptly called the Sunset Coast. Fremantle, 19km (12 miles) southwest of Perth, is a fascinating day trip—take in the colourful maritime heritage, myriad alfresco dining opportunities and specialty shops, and the eclectic weekend markets.

WHAT TO SEE

AQUARIUM OF WESTERN AUSTRALIA

www.aqwa.com.au

This is a great place to see live corals and marine life from Western Australia's 12,000km (7,440 miles) of coastline. Sharks, stingrays, turtles and fish circle a walk-through tunnel.

➕ 271 A2 ✉ 91 Southside Drive, Hillarys Boat Harbour, Hillarys, WA 6025 ☎ 08 9447 7500 🕓 Daily 10–5 🖐 Adult A\$26.50, child (4–15) A\$15 🚆 Warwick then bus 423 🖥 🏛

ART GALLERY OF WESTERN AUSTRALIA

www.artgallery.wa.gov.au

Western Australia's state art collection includes over 15,000 items, of which approximately 10 per cent are on display at any one time. Works include Australian and international paintings, sculpture, prints, photography, craft items and decorative arts. The collection of Aboriginal art is one of the finest in Australia, consisting of more than 2,400 works.

➕ 271 B2 ✉ Perth Cultural Centre, Perth; entry from the city station or Barrack Street via the James Street Mall or William Street ☎ 08 9492 6600 🕓 Wed–Mon 10–5 🖐 Free 🚌 Bus station adjacent 🚆 Perth City 🖥 🏛

Above *The view from one of the lookouts in Kings Park, which has stunning vistas of the city at dusk*

THE BELL TOWER

www.thebelltower.com.au

The Bell Tower is one of the world's largest musical instruments, consisting of 18 change-ringing bells. The bells are housed in a modern concrete, glass and steel tower, opened in 2000, which has seven levels and an 82.2m (270ft) spire. The observation deck on level six has great views over Perth. The ringing chamber is on level two, while level four houses the bells, which you can see in action from behind double-glazed panels. Twelve of the bells originally hung at the Church of St. Martin-in-the-Fields, London, where they rang to mark the homecoming of Captain James Cook in 1771 (▷ 28). The church presented the bells to Perth in 1988.

➕ 271 B3 ✉ Barrack Street, Riverside Drive, Perth, WA 6000 ☎ 08 6210 0444 🕐 10–5, last entry 4.45. Bells ring daily 11.30–12.30 ♨ Adult A$11, child (4–15) A$8 🚌 Free blue CAT bus stops in Barrack Square 🏛

CAVERSHAM WILDLIFE PARK

www.cavershamwildlife.com.au

Caversham Wildlife Park, in the Swan Valley (▷ 271), has more than 2,000 animals representing around 200 species. Most of these are native so this is a good opportunity to see Australian wildlife close up.

➕ Off map 271 C1 ✉ Whiteman Park, Lord Street, Whiteman, WA 6068 ☎ 08 9248 984 🕐 Daily 8.30–5.30 ♨ Adult A$22, child (3–14) A$8 🚌 From Perth to Whiteman 🚆 Whiteman 🅿 🏛 🚌 15km (9 miles) northeast from city

KINGS PARK AND BOTANIC GARDEN

www.bgpa.wa.gov.au

Kings Park has always been a popular playground for the people of Perth, whether for a walk or to enjoy a picnic. Weekends at the park can be crowded with locals so midweek it is usually quieter. It was first reserved in 1872 and originally called Perth Park. The name was changed to Kings Park in 1901 to mark the accession of King Edward VII and the visit to Perth of his son the Duke of Cornwall and Princess Mary (later King George V and Queen Mary).

The park occupies some 400ha (988 acres) of Mount Eliza overlooking the Swan River and the city of Perth, 1.5km (1 mile) to the east. It is mainly natural bushland and partly developed parkland. Of the 470 species of plant recorded in the bushland, almost 300 are native to Kings Park. Spring is a good time to visit, when wild flowers are in bloom. The Western Australian Botanic Garden within the park covers 17ha (42 acres) and has some 1,700 native species.

The main entrance in Fraser Avenue leads to two honour or memorial venues, May Drive and Lovekin Drive, flanked by towering lemon-scented gums. Near the main entrance are the park's shops, bicycle rental outlets, Kings Park Tram (one-hour tours), restaurants and galleries, including the Aboriginal Art and Craft Gallery. The State War Memorial is also close by. Roads, bicycle tracks and trails criss-cross the park and there are picnic areas and playgrounds for families. Self-guiding pamphlets are available at the information office in the Fraser Avenue precinct. The Pioneer Women's Memorial Fountain is a great place to relax. During summer the park is a venue for outdoor theatre, concerts and movies.

➕ 271 A3 ✉ Kings Park, Fraser Avenue, West Perth, WA 6005 ☎ 08 9480 3600 🕐 Daily 24 hours ♨ Free 🚌 37 and 39 from central Perth. The Perth Tram links Kings Park with the city 🚆 The Kings Park Volunteer Guides lead free tours through the bushland and gardens daily at 10am and 2pm (1.5 hours) 🍴 🅿 🏛

LANCELIN

Located about 125km (77 miles) north of Perth, the coastal town of Lancelin is Australia's windsurfing capital. The town lies on the edge of a natural bay, which is protected from the Indian Ocean by outer reefs and islands. The

Above *The Bell Tower holds 18 bells*

Above *Some of the Pinnacles in Nambung National Park*

Below *When Europeans first saw quokkas, they thought they were big rats*

tranquil waters within this shallow inner bay are ideal for novice windsurfers, while experienced board riders can enjoy the more challenging conditions found farther offshore. Local windsurf operators can provide boards for rent as well as expert instruction. Held in early January, the Lancelin Ocean Classic is Australia's biggest windsurfing event. Now more than 25 years old, the four-day event attracts windsurfers from all over the world. Lancelin's main industry is crayfishing. The crayfish that are harvested from here are exported all over the world, a trade worth many millions to the town.

✠ 344 B12 ℹ Tourist Information Office, Lot 102 Gingin Road, Lancelin WA 6044
☎ 08 9655 1100

NAMBUNG NATIONAL PARK
www.naturebase.net

The 17,491ha (43,203-acre) Nambung National Park protects the Pinnacles Desert, a 400ha (988-acre) area where thousands of limestone pillars rise from shifting yellow sand. The pillars come in all shapes and sizes: Some are jagged, sharp-edged columns rising to a point, while others resemble tombstones; many are only ankle high and pencil thin. The largest pillar is nearly 4m (13ft) high and 2m (6.5ft) wide. The park is also renowned for its beaches, coastal dunes, shady groves of tuart trees and low heathland rich in flowering plants. Kangaroo Point has great ocean views and picnic spots, and the sandy beach at Hangover Bay is good for surfing and swimming. Nambung can be seen in a day from Perth—it's a 245km (152-mile), three-hour drive north—but it's worth staying for a couple of days.

✠ 344 B11 ✉ Pinnacles Drive, Cervantes, WA 6511 ☎ 08 9483 1111 🕒 Day: vehicle (up to eight people) A$10, motorcycle A$5, tour or bus passenger A$4. Camping fees extra

THE OLD MILL
On the Mill Point headland across the Swan River from the city is The Old Mill, one of Perth's oldest buildings. The foundation stone was laid by the first governor, James Stirling, in 1835 for the owner, William Kernot Shenton (it is also known as Shenton's Mill). The mill, adjacent miller's cottage and grounds are furnished with relics of the colonial period. Flour milling continued here until 1859.

✠ Off map 271 A3 ✉ Mill Point Road, off Kwinana Freeway, South Perth, WA 6151
☎ 08 9474 0777 🕒 Subject to change

ROTTNEST ISLAND
www.rottnestisland.com

Great beaches and bays, a vibrant past and historic buildings, and native marsupials known as quokkas are the main attractions of Rottnest Island.

About 19km (12 miles) west from Fremantle in the Indian Ocean, Rottnest Island is 11km (7 miles) long and 4.5km (2.8 miles) at its widest point. Before changes in the sea level around 7,000 years ago, Rottnest was attached to the mainland. The Aboriginal people originally referred to the island as Wadjemup: It was named Rottnest in 1696 by Dutch explorers after they mistook quokkas for large rats.

The warm Leeuwin Current flows around Rottnest Island, attracting more than 97 species of tropical fish. The sheltered beaches and bays are ideal for swimming, surfing, snorkelling and scuba diving, especially the Basin, Longreach Bay, Little Parakeet Bay and Mary Cove. Cars are not allowed and some of the best beaches are some distance from the ferry—transportation is either the Bayseeker Bus or bicycle rental. Most accommodation, shops and historic attractions are near the main jetty.

The sea wall was constructed from 1846 to 1849 by men of the Aboriginal penal settlement. Other buildings from the prison period include the Governor's Summer Residence (1840), the Administrator's Cottage (late 1840s), the Moral

Agent's Residence of 1847, the Quod (prison) built in 1864, and the Rottnest Island Chapel built in 1858 as a school house and chapel. The Boys' Reformatory was built in 1881 for the children of European settlers.

The island's museum displays relics of the convict days and shipwrecks. The Oliver Hill Guns and Tunnels, Kingstown Barracks and Bickley Battery belonged to coastal defence during World War II. Rottnest was an internment camp during both world wars.

✚ Off map 271 A3 🛈 Rottnest Island Visitor and Information Centre, Thomson Bay, Rottnest Island, WA 6161 ☎ 08 9372 9732 🕓 Daily 8–5 🚌 Bus service operates around the island ⛴ Ferries from Perth and Fremantle

PERTH HILLS

www.mundaringtourism.com.au

The area known as Perth Hills or Darling Range, about 30km (18.5 miles) east of Perth, encompasses the shires of Mundaring and Kalamunda and is known for its wineries, bushland, orchards, semi-rural villages, galleries, gardens and national parks. Mundaring covers 644sq km (251sq miles), a third of which is state-owned forest—Mundaring was once a major logging centre. The John Forest and Kalamunda national parks contain trails, waterfalls and picnic areas as well as a huge diversity of native wild flowers; John Forest is noted for its jarrah and marri trees. The Mundaring Weir reservoir dates from 1903.

🗺 344 C12 🛈 Mundaring Tourism Information Centre, The Old School, 7225 Great Eastern Highway, Mundaring, WA 6073 ☎ 08 9295 0202 ❓ Visitor centres are available in the other towns

PERTH ZOO

www.perthzoo.wa.gov.au

Perth Zoo is home to more than 1,800 animals, representing 230 indigenous and exotic species. The 19ha (47-acre) zoo has three thematic habitats: the Australian Walkabout (reptiles, an aviary, a penguin area, crocodiles and an Australian bush walk); the African Savannah (lions, rhinos, giraffes, meerkats, hyenas, cheetahs and zebras); and the Asian Rainforest (elephants, orang-utans, otters, gibbons, bears and Sumatran tigers).

🗺 Off map 271 B3 ✉ 20 Labouchere Road, South Perth, WA 6151 ☎ 08 9474 3551 🕓 Daily 9–5 🎟 Adult A$20, child (4–15) A$10 🚌 35 from the City Bus Port 🚢 Regular services from Barrack Street Jetty to South Perth Esplanade, then a short walk to the zoo 🖥 🏛

ROCKINGHAM

www.rockinghamvisitorcentre.com.au

Sea lions, penguins, dolphins and a wealth of bird and marine life abound along Rockingham's coast and nearby islands. The town lies on the bay of Cockburn Sound, a 55km (34-mile) drive south from Perth. Dolphins are regular visitors—boat tours subject to conditions. A boat also leads to Penguin Island, with its colony of fairy penguins—a viewing facility allows close-ups without disturbing the birds.

🗺 344 B12 🛈 Rockingham Tourist Centre, 19 Kent Street, Rockingham, WA 6168 ☎ 08 9592 3464 🚉 From Perth to Fremantle then a bus to Rockingham

SCITECH DISCOVERY CENTRE

www.scitech.org.au

Scitech occupies a modern building about 2km (1.2 miles) northwest of the city centre, and has more than 160 hands-on exhibits. Interactive adventures, exhibitions and theatre shows add to the upbeat educational fun, which appeals to both parents and children.

🗺 Off map 271 A2 ✉ 1st Floor, City West, West Perth; PO Box 1155, West Perth, WA 6005 ☎ 08 9481 6295 🕓 Mon–Fri 9.30–4, Sat, Sun 10–5 🎟 Adult A$14, child (3–15) A$9 🚉 Free train from Perth City to City West on the Fremantle line 🏛

Above *One of the residents of Perth Zoo: a Sumatran orang-utan*
Below *Surfing at Scarborough Beach*

SUNSET COAST

Perth has a fine array of ocean beaches along its seaboard, which is known as the Sunset Coast. Several of these beaches lie within a 15–30 minute drive of the city centre. Most are patrolled by lifeguards throughout the summer, and bathers should always swim between the flags. Conditions are usually better in the morning, before the afternoon breeze springs up. This breeze, known locally as the 'Fremantle Doctor', can be so fierce that beach umbrellas arrive home before their owners.

At the northern end of Perth's beach strip, Mettams Pool is a natural rock pool within the shelter of an encircling reef, ideal for families with small children. At less than 2m deep (6.5 feet) and filled with marine life within no-fishing zone, this is also a popular spot for snorkelling. The more open part of the bay away from the pool is a popular location for surfers, particularly longboarders, who use the full waves to polish their skills.

To the south, Trigg Island Beach is known as one of Perth's best surf breaks. On a warm summer's day, Trigg Island beach swarms with surfers and boogie boarders making the most of the reef break just offshore while swimmers enjoy the turquoise water and pure white sand. The beach also has lawns with barbecues, a kiosk, restaurant and public changing rooms.

One of the city's most popular beaches, the white crystalline sands of beautiful Scarborough Beach attract surfers, sunbathers, windsurfers and kite surfers. Surf conditions are generally better for board riders in the morning, while the afternoon breeze attracts windsurfers. In the evening, the foreshore lights up with restaurants and cafés, at other times of the day the lawns at the back of the beach are popular for picnics.

Although Scarborough and Trigg beaches attract the surf crowd, out of all Perth's pristine beaches, the small scoop of Cottesloe Beach is the loveliest. It's not just the golden sand and the silky surf but also the human ingredient. Cottesloe is a people-watch zone, a place to see and be seen, especially towards sunset. It's also a major food scene, from the zippy concoctions of the Blue Duck Café and Barchetta to the genteel confines of the landmark Indiana Tea House, the mock-Edwardian bathhouse fronting the sea. Don't miss the entertainment sessions at the local hotel overlooking Cottesloe Beach and Hillarys Boat Harbour near Sorrento has good restaurants, shops, the Aquarium of Western Australia (▷ 266), ferries for Rottnest Island, and whale-watching cruises from September to the end of November.

🚹 344 B12 🚹 Tourist Information Office, Sunset Rent a Car, 206 West Coast Highway, Scarborough, WA 6019 ☎ 08 9245 3279 🚉 Currambine from Perth City

Below *Cruising upstream along the Swan River*

SWAN RIVER

www.captaincookcruises.com.au

The Swan River gives Perth much of its appeal, separating the downtown area from the southern suburbs. Locals bicycle, fish and walk along the banks, where the river has habitats for many plants and animals.

The 240km (149-mile) river runs from the foothills of the Darling Range east of Perth, to Fremantle and out into the Indian Ocean. Upriver, the Avon River changes to the Swan at Wooroloo Brook. Moving downstream through Walyunga National Park, the Upper Swan Valley is the state's traditional wine-growing area. The river passes Guildford, Perth's oldest inland suburb, where the riverbanks are dotted with colonial homes.

Near Perth the banks fan out into a wide expanse, on summer evenings you'll see windsurfers taking advantage of the regular winds that pick up late in the day. Before the Swan flows into the Indian Ocean, the river narrows at the port of Fremantle. Take a river cruise from Perth either upstream to the wineries of the Swan Valley or downstream to Fremantle.

🚹 271 B3 🚤 Captain Cook Cruises, Pier 3, Barrack Square, Perth, WA 6000 ☎ Perth 08 93: 3341; Fremantle 08 9336 3311

SWAN VALLEY

www.swanvalley.com.au

The Swan Valley is just an 18km (11-mile) drive northeast from the heart of Perth and follows the Swan River to the foot of the Darling Range. Aboriginal people have inhabited the Swan Valley region for 40,000 years.

Along the river course are small towns and settlements, Guildford (established in 1830) being one of the oldest; the town retains many fine houses, buildings and shops from its colonial past. For landscape and native animals, there is the nearby Caversham Wildlife Park (▷ 267). The region hosts a number of special events, including Spring in the Valley, held in October, and A Taste of the Valley, held in April, many of which are focused on the local food and wine.

There are more than 40 wineries in the region, ranging from third-generation family vineyards to multinational wine producers. As well as cellar door sales, many of the wineries also have restaurants and cafés. The fertile alluvial flats along the Swan River attracted a British expedition in 1827 and the Swan River Colony was founded in 1829. The earliest vineyard, Olive Farm, was established at Guildford at this time and still operates as a winery and café. By 1862 the first commercial wine vintage in Western Australia was made at Houghton Wines. The Houghton Homestead, built in 1863, is a survivor from this period. Sandalford Wines on the Caversham Estate is one of the Valley's most popular

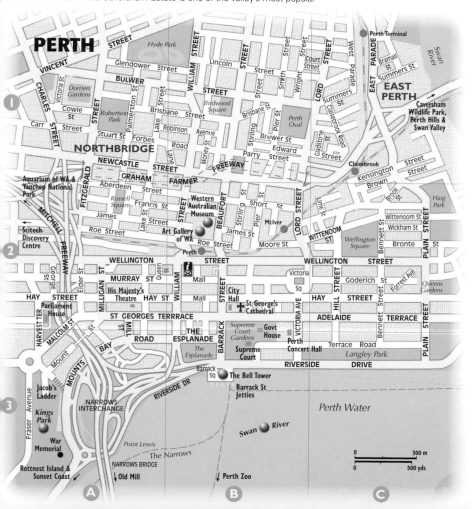

vineyards (daily 10–5). Some cruises up the Swan River (above) include a visit to wineries. The Swan Valley Cheese Company produces gourmet cheeses, the Merrich Estate has olive oil products to taste and buy, while the Margaret River Chocolate Company in West Swan lives up to its name.

The Valley gets very crowded at weekends; mid-week is a better time to visit. The best way to explore the Valley is via signed route 203, which loops up one side of the river and down the other.

✚ 344 C12 ℹ️ Swan Valley Visitors Centre, Cnr Meadow and Swan streets, Guildford, WA 6055 ☎ 08 9379 9400 🕐 Daily 9–4 🚉 Guildford from Perth City

WESTERN AUSTRALIAN MUSEUM

www.museum.wa.gov.au

Set in the heart of Perth's cultural precinct, the museum focuses on the natural history and people of Western Australia. The main collections are Western Land and People, Marine Gallery, Bird Gallery, Diamonds to Dinosaurs and a Mammal Gallery. Head to the Discovery Centre for answers to questions about Australian culture and nature. More recent history is preserved in the 1856 Old Gaol. Keep an eye open for the micro fossils found in the Pilbara, which represent the earliest evidence of life on Earth.

✚ 271 B2 ✉️ Perth Cultural Centre, Perth, WA 6000 ☎ 08 9212 3700 🕐 Daily 9.30–5 ✋ Free 🚌 Wellington Street bus terminal (5-min walk) 🚉 Perth City 💻 🏛️

YANCHEP NATIONAL PARK

www.westernaustralia.com

This 3,000ha (7,410-acre) park is a popular escape for Perth people. It has a large koala colony and is renowned for its native flora and fauna, heritage sites, wetlands and limestone caves. Tuart and banksia woodlands are endemic and wild-flower gardens have a collection of the state's native plants. Crystal Cave on the east side of the park is noted for stalactites. Nyoongar Aboriginal culture is presented at the *Wangi Mia* (Talking Place).

✚ 344 B12 ☎ 08 9405 0759 ✋ A\$11 per car, A\$5 per car for seniors or A\$5 per bus or coach passenger 🚌 Yanchep National Park has day and overnight tours that include pick-up and drop-off from Perth 🚉 Joondalup, then Transperth bus 495 to Yanchep; buses can be irregular 🚌 50km (31 miles) north of Perth off State Route 60; McNess House Visitor Centre is in the main recreation complex 🍴 💻 🏛️

Below *The Swan River sweeps towards the Indian Ocean*

NEW NORCIA

www.newnorcia.wa.edu.au
Australia's only monastic town was founded in 1846 by Benedictine monks as a mission for the Aboriginal people of the Victorian Plains district. The missionary ideal of civilizing and evangelizing turned to a progressive education role for the indigenous children of the state. In the early 20th century the monastic community focused on the care of Western Australia's rural population. The monastery has flourished in recent years, as a place of peace and reflection for citizens, students and tourists. A heritage trail takes in many of the historic buildings. The Museum and Art Gallery houses the monks' art collections, including Spanish and Italian Old Masters paintings.

✚ 3344 C11 ⓘ New Norcia Tourist Information Centre, New Norcia Museum and Art Gallery, New Norcia, WA 6509 ☎ 08 9654 8056 ⓖ Daily 9–4.30

PEMBERTON

www.pembertontourist.com.au
Pemberton, together with Manjimup to the north and Walpole 140km (87 miles) away on the coast, is part of the Southern Forests Region. The attractive small town was built in 1913 for timber workers, and despite art and craft studios and vineries it still has the feel of a timber town. Some of the world's tallest and oldest trees are protected in the national parks around the town. Tall karri trees dominate, though there are also plenty of jarrah and marri trees. The trees in Warren National Park to the southwest stand up to 89m (292ft) high. Gloucester National Park, just east of the town, contains the Gloucester Tree, the highest fire lookout tree in the world at 60m (197ft). Beedelup National Park to the west is known for waterfalls and its karri forest.

For a change of scenery, D'Entrecasteaux National Park on the Southern Ocean has coastal wetlands, dunes and white beaches, and granite outcrops. One of WA's best-known walking tracks, the 1,000km (620-mile) Bibbulmun Track, passes through Pemberton on its route from Kalamunda to Albany on the south coast.

✚ 344 B13 ⓘ Pemberton Tourist Centre, Brockman Street, Pemberton, WA 6260 ☎ 08 9776 1133

PERTH

▷ 266–272.

SHARK BAY

www.sharkbaywa.com.au
Shark Bay is a World Heritage Site because of its unique, rare and superlative natural beauty. The bay is formed by two peninsulas and 1,500km (930 miles) of coastline on the westernmost point of Australia, and covers about 8,000sq km (3,120sq miles). The bay is home to numerous threatened reptile species, rare birds, dugongs and loggerhead turtles. Around the coast the contrast of vast seagrass beds, dunes and blue water is stunning; look for the stromatolites, algae that form dome-shaped fossil-like deposits.

The only town in Shark Bay is Denham, which is the centre of the bay's tourism and fishing industry. At Monkey Mia, 26km (16 miles) northeast of Denham, bottlenose dolphins visit the beach: You can feed them under the supervision of park rangers. Boat excursions and 4WD tours are based at Monkey Mia.

✚ 344 A8 ⓘ Denham and Monkey Mia Visitor Centre, 27 Thornbill Loop, Denham, WA 6537 ☎ 1300 135887

STIRLING RANGE NATIONAL PARK

www.albanytourist.com.au
Encompassed by the 116,000ha (286,520-acre) national park, the peaks of the Stirling Range stretch 65km (40 miles) from east to west. The park is renowned for the mountain landscape, and its wild flowers and bird life. At least 1,500 species of plants and around 140 bird species have been identified. Spring is the prime time to visit when many plants are in flower. Bluff Knoll, at 1,095m (3,592ft), is the highest peak in the southwest

Above *A curious kangaroo at Warren National Park near Pemberton*

of Western Australia. It takes four hours to complete the 6km (4-mile) return climb.

✚ 344 D13 ⓘ Albany Visitors Centre, Old Railway Station, Proudlove Parade Albany ☎ 08 9841 9290 ⓦ A\$11 per vehicle, A\$5 for motorcyles

WAVE ROCK

www.waverock.com.au
Why travel 350km (217 miles) from Perth or elsewhere to see a giant rock formation? Because the 15m (49ft) high, 110m (361ft) long granite cliff really does look like a huge wave about to break. According to geologists Wave Rock was originally vertical but has been sculpted and coloured by the weather for more than 60 million years. The vertical rusty red, ochre and sandy grey bands have been caused by chemicals in the water running off the rock. There are other outcrops nearby, while Mulka's Cave, 21km (13 miles) north from Hyden, preserves Aboriginal hand paintings.

✚ 344 D12 ⓘ Hyden Tourist Information Centre, Wave Rock Wildflower Shoppe, Wave Rock, Hyden, WA 6359 ☎ 08 9880 5022

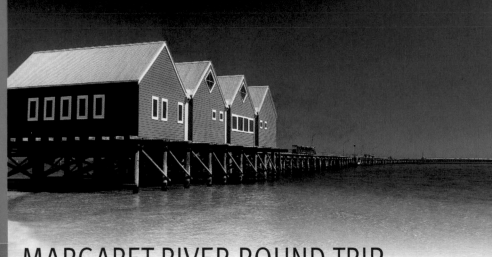

MARGARET RIVER ROUND TRIP

The coastal drive from Perth to Margaret River encounters rolling hills, dramatic forests, fantastic beaches, and wonderful food and wine. While you could drive the whole distance in a day, it is worth staying for a night or two in Margaret River for a more relaxing experience.

THE DRIVE
Distance: 654km (405 miles)
Allow: 2–3 days
Start at: Perth
End at: Perth

★ From Perth take the Old Coast Road (National Route 1) to Bunbury then the Bussell Highway (State Route 10) to Busselton. The towns along the way are worth exploring—including Mandurah, Bunbury and Busselton. From Busselton take Caves Road along the coast to Dunsborough.

❶ Dunsborough is a small resort on the western shores of Geographe Bay. There are good beaches and from June to December opportunities for whale-watching. About 13km (8 miles) farther west (no through road) is the Leeuwin–Naturaliste National Park.

From Dunsborough, travel south for about 8km (5 miles) to Yallingup.

❷ It's worth stopping at Yallingup to look at the pounding surf that breaks on the beach.

Continue south on Caves Road for about 15km (9 miles) through vineyards to the intersection with Hammons South Road.

❸ Many of the Margaret River region's wineries are located along or just off the stretch of road between Yallingup and Gracetown, in the Wilyabrup Valley. Choose a winery or two and drop by for tasting and cellar-door sales. One of the larger wineries is Vasse Felix, on Caves Road near Hammons South Road. The Old Winery Gallery here has regular art exhibitions, showing works by a number of Australian artists including Arthur Boyd, Sidney Nolan and Lloyd Rees as well as a number of less well-known artists.

Just past the Margaret River turnoff (on the left) is the road to Prevelly

Park. Turn right here and take Rivermouth Road, leading to the mouth of the Margaret River and the Indian Ocean.

❹ The mouth of the Margaret River is one of the most popular spots in the area for surfing. The Margaret River Masters international surfing competition is held here in April each year.

Return to Caves Road and continue south to CaveWorks.

❺ The visitor centre at Cave Works explains the caves that riddle the limestone bedrock of this area (▷ 265). There are some 350 caves, but only about a dozen are open to the public. Among them is Lake Cave, which can be entered on a tour from CaveWorks. Just north of CaveWorks is Mammoth Cave. It features a self-guiding system allowing you to explore the cave at your own pace (daily 9–5).

Opposite *Bussleton's Jetty*

About 4km (2.5 miles) south of CaveWorks, turn right on to Boranup Drive, which leads to Boranup Forest.

❻ Tall karri trees, reaching 60m (197ft) or more, dominate Boranup Forest's slopes and valleys. A gravel road, suitable for two-wheel-drive vehicles, winds through the forest past picnic spots. Near the end of the drive, not far before it rejoins Caves Road, is Boranup Lookout.

Rejoin Caves Road and continue south to Bushby Road. Turn left and join the Bussell Highway for the northward journey to Margaret River.

❼ Margaret River township (▷ 264) is the heart of the region and is a good place to spend the night.

Drive north on the Bussell Highway in the direction of Busselton to the small settlement of Cowaramup.

❽ A visit to the Margaret River Regional Wine Centre at Cowaramup provides a chance to learn about the region's wineries. There are also several art and craft galleries. Just north of town, at the junction with Harmons Mill Road, is Fonti Farm, where you can taste local cheeses, ice cream and yogurt (daily 9.30–5).

Continue north on the Bussell Highway to Busselton and Perth.

WHEN TO GO
All year round.

WHERE TO EAT
Wilyabrup Valley: winery restaurants and cafés between Yallingup and Gracetown.
Margaret River: VAT 107, 107 Bussell Highway (daily 9am–late).

PLACES TO VISIT
Augusta, ▷ 259.
Bunbury, ▷ 260.
Margaret River, ▷ 264–265.

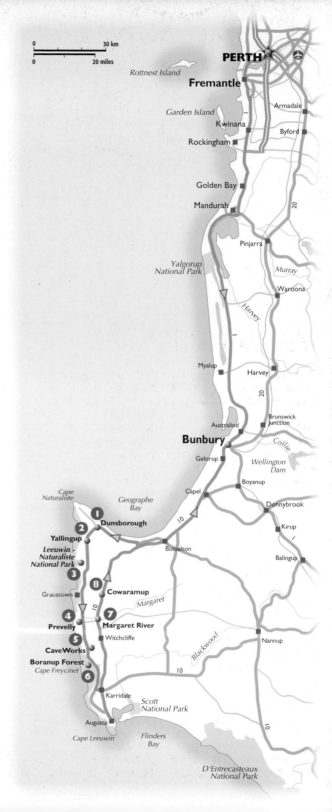

WHAT TO DO

BROOME

PASPALEY PEARLS
www.paspaleypearls.com
At Paspaley Pearls, one of the largest such outlets in Broome (▷ 259), you can buy loose pearls and designer jewellery and learn about pearls and the pearling industry. The shop is in the heart of Chinatown.
✉ 2 Short Street, Broome, WA 6725 ☎ 08 9192 2203 ⊕ Mon–Fri 9.30–5, Sat 9.30–1, Sun 9.30–1

RED SUN CAMELS
www.redsuncamels.com.au
Sunset camel rides on Broome's Cable Beach.
✉ Cable Beach ☎ 08 9193 7423 ⊕ Daily; sunset tours depart 90 minutes before dusk, which ranges from 4 to 5.30 depending on time of year 🚍 Bus to Cable Beach arrives at quarter to the hour 🖐 Adult A$50, child (6–16) A$35, under 6 A$10

SUN PICTURES GARDENS
www.broomemories.com.au
One of the oldest operating outdoor movie theatres. See page 259.
✉ 27 Carnarvon Street, Broome, WA 6725

☎ 08 9192 1077 ⊕ Movies start after dusk 🖵 🍷

BUNBURY

DOLPHIN DISCOVERY CENTRE
www.dolphins.mysouthwest.com.au
Observe dolphins off the coast from December to end April, or swim with them along with the Centre's marine biologist.
✉ Koombana Drive, Bunbury, WA 6230 ☎ 08 9791 3088 ⊕ Oct–end May daily 8–4; Jun–end Aug 9–3 🖐 Centre entry: adult A$8, child A$5; Dolphin watch: adult A$53, child A$45; Swim tour: A$185 per person 🚍 Bus from Bunbury 🖵

CORAL BAY

SWIM WITH MANTA RAYS
www.coralbayadventures.com.au
Snorkelling tours on the Ningaloo Reef and swimming with rays.
✉ Robinson Street, Coral Bay, WA 6701 ☎ 08 9942 5955 ⊕ Daily 7am–6pm 🖐 Adult A$165, child A$90

FREMANTLE

THE CLINK
www.theclink.com.au
The latest music on Friday and Saturday; Sunday is retro.

✉ 14–16 South Terrace, Fremantle, WA 6160 ☎ 08 9336 1919 ⊕ Thu 10pm–3am, Fri, Sat 9pm–5am, Sun 8pm–12am 🖐 A$10 Fri, Sat, A$3 Sun

FREMANTLE MARKETS
www.fremantlemarkets.com.au
Established in 1897, these markets have more than 170 stalls selling everything from food and drinks to crafts, including leather, opals and pottery.
✉ Cnr South Terrace and Henderson Street, Fremantle, WA 6160 ☎ 08 9335 2515 ⊕ Sat–Mon 10–6, Fri 10–8 🚊 Fremantle 🖵

KAILIS AUSTRALIAN PEARLS
www.kailisjewellery.com.au
This pearl farm shop sells pearls and a range of jewellery.
✉ Cnr Marine Terrace and Collie Street, Fremantle, WA 6160 ☎ 08 9239 9330 ⊕ Mon–Fri 9.30–5, Sat, Sun 11–4 🚊 Fremantle

METROPOLIS
www.metropolisfremantle.com.au
A choice of bars and dance floors at Fremantle's biggest and most popular club.

Opposite *Aussie Rules at the Subiaco Oval in Perth*

✉ 58 South Terrace, Fremantle, WA 6160 ☎ 08 9336 1880 🕐 Fri, Sat 9pm–4am 👆 A$10–A$25

MARGARET RIVER
THE CHOCOLATE COMPANY
www.chocolatefactory.com.au
Watch chocolates being made, then buy from a large selection.
✉ Cnr Harman's Mill and Harman's South roads, Metricup, WA 6280 ☎ 08 9755 6555 🕐 Daily 9–5 🖥

JOSH PALMATEER SURF ACADEMY
www.mrsurf.com.au
Learn to surf at Western Australia's most popular surfing destination.
✉ Groups meet at the Margaret River mouth parking area ☎ 08 9757 3850 🕐 Daily 11–1 (closed winter) 👆 From A$45 for a group lesson 🚌 Rivermouth Car Park, at the mouth of Margaret River

MARGARET RIVER REGIONAL WINE CENTRE
www.mrwines.com
Wines from most of the region's winemakers are for sale and available to taste: a good option for those with little time.
✉ 9 Bussell Highway, Cowaramup, WA 6284 ☎ 08 9755 5501 🕐 Mon–Sat 10–7, Sun 10–6

PERTH
ABOUT BIKE HIRE
www.aboutbikehire.com.au
Rent a bicycle to pedal beside the Swan River or off-road; tours of the Munda Biddi Track.
✉ Cnr Plain Street and Riverside Drive, Perth, WA 6000 ☎ 08 9221 2665 🕐 Daily 9–5 👆 Adult from A$10, child A$7, for the first hour 🚌 Red CAT

BLACK BETTY'S
www.blackbettys.com.au
Live music and DJs, light shows and silhouette dancers.
✉ Cnr Aberdeen and Parker streets, Northbridge, WA 6003 ☎ 08 9228 0077 🕐 Wed, Fri, Sat 9–late 👆 A$5 after 10 Thu–Sat 🚌 Perth

BURSWOOD INTERNATIONAL RESORT CASINO
www.burswood.com.au
Perth's casino has nine restaurants, six bars and a theatre.
✉ Great Eastern Highway, Burswood, WA 6100 ☎ 08 9362 7777 🕐 24 hours 🚌 Burswood 🍴 🖥 🍷

CONNECTIONS NIGHTCLUB
www.connectionsnightclub.com
A gay and lesbian club with the latest dance music.
✉ 81 James Street, Northbridge, WA 6003 ☎ 08 9328 1870 🕐 Tue, Wed 10pm–5am, Fri, Sat 10pm–6am 👆 A$12 Fri, A$10 Sat 🚌 Perth

CREATIVE NATIVE
www.creativenative.com.au
This gallery houses the largest range of Aboriginal art and crafts in Western Australia—paintings, boomerangs, didgeridoos and rugs. Authentification certificates are provided.
✉ Shop 58, Forrest Chase, Forrest Place, Perth, WA 6000 ☎ 08 9322 3398 🕐 Mon–Thu 9–5.30, Fri 9–7, Sat 9–5, Sun 11–5 🚌 Red CAT 🚌 Perth

THE DEEN
www.thedeen.com
Live bands, DJs and six bars.
✉ 84 Aberdeen Street, Northbridge, WA 6003 ☎ 08 9227 9361 🕐 Mon, Thu, Fri, Sat 5pm–2am, Wed 5pm–1am 🚌 Perth

FORM CONTEMPORARY CRAFT AND DESIGN
www.craftwest.com.au
Craftwest is the peak professional organization for contemporary craft and design in Western Australia. At its retail outlet you can buy handmade ceramics, glass, jewellery, textiles, woodwork leather and cards.
✉ 357–365 Murray Street, Perth, WA 6000 ☎ 08 9226 2799 🕐 Mon–Thu 9–5.30, Fri 9–6, Sat 9–5 🚌 Red CAT 🚌 Perth

HIP-E-CLUB
www.hipeclub.com.au
Music from the 1970s, 1980s and 1990s; Top 40 on Wednesdays.
✉ 663 Newcastle Street, Leederville, WA

6007 ☎ 08 9227 8899 🕐 Tue 8pm–5am, Wed 10pm–5am, Fri 10pm–5am, Sat 9pm–5am 👆 A From A$5 🚌 Leederville

HIS MAJESTY'S THEATRE
www.hismajestystheatre.com.au
This Edwardian theatre is home to the West Australian Opera and the West Australian Ballet.
✉ 825 Hay Street, Perth, WA 6000 ☎ 08 9265 0900 🚌 Red CAT 🚌 Perth 🖥 🍷

ONYX LOUNGE BAR
www.onyxbar.com.au
Club music into the early hours at this popular after-work bar.
✉ 72 Outram Street, West Perth, WA 6005 ☎ 08 9321 8661 🕐 Fri, Sat 7–late 🚌 City West

PERTH CONCERT HALL
www.perthconcerthall.com.au
This is Perth's main venue for performances of classical music.
✉ 5 St. George's Terrace, Perth, WA 6000 ☎ 08 9231 9900 (tickets: 08 9484 1133) 🚌 Blue CAT 🚌 Perth 🖥 🍷

THE PLAYHOUSE
www.playhousetheatre.com.au
Several theatre companies are based here and it is also used by touring drama and dance groups.
✉ 3 Pier Street, Perth, WA 6000 ☎ 08 9323 3400 🚌 Red CAT 🚌 Perth 🖥 🍷

REGAL THEATRE
www.regaltheatre.com.au
Stages everything from comedy acts and film festivals to musicals and rock bands.
✉ 474 Hay Street, Subiaco, WA 6008 ☎ 08 9388 2066 (tickets: 1300 795 012) 🚌 Subiaco

RISE
www.rise.net.au
One of Northbridge's most popular dance clubs.
✉ 139 James Street, Northbridge, WA 6003 ☎ 08 9226 0322 🕐 Wed, Thu 9pm–4am, Fri, Sat 9pm–6am, Sun 9pm–1am 👆 From A$10 🚌 Perth

SUBIACO OVAL
www.wafootball.com.au
Home to two Australian Rules

football teams, the West Coast Eagles and Fremantle.

✉ Roberts Road, Subiaco, WA 6008
☎ 08 9381 2187 ◷ Matches Apr–end Sep Fri–Sun 🖐 Adult from A$35, child A$11.25 🚌 Transperth park and ride service 🚉 Leederville and Subiaco

UNIVERSAL BAR

www.universalbar.com.au

An open, friendly bar known for its cocktails. Music ranges from funk to traditional blues.

✉ 221 William Street, Northbridge, WA 6003
☎ 08 9227 6771 ◷ Mon–Fri 5pm–late, Sat 5pm–2am, Sun 5pm–12am 🚉 Perth

ZOO CROOZ

www.captaincookcruises.com.au

A combination of a cruise to Fremantle and entry to Perth Zoo plus ferry transfers between cities.

✉ Pier 3, Barrack Square, Perth, WA 6000
☎ 08 9325 3341 ◷ Departs 9.45 and 2pm 🖐 Adult from A$50, child A$27 🚌 Blue CAT 🚉 Perth

SWAN VALLEY
HOUGHTON WINES

www.houghton-wines.com.au

Wine, wine-related products, and locally produced food and crafts are on sale. There's also an art gallery.

✉ Dale Road, Middle Swan, WA 6056
☎ 08 9274 9540, 1800 800 012 ◷ Daily 10–5 🖥

PERTH FAMOUS WINE CRUISE

www.captaincookcruises.com.au

A day tour from Perth to the Swan Valley including wine and cheese tastings and a gourmet three-course lunch.

✉ Captain Cook Cruises, Pier 3, Barrack Square, Perth, WA 6000 ☎ 08 9325 3341 ◷ Departs Perth daily 9.45am, returns 4.45pm 🖐 Adult A$146, child (4–14) A$103

THE VINES RESORT

www.vines.com.au

The resort has two 18-hole courses where many world golf championships have been played.

✉ Verdelho Drive, The Vines, WA 6069
☎ 08 9297 3000 ◷ Dawn–dusk 🖐 From A$50 for 9 holes, A$89 for 18 holes
🍽 🖥 🏆

FESTIVALS AND EVENTS

JANUARY–FEBRUARY
PERTH INTERNATIONAL ARTS FESTIVAL

www.perthfestival.com.au

The Perth International Arts Festival attracts leading artists and performers in music, film, drama, dance, opera, song, jazz and the visual arts.

FEBRUARY
JOHNNIE WALKER CLASSIC

www.johnniewalkerclassic.com

The Johnnie Walker Classic Golf Tournament, in Perth, is Australia's richest golf tournament, with a minimum of A$2.5 million in prize money.

FEBRUARY/MARCH
LEEUWIN ESTATE CONCERT

www.leeuwinestate.com.au

The Leeuwin Estate Concert, at the Leeuwin Estate Winery, attracts top performers.

MARCH/APRIL
FREMANTLE STREET ARTS FESTIVAL

www.fremantlefestivals.com

Timed to coincide with Easter, this lively open-air festival attracts some of the world's best buskers, wandering musicians and performers.

MARGARET RIVER PRO

www.drugawarepro.com

Part of the Association of Surfing Professionals World Tour series, this event brings the cream of the board-riding world to the Margaret River beaches.

JULY–NOVEMBER
NATURAL WILD FLOWER DISPLAYS

See one of the world's great natural wild flower displays at various locations. The season starts in July in the Pilbara (northern) region and heads south until November.

SEPTEMBER
YORK JAZZ FESTIVAL

www.yorkjazz.com.au

The historic town of York hosts the York Jazz Festival.

PERTH ROYAL SHOW

www.perthroyalshow.com.au

The Perth Royal Show showcases agricultural, horticultural, viticultural, rural, technological and mineral resources.

KINGS PARK WILDFLOWER FESTIVAL

www.bgpa.wa.gov.au

The Kings Park Wildflower Festival, in Perth, is an extensive native plant display and wild flower exhibition.

OCTOBER
SPRING IN THE VALLEY

www.emrc.org.au

Spring in the Valley celebrates the produce of the Swan Valley.

DECEMBER–JANUARY
HOPMAN CUP

www.hopmancup.com.au

World-class tennis players compete in national teams in the Hopman Cup in Perth.

Below *The annual Leeuwin Estate Concert*

PRICES AND SYMBOLS

The restaurants are listed alphabetically (excluding Le, La and Les). The prices given are the average for a two course lunch (L) and a three-course dinner (D) for one person, without drinks. The wine price is for the least expensive bottle.

For a key to the symbols, ▷ 2.

BROOME

TIDES GARDEN RESTAURANT AND CHARTERS RESTAURANT

www.mangrovehotel.com.au
Both restaurants are part of the Mangrove Hotel: The Charters is indoors; Tides outdoors. The menu is modern with different dishes each night; seafood is a house special. Vegetarian and children's meals are also available; vegan meals served on request. Reserve ahead.
✉ 47 Carnarvon Street, Broome, WA 6725 ☎ 08 9192 1303 ④ Charters: daily breakfast 6.30–10, dinner 6–9.30, Apr–end Dec. Tides daily 12–3, 6–9.30 🖐 L A$35, D A$55, Wine A$26 🚌 Bus from Broome stops outside the Mangrove

THE OLD ZOO CAFÉ

www.zoocafe.com.au
Set in tropical gardens, this casual café with its splashy colour scheme encapsulates the Broome style. The menu works hard all day, from the mango granola at breakfast to the finger-licking tapas menu later in the day
✉ 2 Challenor Drive, Cable Beach, WA 6726 ☎ 08 9193 6200 ④ Daily 8am–10pm 🖐 L A$25, D A$40, Wine A$29

CAVERSHAM

SANDALFORD RESTAURANT

www.sandalford.com
The Modern Australian menu changes regularly but its most popular dish, locally caught marron (freshwater crayfish), is always available. There's a children's menu as well as vegetarian options. Sandalford wines are sold.
✉ 3210 West Swan, Caversham, WA 6055 ☎ 08 9374 9300 ④ Daily 12–3, Fri 6–late 🖐 L A$55, D A$70, Wine A$29 🚌 Perth central to Midland then 52 bus to Sandalford. The bus runs only every 90 minutes (tel 13 62 13)

DWELLINGUP

HOTHAM VALLEY TOURIST RAILWAY

Every Saturday evening, a 1919 vintage dining car departs Dwellingup Station for a three-hour dinner tour. The five-course meal usually includes soup of the day, roast beef and apple pie.
✉ Dwellingup Railway Station, Dwellingup, WA 6213 ☎ 08 9221 4444 ④ Sat 7.45pm–11.45pm 🖐 D A$70 🚌 Bus departs East Perth Terminal to connect with the tram (A$16.50 fare)

FREMANTLE

CLANCY'S FISH PUB

www.clancysfishpub.com.au
The menu includes seafood chowder, classic fish and chips, fresh shucked oysters, octopus, and cajun calamari served with chips and sweet chilli sauce. Seafood and vegetarian options are available.
✉ 51 Cantonment Street, Fremantle, WA 6160 ☎ 08 9335 1351 ④ Sun–Thu 11.30–9, Fri, Sat 11.30–9.30 🖐 L A$35, D A$45, Wine A$24.50 🚌 CAT bus stops nearby

KAILIS' FISH MARKET CAFÉ

www.kailis.com
The waterfront area comprises a fresh seafood market, a restaurant providing cooked seafood, and a café selling sandwiches, cakes and ice creams. Alcoholic beverages are available only with a meal.
✉ Fishing Boat Harbour, 46 Mews Road, Fremantle, WA 6160 ☎ 08 9335 7755 ④ Daily 8am–late 🖐 Fish and chips A$21, seafood delight A$32 🚌 CAT bus stops nearby

LITTLE CREATURES BREWING

www.littlecreatures.com.au

The dining area has communal tables and leather booths, while the open kitchen is a feature. Its wood-fired oven produces crisp Italian pizzas and specials include prosciutto-wrapped tiger prawns and hand-cut *frites*. Beer is the great attraction here, so the wine list is limited.

✉ 40 Mews Road, Fremantle, WA 6160 ☎ 08 9430 5555 ⊙ Daily 10am–midnight ✋ L A$42, D A$50, Wine A$26 🚉 Fremantle

THE RED HERRING

www.redherring.com.au

The Modern Australian menu changes regularly to take advantage of the seafood available, but crayfish (marron) and fresh oysters are frequent specials. Children's and vegetarian dishes are provided. Popular, so reserve ahead.

✉ 26 Riverside Road, East Fremantle, WA 6158 ☎ 08 9339 1611 ⊙ Daily lunch/dinner 12–late, Sat, Sun and public holidays breakfast 7–11 ✋ L A$55, D A$70, Wine A$26

SAIL AND ANCHOR

www.sailandanchor.com.au

The Sail and Anchor was one of Australia's first pub breweries. Pub and casual meals, such as soup, tapas, salads, fish and potatoes, garlic prawns and pizzas, are served.

Eight beers are brewed here and there is a good selection of Western Australian wines. Reserve for restaurant.

✉ 64 South Terrace, Fremantle, WA 6160 ☎ 08 9431 1666 ⊙ Mon–Thu 11am–12am, Fri, Sat 11am–1am, Sun 11–10 ✋ L A$32, D A$40, Wine A$24.50 🚉 Several buses stop nearby

KALBARRI

BLACK ROCK CAFÉ

www.blackrockcafe.com.au

Modern Australian food is served with a range of special dishes according to the season, but usually featuring seafood. Margaret River-produced Pallandri wines are an additional attraction. Meals for children, vegans and vegetarians are also available. Reserve ahead.

✉ 80 Grey Street, Kalbarri, WA 6536 ☎ 08 9937 1062 ⊙ Tue–Sun 7am–late ✋ L A$25, D A$42, Wine A$25

KALGOORLIE

MP'S

Part of the All Seasons Plaza Hotel, MP's provides Modern Australian cuisine with a range of daily specials and an extensive wine list. Children's and vegetarian meals are available on request. Reservation advised.

✉ 45 Egan Street, Kalgoorlie, WA 6430 ☎ 08 9080 5900 ⊙ Daily 6am–9.30am, 6pm–9.30pm ✋ D A$55, Wine A$28

MARGARET RIVER

1885 RESTAURANT

www.grangeonfarrelly.com.au

Fresh local fish, venison and cheeses are served in the plantation-style interior, along with an excellent selection of Margaret River wines.

✉ Grange Motel, 18 Farrelly Street, Margaret River, WA 6285 ☎ 08 9757 3177 ⊙ Mon–Sat 6.30–9 ✋ D A$55, Wine A$24. Rooms from A$150 🛏 29 🍽

LEEUWIN ESTATE WINERY RESTAURANT

www.leeuwinestate.com.au

The restaurant is popular with both foreign and local visitors to the vineyard. Regional produce is served inside or on the veranda, and includes lamb, venison and seafood; marron is a house special. Wines, of course, come from the estate. For lighter refreshments, come for the morning and afternoon teas. Reservations advised.

✉ Stevens Road, Margaret River, WA 6285 ☎ 08 9759 0000 ⊙ Daily 10–4.30 (L 12–2.30, Sat D 6.30–8.30) ✋ L A$23, D A$75, Wine A$23 🚉 Go 6km (3.5 miles) south from Margaret River on the Bussell Highway, then turn right on to Gnaraway Road

PERTH

ART GALLERY CAFÉ

This licensed café serves moderately priced snacks and meals including reasonable focaccias, salads and lasagne.

✉ Perth Cultural Centre, 47 James Street, Perth, WA 6000 ☎ 08 9328 2372 ⊙ Daily 10–5 ✋ L A$25, Wine A$9.50 🚉 Perth city

BELL'S CAFÉ

Enjoy a coffee and a cake at this café, watching the boats depart from Barracks Jetty for Fremantle and Rottnest Island.

The menu is modern classic with a range of daily specials, such as chicken mandalay and oysters. Children's and vegetarian meals are available. Reservations advised for eating outside.

✉ Jetty 2, Eastern Pavilion, Barrack Street Jetty, Perth, WA 6000 ☎ 08 9221 2344 ⊙ Sun–Thu 8–5, Fri, Sat 8am–late ✋ L A$38, D A$57, Wine A$21 🚉 Blue CAT stop 19 (Barrack Square)

C RESTAURANT LOUNGE

www.crestaurant.com.au

At this revolving restaurant, the Modern Australian cuisine includes seafood, pasta, steak, California rolls and Australian specials such as marron and kangaroo. Vegetarian items available; children's meals on request. The wine list is extensive with top Australian wines.

✉ Level 33, 44 St. Georges Terrace, Perth, WA 6000 ☎ 08 9220 8333 ⊙ Mon–Fri 11am–12am, Sat 5pm–12am, Sun 12–12 ✋ L A$58, D A$96, Wine A$41

FRASER'S RESTAURANT

www.frasersrestaurant.com.au

The cuisine at this restaurant is Modern Australian with an emphasis on seafood, such as wok-fried baby octopus with chilli, ginger paste and bean sprouts, or assorted seafood with tiger prawns in a curry. The wine list runs to more than ten pages. Reservations are essential.

✉ Fraser Avenue, Kings Park, West Perth, WA 6005 ☎ 08 9481 7100 ⊙ Daily 7.30am–late ✋ L A$60, D A$75, Wine A$40 🚉 From central Perth to Kings Park or Blue CAT stop 20 (Mount Hospital)

INDIANA TEA HOUSE

www.indiana.com.au

Come here to watch the sun setting on Cottesloe Beach. Built on the site of the original 19th-century Indiana Tea House, the building recalls the Raj days of palms and cane.

The restaurant is renowned for its Moreton Bay bug salad (Moreton Bay bugs are unique to Australia and taste like lobster). There are fine wines from the Margaret River region. Reservations advised. ✉ 99 Marine Parade, Cottesloe, Perth, WA 6011 ☎ 08 9385 5005 ⏰ Daily 12–late 🍴 L A$48, D A$72, Wine A$37 🚌 72 from central Perth 🚆 Cottesloe then 10-minute walk

MISS MAUD

www.missmaud.com.au
The people of Perth have been feasting on Miss Maud's smorgasbords for over 30 years. The restaurant is part of the Miss Maud Swedish Hotel.

Breakfast smorgasbords include bacon, sausages, eggs, grilled tomatoes, mushrooms, pancakes, Swedish muesli, muffins, pastries, fresh fruit juices, coffee and tea.

Lunch and dinner smorgasbords include king prawns, freshly cooked yabbies, a roast meats carvery, home-made bread, salads, soup, cakes, pastries, coffee and tea. The dinner smorgasbord also has fresh oysters. ✉ 97 Murray Street, Perth, WA 6000 ☎ 08 9325 3900 ⏰ Daily 6.45-10, 12–2.30, 5.30–9.30 🍴 Breakfast smorgasbord A$29.50, L A$39.50, D A$46, Wine A$29 (surcharges Sun and public holidays)

THE OLD SWAN BREWERY RESTAURANT

www.oldswanbrewery.com.au
This historic building beside the Swan River has great views from every seat. The restaurant has a microbrewery with interactive displays and a café.

The menu includes emu and buffalo, as well as the more usual fish, beef and chicken. The café-restaurant has an extensive wine list. Reservations are advised for the restaurant. ✉ 173 Mounts Bay Road, Perth, WA 6000 ☎ 08 9211 8901 ⏰ Mon–Fri 11.30–10 🍴 L A$42, D A$65, Wine A$35 🚌 71 and 72

RESTAURANT AMUSÉ

www.restaurantamuse.com.au
Degustation style dining with a razor's edge is the forté of this handsome, intimate charcoal-toned restaurant, where chef Hadeligh Troy orchestrates one of Perth's top dining experiences. From Tuesday to Thursday, the 11-course degustation menu is throttled back slightly. Excellent wine list. ✉ 64 Bronte Street, East Perth, WA 6005 ☎ 08 9325 4900 ⏰ Tue–Sat 7pm–10pm 🍴 D A$100, Wine A$38

STAR ANISE

www.staraniserestaurant.com.au
Chef David Coomer is a star of long standing on Perth's restaurant scene, testing the boundaries with modern Australian food that is always invigorating and exquisitely presented. For gourmands, the degustation menu is highly recommended. Service is crisp and professional. ✉ 225 Onslow Road, Shenton Park, Perth, WA 6008 ☎ 08 9328 1177 ⏰ Mon–Sat 7pm–10.30pm 🍴 D A$90, Wine A$51

STAYING

PRICES AND SYMBOLS

Prices are for a double room for one night including breakfast, unless otherwise stated. All the hotels listed accept credit cards, unless otherwise stated. Note that rates can vary widely throughout the year.

For a key to the symbols, ▷ 2.

ALBANY

FLINDERS PARK LODGE B&B HOTEL

This sprawling country homestead combines comfort, style and old-fashioned prices with the very nicest of country manners, overlooking Oyster Harbour just outside Albany.
✉ Flinders Park Lodge, Lower King and Harbour roads, Albany, WA 6330
☎ 08 9844 7062 ⊛ All year
✋ A$145–A$340 ① 8

BROOME

CABLE BEACH CLUB

www.cablebeachclub.com
A complex of bungalows and two-floor units, the resort is set in palmy gardens with a chain of canals and little arched bridges. The bright red bungalows are gems—big, comfortable, one- and two-bedroom timber houses with wide verandas, shutters all around and oriental antiques.
✉ Cable Beach Road, Broome, WA 6725 ☎ 1800 199 099 ⊛ All year
✋ A$286–A$1,800 ① 263 ☒ Two outdoor ⬡ ▦ 6km (4 miles) north from Broome

MCALPINE HOUSE

www.mcalpinehouse.com.au
A series of semi-open pavilions set around a pool and buried in tropical greenery, this smart guesthouse evokes the swashbuckling traditions of the Broome pearling masters' houses, accented with Chinese and Indian antiques and bold colours.
✉ 55 Herbert Street, Broome, WA 6725
☎ 08 9192 0510 ⊛ All year ✋ A$380
① 8 ☒ Outdoor

PINCTADA CABLE BEACH RESORT AND SPA

www.pinctadacablebeach.com.au
Set just back from the swathe of Cable Beach, this new resort takes its cues from the cultural mix that lies at the heart of this amiable and relaxed town. Guest rooms are large and luxurious with a clean, minimalist design, and equipped with the latest technology. Dining options include a Mediterranean inspired brasserie, a poolside bar and café, and the sleek NYX Bar. The pool is an asymmetrical design with spa nooks, a cascading water feature and 25m lap lane, lit to an opalescent blue by night.
✉ 10 Murray Road, Cable Beach, Broome WA 6725 ☎ 08 9193 8388 ⊛ All year
✋ A$200–A$320 ① 72 ☒

FREMANTLE

ESPLANADE HOTEL

www.esplanadehotelfremantle.com.au
Most rooms at this hotel have balconies overlooking parklands or tropical gardens. There are two restaurants, two pools, three spas, and a health club.
✉ Cnr Marine Terrace and Essex Street, Fremantle, WA 6160 ☎ 08 9432 4000

Above *The Esplanade Hotel at Fremantle*

All year A\$189–A\$578 259
Two outdoor heated Fremantle CAT
from station

KALBARRI
BEST WESTERN KALBARRI PALM RESORT
www.kalbarripalmresort.com.au
Standard motel suites and family
apartments. Spa and sports facilities.
Porter Street, Kalbarri, WA 6536 08
9937 2333 All year A\$155–A\$250
78 Two outdoor heated
Transfers available from bus station
to resort

MARGARET RIVER
CAPE LODGE
capelodge.com.au
Surrounded by lawns and native
forest, this country estate is built
in a warm, contemporary style that
evokes the finest traditions of the
small, luxury country house hotel.
Rooms come in several styles, some
in the main house, others scattered
around the grounds. There is a
restaurant, as well as an outdoor
pool, tennis court, health and beauty
facilities and vineyard.
3341 Caves Road, Margaret River,
WA 6282 08 9755 6311 All year
A\$475–A\$2,400 22 Outdoor

CHANDLERS SMITHS BEACH COTTAGES
www.chandlerssmithsbeach.com.au
These smart, modern cottages
offer comfortable, self-contained
accommodation at a realistic
price. Furnishings are neat and
simple and each cottage has two
bedrooms, a fully equipped kitchen,
a generous living area with TV and
DVD and sliding doors that open to a
verandah. Smiths Beach—known for
its consistent surf break—is just an
easy stroll away.
50 Smiths Beach Road, Yallingup,
WA, 6282 08 9755 2062 All year
A\$120–A\$155 15 cottages

EMPIRE RETREAT
www.empireretreat.com
Buried in native bushland on
the Empire Estate Vineyard, this
secluded retreat offers a luxurious

cocoon from which guests can
isolate themselves from the rest
of the world. The emphasis is on
restoration and rejuvenation, and
the spa is well equipped. Rooms are
plush and cosy.
Caves Road, Yallingup, WA 6282 08
9755 2065 All year A\$260–A\$550
10

MARGARET RIVER HOTEL
www.margaretriverhotel.com.au
In a prime location, this popular
watering hole and restaurant offers
smart accommodation in traditional
hotel rooms. There are also larger
holiday suites for families.
125 Bussell Highway, Margaret River,
WA 6285 08 9757 2655 All year
A\$130–A\$180 47

PERTH
INTERCONTINENTAL PERTH BURSWOOD
www.burswood.com.au
Hotel, casino, restaurants, bars and
theatre. Health, fitness and beauty
facilities; golf course.
Great Eastern Highway, Burswood,
WA 6100 08 9362 8888 All year
A\$284–A\$1,590, excluding breakfast
413 Indoor and outdoor
Burswood Resort 3km (2 miles) east
from Perth centre

MANTRA ON HAY
www.mantra.com.au
Right in the centre of Perth, all
apartments have private balconies.
The indoor rooftop swimming pool
and gym offer spectacular views of
the city.
201 Hay Street, Perth, WA 6000
1300 987 604 All year A\$228–
A\$328 152 apartments Indoor

MISS MAUD SWEDISH HOTEL
www.missmaudhotel.com.au
This small, charming, independently
owned low-rise hotel sits in an
outstanding location at the heart
of the city. Rooms are modestly
luxurious and are good value. The
smorgasbord breakfast (▷ 281) is
one of the hotel's major drawcards.
97 Murray Street, Perth, WA
6000 08 9325 3900 All year
A\$189–A\$249 52

THE PENINSULA RIVERSIDE SERVICED APARTMENTS
On the banks of the Swan River
looking across to the city, these
stylish apartments are a good choice
for anyone looking for self-catering
accommodation at a moderate price.
53 South Perth Esplanade, South Perth
WA 6151 08 9368 6688 All year
A\$225–A\$400

Below *Perth's Mantra on Hay has serviced apartments with private balconies*

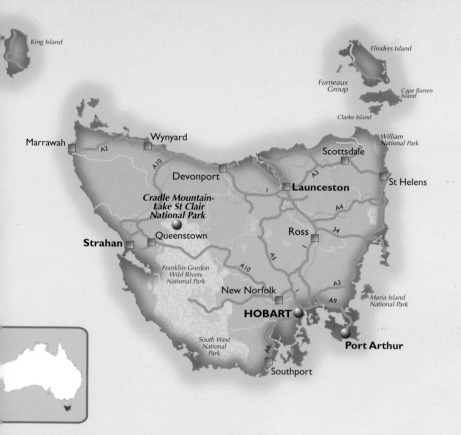

TASMANIA

Tasmania is the smallest of Australia's states, and its slower pace and soothing, rustic manners are valued by those Australians who prefer life out of the fast lane. This is the one state that a visitor could reasonably skim through on a one-week, self-drive holiday.

The island-state was founded as a penal colony for the worst of the criminals deported to New South Wales, a prison within a prison, and the state has a grisly history of crime and punishment that is powerfully evoked by the ruins at Port Arthur, the former penal settlement on the Tasman Peninsula.

The capital, Hobart, is a compact and charming city spread along the estuary of the Derwent River with the booming bulk of Mt Wellington at its back—a peak that is sometimes dusted with snow at the peak of summer. It's also a city with a strong sense of history. After Sydney, Hobart is the second oldest of Australia's capitals, and the city has a rich legacy of historic buildings, especially around its waterfront and the Battery Point precinct.

While it lacks the headline attractions that distinguish the northern states, Tasmania is tailor-made for lovers of brisk outdoor pleasures. Some of Australia's finest walks thread through its mossy forests and along its coast, white-water rafters can lose themselves for days on its wild rivers, the rocky coastline of the Freycinet Peninsula is perfect for sea kayaking and the narrow roads that wind through its tapestry of farms and small villages are ideal for cycle touring. Although its scenery sometimes evokes the green and pleasant countryside of England, Tasmania also has its feral side. The raw and soggy southwest quarter of the state is dominated by untamed rivers, sharp-toothed mountains, glacier-carved lakes, and vast forests with 1,000-year-old trees, and is so rugged that no roads intrude to disturb the primeval silence.

BICHENO

www.bichenopenguintours.com.au

This small fishing port nestles among white sandy beaches on the island's beautiful east coast, sheltered by high granite boulders liberally splashed with bright orange, yellow and green lichens. Eucalypt forests inland and the Douglas-Apsley National Park to the north are great for walking. The port has a history of sealing and whaling; today it's a base for cray boats and abalone divers.

Crayfish and sea horses feature in the Sea Life Centre (daily 9–5), while Bicheno Penguin Tours offer evening trips to watch the native fairy variety. Redbill Beach is the pick of the beaches—lines of swell pour in past pretty Diamond Island.

✚ 355 U17 🚹 Bicheno Penguin Tours, Tasman Highway, Bicheno, TAS 7215 ☎ 03 6375 1333

BURNIE

www.burnie.net

Once a major industrial paper-making town, Burnie is transforming itself into one of the best stops in the northwest. Tourism, cottage industries and a developing café culture are injecting new life into this port. The Emu Valley Rhododendron Gardens (Aug–Feb daily 9–5) on Breffny Road are impressive and open only from August to the end of February, also try the Cheese Tasting Centre (daily 9–5) on Old Surrey Road. Guide Falls, just to the south, is an accessible waterfall and wet forest walk. Creative Paper Mills combines a contemporary gallery and working handmade paper mill (Mon–Fri 9–5, Sat, Sun 9–4).

✚ 355 T17 🚹 Tasmanian Travel and Information Centre, Civic Centre Precinct, Burnie, TAS 7320 ☎ 03 6434 6111 🕐 Daily 8–5

COLES BAY AND FREYCINET NATIONAL PARK

www.parks.tas.gov.au

Coles Bay, at the entrance to the Freycinet Peninsula and just outside the national park, is the jewel of the east coast with the island's most idyllic coastal scenery. Peaceful beach

Opposite *Coles Bay is at the entrance to Freycinet National Park*
Above *Waterfalls, like Liffey Falls near Deloraine, are common in the temperate rainforest*

walks, good food (local oysters) and summer swimming in perfect blue water are all found at the resort.

Tasmanian Aborigines spent summers diving for shellfish and collecting duck eggs from nearby Moulting Lagoon. The remains of their diet are recalled by the middens (shell-refuse mounds) on the coast. French navigator Nicholas Baudin named Freycinet in 1802.

Granite cliffs stretch along the peninsula with a soft fringe of she-oaks (casuarina) on most shorelines. The energetic can enjoy the national park's mountain and coast walks, the rock-climbing and sea-kayaking.

The highlight of the region is Wineglass Bay, on the oceanside of the peninsula. It is a spectacular beach, often ranked among the world's best. It's a moderate climb (1.5 hours round-trip) from Coles Bay for the view, longer (2.5 hours return) to the beach.

✚ 355 U17 ✉ Park via Coles Bay; park rangers based at Freycinet National Park Office ☎ 03 6256 7000 🚗 Vehicle A$24 or A$12 per person

CRADLE MOUNTAIN

▷ 288.

DELORAINE

www.greatwesterntiers.net.au

The 'hippest' town in the north relies less on attractions and more on atmosphere and lifestyle. This rural riverbank settlement has a distinctly English feel allied to a strong creative community. Since the 1970s the beauty of the nearby Western Tiers mountain range and bush has attracted and inspired artists and alternative lifestylers. It hosts Australia's biggest art and craft fair every October and November.

Liffey Falls, a 35km (22-mile) drive south, is the best of many good bush getaways beneath the Western Tiers.

✚ 355 T17 🚹 Great Western Tiers Visitor Centre, 98 Emu Bay Road, Deloraine, TAS 7304 ☎ 03 6362 3471

DEVONPORT

www.devonporttasmania.travel

The Bass Strait ferries from Melbourne and Sydney arrive at this port on the Mersey River, a rural town within reach of wilderness areas such as Cradle Mountain and Walls of Jerusalem. Mersey Bluff is the local highlight, with a sheltered beach, surf club and playground. Walk round Bluff Head to the lighthouse or the Tiagarra Aboriginal Cultural Centre and Museum, close to rock carvings. The Don River Railway operates steam or diesel weekend rail trips in town.

✚ 355 T17 🚹 Devonport Visitor Centre, 92 Formby Road, Devonport, TAS 7310, ☎ 03 6424 4466 🕐 Daily 7.30–5

INFORMATION

www.parks.tas.gov.au
☩ 355 T17 ⓘ Cradle Mountain
Visitor Centre, park entrance, off route
C132 ☎ 03 6492 1110 ⓒ Daily 8–7
✋ Tasmanian National Parks entry
fees: daily (24 hours), adult A\$16.50,
child A\$8.25 🛍 Park shop in the Visitor
Centre: postcards, books, film and
clothing. Some groceries available from
the campsite shop, Cradle Mountain
Lodge Store and Cradle View Restaurant

TIPS

» Avoid December to the end of February
for a purer experience—even the
Overland Track can host a crowd.
» Even if doing only one of the short
walks, be prepared for changes in
weather conditions. Take warm back-up
clothes, even if the sun is hot and the
sky clear.
» Time a trip to the park in late April,
when the autumn reddy-golds of the native
beech dominate the landscape.

Above *Snow can fall on Cradle Mountian
at almost any time of the year*

CRADLE MOUNTAIN–LAKE ST. CLAIR NATIONAL PARK

Tasmania's best-known wilderness attraction has the island's highest peaks and
the deepest lake. Cradle Mountain at 1,545m (5,068ft) overlooks the northern
end of the 85km (53-mile) Overland Track.

Cradle Mountain is a wilderness icon, a dolerite that was squeezed up
through other earth layers 174 million years ago. Its distinctive cradle shape
was caused largely by glacial action 500,000 years ago. The highest peak in
the park, at 1,617m (5,304ft), is Mount Ossa, which can be reached along the
Overland Track to or from Lake St. Clair. The lake, at the southern edge of the
park, is surrounded by other impressive peaks, including mounts Olympus,
Gould and Ida. The weather across this highland region can change very quickly
and heavy dumps of snow can occur, sometimes even in summer.

For shorter visits Cynthia Bay on Lake St. Clair is easily accessed off
the Lyell Highway and, at the northern end of the park, Cradle Mountain is
linked to the Cradle Link Road by a reasonable 7km (4-mile) gravel drive. At
both ends of the park, fantastic rainforest waterfalls and ridgeline lookouts
can be reached by as little as a 30-minute walk. The native wildlife includes
wallabies, wombats, echidnas and sometimes Tasmanian devils. Park rangers,
restaurants and accommodation are available at either end. The Lake St. Clair
Park Centre (tel 03 6289 1172; daily 8–5), has displays on the geology, natural
history and colonization of the highland area. A ferry plies between Cynthia Bay
and Narcissus Bay at the lake's northern end (tel 03 6289 1137).

The Wilderness Gallery at Cradle Mountain Chateau on the road into Cradle
Mountain is packed with Tasmanian crafts and is worth a stop.

BACKGROUND

Tasmanian Aborigines are thought to have used the route of the Overland Track
as a migration path. An Austrian, Gustav Weindorfer, made the sublime beauty of
Cradle Mountain known to the world when he campaigned for it to be protected
in the 1920s. Weindorfer and his partner Kate had come from Melbourne to farm
but fell in love with the remote high country. Waldheim Chalet, where Weindorfer
lived for much of his life, fell into disrepair in the 1970s but has since been rebuilt.
The national park was listed as part of the Tasmanian Wilderness World Heritage
Area in 1982.

EVANDALE
www.evandaletasmania.com
The hub of this village is a 19th-century streetscape. In February, the Evandale Village Fair brings the streets to life, including the National Penny-Farthing Championships. A drink at the central Clarendon Arms (1847) is recommended for local stories. Also refreshing is the Ingleside Bakery for its sweet treats in an original colonial period bakery. Evandale Village Market each Sunday sells antiques and home-made fare. Clarendon House, about 10km (6 miles) south of Evandale, was built in 1838 and is considered Australia's finest grand Georgian mansion (daily 10–4).

355 T17 Evandale Tourism and History Centre, 18 High Street, Evandale, TAS 7212 03 6391 8128

FRANKLIN-GORDON WILD RIVERS NATIONAL PARK
www.parks.tas.gov.au
This is a spectacular World Heritage wilderness, protected by its own very rugged nature and tempestuous climate. Most of it is difficult to access, unless you're really serious about bushwalking or rafting.

The Franklin and Gordon rivers achieved world fame in 1983 when they were saved from a hydroelectric dam project by a massive environmental protest. Visitors to the area need not be cut off by the layers of mountains above 1,200m (3,936ft) and dense temperate rainforest. There are easy walks to waterfalls and vantage points. Less sedate are the guided white-water rafting tours through Franklin's dramatic gorges.

Nelson Falls is a flat, 20-minute return walk through stunning rainforest to a high waterfall; Donaghy's Hill Lookout walk is a moderate 40-minute return climb for views of Frenchmans Cap, the most dramatic peak in the park.

355 T17 North via Lyell Highway (A10) or south via Gordon River Road (B61) 03 6471 2511 or 03 6289 1172 Vehicle A$24 or A$12 per person

HOBART
▷ 290.

LAUNCESTON
www.ltvtasmania.com.au
This small city—Tasmania's second largest—is loaded with charm. Built around the head of the broad Tamar River, many of the central streets are lined with Victorian houses and cottages and graced by the pretty City Park and Princes Square.

Established in 1805, a year after Hobart, Launceston has historically vied with the southern city for capital status. For much of the 20th century, it was a thriving industrial town, with textile factories, the Boags Brewery and mining interests. Tourism is now a mainstay.

All roads lead to the waterfront and a busy yacht basin. You can walk along the banks of the Tamar and the two Esk rivers, which meet in the heart of the city. Quadrant Mall, a historic, cobbled walkway, curves from Brisbane Street to St. John Street, where the clock tower of the post office is a prominent landmark. The Albert Hall is another commanding Victorian building, on the east side of the central district by the entrance to the beautiful City Park. The park has rotundas, a botanical pavilion and a popular macaque monkey enclosure.

On the west side of the city is the remarkable Cataract Gorge, a rocky chasm through which runs the South Esk, a sometimes thundering wild river. A magnificent walkway takes you through the cliffs to parkland, a restaurant and a chairlift. There is also a two-hour return walk to the eroded sandstone Painted Cliffs.

355 T17 Tasmanian Travel and Information Centre, 12–16 St. John Street, Launceston, TAS 7250 03 6336 3133 Mon–Fri 9–5, Sat 9–3, Sun 9–12

MARIA ISLAND NATIONAL PARK/ ORFORD
www.parks.tas.gov.au
No cars, no shops—sometimes no people. Be prepared to walk or take a bicycle to fully enjoy the 11,550ha (28,528-acre) island, which can be explored in two days. You can take your car with you; ferries leave from Triabunna, just north of Orford, for the 25-minute crossing.

Mount Maria at 709m (2,326ft) dominates a coastline of sandstone cliffs, quartzite folds, fossils and sheltered bays. Remains of a penal settlement and a late 19th-century entrepreneurial dream of wine, silk, tourism and cement works survive as ruined buildings, mostly at the former port town of Darlington. Orford, on the mainland, is also rich in history, pretty beaches and fishing spots.

355 U18 Via ferry (near Triabunna Visitor Centre) Ferry booking 0419 746 668 Ferry departs Triabunna Oct–12 Dec Mon, Wed, Fri, Sun 9.30, 4; 13 Dec–19 Apr daily 9.30, 4; 20 Apr–end Sep at 10.30, 3 Ferry round-trip: adult A$50, child (under 15) A$37. Park fees: Vehicle A$24 or A$12 per person Triabunna Visitor Centre, cnr Charles Street and Esplanade, Triabunna, TAS 7190 03 6257 4772

MOLE CREEK
www.greatwesterntiers.net.au
The one street settlement of Mole Creek is central to some of the best attractions in the northern region. Mole Creek Hotel is a good Aussie pub with Tasmanian tiger 'memorabilia'—if the marsupial mystery interests you, this is a good place to ask the locals. Otherwise track down the Trowunna Wildlife Park (daily 9–5). Wombats and wallabies roam the bushy park and keepers show why you should respect the Tasmanian devil's jaws. For a souvenir, try the local Tasmanian leatherwood honey.

There are two limestone caverns open to the public nearby, about 16km (10 miles) west of Mole Creek; Marakoopa Cave has a glow worm display, while King Solomons Cave is rich with great stalactites and stalagmites, and other beautiful cave decorations.

355 T17 Great Western Tiers Visitor Centre, 98 Emu Bay Road, Deloraine, TAS 7304 03 6363 3471

INFORMATION

www.hobarttravelcentre.com.au

➕ 355 U18 ℹ️ Hobart Travel Centre, Cnr Davey and Elizabeth streets, Hobart, TAS 7000 ☎ 03 6238 4222, 1800 979 440 🕐 Mon–Fri 8.30–5.15, Sat, Sun 9–5

HOBART

This small but spectacular harbour city is a dynamic mix of colonial heritage and vibrant contemporary culture. Battery Point is arguably the prettiest urban village in Australia.

Founded in 1804 (16 years after Sydney), Hobart is the second-oldest Australian city and the most southerly. It sits below Mount Wellington, which rises to 1,270m (4,166ft). The majority of interest and nightlife is close to the docks and waterfront warehouses, constructed on land reclaimed by the back-breaking work of the earliest convicts. A great number of colonial buildings survive, especially the warehouses in Salamanca Place and along Sullivans Cove. The state Parliament is close to Sullivans Cove, among many of the busiest pubs, restaurants and galleries. Victoria Dock is packed with the local fishing fleet. At the end of December a food and wine festival around the dock peaks with the finish of the Sydney to Hobart Yacht Race.

WHAT TO SEE

A lively dining precinct lies north of the city on Elizabeth Street. The Republic Bar is home to music, poetry and a radical spirit that gave birth to the world's first green political party.

The city's strong seafaring character is portrayed at the Maritime Museum of Tasmania (daily 9–5), one block up from the waterfront. The Tasmanian Museum and Art Gallery (daily 10–5) around the corner has important colonial paintings. Set on a hill, Battery Point is the old seamen's quarter, with great cafés and restaurants and the Narryna Heritage Museum (Mon–Fri 10.30–5, Sat, Sun 1.30–5) on Hampden Road.

South of the city, via Davey Street, is the historic Cascade Brewery, a tall sandstone building set against a backdrop of bush and Mount Wellington (tours daily 11 and 1).

The Royal Tasmanian Botanical Gardens at Queens Domain, 2km (1.2 miles) northeast from the city, were established in 1818 (daily from 8am).

Below *Hobart's Cascade Brewery has a distinctive silhouette*

MOUNT FIELD NATIONAL PARK

www.parks.tas.gov.au

Mount Field has a range of outdoor experiences, from a picnic just off the track to a 16km (10-mile) drive into the high country; the area is a popular skiing venue in winter and you may need snow chains. Some of the most spectacular features are within easy walking distance of the park entrance.

Originally home to the Big River tribe of Tasmanian Aboriginals, in 1885 Russell Falls was declared Tasmania's first nature reserve, and in 1916 Mount Field became its first national park.

The lower part of the park has a mix of eucalypt and sub-alpine forests, small rivers and often spectacular waterfalls. The upper part of the park is largely rocky alpine moorland, dotted with tarns (small glacial lakes) and the ski-field. A wheelchair-friendly path leads to Russell Falls, an emblem of Tasmania's temperate rainforest environments, and very popular with photographers.

✚ 355 T18 ✉ Via the Gordon River Road (B62/B61) to National Park and park entrance at Mount Field, TAS 7140 ☎ 03 6288 1149 ✋ Vehicle A$24 or A$12 per person

NEW NORFOLK

www.totallysouth.com.au

Just 33km (20 miles) west of Hobart, this classified historic town in the picturesque Derwent Valley is a good stop before the long drive to the west coast. Oast houses (tall drying sheds) in the landscape recall a tradition of hop growing. Local hops continue to enhance the highly regarded Tasmanian beers.

The Bush Inn (1815), overlooking the Derwent River, claims to be the oldest continually licensed hotel in Australia. The river is good for peaceful fishing or a thrilling jet-boat ride over rapids.

The Oast House Museum (daily 9–5) on the east (Hobart) side of town is a working museum.

✚ 355 T18 ✚ Derwent Valley Information Centre, Circle Street, New Norfolk, TAS 7140 ☎ 03 6261 3700

PORT ARTHUR

▷ 292.

RICHMOND

www.richmondvillage.com.au

Richmond is one of Australia's best-preserved historic villages. It is now the hub of a wine region and this is reflected in the town's café culture.

The rural river valley was originally explored by English settlers as early as 1803. It is now a pleasant short stop on the way to Port Arthur. Coal was the initial lure and also wallaby meat; the jail and military barracks soon followed. Richmond Bridge, built 1823–25, is one of the best examples of convict architecture. Richmond Gaol (Bathurst Street; daily 9–5), built in 1825, is Australia's oldest intact prison, and once held Ikey Solomon, supposedly the inspiration for Charles Dickens' Fagin, from *Oliver Twist*.

✚ 355 U18 ✚ Old Hobart Town (brochures only, not a booking office), TAS 7025 ☎ 03 6260 2502

ROSS

www.visitross.com.au

Ross, between Hobart and Launceston, was one of the earliest sites selected for a town in Tasmania in 1821. It remains a hub for one of the island's finest wool-growing areas and the history of this industry is told at the Tasmanian Wool Centre (daily 9–5). After Richmond (▷ 291), Tasmania's other great convict-built bridge (1836) is here, with 186 carvings by convict stonemason Daniel Herbert. The Man O'Ross Hotel (1835), just past the bridge, is a classic pub, with old 'cockies' (sheep farmers) lining the bar.

✚ 355 U17 ✚ Tasmanian Wool Centre, 50 Church Street, Ross, TAS 7209 ☎ 03 6381 5466 ⏰ Daily 9–5

SHEFFIELD

www.discovertasmania.com.au

A rural one-street supply town, Sheffield wound down in the 1980s until locals hit on the idea of painting the town—in fact much of the district—with large murals. Today it thrives as a lunch stop on the way to Cradle Mountain and a place to absorb the Tasmanian lifestyle. The murals tell of pioneering bushmen, farmers and wildlife but there is little to do after viewing them.

✚ 355 T17 ✚ Sheffield Visitor Information Centre, 5 Pioneer Crescent, Sheffield, TAS 7306 ☎ 03 6491 1036

Below *The Tasmanian Wool Centre at Ross tells the story of sheep farming in the district*

INFORMATION

www.portarthur.org.au

✚ 355 U18 ✉ Port Arthur, TAS
7182 ☎ 03 6251 2300 ⊕ Port Arthur
Historic Site information office and
grounds daily 8.30–dusk (dusk); restored
buildings 9–5 ✋ Adult A\$28, child
(4–17) A\$14 ❓ Convict Cemetery Tour
(daily; 30-minute tour), adult A\$12, child
A\$8; Historic Ghost Tour; 90-minute tour
(booking advised), adult A\$20, child A\$12
☕ The Port Café (in information office)
for meals, snacks, beverages; Museum
Coffee Shop (in Asylum building) for light
meals, snacks, beverages 🍴 Felons
(in information office, open evenings),
à la carte restaurant menu based on
Tasmanian ingredients 🏧 Port Arthur
Gift Shop: souvenirs, Tasmanian crafts,
books (daily 9–6)

TIP

» If you're cooking for yourself, be sure
to shop in normal trading hours because
there are no large supermarkets here and
the towns are quiet.

Above *Nubeena is 20 minutes west of
Port Arthur*

PORT ARTHUR AND THE TASMAN PENINSULA

Serenely beautiful today, Port Arthur is a memorial to a grim past when the
prison was a hell on earth for convicts transported from the United Kingdom.
The dramatic Tasman Peninsula first comes into view as you descend to
Eaglehawk Neck, overlooking the spectacular Pirates Bay. The isthmus was once
guarded against convicts escaping from Port Arthur. White pointer sharks along
this coast were also a deterrent to would-be escapees; the surfers don't seem
to care, but you may. The long beach at Eaglehawk Neck is perfect for walking,
surfing and fishing.

CONVICT HISTORY

About 12,000 sentences were served at Port Arthur from 1833 to1877. It was
an experimental prison, where from 1849 reform was sought through extreme
sensory deprivation in solitary cells. This regime of rehabilitation by isolation
was actually worse than the floggings of the early years and drove some
prisoners insane. Other inmates were put to mining coal or felling timber
either for the colony of Van Diemen's Land or the penal settlement itself,
which was almost self-sufficient in producing ships, clothing, bricks, furniture
and food. Decline in numbers started in the mid-19th century with the end of
convict transportation.

WHAT TO SEE

The rugged coast surrounding the settlement is typical of Tasmania. Tall
eucalypt forests are thick across the peninsula right up to the foreshore, and the
highest sea cliffs in Australia run along its eastern flank. Port Arthur Historic Site,
20km (12 miles) south of Eaglehawk Neck, occupies one of the more peaceful
and low-lying bays. Some 40ha (99 acres) of parkland are dotted with more than
30 prison ruins, including a roofless convict-built church (1837), the four-floor
penitentiary, and a stone cottage once occupied by the Irish revolutionary,
William Smith O'Brien. Across the water is the Isle of the Dead, where convicts
were buried. An impressive visitor information office enlivens the ruins.

The aptly named Tesselated Pavement, below the Lufra Hotel at Eaglehawk
Neck, was formed by erosion of the shoreline rocks; the Historic Ghost Tour
at Port Arthur leads you through a heritage of scary happenings. Remarkable
Cave, amid a dramatic cliff coastline, is a 10-minute drive south of Port Arthur,
past Palmers Lookout.

STRAHAN AND WEST COAST

www.westcoast.tas.gov.au
www.discovertasmania.com.au

Try sea-kayaking along the weather-beaten west coast or venture inland to the wilderness of rainforests, mountains and waterfalls.

Tasmania's west coast was one of Australia's most isolated regions until the mid-20th century. Strahan was established only in 1883 as a port on the huge Macquarie Harbour for the mining prospects in the mountains around Queenstown, Zeehan, Rosebery and Tullah.

The Sarah Island penal settlement in Macquarie Harbour (boat from Strahan) pre-dates the port by half a century. This was the most brutal prison in the British Empire. The convicts felled the durable, ship-building timber, Huon pine, unique to western Tasmania. This industry and a lumberjack-style bush culture flourished until the 1960s.

The small settlement of Strahan sprawls around the shores of Long Bay. Rainforest and buttongrass plains border the town and in places come close to the heart of the town. Mount Sorell is a distant backdrop. Rail and steamboat relics dot the shallows of the harbour, and wooden wrecks evoke pioneering times.

The Strahan Woodworks gallery at Morrison's Huon Pine Mill (daily 9–5), the Strahan Visitor Centre and the West Coast Wilderness Railway station are all by the harbour. The Railway's steam trains run through stunning scenery to and from Queenstown (bookings tel 1800 628 288; daily 10.15). River cruises, seaplanes, charter-fishing tours and jet-boats leave from the port, or you can try sea-kayaking under your own steam.

Driving a loop through Strahan, Queenstown and Zeehan is a rewarding day trip. Zeehan has the best museum and Queenstown has dramatically hued mountains as a result of extensive copper mining throughout the 20th century. However, it is Strahan that has comfort, coffee and food. Farther inland, a dense temperate rainforest full of unique species gives way to mountains, waterfalls and the Franklin-Gordon Wild Rivers National Park which can be accessed by cruise boats from Strahan. It is a good idea to study local weather forecasts before every move. The west is dramatic in any weather but heavy rain can make walking unpleasant.

Zeehan verges on a ghost town. The museum (daily 9–5) sits in a row of surviving grand buildings from the boom times—a fascinating capsule of 'wild west' history. A 5km (3-mile) gravel road from Strahan leads to Ocean Beach, Tasmania's longest: 34km (21 miles) of sand, breakers, huge dunes and the chance of a wild sunset.

➕ 355 S17 ℹ️ Strahan Visitor Centre, The Esplanade, Strahan, TAS 7468 ☎ 03 6472 6808 🕐 Daily 10–6 (may vary)

TAMAR VALLEY

www.discovertasmania.com.au
www.tamarvalley.com.au

A meander through the little towns along the broad Tamar River, from Launceston (▷ 289) to the Bass Strait, makes an excellent day or overnight trip. Apples and pears were once the principal produce of the valley but the region is now better known for its vineyards. Some of the best are around Rosevears, and there is a wine route for discerning tasters. The orchards, vineyards and roadside fruit and jams have been joined by a growing number of craftspeople and artists. Batman Bridge is the only link between the east and west banks, crossing near the towns of Deviot and Rowella.

One of Tasmania's earliest settlements was founded in 1804 near Beaconsfield, on the West Tamar. Beaconsfield itself was built around a gold rush in 1869, and one of the mines was reopened in the 1990s; some of the original buildings house the Grubb Shaft Gold and Heritage Museum (daily 9.30–4.30).

Seahorse World at Beauty Point is the world's first commercial sea horse farm with literally thousands on show (daily 9.30–3.30). Farther north near the western side of the Tamar mouth, two beaches dominate uncrowded Narawntapu National Park. Low Head Lighthouse (1833), the second to be built in Tasmania, stands on a headland with dramatic views.

➕ 355 T17 ℹ️ Tamar Visitor Information Centre, Main Road, Exeter, TAS 7275 ☎ 03 6394 4454

WALLS OF JERUSALEM NATIONAL PARK

www.parks.tas.gov.au

A spectacular plateau at 1,250m (4,100ft), part of the World Heritage area, the park provides a full-day walk. The Walls themselves are the dramatic but easily climbed dolerite peaks ringing the area—climb two in a day if you're camping (summer only). To get there from Launceston or Devonport, drive to Mole Creek then on to Lake Rowallan. A steep one-hour climb through dry forest reaches the plateau of the park itself – there are no roads into the park. Beneath the peaks are groves of ancient, gnarled pencil pines. Note: You must be an experienced walker and well equipped to enter the park.

➕ 355 T17 ✉️ Via the B12 west from Deloraine then Mersey Forest Road to Lake Rowallan ☎ 03 6363 5133 🚗 Vehicle A$24 or A$12 per person

WYNYARD

www.discovertasmania.com.au

Wynyard—a small fishing port and rural supply town on the estuary of the Inglis River—is a good place to just retreat. Quiet beaches are overlooked by the Table Cape at the northern edge of town. Typically from late September to mid-October a large tulip farm on top of the cape is in full bloom (open 10–4).

Farther west, Boat Harbour Beach is a special spot in the summer months. Inland, the red volcanic soil produces rich greenery.

➕ 355 T17 ℹ️ Wynyard Visitor Centre, 8 Exhibition Link, Wynyard, TAS 7325 ☎ 03 6443 8383 🕐 Mon–Sat 9–5, Sun 12.30–4.30

WALK

PASSAGE
A STROLL THROUGH
THE HEART OF HOBART

Take in the best of Hobart's historic waterfront, pass through the heart of the attractive residential area of Battery Point, and return through lively Salamanca Place.

THE WALK
Distance: 3.5km (2 miles)
Allow: 1 hour
Start at: Seaward corner of Victoria Dock and Hunter Street
End at: Seaward corner of Victoria Dock and Hunter Street

★ Leave the harbour warehouses and the fishing fleet crammed against the dock and head to the city (▷ 290). Turn at Mures Fish Centre, passing the moored fish punts, cross Davey Street, and go through a parking area to reach Macquarie Street and the Tasmanian Museum and Art Gallery.

❶ The museum and art gallery incorporate the 1808 Commissariat Store, which is Hobart's oldest building. The collections relate to the island's history, including convicts and Tasmanian Aborigines, and there is a good selection of colonial art.
Cross Argyle Street to the Maritime Museum of Tasmania in the Carnegie Building (▷ 290).

❷ The Maritime Museum tells the story of the island's seafaring tradition using objects (including boat models) and photographs. Touring exhibitions are shown in the Carnegie Gallery.

Return to Macquarie Street and turn left up the hill, past the tall General Post Office on the right and the Town Hall on the left, to Franklin Square, which fronts the first Government House. Face the harbour and walk down to Davey Street and turn right to walk along it to St. David's Park.

❸ The park was originally the graveyard of St. David's Cathedral (corner of Macquarie and Murray streets) and on the lowest side some early graves can still be seen. A large band rotunda marks the midpoint of the park.

Emerge at the highest corner of the park, on Harrington Street. Turn left, cross the first intersection, then turn left on to Hampden Road. Follow it to Battery Point, past 19th-century mansions, and cottages to No. 103, the Narryna Heritage Museum.

❹ Narryna Heritage Museum is in one of the area's oldest buildings (1836). Its original fittings include rare colonial Huon pine furniture (▷ 290).

Continue down Hampden Road and turn left into Arthur Circus.

❺ Arthur Circus, a well-preserved circle of small cottages, is built around a village green. St. George's Anglican Church completes the early colonial picture.

Back on Hampden Road, walk a short distance and turn right into Colville Street. Walk for about 100m (109 yards) to a pub called the Shipwrights Arms.

❻ The name of the Shipwrights Arms pub reflects the maritime occupations of the original inhabitants—sailors, boat builders, labourers, sea captains. The 1846 pub is decorated inside with maritime images and historical snippets. The surrounding mariners' cottages made up the hub of the early seafaring community in Hobart.

Go back to Hampden Road. Follow it for another 200m (218 yards) as it changes to the long, sweeping curve of Castray Esplanade around Princes Park.

❼ Stop for a while to take in the harbour views. Princes Park was originally the site of a gun battery that protected the harbour; the suburb was named after the battery. The 1818 signalling station survives.

Continue on Castray Esplanade, with Sullivans Cove on your right, to Salamanca Place.

❽ Salamanca Place is dominated by early colonial warehouses and buildings redolent of the harbour's maritime and commercial origins. They now house art galleries, bookshops, gift shops, cafés, pubs and restaurants. The well-known Salamanca Market is held here on Saturdays.

Princes Wharf, alongside the cove, is the main venue for the Taste of Tasmania Festival around New Year's Day.

Follow the curve of the wharf back to the start at Victoria Dock. Pass the sandstone Parliament House and the modern Brooke Street Pier to the Derwent Ferry departure wharves.

❾ Two ships here give a sense of early Hobart's bustling waterfront. Pride of place belongs to the restored *May Queen*, one of only five wooden boats of its age (1860s) in the world still afloat. Another sailing treasure, the *Lady Nelson*, a colonial square rigger, is moored at nearby Elizabeth Street Pier. The *Lady Nelson* is available for charter and regularly sails the Derwent River in the warmer months. From Elizabeth Street Pier you can return to Victoria Dock.

Opposite *Hobart's Victoria Dock*
Above *Explore the historic area of Battery Point*

WHEN TO GO
All year round.

WHERE TO EAT
Jackman & McRoss Bakery, 57–59 Hampden Road, Battery Point or at 4 Victoria Street, Hobart (daily from 7.30am).

PUBLIC TOILETS
Both museums; Franklin Square; St. David's Park.

Below *Eating out in Salamanca Place*

DRIVE

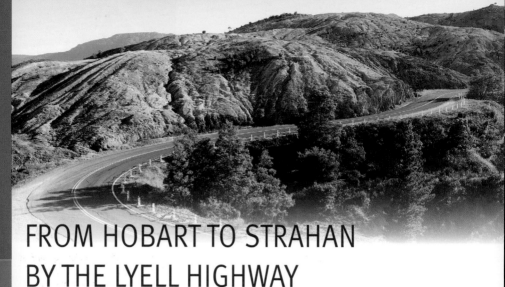

REGIONS

FROM HOBART TO STRAHAN
BY THE LYELL HIGHWAY

This east–west drive across Tasmania (▷ 286–293) samples a cross-section of the island's landscapes, from farmland to wild mountains. Journey's end is beautiful Strahan, gateway to the remote West Coast.

THE DRIVE
Distance: 350km (217 miles)
Allow: 2 days
Start at: Hobart
End at: Strahan

★ From Hobart, drive northwest on the Brooker Highway (National Highway 1). At Granton, the Lyell Highway (A10) takes over from the Brooker and leads through rural scenery along the Derwent River to New Norfolk.

❶ New Norfolk is the major town of the Derwent Valley, and a former hub for hop-growing (▷ 291). The Bush Inn is a good place to stop for refreshments, and there are walks along the riverside.

Continue on the Lyell Highway to the town of Hamilton, passing poppy fields, old hop-drying oast houses, scattered farms and one-pub hamlets like Gretna.

Above *The bare hills of Queenstown*

❷ Stroll around the wide streets of Hamilton to admire the historic sandstone buildings. The town grew rapidly in the early 1800s, but stagnated from the middle of the 19th century. The lack of subsequent development preserved many of the town's early buildings.

Soon after Hamilton, the highway climbs to higher, wilder country. Native vegetation takes over from farmland until eventually all signs of agriculture vanish. Drive to Derwent Bridge, passing through the buttongrass plains that characterize Tasmania's southwest highlands.

❸ Approaching the hamlet of Derwent Bridge, you can see some of the many peaks of the central highlands and the southwest. Mount Olympus (1,447m/4,746ft) rises to the northwest and marks the western corner of Lake St. Clair. A 5km (3-mile) side road going north from the middle of the settlement leads to the lake, at the southeastern

end of Cradle Mountain–Lake St. Clair National Park (▷ 288). Cynthia Bay is well worth a visit, as are the nearby café and interpretation office. Derwent Bridge is a good area for an overnight stop. Before leaving, top up the fuel tank, as it is the last filling station for the next 83km (51 miles).

Return to the highway and drive west into the mountains. After about 15km (9.5 miles) the dramatic peak of Mount King William I rises south of the road to 1,324m (4,343ft). There are several stopping points for lookouts and nature trails along this part of the highway, the first one being King William Saddle.

❹ King William Saddle Lookout gives great views of this mountainous country, much of which is encompassed by Cradle Mountain–Lake St. Clair National Park to the north, and Franklin-Gordon Wild Rivers National Park to the south. The saddle marks a change in vegetation: The

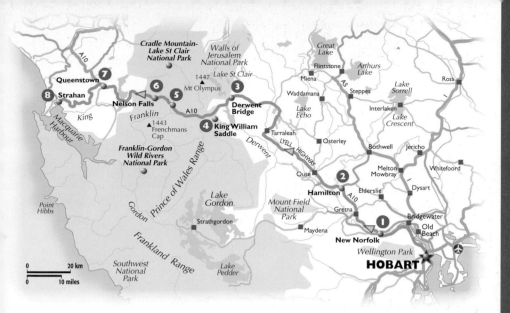

distinctive west coast temperate rainforest—notable for king billy pines and pandani—takes over from the eucalypts and buttongrass of the east. A short drive away is the Surprise Valley Lookout, which has wonderful views of the U-shape glacial valley and Frenchmans Cap to the southwest.

Continue west, descending steeply by the Mount Arrowsmith pass. Pull in where the highway crosses the Franklin River.

❺ The Franklin River Nature Trail starts here, and leads for an easy 1km (0.6 mile) into temperate rainforest.

After the walk, drive a few kilometres west along the highway to Donaghy's Hill, where a moderate 40-minute return climb takes you to Donaghy's Hill Lookout. There are magnificent views from here southwest to Frenchmans Cap, which at 1,443m (4,733ft) is the most inspiring peak of the region.

Drive on for several kilometres, descending the Victoria Pass. Cross the Nelson River Bridge, and turn into the parking area for Nelson Falls.

❻ Nelson Falls is a level 20-minute walk through jungle-like temperate rainforest. Colourful fungi and a tangle of creeping vines and ferns predominate. The falls are spectacular after good rains.

On from here, the Bradshaw Bridge takes the Lyell Highway across Lake Burbury, with mountains and high ridges rising from its shores. A few kilometres farther on are the small towns of Gormanston and Linda and then Queenstown just beyond.

❼ Gormanston and Linda are fascinating run-down mountain towns that evoke the heyday of the mining boom during the late 19th century. The once-thriving Royal Hotel by the side of the highway at Linda is now, sadly, derelict. This is strange-looking country—mountainous, but with the worked-over appearance of a vast quarry.

A winding descent along the highway brings you to Queenstown. After so much wilderness, Queenstown comes as a shocking yet fascinating contrast, as more than 100 years of mining have stripped the vegetation and soil on hills around the town to bare rock. Queenstown itself has a number of

Victorian buildings, including the Eric Thomas Galley Museum, housed in a former hotel, telling the town's story in photographs. Steam trains of the West Coast Wilderness Railway run from Queenstown to Strahan on a rugged and scenic route.

The last stage is a winding 40-minute drive to Strahan.

❽ The town and port of Strahan have much to offer the visitor, including museums, restaurants, bushwalks and cruises on Macquarie Harbour (▷ 293).

WHEN TO GO
All year round. October to the end of April are the ideal, warmer months; other times are beautiful, if cool to cold.

WHERE TO EAT
Derwent Bridge: Lake St. Clair Visitor Centre; Derwent Bridge Hotel; Derwent Bridge Roadhouse (fuel stop).

PUBLIC TOILETS
At Derwent Bridge or Lake St. Clair. There's a basic composting toilet at the Franklin River Nature Trail (stop No. 5), between Derwent Bridge and Queenstown.

WHAT TO DO

BRUNY ISLAND
BRUNY ISLAND CRUISES
www.brunycruises.com.au
These fast-moving eco cruises take visitors on half and full day tours of the astonishing coastline of Bruny Island, with seals, muttonbirds, albatross and sometimes (May to July and September to November) whales for company.
✉ 915 Adventure Bay Road, Adventure Bay, Bruny Island, TAS 7150 ☎ 03 6293 1465 ♿ Adult A$100, child S$55 (half day), adult A$150, child A$110 (full day)

BURNIE
BEACH HOTEL
This lively, friendly pub, within a stone's throw of the beach, has occasional live music.
✉ 1 Wilson Street, Burnie, TAS 7320 ☎ 03 6431 2333 ⏰ Sun–Wed until late, Thu–Sat until 2am ♿ Free

CRADLE MOUNTAIN
THE WILDERNESS GALLERY
www.thewildernessgallery.com.au
Tasmania's wild landscapes and unique plant and animal life have inspired many photographers. This gallery features the work of the best of them, and a shop sells cards and prints.

✉ Cradle Mountain Chateau, Cradle Mountain Road, Cradle Mountain, TAS 7306 ☎ 03 6492 1404 ⏰ Daily 10–5 ♿ A$5

DELORAINE
ASHGROVE CHEESE
www.ashgrovecheese.com.au
A short drive west of Deloraine is this farmhouse shop run by the Bennett family, who make traditional, English-style hard cheeses, including tasty Cheddars, Cheshire, Gloucester and Wensleydale with milk from their own cows. Tasmanian native bush peppers flavour some varieties.
✉ 6173 Bass Highway, Elizabeth Town, TAS 7304 ☎ 03 6368 1105 ⏰ Daily Oct–Apr 7.30–6, May–Sep 7.30–5

DEVONPORT
ALLGOODS
www.allgoods.com.au
This shop has a wide choice of quality equipment for adventure adventures including clothing, footwear, wet-weather and camping gear. The staff is an excellent source of information on all outdoor activities throughout the island.
✉ 6 Formby Road, Devonport, TAS 7310 ☎ 03 6424 7099 ⏰ Mon–Fri 9–5.30, Sat 9–4, Sun 10–2

CMAX CINEMAS
www.cmax.net.au
A modern movie-theatre complex with first-release films.
✉ 5–7 Best Street, Devonport, TAS 7310 ☎ 03 6420 2111 ⏰ Daily ♿ Adult A$13.50, child A$9.50

FORTH BRIDGE HOTEL
www.forthpub.com.au
Bands play here regularly at the Bridge Hotel, a short drive west of Devonport.
✉ Main Road, Forth, TAS 7310 ☎ 03 6428 2239 ⏰ Daily, Thu–Sat until 12am or 2am ♿ Free most nights

WAREHOUSE NITECLUB
This popular place is an Aussie beer-barn style of nightclub. Touring bands sometimes play here.
✉ 18–22 King Street, Devonport, TAS 7310 ☎ 03 6424 7851 ⏰ Wed–Thu, 8pm–12am, Fri, Sat 7pm–5am ♿ A$5

FRANKLIN
WOODEN BOAT DISCOVERY CENTRE
Tasmania has a long history of wooden boat building and this

Above Don't miss the Saturday market at Salamanca Place

fascinating centre is dedicated to maintaining the traditional skills of the shipwright. The centre displays tools and the boats that are made in the adjacent Wooden Boat Centre, which uses native Tasmanian timbers to build small boats.
✉ Main Road, Franklin, TAS 7113 ☎ 03 6264 1838 ⏰ Daily 9.30–5

HOBART

AURORA STADIUM
www.aurorastadium.com
Australian Rules football is Tasmania's premier sport, and watching one of these fast, exciting games is highly recommended. Aurora Park is the state's main venue for both national (AFL) and Tasmanian league games.
✉ York Park, Launceston, TAS 7250 ☎ 03 6323 3666 or 03 6323 3213 (tickets), 03 6323 3383 (general enquiries) ⏰ Matches (Apr–end Oct only) Fri, Sat, Sun ✋ From A$35 adult, $14 child 🚌 Just north of the city centre, across the North Esk River

BELLERIVE OVAL
www.tascricket.com.au
This attractive ground by the Derwent River hosts the main inter-state cricket competition (the Pura Cup), as well as an international one-day game in January. Guided tours of the 16,000-seat stadium are available on Tuesdays.
✉ Derwent Street, Bellerive, TAS 7018 ☎ 03 6211 4000 ⏰ Tasmania play four- and one-day inter-state matches Nov–end Mar ✋ From A$8 per day 🚌 Metro bus

DERWENT ENTERTAINMENT CENTRE
www.derwent.com.au
Star names perform at this modern auditorium, Tasmania's biggest live venue.
✉ Brooker Highway, Glenorchy, TAS 7010 ☎ 03 6273 0233 ⏰ Dependent on shows ✋ Most concerts A$45–A$80 🚌 Metro bus 🚌 🍴

FEDERATION CONCERT HALL
www.tso.com.au
The Tasmanian Symphony Orchestra performs at this modern concert hall on Hobart's waterfront.

✉ Adjacent to Grand Chancellor Hotel, Davey Street, Hobart, TAS 7000 ☎ 03 6235 3633 (box office) ⏰ Check website for dates ✋ Adult A$50–A$80

FISH WILD TASMANIA
www.fishwildtasmania.com
Fish Wild's guided trips include sea-fishing for salmon and bream, and fly-fishing for trout in highland lakes.
✉ 115A King Street, Sandy Bay, TAS 7005 ☎ 0418 348 223 or 03 6223 8917 ⏰ Fishing all year; closed seasons for different fisheries (trout closed from end Apr–beg Aug) ✋ From A$285 for one day 🚌 Sandy Bay

JAM PACKED
www.jampacked.com.au
Sit under a dramatic glass atrium and enjoy coffee, tasty home-made treats, and delicious chocolates at this first-rate store and café.
✉ 27 Hunter Street, Hobart, TAS 7000 ☎ 03 6231 3454 ⏰ Daily 8–5.30 🚌 Metro bus

PEACOCK THEATRE
www.salarts.org.au
Part of the Salamanca Arts Centre, the theatre stages innovative dance, drama, debates and recitals.
✉ Salamanca Arts Centre, 77 Salamanca Place, Hobart, TAS 7000 ☎ 03 6234 8414 ✋ A$30–A$55 🚌 Salamanca, Metro bus 🍴

REPUBLIC BAR AND CAFÉ
www.republicbar.com
Hobart's best pub-music venue hosting live blues, roots and jazz.
✉ 299 Elizabeth Street, Hobart, TAS 7000 ☎ 03 6234 6954 ⏰ Daily until 2am ✋ Variable; bar free before bands start 🚌 North Hobart

SALAMANCA MARKET
www.salamanca.com.au
Spend a few hours or a whole day browsing the stalls of this open-air market, which fills three waterfront blocks. Many of Tasmania's artisans display their wares and there's plenty of good food and music.
✉ Salamanca Place, Hobart, TAS 7000 ☎ 03 6238 2843 ⏰ Sat 8.30–3 🚌 Salamanca Place, Metro bus

SYRUP
www.syrupclub.com
Syrup is Hobart's best dance club, with a pulsating atmosphere and high-profile visiting DJs. You can dance till dawn.
✉ 39 Salamanca Place, Hobart, TAS 7000 ☎ 03 6224 8249 ⏰ Thu–Sat 8pm–3 or 5am ✋ From A$10

TASAIR
www.tasair.com.au
Take a scenic flight over the vast wilderness and coastal areas, including remote Bathurst Harbour in the southwest.
✉ Hobart International Airport ☎ 03 6248 5088 ⏰ All year, weather permitting 🚌 Hobart Airport ✋ 30-minute scenic flight over Hobart area A$115; 2.5-hour scenic flights over southern Tasmania A$298 📍 17km (10.5 miles) northeast of Hobart

TASMANIAN MAP CENTRE
www.map-centre.com.au
This one-stop shop two blocks north of Hobart Mall has an extensive selection of maps and guidebooks for Tasmania and other destinations, and other guides for camping, walking and off-road driving.
✉ 100 Elizabeth Street, Hobart, TAS 7000 ☎ 03 6231 9043 ⏰ Mon–Fri 9.30–5.30, Sat 10.30–3.30

Below The haunted auditorium at Hobart's Theatre Royal

THEATRE ROYAL

www.theatreroyal.com.au

Completed in 1837, this architectural gem is Australia's oldest working theatre (with a resident ghost).

✉ 29 Campbell Street, Hobart, TAS 7000 ☎ 03 6233 2299 🕓 Box office: Mon–Fri 9–5, Sat 9–1 ✋ A$35–A$85 🚌 Metro bus

WREST POINT HOTEL CASINO

www.wrestpoint.com.au

This large complex just outside the city centre includes Hobart's casino, restaurants, five bars and two entertainment venues. The Showroom features intimate cabaret and comedy acts, while the Entertainment Centre stages larger shows.

✉ Sandy Bay, Hobart, TAS 7005 ☎ 03 6225 0112 🕓 Daily, casino to 2am Sun–Thu, 4am Fri, Sat. Call for details of performance times ✋ Casino free, shows from A$33 🚌 Metro bus to Wrest Point

Below *Evandale hosts the annual National Penny Farthing Campionships every February*

LAUNCESTON

BOAGS BREWERY

www.boags.com.au

Situated on the river Esk in Launceston, Tasmania, Boag's Brewery is a great place to sample traditional-style bitters, ale and lager that display the real craftsmanship treasured by connoisseurs. The 90-minute brewery tours include a beer and cheese tasting. Bookings are essential.

✉ 39 William Street, Launceston, TAS 7250 ☎ 03 6332 6300 ✋ Adult A$25, child A$22

DESIGN CENTRE OF TASMANIA

www.designcentre.com.au

The Design Centre displays the work of some of Tasmania's best craftworkers and designers. Its Tasmanian Wood Design Collection is a world-class assemblage of contemporary woodwork that uses timber native to Tasmania. Pieces range from elegant items of furniture to delicate smaller items.

✉ Cnr Tamar and Brisbane streets,

Launceston, TAS 7250 ☎ 03 6331 5506 🕓 Mon–Fri 9.30–5.30, Sat, Sun 10–2 ✋ Adult A$5, child under 18 free

EARL ARTS CENTRE

www.theatrenorth.com.au

A small venue staging experimental productions, music recitals and touring shows.

✉ 10 Earl Street, Launceston, TAS 7250 ☎ 03 6323 3666 ✋ A$15–A$40

PRINCESS THEATRE

www.theatrenorth.com.au

This 19th-century theatre hosts an intermittent schedule of theatre and dance.

✉ 57 Brisbane Street, Launceston, TAS 7250 ☎ 03 6323 3666 🕓 Box office: Mon–Fri 9–5.30, Sat 9.30–1 ✋ A$25–A$90

COUNTRY CLUB TASMANIA

www.countryclubtasmania.com.au

This is one of the very few late-night options in Launceston. It's a 10-minute taxi ride from the city centre.

✉ Country Club Avenue, Prospect, near Launceston, TAS 7250 ☎ 03 6335 5779

Nightly, generally to 1am Sun–Fri, 3am Sat Free

COUNTRY CLUB TASMANIA GOLF COURSE

www.countryclubtasmania.com.au
A ritzy country club with a demanding 18-hole course.
Country Club Avenue, Prospect, TAS 7250 03 6335 5777 Summer daily 7.30am–9pm; winter 8–6 18 holes A$60, 9 holes A$40

TASMANIAN EXPEDITIONS

www.tas-ex.com
Choose from about 25 itineraries—paddling, bicycling and walking. Tours are three to thirteen days, or go on a half- or full-day climb.
PO Box 5010, Launceston, TAS 7250
03 6339 3999 or 1300 666 856
Longer trips Oct–end Apr; three-day walking trips (Cradle Mountain, Freycinet National Park) all year seven-day walk and bicycle: A$1,850 (costs and equipment); three-day walks: A$890 all-inclusive; three-day kayaking A$1,995

AQUARIUS ROMAN BATHS

www.romanbaths.com.au
These baths follow the layout of a Roman bath, in which bathers enter a number of hot rooms in turn, and then warm and hot baths before a cold plunge. Massages, a beauty clinic, café, solarium and gymnasium complete the complex.
127–133 George Street, Launceston, TAS 7250 03 6331 2255 Mon–Fri 7–8, Sat, Sun 9–6 Baths from A$26; massage from A$52

PORT ARTHUR

TASMAN GOLF CLUB

There's a trust system for green fees and a famous eighth hole over cliffs to the sea at this 9-hole course.
Point Puer Road, Port Arthur, TAS 7182 03 6250 2444 Course: daily; Clubhouse/bar: Sun, Tue Green fees A$15 per day

STRAHAN

STRAHAN VISITOR CENTRE

www.roundearth.com.au/ship.htm
Every night sees an amusing performance of The Ship that

FESTIVALS AND EVENTS

DECEMBER–JANUARY

HOBART SUMMER FESTIVAL

www.hobartsummerfestival.com.au
The biggest festival in Tasmania. The highlight is the Taste of Tasmania, a food and wine festival that coincides with the arrival of the yachts in the Sydney-to-Hobart ocean classic.

JANUARY

CYGNET FOLK FESTIVAL

www.cygnetfolkfestival.org
Fans of folk and world music descend on the small coastal town of Cygnet, 50km (31 miles) south of Hobart for the Cygnet Folk Festival. Local, interstate and international musicians attend.

FEBRUARY

FESTIVALE

www.festivale.com.au
Launceston stages its biggest event, Festivale, over three days in mid-February. City Park is filled with food and wine stalls, drama and music.

AUSTRALIAN WOODEN BOAT FESTIVAL

www.australianwoodenboatfestival.com.au
Hundreds of wooden boats drop anchor in Hobart's Constitution Dock and Sullivans Cove for the biennial Wooden Boat Festival. There are also boat-building exhibitions, model-boat displays, street drama and food stalls. The festival takes place in odd-numbered years.

Never Was, with plenty of audience participation.
The Esplanade, Strahan, TAS 7468
03 6471 7622 Daily 5.30pm
Adult A$17.50, child A$7.50, under 13s free

SWANSEA

KATE'S BERRY FARM

www.katesberryfarm.com

EVANDALE VILLAGE FAIR

www.evandalevillagefair.com
Each February, bicyclists from around the world take part in the National Penny-Farthing Championships, the highlight of the Evandale Village Fair.

APRIL

TEN DAYS ON THE ISLAND

www.tendaysontheisland.org
A major arts festival, staged in odd-numbered years, that showcases the best visual and performance art from island cultures around the globe. Venues are across the state.

TARGA TASMANIA

www.targa.org.au
The fastest touring, sports and GT cars in the world race in stages across the state for the six days of Targa Tasmania.

MAY

AGFEST

www.agfest.com.au
Agfest, staged near Launceston over three days, is a huge agricultural trade show and fair.

OCTOBER–NOVEMBER

TASMANIAN CRAFT FAIR

www.tascraftfair.com.au
The Tasmanian Craft Fair at Deloraine is Australia's largest. It takes place over four days.

On a hillside just south of Swansea, this pretty farm grows luscious berries that explode in the mouth. Out of season there are all-natural berry flavourings, jams sauces, chocolates and delicious berry ice creams. Try one of Kate's home-made fruit pies at the on-site café.
12 Addison Street, Swansea, TAS 7190
03 62578 428 Daily 9.30–4.30

EATING

PRICES AND SYMBOLS

The restaurants are listed alphabetically (excluding Le, La and Les). The prices given are the average for a two-course lunch (L) and a three-course dinner (D) for one person, without drinks. The wine price is for the least expensive bottle.

For a key to the symbols, ▷ 2.

CAMBRIDGE
MEADOWBANK ESTATE VINEYARD RESTAURANT

www.meadowbankwines.com.au
This winery, a short drive from Hobart, is also home to an acclaimed restaurant. The regularly changing menu relies on Tasmania's fine seasonal produce, with dishes such as local Barilla Bay oysters, Flinders Island lamb and Spring Bay scallops. The excellent food can be accompanied by Meadowbank's own cool-climate red and white wines, and there are great views over the vineyards and surrounding countryside.
✉ 699 Richmond Road, Cambridge, TAS 7170 ☎ 03 6248 4484 🕐 Daily 12–3 (also wine tasting 10–5) 🖐 L A$45, Wine A$26.50 🚍 A 15-minute drive northwest of Hobart, on the way to Richmond

COLES BAY
EDGE OF THE BAY

www.edgeofthebay.com.au
With a wonderful setting on Coles Bay looking across to the Hazards Mountains, this innovative restaurant is run by four friends who ensure an intimate and friendly atmosphere.

The imaginative, modern cuisine includes game and wallaby in winter and fresh local seafood in summer. Vegan and vegetarian meals are available. The wine list focuses on Tasmanian and Australian wines with a list of cellar specials. It is best to reserve ahead.
✉ 2308 Main Road, Coles Bay, TAS 7215 ☎ 03 6257 0102 🕐 Daily from 6.30 🖐 D A$29, Wine A$68 🚍 On the main road into Coles Bay

CRADLE MOUNTAIN
WEINDORFERS

Hearty home cooking with a Swedish influence makes this restaurant, within sight of Mount Roland, an excellent lunch stop.

There is a strong emphasis on local farm produce aided by a good range of local wines as well as Tasmanian beers. Vegan, vegetarian

and children's meals are available. Reserve ahead.
✉ Wellington Street, Gowrie Park, TAS 7306 ☎ 03 6491 1385 🕐 Daily 10–10, group bookings only during winter months 🖐 L A$25, D A$40, Wine A$24.50 🚍 15km (9.5 miles) southwest from Sheffield on the C136 to Cradle Mountain

DELORAINE
CHRISTMAS HILLS RASPBERRY FARM CAFÉ

www.raspberryfarmcafe.com
The country-style menu makes innovative use of raspberries and the sweets menu is very popular. Vegan, vegetarian and children's meals are available. The wine list favours Tasmanian vineyards.
✉ 9 Christmas Hills Road, Bass Highway, Elizabeth Town, TAS 7304 ☎ 03 6362 2186 🕐 Daily 7–5 🖐 L A$20, Wine A$23 🚍 15km (9.5 miles) northwest from Deloraine on Highway 1 to Devonport

HOBART
FISH FRENZY

www.fishfrenzy.com.au
Set on the waterfront, this is arguably Tasmania's best fish and chip café. The calamari salad is invariably superb.

Opposite *The Meadowbank Estate Vineyard Restaurant at Cambridge*

✉ Elizabeth Street Pier, Hobart, TAS 7000
☎ 03 6231 2134 🕑 Daily 11–9
🖐 L A$22, D A$35, Wine A$22

JACKMAN & McROSS

This prominent café on Battery Point is an exceptional bakehouse with some of the friendliest service in Hobart. For light meals expect pastries, pizzas, pies and rich sweets; try a breakfast of strong coffee and a half-size buttermilk fruit loaf. Credit cards are not accepted.
✉ 57–59 Hampden Road, Battery Point, Hobart, TAS 7004 ☎ 03 6223 3186
🕑 Mon–Fri 7.30–6, Sat, Sun 7.30–5. Closed public holidays 🖐 A$19 per person

LEBRINA RESTAURANT

A series of small, elegant rooms in a historic cottage is the refined showcase for the talents of Chef Scott Minervini, who brings skill and finesse to the classics of the French and northern Italian kitchen.
✉ 155 New Town Road, New Town, TAS 7008 ☎ 03 6228 7775 🕑 Tue–Sat 7–9.30 🖐 D A$75, Wine A$33

MALDINI

www.maldini.com.au
This café-restaurant's menu includes pastas and other Italian dishes.
✉ 47 Salamanca Place, Hobart, TAS 7000 ☎ 03 6223 4460 🕑 Daily 8am–late
🖐 L A$45, D A$60, Wine A$29.50

MURES UPPER DECK

www.muresupperdeck.com.au
A long-standing favourite on the local food scene, this dockside restaurant serves up a seafood feast, with the sound of seagulls and the local fishing fleet as a backdrop. Delicious fresh fish.
✉ Victoria Dock, Hobart, TAS 7000
☎ 03 6231 1999 🕑 Daily 12–3, 6–11
🖐 L A$45, D A$55, Wine A$32.50

RETRO CAFÉ

A good place to watch life on the waterfront, where there are simple but good-tasting breakfast and light meals for lunch.

✉ 33 Salamanca Place, Hobart, TAS 7000
☎ 03 6223 3073 🕑 Mon–Sat 8–6, Sun 8.30–6 🖐 L A$33

LATROBE (DEVONPORT)
HOUSE OF ANVERS

www.anvers-chocolate.com.au
At this Belgian chocolate factory there are indoor and outdoor cafés, and you can also watch the chocolate-making process. Igor Van Gerwen, the proprietor, swears that Tasmanian butter is the richest he has tasted. That and 64 per cent cocoa content make for very rich chocolate. Try the French-Belgian breakfast consisting of chocolate croissant or brioche. Truffles are another house special.
✉ 2025 Bass Highway, Latrobe, TAS 7307 ☎ 03 6426 2703 🕑 Daily 7–7
🖐 L A$28 🚗 10km (6 miles) southeast from Devonport on Highway 1 to Launceston, 5km (3 miles) from Latrobe, on the right side of the road

LAUNCESTON
THE GORGE RESTAURANT

Originally set up as a tea room in 1892, this restaurant has a most romantic setting in the Cataract Gorge and Cliff grounds. At night the cries of peacocks echo through one of Launceston's oldest gardens. View Cataract Gorge cliffs by moonlight or wander around the gently lit paths and rotunda. The meals are traditional and sumptuous, with meat and seafood dishes complemented by a strong wine list.
✉ Cataract Gorge Cliff Grounds, Launceston, TAS 7250 ☎ 03 6331 3330
🕑 Tue–Sun 12–2.30, Tue–Sat 6.30–9. Kiosk daily 9–5 for Devonshire teas
🖐 L A$35, D A$45, Wine A$28 🚗 Cross Kings Bridge and drive to top of Trevallyn

HARI'S CURRY

Value eating with Bollywood classics playing on the TV. Northern Indian favourites: Tandoori a house special. Vegetable curry is available, but there are no vegan dishes on the menu. BYO wine.
✉ 150–152 York Street, Launceston, TAS 7250 ☎ 03 6331 6466 🕑 Daily 5–10
🖐 D A$33

MUD BAR AND RESTAURANT

www.mudbar.com.au
Casual, stylish and very popular, patrons come for the excellent coffee and cocktails, as well as the keenly priced Modern Australian cuisine and the comprehensive wine list.
✉ 28 Seaport Boulevard, Launceston, TAS 7250 ☎ 03 6334 5066 🕑 Daily 11am–12am 🖐 L A$45, D A$70, Wine A$35

STILLWATER AT RITCHIE'S MILL

www.stillwater.net.au
By day this is an informal café, but in the evening it becomes one of Australia's best creative restaurants. Set inside a picturesque 19th-century flour mill on the banks of the River Tamar, it has good views of the yacht basin. The mill gallery sells gifts. Freestyle Modern Australian food can be ordered as a series of small courses instead of one main course. Local seafood and game are specials. The wine list has over 300 choices with a Tasmanian bias. Reserve ahead.
✉ Paterson Street, Launceston, TAS 7250 ☎ 03 6331 4153 🕑 Mon–Sat 8.30am–late, Sun 8.30–3 🖐 L A$40, D A$85 (three courses), A$105 (six-course tasting menu), Wine A$32

STRAHAN
FRANKLIN MANOR

www.franklinmanor.com.au
Established gardens and timber verandas mark this luxurious restaurant, close by the harbour and near Regatta Point. The menu is a harmonious marriage of French and Australian cuisines using local seafood. Specials are crayfish, abundant on the west coast, scallops and oysters. A seven-course tasting dinner with matching wines to each dish is also available. The extensive wine list is excellent. It is a good idea to reserve ahead.
✉ The Esplanade, Strahan, TAS 7468
☎ 03 6471 7311 🕑 Daily from 6.30
🖐 D A$110, Wine A$39 🚗 150m (164 yards) from town centre, around harbour to Regatta Point

PRICES AND SYMBOLS

Prices are for a double room for one night including breakfast, unless otherwise stated. All the hotels listed accept credit cards, unless otherwise stated. Note that rates can vary widely throughout the year.

For a key to the symbols, ▷ 2.

CRADLE MOUNTAIN
CRADLE MOUNTAIN LODGE

www.cradlemountainlodge.com.au
Luxurious wood-cabin retreat.
✉ Cradle Mountain Road, TAS 7306
☎ 03 6492 2103 (general enquiries),
1300 806 192 (reservations) ⊕ All year
♨ A$270–A$750 ① 88 🚍 82km
(51 miles) southwest from Devonport via
B14 to Sheffield then C136 and C132 roads

DERWENT BRIDGE
DERWENT BRIDGE CHALETS AND STUDIOS

www.derwent-bridge.com
Chalets with kitchens.
✉ 15478 Lyell Highway, east end of

Derwent Bridge, TAS 7410 ☎ 03 6289
1000 ⊕ All year ♨ A$145–A$365 ① 8
🚍 170km (105 miles) from Hobart via the
Lyell Highway

HOBART
HOTEL GRAND CHANCELLOR

www.ghihotels.com/hgc
Modern waterfront hotel.
✉ 1 Davey Street, Hobart, TAS 7000
☎ 03 6235 4535 ⊕ All year
♨ A$150–A$190 excluding breakfast
① 240 ⊕ ⊠ Indoor ☕

HENRY JONES ART HOTEL

www.thehenryjones.com
Classy and well located on the
Hobart waterfront (pictured above).
✉ 25 Hunter Street, Hobart, TAS
7000 ☎ 03 6210 7700 ⊕ All year
♨ A$230–A$750 ① 55

PORT ARTHUR
STEWARTS BAY LODGE

www.stewartsbaylodge.com.au
Eighteen waterfront cabins settled

within 9ha (22 acres) of protected
bushland with abundant wildlife.
✉ Arthur Highway, Port Arthur, TAS
7182 ☎ 03 6250 2888 ⊕ All year
♨ A$175–A$415 excluding breakfast
① 18

STRAHAN
RISBY COVE

www.risby.com.au
Small waterfront resort, 2km
(1.6 miles) from the village centre.
✉ The Esplanade, Strahan, TAS 7468
☎ 03 6471 7572 ⊕ All year ♨ A$110–
A$244 ① 8

WESTBURY
ELM WOOD BED & BREAKFAST

www.elmwood.com.au
Set in Tasmania's Golden Valley, this
Victorian gothic-style house was
purpose built as a guesthouse.
✉ 10 Lonsdale Promenade, Westbury,
TAS 7303 ☎ 03 6393 2169 ⊕ All year
♨ A$175–A$360 including breakfast ① 4
🚍 35km (22 miles) from Launceston

PRACTICALITIES

Practicalities gives you all the important practical information you will need during your visit, from money matters to emergency phone numbers.

ESSENTIAL INFORMATION

PRACTICALITIES ESSENTIAL INFORMATION

WEATHER

WEATHER DOWN UNDER

Australia is in the southern hemisphere, so its seasons are the opposite to those in Europe and North America. Summer is from December to the end of February, and winter, which in most places is mild rather than cold, lasts from June to August. The north is tropical while the south is temperate. In the tropical regions very high humidity is confined to the wet season (Nov–end Mar). The country as a whole does not suffer extreme cold, most snow falling in the ski fields in the southeast and in Tasmania. Overall the climate is well suited to outdoor activities for most of the year.

New South Wales, ACT

The climate of New South Wales is temperate, with hot summers and mild temperatures for the rest of the year. It is seldom very cold, especially by the coast, and extreme weather is rare. Rainfall is generally moderate.

The Canberra region, in the south, is sunny for most of the year.

Summer is hot and dry, autumn mild, and winter is cold with occasional snow.

Victoria

Victoria has four distinct seasons: sunny, but changeable, hot summers; a vivid-hued autumn with moderate temperatures; cold winters with snow in the mountains; and fresh, bright spring days.

Queensland

Tropical Queensland has very hot sun, even during the winter, and high humidity on the coast; rain is rare during this period. Monsoonal rains fall in summer (Dec–end Feb), particularly in the north and this period is the cyclone season in north Queensland.

South Australia

One of the driest regions of Australia, the state enjoys mild winters and hot to very hot summers. Some rain falls in the summer, but frost has never been recorded in Adelaide.

Northern Territory

The northern part of the Territory (Top End) is a tropical region, with two seasons. The wet (summer) season can have heavy rainstorms, especially around the coast, with some flooding, while the dry (winter) season is hot.

The southern part of the state, however, is desert, with little rain. Days are hot and sunny—over 40°C (104°F) in the summer—but the nights are cold.

TIME ZONES		
Australia is covered by three time zones:		
Eastern Standard Time		
New South Wales		
Queensland		
Tasmania		
Victoria		
Central Standard Time		
Northern Territory		
South Australia		
Western Standard Time		
Western Australia		

CAIRNS

TEMPERATURE

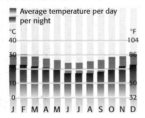

ALICE SPRINGS

TEMPERATURE

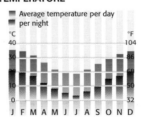

PERTH

TEMPERATURE

RAINFALL

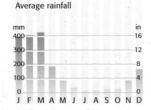

RAINFALL

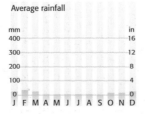

RAINFALL

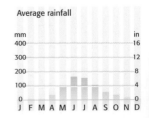

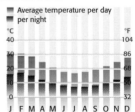

Western Australia

Accounting for approximately one-third of the total landmass of the country, Western Australia has a number of different climatic zones. The north receives heavy rains in the wet (summer) season; the interior is drier and hotter; and the southwest has a more temperate climate, with occasional snow on the Stirling Range.

Tasmania

The island has a temperate climate. At sea level, summers are mild, and winters generally cool to mild. Mountainous areas have cold winters, and snow may fall even in summer.

EXTREME WEATHER

» The tropical north experiences intense storms called tropical cyclones between about December and the end of February. Damage by cyclones can be very severe.
» Snow falls mainly in the southeast of Australia on the Snowy Mountains and northern tablelands of New South Wales, Victoria and, rarely, in parts of Queensland. Tasmania also has snow in the summer on areas over 1,400m (4,592ft).

SYDNEY
TEMPERATURE

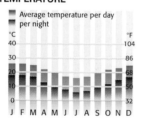

RAINFALL

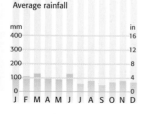

» The Australian sun is dangerous, causing skin damage and, perhaps, skin cancer. Temperatures, can reach 40°C (104°F) or more. In high summer, burning can happen in about 10 minutes even in overcast conditions. Problems can arise years after the sunburn actually happens.

WEATHER INFORMATION

Newspapers, radio and television all carry forecasts. Several websites provide information.
» www.bom.gov.au—the national Bureau of Meteorology has information down to local level and specialized forecasts.
» www.weather.com—this American site has great detail on Australian weather, including useful 10-day forecasts.
» www.meto.gov.uk—this British site has comprehensive information about the Australian climate and five-day forecasts.
» www.wunderground.com—hundreds of Australian towns are on this site, with daily forecasts.

SUMMER DAYLIGHT SAVING		
	HOUR FORWARD	**HOUR BACK**
NSW	Oct last Sun	Mar last Sun
ACT	Oct last Sun	Mar last Sun
Vic	Oct last Sun	Mar last Sun
Qld	no change	no change
NT	no change	no change
SA	Oct last Sun	Mar last Sun
WA	no change	no change
Tas	Oct first Sun	Mar last Sun

Most states observe daylight saving in the summer, advancing clocks by one hour at the start and putting them back one hour at the end.

BEST TIME TO VISIT	
NSW	All year. Jan–end Feb can be very hot
ACT	All year. Jan–end Feb can be very hot
Vic	Most of year. Jan/Feb can be very hot and Jun–end Aug cold and wet
Qld	Southern areas all year. Avoid the tropical north Dec–end Mar when humidity is extremely high
NT	Central Australia is best Jul–end Sep when temperatures are bearable— outside these times avoid strenuous exercise during heat of the day. In the tropical north avoid the wet season Dec–end Mar when many roads and attractions are closed
SA	Most of year. Summer months can be uncomfortably hot
WA	Most of year—coastal areas are cooled by afternoon sea breezes. Outback hot all year
Tas	Best Nov–end Mar. Be prepared for snow on the mountainous interior all year

TIME DIFFERENCES				
	GMT 12PM	**WST**	**CST**	**EST**
Western Standard Time	8pm	0	+1.30	+2
Central Standard Time	9.30pm	+1.30	0	+0.30
Eastern Standard Time	10pm	+2	+0.30	0
San Francisco	4am	+16	+17.30	+18
Chicago	6am	+14	+15.30	+16
New York	7am	+13	+14.30	+15
London	12pm	+8	+9.30	+10
Paris	1pm	+7	+8.30	+9
Johannesburg	2pm	+6	+7.30	+8
Tokyo	9pm	-1	-0.30	+1
Berlin	1pm	+7	+8.30	+10

weapons, ammunition, protected wildlife and products made from them, and some medicinal products, including performance-enhancing drugs. You must declare if you are carrying medication: It is wise to take a letter or a prescription from your doctor describing the medication and your medical condition. Food items, particularly fruit and meat, cannot be taken into the country and will be confiscated on arrival. Some particular foodstuffs, including fruit and honey, cannot be taken across some state borders.

TOURIST REFUND SCHEME (TRS)

It is possible to claim a refund of the Goods and Services Tax (GST) and Wine Equalisation Tax (WET) paid on goods bought in Australia. The refund only applies to goods carried as hand luggage or worn when you leave the country. The refund is paid on goods costing A$300 or more, bought from the same store, no more than 30 days before you leave. You may buy goods from several stores, provided each store's tax invoice totals at least A$300 (GST inclusive).

When leaving Australia through an international airport, look for the TRS booth in the departures area after you have passed through passport control. The booths are also at cruise liner terminals. You must produce the relevant goods (to prove you are taking them out of the country), the tax invoice from the retailer, and your passport and international boarding pass. You will then be paid the refund.

DOCUMENTATION
PASSPORTS AND TOURIST VISAS

All visitors to Australia must carry a valid passport and visa. Ensure next of kin details are written in the back of your passport. Tourist visas cost between A$20 and A$105 and for many countries are now available in an electronic format—an ETA (Electronic Travel Authority). ETAs are no additional charge. These can be obtained from travel agents or via the web from www.immi.gov.au and they are generally valid for three months within the year after the visa is issued. They should be applied for at least two months before travelling; and they cannot be obtained at Australian airports.

If you want to stay for more than three months then apply for a longer-term visa from the local Australian Embassy or High Commission. If your visit to Australia is unexpectedly extended you must apply for a further visa at an Australian visa office before your ETA expires.

WORKING VISAS

Applicants must be aged 18 to 30, single or married without dependent children. You have to show that any work is to support yourself while on holiday. You must also have a return ticket, or sufficient funds for a return fare and the first part of your stay, and show that you intend to leave Australia at the end of the authorized stay. The maximum stay is generally 12 months from the date of initial entry to Australia, whether or not you spend the whole period in Australia. In addition you cannot work longer than three months with one employer. A charge, currently A$180, applies to the application.

For more information see www.immi.gov.au.

If you intend to earn a salary in Australia you will need a tax file number. To get this you must open an Australian bank account. You'll need your passport, plus additional identification such as a driving licence. See also page 309.

DRIVING LICENCE

If you plan to drive a car in Australia you will need to take your driving licence. An International Driving Permit (IDP) is not essential but in some states it can be useful; apply via your motoring organization.

CUSTOMS REGULATIONS

Australia has laws controlling the importation of illegal drugs, firearms,

DUTY-FREE GOODS
You can bring the following into Australia:
A$900 of goods (including gifts) excluding tobacco or alcohol (A$450 for travellers under 18)
2.25 litres alcohol (18+ only)
250 cigarettes, or 250 grams of cigars or tobacco (18+ only)
Personal items and also goods owned for at least a year
More information at: www.customs.gov.au

MONEY

CHANGING MONEY

It is easy to change money in Australia. Banks and exchange bureaux often charge a commission, but the rates will be better than in airports, hotels and the smaller money exchange shops. It is sensible to have some Australian currency before arriving. Traveller's cheques may seem unnecessary in the age of credit cards, but their benefit is that they can be refunded if they are lost or stolen. Exchange rates for traveller's cheques can be better than for foreign cash. Note that identification—usually your passport—may be required when cashing traveller's cheques or exchanging currency.

CREDIT CARDS

MasterCard and Visa are the most useful cards in Australia, followed by Bankcard (issued by banks in Australia), American Express and Diners Club. Should you lose your card, contact the issuer listed in the table above.

CASH MACHINES

If the bank issuing your credit or debit card is part of the Plus, Cirrus or Visa networks, there will be plenty of ATMs (automatic teller machines) for withdrawing money. But always check with your bank to confirm you can use your card in Australia: It may be necessary to change your PIN or even have a new card issued.

EFTPOS

Most Australian shops, hotels, restaurants and fuel stations use EFTPOS (electronic funds transfer at point of sale) at their cash tills, which accept Australian credit or debit cards. These cards can also be used to withdraw cash.

If you intend to stay in Australia for a length of time it would be worthwhile opening an Australian bank account, which is necessary to access EFTPOS. In remote country areas, however, EFTPOS is less common.

TIPPING

In general, Australians do not tip excessively. In an expensive restaurant 10 per cent is acceptable, but a tip is not expected in pubs, bars or cafés. In taxis it is usual to round up the fare, and hotel porters might expect A$1–A$2 per bag.

No offence will be taken if you do not tip, and only tip if you have been given good service.

DISCOUNT CARDS

Student cards allow reduced-price admission to museums and other attractions, and often provide discounts on transport. Most useful is the International Student Exchange card (ISE; www.isecard.com), but other options are the International Student, Youth and Identity cards that can be used by students and teachers in full-time education and by anyone under 26.

The Hostelling International Membership Card (www.hostel-booking.com) is a good option for travellers on a budget, and there are other cards available from hostels.

Particularly useful is the VIP Card (www.vipbackpackers.com) that not only provides hundreds of discounts, but also functions as a rechargeable phonecard.

The Tourist Australia Travel Card (www.touristaustralia.com.au) provides discounts in exchange for a year's membership.

Pensioners may be able to obtain discounts by showing their card from home, but most of these discounts are limited to Australian citizens.

If travelling by car you can buy a pass to all the charging national parks in each state, which may give a considerable saving on paying the full price each time. See the national park websites, ▷ 316.

BANKS

» Most banks open Mon–Thu 9.30–4, until 4.30 Fri. Some banks open Sat morning.

The major banks are given in the table below.

LOST/STOLEN CREDIT CARDS

American Express
1300 132 639
www.americanexpress.com.au

Diners Club
1300 360 060
www.dinersclub.com.au

MasterCard
1800 120 113
www.mastercard.com.au

Visa
1800 450 346
www.visa.com.au

EXCHANGE RATES

At time of publication	
US $10	A$10.95
Canada $10	A$10.32
UK £10	A$17.80
New Zealand $10	A$7.95
Euro €10	A$15.98
See www.xe.com for the latest rates.	

10 EVERYDAY ITEMS AND HOW MUCH THEY COST

Takeaway (takeout) sandwich	A$4.50
Bottle of water (1 litre)	A$3.50
Cup of tea or coffee	A$3.50
Glass of beer (425ml)	A$5.50
Glass of wine	A$7.50
Daily newspaper	A$1.20
Camera film (36)	A$9.00
Cigarettes (20 pack)	A$14.50
Petrol (gas) (1 litre)	A$1.30
Can of Coke	A$2.00

BANKS

NAME	TELEPHONE	WEBSITE
Commonwealth Bank	Tel 13 22 21	www.commbank.com.au
National Australia Bank	Tel 13 22 65	www.nab.com.au
ANZ Bank	Tel 13 13 14	www.anz.com
Westpac Bank	Tel 13 20 32	www.westpac.com.au

HEALTH

MEDICAL ADVICE

You should see your doctor four to six weeks before you go to ensure you have any necessary vaccinations. Alternatively you could visit a specialist Travel Clinic. These clinics provide professional advice about all travel health recommendations. It is a good idea to know your blood group before you travel, as this will save time in case of an emergency.

For your own safety, it is recommended that your polio and tetanus inoculations are up to date; if they are more than 10 years old, get a booster injection. Hepatitis A and typhoid inoculations are not absolutely necessary, but it is wise to have them, particularly if you are also visiting Asian countries. Yellow fever vaccination certificates are required only if you have visited a country where it is endemic before arriving in Australia.

AVOIDING JET LAG

» On the flight, drink sufficient fluid to prevent dehydration.
» If you want to sleep during the flight, only do so if it coincides with night time at your destination.
» Gradually adjust your body clock on arrival. On the first day be active in bright light between 12pm and 6pm and relax between 4am and 10am local time. On the second day go out between 10am and 4pm and relax between 2am and 8am. On the third get out between 8am and 2pm and relax between 12am and 7am.

HEALTH CARE IN AUSTRALIA

Australia's health-care system is called Medicare and includes both public and private hospitals. The costs of health care are comparable to those in other developed countries. You should obtain adequate health insurance to cover the costs of any unexpected treatment during a visit to Australia.

Australia has Reciprocal Health Agreements with nine countries, but the benefits vary. For more information visit: www.hica.com.au.

These agreements do not cover overseas students studying in Australia, who need to take out Overseas Student Health Cover. See www.health.gov.au, then go to A–Z Index.

The Reciprocal Health Agreements do not cover dental treatment, private medical care, ambulance cover, treatment that is not immediately necessary, medical evacuation to your home country or funeral expenses; additional health insurance should account for these risks.

If you require treatment, state that you wish to be treated as a Medicare public patient under a Reciprocal Health Agreement. Any Medicare office (tel 13 20 11 within Australia) will confirm what documentation is required.

PHARMACIES

Pharmacies (chemists) are widely distributed. The main chains are Amcal Chemists and Chemmart. They sell a similar range of over-the-counter medicines as British or American pharmacies, and they also dispense prescription medicines.

Local hotels and telephone directories usually have lists of pharmacies open outside normal trading hours.

SURGERIES

Surgeries are common in populated areas. If your accommodation cannot recommend one, ask at the local pharmacy or check a phone book.

In suburban areas surgeries are often found in shopping malls.

Most surgeries will expect payment at the time of treatment: Keep the receipt for claiming insurance or, if you are eligible, Medicare.

DENTAL SURGERIES

Dentists are plentiful and the standard of treatment is high—as are the bills. In an emergency go to the casualty wing of a local hospital, or locate a dentist from the phone book. Medical insurance is essential for visitors from overseas.

EMERGENCY—CALL 000

You are likely to be billed for using an ambulance. Again, this should be refunded by your insurance company on production of a receipt.

HEALTH RISKS IN AUSTRALIA

Road Accidents

Vehicle accidents form the greatest risk overall, in Australia as in other countries. Accidents on holiday are often more complicated to deal with, so it is important to follow the obvious safety rules, such as wearing a seat belt, keeping to the speed limit, wearing a crash helmet on a scooter or motorcycle, and not drinking and driving.

Sun Protection

Take care in the sun when visiting any part of Australia—sunburn or even sunstroke can ruin your holiday. Follow the sensible advice of the Slip, Slop, Slap campaign:
» Slip on a shirt.
» Slop on some sunscreen.
» Slap on a hat.
Sunscreen creams are inexpensive in Australia. It is advisable to use high-factor sunscreen on all exposed skin: SPF 30+ is recommended for adults and total blockout for children. In hot sun you should also wear loose clothing, avoid vigorous exercise and drink plenty of water.

If walking in the heat, try to drink at least 1 litre (1.75 pints) of water per hour. Wear good-quality sunglasses in strong sunshine to protect your eyes.

Diarrhoea

The most common travel illness is diarrhoea, caught from contaminated food or water. Food and water in populated areas should be safe—check with locals about water quality in outback areas.

There are several good antibiotics available to take with you, and it is also important to ensure that you drink plenty of fluids with the treatment.

Mosquito-borne Diseases

Malaria is very rare in Australia, but international travel increases the risks of it spreading. There are other mosquito-borne diseases to beware of, such as Ross River fever and Murray River encephalitis. The main risk, however, is dengue fever, which can be caught in northern Queensland and the Torres Strait Islands. It is an unpleasant, flu-like illness that can last at least a week. The mosquitoes that carry this virus bite during the day.

Protection from mosquito bites involves avoiding swampy, stagnant water; watching for insects around dusk; using insect repellent; and wearing long-sleeved shirts and long trousers in areas where dengue fever is a risk.

Poisonous Creatures

Australia is home to a good number of poisonous creatures. Treat all snakes with caution. Generally, snakes will not attack you unless you threaten them or catch them unawares. They are rarely seen in populated areas.

The best advice is to look where you are walking; walk noisily so they can feel you coming; step on to fallen tree trunks rather than stepping over them; wear long trousers and robust shoes when walking through grass or bush; and do not put your hands into dark crevices. It is also a good idea to carry a crepe bandage and a mobile phone, so that if you or a companion is bitten, you can apply the bandage to slow the spread of the venom while help is summoned.

Sydney funnel web spiders found on the New South Wales coastline also have a poisonous bite, and it is important to get rapid treatment with anti-venom.

Some other poisonous creatures live in the sea. Around much of the coast of Australia jellyfish can give a very painful sting. In the tropics, you will see signs warning of the box jellyfish for several months of the year. Take heed of the signs as this species has tentacles many metres long and the sting can be fatal. There are also some brightly hued sea snakes that are not usually aggressive, but which have a deadly venom. Blue-ringed octopus live in rockpools around the coast. Small and well camouflaged, they are extremely dangerous and should never be touched.

Dangerous Animals

Sharks swim off the coasts of Australia but they rarely attack swimmers. Where there is particular risk, warning notices are posted on the beaches.

In northern areas, saltwater crocodiles are also dangerous and occasionally attack and kill people. They move very quickly, so make sure you know where they are likely to be found. The crocodiles frequent marine estuaries, rivers and lagoons, and are most dangerous during the breeding season (September to the end of April). Despite their name, saltwater crocodiles also inhabit freshwater rivers. There may be warning notices, but it is always wise to keep away from places where they may lurk, including beach areas.

FLYING DOCTOR

The Royal Flying Doctor Service is a charitable service that provides medical emergency and primary health-care services, together with communication and education assistance, to people who live, work and travel in regional and remote Australia. They have 20 base stations, some of which can be visited, and they offer practical advice to those planning a trip to the outback. In particular they advise taking a high-frequency radio compatible with the Flying Doctor service; see www.rfds.org.au.

BASICS

PACKING

Before you leave, ensure that someone at home has your detailed itinerary. It may also be useful to establish an email account that you can access through the internet anywhere. And re-confirm your flights just in case they are overbooked. Make a list of the following before you leave:
» Passport number and date issued.
» Serial numbers of tickets.
» Credit card numbers and emergency number.
» Serial number of travel insurance policy and emergency contact number.
» Driving licence number.
» Serial numbers of traveller's cheques.
» Serial numbers of valuables.
» Copies of prescriptions for spectacles/contact lenses.
Give one copy to someone you can reach in an emergency, and keep one yourself separate from your luggage. In addition, it is worth taking a photocopy of your passport, travel insurance, tickets and other important documents.

WHAT TO WEAR

Most people in Australia dress casually, wearing lighter clothing in the summer months of December, January and February, and heavier clothing in the winter months of June, July and August. In the more northern latitudes most days are warm. Australians may dress up to go to the opera, or for formal occasions, but the best guide is to wear whatever feels comfortable, although most establishments require reasonable footwear. Remember that it gets very cold at night in the desert areas. Take a good sun hat with a wide brim and sunglasses. Sunscreen is a must. If you will be walking take good boots, a torch (flashlight) and a compass.

METRIC CONVERSIONS

Australia uses the metric system, and the basic conversions are as in the table, right.

ELECTRICAL DEVICES

Australian electricity is generally 240V as in Britain, though the three flat-pin plug sockets are of a different form. North America uses 110V, so it will be necessary to use a voltage plug adapter, or a separate power cord with an Australian plug.

Be careful if you are taking a DVD player. A DVD made for one region is not necessarily compatible with a DVD player in any other region. The USA is region 1, Australia is region 4, and Europe is region 2.

TRAVEL INSURANCE

Travel insurance is important and you should look for a policy that covers all the activities you expect to enjoy in Australia. You should also look for good medical cover as not all aspects of medical care are covered by Reciprocal Health Agreements (▷ 310).

COMFORT AND SAFETY

Feeling comfortable and secure on holiday is more often a matter of taking sensible precautions.
» Keep money and other valuables secure from pickpockets, or alternatively locked in a safe.
» The most serious danger on holiday is traffic accidents. Take as much or more care than you do at home; don't drink and drive; and keep in mind the road conditions in Australia. Roads in the outback are often just tracks, so you will often need to use a 4WD if you plan to travel there.
» Try not to drive outside populated areas at night, dawn or dusk as many animals are attracted to headlamps—and hitting a kangaroo, wombat or other large animal can seriously damage your vehicle.
» Road trains are another hazard—keep well out of their way, and make sure you allow at least 1km (0.6 mile) of clear, straight road to overtake them.
» Australia is home to a number of poisonous and dangerous creatures. So long as you are aware of the risks (▷ 311) and don't touch or threaten them, you should not be harmed.

LOOKING AFTER CHILDREN

Australia has plenty of attractions for children to enjoy. There are many family-orientated hotels, motels, camping parks and restaurants that provide special meals and arrangements. Baby-changing facilities are available in some public toilets.

All the advice about living in a hot climate applies especially to children. In particular, protect them from the sun.
» Remember Slip, Slop, Slap: Slip on a shirt, Slop on some sunscreen and Slap on a hat.
» Ensure children drink plenty of water, and keep them within view when near the sea, rivers, lakes and swimming pools.
» Teach your children to be careful about spiders, jellyfish, snakes, bees and wasps, ants, cane toads and dingoes. Apart from remote areas in general, dangerous creatures lurk around rock pools or ponds.
» Kangaroos will defend if cornered, but may be attracted to food at barbecue or picnic areas, and occasionally become nosey.
» Any toys left outside overnight must be thoroughly checked in the morning for dangerous creatures.

CONVERSION CHART

FROM	TO	MULTIPLY BY
Inches	Centimetres	2.54
Centimetres	Inches	0.3937
Feet	Metres	0.3048
Metres	Feet	3.2810
Yards	Metres	0.9144
Metres	Yards	1.0940
Miles	Kilometres	1.6090
Kilometres	Miles	0.6214
Acres	Hectares	0.4047
Hectares	Acres	2.4710
Gallons	Litres	4.5460
Litres	Gallons	0.2200
Ounces	Grams	28.35
Grams	Ounces	0.0353
Pounds	Grams	453.6
Grams	Pounds	0.0022
Pounds	Kilograms	0.4536
Kilograms	Pounds	2.205
Tons	Tonnes	1.0160
Tonnes	Tons	0.9842

BEACH SAFETY

One of the great attractions of Australia is the sunny weather, but treat the sun with respect, particularly on the beach.

» Wear sunscreen, sun hat, shirt and sunglasses.

» Swim or surf only at places patrolled by lifeguards, or check with locals first. If you are unsure whether sea conditions are safe, then ask a lifeguard.

» Swim only between the yellow and red flags.

» Don't swim after a meal or under the influence of alcohol or drugs.

» If you get into trouble, don't struggle against the current—raise an arm and wait for help or swim parallel to the beach.

OUTBACK SAFETY

It is undeniably an exciting holiday adventure to explore the Australian outback. But all trips must be planned carefully.

» Wear appropriate clothing and walking shoes; take some warm clothes as it can get cold at night.

» Take a hat, sunscreen and insect repellent.

» Take plenty of water—1 litre (1.75 pints) per hour if walking—stored in several containers.

» Do not pack too much on your vehicle's roof rack.

» Pack a first-aid kit.

» Carry a high-frequency radio compatible with the Flying Doctor Service. Mobile phones and CB radios may not work in more remote areas.

» Plan your route carefully and tell others where you are going.

» If you break down, you must stay with the car—it is far easier for rescuers to see a car than a person. Never try to walk out of a remote area. Set up some type of shelter and remain in the shade.

PUBLIC TOILETS

Public toilets are common in Australian cities and are clearly marked. Remote areas are also well served with toilet facilities, but do check for wildlife. The website

www.toiletmap.gov.au lists 13,000 public toilets, with access details for people with disabilities.

WOMEN ON HOLIDAY

Generally, Australia is a safe place for female travellers. It is always worthwhile, however, taking standard precautions.

» Avoid walking alone late at night in dark streets in either cities or rural areas.

» Be careful if staying or drinking by yourself in pubs.

» Do not hitch-hike alone.

» If you are going to be out late, arrange for a lift or taxi home. Australia has only reputable, clearly marked, licensed taxis.

» If you are driving alone, carry a mobile (cell) phone, lock the car doors when stationary, particularly at night, and never pick up hitch-hikers.

» Sit near the driver or conductor on buses, and avoid empty carriages (cars) on trains.

FINDING HELP
LOST PROPERTY

» Rather than take risks, leave valuable belongings in a secure place, such as a hotel safe.

» For items lost in transit, contact the transportation operator.

» Contact the local police station for items lost in Australia.

» The website noticeboard www.internetlostandfound.com.au is a useful way to advertise lost goods or search for found items. In small towns, stores and supermarkets usually have a noticeboard where signs can be posted for no charge.

MONEY PROBLEMS

Relatives and friends can send you extra money in an emergency.

EMERGENCY

POLICE 000
AMBULANCE 000
FIRE 000

This number is free on all payphones and mobile (cell) phones.

Western Union Money Transfer can quickly supply funds across a global network to the nearest bank; www.westernunion.com.

CONSULATES

In an emergency the consul can help in a number of ways, but not necessarily financially. Work permits *cannot* be arranged through the consul.

» Accidents—relatives and friends can be contacted, and advice given on procedures for repatriation if necessary.

» Financial—although they will advise on how to transfer funds, they will not pay your outstanding bills. In emergencies they may give a limited loan for repatriation.

» Legal—legal advice *cannot* be provided, but they can supply a list of local lawyers.

» Medical—a list of local doctors can be supplied, but they cannot help to get improved medical care, or pay medical bills.

» Passports—they can issue emergency passports.

THE LAW

Always avoid trouble as the police can be very strict. Various states are increasingly strict about speeding and drink-driving. If you are stopped or arrested, the following advice may be useful.

» Fines for minor offences are paid by post or to the clerk of the court. You will not be asked to pay the police officer, and do not offer to do so under any circumstance.

» If you are arrested, give your name and address, but otherwise say nothing before contacting your consul or a lawyer.

» Remain calm and polite—do not become abusive.

» Your rights will be explained to you by the police. It is your right to contact your consul.

» You will be allowed to make one telephone call; contact a relative or friend who can organize assistance.

» You can be held for a reasonable time (usually four hours) before you must be charged or released.

COMMUNICATION

TELEPHONES

Calls to Australia

» The code for calling Australia is 61. However, the dial code depends on the country you are calling from. So, to call Australia from these countries, dial:

Canada	011-61
New Zealand	00-61
United Kingdom	00-61
USA	011-61

This is followed by the state code, omitting the 0, then the subscriber number.

Calls in Australia

» There are two main telephone operators in Australia, Telstra (www.telstra.com) and Optus (www.optus.com.au).

» For telephone calls within the country it is best to use a local phonecard, available from post offices and newsagents. The minimum charge for a local call is 40 cents.

» You can also buy phonecards for international calls.

TELEPHONE CODES IN AUSTRALIA

If you are dialling from one state to another use these codes:

Australian Capital Territory	02
New South Wales	02
Victoria	03
Queensland	07
Northern Territory	08
South Australia	08
Western Australia	08
Tasmania	03

Other phone codes:

Freephone	1800
Calls charged at local rate	13 or 1300
Premium rate calls	190

Other useful numbers:

Operator	1234
Australian directory enquiry	1223
International directory enquiry	1225

You can also find telephone numbers using the White Pages and Yellow Pages websites (www.whitepages.com.au; www.yellowpages.com.au).

MOBILE PHONES

» Australia uses the same Global System for Mobile (GSM) as the rest of the world (except for North America and Japan) at 900MHz and 1800MHz. However, some American GSM phones designed for 1900MHz can also handle standard GSM. CDMA (Code Division Multiple Access) phones are more likely to be compatible from one country to another; but check in advance. Even if your phone is compatible, check the recharger to make sure that it too will work in Australia.

» Coverage is good in most urban areas but can be poor or non-existent in remote areas. If you plan to travel away from the major population centres or off the main highways, you should check the network coverage maps provided by Telstra: See www.telstra.com. The Telstra website also has information about the various types of mobile phone.

» A mobile phone is an expensive means to phone home.

EMAIL

» Email is an excellent way to contact people at home and other travellers abroad. A number of internet email accounts (such as www.hotmail.com) can be accessed from any terminal. These accounts can get clogged up with junk mail. If you sign up with an Australian ISP provider, make sure that calls are charged at the local rate.

» www.world66.com has a large list of internet cafés, and www.yellowpages.com.au is also useful. Minimum café charges range from A$2 to A$12 per hour depending where you are.

INTERNATIONAL DIALLING CODES FROM AUSTRALIA TO

Canada	0011-1
France	0011-33
Germany	0011-49
Ireland	0011-353
New Zealand	0011-64
United Kingdom	0011-44
USA	0011-1

» Public libraries provide free internet links but these are often intended for research, although some libraries have computers for accessing emails. Many hostels have internet links.

» WiFi HotSpots also provide access to internet email accounts and the internet itself. The HotSpots are often located in cafés, hotels, transportation terminals and stores. You can use your own WiFi enabled laptop or PDA (personal digital assistant)—most recent equipment is enabled—via a WiFi provider.

» For worldwide HotSpots and providers see www.wifi411.com or the websites of the major telecommunications companies.

» If you are taking a laptop with you there are a number of things to check. You should use a global PC card modem, or buy a local PC card modem in Australia. RJ-45 and Telstra EX1-160 four-pin telephone plugs are used. An Australian plug adapter and an AC adapter will also be needed. Remember that laptops are easily stolen, so take care.

MAIL

» Post offices open Mon–Fri 9–5; some also open Sat 9–12.

» Stamps can be bought from post offices or post office agencies in newspaper shops, or from Australia Post shops.

» Major post offices will hold mail for visitors by arrangement, but it will be necessary to provide identification before it can be collected.

» Postal deliveries are made to hotels and private addresses on Mondays to Fridays; there are no deliveries on Saturdays.

POSTAGE RATES OUTSIDE AUSTRALIA:

Postcards and greetings cards	A$1.40
Air mail letters	
under 50 grams from:	A$2.10
Parcels up to	
250 grams air mail: from	A$9.30
sea mail/economy air:	A$6.80
See Australia Post www.auspost.com.au.	

OPENING HOURS

PUBLIC HOLIDAYS

Australia has 9 national public holidays. In addition, each state has some public holidays of its own, and some grant additional public holidays for major events.

January	1	New Year's Day
	26	Australia Day
March	1st Monday	Labour Day (WA)
	2nd Monday	Eight Hour Day (Tas)
		Labour Day (Vic)
	3rd Monday	Canberra Day (ACT)
March/April	Easter	(Good Friday to Easter Monday)
April	25	Anzac Day
May	1st Monday	May Day (NT)
		Labour Day (QLD)
	3rd Monday	Adelaide Cup Day (SA)
June	1st Monday	Foundation Day (WA)
	2nd Monday	Queen's Birthday (not WA)
August	1st Monday	Picnic Day (NT)
September	Last Monday	Queen's Birthday (WA)
October	1st Monday	Labour Day (NSW, ACT, SA)
November	1st Tuesday	Melbourne Cup Day (Melbourne)
December	25	Christmas Day
	26	Boxing Day

OPENING TIMES

There are no standard opening times across Australia. Places in large cities tend to have longer opening hours, and the smaller and more remote places are more limited. The times below give a general guide.

Business hours	Mon–Fri 8.30–5
Banks	Mon–Thu 9–4, Fri 9–4.30, Some banks Sat 9–12
Post offices	Mon–Fri 9–5, (some) Sat 9–12
Stores	Mon–Fri 8.30–5, Sat 9–1
City stores late night	Thu or Fri until 9,
	City stores may open all day Sat, Sun
Bigger supermarkets in large cities	Daily 24 hours
Tourist information	Major cities daily 9–5. Smaller places may close earlier and open fewer hours Sat, Sun

SCHOOL HOLIDAYS

Most Australian schools run on a four-term academic year, with the school year starting in February.

January	Much of the month in most states
March/April	Easter (one or two weeks)
June/July	Two weeks
December	Two weeks from mid-December

Shop opening hours are determined by each state government, and visitors will find slight variations as they travel around the country.

In capital cities and major tourist areas such as Cairns and Alice Springs, shops open all weekend. Supermarkets tend to have longer opening hours than other shops. In rural towns and even smaller inland cities, shops will often close between midday Saturday and Monday morning.

In country areas throughout Australia petrol stations are often closed after 6pm. This won't happen on major highways although not all petrol stations will stay open all night. However if you plan on a long night drive on lesser highways, you might find yourself stranded. Be aware that, for reasons of safety in excessively hot desert conditions, petrol stations may not sell fuel during the extreme heat of the day.

TOURIST INFORMATION

TOURISM AUSTRALIA
The offices of Australia's official tourist commission are a useful stop for research and free information before you travel. Ask for a copy of the latest Travellers' Guide brochure.
www.australia.com

UK
Australia Centre
Australia House, 6th Floor
Melbourne Place, The Strand
London WC2B 4LG
Tel 020 7438 4601

USA
6100 Center Drive, Suite 1150
Los Angeles, CA 90047
Tel 310/695-3200

AUSTRALIA
GPO Box 2721, Sydney, NSW 2001
Tel 02 9360 1111

PLACES OF WORSHIP
Local churches, mosques, temples and synagogues are listed in phone books, or see www.yellowpages.com.au, or contact the nearest tourist office.

Anglican Church
The General Secretary
PO Box Q190, QVB Post Office, Sydney, NSW 1230; tel 02 8267 2700; www.anglican.org.au

Buddhism
www.buddhanet.net/
Australian organizations are listed on the website.

Catholic Church
The Australian Catholic Bishops Conference
GPO Box 368, Canberra, ACT 2601; tel 02 6201 9845; www.catholic.org.au

Hinduism
Hindu Council of Australia
17 The Crescent, Homebush, NSW 2140, tel 02 8208 9810; www.hinducouncil.com.au

Islam
Australian Federation of Islamic Councils (AFIC)
932 Bourke Street, Zetland, NSW 2015; tel 02 9319 6733
Search for mosques and prayer times at www.afic.com.au.

Judaism
The Great Synagogue, Sydney
166 Castlereagh Street, Sydney, NSW 2000; tel 02 9267 2477; www.greatsynagogue.org.au
Search for synagogues at www.synagogues.com

Uniting Church
PO Box 2178, Sydney South, NSW 1235; tel 02 8267 4300; www.uca.org.au
In Australia, the Congregational, Methodist and Presbyterian denominations combined to form the Uniting Church in 1977.

NATIONAL TRUST
The Australian National Trust cares for some 300 historic properties.

Australian Council of National Trusts
✉ 14/71 Constitution Avenue, Campbell, ACT 2612
PO Box 413, Campbell, ACT 2612
☎ 02 6247 6766
www.nationaltrust.org.au

ACT
☎ 02 6230 0533
www.nationaltrustact.org.au

New South Wales
☎ 02 9258 0123
www.nsw.nationaltrust.com.au

Victoria
☎ 03 9656 9800
www.nattrust.com.au

Queensland
☎ 07 3223 6666
www.nationaltrustqld.org

Northern Territory
☎ 08 8981 2848
www.nationaltrustnt.org.au

South Australia
☎ 08 8212 1133
www.nationaltrustsa.org.au

Western Australia
☎ 08 9321 6088
www.ntwa.com.au

Tasmania
☎ 03 6344 6233
www.nationaltrusttas.org.au

NATIONAL PARKS

New South Wales
National Parks and Wildlife Service
☎ 1300 361 967 or 02 9995 5000
www.nationalparks.nsw.gov.au

Visitor Information Centre
✉ 110 George Street, The Rocks, Sydney, NSW 2000
☎ 02 9247 5033

Parks Victoria
☎ 13 19 63
www.parkweb.vic.gov.au

Queensland Parks and Wildlife Service
☎ 13 13 04
www.epa.qld.gov.au

Parks and Wildlife Commission of the NT
☎ 08 8999 5511
www.nt.gov.au/nreta/parks

South Australian Department for Environment and Heritage
☎ 08 8204 1910
www.environment.sa.gov.au/parks

Western Australian Department of Conservation and Land Management
☎ 08 6467 5000
www.dec.wa.gov.au

Tasmania Parks and Wildlife Service
☎ 1300 135 513
www.parks.tas.gov.au

TOURIST INFORMATION IN AUSTRALIA

There are tourist information centres in most towns and resorts. The main state offices and those for the larger and more popular places are given here.

AUSTRALIAN CAPITAL TERRITORY

Canberra and Region Visitors Centre

✉ 330 Northbourne Avenue, Dickson, ACT 2602
☎ 02 1300 554 114;
www.visitcanberra.com.au
🕐 Mon–Fri 9–5.30, Sat, Sun 9–4

NEW SOUTH WALES

Tourism New South Wales

☎ 13 20 77;
www.seesydney.com.au
www.visitnsw.com.au

Sydney Visitor Centre

✉ Cnr Argyle and Playfair streets, The Rocks, Sydney, NSW 2000
☎ 9240 8788 or 1800 067 676;
www.sydneyvisitorcentre.com.au

Blue Mountains Heritage Centre

✉ Govetts Leap Road, Blackheath, NSW 2785
☎ 02 4787 8877

Byron Bay Visitor Centre

✉ The Old Station Master's Cottage, 80 Jonson Street, Byron Bay, NSW 2481
☎ 02 6680 8558;
www.visitbyronbay.com

Coffs Coast Visitor Information Centre

✉ Cnr Pacific Highway and McLean Street, Coffs Harbour, NSW 2450
☎ 02 6648 4990;
www.coffscoast.com.au

Port Macquarie Visitor Information Centre

✉ Cnr Gordon and Gore streets, Port Macquarie, NSW 2444
☎ 02 6581 8000;
www.portmacquarieinfo.com.au

VICTORIA

Tourism Victoria

✉ 356 Collins Street, Melbourne, VIC 3000
☎ 13 28 42;
www.visitvictoria.com.au

Melbourne Visitor Centre

✉ Federation Square, Melbourne, VIC 3000
☎ 03 9658 9658;
www.visitmelbourne.com

Great Ocean Road Visitor Information Centre (Geelong)

✉ Stead Park, Princes Highway, Corio, VIC 3214
☎ 1800 620 888 or 03 5275 5797;
www.greatoceanroad.org

QUEENSLAND

Tourism Queensland

www.queensland-holidays.com.au

Queen Street Mall Visitor Information Centre

✉ Queen Street, Brisbane, QLD 4000
☎ 07 07 3006 6290;
www.visitbrisbane.com.au

Tourism Tropical North Queensland Gateway Discovery Centre

✉ 51 The Esplanade, Cairns, QLD 4870
☎ 07 4051 3588;
www.tropicalaustralia.com.au

NORTHERN TERRITORY

NT Tourist Commission

✉ 43 Mitchell Street, Darwin, NT 0800
☎ 08 8999 3900;
www.tourismnt.com.au

Tourism Top End

✉ Knuckey Street, Darwin, NT 0800
☎ 08 8980 6000;
www.tourismtopend.com.au

Central Australian Tourism Industry Association

✉ 60 Gregory Terrace, Alice Springs, NT 0870
☎ 08 8952 5800;
www.centralaustraliantourism.com

Uluru-Kata Tjuta National Park Cultural Centre (Ayers Rock)

✉ Yulara Drive, Yulara, NT 0872
☎ 08 8956 1100;
www.environment.gov.au/parks/uluru

SOUTH AUSTRALIA

South Australian Visitor and Travel Centre

✉ 18 King William Street, Adelaide, SA 5000
☎ 1300 764 227 or 08 8463 4547;
www.southaustralia.com
www.adelaide.southaustralia.com

Kangaroo Island Gateway Visitor Information Centre

✉ Howard Drive, Penneshaw, Kangaroo Island, SA 5222
☎ 08 8553 1185 or 1800 811 080;
www.tourkangarooisland.com.au

WESTERN AUSTRALIA

Western Australian Visitor Centre

✉ Albert Facey House, Forrest Place, Perth, WA 6000
☎ 1800 812 808;
www.wavisitorcentre.com

Albany Visitor Centre

✉ Old Railway Station, Princess Royal Drive, Albany, WA 6332
☎ 08 9841 9377;
www.albanytourist.com.au

Kalbarri Visitor Centre

✉ Grey Street, Kalbarri, WA 6536
☎ 08 9937 1104;
www.kalbarriwa.info

Broome Visitor Centre

✉ Broome Highway, Broome, WA 6725
☎ 08 9192 2222 or 1800 883 777;
www.broomevisitorcentre.com.au

TASMANIA

Hobart Travel Centre (general information)

✉ 20 Davey Street, Hobart, TAS 5000
☎ 03 6238 4222 or 1800 990 440;
www.hobarttravelcentre.com.au

Tasmanian Travel Centre (holiday bookings)

☎ 1300 827 743;
www.discovertasmania.com

USEFUL WEBSITES

There are thousands of sites on the internet with information about Australia, but, as elsewhere in the world, not all are reliable.

The select list below includes the addresses of organizations that are of main value to visitors, and these often have links to related websites.

Backpackers

» www.yha.com.au; backpackers and youth accommodation and travel.
» www.bugaustralia.com; concise, practical information.
» www.vipbackpackers.com; useful hostel search.
» www.world66.com/netcafeguide; comprehensive listing of internet cafés.

Banks

» www.anz.com
» www.commbank.com.au
» www.nab.com.au
» www.westpac.com.au

Communication

» www.auspost.com.au; includes information on the cost of sending items by post.
» www.telstra.com; information about mobile (cell) phones and landlines.
» www.whitepages.com.au; online directory enquiries.
» www.yellowpages.com.au; indispensable for directory assistance on products and services.

Documentation and Visas

» www.australia.com; Tourism Australia website with advice on all aspects of travel to Australia.
» www.eta.immi.gov.au; apply here for an electronic visa.
» www.fco.gov.uk; Britain's Foreign and Commonwealth Office, with advice on visas, consulates, and how to get help abroad.
» www.immi.gov.au; Department of Immigration and Multicultural and Indigenous Affairs, with application forms.
» www.travel.state.gov; US Department of State Bureau of Consular Affairs.

Embassies and Consulates

» Canada: www.dfait-maeci.gc.ca/australia
» Germany: www.germanembassy.org.au
» South Africa: www.sahc.org.au
» UK: www.ukinaustralia.tco.go.uk
» USA: www.canberra.usembassy.gov
» For details of other embassies and consulates see www.embassyworld.com.

Tourist Information

» www.access-able.com; an American site with good information for travellers with disabilities.
» www.airportsaustralia.com; compendium of travel resources.
» www.atn.com.au; hotels and tourist attractions by state.
» www.ausemade.com.au; online travel booking.
» www.babs.com.au; bed-and-breakfast in Australia.
» www.dec.wa.gov.au; Western Australian Department of Conservation.
» www.citysearch.com.au; listings for all major cities and tourist areas.
» www.coastalwatch.com.au; surfing conditions, information and events.
» www.customs.gov.au; what you can and cannot take into and out of the country.
» www.deh.gov.au; Department of the Environment and Heritage.
» www.nationaltrust.org.au; the main site for the National Trust of Australia, with links to the National Trusts for each state.
» www.toiletmap.gov.au; valuable information covering all Australia.
» www.traveldownunder.com.au; online travel booking.
» www.virtualtourist.com; personal opinions on attractions.

Health

» www.who.int/en; comprehensive health advice for all countries from the World Health Organization.
» www.cdc.gov; health advice for American travellers.
» www.fco.gov.uk; includes health advice for UK travellers abroad.

» www.health.gov.au; details of health cover for overseas students.
» www.masta-travel-health.com; British clinics providing travel medicine.
» www.flyingdoctor.net; information about Australia's Royal Flying Doctor Service.
» www.tmb.ie; the Tropical Medicine Bureau in Ireland.

Media

» www.abc.net.au; ABC radio and television channels.
» www.couriermail.news.com.au; Queensland's Courier-Mail.
» www.dailytelegraph.news.com.au; Daily Telegraph and Sunday Telegraph.
» www.seven.com.au; Television Network 7.
» www.ntnews.com.au; Northern Territory News.
» www.ninemsn.com.au; Television Network 9.
» www.ten.com.au; Television Network 10.
» www.theaustralian.news.com.au; The Australian newspaper.
» www.smh.com.au; Sydney Morning Herald.
» www.theadvertiser.news.com.au; South Australia's The Advertiser.
» www.theage.com.au; Victoria's The Age.
» www.themercury.news.com.au; Tasmania's The Mercury.
» www.thewest.com.au; The West Australian.

Motoring Organizations

See page 46.

Weather

» www.bom.gov.au; Australia's national Bureau of Meteorology, with comprehensive weather information and forecasts.
» www.news.bbc.co.uk/weather; this British site has information about the Australian climate and gives five-day forecasts.

Working Holidays

» www.immi.gov.au; information on visas, etc., for those planning to work their way round Australia.

NEWSPAPERS

Most Australian newspapers are state-oriented; there is only one national newspaper, *The Australian*.

Most of the major papers have websites (see table ▷ below). These can give you a feel for the local area and usually carry listings of what's on.

You can buy some international newspapers at larger newsstands across Australia but these are likely to be a day or two out of date because of the distance and time difference.

MAGAZINES

As in most countries, there are hundreds of magazines in Australia catering for all interests. Many well-known international titles have editions in Australia, but there are also widely read Australian magazines (see table ▷ below) which are also exported widely in the Asia-Pacific region.

TELEVISION

There are five terrestial TV networks and a growing number of cable or satellite pay-to-view channels (see table ▷ 320). Not all channels are available in all regions; in remote parts of the country there is likely to be a very limited choice.

All channels broadcast commercials, except for the Australian Broadcasting Corporation (ABC TV).

RADIO

The national stations are run by the Australian Broadcasting Corporation, ABC (www.abc.net.au). The main frequencies are shown in the table below, but these vary in the regions; check the local press for details. In addition there are dozens of commercial radio stations broadcasting across Australia.

Special Broadcasting Service (SBS) Radio www.sbs.com.au broadcasts multicultural programmes in 68 languages. There is a different language programme every hour 6am–12am, covering home and international news, culture, music and sport.

SBS RADIO

Sydney	97.7 FM, 1107 AM
Melbourne	93.1 FM, 1224 AM
Brisbane	93.3 FM
Perth	96.9 FM

NEWSPAPERS AND MAGAZINES

NEWSPAPERS

National

The Australian		www.theaustralian.news.com.au
The Weekend Australian		
Australian Financial Review		www.afr.com
Australian Capital Territory		
Canberra City News		www.citynews.com.au
Canberra Times		www.canberratimes.com.au
New South Wales		
Daily Telegraph	Thursday entertainment listings	www.dailytelegraph.news.com.au
Sydney Morning Herald	Friday entertainment listings	www.smh.com.au
Victoria		
The Age	Friday entertainment listings	www.theage.com.au
Herald Sun	Thursday entertainment listings	www.heraldsun.news.com.au
Queensland		
Courier-Mail		www.couriermail.news.com.au
Northern Territory		
Northern Territory News		www.ntnews.com.au
The Guide	Free, monthly	
Alice Springs News	Every Wednesday	www.alicespringsnews.com.au
Centralian Advocate	Twice-weekly in Alice Springs	
South Australia		
The Advertiser	Thursday entertainment listings	www.theadvertiser.news.com.au
Western Australia		
The West Australian		www.thewest.com.au
Sunday Times		www.perthnow.com.au
Tasmania		
The Mercury	Thursday entertainment listings	www.themercury.news.com.au
Tasmanian Travelways	Free paper with accommodations	

MAGAZINES

National

Australian Geographic	Illustrated nature and wildlife	www.ausgeo.com.au
Australian Gourmet Traveller	Popular food and travel	www.gourmet.ninemsn.com.au
Business Review Weekly	Authoritative business news	www.brw.com.au
Outdoor Australia	Illustrated outdoor adventure	www.outdooraustralia.com
Wild	Wilderness adventure	www.wild.com.au

TELEVISION

ABC	Publicly funded: news, current affairs and cultural programmes	www.abc.net.au
7 Network	Largest commercial channel: news, current affairs and entertainment	www.seven.com.au
9 Network	News, entertainment and sport	www.ninemsn.com.au
10 Network	Repeats and bought-in programmes	www.ten.com.au
SBS	Publicly funded, multicultural channel: good news programmes	www.sbs.com.au

PAY TO VIEW

Optus	Covering Sydney, Melbourne and Brisbane	www.optus.com.au
Foxtel	Covering Sydney, Melbourne, Brisbane, the Gold Coast, Adelaide and Perth	www.foxtel.com.au
Austar	Darwin	www.austar.com.au
Imparja	Channel for Aboriginal viewers	www.imparja.com.au

ABC RADIO

	CANBERRA	SYDNEY	MELBOURNE	BRISBANE	DARWIN	ADELAIDE	PERTH	HOBART
NewsRadio	103.9 FM	630 AM	1026 AM	936 AM	102.5 FM	972 AM	585 AM	747 AM
	Continuous news							
Radio National	846 AM	576 AM	621 AM	792 AM	657 AM	729 AM	810 AM	585 AM
	Social, cultural and political issues							
Triple J	101.5 FM	105.7 FM	107.5 FM	107.7 FM	103.3 FM	105.5 FM	99.3 FM	92.9 FM
	New music for young Australians							
Classic FM	102.3 FM	92.9 FM	105.9 FM	106.1 FM	107.3 FM	103.9 FM	97.7 FM	93.9 FM
	Classical, jazz and contemporary music							
Local Radio	For local frequency see www.abc.net.au/radio/localradio							
	News, local issues, sport, talkback							
Radio Australia	For local frequency see www.abc.net.au/ra							
Asia-Pacific audience	DiG Radio	www.abc.net.au/dig						
	New and popular music on the internet							

BOOKS AND FILMS

BOOKS

Understanding Australia's history and culture enhances any visit to the country. It has a rich literary tradition, but it does not take itself too seriously. These books are enjoyable to read and will help to inform any holiday there.

Literature

Bill Bryson, **Down Under/In a Sunburned Country** (2000)—the entertaining story of his walk across Australia, trying to discover why Australians are so laid-back.
Peter Carey, **Oscar and Lucinda** (1988)—partly set on an ocean liner sailing to Australia.
Peter Carey, **True History of the Kelly Gang** (2000)—novel in the form of Ned Kelly's diary.
Albert Facey, **A Fortunate Life** (1981)—the award-winning autobiography of an ordinary man as a manual worker, soldier and family man.
Kate Grenville, **The Secret River** (2005)—Set in the early 19th century on the frontier of white settlement where normal rules don't apply.
Robert Hughes, **The Fatal Shore** (1986)—an epic description of the transportation of men, women and children from Georgian Britain into a horrific penal system.
Thomas Keneally, **The Chant of Jimmie Blacksmith** (1972)—the tragic consequences of a 19th-century white girl's marriage to an Aborigine, by the author of *Schindler's List*.
D. H. Lawrence, **Kangaroo** (1923)—classic story of early settlers' conflicts.
David Malouf, **Remembering Babylon** (1993)—lyrical story about the hostility between early British settlers and Aboriginal people.
Jan Morris, **Sydney** (1992)—evocative portrait of the city.
Banjo Paterson, **The Man from Snowy River** (1895)—High Country bushman's poem by the writer of 'Waltzing Matilda'.
Nevil Shute, **A Town Like Alice** (1950)—book and memorable film

about English girl meeting Australian soldier in Alice Springs.
Patrick White, **Voss** (1957)—epic about a 19th-century explorer in the outback.
Tim Winton, **Dirt Music** (2001)—a love story set in the remote north of Western Australia. Winner of the Miles Franklin Award, 2000.

Aboriginal Culture and Issues

Bruce Chatwin, **The Songlines** (1987).
James Cowan, **Aborigine Dreaming** (2002).
Josephine Flood, **Archaeology of the Dreamtime** (1983).
Matthew Kneale, **English Passengers** (2000).
Christobel Mattingley and Ken Hampton (ed.), **Survival in Our Land** (1988).
Henry Reynolds, **The Other Side of the Frontier** (1982).

Reference

Ivan Holliday: **A Field Guide to Australian Trees** (3rd edition, 2002, New Holland).
The Mammals of Australia (rev. edition, 2002, New Holland).
Penguin Good Australia Wine Guide (2010, Penguin Books Australia).
Ken Simpson and Nicolas Day: Field Guides to Birds of Australia (7th edition, 2004, Viking Australia).
Traveller's Atlas of Australia (2010, Explore Australia).

Children's books

Graeme Base's picture books.
May Gibbs, **Snugglepot and Cuddlepie** (1918).
Paul Jennings—any of his stories.
Norman Lindsay, **The Magic Pudding** (1918).
Juli Vivar and Mem Fox, **Possum Magic** (1983).

FILMS

The Australian film industry is internationally regarded as being in the first rank of creative and technical excellence. Actors, such as Nicole Kidman, work on the world stage and receive the highest

awards. To understand the nature and character of the country there are a number of popular films that repay watching.

Crocodile Dundee (1986)—hugely entertaining film, set in the Top End.
Dead Calm (1989)—the thriller that launched Nicole Kidman's career.
The Dish (2000)—Sam Neill stars in the story of Australia's contribution to landing a man on the moon.
Evil Angels (A Cry in the Dark) (1988)—story of the mother who's baby was taken by a dingo, starring Meryl Streep.
Gallipoli (1981)—an early Mel Gibson film about the horrors of the infamous World War I battle.
Japanese Story (2003)—A feisty geologist and a Japanese businessman strike up a transitory friendship in outback Western Australia.
Mad Max I, II and III (1979, 1981, 1985)—George Miller's post-apocalyptic adventures brought Mel Gibson international stardom.
Muriel's Wedding (1995)—comedy starring Toni Collette (Muriel) who moves from small-town Australia to start a new life in Sydney.
Ned Kelly (1970 and 2003)—The former stars Mick Jagger; the latter Heath Ledger.
Picnic at Hanging Rock (1975)—a schoolgirls' picnic goes wrong when some of them disappear in the bush.
Priscilla, Queen of the Desert (1994)—comedy starring Terence Stamp and Guy Pearce: drag queens drive a bus through the outback.
Rabbit Proof Fence (2002)—three Aborigine girls walk thousands of miles to find their mother.
Shine (1996)—virtuoso Australian pianist struggles with mental illness.
Story of the Kelly Gang (1906)—the world's first full-length feature film.
Ten Canoes (2006)—Opened the nations's eyes to Aboriginal traditions, culture and spirituality by bringing together fantasy, comedy and drama.

Opposite *Still from* Priscilla, Queen of the Desert

SHOPPING

There is fierce competition between the capital cities in each state to woo the committed shopaholic. Although most would agree that the best shopping on offer is in Sydney and Melbourne, you will find an excellent range of shopping options in all of Australia's major cities.

Airlines once ran shopping tours to the Victorian capital from all around Australia, so if you plan to shop in Melbourne you can't go far wrong.

The best selection of shops are found in the central business districts (CBDs) of all the capital cities. Here the major department stores, boutiques and speciality shops line the main streets or shelter in arcades.

BARGAIN TIME

Like shoppers all over the world, Australians like to take advantage of the great end-of-season sales. Discount retail parks, which are big in many parts of the world, are not well established in Australia so bargains are found mostly during the sales.

However, Melbourne and Sydney excel in factory outlets selling seconds, out-of-season and discontinued lines. In Melbourne, these outlets are in Bridge Road and Swan Street, Richmond.

In Sydney the clothing trade is based mainly in the cosmopolitan, inner-city suburb of Surry Hills. Scores of small, intersecting streets house factory outlets and wholesalers selling men's and women's clothing and accessories. The area around Regent and Redfern streets, a few minutes south of Sydney's central business district, is another mine for bargains.

CHAIN STORES

Australia has two main department stores, Myer and David Jones, and three large discount stores: Big W, Target and K Mart. There are also two major supermarket chains, Coles and Woolworths.

Smaller chain stores specialize in everything from clothing to jewellery. The range of goods found in these stores depends on their location. One of the best times to shop is at the end of December and the end of June, when they all have end-of-season sales.

The largest branches of Myer and David Jones are in Sydney and Melbourne; the other branches in suburban and regional shopping malls offer similar products but lack the range. K Mart and Target have a good spread of shops in Australia. If you're searching for name brands, the department and specialist stores are better, but if price is a main factor then discount stores provide an extensive range of goods.

The range and size of goods on offer in supermarkets also varies with location. In regional areas, supermarkets often have more general merchandise than their city counterparts. Supermarkets that serve large regional areas can have a range of general and 'tourist' items.

Many locals do their shopping at the large shopping malls in suburban and rural areas because of the array of shops available—many national boutiques and larger stores are found in these centres—and because it is easier to park.

CULTURED GIFTS

Australia's multicultural population makes it a great shopping spot for art and crafts. Markets are full of tubular wind chimes, intricate stained-glass panels, bowls carved from native timber, natural crystal, jewellery dripping with local gemstones, original T-shirt designs and framed pen-and-wash sketches of city or outback scenes. Most craft galleries show locally made pottery, jewellery and other handmade goods.

Aboriginal art is becoming more popular. All the major cities have galleries devoted exclusively to the products of Aboriginal Australians—dot paintings, boomerangs and didgeridoos. Many Aboriginal-based attractions also sell traditional items, and in some cases the items have been made on the premises.

If you want to buy a major piece of Aboriginal art, try to ensure that it is the real thing. To prevent the sale of fake Aboriginal art, Australia's indigenous people have developed the Label of Authenticity, a symbol that helps guarantee Aboriginal and Torres Strait Islander art and other cultural products as authentic. Each label has a serial number that can be traced to the maker of the artwork or craft item.

MARKETS

The many markets held all around Australia have opportunities for the devout bargain-hunter. Some open on weekdays but most are run on weekends.

In Sydney, Paddy's Market, which is more than 150 years old, is a compendium of about 800 stalls, selling everything from clothes to potatoes. Queen Victoria Market, in Melbourne, offers an equally, if not more, impressive range. St. Kilda Market, along the beachfront Esplanade on Sundays, is known for art and crafts, while the Sunday Arts Centre Market at 100 St. Kilda Road sells traditional and contemporary ceramics, handmade picture frames and jewellery. Open-air shopping at Brisbane's weekend markets is a summer delight. Riverside Markets,

along Eagle Street, features art, jewellery, fabric painting and wood-carving. South Bank Craft Markets has more than 100 stalls. In Cairns, the weekend Mud Markets at the Pier, and Rusty's Bazaar Markets, on Fridays and Saturdays, deal in a complete range of art and crafts. Adelaide's Central Market in Grote Street runs on Tuesdays and Thursdays to Saturdays and has scores of stalls selling fruit, craftwork and jewellery. Hobart's Salamanca Market, held on Saturdays features a good selection of craftwork made from native woods, pottery and glass.

NATURAL FINDS

Australia is a natural source of gold, diamonds, sapphires and other precious stones, as well as around 95 per cent of the world's opal deposits. White opals are mined from the fields of Andamooka and Coober Pedy in South Australia. Boulder opals come from Queensland, and black opals from Lightning Ridge and White Cliffs. Stores selling opal jewellery abound in all Australian cities, including duty-free shops. Australia also possesses an abundance of pearls. Pearls produced in the waters off Broome, Western Australia are known by the trade name South Sea. Several shops in Broome sell them, but don't expect bargains—pearls are always expensive.

SHOPPING—LOCAL GOODS

Clothing, opal jewellery and Aboriginal items are often high on the list of unique presents or souvenirs. Of course, you will also have no problem finding souvenirs ranging from tea towels to fridge magnets, but as most are not made in Australia, always check the labels first for an authentic item.

SHOPPING PRECINCTS

Many locals shop at large suburban shopping malls and specialist shopping streets. Melbourne has many such streets, including Greville Street, and Prahran and

Chapel streets, South Yarra, where Australia's young and upcoming designers show their work.

In Sydney, the Paddington end of Oxford Street has some of the best Australian fashion and food on offer. Other popular shopping spots are the Strand Arcade and Queen Victoria Building, Pitt Street Mall and Darling Harbour.

In Darwin the locals go to the Smith Street Mall, the Casuarina Shopping Centre, Parap Shopping Village and the Fannie Bay Shopping Centre. Most Brisbane shoppers browse the Queen Street Mall, Wintergarden, Roma and Brisbane arcades, the South Bank and Paddington. In Cairns there's Broadbeach Mall, Orchid Plaza and The Conservatory Shopping Village. Adelaide has the Rundle Mall, Southern Cross and Adelaide Arcade and Glenelg. In Hobart try the Elizabeth Street Mall, the Cat and Fiddle Arcade and Gasworks Village. Perth's shopping includes the Hay Street and Murray Street malls, the Forrest Chase complex, London Court, the Carillon Centre and Piccadilly Arcade.

WEARING OUT

It doesn't cost a lot to pick up a genuine Australian souvenir. Surfing gear, wool and sheepskin products, Drizabone oilskin raincoats, Akubra hats (wide-brimmed and usually made of felt) and bushwear are all unmistakeably Australian. You can find them in all the major cities and in most larger country towns

Australia has a distinct style of clothing, from vibrant and challenging to simple and classic. Good names include Trent Nathan, Country Road, Covers, Perri Cutten, Scanlan & Theodore and Collette Dinnigan. Also distinctively Australian is wearable art in the form of swimwear, fashion garments, fabrics and souvenirs including Ken Done (the artist and designer) and Desert Designs. Knitwear, from vivid children's clothing to Jumbuk-brand greasy wool sweaters, is available in major shopping areas.

ENTERTAINMENT AND NIGHTLIFE

Culture addicts will not be deprived in Australia. Or at least, not in the main cities and towns. Each capital and many of the large provincial cities have excellent arts venues where you can enjoy everything from international stars to local theatre companies. And all the states have at least one festival, often several, devoted to the performing arts, featuring both Australian and international talent.

OK, it's a cliché, but many young Australians do work hard and party hard. As a result, every major city and many country towns have plenty of fun for all tastes and budgets after dark. Many hotels, clubs and restaurants also offer live music, especially at weekends.

During the summer months many leading stars also perform outdoors. The Leeuwin Estate, a winery in Western Australia, was one of the first to introduce outdoor performances and has attracted such stars as Dame Kiri Te Kanawa, Shirley Bassey and Tom Jones. Many vineyards have followed suit, providing a night of great wine and entertainment.

TASTE FOR MUSIC

A number of world-recognized performing arts companies are based in Sydney, but all state capitals have their own symphony orchestras and theatre groups, and many states have youth orchestras and other specialist music groups. It's not essential to travel to a city for a night of entertainment. The leading companies frequently tour around the country, performing everywhere from the grandest theatres to parks.

Less formal are the many free concerts in local parks during the summer months. These cater for all musical tastes from jazz to Latin American, but they are also popular with Australia's top performance companies. Audiences usually take along picnics to enjoy while listening to the music.

Opera Australia presents more than 260 performances a year, from traditional to contemporary. It performs at the Sydney Opera House for eight months of the year and resides under the spire at The Arts Centre, Melbourne.

THEATRE LIGHTS

Mel Gibson, Cate Blanchett, Geoffrey Rush and Judy Davis are just some of the cast of actors who began their careers in Australian theatre. The Sydney Theatre Company is a major force in Australian drama, operating from its home venue, The Wharf, on Sydney's harbour, and there's also the Drama Theatre and the Playhouse of the Sydney Opera House.

Expect style and passion at The Arts Centre, the usual home of the Melbourne Theatre Company. Performances range from classic and contemporary Australian to international plays.

Many of the world's hit musicals, such as *The Lion King*, are staged in Australia.

DANCE

The Australian Ballet is the largest ballet company in the country, with more than 60 dancers and giving about 200 performances each year. Based in Melbourne, the company performs regionally, nationally and internationally. The West Australian Ballet is based in Perth and tours extensively. Queensland Ballet is based at the historic Thomas Dixon Centre in Brisbane's West End.

The Sydney-based Bangarra Dance Theatre blends traditional Aboriginal and Torres Strait Islander history and culture with international contemporary dance influences; its home is The Wharf, on Sydney's harbour. The Tjapukai Dance Theatre, based near Cairns, also showcases Aboriginal dance.

MAKING AN ENTRANCE

Daily newspapers are the best way to find out about upcoming performances, or visit the website of the local state tourist authority (▷ 317).

Australia's two major ticket booking agencies can provide information on events and take bookings: Ticketek, tel 13 28 49; www.ticketek.com.au; Ticketmaster, tel 13 61 00; www.ticketmaster.com.au. Tickets to opera, ballet and big-time shows are sometimes hard to obtain, so book as early as possible.

Performance starting times at more formal events are taken literally—latecomers are not admitted until there's a suitable break in the performance. Dress code is not strict. Either suits or casual dress is acceptable.

PARTY HARD

Like many countries, Australia has embraced the lifestyle of nightclubs and discos, and many of the older establishments are still going strong. And, just like everywhere else, the most popular venues are the ones with the longest wait.

Dance parties are also popular in the major cities, many of them all-night events, with various Australian DJs plus visiting international names.

ON STAGE

Australians have a long tradition of going to their local hotel or pub to listen to up-and-coming bands. Some of Australia's best-known international performers started on the local hotel and pub scene. The tradition is still just as strong, but it's not all rock, grunge and techno—there's ample jazz, blues and acoustic, too. Attending pub venues is also a great way to meet the locals, and many hotels provide good food, allowing partygoers to make a night of it.

Although many restaurants offer live music, the style is generally more sedate and not quite as loud as it can be in the pub. Venues, acts and attractions are listed in guides published in each state's metropolitan daily newspapers, usually on Thursday or Friday.

BAR ICE

There are, of course, those who want to enjoy a night without being blasted out by loud music. Stylish bars, clubs and lounges are common in all state capital cities, where the emphasis is on providing great drinks and a friendly environment. Such bars and clubs are particularly popular after work on week nights with businessmen and

women; at weekends the dress code is less formal.

Growing in popularity are bars attached to boutique breweries, where a range of local beers are on tap, together with traditional drinks.

GAY LIFE

The large gay, lesbian, bisexual and transgender community in Australia ensures plenty of bars and clubs catering specifically for these groups. Sydney and Melbourne have the most, and many clubs are found within specific suburbs.

In Sydney the heart of all things gay can be found on Oxford Street, taking in the suburbs of Darlinghurst, Surry Hills and Paddington. The inner west suburbs of Newtown, Erskineville and Leichhardt also have a burgeoning pub/bar scene with a strong gay and lesbian background.

Sydney's downtown and Darling Harbour precincts also have an enormous range of gay and straight chic bars and nightclubs.

Among Melbourne's gay and lesbian precincts are the northern suburbs of Fitzroy and Collingwood, and south of the city in Prahran, South Yarra and St. Kilda.

A GOOD BET

Many night-owls frequent the country's casinos, which offer everything from gambling to live shows to movies.

Casinos can be found in Hobart, Perth, Launceston, Alice Springs, Darwin, Surfers Paradise, Adelaide, Canberra, Melbourne, Townsville, Cairns, Sydney and Brisbane.

Dress codes usually apply at clubs and casinos. People wearing blue jeans, sandshoes (sneakers), thongs (flip-flops) or singlets (sleeveless T-shirts) will not be admitted. The smarter the establishment the stricter the dress code. Some of the more popular nightspots have 'minders' who control who is admitted.

The legal alcohol level for driving is 0.05 per cent in most states, and the police strictly enforce this law with random breath testing.

PRACTICALITIES | **WHAT TO DO**

SPORTS AND ACTIVITIES

If there's one thing Australians love, it's cheering their chosen teams or sports stars. Over the years they have had plenty to shout about. The Australian love affair with sport goes way beyond just watching it. With more than 120 national and thousands of local, regional and state sporting organizations, it's estimated that 6.5 million people in Australia are registered sport participants. Not bad from a population of only 19 million. For visitors, there's no reason not to join in and continue your exercise regime while on holiday.

Outback plains, mountains, rainforests, wild rivers and the world's largest coral reef—Australia is adventure. But you don't need to go far off the beaten track for a challenge: Zip across Sydney Harbour in a jet-boat, ski down one of Australia's challenging ski slopes, or ride a Harley-Davidson motorcycle along the Great Ocean Road.

ADVENTURE ACTIVITIES

If you have a head for heights, hot-air balloon flights are available in many parts of Australia. Or there is skydiving and bungee-jumping. And if you are into hang-gliding, then head for Queensland's Sunshine Coast and Mount Tamborine, New South Wales's Taree, Western Australia's Albany, and Victoria's Ararat. Australia also has around 100 gliding clubs, and joy flights can be taken with experienced pilots.

There is no shortage of places to go abseiling (rappelling) and rock-climbing or horseback riding and bushwalking. If you want the wilderness experience without the work, then a 4WD drive adventure is a good option—rent a vehicle or join one of a number of tours.

White-water rafters have lots of choices, but many head to the Tully River in Queensland and the Franklin in Tasmania.

If you prefer a more leisurely pace there's kayaking. A quiet paddle down the Northern Territory's Katherine Gorge is memorable, as is kayaking alongside dolphins in Byron Bay, New South Wales.

Many visitors combine a trip to Australia with the chance to learn to dive. The deep-sea diving off the New South Wales and Queensland coasts is spectacular, and the Ningaloo Reef off Western Australia is just a short swim from the beach. Or swim with the whale sharks—they come to Exmouth at the end of summer.

AUSTRALIAN RULES FOOTBALL

Talk to many sports lovers from Melbourne, Adelaide and Perth and they'll tell you that there's only really one winter sport—Australian Rules Football. In truth, there is also nothing quite like attending Melbourne Cricket Ground when 90,000 fans are all screaming for their teams. While it obviously helps to understand the rules, the game is spectacular enough to ensure an enjoyable afternoon even if you don't.

GOLF

Australians have a passion for golf. Hundreds of courses are dotted all around Australia, and just about every town seems to have a course or is near one. In the past the best courses were private, but more new courses are opening that are top-notch and welcome the public. Many courses also offer accommodation. Naturally, the more popular courses are more expensive.

Ausgolf (www.ausgolf.com.au) lists more than 1,500 courses around Australia, along with the cost of playing a round.

HORSE RACING

In autumn and spring, sport attention turns to horse racing. Races are held all around the country. The most famous is the Melbourne Cup, part of the Spring Racing Carnival that features many of Australia's top racehorses. Some of the same horses try again in Sydney's Golden Slipper and Sydney Cup in March.

JOGGING/BICYCLING

For many Australians, a morning or afternoon run or walk is the most popular form of exercise. Every capital city has special walking/bicycling tracks that take in the most scenic attractions. The tracks around Melbourne, Perth and Sydney's Botanic Gardens, Canberra's Lake Burley Griffin, Brisbane's river and Darwin's harbour provide spectacular routes for a daily jog.

The same tracks are equally popular with bicyclists, especially at weekends; bicycle rental establishments are available near the most popular bicycling routes.

Generally it's safe to walk and run during the day, but after dark you should be careful, more so if you head off the beaten track or are in unlit or badly lit areas.

MOTORSPORTS

Melbourne also hosts another major event on the sporting calendar, the Formula One Grand Prix, held around Albert Park Lake, usually in March. Racing enthusiasts agree that the first two days of the race are the best time to attend as competitors are more relaxed and the crowds aren't as large.

Phillip Island, which lies 140km (87 miles) southeast of Melbourne, also stages a Grand Prix, but for motorcycles. The race is held in October, the same time as the

Indy300 international motor race is staged on Queensland's Gold Coast. General admission tickets for both Victorian events can be purchased at the venue. Grandstand tickets need to be pre-purchased.

RUGBY

Australian Rules is played in New South Wales and Queensland, but most sports lovers in these states are fans of rugby league (rugby union is less popular). On most weekends between April and the end of September rugby union, rugby league and Australian Rules Football matches are played around the country. To see one of these matches, often all you need do is turn up at the venue to be sure of a ticket, although when top teams are playing at some of the smaller stadiums it's a good idea to book ahead, as some matches sell out. Tickets for these and other sports can be booked on the telephone or via the web.

SOCCER

While support for soccer isn't as strong in Australia as elsewhere in the world, there are many fans out there, especially during World Cup time or at international friendly games. Western Australian soccer matches attract the biggest crowds, in no small part due to the many British-born residents of Perth.

SPORTS CENTRES

Local councils and the *Yellow Pages* (www.yellowpages.com.au) have listings and information on the many gyms around the country. Most gyms have casual entry and many have a range of classes, such as aerobics. Some have squash courts, and there are also many stand-alone squash courts that are open to the public.

Some tennis clubs are open to members only, but two of Australia's most famous tennis stadiums—Melbourne Park, home of the Australian Open, and the Sydney Olympic Tennis Centre—are open to the public all year round.

SUMMER SPORT

Cricket, tennis and golf take over the sporting calendar in summer. Australia's best cricketers play in the local state competition (although many of the national team now play in fewer state matches) and at international level. There is rarely a problem getting a seat to watch state cricket, but given the popularity of the national team, it's wise to book ahead if you want to attend an international game.

The main tennis season starts around December, and finishes in late January with the staging of the Australian Open in Melbourne. One of the best times to attend the Open is in the first week. A ground pass takes you to the outside courts where you can see champions in action playing lesser-known opponents or practising.

Many of the world's top golfers head to Australia during the summer to take part in major tournaments.

WATERSPORTS

Given that Australia has about 36,735km (22,776 miles) of coastline, it's no surprise that swimming is a popular recreational sport for many.

Although some beaches are perfect for swimming all year round, care must be taken at others. You must not swim off the northern Australian coastal beaches from around November to the end of April because of the presence of potentially deadly box jellyfish. In the very far north, saltwater crocodiles can also be a (possibly fatal) problem.

The more energetic culture of surfing is alive and well all around Australia, and keen surfers will find plenty of challenges. Novice surfers can enrol at a 'learn to surf school' where you will be taught all the skills to impress your friends. Shops near the most popular surfing spots rent out surfboards and all the gear you might need.

If you plan to swim at one of Australia's many surf beaches you must swim between the warning flags and heed the advice of the surf lifesavers as these waters can be very dangerous.

For those who prefer the safety of a local swimming pool there are plenty of options. Most councils in the major cities and many country towns maintain public swimming pools. Some offer indoor and outdoor pools, while some pools close during the winter. One of the most famous pools is the Sydney Aquatic Centre, which hosted the 2000 Olympics swimming competition. The price of a swim depends on the facilities and location. Local councils or the *Yellow Pages* (www.yellowpages.com.au) are good sources of information.

HEALTH AND BEAUTY

It could be argued that Australians were slow to recognize the benefits of looking after their minds and bodies with a little pampering, but they have now caught up with the rest of the world.

Getting that essential facial or relaxing massage is easier than ever, especially in Sydney, Melbourne and Brisbane. Many of Australia's five-star hotels in the state capital cities and major tourist areas have spas.

Increasingly popular are day spas run by cosmetic or skin-care product manufacturers, or specialized spa operators such as Aveda, Jurlique, Angsana and Spa Chakra.

Australia's health retreats are often situated in tranquil, idyllic surroundings—for example, immersed in rainforests or beside beaches, where the environment is conducive to rest and relaxation.

If you take your health and relaxation seriously, Camp Eden is worth considering. Located in the lush hinterland behind the Gold Coast, it is one of Australia's

leading holistic health retreats.

The Daintree Eco Lodge provides elegant luxury and effective treatments in the heart of the Wet Tropics of Queensland World Heritage Area, the world's oldest living rainforest.

Or combine pampering with sightseeing at Lilianfels in New South Wales's Blue Mountains, near Sydney.

FOR CHILDREN

Fascinating zoos and wildlife parks, fun museums, numerous outdoor activities and child-friendly accommodation make Australia a great place for families. Australian operators are aware of the importance of families and go out of their way to cater for them, with family passes and plenty of activities for youngsters.

ADVENTURE ACTIVITIES
Away from the coast, horseback riding, bushwalking and other sporting activities keep even the most energetic challenged. Many families choose to stay at the growing number of hotels with children's clubs, which provide activities for children of all ages. Australia's beaches are wonderful places for kids to be fully entertained.

MUSEUMS
The days of going to a museum and looking at exhibitions behind glass cases are gone: Hands-on learning is the go in all the major museums in Australia. Sydney's Darling Harbour (▷ 71) is a child's delight due to such attractions as the Powerhouse Museum and the Australian National Maritime Museum. Questacon, the National Science and Technology Centre in Canberra (▷ 112), where learning is combined with activities.

THEME PARKS
Queensland's Gold Coast has the reputation as Australia's theme park

capital, though many other states can also provide a fun day out.

Victoria's Sovereign Hill, built on a former gold-mining site in Ballarat (▷ 133), re-creates the dusty life of the 1850s, when gold was king. Children can pan for gold and keep their finds.

Rides are a great attraction at Queensland's Gold Coast theme parks: Sea World, Warner Bros. Movieworld, Dreamworld and Wet'n'Wild (▷ 181). In addition, Sea World is known for its dolphin and sea-lion shows. At Warner Bros. Movie World you can see real movies being made, watch stunt shows and experience virtual reality. At Dreamworld there are rare Bengal tigers on Tiger Island, the Thunder River Rapids Ride (you'll get wet), movies on a massive IMAX screen, a steam train ride, koalas, and the rather messy Slime Bowl.

TRAIN RIDES
Families on holiday in Victoria often combine a trip to Phillip Island with a ride on the Puffing Billy steam train

in the Dandenongs (▷ 134). Many of the other states also have rides in restored trains. The Blue Mountains in New South Wales has one of the world's steepest railways, the Zig Zag (▷ 108).

ZOOS AND WILDLIFE PARKS
Children love seeing Australia's cuddly koalas and patting a kangaroo. Australian zoos and wildlife parks have made great efforts to allow visitors to get as close as possible to the animals and now many offer walk-through enclosures. The wildlife parks are a good way to see local wildlife—the parks near Alice Springs and Darwin are world famous. At Monkey Mia in Western Australia, children can get close up to dolphins. In southeastern Queensland, Currumbin Sanctuary is home to hundreds of rainbow lorikeets. On Victoria's Phillip Island you can watch fairy penguins walk each night from the water to their sandy burrows. And if you're too young to go deep-sea diving, try the Sydney Aquarium at Darling Harbour.

FESTIVALS AND EVENTS

The larger capital cities vie for the title of 'event capital of Australia', so it's not surprising that the Australian calendar is filled year-round with a huge array of festivals and events. There's everything from a horse-race that stops the nation to the more usual artistic and musical festivals. Australia's multiculturalism is evident through various festivals—every Chinatown around the country comes alive at Chinese New Year, and other groups celebrate important days with equal gusto.

To start the year, firework displays and celebrations are held around the country on New Year's Eve; most people agree that the Sydney foreshore is one of the best places to be. Regular major capital city events in January include the Sydney Festival, which covers street theatre, art shows, amusement parks, poetry readings, international drama and a free concert series. Hobart's similar festival celebrates its art and culture and Tasmania's great food. The performing arts and culture of Western Australia are highlighted at the Perth International Arts Festival.

Adelaide hosts one of the country's most extensive arts events. Held biennially in even-numbered years in late February and early March, the Adelaide Festival involves hundreds of Australian and international performers. The Adelaide Fringe Festival runs parallel to the main event, beginning a week earlier with performances in venues across the city, ranging from the crazy to the bizarre to the seriously intellectual.

One of Sydney's largest festivals, the Sydney Gay and Lesbian Mardi Gras, is held in March. This has prime place in the world's gay calendar, and a highlight is the fun-filled, provocative parade along Oxford Street.

March in Melbourne brings the Australian Grand Prix, the Melbourne International Comedy Festival, the Wine and Food Festival, and Moomba, known for its fireworks, music and river pageants.

Meanwhile in Canberra, Taste—Celebrating Food, Wine and the Arts—is staged. The festival highlights Canberra's and the surrounding region's food producers, chefs and artistic performers. The Hot Air Balloon Fiesta—the biggest in the southern hemisphere—is also held in Canberra in March. Around 50 balloons of all shapes and sizes fill the sky.

Early April is the time for the Melbourne International Flower and Garden Show (www.melbflowershow.com.au). Held at the Royal Exhibition Building and Carlton Gardens, it's a must for keen gardeners. Wine lovers head to the Barossa Vintage Festival at Barossa in South Australia.

In June it is the turn of Brisbane's gay and lesbian community to host their festival, while in Sydney cinema-goers can enjoy the glamour of the Sydney Film Festival. If you miss this, Melbourne has a film festival in July and August.

Spring is the signal for one of Canberra's most popular events, Floriade (www.floriade australia. com). From mid-September to the end of October thousnds of visitors arrive to admire the amazing displays of bulbs and annuals.

In October and November Melbourne puts on its party face to celebrate the Spring Racing Carnival and the horse-race that brings the entire nation to a standstill, the Melbourne Cup. The Melbourne Festival, and the Australian Motorcycle Grand Prix at the Phillip Island Grand Prix Circuit, make October a busy month in Victoria.

One of the world's classic blue-water yacht races starts on Boxing Day in Sydney, in front of a vast crowd, and culminates in a lively party in Hobart, Tasmania.

What these events are to the major cities, agricultural shows are to many of the country towns. As well as providing family fun, displays of crafts, produce and livestock, and demonstrations of horseback riding, sheep shearing and wood chopping give an insight into rural Australia.

In each state capital city the country comes to the city at least once a year in the form of Royal Agricultural shows.

EATING

As people of an immigrant nation Australians have adopted the cuisines of their countries of origin. As a result many Aussies cannot describe the cooking style of their country, where the traditions of early English, Welsh, Scots and Irish settlers have fused with the tastes of later immigrants and international styles.

BOUNTIFUL AUSTRALIA

No visitor to Australia need go hungry. Inexpensive meals are available at pubs in almost every town, while major cities have everything—Spanish tapas bars, restaurants offering every national cuisine, brasseries, bistros, cafés and hotels. Even motels serve Continental or filling English/American breakfasts. You can find basic food at roadside filling stations, museums, universities and some wineries, while American-influenced burger, chicken and pizza outlets abound.

Most metropolitan city shopping complexes and major markets have food halls offering inexpensive dishes from around the world. Or try Australian bakeries, or hot-bread shops, whose breads now range from focaccia to French-inspired Vietnamese. Pies, quiches and sweet treats can be enjoyed at alfresco tables outside some bakeries and they are certainly a good source for picnics and barbecues.

HOME-GROWN

Australia is rich in meat, seafood, fish, vegetables and fruit, including tropical varieties such as mangoes, bananas, rambutan, custard apples, papayas and avocado. There are macadamia nuts in tropical Queensland and cold-climate produce in the apple isle, Tasmania. Citrus fruits—oranges, mandarins, lemons and limes—grow from South Australia's Riverland on the Murray River to Queensland.

ABORIGINAL FOOD

You can experience the food of Australia's Aborigines—traditional hunters and gatherers—at places such as Adelaide's Tandanya (▷ 238). On any tour to discover Aboriginal culture, you are inevitably introduced to bush tucker, sustenance for thousands of years. Kangaroo, the world's healthiest meat, may be on the menu, as will the long-legged bird, the emu. More likely you'll be shown how to eat berries and leaves in the bush and how to get early morning water from dew-fresh leaves—survival stuff for the stranded.

TRADITIONS

Until the 1960s the typical Australian evening meal followed the then

British tradition: meat (usually roasted or stewed) and two or three vegetables. Dining out was uncommon for everyone except commercial travellers (travelling salesmen), who stayed and dined at country pubs. Lunch was a sandwich, a meat pie with tomato sauce, or a pasty.

The pasty (or pastie, an envelope of pastry filled with meat and vegetables) is still revered among the Yorke Peninsula Copper Triangle towns of South Australia, where it was imported by miners from Cornwall. These pioneers–and their cuisine–are commemorated at Kernewek Lowender, the world's biggest Cornish festival, held in odd-numbered years.

Meat pies, too, are still very popular takeout meals. You may be lucky enough to find shops selling gourmet varieties. One of these, Fredo Pies, at Frederickton on the north coast of New South Wales, sells some 100 varieties, including emu and crocodile. South Australia went one step further and created the pie floater (a meat pie in pea soup or gravy). Pie floaters are sold from pie carts outside Adelaide's general post office, the train station and casino, and in suburban Norwood.

CHEFS OF THE WORLD

Early travellers to the old country—Britain—found French flavours in London and Paris. On their return French restaurants emerged slowly, but initially catering only for the wealthy. Cantonese cooks—assiduous vegetable gardeners—arrived during the gold rushes of the 1800s. They opened small establishments where the adventurous tried 'chow food'—fried rice and chicken chow mein. Meanwhile German pioneers established vineyards from the 1840s and brought their food heritage with them.

After World War II large-scale migration brought more Europeans, particularly Italians and Greeks. Their presence revolutionized Australian cooking. Mediterranean aromas wafted from their kitchens and gradually Anglo-Saxon Australians entered new Italian restaurants.

Asian food has also impacted greatly on Australia. Japanese food arrived in the early 1960s, followed by Thai and Vietnamese.

Australia is no longer content with steak, eggs and chips, though damper (bread baked in fire ashes), and hearty camp stews and barbecues are still traditional on 4WD bush or outback tours. Now you can dine in every capital city on any cuisine. Fusion food, also called Modern Australian, combines East and West and is the popular choice in many fine restaurants.

TIPPING

A service charge, from 10 to 15 per cent, is included at all upscale eateries in Australia. In other restaurants you can reward good service with a 10 per cent tip, but it is not compulsory.

SMOKING

All states have passed laws banning smoking from restaurants and other enclosed places. Some establishments may have outside smoking areas—check when booking if you want to smoke.

DRESS CODE

Although Australians may dress up for formal occasions, for socializing and dining they dress casually. It's polite, however, to wear reasonable footwear to restaurants.

A QUICK GUIDE TO AUSTRALIAN FOOD
NEW SOUTH WALES AND ACT

Sydney's restaurants, brasseries, bistros, bars, hotels and coffee shops serve all types of food. But it's Australia's most expensive dine-out city: Prices start at around A$50 and A$110 for lunch and dinner respectively, and are often higher. Then add beverages.

The *Sydney Morning Herald Good Food Guide* has excellent suggestions, with prices. Look for Sydney rock oysters, small but tasty. Hit suburban pubs for great steak with veg or salad counter lunches and dinners from about A$15.

Canberra, Australia's capital and host to international diplomats, has similar eating options to Sydney's though prices are slightly lower. There are many foreign restaurants, and outlets for the grain-fed beef, lamb and south-coast seafood of New South Wales. Major dining areas are the CBD, Dickson and cosmopolitan Manuka. Wine bars offer lunches that are the equal of their wines.

VICTORIA

Melbourne—in competition with Sydney—has hundreds of cafés, restaurants, bistros, brasseries and delis. Take your pick by the Yarra River—a mid-market two-course meal is from A$40 to A$60. In suburban Richmond you can opt for Greek and Vietnamese, in Carlton go Italian or Greek. The *Age Good Food Guide* has recommendations with prices. Excellent restaurants aren't just near the city, you'll find good options out in the suburbs.

Australia's smallest mainland state is dairy-rich. From regional Gippsland a gourmet-deli trail loops east along the Princes Freeway for 145km (90 miles), well-signed from the Baw Baw turnoff. Finish at Yarragon with tea rooms and produce stores.

In the central north of the state, one-time Ned Kelly territory, Milawa Gourmet Country merges with one of Australia's oldest wine-growing areas, around Rutherglen, where wineries serve Modern Australian lunches. Victoria is a fish state too: A huge fishing fleet sails out of the town of Lakes Entrance on the southeast coast.

QUEENSLAND

Almost the size of western Europe, Queensland has everything from hinterland beef (Rockhampton is Australia's beef capital) to scallops and mud crabs. Try the mud crabs in ravioli or just break them apart as locals do. The nation's sugar industry is based here too, so don't be surprised when chefs caramelize fish and vegetables. Prices are just above South Australia's—so are relatively low.

NORTHERN TERRITORY

There are various menus on the long route from Darwin to Alice Springs—expect crocodile and camel meat particularly, barramundi (a tender fish), water buffalo, magpie geese and bush tucker; kangaroo or emu are gourmet tucker.

Alice Springs restaurants vary from Irish late-night premises with Indian influences to an inexpensive—from A$25—dinner at a Turkish café. In the dry season at Darwin's Mindil Beach Thursday markets, food stalls display inexpensive treats from Brazilian to Balinese, and Laotian to Portuguese, with almost all national dishes in among them.

SOUTH AUSTRALIA

South Australia is the festival state. Most festivals focus on food, from German to Greek, via Italian, Spanish and Polish. The January Tunarama Festival at Port Lincoln on the Eyre Peninsula not surprisingly features tuna. The Peninsula also yields Australia's biggest oysters and famed King George whiting.

Per capita, South Australia has more eateries than any state and is probably the nation's cheapest. And it produces Australia's finest wines, recognized internationally. The most famous are from the Barossa Valley, and they often accompany a cuisine known as Barossan, based on the traditional food of the 19th-century German immigrants and refined with fresh produce.

Many wineries have restaurants, as do the wine-growing areas of McLaren Vale, Clare Valley, citrus-rich Riverland, Coonawarra (revered for its reds) and cool-climate wineries in the Adelaide Hills. The last area also produces great olives and berry fruits. Kangaroo Island's own wine industry is catching up,

MENU READER

Abalone: marine mollusc
Anzac biscuits: biscuits made with flour, oats, coconut and golden syrup
Balmain bug: crayfish (crawfish), named after a Sydney suburb
Barbie: barbecue
Barramundi: or barra, a large freshwater fish found in the northern and western states
Bunya Bunya nuts: similar to macadamia nuts
BYO: Some restaurants allow you to 'Bring Your Own' wine, but usually charge corkage of A$3–A$5 per person or bottle
Capsicum: sweet pepper
Damper: unleavened bread baked in a camp oven
Eggplant: aubergine
Flake: shark, as served in fish and chip takeaways (takeouts)
Kakadu plums: native plums, used in pies or as a preserve

Lamington: sponge cake with a chocolate and coconut topping
Lemon myrtle: tree whose lemon-scented leaves are used in cooking
Lilly-pilly: berries of a native tree eaten as bush tucker
Marron: freshwater crayfish native to Western Australia
Middy: medium-size glass of beer, usually 0.285 litre (0.5 pint) but can be larger
Moreton Bay bug: crayfish again, found in Queensland and the north
Pie floater: meat pie in pea soup or gravy
Quandong: small native fruit often served in pies or tarts or as a preserve
Schooner: large glass of beer, usually 0.425 litre (0.75 pint)
Stubby: small bottle of beer
Tinnie: can of beer
Witchetty grub: a grub or larva traditionally eaten by Aborigines
Yabby: freshwater crayfish
Zucchini: courgette

and there is a food culture here based on corn-fed chicken, seafood, including marron (freshwater crayfish), and fine cheeses, including brie and camembert.

WESTERN AUSTRALIA

The state occupies a third of the continent, its southern corner punctuated by orchards and farms. Wonderful wine comes from the Margaret River region, but beer is the beverage of choice in outback regions, often accompanying sensational seafood and steaks transported inland. Seafood-lovers can look forward to blue manna crabs, prawns and salmon, as well as local lamb, goat's cheese, White Rocks veal and marron.

Perth suburb Northbridge has a large migrant population and one of the nation's greatest concentrations of restaurants. For alfresco dining head to the port of Fremantle. In

these areas, you are likely to spend A$45 to A$60 for two courses.

TASMANIA

Tasmania, 200km (124 miles) from Melbourne across the Bass Strait, has clung to British food traditions and is known as the gourmet isle. Devonshire tea rooms are everywhere, serving fresh scones, jam and cream, adopted from Devon, England. Local seafood, from oysters to Tasman Peninsula salmon, is among the highlights around Hobart's harbour, where fish punts, pubs, restaurants, cafés and sushi bars serve at considerably less than Melbourne prices. For Thai, Indonesian, Indian, Lebanese and Italian foods, walk to North Hobart. Mutton-bird pâté is unique to the island. Tasmania also produces good wines though they are fairly expensive. King Island, offshore to the north, is famed for its cheeses.

STAYING

Camping off-road in the barren outback may be the cheapest and most basic option, but Australia also offers a wide range of accommodation for all budgets.

WHAT IS AVAILABLE?
Australia has accommodation options to suit every pocket, from basic camping grounds to exclusive luxury resorts. Other than during the Christmas and January summer school holiday period, it is usually easy to find somewhere to stay on arrival in a destination, but if you reserve ahead you might be able to negotiate a special deal. Tourist offices can help you find a bed for the night, and most places are listed on the internet.

PITCH HERE
Caravan and camp grounds are everywhere—look for shaded sites that provide relief from the sun. Caravan pitches start at about A$22 and tent pitches at A$12. Often, basic supplies can be bought. Many parks rent on-site caravans (trailers) from A$40, or cabins with cooking facilities from A$45. Check if bed linen can be hired. Remember that distances between towns can be vast, so never venture into the outback without sufficient water, fuel and provisions. Always allow for the risk that your vehicle could break down in hot, isolated areas.

BACKPACK
Backpacker hostels, often former old hotels, some brightly painted with big signs, are widespread. Look for backpacker handbills at airports, train stations and bus terminals or local tourist offices. Average nightly cost is about A$18. At these prices expect shared dormitories, rooms and bathrooms.

MOTELS
Some country pubs offer accommodation but often they have given way to motels. Expect to pay about A$60–A$80 for a double/

twin per night with bathroom and tea/coffee facilities. All have fans or air-conditioning and heating, and many have swimming pools. Breakfast, delivered to your door, from Continental to full English, is extra. Some motels have excellent dining rooms. Children are accommodated, sometimes at no extra cost, depending on their age. Away from cities, many fully booked establishments will even telephone rivals to find available rooms or direct you elsewhere.

HOTELS
The usual range of hotels is available in the populated parts of the country and prices can range from A$130 to over A$1,000 per night for a double room. Luxury hotels, including Hilton, Hyatt, Marriott, Oberoi, Sheraton and Stamford abound in the capital cities and popular resorts. Queensland dominates in resort hotels, mainly on islands—there are 74 in the Whitsundays alone. Resorts are set on several hectares, usually by a beach. Accommodation is motel-style, often smart, with pool, and most hotels have a spa and walking areas. Some offer sports, from snorkelling and diving to tennis and golf.

SERVICED APARTMENTS
You can book serviced apartments in most of the major cities for stays of a few nights to many months. Prices range considerably from about A$200 upwards.

B&B
Bed-and-breakfast establishments are widespread. Most are now smart, some charging as much as luxury hotels. If you are looking for an inexpensive option then it might be best to book a motel, as B&B

prices usually range from A$125 per double in a modest B&B to more than A$450 per double.

B&Bs may be restored pioneer cottages, deconsecrated churches or fine country houses. In country areas there are farmstays, where you can reside in-house with the family or in separate premises.

OUTBACK LODGES
Australia has a growing number of lodges that offer a base for exploring Australia's more remarkable wilderness areas. While some offer luxurious accommodation and facilities, due to their remoteness, many provide only basic accommodation, although the price may be well above five-star rates. It's the experience that counts, and the memories you will take away from such a stay are often priceless. The Outback Encounter website (www.outbackencounter.com) provides a good overview.

TIPPING
Australians are not great tippers. Only in luxury hotels is a tip expected, by the person who carries luggage to and from your room. A A$2 coin will suffice but some may anticipate a A$5 note. In-house hairdressers do not expect tips.

MINIBARS
Hotel minibars are expensive, usually double the high street retail prices.

TELEPHONE CALLS
Telephone charges from modest motel to top hotel are expensive, from 50 to 100 per cent more from your room. Calling from a phone booth with coins or a phonecard (available from post offices) is much cheaper (▷ 314).

Sir Joseph Banks (1743–1824)
Botanist accompanying James
Cook on Endeavour voyage of 1768
William Barak (1823–1903)
Aboriginal elder and painter of the
Yarra Yarra tribe of Victoria
Sir Edmund Barton (1849–1920)
Australia's first prime minister,
1901–03
George Bass (1771–1803) English
surgeon and explorer who, with
Matthew Flinders, discovered
Bass Strait
Arthur Boyd (1920–99) Australian
artist
John Job Crew Bradfield
(1867–1943) Civil engineer and
designer of the Sydney Harbour
Bridge
Sir Don Bradman (1908–2001)
Cricketer, regarded as Australia's
greatest batsman

Robert O'Hara Burke (1821–61)
Irish-born explorer who died
on the return trip from the first
south–north crossing of Australia
Martin Cash (1810–77) Irish-born
bushranger
Joseph Benedict Chifley (1885–
1951) Prime Minister 1945–49
Caroline Chisholm (1808–77)
English-born philanthropist, known
for work with immigrant women
Captain James Cook (1728–79)
English navigator and explorer who
first mapped the east coast of
Australia in 1770 in the *Endeavour*
Edith Dircksey Cowan (1861–1932)
First Australian woman Member of
Parliament
William Dampier (1651–1715)
English explorer who landed in
northwestern Australia in 1688
and 1699

Sir William Dobell (1899–1970)
Portrait painter and winner of
Archibald Prize in 1943, 1948 and
1959
Sir George Russell Drysdale
(1912–81) English-born landscape
artist
Edward John Eyre (1815–1901)
English-born explorer of
southwestern and central Australia
Dr Tim Flannery (1956–) Earth
scientist and best-selling author on
environmental-science topics.
Matthew Flinders (1774–1814)
English explorer; first to
circumnavigate Van Diemen's Land
(Tasmania)
Emanuel Phillips Fox (1865–1915)
Australian artist and one of the
founders of Melbourne Art School
Vida Jane Mary Goldstein (1869–
1949) Feminist and suffragist

Francis Howard Greenway (1777–1837) Convict architect, later Sydney's civil architect in 1816

Sir Walter Burley Griffin (1876–1937) US architect who designed the city of Canberra

Sir Roy Burman Grounds (1905–81) Architect of The Arts Centre and Australian Academy of Science in Canberra

Sir Hans Heysen (1877–1968) German-born landscape artist and nine-times winner of the Wynne Prize

Ned Kelly (1855–80) Bushranger and leader of the Kelly Gang

Sir John Robert Kerr (1914–91) Governor-General who dismissed the Whitlam government in 1975

John Simpson Kirkpatrick (1892–1915) English-born Australian soldier at Gallipoli who rescued the wounded with a donkey

Emily Kame Kngwarraye (1910–96) Aboriginal artist

Peter Lalor (1827–89) Irish-born leader of the Eureka rebellion in 1854 and later elected to Victorian parliament

George Washington Thomas Lambert (1873–1930) Russian-born painter and war artist

William Light (1786–1839) Naval captain and surveyor who founded Adelaide

Lady Joan Lindsay (1896–1984) Artist and novelist, author of *Picnic at Hanging Rock* (1967)

Norman Lindsay (1879–1969) Influential literary figure, artist and author of the children's book *The Magic Pudding* (1918)

Frederick McCubbin (1855–1917) Landscape painter and one of the founders of the Heidelberg School

Saint Mary Mackillop (1842–1909) Australia's first saint, canonized in 2010

Lachlan Macquarie (1762–1824) Governer of New South Wales 1810–24, responsible for many public works

Sir Douglas Mawson (1882–1958) One of Shackleton's Antarctic expedition and leader of the Australian expedition of 1911–12

Sir Robert Gordon Menzies (1894–1978) Australia's longest-serving Prime Minister 1939–41 and 1949–66

Albert Namatjira (1902–59) Watercolourist who was the first Aboriginal artist to win international acclaim

Arthur Phillip (1738–1814) British naval officer and captain general of the First Fleet

Tom (Thomas William) Roberts (1856–1931) Landscape artist of the Heidelberg School

Sir Arthur Streeton (1867–1943) Autralian landscape painter and co-founder of the Heidelberg School

Sir Paul Edmund de Strzelecki (1797–1873) Polish-born explorer and scientist

John McDouall Stuart (1815–66) Scottish-born explorer of central Australia

Charles Sturt (1795–1869) Indian-born explorer of eastern Australia and Darling River area

Abel Janszoon Tasman (1602–59) Dutch navigator who 'discovered' the island (now Tasmania), that he named Van Diemen's Land

Truganini (1812–76) The last surviving full-blooded Tasmanian Aboriginal woman

William Charles Wentworth (1790–1872) Explorer and politician

Brett Whiteley (1939–92) Prolific and outrageous Australian painter

(Edward) Gough Whitlam (1916–) Prime minister 1972–75

William John Wills (1834–61) English-born explorer of central Australia who perished on the 1860–61 expedition with Robert O'Hara Burke

Left Abel Tasman, his wife and daughter *by Jacob Gerritsz Cuyp*

Below left *Charles Sturt and some of his follow explorers at Depot Creek*

Below right *Sir Joseph Banks*

AUSTRALIAN COLLOQUIALISMS

Australia has some very colourful words, some of which are becoming known outside the country. Others, however, can cause much bafflement and some English-speaking visitors to Australia can have trouble understanding Australians, even after they've got used to the accent.

Adrians....................................drunk
arvo .... afternoon
Aussie salute ....flicking off flies
back of Bourke .... any remote place
bandicoot .... small marsupial
banksia .... coastal plant
barbie ....barbecue
barrack .... support a sports team
bathers ....swimming costume
better than a poke in the eye with a blunt stick....... better alternative
billabong ....waterhole
Bluey .... a nickname for a redhead
bonzer .... excellent
Buckleys .... no chance
bunkum .... utter nonsense
have a burl .... have a go
bush   loose term for anywhere rural
cark it ....to die
cheapie inexpensive or inferior item
chillybin .... portable icebox
chuck a uey .... make a U-turn
chunder .... to vomit
ciggie ....cigarette
coldie ....a can or bottle of cold beer
corker .... an astonishingly good thing or person
crook ...... badly made or feeling sick
croweater ..... someone from South Australia
dag ....an odd or amusing person
damper .... a bread made from flour, salt and water
digger ....an Australian soldier, particularly one who served in World War I
dingbat ...... an eccentric or peculiar person
dingo ..... species of dog introduced by Aboriginal people
dinkum .... genuine, as in the term fair dinkum
dead horse ....tomato sauce

doona ....duvet or quilted eiderdown
drongo ....stupid
drop-kick .... a stupid person
dunny ....a toilet
Enzed ....New Zealand
esky .... portable ice box
fang it . exert force so that someone will lend you something, take what's not yours, or go extremely fast
flake ....fillet of shark
footie .... football (soccer)
furphy ....rumour
galah ......a small cockatoo, or a silly person
garbo .... garbage collector
gone troppo ....
moved to tropical Australia, or crazy because of drink or the heat
greenie .... an environmentalist
grog ... alcohol—beer, wine or spirits
grouse ....very good
gum boots .... wellington boots
gum tree .... eucalyptus tree
hard yacker ....hard work
hoo-roo ....good-bye
humbug ....to ask for drinks or cigarettes from someone
illywhacker .. a con man who would take advantage of the gullible
jarmies .... pyjamas
Joe Blake..............................snake
jumbuck .... sheep
kelpie Australian sheep or cattle dog
king brown Mulga snake, or a large bottle of beer
lairy .... vulgar
larrikin .... a mischievous young person
lemon ...something shoddy or faulty
lippy .... lipstick
lollies .... sweets or candy
middy .... a medium-sized glass, usually of beer
milk bar .... corner shop/ convenience store
nipper .... young child
nix .... nothing; zero
nong .... idiot
ocker ... boorish Australian workman
open slather .... free-for-all
pokie .... a slot machine
poddy-dodger .... someone who steals unbranded calves

pom .... an English person
pressie .... present
not the full quid someone not quite on the ball
rack off .... go away
ridgy-didge ....genuine
ripper .... terrific
roo bar ... strong safety bar attached to the front of a vehicle
rug rat ....a small child
sanger ....sandwich
schoolies' week ....boisterous end-of-year fun for school leavers
schooner .... large glass (of beer)
seppo .... American
shark biscuit .... surfer with no experience
she'll be apples ... everything is fine
skite ....brag
slab .... a box of 24 beer cans
snag .... sausage
spine bashing ....loafing about
spit the dummy baulk at something
station (cattle/sheep)............ ranch
stickybeak ....a person who pries or interferes
stinker ....a very hot day
strawbs.........................strawberries
stubby ..small bottle, usually of beer
sundowner ....a workman who arrives at a house in the evening and gets shelter for the night
surfie .... a surfboard rider
tall poppies ....high achievers
tin lizzie .... old car
tinnie ....a can of beer
togs .... bathing suit or clothing in general
tops .... excellent or outstanding
true-blue .... faithful or genuine
U-ie/U-turn .... a turn that completely reverses the direction of travel
ute ....a pick-up truck
veggies ....vegetables
verbal diarrhoea ..... ceaseless flow of talk
walkabout ..... wandering, generally in relation to Aboriginal people
wax-head............................... surfer
wowser .... prudish person
yahoo ....a lout

GLOSSARY OF TERMS FOR US VISITORS

anticlockwise ...... counterclockwise
aubergine .... eggplant
autumn .... fall
big wheel .... Ferris wheel
bill .... check (at restaurant)
biscuit .... cookie
bonnet .... hood (car)
boot .... trunk (car)
bottle shop .... liquor store
bowls .... lawn bowls
busker .... street musician
caravan .... trailer house
car park .... parking lot
carriage .... car (on a train)
casualty .... emergency room
(hospital department)
chemist .... pharmacy
chips ....french fries
coach .... long-distance bus
corridor ....hall
crèche .... day care
directory enquiries........... directory
assistance
dual carriageway.............. two-lane
highway
en suite ....a bedroom with its own
private bathroom; may also

just refer to the bathroom
fireworks...................... firecrackers
full board .... a hotel tariff that
includes all meals
garage .... filling station
GP.................................... doctor
half board .... hotel tariff that
includes breakfast and either
lunch or dinner
handbag .... purse
high street .... main street
hire .... rent
jelly .... Jello™
junction .... intersection
layby .... rest stop
level crossing .... grade crossing
licensed .... a café or restaurant
that has a licence to serve
alcohol (beer and wine only
unless it's 'fully' licensed)
lift... elevator
main line station ...... a train station
as opposed to an underground or
subway station (although it may be
served by the underground/subway)
mobile phone .... cell phone
motor home .... RV

nappy .... diaper
pavement .... sidewalk
petrol ....gas/fuel
phone box .... phone booth
pudding .... dessert
purse....................... change purse
return ticket.............roundtrip ticket
rocket (salad)...................... arugula
roundabout ... traffic circle or rotary
self-catering........... accommodation
including a kitchen
single ticket.............one-way ticket
surgery .... doctor's office
tailback, traffic jam ...... stalled line
of traffic
takeaway .... takeout
taxi rank.................... taxi stand
ten-pin bowling .... bowling
T-junction...... an intersection where
one road meets another at
right angles (making a T-shape)
toilets ....restrooms
torch .... flashlight
trolley... cart
trousers .... pants
way out .... exit

GLOSSARY OF AUSTRALIAN WORDS

Anzac .... an Australian or
New Zealand soldier
BYO ....Bring Your Own:
A form of licensing that allows you
to take alcohol purchased elsewhere
into a restaurant
corroboree .... an Aboriginal
gathering
dasyurid .... carnivorous and
insectivorous marsupial such
as the Tasmanian devil
echidna .... spine-covered
egg-laying mammal
eucalyptus ..... a group of about 600
species of tree
First Fleet .... the ships bringing
convict settlers in 1788
fossick .... to hunt for gems
gibber .... plain littered with rounded
stones found in arid parts
glider .... an arboreal marsupial
with a parachute-type
membrane allowing it to

glide from one tree to another
Gondwana .... the southern-
hemisphere supercontinent that
began to split and drift apart 150
million years ago
kookaburra .... world's largest
kingfisher, well-known for its
laughing call
lorikeets .... nectar-eating parrots
macropod .... superfamily of
herbivorous marsupials including
kangaroos and wallabies
mallee .... woody plants that
grow with multiple stems from
underground lignotubers
marsupial ......animals with pouches
for developing the young such as the
koala and kangaroo
monotreme .. animals that lay eggs
such as the platypus and echidna
platypus ... egg-laying mammal that
looks a bit like a small otter
possum...........................a family of

herbivorous arboreal marsupials
quokka .... small wallaby found on
Rottnest Island, WA
quandong .... native tree or its
edible fruit
rosellas .. brightly hued parrots living
in forested areas
Southern Cross .... a constellation
in the southern sky represented
on the Australian flag
spinifex .... prickly, clumping
grass found widely in
central Australia
squatter .... wealthy sheep farmer
Top End .... northern part of the
Northern Territory
wallaby .... a macropod smaller
than a kangaroo or wallaroo
wattle .... common name for 900
species of trees and
shrubs in the genus *Acacia*
wombat .... stocky, burrowing
nocturnal marsupial

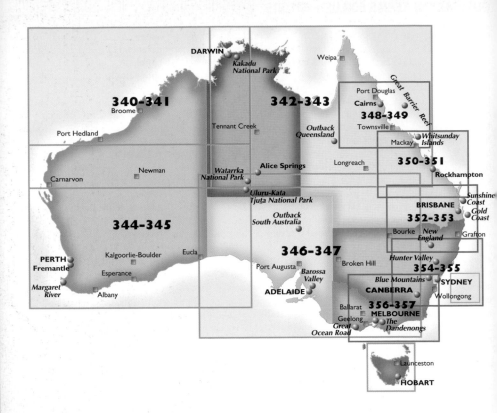

- DARWIN
- Kakadu National Park
- Weipa
- Port Hedland
- Broome
- **340-341**
- Tennant Creek
- **342-343**
- Great Barrier Reef
- Port Douglas
- Cairns
- **348-349**
- Outback Queensland
- Townsville
- Mackay
- Whitsunday Islands
- **350-351**
- Rockhampton
- Carnarvon
- Newman
- Watarrka National Park
- Alice Springs
- Longreach
- Uluru-Kata Tjuta National Park
- Sunshine Coast
- BRISBANE
- Gold Coast
- **352-353**
- **344-345**
- Outback South Australia
- Bourke
- New England
- Grafton
- Kalgoorlie-Boulder
- Eucla
- PERTH
- Fremantle
- Esperance
- Port Augusta
- Barossa Valley
- Broken Hill
- Hunter Valley
- **354-355**
- Margaret River
- Albany
- **346-347**
- Blue Mountains
- SYDNEY
- CANBERRA
- Wollongong
- ADELAIDE
- Ballarat
- **356-357**
- MELBOURNE
- Geelong
- The Dandenongs
- Great Ocean Road
- Launceston
- HOBART

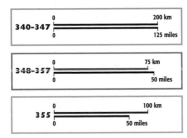

| **340-347** | 0 | 200 km |
| | 0 | 125 miles |

| **348-357** | 0 | 75 km |
| | 0 | 50 miles |

| **355** | 0 | 100 km |
| | 0 | 50 miles |

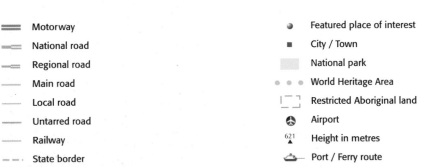

≡≡≡ Motorway

⊏≡ National road

⊏≡ Regional road

— Main road

— Local road

— Untarred road

— Railway

– – – State border

● Featured place of interest

■ City / Town

National park

● ● ● World Heritage Area

⌐ ⌐ Restricted Aboriginal land

✈ Airport

621 ▲ Height in metres

⛴ Port / Ferry route

MAPS

Map references for the sights refer to the atlas pages within this section or to the individual town plans within the regions. For example, Perth has the reference 344 B12, indicating the page on which the map is found (344) and the grid square in which Perth sits (B12).

A B C D E

1
2
3
4
5
6
7
8

BE[A]

Coulomb Point
National Reserve

Broome

GREAT NORTHERN HIGHWAY

Port
Hedland

138

95

Dampier
Archipelago

Barrow Island

Dampier

Karratha

YANDEYARRA

138

**Millstream-
Chichester
National Park**

Point
Murat

Onslow

Pannawonica

Pilbara

Mungaroona
Range National
Reserve

Cape Range
National Park

Exmouth

1129
Mount Brockman

Ningaloo
Marine Park

Tom Price

**Karijini
National Park**

1215
Mount
Meharry

JIGALONG

Barlee Range
National
Reserve

136

344

Paraburdoo

Newman

Tropic of Capricorn

Mount Augustus
National Park

Collier
Range
National Park

*Little Sandy
Desert*

1106
Mount
Augustus

8

Point
Quobba

Carnarvon

A B C D E

WESTE[RN]

340

Shark Bay

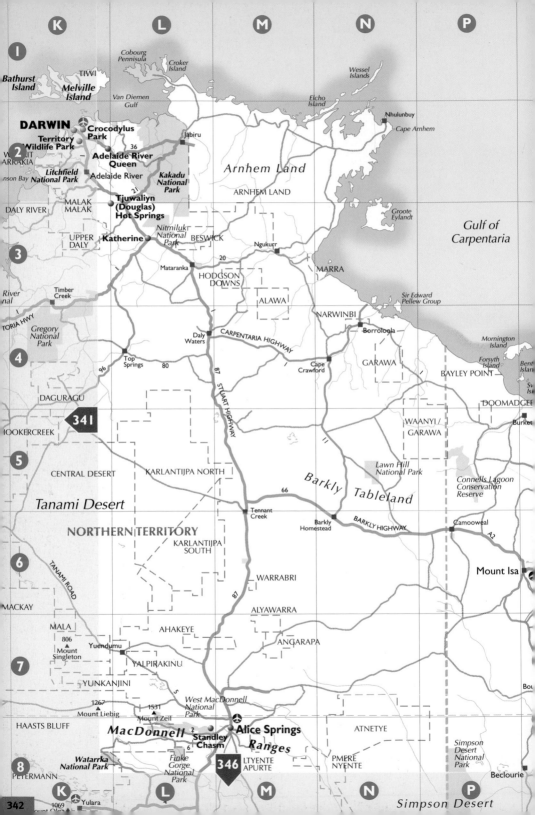

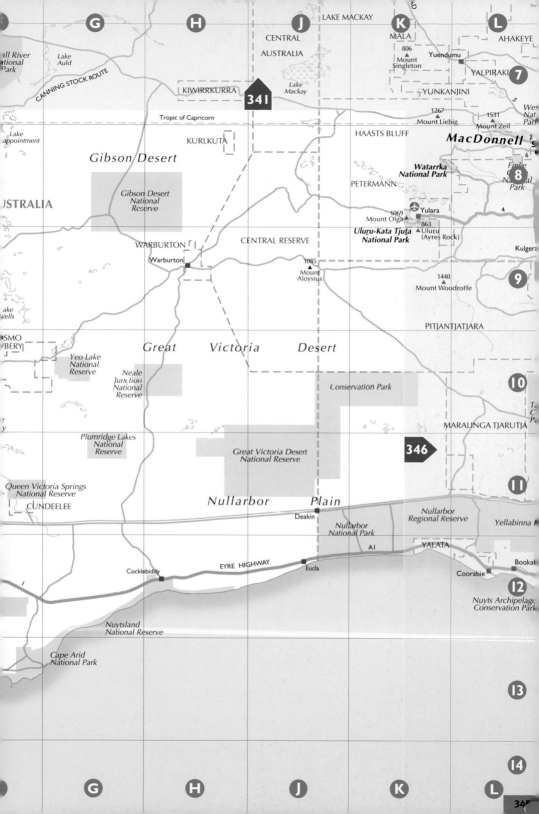

LAKE MACKAY

CENTRAL

AUSTRALIA

K MALA

806
Mount
Singleton

Yuendumu

AHAKEYE

YALPIRAKI

7

CANNING STOCK ROUTE

all River
National
Park

Lake
Auld

Lake
appointment

KIWIRRKURRA

341

Lake
Mackay

YUNKANJINI

1267
Mount Liebig

1531
Mount Zeil

Wes
Nat
Par

Tropic of Capricorn

KURLKUTA

Gibson Desert

HAASTS BLUFF

MacDonnell

2

USTRALIA

Gibson Desert
National
Reserve

PETERMANN

Watarrka
National Park

Finke
G
Na al
Park

8

Lake
wells

WARBURTON

Warburton

CENTRAL RESERVE

1069
Mount Olga

Yulara

863

Uluru-Kata Tjuta
National Park

Uluru
(Ayres Rock)

4

Kulgera

ake
ells

1085
Mount
Aloysius

1440
Mount Woodroffe

9

SMO
BERY

Great   Victoria   Desert

Yeo Lake
National
Reserve

Neale
Junction
National
Reserve

PITJANTJATJARA

Conservation Park

10

T
C
Pa

Plumridge Lakes
National
Reserve

Great Victoria Desert
National Reserve

MARALINGA TJARUTJA

346

Queen Victoria Springs
National Reserve

CUNDEELEE

Nullarbor   Plain

Deakin

Nullarbor
National Park

Nullarbor
Regional Reserve

Yellabinna

11

YALATA

EYRE   HIGHWAY

Cocklebiddy

Eucla

A1

Coorabie

Bookab

12

Nuytsland
National Reserve

Nuyts Archipelago
Conservation Park

Cape Arid
National Park

13

14

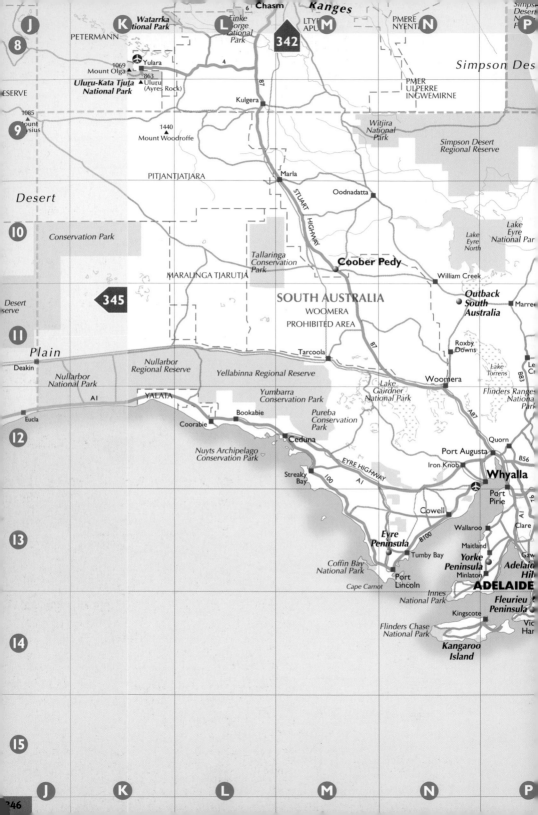

8

PETERMANN

Watarrka National Park

Finke Gorge National Park

6 Chasm

Ranges

LTYE APU

PMERE NYENT

Simps Deser N

342

1069 Mount Olga ▲ Yulara

863 ▲ Uluru (Ayres Rock)

Uluṟu-Kata Tjuṯa National Park

4

Kulgera

87

PMER ULPERRE INGWEMIRNE

Simpson Des

ESERVE

9

1085 ount ysius

1440 ▲ Mount Woodroffe

PITJANTJATJARA

Marla

Oodnadatta

STUART HIGHWAY

Witjira National Park

Simpson Desert Regional Reserve

Desert

10

Conservation Park

Tallaringa Conservation Park

Lake Eyre North

Lake Eyre National Par

Desert eserve

345

MARALINGA TJARUTJA

Coober Pedy

William Creek

Outback South Australia

Marre

11

SOUTH AUSTRALIA

WOOMERA

PROHIBITED AREA

87

Roxby Downs

Lake Torrens

Le Cr

Plain

Deakin

Nullarbor Regional Reserve

Yellabinna Regional Reserve

Tarcoola

Woomera

A87

Flinders Ranges Nationa Park

B83

Nullarbor National Park

12

Eucla

A1

YALATA

Yumbarra Conservation Park

Lake Gairdner National Park

Nuyts Archipelago Conservation Park

Coorabie

Bookabie

Ceduna

Pureba Conservation Park

Quorn

B56

Port Augusta

Iron Knob

Whyalla

Port Pirie

Streaky Bay

100

A1

EYRE HIGHWAY

Cowell

Wallaroo

Clare

A1

76

13

Eyre Peninsula

B100

Tumby Bay

Maitland

Yorke Peninsula

Gaw

Adelaid Hil

Coffin Bay National Park

Port Lincoln

Minlaton

ADELAIDE

Cape Carnot

Innes National Park

Fleurieu Peninsula

14

Flinders Chase National Park

Kingscote

Vic Har

Kangaroo Island

15

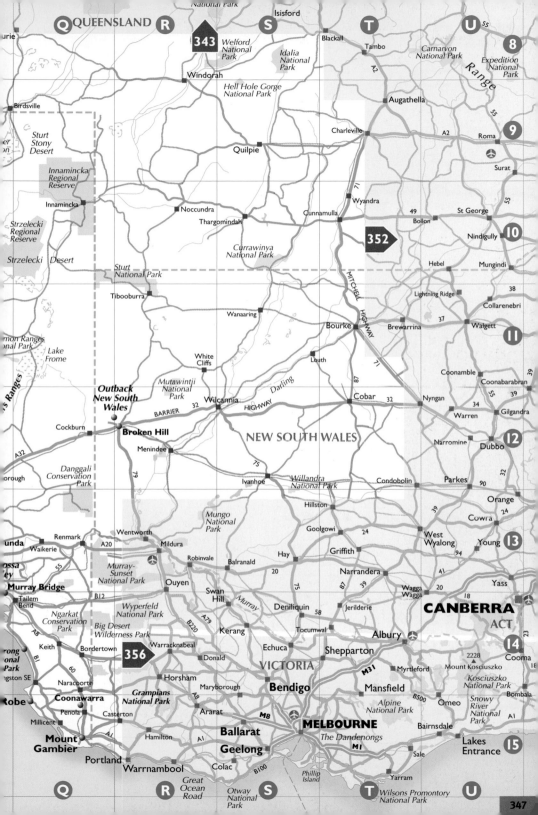

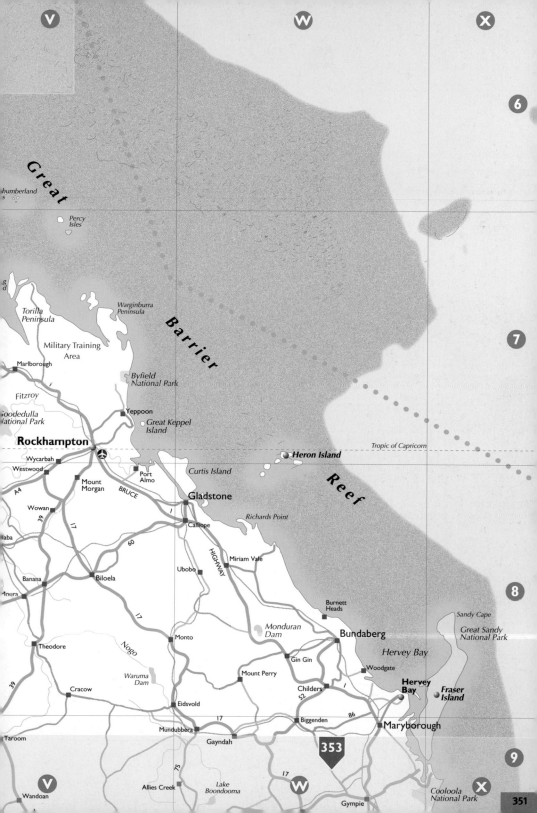

Great

Barrier

Reef

humberland
s

Percy
Isles

d

Torilla
Peninsula

Warginburra
Peninsula

Military Training
Area

Marlborough

Fitzroy

Byfield
National Park

Goodedulla
National Park

Yeppoon

Great Keppel
Island

Rockhampton

Wycarbah

Port
Almo

Westwood

A4

Mount
Morgan

BRUCE

Curtis Island

Heron Island

Tropic of Capricorn

Wowan

39

17

Gladstone

60

Calliope

Richards Point

Iaba

1

aba

Banana

Biloela

HIGHWAY

Ubobo

Miriam Vale

Moura

17

Burnett
Heads

Theodore

Monto

Monduran
Dam

Bundaberg

Sandy Cape

Great Sandy
National Park

Nogo

Gin Gin

Hervey Bay

Cracow

Waruma
Dam

Mount Perry

Woodgate

39

Eidsvold

Childers

52

**Hervey
Bay**

*Fraser
Island*

Taroom

Mundubbera

17

Biggenden

86

Maryborough

Gayndah

353

Wandoan

Allies Creek

Lake
Boondooma

17

Cooloola
National Park

Gympie

New England

Guyra

Mitchell

Woolgoolga

PACIF

Warrabah
National
Park

Armidale

Cathedral Rock
National Park

Dorrigo
National
Park

Dorrigo

Coffs Harbour

78

78

Bellingen

Urunga

Nambucca Heads

Macksville

South West Rocks

353

New England
National Park

Oxley Wild
Rivers
National Park

Macleay

Walcha

Apsley

Kempsey

Hat Head
National Park

Werrikimbe
National
Park

Crescent Head

15

MacDonald

34

Hastings

Wauchope

Port Macquarie

Comboyne

Wingham

Harrington

Taree

Barrington Tops
National Park

Gloucester

Tuncurry
Forster

Wallis
Lake

Bulahdelah

Singleton

Hunter

Myall Lakes
National Park

Maitland

Raymond
Terrace

Port Stephens

Cessnock

Nelson Bay

Newcastle

Lake
Macquarie

Central
Coast

Toukley

The
Entrance

Ku-ring-gai
Chase National Park

Hornsby

Manly

Port Jackson

Botany Bay

Melbourne

16

Three Hummock
Island

Hunter
Island

Walker Island
Robbins Island

Palana

Furneaux
Group

Flinders
Island

Emita

Prime Seal
Island

Whitemark

B85

Lady Barron

Cape Barren
Island

Clarke Island

Banks Strait

Cape Portland

Smithton

Stanley

Mount William
National Park

Marrawah

A2

Somerset

Wynyard

Burnie

Ulverstone

Port
Sorell

George
Town

Bridport

B82

Eddystone
Point
Bay of Fires

17

Arthur Pieman
Conservation
Area

Arthur

A10

Devonport

Latrobe

Tamar
Valley

A7

Beaconsfield

Derby

Scottsdale

St Helens

Sandy
Cape

Savage River

Waratah

Sheffield

Mersey

Deloraine

Launceston

Ben Lomond
National Park

St Marys

Pieman

Rosebery

Mole Creek

Evandale

A4

Fingal

Douglas Apsley
National Park

Zeehan

Cradle
Mountain-
Lake St Clair
National Park

Walls of Jerusalem
National Park

Great
Lake

TASMANIA

B51

Arthurs
Lake

Bicheno

Strahan

Queenstown

Lake
St Clair

Lake
Burbury

Derwent
Bridge

Lake
Echo

B34

Campbell
Town

Ross

Swansea

Coles Bay
Freycinet
National
Park

Cape
Sorell

Franklin-Gordon
Wild Rivers
National Park

Lake
King William

Tarraleah

A10

Bothwell

A5

Oatlands

A3

Triabunna

Great
Oyster
Bay

Freycinet
Peninsula

Point
Hibbs

Gordon

Strathgordon

B61

Hamilton

Kempton

Derwent

Orford

Darlington

Maria Island

South
West
Conservation
Area

Lake
Gordon

Lake Pedder

Mount Field
National Park

Maydena

Bridgewater

Gretna

New Norfolk

Richmond

Sorell

A9

Maria Island
National Park

Forestier
Peninsula

HOBART

Lauderdale

Huon

Geeveston

Huonville

Port Arthur

Tasman Peninsula

Dover

A6

Storm
Bay

Cape
Raoul

Cape
Pillar

Point
St Vincent

South West
National Park

Southport

Bruny Island

South Bruny
National Park

South West Cape

Maatsuyker
Group

South East
Cape

355

ACKNOWLEDGEMENTS

The Automobile Association wishes to thank the following photographers and organisations for their assistance in the preparation of this book.

Abbreviations for the picture credits are as follows – (t) top; (b) bottom; (l) left; (r) right; (c) centre; (AA) AA World Travel Library

2 AA/Simon Richmond;
3t AA/Steve Watkins;
3tc AA/Bill Bachman;
3bc AA/Mike Langford;
3b Australian Tourism Commission;
4 David Hannah/Photolibrary.com;
5 Rob Henderson/Ticket/Photolibrary. com;
6 Marc Anderson/Alamy;
7 Getty Images;
8 AA/Mike Langford;
10 AA/Simon Richmond;
11t AA/Mike Langford;
11b Australian Tourist Commission;
12 Blue Mountains Tourism Limited;
13 Peter Harrison/Photolibrary.com;
14 Courtesy of Tourism Queensland;
15t Greg Price/Ticket/ Photolibrary.com;
15b Peter Harrison/Ticket/ Photolibrary.com;
16 The Art Archive/Musée des Arts Africains et Océaniens/Alfredo Dagli Orti;
17l AA/Steve Watkins;
17r Ian McIlgorm/Rex Features;
18 Lions Camel Cup Committee/ Moving Pictures/2009 Lions Imparja Camel Cup;
19t Ozimages/Alamy;
19b Getty Images;
20 Jeff Busby/Sydney Dance Company;
21t Austral Int./Rex Features;
21b Humberto Carreno/Rex Features;
22 AA/Bill Bachman;
23t AA/Steve Watkins;
23b James Derrick/Alamy;
24 Courtesy of Tourism Queensland;
25 eye ubiquitous/Robert Harding;
26 AA;
27t Bill Bachman/Alamy;
27b AA;
28 AA/Steve Day;
29t imagebroker/Alamy;
29b AA ;
30 AA/Bill Bachman;
31l AA/Bill Bachman;

31r AA;
32 From the collection of the National Archives of Australia;
33t AA;
33b AA/Bill Bachman;
34 Getty Images;
35t AA/Adrian Baker;
35b Getty Images;
36 Stephen P Graham/Tips Italia/ Photolibrary.com;
37 AA/Andy Belcher;
38 Perth Airport;
40 AA/Mike Langford;
41 P&O Cruises;
42 AA/Mike Langford;
45 Courtesy of Britz;
46tl AA/Andy Belcher;
46tcl AA/Mike Langford;
46tcr AA/Andy Belcher;
46tr AA/Mike Langford;
46bl AA/Mike Langford;
46bc AA/Mike Langford;
46br AA/Mike Langford;
48 AA/Mike Langford;
49 Rob Walls/Alamy;
51 David Moore/Victoria/Alamy;
53l South Australia Tourist Commission;
53r Jason Smith Photography/Transit Australia Group;
54 Metro Transport Sydney;
56 AA/Andy Belcher;
59 AA/Bill Bachman;
60 Ken Gillham/Robert Harding;
66 Bjanka Kadic/Alamy;
67 Mark Sunderland/Alamy;
68 Australian National Maritime Museum;
69 AA/Mike Langford;
70 AA/Steve Day;
71 Metro Transport Sydney;
72l AA/Steve Day;
72r AA/Steve Day;
73 Leisa Hale/Alamy;
74 Museum of Contemporary Arts;
75 J Marshall - Tribaleye Images/ Alamy;
76 Ken Gillham/Robert Harding;
77 AA/Mike Langford;

78 Chad Ehlers/Photolibrary.com;
79 AA/Mike Langford;
81 D H Webster/Robert Harding;
82 Iain Baker/Alamy;
83 Australian Tourist Commission;
84 Thien Do/Ticket/Photolibrary.com;
85l AA/Mike Langford;
85r Bill Bachman/Alamy;
86 John Warburton-Lee Photography/Alamy;
87 AA/Steve Day ;
88 AA/Mike Langford;
91 AA/Mike Langford;
93 Trent O'Donnell/ Sydney Festival;
94 Murray Fredericks/Opera Bar;
96 Tetsuyas;
98 Hilton Sydney;
101 The Westin Sydney;
102 Ken Stepnell/Ticket/Photolibrary. com;
104 AA/Adrian Baker;
105 Blue Mountains Tourism Limited;
106l Tourism New South Wales;
106r AA/Simon Richmond;
107 Blue Mountains Tourism Limited;
108 Blue Mountains Tourism Limited;
109 AA/Paul Kenward;
110l AA/Paul Kenward;
110r George Serras/National Museum of Australia. Designed by Howard Raggatt of Ashton Raggatt McDougall and Robert Peck von Hartel Trethowan;
111 Rob Blakers/Ticket/Photolibrary. com 112r Tourism New South Wales;
112l AA/Paul Kenward;
113 Tourism New South Wales;
114 AA/Steve Day;
115l AA/Adrian Baker;
115r Tourism New South Wales;
116 Tourism New South Wales;
117 Tourism New South Wales;
118 AA/Adrian Baker;
120 AA/Adrian Baker;

121 Blue Mountains Tourism Limited;
122 William Hall/Canberra Theatre Centre;
124 Lilianfels;
127 Ken Martin/Ulladulla Guesthouse;
128 Hyatt Hotels and Resorts;
130 Chad Ehlers/Nordic Photos/Photolibrary.com;
132 AA/Bill Bachman;
133 AA/Bill Bachman;
134 AA/Bill Bachman;
135 Cubo Images/Robert Harding;
136 Robert Francis/Robert Harding;
138 AA/Bill Bachman;
139 Jochen Schlenker/Robert Harding;
140 Wayne Fogden/Ticket/Photolibrary.com;
141 AA/Bill Bachman;
142t The National Trust of Australia's (Victoria) Como House & Garden, from the Trust's photo collection;
142b Wayne Fogden/Ticket/Photolibrary.com;
143t AA/Bill Bachman;
143b AA/Bill Bachman;
144t AA/Bill Bachman;
144b SDP Photos/Melbourne Cricket Club;
145t Photo courtesy of Melbourne Zoo;
145b AA/Bill Bachman;
146t AA/Christine Osbourne;
146b AA/Bill Bachman;
147t AA/Bill Bachman;
147b AA/Bill Bachman;
150 Phillip Island Nature Parks;
151 AA/Bill Bachman;
152 Robert Francis/Robert Harding;
154 AA/Bill Bachman;
155 AA/Mike Langford;
156 AA/Blll Bachman;
159 AA/Bill Bachman;
161 Bill Bachman/Alamy;
162 Lake House, Daylesford;
164 Healesville Hotel;
166 The Queenscliff Hotel;
168 Adina Tovy/Robert Harding;
170 AA/Lee Karen Stow;
171 Courtesy of Tourism Queensland;
172 David Messent/Ticket/Photolibrary.com;
173 David Wall/Alamy;
174t Mark Rayner/Newstead House;

174b AA/Adrian Baker;
177 Andrew Watson/Ticket/Photolibrary.com;
178 TravelInk/Robert Harding;
179 Dave and Sigrun Tollerton/Alamy;
180 Andrew Watson/John Warburton-Lee Photography/Photolibrary.com;
181 AA/Andy Belcher;
182 Courtesy of Tourism Queensland;
183 Ken Stepnell/Ticket/Photolibrary.com;
184t imagebroker/Alamy;
184b Chris McLennan/Alamy;
185 AA/Rob Moore;
186 AA/Andy Belcher;
187 Courtesy of Tourism Queensland;
188 Ken Gillham/Robert Harding;
189 Peter Harrison/Ticket/Photolibrary.com;
191 Ken Gillham/Robert Harding;
192 Bjanka Kadic/Alamy;
193 Courtesy of Tourism Queensland;
194 AA/Andy Belcher;
196 AA/Lee Karen Stow;
198 AA/Michael Moody;
202 Summit Restaurant;
204 French Quarter Resort/Mantra Group;
206 Ken Wilson/Robert Harding;
208 Ken Stepnell/Ticket/Photolibrary.com;
209 Courtesy of Crocodylus Park;
210 Australian Tourist Commission;
211 Lisa Mckelvie/Ticket/Photolibrary.com;
212 Botanica/Photolibrary.com;
213 Ted Mead/Ticket/Photolibrary.com;
214 Dave Watts/Alamy;
215 AA/Simon Richmond;
216 eye ubiquitous/Robert Harding;
217 AA/Adrian Baker;
218l AA/Simon Richmond;
218r Courtesy of Ayers Rock Resort;
219 AA/Simon Richmond;
220 Ingo Schulz/imagebroker/Photolibrary.com;
221 Jochen Schlenker/Robert Harding;
222 Graham Monro/Ticket/Photolibrary.com;

223 Jochen Schlenker/Robert Harding;
224 Outback Ballooning;
226 Courtesy of Voyages Hotels & Resorts;
228 Hamilton Lund/Crown Plaza Darwin;
229 The Gagudju Crocodile Holiday Inn;
230 Anne Montfort/Photononstop/Photolibrary.com;
232 Paul Kingsley/Alamy;
233 Milton Wordley/Photolibrary.com;
235t Courtesy of Zoos SA;
235b South Australia Tourist Commission;
236t David Wall/Alamy;
236b Adrian Lyon/Alamy;
237l Milton Wordley/Photolibrary.com;
237r Adrian Lyon/Alamy;
238t Sam Sangster/Alamy;
238b David Moore/South Australia/Alamy;
239 Superstock/Photolibrary;
240 AA/Matthew Cawood;
241 Thorsten Milse/Robert Harding;
242 South Australia Tourist Commission;
243 South Australia Tourist Commission;
244 David Wall/age fotostock/Photolibrary.com;
245l Courtesy of the Botanic Gardens of Adelaide;
245r Neale Clark/Robert Harding;
246 Gary Lewis/Photolibrary.com;
247 Paul Wallace/Photo courtesy of the National Trust of South Australia;
248 South Australia Tourist Commission;
250 King William Road;
251 Tony Lewis/Womadelaide;
252 The Poplars at Chardonnay Lodge;
254 The North Adelaide Heritage Group;
255 Prarie Hotel;
256 David Jacobs/Robert Harding;
258 Sergio Pitamitz/Robert Harding;
259 AA/Steve Watkins;
260 Dattatreya/Alamy;
261 Jochen Schlenker/Robert Harding;
262 Peter Scholey/Robert Harding;

263 AA/Adrian Baker;
264 Bill Alexander/Ticket/
   Photolibrary.com;
265l AA/Mike Langford;
265r AA/Mike Langford;
266 Michael Willis/Alamy;
267 The Swan Bells;
268t Ken Gillham/Robert Harding;
268b Rottnest Island Authority;
269t Perth Zoo;
269b AA/Mike Langford;
270b AA/Mike Langford;
272 Simon Pennie/Alamy;
273 Western Australian Tourist
   Commission;
274 Christian Fletcher/Busselton
   Jetty Marketing;
276 Sheldon Levis/Alamy;
278 Leeuwin Estate;
279 Frasers Restaurant;
281 The Old Brewery Restaurant;
282 The Esplanade Hotel;
283 The Mantra on Hay;
284 Japan Travel Bureau/
   Photolibrary.com;
286 Julian Love/John Warburton-Lee
   Photography/Photolibrary.com;
287 Ted Mead/Ticket/Photolibrary.
   com;
288 Australian Tourism Commission;
290 Robin Smith/Ticket/Photolibrary.
   com;
291 Courtesy of Tasmanian Wool
   Centre;
292 Robert Francis/Robert Harding;
294 Richard Cummins/Robert
   Harding;
295t Robert Francis/Robert Harding;
295b Wayne Fogden/Ticket/
   Photolibrary.com;
296 Schuler Bernd/Sodapix AG/
   Photolibrary.com;
298 John Warburton-Lee
   Photography/Alamy;
299 Photography provided by the
   Theatre Royal Hobart;
300 The Evandale Village Fair;
302 The Meadowbank Estate
   Vineyard Restaurant;
304 Henry Jones Art Hotel;
305 Wayne Fogden/Ticket/
   Photolibrary.com;
307 AA/Lee Karen Stow;
308 ANZ Bank;

315 AA/Mike Langford;
319 AA/Bill Bachman;
320 AFFC/RGA;
322 Photodisc;
324 AA/Bill Bachman;
327 AA/Steve Watkins;
329 AA/Mike Langford;
330 Lisa Mckelvie/Ticket/
   Photolibrary.com;
334 Abel TASMAN, His Wife and
   Daughter, c. 1637 by Jacob
   Gerritsz Cuyp. The Art Archive/
   National Library of Australia;
335 right AA;
335 left AA;
339 AA/Matthew Cawood.

AUSTRALIA

ACKNOWLEDGEMENTS

CREDITS

Managing editor
Sheila Hawkins

Project editor
Strange Editorial Services

Design
Low Sky Design Ltd

Picture research
Paula Boyd Barrett

Image retouching and repro
Sarah Montgomery, Jackie Street

Main contributors
Judith Bamber, Jenny Burns, Michael Buttler, Rick Eaves, Michael Gebicki, Jane Gregory, Kerry Kenihan, Anne Matthews, Sue Neales, Ingrid Ohlsson, Rod Ritchie, Pamela Wright

Updater
Michael Gebicki

Indexer
Marie Lorimer

Production
Lorraine Taylor

Mapping
Maps produced by the Mapping Services Department of
AA Publishing

Published by AA Publishing, a trading name of AA Media Limited, whose registered office is
Fanum House, Basing View, Basingstoke, RG21 4EA. Registered number 06112600.
A CIP catalogue record for this book is available from the British Library.

ISBN 978-0-7495-6754-5

KeyGuide is a registered trademark in Australia and is used under license.
Colour separation by AA Digital Department
Printed and bound by Leo Paper Products, China

We believe the contents of this book are correct at the time of printing. However, some details, particularly prices, opening times and telephone numbers do change. We do not accept responsibility for any consequences arising from the use of this book.
This does not affect your statutory rights. We would be grateful if readers would advise us of any inaccuracies they may encounter, or any suggestions they might like to make to improve the book. There is a form provided at the back of the book for this purpose, or you can email us at travelguides@theaa.com

A04201
Mapping produced from map data © New Holland Publishing (South Africa) (PTY) Ltd 2010
Weather Chart statistics supplied by Weatherbase © Copyright 2003 Canty and Associates, LLC
RACV assistance with distance/time charts gratefully acknowledged
Transport map © Communicarta Ltd, UK

Find out more about AA Publishing and the wide range of travel publications and services the AA provides by visiting our website at
theAA.com/shop

READER RESPONSE

Thank you for buying this KeyGuide. Your comments and opinions are very important to us, so please help us to improve our travel guides by taking a few minutes to complete this questionnaire.

You do not need a stamp (unless posted outside the UK). If you do not want to cut this page from your guide, then photocopy it or write your answers on a plain sheet of paper.

Send to: **KeyGuide Editor, AA World Travel Guides**
FREEPOST SCE 4598, Basingstoke RG21 4GY

Find out more about AA Publishing and the wide range of travel publications the AA provides by visiting our website at www.theAA.com/bookshop

ABOUT THIS GUIDE

Which KeyGuide did you buy? ....

Where did you buy it? ....

When? ....month .... year

Why did you choose this AA KeyGuide?
☐ Price ☐ AA Publication
☐ Used this series before; AUSTRALIA
☐ Cover ☐ Other (please state)

Please let us know how helpful the following features of the guide were to you by circling the appropriate category:
very helpful (VH), helpful (H) or little help (LH)

Size	VH	H	LH
Layout	VH	H	LH
Photos	VH	H	LH
Excursions	VH	H	LH
Entertainment	VH	H	LH
Hotels	VH	H	LH
Maps	VH	H	LH
Practical info	VH	H	LH
Restaurants	VH	H	LH
Shopping	VH	H	LH
Walks	VH	H	LH
Sights	VH	H	LH
Transport info	VH	H	LH

What was your favourite sight, attraction or feature listed in the guide?

Page.................Please give your reason ....
....

Which features in the guide could be changed or improved? Or are there any other comments you would like to make?

....
....

ABOUT YOU

Name (Mr/Mrs/Ms)..

Address ....

....

....

....

Postcode... Daytime tel nos..

Email...
Please only give us your mobile phone number/email if you wish to hear from us about other products and services from the AA and partners by text or mms.

Which age group are you in?
Under 25 ☐   25–34 ☐   35–44 ☐   45–54 ☐   55+ ☐

How many trips do you make a year?
Less than1 ☐   1 ☐   2 ☐   3 or more ☐

ABOUT YOUR TRIP

Are you an AA member?   Yes ☐ No ☐

When did you book?.............. month................. year

When did you travel?..............month................. year

Reason for your trip?   Business ☐ Leisure ☐

How many nights did you stay? ....

How did you travel?   Individual ☐ Couple ☐ Family ☐ Group ☐

Did you buy any other travel guides for your trip?..

If yes, which ones?...

Thank you for taking the time to complete this questionnaire. Please send it to us as soon as possible, and remember, you do not need a stamp (unless posted outside the UK).
AA Travel Insurance call 0800 072 4168 or visit www.theaa.com

AUSTRALIA is in the KeyGuide series:

Australia, Barcelona, Berlin, Britain, Brittany, Canada, China, Costa Rica, Croatia, Florence and Tuscany, France, Germany, Ireland, Italy, London, Mallorca, Mexico, New York, New Zealand, Normandy, Paris, Portugal, Prague, Provence and the Côte d'Azur, Rome, Scotland, South Africa, Spain, Thailand, Venice, Vietnam, Western European Cities.

AA Travel Insurance call 0800 072 4168 or visit www.theaa.com